PC Hardware: A Beginner's Guide

RON **GILSTER**

Osborne/**McGraw-Hill**
New York Chicago San Francisco
Lisbon London Madrid Mexico City
Milan New Delhi San Juan
Seoul Singapore Sydney Toronto

Osborne/**McGraw-Hill**
2600 Tenth Street
Berkeley, California 94710
U.S.A.

To arrange bulk purchase discounts for sales promotions, premiums, or fund-raisers, please contact Osborne/**McGraw-Hill** at the above address. For information on translations or book distributors outside the U.S.A., please see the International Contact Information page immediately following the index of this book.

PC Hardware: A Beginner's Guide

34567890 DOC DOC 01987654321

ISBN 0-07-212990-5

Publisher
Brandon A. Nordin
Vice President & Associate Publisher
Scott Rogers
Acquisitions Editor
Michael Sprague
Project Editor
Patty Mon
Acquisitions Coordinator
Paulina Pobocha
Technical Editor
Gregg Rochman
Copy Editor
Sally Engelfried
Proofreader
Susie Elkind
Indexer
Valerie Robbins
Computer Designers
Melinda Moore Lytle
Carie Abrew
Roberta Steele
Illustrators
Michael Mueller
Lyssa Sieben-Wald
Series Design
Peter F. Hancik

This book was composed with Corel VENTURA™ Publisher.

ABOUT THE AUTHOR

Ron Gilster, one of the top best-selling authors of hardware and certification books, has been involved with computer hardware and software for over 33 years. His professional career includes experience as a technician, supervisor, manager, executive, consultant, trainer, teacher, developer, merchant, and end-user. He is the author of several books on PC hardware, A+ certification, and many other information technology and computing topics, including several books on networking, the Internet, computer and information literacy, and programming.

**This book is dedicated to George Price, my Dad,
as a small thanks for his love
and his belief in me.**

CONTENTS

Part IV

System Care and Troubleshooting

ACKNOWLEDGMENTS

My thanks to Dan Caldwell, Mike Glencross, Brian Huddell, and Greg Notske for their contributions to this book and Diane McMichael Gilster for her great photography.

I would also like to acknowledge the patience and support of the crew at Osborne: Michael Sprague, Patty Mon, and Paulina Pobocha.

And special thanks to the following companies and organizations for the use of their product images, illustrations, and information:

3M Corporation (www.3m.com)
ATOP Technologies (www.atop.com.tw)
American Megatrends, Inc. (www.ami.com)
AOpen America, Inc. (www.aopen.com)
Belkin Components (www.belkin.com)
Boundless Technologies (www.boundless.com)
COLORCASE, a division of Rainier Company (www.colorcase.com)
Delkin Devices, Inc. (www.delkin.com)
Desco Industries, Inc. (www.desco.com)
Enlight Corporation (www.enlightcorp.com)
Epson Corporation (www.epson.com)
Gateway, Inc. (www.gateway.com)
Hewlett-Packard Company (www.hp.com)
Hungtech Industrial Co., Ltd. (www.hungtech.com.tw)
IBM Corporation (www.ibm.com)
Ines, Inc. (www.ines.com)
Intel Corporation (www.intel.com)
In Touch Systems (www.magicwandkeyboard.com)
In-Win Development, Inc. (www.in-win.com)
Iwill USA (www.iwillusa.com)
Kingston Technology Company, Inc. (www.kingston.com)
Lexmark International, Inc. (www.lexmark.com)
Linksys Corporation (www.linksys.com)
Logitech Inc. (www.logitech.com)
Niagara Technology (www.niagaratech.com)
Nidec America Corporation (www.nidec.com)
Nokia USA Corporation (www.nokia.com)
Oki Data Americas, Inc. (www.okidata.com)
PC Power and Cooling, Inc. (www.pcpowercooling.com)
Saitek Industries (www.saitekusa.com)
School Technologies, Inc. (www.schooltechnologies.com)
Silicon Integrated Systems, Inc. (www.sis.com)
Super Micro Computer (www.supermicro.com)
The Computer Garage (www.computergarage.org)
Tecpel Co., Ltd. (www.tecpel.com)
ViewSonic Corporation (www.viewsonic.com)
Xantrex Technology Inc. (www.xantrex.com)

There is another group of people that made the final product of this book possible. To my parents for giving me life, I hope I have made you proud. To Richard, Mike, Lee, and Joseph who helped me gain the wisdom to write this book. To Johnny Huffman for all his words of switching wisdom and fine photography, thanks. To Craig Dunton and Mary Beth Lesko for their additional edits and comments. To Harry Newton and his Telecom Dictionary—it never hurts to have a second opinion. To Creative Labs, Pinnacle Software, Vivo, Voice Information Systems, Teltone, and ACS for providing insider information about the industry. And finally to anyone that I might have forgotten.

INTRODUCTION

Everyday we are challenged with new technology and new adaptations of existing technology with the result that we are continually all beginners. While this book is written primarily for people who wish to know more about personal computer (PC) hardware, it may also prove to be helpful to people who wish to expand their knowledge of the PC's hardware.

It is remarkable that a personal digital assistant, such as the Handspring Visor or the Palm Pilot, holds more raw computing power than existed in the entire world only 20 years ago. It is also remarkable that the basic structure of the personal computer over this same 20 years has not changed all that much. The essential components that make a PC are the same today as they were in 1981. What has changed is the integration scale, the ability of the peripherals, and the size and capabilities of the software.

I have included all of the technology with which a PC user comes into contact and explain its function and interactions with the other components and technologies in the PC. While the details of all of the PC's components is included in the book, additional information has been included for the areas to which the beginning user has more contact, such as the audio/visual systems, CD-ROM and DVD drives, hard disk drives, keyboard, mouse, and others.

This book is intended to provide an in-depth introduction to the hardware and technology of the personal computer and to answer your questions about how it all works. I sincerely hope you enjoy the book and learn from it. If you have any feedback or questions, please contact me at feedback@rongilster.com.

PART I

The Basics

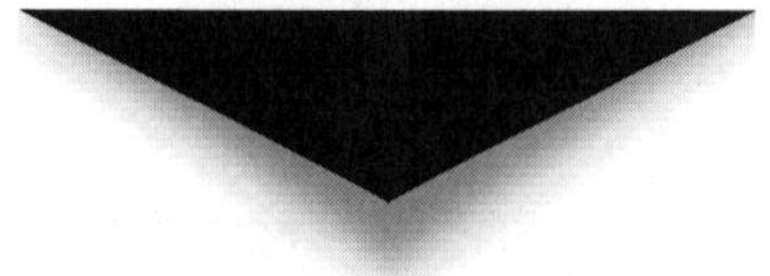

CHAPTER 1

The Personal Computer

Today's personal computer, like the one shown in Figure 1-1, is a much more powerful computer than the PCs of just five years ago. Not to mention how different the PC is from computers way back in the early days of its development. Remember that the whole of the computer's history is compacted into a little more than 50 years and the personal computer has only been around for a little over 20 years. In fact, the PC's most spectacular development has probably been made in just the past five to ten years. It is also safe to say that the computer of today will be nothing compared to what we'll have in five to ten more years. The one bit of good news in all of this is that the PC will most likely continue to have the same basic hardware components.

A BRIEF LOOK AT THE EVOLUTION OF COMPUTERS

Twenty-five years ago, it was virtually unthinkable that somebody would want to have a computer on their desk. Many of the "big" thinkers of the time could not even conceive of what anyone would possibly do with such a thing. It was a time of mainframes and minicomputers, which served the needs of corporations, companies, and departments. The idea that a single person could possibly have use for a computer all to themselves was just unthinkable.

Figure 1-1. Personal computers come in several styles

Mainframe Computers

Until the dawn of the personal computer in the early 1980s, computers were large, multiple cabinet affairs that required special room conditions and trained operators and programmers. *Mainframe computers*, the larger of the computers (see Figure 1-2) can literally fill a room. These large computers, sold by IBM, Amdahl, Unisys, Hitachi, and others, are used to fulfill the computing needs of large companies and corporations and are also used in large telecommunications centers. They are very powerful with huge amounts of storage and processing capability. The drawbacks to the mainframe computer for use as a personal computer are its size, its immense amount of computing power, and its price, which can run into the millions of dollars.

Before the personal computer, each mainframe user worked at a *terminal*, which is a device (see Figure 1-3) that combines a display monitor with a keyboard and is attached directly to the mainframe computer by a dedicated cable. The terminal, so called because it terminates the connection line, allows the user to send large blocks of data—the contents of the entire display screen, actually—to the mainframe for processing, and the results are displayed on the terminal's monitor. The early mainframe user did not have use of a mouse, and all data was entered as text. Graphical user interfaces (GUI) such as Microsoft Windows or X Windows were yet to come. Today's mainframe user is more likely to be connected to the mainframe over a local network and to use a PC as a terminal device.

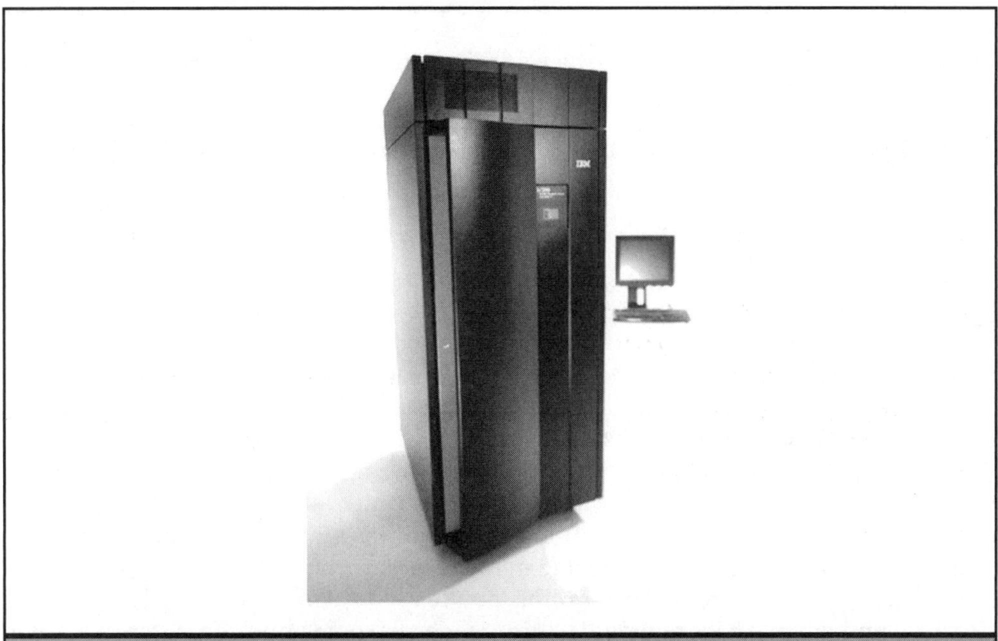

Figure 1-2. Mainframe computers provided computing for entire companies

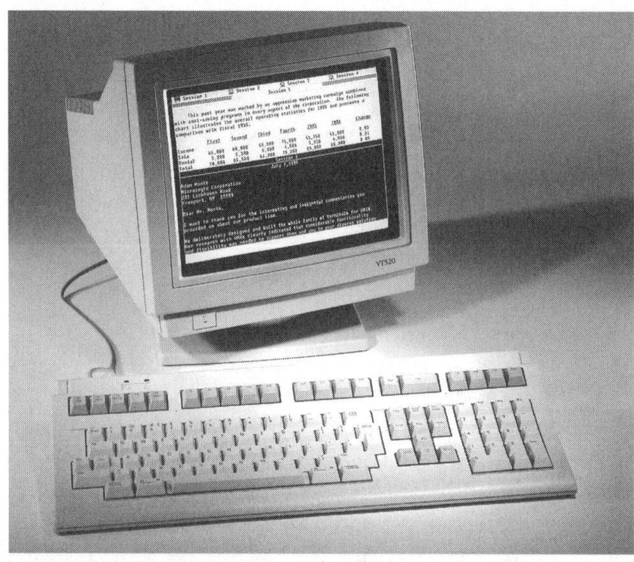

Figure 1-3. Terminals, like the VT 520, are one way to connect to a mainframe. Photo courtesy of Boundless Technologies

For more information on the history of the mainframe and its uses today, visit the following Web sites:

- **Rock Painter's Mainframe Links** www.texasrock.com/oem.shtml
- **Techweb Encyclopedia** www.techweb.com/encyclopedia
- **The Machine That Changed the World** ei.cs.vt.edu/~history/TMTCTW.html
- **Stanford University** gobi.stanford.edu/computer_history/

Minicomputers

The *minicomputer* (see Figure 1-4) was developed to serve the computing needs of smaller companies and the larger departments of corporations. The minicomputer, also known today as a midrange computer, has essentially the same functionality of the larger mainframe computer but on a smaller scale—and not much smaller, at that. The minicomputer was developed largely to open new markets for computers after most of the larger companies had purchased mainframes. The mainframe was scaled into a smaller package with most of its functions remaining and a little less storage and processing power, sold at a reduced price. There are computing devices today, made by Hewlett Packard, Compaq, and others, that are manufactured under the name minicomputer that are in fact midlevel computers that are more powerful than personal computers and less powerful than a mainframe. Because of advances in technology, today's minicomputer can

Figure 1-4. Minicomputers were as powerful as mainframes, only smaller

fulfill the entire computing needs of a small- to medium-sized company as well as serve as a very powerful communications server. Minicomputers are much too big, in terms of processing power and size, not to mention price, to be used as a personal computer.

For more information on the minicomputer, visit the following Web sites:

- **Minicomputer** www.whatis.com/minicomp.htm
- **Stanford University** gobi.stanford.edu/computer_history/mini.htm
- **SPARC Directory** www.sparcproductdirectory.com/history.html

Other Computers

You may have heard of a couple of other computer classifications: the supercomputer and the embedded computer. A *supercomputer,* like the one pictured in Figure 1-5, is an extremely powerful computer used mostly in research and space, military, and governmental applications. A supercomputer, which can cost tens of millions of dollars, contains the equivalent of thousands of personal computers that share in the processing load to solve very large and complex problems in hours or days instead of weeks, months, or years. A supercomputer is the largest and most powerful computer, sometimes equaling the power of several mainframes combined. For example, the Massachusetts Institute of Technology (MIT) is using a supercomputer to calculate the value of the mathematic

Figure 1-5. A supercomputer is the most powerful of the computer family

value *pi* to over a million decimal places, so far. Although it is the stuff dreams are made of, a supercomputer is way beyond consideration as a personal computer.

It seems as if virtually all electronic devices have a computer built into them in some way. These very small and single purpose processors are classified as *embedded computers*. An embedded computer is built into another device to control, monitor, or manage some activity for the device. The controls of a microwave oven, the carburetion on your car, the function of your electronic alarm clock, even your wristwatch most likely, all have at least one, and probably more, embedded computers. While it is true that a personal computer also has an embedded computer in its microprocessor (more on this later), the PC's processor is a multifunction device capable of controlling more than a single process or activity.

For more information on supercomputers and embedded computers, visit the following Web sites:

Supercomputers:

- **Ohio Supercomputer Center** www.osc.edu
- **Top500 Supercomputer List** www.hoise.com/vmp/examples/top500/

Embedded computers:

- **Technologic Systems** www.t-systems.com/sbc/
- **Gary's Encyclopedia** members.aa.net/~swear/pedia/embedded.html
- **DMOZ Open Directory** dirt.dmoz.org/Computers/Hardware/Embedded_Systems/

The Evolution of Personal Computers

There is some argument about what was actually the very first personal computer. Some say it was the MITS Altair 8800 (see Figure 1-6), and others claim it was the Apple. It may depend on the definition you use for just what a personal computer is, or was.

The Altair 8800 was a kit computer that fast became the favorite of hobbyists looking to get a computer all their own. Ed Roberts and his company, MITS (Model Instrumentation Telemetry Systems), developed this early personal computer kit, which was named the Altair by his daughter after a planetary destination on the TV show *Star Trek*. The software for the MITS was a BASIC programming language written by a fledgling company called Microsoft. However, like nearly all early personal computers, the Altair 8800 did not have off-the-shelf application software, and users had to write their software themselves using the BASIC language interpreter. While this was a challenge, to those kindred spirits looking to get in on the computing craze, it wasn't a problem.

In 1978, after seeing a demonstration of the Altair 8800, two young computer enthusiasts, Steve Jobs and Steve Wozniak, set out to build their own computer and developed a computer they named the Apple I. Like its predecessors, the Apple I established a following that encouraged its young developers to continue. The Apple II soon followed (see Figure 1-7), bolstered by what may have been the first killer application, an early spreadsheet program called VisiCalc, and became a commercial success.

It wasn't long before nearly every mainframe and minicomputer manufacturer leaped into the personal computer market. IBM, Digital Equipment, and others soon had their own PCs in the marketplace. The IBM PC and its extended technology (XT) and advanced technology (AT) versions soon became the standard for computers using Intel microprocessors,

Figure 1-6. The Altair MITS is thought to have been the first personal computer

Figure 1-7. The Apple computer was the first commercially successful personal computer

while Apple Computer continued to carve its own niche. The IBM PC AT (see Figure 1-8) and the Apple Macintosh (see Figure 1-9) represent commercially successful PCs that largely defined the personal computer in terms of its size, shape, and functions—a standard that has continued until today. This is the point at which we will begin looking at the technology of the PC and its hardware.

If you wish to learn more about some of the earliest computers and the pioneers who developed them, visit the following Web sites:

- **The Obsolete Computer Museum** www.obsoletecomputermuseum.org/
- **Jones Telecommunications and Multimedia Encyclopedia** www.digitalcentury.com/encyclo/update/pc_hd.html
- **The Mary Butterworth School** www.marybutterworth.net/historyofpc.html

The PC over the Years

Here is a list of some of the key events that have lead to the personal computer as we know it today. Each of these events was instrumental in either the development of the hardware of the PC or its software.

Figure 1-8. The IBM PC AT established the standard for Intel-based personal computers

Figure 1-9. The Apple Macintosh established a strong niche market early on

Year	Event
1961	Fairchild Semiconductor releases the first commercially available integrated circuit.
1963	Douglas Engelbart patents the mouse pointing device.
1970	Intel introduces the 4004 microprocessor.
1971	IBM introduces the floppy disk.
1974	Intel releases the 8080 microprocessor.
1975	MITS Altair 8800 sells in kit form for $375.
1976	Steve Wozniak and Steve Jobs build Apple I.
1977	Microsoft Corporation formed by partners Bill Gates and Paul Allen. Apple Computer produces Apple II.
1978	Intel produces the 8086 microprocessor.
1979	VisiCalc, the first killer application, is released. Intel produces the 8088 microprocessor.
1980	Apple III computer is introduced. The Radio Shack TRS-80 is introduced.
1981	IBM 5150 PC released featuring PC DOS (MS-DOS) 1.0.
1982	Commodore 64 computer is introduced. Intel produces the 80286 microprocessor. The Compaq Portable PC is introduced.
1983	Lotus 1-2-3 application is released. IBM PC XT is introduced. MS-DOS 2.0 is released.
1984	Hewlett Packard releases the LaserJet printer. Phoenix ROM BIOS is released.
1985	Intel releases the 80386DX. Microsoft Windows 1.0 is released. PC CD-ROM drives are made available.
1986	The first 80386 PC is produced.
1987	Apple Macintosh computer is introduced. IBM introduces PS/2 computers featuring OS/2 and VGA graphics.
1988	Intel releases the 80386SX microprocessor. Steve Jobs introduces the NeXT computer.
1989	Intel announces the 486 microprocessor.
1990	Microsoft Windows 3.0 is released.

Year	Event
1991	AMD releases its clone of the 386 microprocessor.
1992	Intel releases the 486DX2 microprocessor. Windows 3.1 is released.
1993	The Intel Pentium microprocessor is announced.
1994	Netscape Navigation browser is released. Iomega introduces the Zip drive.
1995	Pentium Pro microprocessor is introduced.
1998	Pentium II microprocessor is released.

As you can see, many separate events, all of them loosely related, were instrumental in the development of the personal computer as it exists today. The general structure of the PC has changed very little since its beginnings in the late 1970s. However, its speed, capacities, and power have increased nearly exponentially.

For a more fully detailed listing of the timeline and events in the history of the personal computer, visit the following Web sites:

- **The Microcomputer Timeline** www.islandnet.com/~kpolsson/comphist/
- **Computer History** www.komkon.org/fms/comp/
- **The Home Computer Hall of Fame** www.gondolin.org.uk/hchof/
- **The Historical Computer Society** www.cyberstreet.com/hcs/

INTEL VERSUS APPLE

In what has been compared to a religious war at times, the debate has raged for years between IBM clone users and Macintosh users. The term *IBM clone* refers to personal computers based on the IBM PC AT architecture, an open architecture that was shared with other computer manufacturers and became the standard for computers with Intel microprocessors. Often the "clone" part of the name is dropped and people refer to "IBM computers" (regardless of their true manufacturer).

With several hundred different manufacturers of IBM-type computers, sales of the clone have far exceeded the sales of the Apple computers. So much so that the term PC has come to mean non-Apple computers; although technically Apple computers are personal computers as well, it is common to hear a distinction made between an Apple computer and a PC.

In 1971, two pioneering engineers, Robert Noyce and Gordon Moore, formed Intel to develop and manufacture microprocessors. One of their first microprocessors, the 8080 (see Figure 1-10), was used in many of the early computers, including the Altair 8800 and IMSAI 8080, another popular early PC. Over the years, Intel microprocessors have emerged as the market leader. While other manufacturers such as AMD, Cyrix, and Zilog

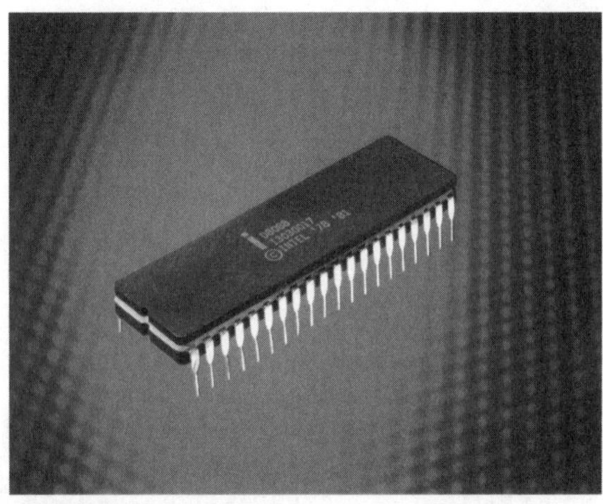

Figure 1-10. The Intel 8080 microprocessor. Photo courtesy of the Intel Museum Archives and Collections

have competed with Intel, Intel has managed to dominate the market with its x86 and Pentium microprocessors (see Chapter 3 for more information on the microprocessors used in PCs).

While other developers were adopting the Intel chips, Steve Wozniak chose to use the 6502 microprocessor in the Apple I and II computers. He did this for several reasons, not least of which was that it cost less than $100. He also favored this processor because its disassembler allowed the user to play around with the system. Figure 1-11 shows the Apple I motherboard with the 6502 processor (the large white chip on the center of the board).

The debate as to which system, the PC or the Macintosh, may be better is certainly a matter of preference and will probably continue for as long as the two platforms are manufactured and sold. Essentially, the hardware, the focus of this book, is and performs about the same (although even this very general statement could start an argument). Some believe the Macintosh computer to be better for artistic uses and graphics and the PC to be better for number crunching and applications, but these differences are largely because of the software developed for each.

The examples we show in the figures and illustrations of this book focus on personal computer systems based on Intel processors. This is not meant to indicate that one type of computer is better or worse than another. Our choice is based strictly on the fact that the PC has dominated the market and that you are more likely to have an Intel-based computer than not.

Figure 1-11. Apple I motherboard with the Intel 6502 microprocessor

AN OVERVIEW OF SYSTEMS AND COMPONENTS

Okay, let's take a quick tour of a typical personal computer's hardware. Study Figure 1-12 and take note of each of the items in the illustration.

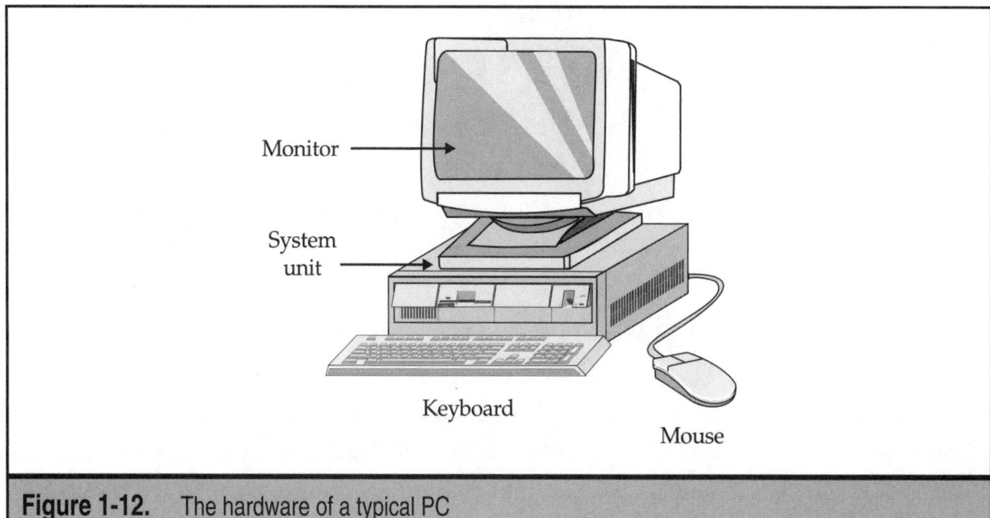

Figure 1-12. The hardware of a typical PC

The items in Figure 1-12 correspond to the following:

- The monitor, which is also called the display, the visual display unit (VDU), or the screen
- The keyboard
- The system unit, which contains the motherboard, disk drives, expansion cards, and input/output ports
- The mouse

The desktop computer in Figure 1-12, where the monitor sits on top of the system unit, is a very common configuration for personal computers. Other popular PC configurations are the tower and minitower computers, in which the system units sits on the floor or other surface and the monitor sits separately on a desktop or wherever. Figure 1-13 shows a tower-style computer.

Computers also come in small packages. The notebook computer (see Figure 1-14) has made power-computing very portable. The pocket-sized palmtop computer, such as the Casio Cassiopia (Figure 1-15), and the personal digital assistant (PDA), such as the 3Com Palm Pilot or the Mindspring Visor (see Figure 1-16), has the ability to perform many personal productivity applications.

Figure 1-13. A personal computer with a tower case. Photo courtesy of IBM Corporation

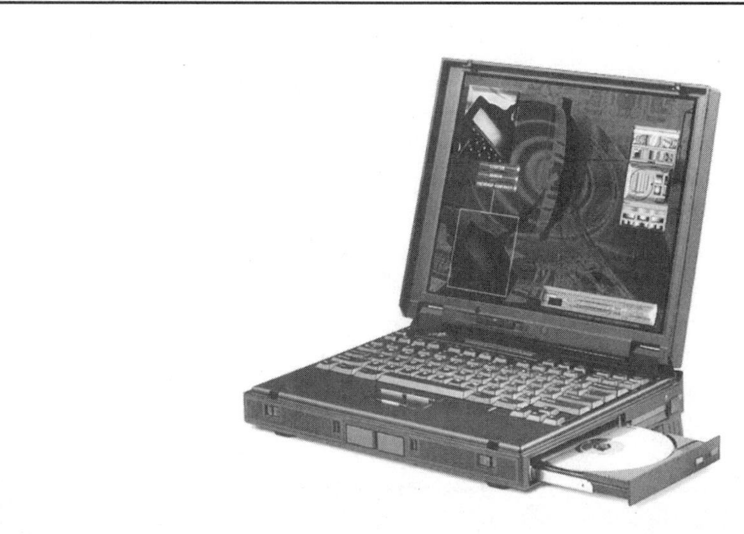

Figure 1-14. A notebook computer

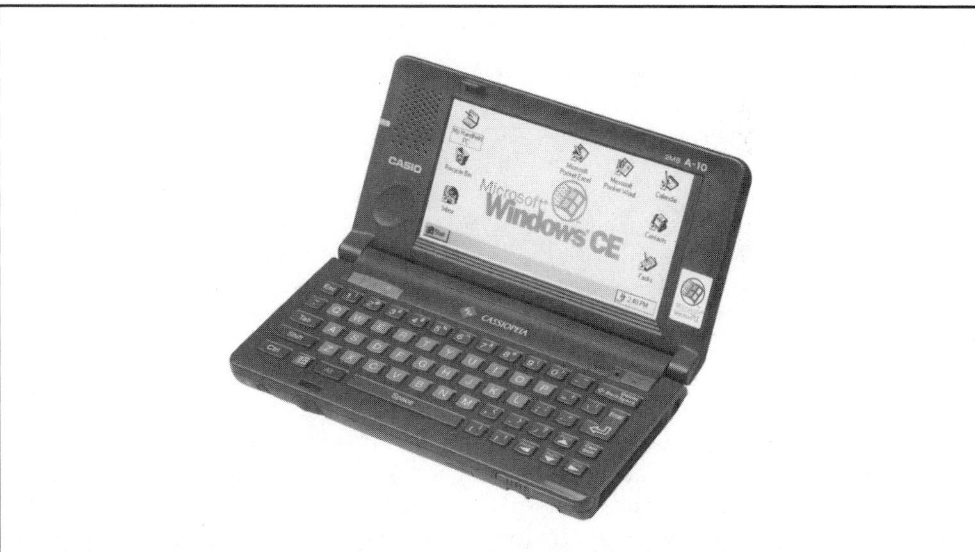

Figure 1-15. An example of a palmtop computer. Photo courtesy of Casio

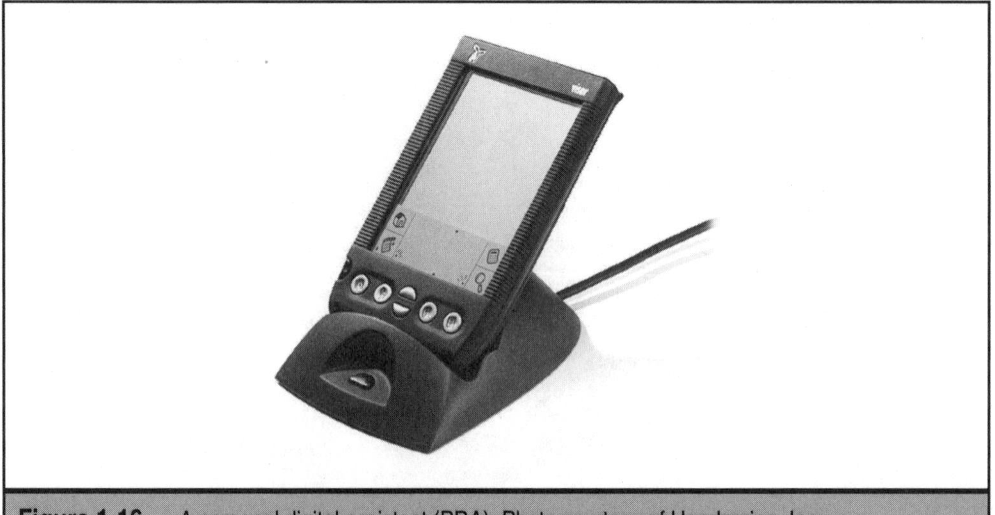

Figure 1-16. A personal digital assistant (PDA). Photo courtesy of Handspring, Inc.

Regardless of the size of the package, personal computers all have the same six groups of hardware components:

- Input devices
- Output (display) devices
- Processor/motherboard
- Storage devices
- Adapters/peripherals
- Power supply

Input Devices

Computers process data into information; simulate an action or animation; and, among other actions, replicate hand motions to draw an image. What each of these actions or processes has in common is that each requires some form of interaction with an operator. At least so far, the operator is generally human and the human needs to provide instructions, data, or other stimuli (called inputs) to the computer so it can do its thing. To facilitate this interaction, the computer must provide devices that the operator can use to give it its inputs. Reasonably enough, these devices are called *input devices*.

Over the years, the most common input device has been the keyboard. However, in the past few years, it has been a dead heat between the keyboard and mouse (see Figure 1-17) because virtually every computer sold has both devices. Newer hybrid devices now even

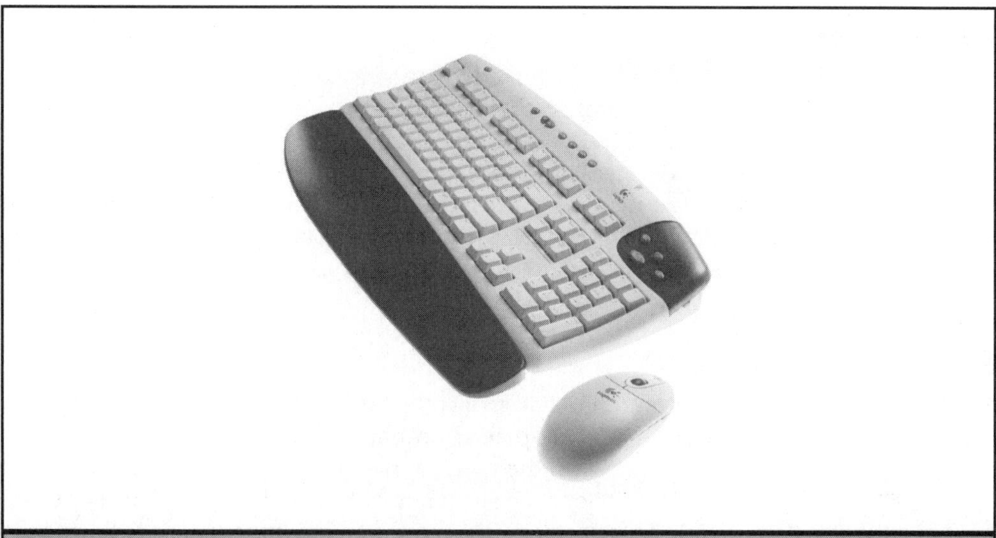

Figure 1-17. A standard keyboard and mouse. Photo courtesy of Logitech International

combine the two, replacing the mouse with a touchpad built right into the keyboard. This hybrid style is very common on notebook computers, as shown in Figure 1-18. See Chapter 18 for more information on keyboards and other input devices.

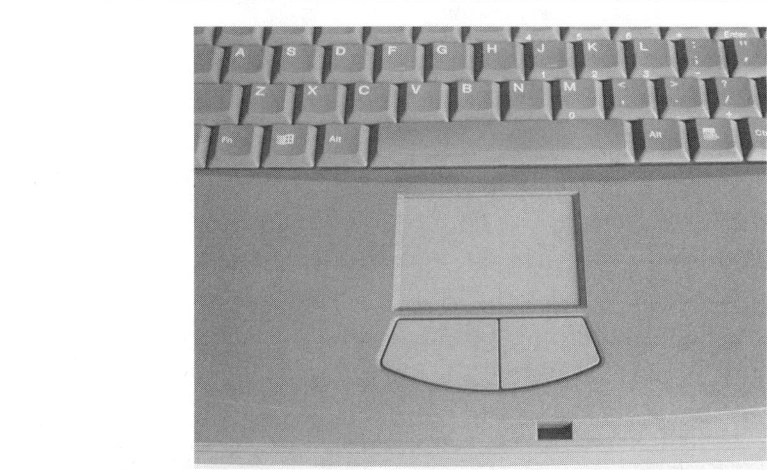

Figure 1-18. The touchpad and keyboard on a notebook computer

Output Devices

The output devices of any computer are linked to the senses of its human operator. If you haven't made this connection before, give it some thought. The computer must communicate with its operator through one of their senses, most likely sight and sound. These two human senses allow the operator to see and hear the outputs produced by the computer. The other human senses could be used, but at least so far the computer has not had much success with using the operator's senses of touch, taste, and smell. (You know systems that produce real-time smells can't be too far into the future, and there are already printers that can produce their output in Braille for sight-impaired users.)

Printers and Displays

The human sense of sight is by far the sense most often used to view a computer's output. Text and graphics can be permanently placed on paper by a printer (like the one in Figure 1-19) or viewed temporarily on the monitor (see Figure 1-20). Some outputs of the computer, some of which may not even seem like outputs—like the Windows desktop—do not need to be printed for permanent reference, while others need to be printed so they can be viewed away from the computer and shared with others. See Chapters 16 and 17 for more information about displays and printers, respectively.

Sound Devices

The other common output from a personal computer is sound. Whether it is as simple as the beep codes produced through the system speaker when the computer is started up or the

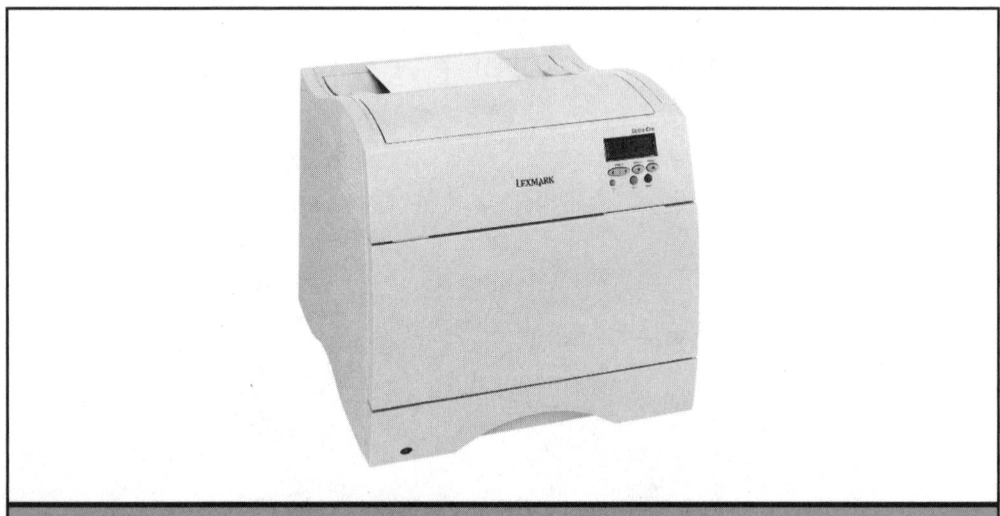

Figure 1-19. A laser printer. Photo courtesy of Lexmark International

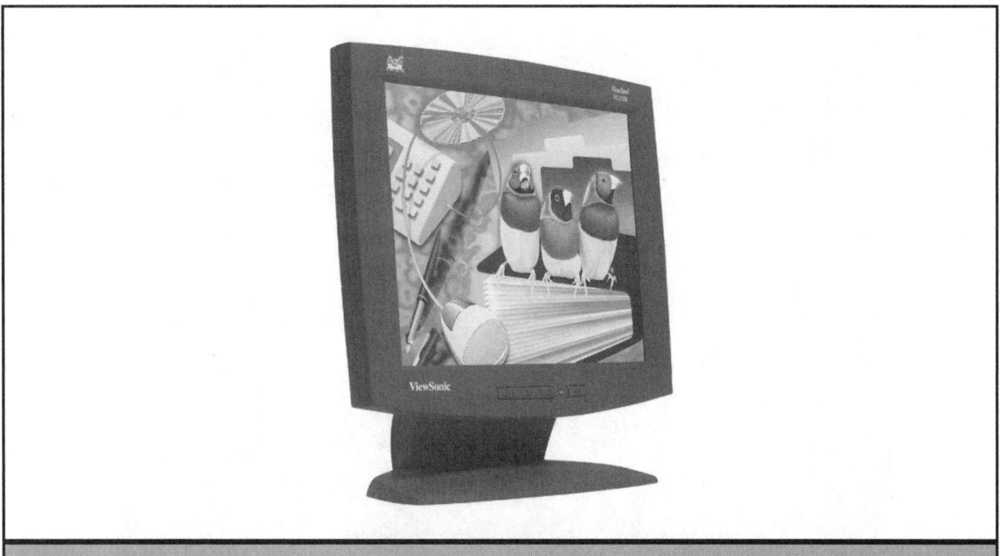

Figure 1-20. A flat-panel monitor. Photo courtesy of ViewSonic, Inc.

near-high fidelity sounds produced from a CD-ROM or DVD, digital systems and sound are a match made in audio heaven. See Chapter 21 for more information on sound devices.

Inside the System Case

The system case encloses most of the key electronic components of the personal computer, including the motherboard, power supply, and expansion cards. The motherboard, an example of which is shown in Figure 1-21, holds the microprocessor, memory, ROM, and most of the other electronic components that allow the computer to function. These vital components are covered in detail in Part II of this book.

Don't think of the system case as just a plastic or metal box into which all of these components are placed just so they won't get damaged or lost. The system case plays a very vital role in both the electrical and ventilation systems engineered into the PC. Chapter 15 details the functions and purpose of the system case.

It All Works Together

The amount of accumulated engineering time over the years that has gone into perfecting the way in which the personal computer's components work together is immense. The way the parts fit and function together to allow you to write a letter, play a game, or find Wal-Mart's online shopping page is no accident. If you are like most computer users, you rarely wonder about or consider how the components interact to create the function of the computer.

Figure 1-21. A microcomputer's motherboard. Photo courtesy of Iwill USA

Not counting the millions of transistors crammed into a computer's microprocessor, there are literally thousands of interacting parts in a computer. All of these parts must be coordinated, controlled, and managed so that the computer's actions fulfill the desire of its user. However, the PC is much more than just hardware. In order for the computer to accomplish something useful and of value, it must also have software to instruct the hardware on what to do, data to be processed, and a person to either develop the instructions or enter the data (and to place value on the output). If any one of these components is missing, nothing of value or use can happen. Without hardware, software is useless and vice versa. Without data, what is there to do? And without a person, who enters the data or views the output?

As important as each of these components is, this is not the beginner's guide to software, people, or data. In this book, you will find an in-depth introduction and guide to the hardware of the personal computer. The focus in this book is on explaining how, when, and why components, parts, and features are used, as well as some tips on what to do when they don't work correctly or need to be replaced or updated.

IN THIS BOOK ...

The contents of this book are structured so that you can focus on a particular group of the parts of the PC.

This part of the book (Part I—The Basics) also contains an introduction to some of the underlying concepts and principles of the PC, including digital logic, electronics, and electricity.

Part II (Internal Components) looks at the electronics and other components found inside the system case. This is where all the mysterious stuff goes on and is a very good place to start your reading.

Part III (External Components) covers the devices found outside the system case (including the system case itself) that connect to the computer through its interface ports.

Finally, Part IV (System Care and Troubleshooting) is a guide to how to care for your computer and figure out what is wrong when the PC is not working as it should.

We hope you enjoy this book. When you have completed it, you will be an ex-beginner.

CHAPTER 2

Basic PC Concepts and Terminology

Like a blender or any other electrically powered appliances, the computer runs on electricity. Without electricity, a computer is just a slick looking collection of rather expensive chunks of plastic, glass, and metal that have little value beyond keeping your desk from floating away. However, the computer uses electricity (actually, electrical charges) in ways the blender can't—at least not your everyday ordinary blender.

To store data, a computer also uses a few numbering systems. Numbering systems, such as binary and hexadecimal (more on these later in this chapter), allow the computer to take advantage of the some basic properties of electricity to create, store, and process data. To understand what makes a computer tick, buzz, whir, and, of course, compute, you should have a basic understanding of how electricity and the numbering systems are used in the computer—which is exactly what we provide you in this chapter. It may seem like a math lesson at times, but it's painless, and you'll be better informed for having read it.

AN INTRODUCTION TO DIGITAL LOGIC

You have most likely heard the term *digital* used with watches, clocks, calculators, and other common items, but have you ever stopped to think about just what that meant? Digital doesn't mean that a device displays its information in digits, it means the device creates, stores, and processes data using the two states of electricity—positive and negative (technically, it's nonpositive, but more on that later). In effect, anything digital uses some form of automated computation to operate. And yes, this definitely includes the computer.

The opposite of digital is analog. An analog device expresses data as a continuing electrical wave that usually has a varying frequency or amplitude that is sent over a carrier wave. Your home telephone is most likely an analog device that carries the sound of your voice over the telephone wires with an analog signal wave. Other common analog devices are radios and televisions (not counting High Definition Television—HDTV, which is a digital device).

On the other hand, digital devices transmit, store, and process data using the two-state properties of electricity. There are many digital devices around, such as CD players, HDTV, and most of the stuff at Radio Shack and the Sharper Image stores.

Digital versus Analog

Figure 2-1 illustrates the difference between a digital signal and an analog signal. The digital signal is either one value or another; there are no in-between values. The digital signal shown in Figure 2-1 illustrates this principle. Notice that the horizontal parts of the wave line are either near the top or near the bottom with the wave line connecting either straight up or straight down. When one value stops, the transition is immediate and the other begins. As we will be discussing in the next few sections, the computer, because it is an electrical appliance, is capable of storing only digital values, and as a result, is a digital device.

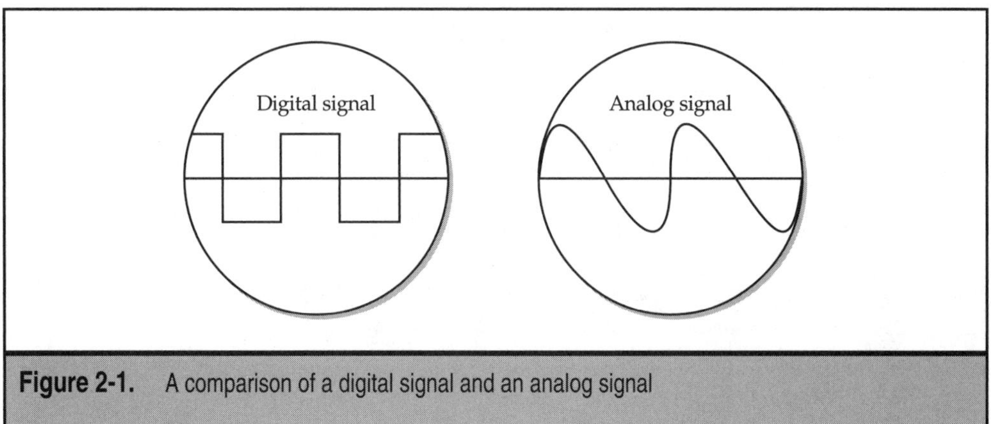

Figure 2-1. A comparison of a digital signal and an analog signal

As pictured in Figure 2-1, the analog signal fluctuates among a series of values, all of which are represented on the wave line. This could represent the rise and fall of a sound wave or any other event made up of a series of related increasing or decreasing values.

Computing in Binary Numbers

The primary storage device inside the computer is the transistor. Yes, the same device that made radios small enough to fit in your shirt pocket in the 1960s is the same miracle of science that allows your computer to store and process millions of bits of data. A single transistor is capable of holding an electrical charge that is either positive or nonpositive. Since the objective of the computer is to manipulate data, the electrical states of the transistor (positive and nonpositive) are assigned the numerical values of 1 and 0 (zero). It may seem that you can't do very high math, or even low math for that matter, with only a 1 and a 0, but using the binary number system, the computer is fully capable of performing all of its magic. Figure 2-2 shows the two values of binary in contrast to the two states of the transistor.

The Binary Number System

The binary (the prefix *bi* meaning two) number system uses only the two values: 0 and 1. This matches the capabilities of the transistor perfectly, as the transistor can also have only two states or values. As shown in Figure 2-2, the two values of the binary number system and the two states of the transistor can be paired up so that the transistors positive state represents the value 1 and its nonpositive state represents the value 0. The bonding of these two systems allows the computer to use the binary number system.

The computer stores a single binary numeral (either a one or a zero) in a single transistor. In fact, the word *bit* in computer lingo is a short form of *binary digit*. Each transistor holds a single electrical charge that is either positive or nonpositive, which in turn represents a 1 or a 0. As we will discuss in Chapter 7, eight bits are grouped together to form

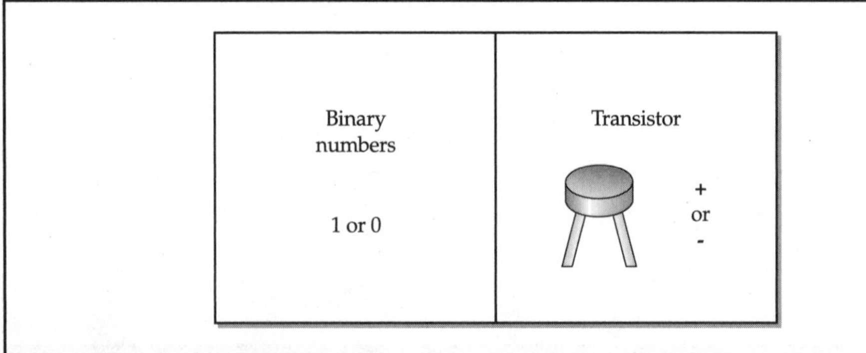

Figure 2-2. The binary number system and the transistor each have two values or states

what is called a *byte*. A byte can store smaller integer numbers or a single character. The eight bits of a byte can create 255 different values in the binary number system.

So, what is the binary number system, that is, beyond its one and zero values? The binary number system is a base-two number system and represents values as exponential values of two. Compare this to decimal, which is a base-ten number system. Perhaps the best way to explain binary to you is to refresh your knowledge of decimal.

Decimal numbers, such as 101, are really a combination of individual values, each of which is expressed as a power of ten. In the case of the number 101, it really means 1 plus no 10s plus one 100. Everyone knows that, right? However, technically speaking, 101 really represents 1 times 10 to the zero power plus 0 times 10 to the first power plus 1 times 10 to the second power:

$$(1 * 10^2) + (0 * 10^1) + (1 * 10^0) = 101$$

Likewise, the number 221 represents

$$(2 * 10^2) + (2 * 10^1) + (1 * 10^0) = 221$$

Decimal values have ten numerals (0 to 9) to express how many of a particular power of ten is included in a number. The word *decimal* is derived from the word ten.

The binary number system works just like the decimal system with two exceptions: each place in a binary number represents a power of two, and the binary system has only two numerals (0 and 1) it can use to express how many of a particular power of two is included in a value. Other than that, the binary system works just like the decimal.

Probably the best way to think about how a power of two value is expressed in binary is that a one turns on a particular value, and the zero turns it off. For example, the binary number 101 represents the decimal value 5. Here's why:

$$(1 * 2^2) + (0 * 2^1) + (1 * 2^0) = 5$$

In this example, one times two to the second power plus one times two to the zero power adds up to the decimal number five.

Each numeral in the number represents a power of two, which gets bigger by one (starting from 0) moving to the left. However, if you tried inserting our decimal example of 4,321 into the binary number, it won't be a direct fit. Remember that binary has only the numerals 0 and 1 to use to express how many of a particular power of two value is included in the value. In this case, you would need to substitute the actual values to represent this decimal number. Table 2-1 lists the first eight powers of two.

Converting Decimal to Binary

To convert the decimal number 221 to binary, power of two values are subtracted from the number and a one is placed in the power of two position for that value. Like this:

1. The largest power of two value that is not greater than 221 is 128 (the next power of two value is 2^8 or 256): 221 – 128 = 93. The binary number at this point is 10000000, which represents the decimal value 128.
2. The largest power of two value that is not greater than 93 is 64 (see Table 2-1): 93 – 64 = 29. The binary number is now 11000000, which represents the decimal value of 192 (128 + 64).
3. The largest binary value that is not greater than 29 is 16 or 2^4: 29 – 16 = 13. The binary number is now 11010000. Remember that we did not use the 2^5 (32) position.
4. The largest binary value that is less than 13 is 8 or 2^3: 13 – 8 = 5. The binary number at this point is 11011000, which represents the decimal value of 216 (128 + 64 + 16 + 8).
5. To complete the conversion, turn on the binary values for 4 and 1, which results in the binary number 11011101, which represents the decimal value of 221 (128 + 64 + 16 + 8 + 4 + 1).

If you're thinking that the number 11011101 would take more space in the computer to store than the number 221, remember that the computer can only store the binary values of 1 and 0. It can't store, work with, manipulate, add, or use any value not expressed as a binary number. There just isn't any way to store a 2, a 4, or a 9 in a single bit.

Power of Two	Calculation	Decimal Equivalent
2^0	2 * 0	1
2^1	2 * 1	2
2^2	2 * 2	4
2^3	2 * 2 * 2	8
2^4	2 * 2 * 2 * 2	16
2^5	2 * 2 * 2 * 2 * 2	32
2^6	2 * 2 * 2 * 2 * 2 * 2	64
2^7	2 * 2 * 2 * 2 * 2 * 2 * 2	128

Table 2-1. Power of Two Values

THE HEXADECIMAL NUMBER SYSTEM

Another number system you should be aware of is the hexadecimal number system. Hexadecimal means six and ten or a base-16 number system. Since, after reading the preceding section on binary numbers, you are now a number system expert, hexadecimal should be a piece of cake for you.

Why hexadecimal? Good question! Many of the addresses and configuration values you work with on the PC are expressed as hexadecimal numbers because very large numbers can be expressed in fewer characters. Hex, as its friends call it, uses a combination of 16 values: the decimal numbers 0 through 9 for the first 10 values and the six letters A through F to represent the decimal values of 11–15 (see Figure 2-3).

Hexadecimal numbers can represent much larger numbers in the same number of digits as a decimal number, but where a decimal number is stored in binary in 8, 16, 32, or 64 bits, each hexadecimal digit uses 4 bits. The four bits have the binary values ranging from 2^0 in the right-most position and 2^3 in the left-most position. When all four bits have a one, the total decimal value is 15 or the equivalent of the hexadecimal F. This four-bit bit cluster is called a *nibble* and it can express the hexadecimal numerals 0–F.

Hexadecimal helps to solve the problem of how to store numbers like 11 or 15 as a single character, which ultimately saves characters when working with large numbers. You really don't need to master hexadecimal to the point that you can readily convert it back and forth to decimal, but you should have some idea of what a hexadecimal number represents in terms of decimal values.

Our friendly number 101, which was one hundred and one in decimal and five in binary, represents the decimal value 257 in hexadecimal. This illustrates how larger numbers can be stored in hexadecimal. Another example is that the hexadecimal value

Hexadecimal value	0	1	2	3	4	5	6	7	8	9	A	B	C	D	E	F
Decimal value	0	1	2	3	4	5	6	7	8	9	10	11	12	13	14	15

Figure 2-3. The values of the hexadecimal number system

ABCDEF represents 11,259,375 in decimal. It is unlikely that you will see hex numbers like 101 or ABCDEF; it is far more likely you will see something like 12C3F (76,863).

As you read this book, especially the chapters covering storage and system resources, you will encounter references to hexadecimal and binary values. Should you have trouble later with the number systems, just return here and review, but remember that it is not mandatory that you have an advanced degree in binary or hexadecimal to understand and work with the hardware of the PC. However, a good understanding of them will certainly help you.

Working with Number Systems on the PC

Here's a tip: when working with numbers on the computer, a very valuable tool to know and use is the Windows Calculator in its Scientific view, shown in Figure 2-4. This tool allows you to enter a hexadecimal number and then change the base to decimal and get its equivalent value.

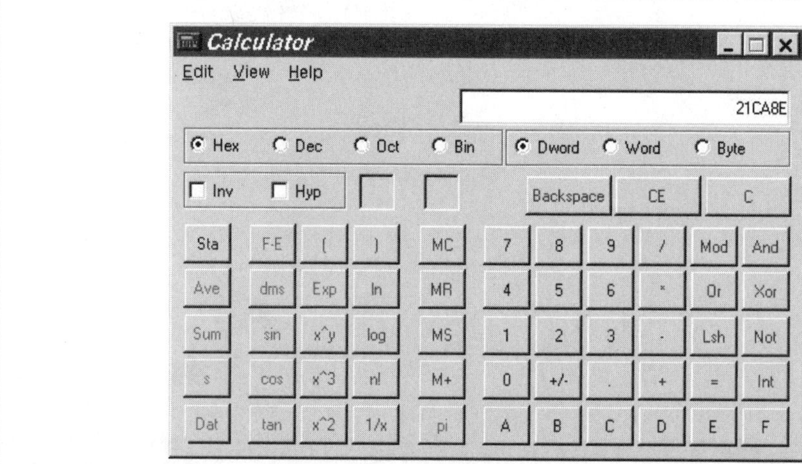

Figure 2-4. The Windows Calculator in its scientific view

ELECTRICITY AND THE PC

A basic understanding of the properties of electricity is necessary to be able to understand how a computer operates. There is a well-used analogy involving water through a pipe that can be helpful in understanding the fundamentals of electrical properties.

Electricity flows through a circuit in much the same manner as water flows through a pipe or hose. This concept is illustrated in Figure 2-5. When water is flowing through a pipe, it is pushed along by a measurable rate of pressure. A good experiment is to go out into your yard and water your garden with a hose. With the water turned on about halfway the flowers bend a bit as the water hits them, but it does not push them over. If you then turn the water up full blast, it not only pushes the flowers over, but the water pressure—the force of the flow—may even damage them. Electricity also flows through a circuit with a measurable pressure. This pressure is measured in units called *volts*. Don't attempt the same experiment with electricity in your garden, unless you are searching for earthworms.

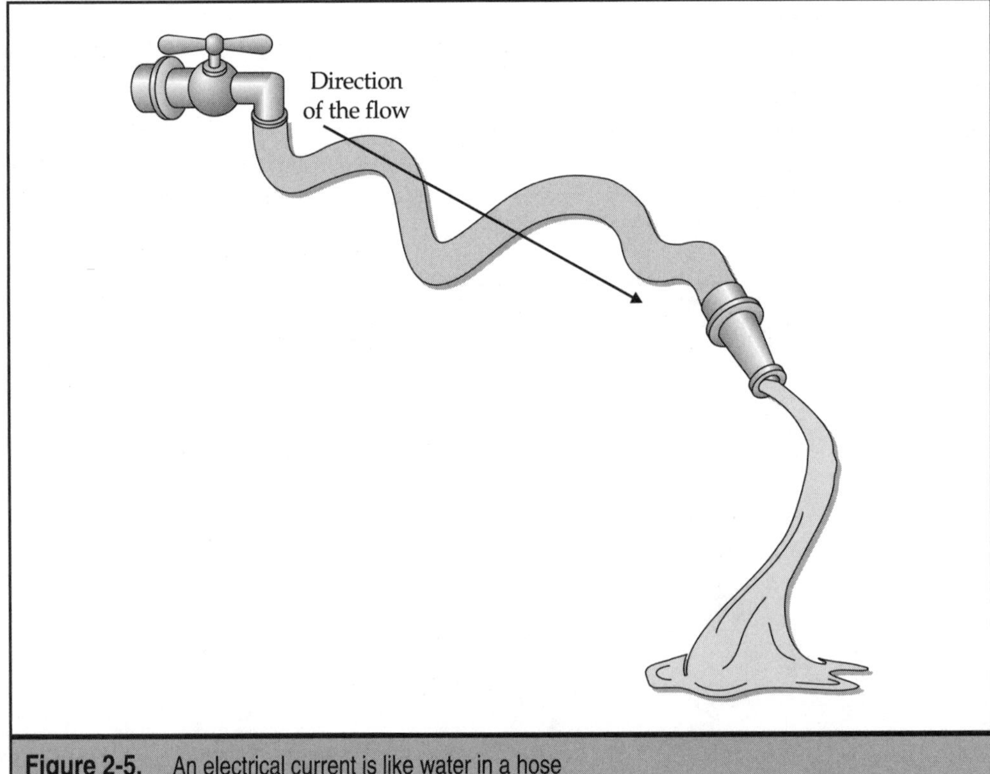

Figure 2-5. An electrical current is like water in a hose

While the water is flowing through a pipe or hose, it experiences some loss of pressure through friction. The same thing happens to electricity as it flows through a circuit: there is friction that causes a loss in pressure. This friction is called *resistance* and is measured in units called *ohms*. The amount of water that flows through a pipe for a specified length of time, such as the gallons-per-minute, is called the *volume* of the water flow. For an electrical current, volume, or the rate of flow, is measured in *amps*.

Another electrical term you should know is *watt*. The amps (rate of electrical flow) in combination with the volts (pressure in a circuit) form the watts, or the electrical power in a circuit. When an electrical circuit is open, there is no current or flow in the electricity. However, there can still be pressure (volts) in the circuit. A standard household electrical outlet has voltage (electrical pressure) just waiting for you to plug in a household appliance, which completes the circuit and starts the flow. This is why you don't want to stick your finger into an electrical outlet. You would be supplying the extra circuitry to close the circuit and cause the electricity to flow—through you, in this case. And because you are not well insulated and you don't make a particularly good conductor of electricity, you feel the electricity flowing through you as a shock. The degree of shock you feel when you close the circuit depends on the watts, or electrical power in the circuit. Please do not try this at home (or work or on vacation, for that matter); this is one of those facts of nature you should just accept as fact without question. Chances are you have already tested it anyway.

AC Power and DC Power

An electrical *current* is a movement of electrons through a copper wire or some other conducive property (more on this topic later). There are two types of electrical currents: alternating current (AC) and direct current (DC). *Alternating current* (AC) changes the direction of the electrical flow at a rate of about 60 times per second. The voltage changes from a positive charge to a negative charge, causing the electrical flow to change directions. The electrical flow in a *direct current* (DC) keeps a constant pace and flows in the same direction all the time. Direct current flows from a negative charge to a positive charge and does not fluctuate. AC power is what you very likely have at your standard household electrical outlets (at least in the United States and Canada), but DC is what the computer must have to operate properly. Let me repeat this for you: the computer needs DC power, but your wall outlet provides AC power. What's wrong with this picture?

Inside your PC is a module called the *power supply*, which converts the electricity in your household circuit (HC) from AC power into the DC power that the computer needs. Yes, this means that the HC provides AC, but the PC needs DC. All of the circuitry, the electronics on the motherboard, including the microprocessor, the disk drive motors, and all other electrical parts, require DC power to operate. It is the function of the power supply to convert the AC power to DC power. Chapter 14 covers the power supply in shocking detail.

External Power Issues

The PC's power supply solves the internal power issues for the computer, but many of the PC's power problems are caused by the original power source. Although we tend to take electrical power for granted most of the time, that is, until it is not there, electrical power can be a very unstable, damaging force that the PC needs to be protected against. Chapter 23 covers the many ways that the PC can be protected, but this is a serious enough problem that it bears mention here as well.

Electrical power tends to fluctuate in its voltage. While its normal operating range can vary, it is usually between 95 and 125 volts. On occasion though, the current spikes above or drops below its normal range and causes damage to a PC that is unprotected from sudden changes in the current. The best way to protect your PC is with a surge suppressor or an uninterruptible power supply (UPS). Chapter 23 will explain these devices in more detail.

Protecting Against ESD

One of the most insidious destroyers of PC circuits is *electrostatic discharge* (ESD), which can occur when you touch the fragile electronic components of the PC. *Static electricity* is what makes your hair stand straight up when you rub a balloon on it, or it gives you a shock after you walk across the carpet and grab the doorknob. Certain fabrics, fibers, and materials naturally generate static electricity, and the human body has a tendency to absorb and hold it until it finds a way to discharge it as an electrical flow. Except for the tingle in your hand, this is usually a fairly innocent and undamaging phenomenon. However, when it is the electronic components on your PC's motherboard or any of its other circuits, such as adapter cards, that receives the spark, it is more than likely that some damage has taken place.

Just because you can't feel, see, or hear ESD, doesn't mean it won't damage your computer. You can feel an electrostatic discharge of around 3,000 volts, but it only takes 30 volts to fry some of the electronics on an electronic circuit card, including the motherboard. Most of the electronics inside the computer are made to use from 1 to 12 volts of DC power, so it is no wonder that a charge with higher voltage may do damage. (Just for the record, any ESD that you can see has around 20,000 volts, which is why it hurts.)

To protect your computer, always follow the ESD safety guidelines for your PC. The safest thing to do is to always wear an antistatic wrist strap (see Figure 2-6) anytime you open your computer case. Other precautions are available, but wearing a wrist strap is probably the easiest and safest way to protect your computer. Chapter 23 covers some of the other ways you can protect your PC.

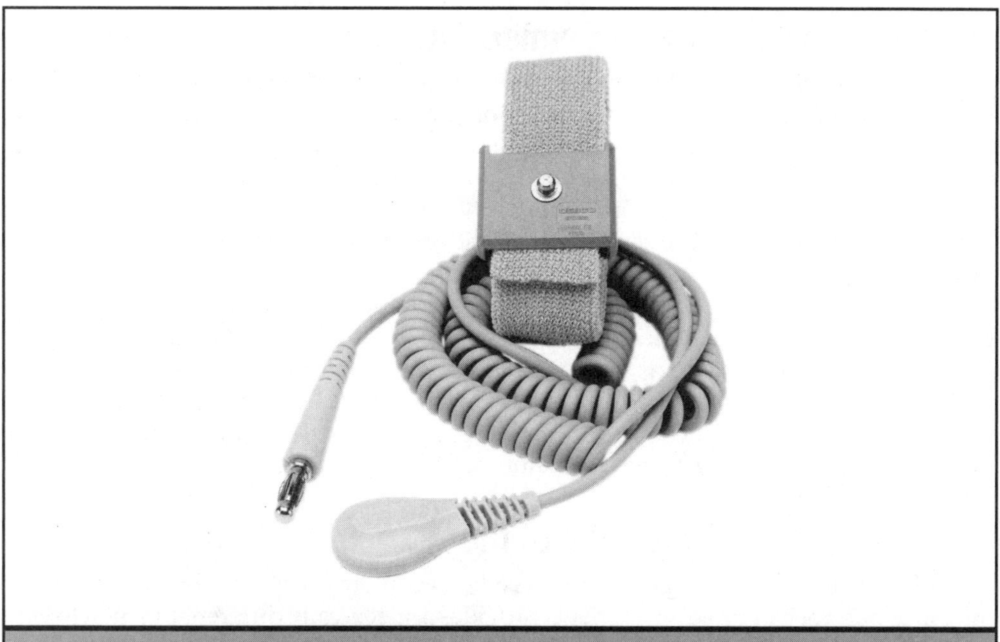

Figure 2-6. A wrist strap protects your PC against electrostatic discharge (ESD) damage. Photo courtesy of Desco Industries, Inc.

A QUICK OVERVIEW OF THE ELECTRONICS OF THE PC

The electronic components of your computer create a series of digital circuits that, while each has a logical objective, work together to process your data, play your game, or communicate with the world. A *digital circuit* is a group of electronic components that accept and process binary data and then apply Boolean algebra to reach a result. Don't worry; you don't need to learn algebra all over again. Boolean algebra is the logic mechanism that applies certain rules (AND, OR, and NOT) to binary values to determine an answer. Exactly how this happens is very important to programmers and engineers, but it's not too important to hardware technicians, especially beginners.

Conductors, Insulators, and Semiconductors

The DC electrical flow inside the computer, or outside for that matter, travels over a *conductor*, which is any material, such as copper or gold, that readily carries electricity without much resistance. It is common that a conductor is wrapped or coated by another material, called an *insulator*, such as rubber, that is not a good conductor of electricity. A good and easily found example is the cord to your lamp. Most likely it is a rubber cord with copper wires inside. The copper wire is the conductor and the rubber coating is the insulator.

Many of the electronic components inside the computer are neither conductors or insulators. They are made of materials, such as silicone, that is both and neither a conductor or an insulator. These materials, which can be made chemically and electronically to be either conductive or insulating, are called *semiconductors*. Depending on the type and purpose of a circuit, a semiconductor can be set to provide the right action. A semiconductor could also be called a semi-insulator, but so far this name hasn't caught on.

The Electronic Building Blocks of the PC

Four primary electronic components are used on virtually every electronic circuit inside the computer. Each of these components provides a specifically different function to each circuit. These components are resistors, capacitors, diodes, and transistors.

- A *resistor* slows down the flow of electrical current in a circuit.
- A *capacitor* is used to store electrical charges. Most of the computer's capacitors are small, but there are some large capacitors in the computer that hold enough charge to kill you, such as those in the monitor and power supply.
- A *diode* forces the electricity to flow in one way only.
- A *transistor,* which was mentioned earlier in the chapter, stores a single binary digit (bit).

Another basic electronic component found in the circuitry of the PC is the logic gate. A *logic gate* is created from a combination of resistors, capacitors, diodes, and transistors. Circuits are made up of logic gates and electronic systems are made up of circuits.

Perhaps the most important electronic component in the computer is the microprocessor. The microprocessor controls the function of virtually all other electronic components of the computer. Chapter 3 covers the various processors, past and present, used in PCs.

PART II

Internal Components

CHAPTER 3

Microprocessors

Everything a computer can do for you, that is, all of its magic, is controlled by its *microprocessor*. At the heart of every computer is a microprocessor, which is designed to perform all of the arithmetic, logic, and other basic computing steps that make up the actions of your PC. What you see as a word processor, a computer game, a World Wide Web browser, your e-mail, or any of the other software programs you perform on your PC, are in fact hundreds, even thousands of instructions that the microprocessor executes one at a time to carry out the actions of each program. The *processor*, which is short for both microprocessor and *central processor unit (CPU)*, is a piece of electronic circuitry that uses digital logic to perform the instructions of your software.

In this chapter, you are introduced to the processor and its functions. Included in this discussion are the following topics:

- Digital logic
- The binary number system
- The construction and manufacturing of a microprocessor
- The development and evolution of the microprocessor

AN INTRODUCTION TO DIGITAL LOGIC

Before you get too deep into the digital circuits and logic of the processor, you must first understand some fundamentals that underlie the way the computer and the processor use electricity. It is perfectly normal for you to think of the computer as just another electrical appliance, like a refrigerator, television, vibrating recliner, and so on. Sure, you plug it in, turn it on, and it works. What could be simpler? Ah, but there's a catch: it really isn't that simple.

Two-State Logic

Like the light switch on the wall, the electricity in the computer is either on or off. Data is stored in the computer with electrical charges that are either on or off. In the early days of the computer, *vacuum tubes*, which were about the size and shape of small light bulbs, stored data by turning individual tubes on or off. In today's computers, this same concept is applied on a much smaller scale with the transistor. Like the vacuum tube, the *transistor* holds an electrical charge that is—yes, you guessed it—on or off.

Actually, the electrical charge in a transistor is one of two distinct electrical voltage levels. A higher voltage level represents one value, and a lower voltage level represents another value. Because the computer has only these two electrical states in which to store data, the data has to be either very simple, or some means must be used to allow multiple transistors to be grouped to represent more complex data.

If all you ever need to store in the computer is on or off, true or false, yes or no, this or that, ying or yang—two-state values that can be represented as two voltage levels—then the computer and processor will work just fine without any additional complexity. But, what if you wish to store names, dates, facts, numbers, and other more complicated data in the computer? What then?

Binary Data

The term *binary* loosely means "two numbers," and the two numbers associated with binary are 1 and 0. Simply by assignment, the two voltage levels in the computer can represent these two binary values, with the lower voltage level equaling 0 and the higher voltage level equaling 1. Given this, then it shouldn't be too hard to understand that a transistor can store either the voltage representing a 1 or a 0. When a transistor is assigned a binary value this way, it becomes a *binary digit*, or *bit*, for short. Refer back to Chapter 2 for a review on how binary values are formed.

Now you know that the computer can store numbers, at least two numbers, anyway. But, once again, how do you store other numbers, words, or formulas in the computer?

Bit Groupings

To store data larger than a single bit, groups of bits are combined. These groupings all have names (some are very odd names), and each is capable of storing a different maximum binary value. Here are some of the key digital elements involved with the digital logic of the computer:

- A *bit* (binary digit) is a single binary number that can be either 1 or 0.
- A *binary word* is one or more bits and usually ranges from 4 to 64 bits.
- A *byte* (pronounced "bite"; the common 8-bit binary word), depicted in Figure 3-1, is probably the computer storage unit you hear the most about. The memory and storage on the computer are normally expressed in bytes. As you will see later in this chapter ("Storing Data in a Byte"), a single byte can hold the binary values equal to 0 to 255 in decimal.

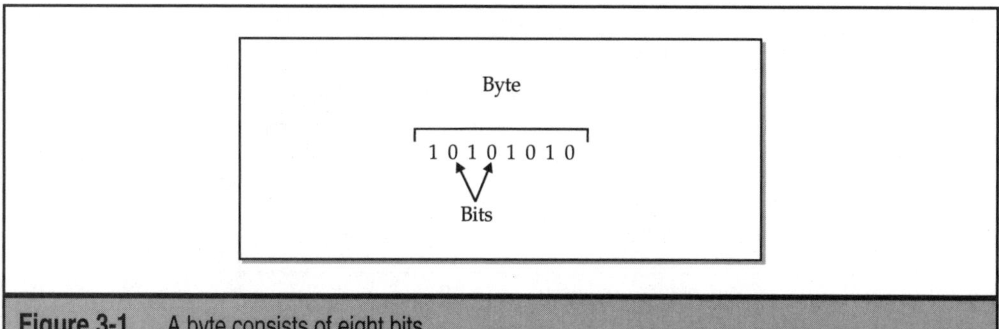

Figure 3-1. A byte consists of eight bits

- A *nybble* (pronounced "nibble"), shown in Figure 3-2, is a 4-bit binary word. It holds the binary equivalent of the decimal values 0 to 15. An 8-bit binary number is divided into two nybbles so it can hold two hexadecimal numbers (see "The Hexadecimal System" later in the chapter).
- A *machine word* is the number of bits that are required to hold the largest binary number a microprocessor can process. The machine word is commonly used to refer to the bit size of the processor. For example, computers are often described as having a 16-bit processor, a 32-bit processor, or a 64-bit processor.

Storing Data in a Byte

The byte is used on the computer to store many types of data. The eight bits of the byte can hold the decimal values 0 to 255. If it seems odd to you that eight bits must be used to store from one to three digits, remember that only binary 1s and 0s can be stored in the byte's bits. How these values are stored in a byte is by assigned each bit a different power of two value. Table 3-1 shows the binary values assigned to each bit in the byte.

Understand that the first bit (bit 1 in Table 3-1) is the right-most bit in the byte. If you add all of the decimal values for each bit in Table 3-1, the total is 255. The binary number 00000000 (the eight bits in a byte) represents 0 because none of the power of two values is used in the number. To put it another way, none of the power of two values was turned on. On the other hand, the binary value 11111111 represents 255 because all of the power to two values are turned on and therefore included in the number represented. I'll talk about this more in Chapter 7 when I cover how alphabetic and special characters are stored in memory.

If you wish to store a number larger than 255, you use more bits. This is where the machine word comes in. You can store the number 32,767 in 16 bits; 32 bits can hold the number 2,147,483,647; and 64 bits can represent the number 92,23,372,036,854,775,808 (my lucky number, by the way). If you aren't convinced of the power of binary to represent very large numbers, calculate the number that could be represented in 128 bits. Wow, now *that's* a large number!

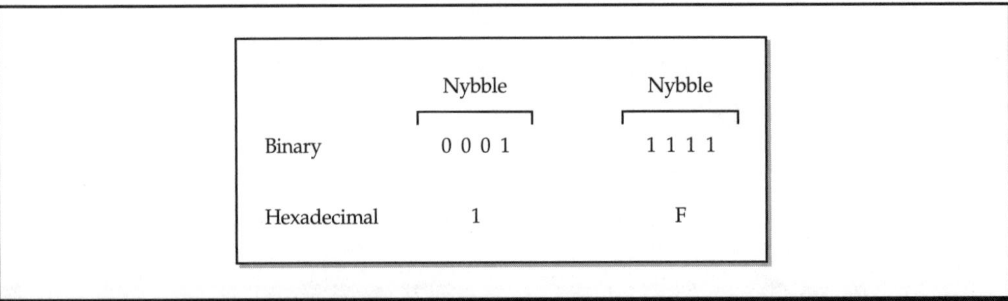

Figure 3-2. A nybble holds a 4-bit hexadecimal value

Bit	Power of Two	Decimal
1	2^0	1
2	2^1	2
3	2^2	4
4	2^3	8
5	2^4	16
6	2^5	32
7	2^6	64
8	2^7	128

Table 3-1. The Bit Values in a Byte

Converting Decimal to Binary

Here's a quick way to convert a decimal number into a binary number:

1. Divide the decimal number by 2 and keep the answer. Write down the remainder (you may want to start writing down the remainders on the right side of the paper); it will be either a 1 or a 0.
2. Divide the answer by 2 and record the remainder to the left of the first remainder.
3. Repeat step 2 until the number in the answer is either a 1 or a 0 and record it to the left of the last remainder.

For example, if you used the above procedure to convert the number 2,469 to a binary number, it would go like this:

1. 2,469 divided by 2 equals 1,234 with a remainder of 1
2. 1,234 divided by 2 equals 617 with a remainder of 0
3. 617 divided by 2 equals 308 with a remainder of 1
4. 308 divided by 2 equals 154 with a remainder of 0
5. 154 divided by 2 equals 77 with a remainder of 0
6. 77 divided by 2 equals 38 with a remainder of 1
7. 38 divided by 2 equals 19 with a remainder of 0
8. 19 divided by 2 equals 9 with a remainder of 1

9. 9 divided by 2 equals 4 with a remainder of 1
10. 4 divided by 2 equals 2 with a remainder of 0
11. 2 divided by 2 equals 1 with a remainder of 0
12. 1 divided by 2 equals 0 with a remainder of 1

If you now record the remainders beginning with step 1 and the remainder of each step to the left of the first one, you will get the binary value of 100110100101 or 2,469. If you want to verify this, use the Windows Calculator in its Scientific view. Click on the Dec button and enter the decimal value, then click on the Bin button to display the binary equivalent. I guess that's an even easier way to convert a binary number, isn't it?

Just for Fun

Some of the other names used for other binary words are listed in Table 3-2.

Binary Logic Operations

Processors use binary numbers for addressing, arithmetic, and to make comparisons, such as equal to, less than, greater than, not equal to, not less than, or not greater than. Beyond addressing (see Chapter 7) and arithmetic, a processor performs logical (comparison) and data shift operations using three functions: AND, OR, and EXCLUSIVE OR. These three binary functions are a part of *Boolean algebra,* which is used to test two values to produce a third.

AND Operations

The AND Boolean (pronounced boo-lee-un) algebra operation has a very simple set of rules:

- Only two truths equal a truth
- A false always makes a false

Size	Name(s)
2 bits	Crumb or tayste
5 bits	Nickel
10 bits	Deckel
16 bits	Playte or chawmp
32 bits	Dynner
48 bits	Gawble

Table 3-2. Other Binary Words

When this operation is used, which is called *anding*, two bit values are combined (compared) to produce a result. For example, if the two bit values are both 1s, the result is 1. The value 1 represents true. Applying the two rules, two 1s make a 1. The logic is this and that must be true. Trust me on this. However, if one of the bits contains a 0 (false), then one truth and one false would result in a false. This is the basic logic used in electronic logic circuits.

OR Operations

The OR Boolean algebra operations have only one rule: if either of two values is a 1 (true), then the result is a 1. The logic here is this or that can be true.

Exclusive OR Operations

An Exclusive OR (also known as an XOR) operation requires one, and only one, of the two bit operands to be true, exclusive of the other bit's value. So, in an XOR logical operation, if one and only one bit is true (1), then the pair results in a true. If both or neither of the bits is true, the result is false (0). Exclusive OR operations are used to produce the complement of a number.

The Hexadecimal System

Another number system that is also used with the PC to express large numbers and addresses: hexadecimal numbers. *Hexadecimal* means six and ten or a radix of 16. Hex, as it is commonly called, uses 16 values to express its values—the decimal numbers 0 through 9 and the six letters A through F to represent the decimal values of 11–15.

Hexadecimal numbers use four bits, or a nybble, to store each of its digits. In its four bits, a nybble can represent the decimal values 0 to 15 or the hexadecimal values 0 to F. Because of its larger radix (16), hexadecimal is able to store each of the values 11 through 15 as a single character.

The number 101, which is one hundred and one in decimal and five in binary, is now worth 257 in hexadecimal. This shows how well larger values are stored in hexadecimal. Another example is that the hexadecimal value ABCDEF is the equivalent of 11,259,375 in decimal. For more information on hexadecimal, see Chapter 2.

SEMICONDUCTORS

A microprocessor is constructed of layer upon layer of electronic circuits that are literally carved out of silicon. *Silicon* is a very commonly found element in the world. In fact, after oxygen, there is more silicon available than any other element, and you can find it easily on the beach in rocks and sand. However, the silicon used for manufacturing integrated circuits is found in white quartz.

Silicon is the primary building material used in manufacturing the electronic integrated circuits (chips) that are used to construct the processor and ultimately the computer. It is used in electronic circuits because it is an excellent semiconductor. A *semiconductor* is a material that is neither a conductor nor an insulator but can be chemically altered to be either one.

You may have noticed that many of the places where high-tech manufacturing companies are located have taken on nicknames like Silicon Valley (California), Silicon Alley (New York), and Silicon Glen (Scotland).

Conductors and Insulators

A material that is a *conductor* allows electrical current to pass through it. Without getting too technical, materials like copper, aluminum, or gold are good conductors of electricity because they have free electrons through which the current can pass.

On the other hand, a material that does not allow an electrical current to pass through it is called an *insulator*. Insulators like rubber, wood, or glass do not have many free electrons through which the current can pass.

Those materials that, depending on their chemical make-up, will or will not allow electricity to pass are called *semiconductors,* which means they can be altered chemically to be either a conductor or an insulator. Silicon is a semiconductor. However, when it is combined with phosphorus, it picks up some extra electrons and becomes a conductor; when it is combined with boron, which lacks electrons, it becomes an insulator. By mixing silicon with phosphorus or boron, it can be either a conductor or an insulator, which makes silicon the perfect material for transistors and other electronic components.

How an IC Is Made

The creation of a microchip is a very involved chemical process. If you want an excellent explanation and look at how an integrated circuit is manufactured, visit the "How Microchips are Made" Web site provided by the Intel Corporation at **www.intel.com/home/howto/basics/chips/**. However, here is a brief summary of what happens in this process:

1. A seed crystal is slowly dipped into a molten silicon bath. As it is slowly extracted, it grows into an ingot of pure silicon that is ground into a perfect cylinder. A very thin wafer is sliced from the cylinder and polished.
2. The wafer is exposed to some gases at very high heat. This allows a very thin layer of silicon dioxide, like rust on metal, to form on the wafer.
3. The wafer is coated with a chemical called *photoresist*, which is resistant to ultraviolet (UV) light, and then dried. The photoresist softens when exposed to UV light.
4. A stencil mask is placed over the wafer, and it is exposed to UV light. The parts of the wafer that are not shielded by the mask become soft and gooey. Solvent is used to remove the soft photoresist material, leaving behind the pattern created by the mask.
5. The exposed silicon diode is removed with other chemicals, which exposes the base silicon wafer in those places left open by the mask. The remaining

photoresist is removed, which leaves ridges of silicon diode where the mask shielded the wafer.

6. The wafer is covered with a layer of a conductive material called *polysilicon*, which is used to connect the layers of the circuit being developed.
7. Another layer of photoresist covers the wafer and is bathed in UV light through another mask. When the photoresist is removed, it exposes areas of the silicon diode and polysilicon.
8. The wafer is blasted with ions (charged atoms), a process called *doping*, which changes the exposed areas of the wafer to either conductors or insulators.
9. Steps 3 through 8 of this process are repeated as many as 20 times, depending on the complexity of the circuit, with small windows left open between the layers.
10. Metal is applied to the circuit, which flows down into the open windows and connects the layers.

The circuit wafer actually contains hundreds of separate circuits. The last step of the process is to cut the wafer into the microchips. The chips are then packaged with wiring to connect the chip to the pins (legs) of the packaging, and the integrated circuit (IC) is now ready for use.

For a more detailed explanation of how a microchip is manufactured, plus some other very good information about the history of integrated circuits, visit the **www.techweb.com/encyclopedia/** Web site and search for *chip*.

THE TRANSISTOR

The size of microprocessors, relative to their computing power, is shrinking every day. This is largely possible because of the technology advances that allow an increasing number of microscopic transistors to be placed closer together on a circuit. In the 1960s, the transistor paved the way for radios, calculators, and other electronic devices to become very small. Where the earliest computers filled up gymnasiums and had tens of thousands of vacuum tubes, today a billion transistors would fit into a single vacuum tube.

The *transistor* is the primary circuit in a microprocessor and is used in several different ways, but its basic function is to store the electrical voltage that represents one bit. A transistor works something like an electric light switch, in that it either has a high electrical charge (on) or a low electrical charge (off). However, unlike the light switch, the transistor has no moving parts; its charge is set electrically on or off to represent the 1s and 0s of binary values (see the section "Binary Data" earlier in the chapter).

The number of transistors included in its circuitry determines the capacity of the processor. Modern microprocessors include millions of transistors, which is the source of their computing power. For example, the Intel Pentium III contains nearly ten million transistors, and the processors used in larger mainframes and supercomputers have billions of transistors.

Storing Electricity

Transistors store a bit value as electrical voltage. The amount of electrical power used in a transistor is not very large. Most of the earliest microprocessors used 5 volts of direct current (DC), and the newer processors now use as little as 2.2 volts DC (VDC). A transistor stores data by switching between high and low voltage, which represents the binary 1s and 0s, respectively. For example, in a 5 VDC processor, a charge of +5 volts is the high voltage and represents a binary 1, and a charge of –5 volts is the low voltage and represents the binary 0.

One problem with using a higher voltage level to store a value in a transistor is that switching between these two voltage values, as much as 10 volts total, does take a certain amount of time. By reducing the voltage, to 2.2 VDC for instance, the range of change is smaller, it takes less time, and the microprocessor can do more.

By decreasing the voltage of a microprocessor from 5 VDC to as low as 2.2 volts, Intel and other manufacturers were able to dramatically increase the speed of their systems. Another benefit of reducing the voltage is that it reduces the amount of power needed to run the computer—very important for portable computers—and reduces the heat generated by all those transistors.

Integrated Circuit

I have used the term integrated circuit a few times in this chapter and it's time for a brief description of just what that is. An *integrated circuit (IC)* is a combination of electronic components, such as transistors, capacitors, and resistors. An IC is designed to fulfill some logical function and can be built to be a timer, counter, a bank of computer memory, or even a microprocessor.

The basic building block of an IC is a logic gate. A *logic gate* performs the Boolean algebra AND operation by testing two input signals (each stored in a transistor). If both are positive (representing true or 1), it sets the signal of a result value to positive. Otherwise, the value is set to negative (representing false or 0).

THE MICROPROCESSOR

The microprocessor is a multifunction integrated circuit that is, in essence, the computer. The processor, which is also called the central processing unit (CPU), is made up of several parts. These parts work together to carry out the instructions and actions that translate to a word processing system or a game on your PC.

The primary parts of the CPU, as illustrated in Figure 3-3, are as follows:

- **Control Unit (CU)** At the risk of being obvious, the control unit *controls* the functions of the CPU. It is kind of like the manager who coordinates the activities between the different parts of a factory. It tells the other parts of the CPU how to operate, what data to use, and where to put the results.

- **Protection Test Unit (PTU)** This part of the CPU works with the control unit to monitor whether or not functions are carried out correctly. It is like the quality control department of the CPU. If it detects something is not done properly, it generates an error signal.
- **Arithmetic and Logic Unit (ALU)** The ALU performs all of the calculations and comparative logic functions for the CPU, including all add, subtract, divide, multiply, equal to, greater than, less than, and other arithmetic and logic operations.
- **Floating Point Unit (FPU)** The FPU goes by several other names, including the math coprocessor, the numerical processing unit (NPU), and the numerical data processor (NDP). It handles all floating point operations for the ALU and CU. *Floating point* operations involve arithmetic on numbers with decimal places and high math operations like trigonometry and logarithms.
- **Memory Management Unit (MMU)** The MMU handles the addressing and cataloging of where data is stored in system memory. Whenever the CPU needs something from memory, it requests it from the MMU. The MMU manages memory segmentation and paging allocations and translates all logical addressing into physical addressing (see Chapter 7 for more information on memory addressing).
- **Bus Interface Unit (BIU)** The BIU supervises the transfer of data over the bus system between the other components of the computer and the CPU. It also serves as the interface point for the CPU and its external bus, as well as handling all data transfers out of the control unit.
- **The Prefetch Unit** This unit preloads the instruction registers of the CPU with instructions from memory whenever the BIU is idle. This allows the CPU to look ahead at future instructions. The prefetch unit does not analyze instructions, so on occasion it may bring in an unnecessary instruction because it assumes that the instructions will be carried out one after the other without branching or jumps.
- **Decode Unit** Many instructions are actually combinations of simpler instructions. The decode unit does just about what its name suggests. It decodes incoming instructions to their simplest form. While the prefetch unit retrieving more instructions, this unit decodes them to get them ready for the control unit.
- **Registers** Built into the CPU are a number of holding areas and buffers that are used to temporarily hold the data, addresses, and instructions being passed around between the CPU's components. These are the registers.

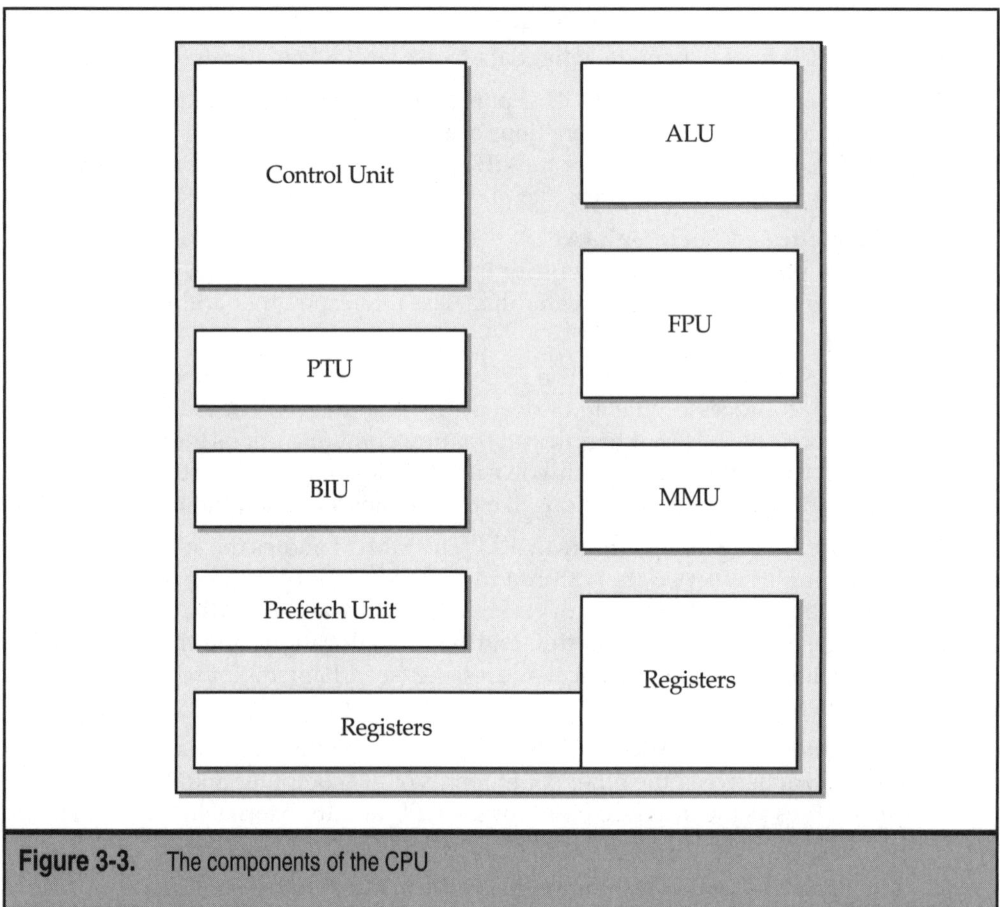

Figure 3-3. The components of the CPU

CPU's Bus System

The *bus,* as it relates to the pathways on the computer and in the processor, carries the various signals, addresses, and data (remember, *data* is plural) that are transferred around the computer between its components. Although quite dissimilar, it can be related to the routes of your local transit company in many ways.

On the computer, a bus structure is a group of electronic transmission lines that connect the various components of the CPU, motherboard, and expansion cards to each other. Bus structures have different sizes, ranging from 16 to 64 bits on modern microprocessors, and their size determines the amount of data that can be transmitted. Obviously, a 64-bit bus carries more data than a 16-bit bus.

Within the computer, there are several bus structures, as illustrated in Figure 3-4. The most important of these are as follows:

- **Data bus** Carries information to and from the CPU.

- **Address bus** Carries the address from where data is to be read to where data is to be written.
- **Control bus** Carries the signals used by the CPU and the other components of the computer to communicate with each other, including when data is ready to be read, when another device wishes to use the bus, and the type of operation to be performed (read, write, interrupt).

Packaging

When you look at a microprocessor, like the Pentium shown in Figure 3-5, it is the packaging that you see rather than the microprocessor itself that is packaged inside the ceramic or plastic outer shell.

The outer covering of the processor (see Figure 3-6), protects the core that contains the microchip and the wiring that connects the chip to the processor's pin grid array (PGA). The pins of the PGA are inserted into the mounting socket or the slot edge connectors. Older packaging designs were often in ceramic, which has excellent heat resistance and dissipation properties, but most of today's processors are mounted in plastic-encased SECC (single-edge contact cartridge) cards. SECC packaging features built-in mountings for a heat sink and a fan (which are used to cool the processor—more information on that in the next section), easy upgrading, and high-speed access by the motherboard to the CPU.

Cooling the Processor

Before the Intel 486, microprocessors were cooled largely by the airflow inside the case created by the system fan. This was called *radiant cooling*. Any heat radiated by the pro cessor was cooled by air being sucked into the system case by the fan in the power supply.

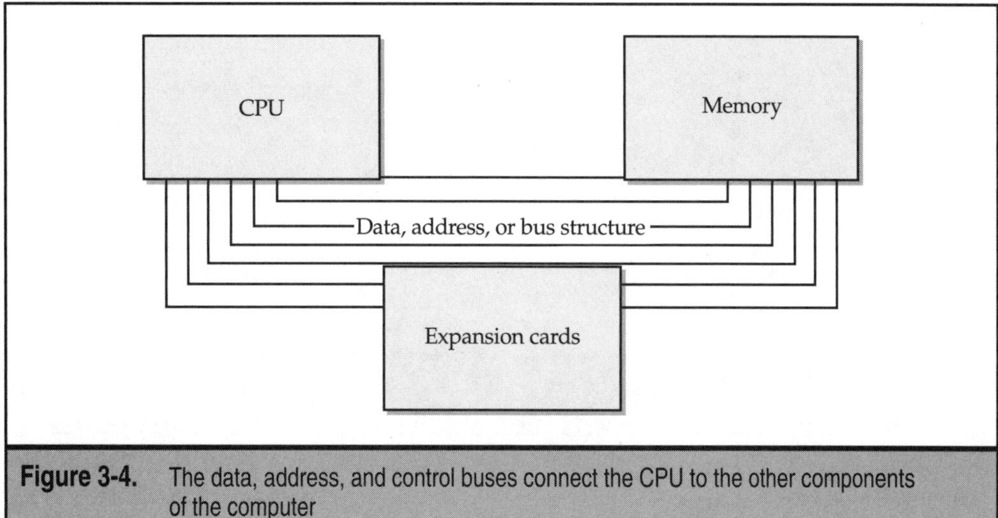

Figure 3-4. The data, address, and control buses connect the CPU to the other components of the computer

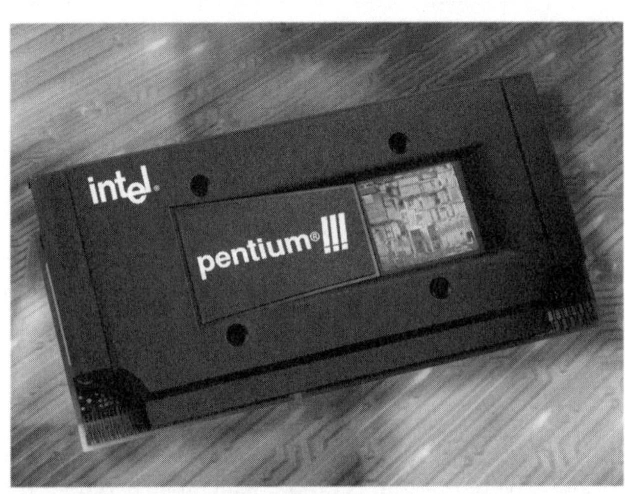

Figure 3-5. The packaging on a Pentium microprocessor. Photo courtesy of Intel Corporation.

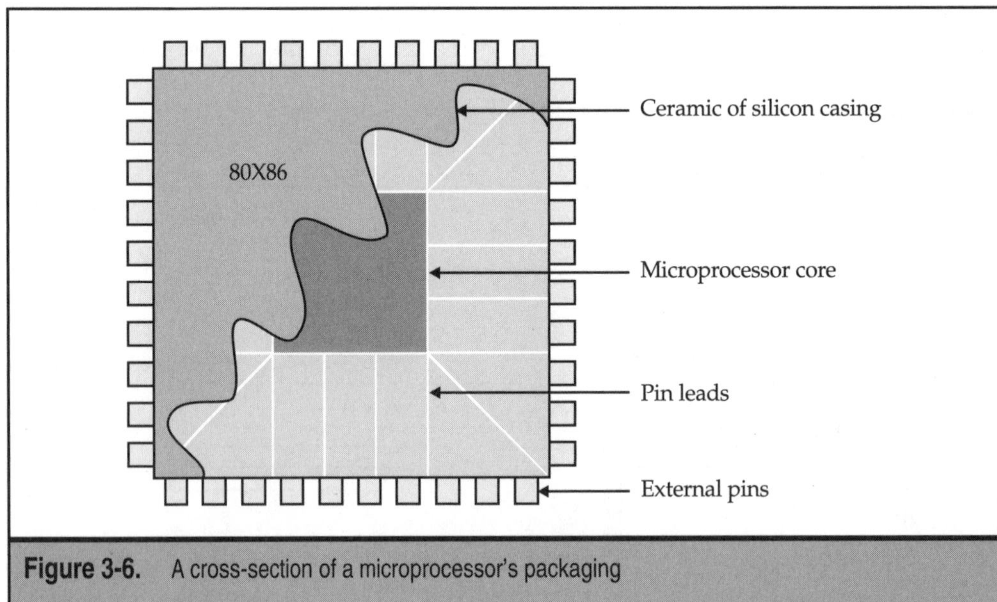

Figure 3-6. A cross-section of a microprocessor's packaging

Beginning with the 486, processors were cooled with a *heat sink* or *processor cooling fan* (see Figure 3-7) or both, attached directly to the surface of the processor. In addition, the system fan was reversed to extract the heated air from inside the computer case and force it out.

The Pentium processor is meant to operate at 185 degrees Fahrenheit (85 degrees Celsius). The Pentium III processor should operate at 100 degrees Celsius (about 212° Fahrenheit), which is pretty hot. It is very important that a processor's cooling system is kept at or near its designed operating temperature. At too-high operating temperatures, processors begin to perform poorly, shut down, or become permanently damaged. *Heat sinks*, like the one shown in Figure 3-8, and fans (see Figure 3-7) are designed to draw the heat up and out of the processor's packaging and carry it away on the tines of the heat sink and the airflow of the fan.

On the 486, Pentium, and Pentium Pro processors, heat sinks and fans are either clipped to the processor or attached with a dielectric gel, also called *thermal grease* or both. Later Pentium models, including the Celeron, the Pentium II, and the Pentium III, all of which use SECC (single-edge contact cartridge) packaging, include mounting points for fans and heat sinks as part of their design.

Commonly, the processor is not the only high-heat device inside the computer case. Other high-performance devices, such as accelerated video cards and high-speed hard disk drives, can also produce significant heat. Computer case designs should provide for enough ventilation to allow cool air to be drawn in and hot air to be expelled. Otherwise, the computer's lifespan will be dramatically shorter.

Figure 3-7. A cooling fan for a Pentium III microprocessor

Figure 3-8. A microprocessor heat sink

Sockets and Slots

Microprocessors are attached to the motherboard of the computer (see Chapter 4). There are two general types of mountings used to connect the processor onto the motherboard: sockets and slots. Some processors are available in only one mounting type; others, such as the Intel Celerons, are available with both types of mountings. Which type is used is largely a matter of preference on the part of the processor manufacturer. The two types look very different, but functionally their differences are small.

Socket Types

Here are ten of the most commonly used socket types:

- **Socket 0** A 168-pin inline-layout processor connector for 5V 486DX processors.
- **Socket 1** A 169-pin inline-layout processor connector for 5V 486DX and 486SX processors.
- **Socket 2** A 238-pin inline-layout processor connector for 5V 486DX, 486SX, and 486DX2 processors.
- **Socket 3** A 237-pin inline-layout processor connector supporting 3 and 5V 486DX, 486SX, 486DX2, and 486DX4 processors.

- **Socket 4** A 273-pin inline-layout processor connector supporting 5V Pentium 60 and Pentium 66 processors.
- **Socket 5** A 320-pin staggered-layout connector supporting early 3V Pentium processors.
- **Socket 6** A 235-pin inline-layout processor connector for 3V 486DX4 processors.
- **Socket 7** A 321-pin staggered-format socket created to support later Pentium processors. It used a common interface between the L2 cache bus and the main system bus. This common interface typically limited the bus's clock speed. AMD K6, Cyrix 6x86, and IDT processors also use this socket format. This design also provided for a Voltage Regulator Module to allow different voltage levels to be implemented by the socket (see Figure 3-9).
- **Super 7 Sockets** An extension of the Socket 7 design to support 100MHz bus speeds on AMD K6-2 and K6-3 processors allowing them to see an almost 50 percent increase in bandwidth and get around the limitations of the Socket 7.
- **Socket 8** A 386 pin staggered ZIF-socket format for the Pentium Pro processor.
- **Socket 370** The original Celeron main board connection. This supported the early Celerons in the Plastic Pin Grid Assembly (PPGA) format (see Figure 3-10).

Figure 3-9. A Socket 7 microprocessor socket

Figure 3-10. A Socket 370 mounting on a motherboard. Photo courtesy of AOpen America, Inc.

Slot Types

There are four types of slot mountings used to attach microprocessors to motherboards:

- **Slot 1 (SC-242 connector)** A proprietary Intel connector supporting Celeron SEPP, Pentium II SECC (single-edge contact cartridge), Pentium II SECC2, and Pentium III processors. It has a 242-pin edge interface and allows higher bandwidth than the original socket designs.
- **Slot 2 (SC-330 connector)** Another Intel processor bus connector style for the high performance Pentium II Xeon and Pentium III Xeon chips. These processors are designed for Symmetric Multiprocessing (multiple processors working together), and this slot style enhances this interaction.
- **Slot A** Used by the AMD Athlon processors. It is physically the same as a Slot 1 connector but has incompatible pin-outs.
- **Slot M** Connectors are planned for the upcoming 64-bit Intel Itanium processor.

The Evolution of the PC Microprocessor

Other manufacturers, such as AMD, VIA Cyrix, and others, make excellent processors, but Intel is by far the leading manufacturer of PC microprocessors. Intel has consistently set the standard by which all processors are measured.

Intel 8086 and 8088

In 1978, Intel introduced the 8086 microprocessor, which had a clock speed of 4.77MHz (megahertz). The *clock speed* of a processor is the speed at which the CPU operates. Clock speeds are rated in megahertz or millions of electronic cycles per second. A computer rated at 5MHz has five million processing cycles per second. The more cycles per second a computer supports, the more instructions it can execute. Remember that most instructions, because they include many processing steps, including memory transfers, ALU operations, etc., require more than a single CPU cycle to complete. The 8086 was capable of running about 0.33 MIPS (million of instructions per second). MIPS is a standard used to measure the processing power of a processor. The 8086 processor, which included 29,000 transistors, was a 16-bit processor (its data bus was 16-its wide) and had an address bus of 20-bits. It could address 1MB (megabyte) of memory, which was an incredible amount at the time. The 8086 was not a popular choice for PCs, but it did create a baseline for all future Intel 80x86 processors.

A year later, Intel reduced the data bus of the 8086 to eight bits and released the 8088 that still had a 20-bit address bus. In all other respects, the 8088 was a clone of the 8086, including the number of transistors and its clock speed. IBM chose to use the 8088 for its first personal computer, the IBM PC-XT.

As shown in Figure 3-11, the 8088 (and 8086) were packaged in a 40-pin dual inline package (DIP) integrated circuit. Figure 3-11 also shows how each of the pins was designated to a particular value or function. This is common on microprocessors and integrated circuits.

A second version of the 8088 was released later that added the Turbo feature and allowed the processor to run at two clock rates, the regular 4.77MHz and a new Turbo at 8MHz.

Intel 80286

Computer manufacturers largely skipped over the next Intel microprocessor generation, the 80186, to adopt the Intel 80286 (see Figure 3-12). IBM chose the 80286 for its next PC release, the PC AT. The 286 processor, as it was commonly known, was released in early 1982 with a 6MHz clock speed, 134,000 transistors, and nearly three times the power of the 8086 with 0.9 MIPS. The 286 was able to address 16MB of memory with its address bus expanded to 24 bits. Its data bus was also backward compatible to the 8086's original 16 bits. Later 286 versions had clock speeds of 10MHz and 12MHz.

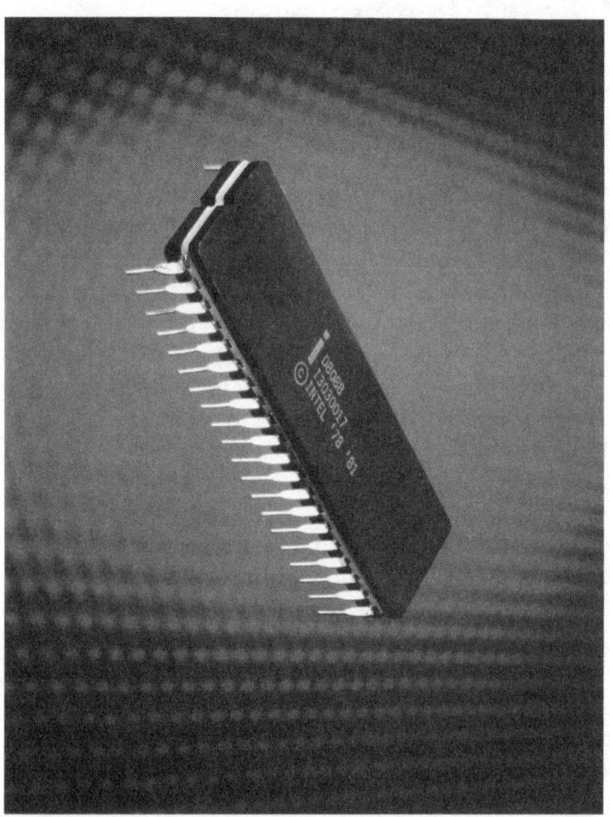

Figure 3-11. The Intel 8088 microprocessor. Photo courtesy of Intel Corporation

Intel 80386, 80386DX, and 80386SX

Intel released the 16MHz 80386, commonly called the 386, in 1985. The 386 microprocessor was a full 32-bit processor packaged in a 132-pin PGA package. The 386 had 275,000 transistors and had the clock speed to support over 5 MIPS.

While it had a 32-bit mode, which meant it was able to move data in bytes, 16-bit words, or 32-bit double words (or *dwords*). Two features provided by the 386 were improved virtual memory capabilities that allowed large amounts of memory to be temporarily stored on the hard disk and instruction pipelining, a process that preloads and pre-evaluates complex instructions, which results in faster processing speeds. The Intel 386 had versions with clock speeds ranging from 16MHz to 33MHz. However, other manufacturers, specifically AMD and Cyrix, had competing processor versions with speeds up to 40MHz.

Figure 3-12. The Intel 80286 microprocessor. Photo courtesy of Intel Corporation

The 386DX

The first of the 386 processors introduced by Intel was the 386DX. The 386 was a true 32-bit processor and included 32-bit internal registers, a 32-bit internal data bus, and a 32-bit external data bus. It was built with a new technology called VLSI (Very Large Scale Integration) with 275,000 transistors. The 386 used less power than its predecessors, including the 8086, because it was constructed of CMOS (Complementary Metal Oxide Semiconductor) materials, a way of manufacturing transistors that reduces the amount of power required when idle.

The 386DX could address up to 4 gigabits of system memory, but its built-in virtual memory management (VMM) system allowed VMM-enabled software access a virtual memory store of the equivalent of 64 terabytes (TB) of memory (a *terabyte* is a trillion bytes of memory).

The 386SX

Intel also released a lower-cost version of the 386 processor called the 386SX. The primary difference between the 386SX and the 386DX was that the SX model had only a 16-bit external data bus and a 24-bit address bus, which made it backward compatible to the 286 processor. The 386SX was released to fill a market need, which was a lower-priced processor with the power of the 386DX at the cost of the 286.

The 386SL

Intel released the 386SL, which was a 20MHz processor, in 1990. The SL version was similar to the 386SX, but it was specifically designed for portable computers, featuring improved power management functions.

Intel 80486DX and SX

Processors did not break the one million-transistor barrier until Intel released the 25MHz 486DX microprocessor in early 1989. This processor had over 1.2 million transistors and generated 20 MIPS. This processor also introduced a number of innovations, including the inclusion of processor cache (Level 1 cache) on the processor chip, the introduction of burst-mode memory access, and for the first time, an integrated math coprocessor. Before the 486DX, if a user wished to speed up the math functions on a PC, a separate math coprocessor had to be installed. The 486 was packaged in a 168-pin Ceramic Pin Grid Assembly (CPGA) package that required a processor-mounted fan to cool it. Processors before the 486DX had relied on the system fan in the PC's power supply for cooling.

As it had done with the 386, Intel released a 486SX model in 1991 to provide a low-cost processor. The primary difference between the DX and the SX models was that the SX model did not have a built-in math coprocessor.

Intel 80486DX2/DX4

The next model of the 486 was released in 1992 as the 80486DX2. The "2" designation referred to a technique called *overclocking* that allows a processor's clock speed to be doubled. The DX2 was first released as a 50MHz version, which doubled the DX's 25MHz bus speed, and was followed by a 66MHz version (33MHz bus times 2).

The 486DX4 was a product of overclocking as well. The 486 25MHz and 33MHz processors were overclocked to produce triple their normal clock speeds. This resulted in the DX4 processor available with 75MHz (25MHz times 3) and 100MHz (approximately 33MHz times 3) clock speeds.

Overclocking is the result of resetting a PC so its microprocessor runs at a higher clock speed than its manufacturer-specified speed. Although this sounds like it must be illegal, it is and can be done, especially on Intel processors, because Intel is more conservative in setting the labeled speed of its processors. If you'd like more information on overclocking, visit this Web site: **www5.tomshardware.com/guides/overclocking/**.

AMD 5x86

Intel did not have much competition until Advanced Micro Devices (AMD) released its 75MHz 5x86 microprocessor. The AMD 5x86 processors were compatible with 486 motherboards but had similar power to the early Pentium processors.

Cyrix 5x86

The Cyrix 5x86, also known as the M1SE, was intended to compete with the Intel 486 with which it was socket compatible. Like the AMD 5x86, the Cyrix processor was able to compete with early Pentium processors.

The Pentium

Although it was known in its early development as the 80586, by 1992, Intel had discovered that model numbers could not be copyrighted. So, instead of the number, they used a trademark name, Pentium, for their next processor. This new processor, shown in Figure 3-13, included many new features, including separate 8-bit caches for data and instructions and a very fast FPU. The Pentium kept the 32-bit address bus of the 486 but added a 64-bit data bus. It also included *superscalar* architecture, which is a processor technology that allows more than one instruction to be executed in a single clock cycle. The clock speeds of the Pentium processor ranged from 60MHz to 200MHz.

MMX Technology

The next version of the Pentium processor was the Pentium MMX, which had clock speeds from 166MHz to 233MHz. This version of the Pentium processor added MMX (Multimedia Extensions) technology to the Pentium along with some improved internal clock speeds. MMX technology is a set of instructions that uses matrix math (another meaning for MMX) to support graphic compression and decompression algorithms (such as JPEG, GIF, and MPEG) and 3D graphic renderings. MMX allows the FPU to act on several pieces of data simultaneously through a process called SIMD (single instruction multiple data).

Cyrix 6x86 Processors

Cyrix, which is now VIA Cyrix, produced a family of Pentium clone processors that were designated as the 6x86-P series. The "P" value in the model name was a performance rating indicator. The 6x86-P200 indicated that the Cyrix processor with that model number had the performance equivalent of a Pentium 200MHz processor. Cyrix produced models ranging from its 6x86-P120 to the 6x86-P200. The 6x86-P series had overheating problems as well as some incompatibility issues, which prompted Cyrix to produce a low-power, low-temperature version, the 6x86L.

Other Pentium Clones

Two other manufacturers produced processors to compete with the Pentium. The AMD K5 processor, with versions of 75MHz to 166MHz, unfortunately suffered from its own complexity, which affected its processing speeds. The Integrated Device Technology

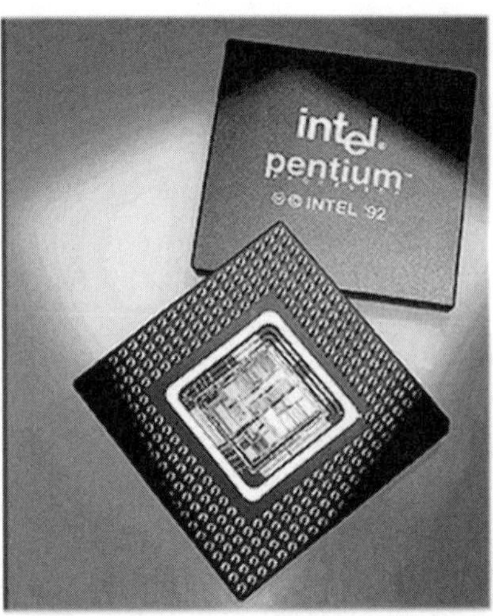

Figure 3-13. The Pentium microprocessor. Photo courtesy of Intel Corporation

(IDT) Centaur WinChip C6 includes MMX extensions, has a large L1 cache, and is less expensive than the 200MHz Pentium MMX. The WinChip C6, which is popular outside of the U.S., is available in 180MHz to 240MHz versions. Of the MMX clones, the WinChip C6 is the one most similar to the Intel Pentium MMX in capability and speed.

Intel Pentium Pro

Shown in Figure 3-14, the Pentium Pro, the next in the Pentium line, was developed as a network server processor. To support the demands put on a network server, the Pentium Pro has 1 megabit of advanced second level (L2) cache. The Pentium Pro 200MHz version was specially designed to support 32-bit network operating systems, such as Windows NT, and to be used in configurations of one, two, or four processors.

The Pentium II

The Pentium II, shown in Figure 3-15, is the Intel Pentium Pro with MMX technology added. The PII, as it is commonly referred to, is available with clock speeds of 233MHz, 266MHz, and 300MHz. It is excellent for multimedia reproduction that requires support for full-motion video and 3D images.

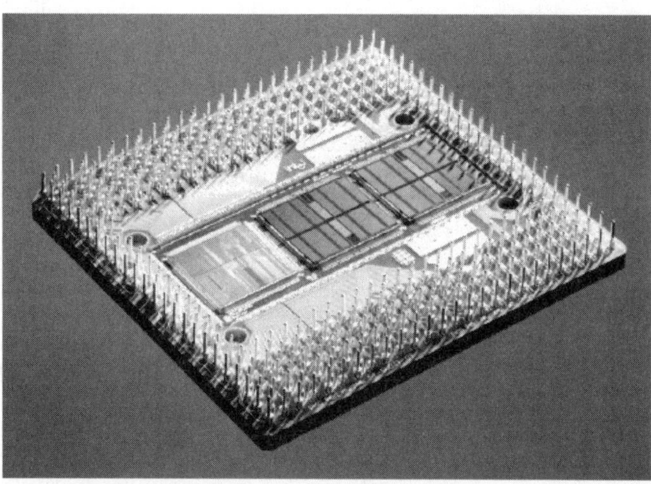

Figure 3-14. The Intel Pentium Pro microprocessor. Photo courtesy of Intel Corporation

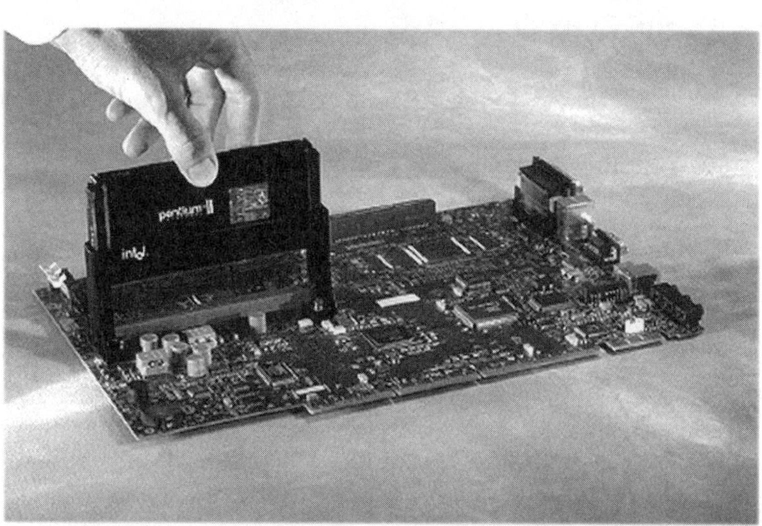

Figure 3-15. The Intel Pentium II microprocessor in the Slot 1 package. Photo courtesy of Intel Corporation

Celeron

Developed from use in desktop and portable computers, the Celeron microprocessor, shown in Figure 3-16, is the low-cost model of the Pentium II processor series. It features two choices for mountings, the Pentium II's Slot 1 and a socket style named after the number of pins in use, Socket 370, shown in Figure 3-16. The Celeron is released in versions with clock speeds of 333MHz to 500MHz, with newer models, built on the Pentium III core, to offer clock speeds of 566MHz or faster.

Xeon

Figure 3-17 depicts the Pentium II Xeon processor, which is the successor to the Pentium Pro as a network server processor. To enhance its ability as a network server microprocessor, the Xeon features a range of L2 cache size choices, ranging from 512K, 1MB, and 2MB. The Xeon is capable of addressing and caching up to 64GB of memory with its 36-bit memory address bus. The PII Xeon can be configured with four to eight CPUs in one server.

AMD K6

Developed to compete with the Pentium MMX, the AMD K6 outperforms it in speed and price. It is available in 166MHz, 200MHz, 233MHz, 266MHz versions, and a 300MHz model that mounts in a Super 7 socket.

Cyrix 6x86MX and Cyrix III

Also known as the MII, the Cyrix 6x86MX processor contains an MMX instruction set. The 6x86 MX has a performance rating (PR) of P-166 to P-366. Cyrix, which is now owned by VIA Technologies, now also offers the 6x86 in a P-433 version as well.

The Cyrix III microprocessor (see Figure 3-18) runs at clock speeds of 433, 466, 500, and 533MHz. It supports Intel's MMX and 3DNow, the AMD equivalent of multimedia extensions. The Cyrix III processor, technically the VIA Cyrix III, is the equivalent of an Intel Pentium II Celeron processor.

AMD K6-2 and K6-III Processors

To compete with the MMX technology of the Pentium processors, the AMD K6-2 processor, shown in Figure 3-19, has an added 3DNow, a set of 3D graphic instructions that extend the MMX instructions already incorporated into the K6 design. The K6-2 processors are available with clock speeds from 266MHz to 550MHz. A newer model of the AMD K6 line is the K6-2+, which has additional L2 cache on the processor chip and some new power control features.

The K6-III processor features 256K of L2 cache and clock speeds from 400MHz to 600MHz. A newer model, the K6-III+ includes 1MB of cache and runs at the clock speeds of the K6-III.

Figure 3-16. The Intel Celeron microprocessor in the Socket 370 configuration. Photo courtesy of Intel Corporation

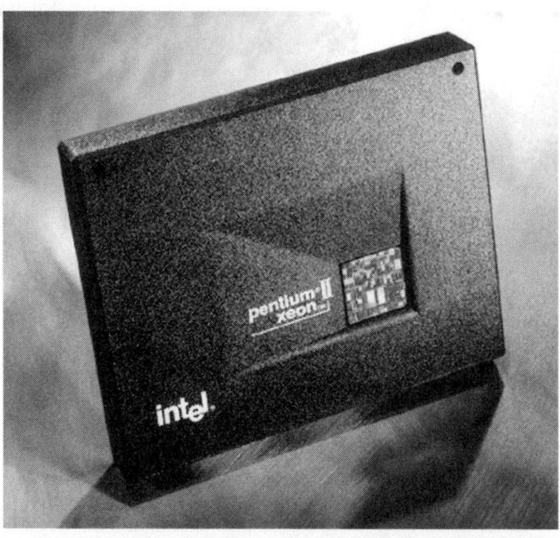

Figure 3-17. The Intel Pentium II Xeon processor. Photo courtesy of Intel Corporation

Figure 3-18. The VIA Cyrix III microprocessor. Photo courtesy of VIA Technologies, Inc.

Intel Pentium III

The Pentium III processor features 9.5 million transistors, a 32K L1 cache, and 512K of L2 cache. The Pentium III is available with clock speeds of 450MHz to 1GHz and is packaged in a second-generation single-edge connector package called the SECC2, shown in Figure 3-20. The SECC2 package, which fits into the Slot 1 bus, is designed to conduct and remove heat better than earlier single-edge packages.

Figure 3-19. The AMD K6 Processor. Photo courtesy of Advanced Micro Devices, Inc.

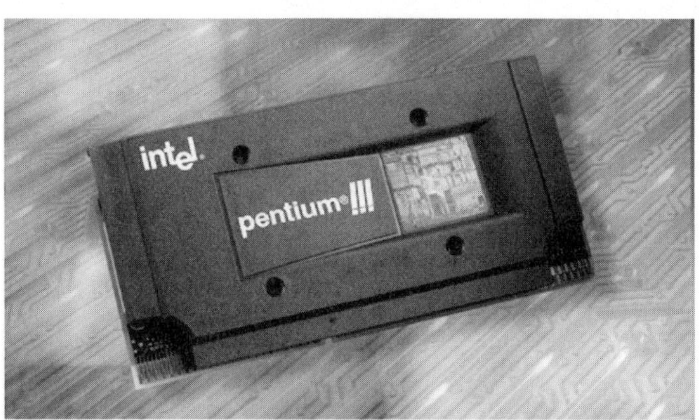

Figure 3-20. The Pentium III processor in the Slot 1 SECC2 package. Photo courtesy of Intel Corporation

Most motherboards that support a Pentium II processor can be upgraded to a Pentium III; however, it may require a flash BIOS (see Chapter 4) upgrade. A newer version of the PIII, which sports 256K of L1 cache and a 133MHz bus speed is to be packaged in the less expensive Slot 370-like FC-PGA (Flip Chip-Pin Graphics Assembly) (see Figure 3-21).

Figure 3-21. The Pentium III in the FC-PGA socket package. Photo courtesy of Intel Corporation

AMD Athlon

The honor of having the new powerhouse processor may have moved to AMD with the release of its 1GHz AMD Athlon, pictured in Figure 3-22. The Athlon boasts 22 million transistors, support for Intel's MMX and AMD's 3DNow, and improved FPU functions. It also has the power to decode more instructions simultaneously than the Pentium III, with 256KB of L2 cache and 128KB of L1 cache on the chip. The Athlon is plug compatible with the Slot 1 connector, but it is designed for AMD's Slot A bus, which runs at bus speeds of 200MHz to 400MHz.

A derivative of the Athlon is the AMD Duron. The AMD Duron processor is designed for general computing, including business, home user, and portable applications. The Duron processor is available at clock speeds of 600MHz, 650MHz, and 700MHz.

Intel Pentium 4

The latest of the Intel processors is the Intel Pentium 4 (Figure 3-23), which is available with processor speeds of 1.3 to 1.5 GHz (gigahertz). The Pentium 4 uses a new proprietary micro-architecture called Net-Burst, which features a 400 MHz system bus, advanced on-board caching, enhanced floating point math and multimedia support, and hyper-pipelining technology. The Pentium 4 also supports the use of dual-channel RDRAM.

Figure 3-22. The AMD Athlon microprocessor. Photo courtesy of Advanced Micro Devices, Inc.

Figure 3-23. The Pentium 4 microprocessor. Image courtesy of Intel Corporation

CHAPTER 4

Motherboards

The motherboard is easily the most important part of the computer. Although there are a number of components that a PC cannot function without, it's the motherboard that ties them all together and turns them into a personal computer.

The *motherboard*, or mainboard, of a PC is a large printed circuit board that is home to many of the most essential parts of the computer, including the microprocessor, chipset, cache, memory sockets, expansion bus, parallel and serial ports, mouse and keyboard connectors, and IDE, EIDE, or SCSI controllers, among other components of the PC. The motherboard binds the PC's operational components together. Even devices like printers, hard disks, CD-ROMs, and the like, either connect to or are controlled by the devices or controllers on the motherboard.

There is a wide variety of shapes, sizes, and types of motherboards available. There is at least one motherboard design from at least one manufacturer to fit just about every PC still running. Manufacturers attempt to set their motherboards apart from the others and to increase their value by incorporating more or fewer controllers, expansion buses, processor sockets, external connectors, and memory slots. As a consumer of PC motherboards, this is to your benefit because there is a very wide range of motherboards with a long list of features that will fit into an even wider range of PCs. This wide range of selection is also the bad news. If you don't do your homework before buying a new motherboard, you can end up with lower quality components than you may desire.

In most situations, a motherboard is just something that comes with the computer. More often than not, a completely new PC is purchased instead of the motherboard being upgraded. However, as I will discuss later in this chapter, the standards that have emerged for motherboards provide a lower-cost path to upgrading a PC's performance and power.

MOTHERBOARD DESIGNS

Not all motherboards are created equal. To begin with, two different design approaches are used for PC mainboards: the motherboard style and the backplane style.

Motherboards

A *motherboard* (also known as a mainboard, system board, or a planar) aggregates all of the PC's primary system components on a single printed circuit board (PCB). In the motherboard's single board design, all of the PC's electronic circuitry that provides the conduit through which all operations flow is located on the motherboard.

Backplanes

Backplane-style mainboards are less popular today than they were in the mid- to late 1980s, but they are still around. Backplane mainboards are common in large PC network servers and on other computers on which the processor is upgraded frequently.

In its basic form, a *backplane* mainboard contains very little in the way of intelligence and storage capabilities. It is merely a receptacle board into which processor cards, memory cards, and other component boards are inserted to add capability to a PC. This type of backplane board is called a *passive backplane*. Processor cards, containing the CPU and its support chips, and I/O (input/output) cards, with bus and device interfaces, which are referred to as *daughterboards*, are plugged into open slots on the backplane board. The backplane provides the bus and data buffering that interconnects the daughterboards. The passive backplane design is popular on network servers because it is easily upgraded or repaired. With this type of mainboard, a server can be back online much quicker since typically only a single card needed to be replaced, instead of an entire mainboard!

The other type of backplane is the *active backplane*. This mainboard design is also referred to as an intelligent backplane because it adds capability to the main backplane board to help speed up processing. The CPU, controllers, and other components are still on their own daughterboards. Actually, this type of backplane is being replaced by newer motherboards that have Slot 1 or Slot 2 sockets for Pentium II and Pentium III Xeon processors. The motherboard is much like the active backplane with the PII and PIII Singe Edge Connector packaging acting much like a daughterboard, which also offers the same utility and advantage of the active backplane.

In this book, whenever I refer to the mainboard, the system board, or the motherboard, I will be referring to the motherboard type of PC mainboard. When I am discussing a backplane board, which I rarely do, I will specifically say so.

MOTHERBOARD FORM FACTORS

The original IBM PC desktop computer, which was introduced in 1981, had a simple motherboard (compared to today's designs) that featured an 8-bit processor (the Intel 8088), five expansion slots, a keyboard connector, memory banks for 64K to 256K of RAM, a chipset, a BIOS ROM chip, and a cassette tape I/O adapter. The layout and size of the IBM PC's system case controlled the size of its motherboard and set the first form factor. Essentially, a *form factor* defines a motherboard's size, shape, and how it is mounted to the case. However, form factors now include the size, shape, and function of the system case; the type, placement, and size of the power supply; the system's power requirements; the location and type of external connectors, and the case's airflow and cooling systems. Table 4-1 lists the more common PC form factors used in PCs.

In case you are wondering why Apple Computer motherboards aren't listed, Apple was never an *open architecture*, which means that its designs weren't shared with other manufacturers. Apple motherboards only worked in Apple computers and each successive model of the Apple II and Macintosh computers had its own distinctive motherboard. Apple computers may have had form factors, but they were not industry standards.

Form Factor	Width (in inches)	Length (in inches)	Design Type	Case Type
IBM PC	8.5	13	Motherboard	IBM PC
IBM PC XT	8.5	13	Motherboard	IBM PC XT
AT	12	11-13	Motherboard	AT Desktop or Tower
Baby AT	8.5	10-13	Motherboard	Baby AT Desktop or Tower
LPX	9	11-13	Backplane	Low profile
Micro-AT	8.5	8.5	Motherboard	Baby AT Desktop or Tower
ATX	12	9.6	Motherboard	ATX Desktop or Tower
Mini-ATX	11.2	8.2	Motherboard	Smaller ATX Desktop
Mini-LPX	8-9	10-11	Backplane	Low profile
Micro-ATX	9.6	9.6	Motherboard	Low profile
NLX	8-9	10-13.6	Backplane	Low profile
Flex-ATX	9	7.5	Motherboard	Flexible design

Table 4-1. Motherboard Form Factors

The IBM PC XT

The successor to the IBM PC was the IBM PC XT (Extended Technology). The motherboard of the PC XT was about the same size, but it included three more expansion slots (eight compared to five) and replaced the cassette tape with a 5.25-inch floppy disk drive.

The IBM PC AT

IBM next introduced its 16-bit PC AT (Advanced Technology) that included enough additional circuitry that its motherboard (and case) was expanded in size. It was also the size, shape, and mounting placements of the AT's case that was chosen by clone manufacturers for their XT-upgrade motherboards. The popularity of the AT established it as the first real motherboard form factor standard.

The Baby AT Form Factor

Following the success of the IBM PC AT, clone manufacturers began releasing their own 16-bit PCs. Higher integration technology reduced the space required by support chipsets and circuits allowing for a smaller motherboard. This smaller motherboard, which trimmed 3.5 inches off the width and as much as two inches off the height, became known as the Baby AT, shown in Figure 4-1. The Baby AT, so called because it would mount in AT cases using the AT form factor's mountings, became very popular because of its flexibility and quickly surpassed the AT as the form factor of choice. Most of the computer cases manufactured between 1984 and 1996 were Baby AT form factors.

Figure 4-1. The Baby AT motherboard

Micro-AT Form Factor

Further high-scale integration of processor chipsets and supporting components lead to the development of a motherboard size even smaller than the Baby AT. The Micro-AT motherboard, which fit in both the AT and Baby AT system cases, was nearly half the size of the Baby AT main board.

LPX and Mini-LPX Specifications

The LPX and Mini-LPX motherboard specifications are not actually form factors because they lack a specific motherboard standard; they are more of a general motherboard design. Originally developed by Western Digital as a part of their effort to slim down computer cases, the LPX and Mini-LPX have been copied by many other companies, each giving the design their own variation of the original specification. Packard Bell and Compaq, among other computer manufacturers, have used their own proprietary configurations of the LPX or Mini-LPX motherboards in their PCs. Because there is no industry-wide standard for this board, the users who purchase these systems could not upgrade their PCs without changing out the motherboard.

A daughterboard (riser board) that plugs into a mounting slot that runs down the middle of the motherboard characterizes the LPX-style motherboard. The daughterboard contains two or three peripheral expansion slots, depending on the size of the daughterboard and whether it has slots on both sides. Because the expansion cards are mounted sideways on the daughterboard, less space is required and the case size is smaller.

The LPX-style also integrates device controllers on the motherboard, including controllers for IDE (Integrated Drive Electronics), video, and sound devices. This also helps to reduce the case size by reducing the number of expansion slots required on the daughterboard.

The external connections on the LPX-style boards are mounted in a row (see Figure 4-2). This allows for easy access to keyboard and mouse connectors, serial ports, parallel ports, and video and audio connectors. Some LPX versions also include USB (Universal Serial Bus) connectors or an onboard NIC (network interface card).

In spite of the fact that many of the LPX motherboard's design features were very innovative, the lack of a standard form factor that would allow for easy upgrade made it unattractive to users. However, the best innovations of the LPX were incorporated into the next-generation form factors, the ATX and NLX boards, which are discussed in the following sections.

ATX Form Factor

The ATX form factor, released by Intel in 1995, was an improvement over the LPX form factor because it is a published and continuously maintained specification for motherboards, cases, and power supplies. All ATX cases and boards are guaranteed compatibility among all adopters of the standard.

The ATX form factor is generally based on the smaller Baby AT motherboard size. However, size is about the only thing they have in common. ATX is a completely new design

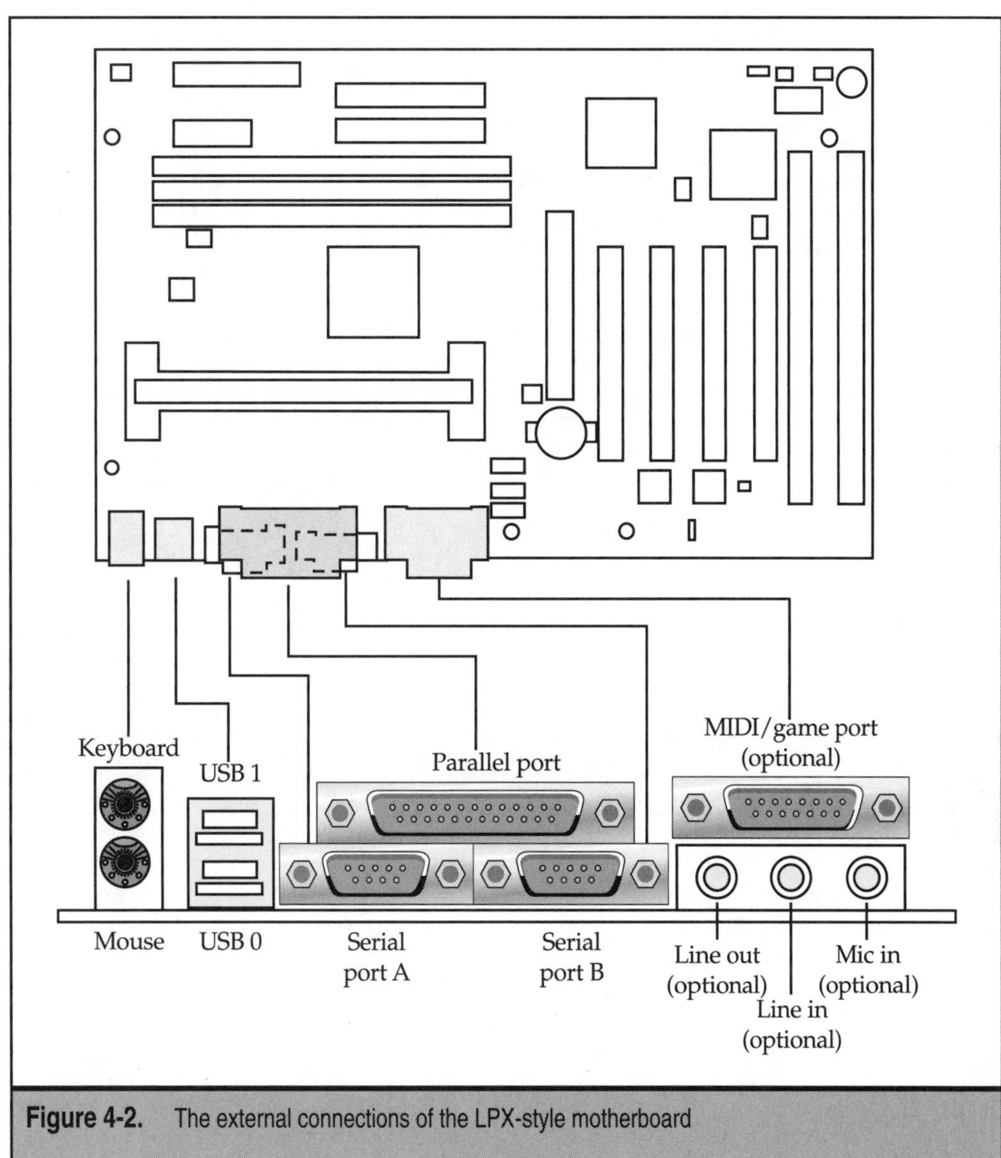

Figure 4-2. The external connections of the LPX-style motherboard

that rotates the motherboard's orientation by 90 degrees and incorporates a new set of mounting locations and power connections. All of the I/O connections on an ATX motherboard are in a two-row block on the back of the PC.

The standard placement of the I/O connectors on an ATX motherboard is shown in Figure 4-3. The top row includes a PS/2-type keyboard or mouse connector, a parallel

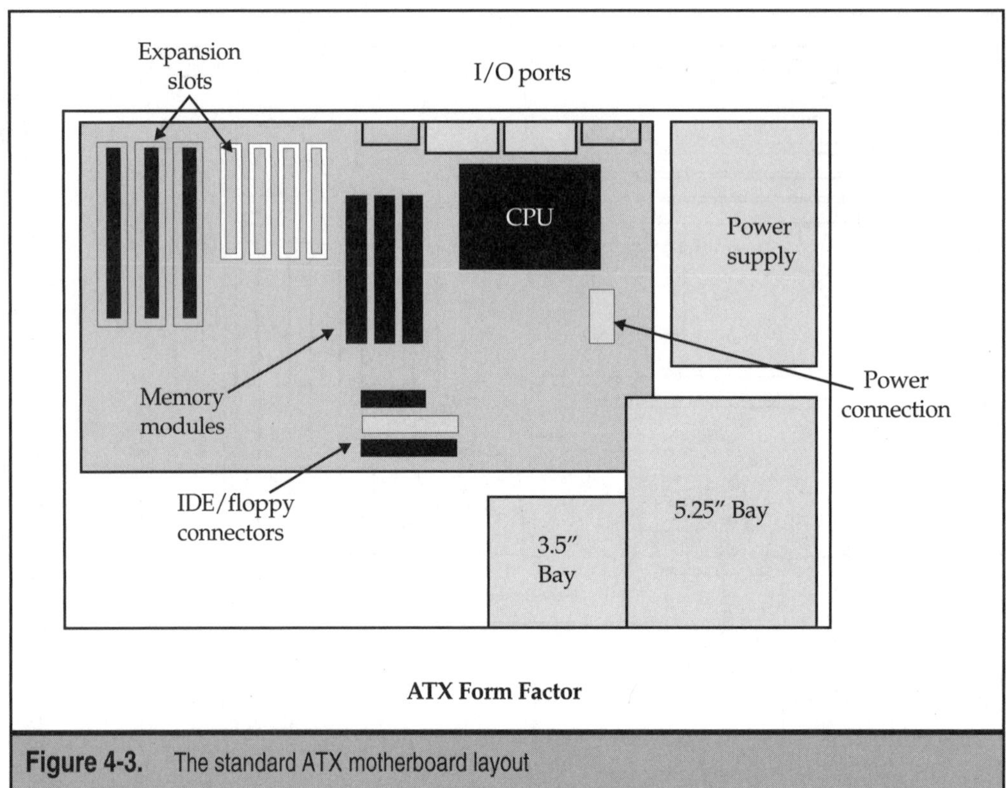

Figure 4-3. The standard ATX motherboard layout

port, and a blank slot that could be used for a second parallel port. The bottom row includes a second PS/2-type keyboard or mouse connector, two serial ports, and a series of blank ports that might be used for sound or video card connectors. The defined size of the connector area on an ATX motherboard is small (6.25 inches by 1.75 inches), which helps eliminate the clutter of cables found near the rear panel of a Baby AT motherboard.

The ATX form factor is a result of the lessons learned from Baby AT and LPX motherboards. The ATX locates the CPU and RAM mountings away from the expansion cards and close to the power supply fan, as shown in Figure 4-3. This arrangement improves the airflow available to cool the CPU and RAM chips. Originally, the ATX specification had the power supply's fan pulling air into the case, over the CPU, and out the vents on the case, in an effort to eliminate the need for a separate CPU fan. This design resulted in dust and other airborne particles (like chalk dust, metal filings, and more) being pulled into the case and settling inside. Instead of eliminating fans, the result was that the case actually required additional fans to cool the CPU properly, not to mention clogged up and shorted out PCs. Newer ATX versions now have the fan venting the case. The ATX design also allows for additional case fans, which are recommended for PCs with 3D video accelerators, other high-heat producing cards, or multiple hard disk drives.

Figure 4-4. An ATX motherboard. Photo courtesy of AOpen America, Inc.

The ATX design (see Figure 4-4) also incorporates a number of features into the power supply. The power on and off functions can be controlled by the motherboard, a feature called *soft switching*. Power supply connectors are a one-piece keyed fit that cannot be connected incorrectly, preventing the possibility of a fried motherboard and personal injuries. The ATX power supply also supplies *split voltage*, which is a range of voltages, usually 12v, 5v, and 3.3v, to the motherboard, eliminating the need for a voltage regulator on the motherboard.

Mini-ATX

A subspecification of the ATX spec is the mini-ATX. Despite its name, this form factor is only slightly smaller than the ATX form. Other subspecifications of the ATX form factor you may encounter are the Micro-ATX and the Flex-ATX.

NLX Form Factor

A new standardized form factor is the NLX low-profile motherboard, shown in Figure 4-5. This board design supports many current and emerging technologies as well as support for AGP (Accelerated Graphics Port) video adapters and tall memory modules. The design goals of the NLX form are easy removal and replacement of the motherboard without tools and to provide more flexibility for system-level functions. The NLX uses the backplane design approach that includes a riser board for expansion cards.

Figure 4-5. An NLX motherboard and riser board. Photo courtesy of Intel Corporation

A consortium of computer and component manufacturers developed the NLX specification. This standard is published for all to use. The hope is that by sharing information, the problems associated with the LPX form factor can be avoided.

There were three primary focuses of the NLX standard: processor and system cooling, the number of connectors for multimedia hardware, and reducing the clutter of interior cables. The NLX specification features a redesigned airflow for its slim line case. The size and high operating temperatures of newer and more powerful microprocessors and high-performance graphics adapters necessitated a new approach to the cooling system of the PC case. The NLX also addresses the requirement from multimedia systems for additional I/O connectors on the motherboard and the need to reduce the cable clutter in the system case that impedes repairs and upgrades.

THE COMPONENTS OF THE MOTHERBOARD

The motherboard is the foundation on which a PC is built. It provides the interconnecting circuitry through which the primary components of the motherboard receive their power and pass control signals, data, addresses, and instructions to each other. In short, with a microprocessor installed on the motherboard, it is essentially the computer. Figure 4-6 shows where the major components are found on a typical motherboard.

Figure 4-6 identifies each of the following major parts of the motherboard:

- **CPU slot and socket** The CPU mounts to the motherboard through either a slot or socket mounting. See Chapter 3 for information on CPU mountings.
- **Chipset** Many of the circuit and CPU level functions are contained in the chipset. See Chapter 5 for information on chipsets.
- **Memory sockets** Depending on the age of the PC, its memory is mounted on the motherboard as individual memory chips that fit into separate DIP (dual inline packaging) sockets or as memory modules, such as a SIMM (single inline memory module) or a DIMM (dual inline memory module), that snap into edge connector mountings. See Chapter 7 for more information on memory systems.
- **BIOS ROM** The BIOS (Basic Input/Output System) is stored as firmware on a read-only memory (ROM) chip. The BIOS is used to start the PC up when the power is turned on and provides a link for the CPU to the PC's peripheral devices. See Chapter 6 for more information on PC BIOS.

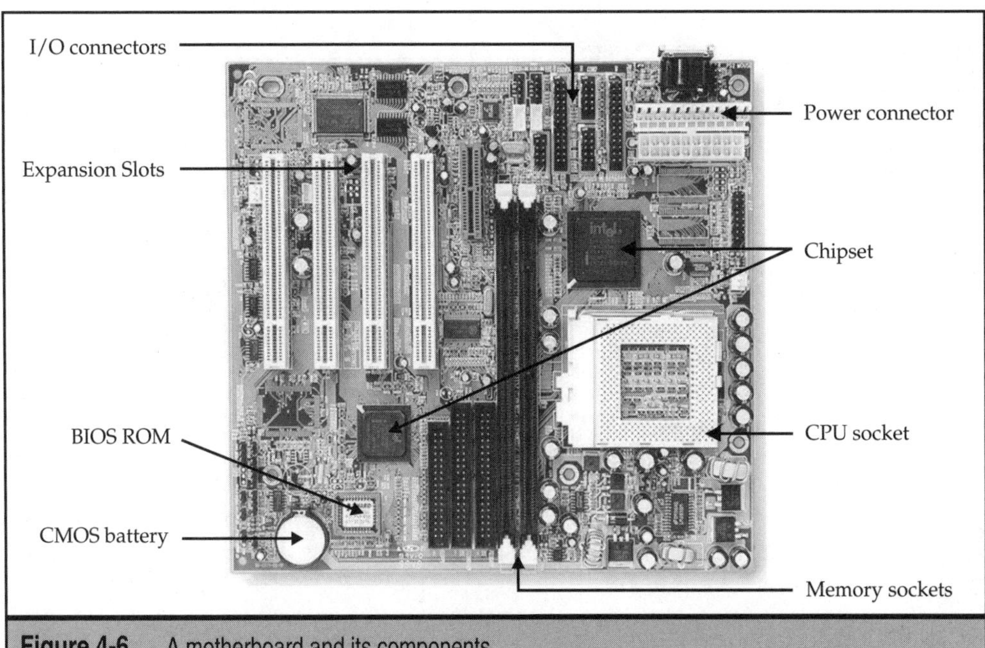

Figure 4-6. A motherboard and its components

- **CMOS battery** The configuration of a PC at the systems level is stored in a type of memory, CMOS (Complementary Metal Oxide Semiconductor), that requires very little power to hold its contents. The CMOS battery supplies a steady power source to store the system configuration for use during the PC's boot sequence. See Chapter 6 for more information on the BIOS and the information stored in CMOS.
- **Power connector** A connection must be made to the power supply so that power is available to the circuitry on the motherboard. Motherboards use different voltages of power for different components on the board. See Chapter 14 for more information on the power supply and the voltage requirements of the PC.
- **I/O connectors** The motherboard includes a variety of external I/O connectors that allow external devices to communicate with the CPU. See Chapter 19 for information on the ports and connectors found on the motherboard and PC.
- **Expansion slots** External peripherals and internal devices are interconnected into the motherboard and CPU through the expansion bus. The motherboard features a variety of expansion slots that usually include three or more of the different expansion buses available. See Chapter 11 for more information on the expansion buses and expansion cards.

UPGRADING A MOTHERBOARD

If your old PC isn't quite as fast or as powerful as your friends' computers and you'd really like to move up, you have two choices: buy a whole new computer or upgrade the motherboard (and possibly some of your PC's peripheral devices). Depending on the upgrade you do, in general, upgrading your motherboard and CPU will cost you a whole lot less than a brand new computer. The cost may not be the deciding factor though; you may just want to upgrade for the fun and satisfaction of doing it.

Here is a list of the critera you should consider when evaluating your PC and deciding how to upgrade it:

- **The CPU** Which CPU you use with your current motherboard depends mostly on the motherboard itself. While nearly all motherboards can be upgraded with a new processor and chipset, exactly which CPU and chipset is totally dependent on the configuration of the motherboard. If you have a Pentium 75 MHz processor and wish to move up to a Pentium III Xeon, you can count on replacing the motherboard and CPU and perhaps the power supply and more. However, if you merely want to step up to the next level of processor, as long as the processor you wish to move to is within the specification of the motherboard, the move should be fairly effortless. There are some processors, such as the

Pentium Pro and Pentium II processors, which have unique motherboard configurations and aren't typically compatible with other Pentium-based motherboards. Check your motherboard's documentation or check with your PC's manufacturer to be sure of your choices.

- **Sockets and slots** Most upgrade and third-party motherboards have at least one ZIF (zero insertion force) socket. The most common socket style on newer computers is the Socket 7 mounting, although processors in the SEC (Single-Edge Connector) packaging have either a Slot 1 or Slot 2 type processor connection. The specifications for the CPU you wish to move up to should specify its socket or slot requirements. Trust me, you won't confuse a socket for a slot mounting. See Chapter 3 for more information on processors and their mountings.
- **Bus speed** The bus speed supported on a motherboard must be matched to the processor. There is usually a direct relationship between the processor speed and the motherboard speed. In addition to the processor, most of the other motherboard components, and especially the cache memory, must also be matched to the maximum allowable motherboard speed.
- **Cache memory** While virtually all Pentium motherboards have between 256K to 512K of Level 2 cache memory on the board, most Pentium Pro and higher processors also include Level 2 cache on the chip. Additional Level 2 cache can be added to the motherboard to improve performance. In fact, on Pentium II processors and above, most motherboards already have this cache. If you wish to add cache to your motherboard, remember that it must be matched to the motherboard's bus speed.
- **Memory modules** All Pentium and higher motherboards use either the 72-pin SIMM (Single Inline Memory Module) or the 168-pin DIMM (Dual Inline Memory Module). DIMMs can be installed individually, but, because of the 64-bit buses on these motherboards, 72-pin SIMMs must be installed in matched pairs. Before you start cramming memory modules into open slots, verify the total amount of memory supported by your motherboard and the type of memory supported by the processor and chipset.
- **Expansion bus** Consider your current expansion cards and what controllers or adapters may be built into your new motherboard. You will need to match your expansion card needs to the number of bus slots available on the motherboard. If your new motherboard has only one PCI slot and you need three, there is no retrofit to help you. Here's a tip on expansion slots on generic motherboards: make sure that none of the expansion slots, when occupied, block access to a memory socket, the ROM BIOS, the password-clear jumper, or the CMOS battery. This can be a hassle later for maintenance or repair.

- **BIOS** The motherboard should use an industry-standard BIOS such as those from AMI, Phoenix, or Award. Preferably, the BIOS chip should be the flash ROM (EEPROM) type. If you have the choice, choose a BIOS that supports Plug and Play (PnP), Enhanced IDE, and Fast ATA. A BIOS that supports the newer power management standards, such as APM and SMM, is a good choice.
- **Chipset** There are reasons to upgrade the chipset on a PC (see Chapter 5), but the rule of thumb is that the chipset must be matched to the processor and the motherboard. The chipset enables and supports such motherboard functions as ECC memory and parity checking, USB ports, multiple CPUs, and other performance issues.
- **Form factor** If you aren't changing your case, then you are stuck with the motherboard form factor that will fit it. Typically, you are looking at an ATX or NLX case and motherboard, unless your system is older, in which case (no pun intended), it is likely a Baby AT. As discussed earlier in this chapter, many of the different form factors share mounting placements, so you can upgrade to any form factor that fits your case. Remember that the power supply is also a component of the form factor and you may want to consider upgrading it as well. If you go that far, consider replacing the case as well.
- **Built-in controllers and interfaces** There are those who prefer that the motherboard have as many built-in controllers and plugs as possible, and there are those who dislike the "all-in-one" nature of these boards. If one of the built-in controllers fails, which rarely happens, the entire motherboard must be replaced. This can be much more costly than replacing a single expansion card. On the other hand, there is no worry about compatibility among the integrated controllers and interfaces on a motherboard featuring this design.
- **Documentation** This is an excellent consideration when choosing a motherboard. All things equal, the motherboard with the best documentation should win. Remember that documentation available over the Internet counts.

CHAPTER 5

Chipsets and Controllers

Without question, the most important component of a PC is the motherboard. Among the components on the motherboard contributing to its importance are the chipset and its associated controllers. This group of devices provides much of a PC's functionality and its ability to accept, display, and move data. The logic circuits of the chipset and controllers give the motherboard its intelligence and its ability to function. The chipset and controllers also control the movement of data on the system buses so that data and instructions can move about the PC, between the CPU, cache memory, and peripherals. The system chipset plays a major role in a PC's function, feature set, and speed. Unless data and instructions are able to flow between one component of the PC and another, there isn't much point to even powering up the PC.

INTRODUCTION TO CHIPSETS

The chipset, like the one shown in Figure 5-1, is technically a group of chips that helps the processor and other components on the PC communicate with and control all of the devices plugged into the motherboard. The chipset only contains enough instructions to perform its functions at the very most rudimentary level. Most of the function that occurs between the chipset and a device is actually provided by the device's device driver reacting to the basic commands communicated to it from the chipset.

The chipset controls the bits (data, instructions, and control signals) that flow between the CPU, system memory, and over the motherboard's bus. The chipset also manages data transfers between the CPU, memory, and peripheral devices and provides support for the expansion bus and any power management features of the system.

Figure 5-1. The Intel 820E chipset. Image courtesy of Intel Corporation

Socket Type

The socket type used to mount the CPU on the motherboard is the most common grouping for chipsets. You will find Socket 7 chipsets in one group, Socket 8 chipsets in another, Socket 1 and 370 chipsets in a third, and Slot A chipsets in another. There are chipsets that do not conform to this grouping technique, such as AMD's K7 chipset and others that generally form their own separate groupings. See Chapter 3 for more information on processor mountings.

North Bridge and South Bridge

Another characteristic that sets one chipset apart from another is whether it has one, two, or more chips in the set. The two-chip chipset, which contains what is called the north bridge and the south bridge, is the most common, but some manufacturers, such as SiS and VIA, produce mostly single chipsets today. Other chipsets have as many as six chips in the set. Figure 5-2 illustrates the relationship of these two elements.

The north bridge is the major bus circuitry that provides support and control for the main memory, cache memory, and the PCI bus controllers. The north bridge is typically a single chip (usually the larger of a two or more chipset), but it can be more than one chip. In a chipset, the north bridge supplies the chipset its alpha designation and distinction in a chipset family. For example, the chip *FW82439HX* is the north bridge chip of the Intel 430*HX* chipset.

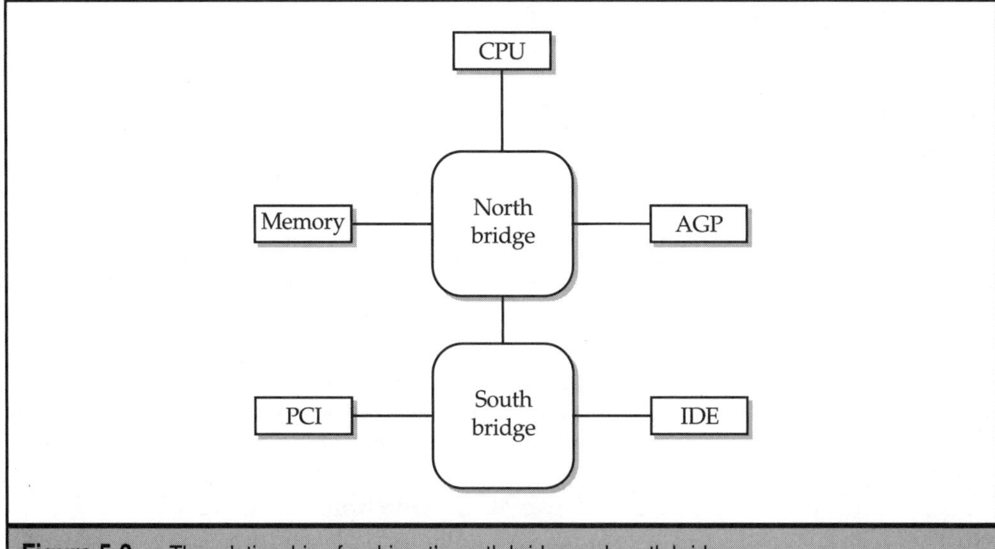

Figure 5-2. The relationship of a chipset's north bridge and south bridge

The south bridge includes the controllers for the peripheral devices and any controllers not essential to the PC's basic functions, such as the EIDE (Enhanced Integrated Device Electronics) controller and the serial port controllers. The south bridge is typically only one chip and is common among all variations in a chipset family and even between manufacturers, such as the SiS 5513 and the Intel PIIX south bridge chips.

Processor Generations

Another grouping technique that is fading away is the chipset's, and processor's, generation. As processors have evolved from the early days, processors have been grouped by their evolutionary generation. For example, the 8088 was a first-generation processor, the 386 a third-generation processor, the 486 a fourth-generation processor, the Pentium a fifth-generation processor, and so on. When Intel was the dominant processor manufacturer, the generations were much easier to follow, but now that AMD and VIA Cyrix processors have gained a foothold in the market, the generation of processors is more fuzzy. Chipsets emerged on the processor's fourth generation, and you will see some legacy chipsets categorized to the generation of the processor it supports.

At one time, a chipset was several smaller single-purpose controller chips. Each separate controller, which could be one or more chips, managed a single function, such as controlling the cache memory, handling interrupts, managing the data bus, and the like. Today's chipset combines this set of controller functions into one or two larger, multifunction chips, as shown in Figure 5-1.

Chipset chips are also referred to as *Application Specific Integration Circuits,* or *ASICs* (pronounced "a-six"), but not all ASICs are chipsets; some are timers, memory controllers, bus controllers, digital sound processors, and more, so avoid this generic classification. Manufacturers of video graphics cards also use the term chipset for the function set on their video cards, but don't confuse the two—one cannot be substituted for the other (see Chapter 12 for more information on video card chipsets).

CONTROLLER CHIPS

Generally, a chipset does not incorporate all of the controllers used to direct the actions of every peripheral device on the PC. In addition to the chipset, there are at least two, and possibly more, controllers mounted directly on the motherboard. In most cases, the motherboard will have at minimum a keyboard controller and an I/O controller (a.k.a. the Super I/O controller). Some expansion cards, such as video adapters, sound cards, network interface cards (NICs), and SCSI (Small Computer System Interface) adapters, have built-in controller chips. Individual controller chips come in all sizes and shapes, as illustrated in Figure 5-3.

A controller chip controls the transfer of data to and from a peripheral device, such as a disk drive, the monitor, the keyboard, or a printer. All of these devices depend on a device controller to interact with the CPU and the rest of the PC. For the most part, PC users

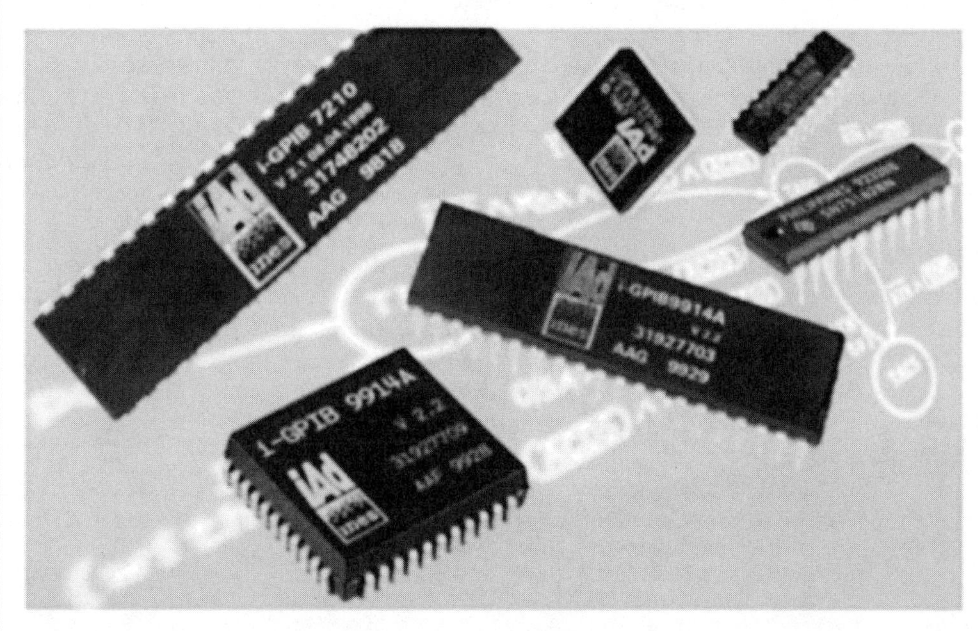

Figure 5-3. Controller chips control individual I/O or devices. Photo courtesy of Ines, Inc.

don't ever think about controller chips on their systems. In fact, most users probably don't even know they exist. How data gets to and from the keyboard is not of concern, only that it does.

On a PC, a controller is typically a single chip that either mounts directly on the motherboard or on a card that is inserted in an expansion slot on the motherboard. Because they control the flow of data to and from peripheral devices, controllers must be matched to the bus architecture of the PC.

Bus Architectures

The bus architecture of the PC is made up of the wires, connectors, and devices that move data and instructions around the PC (see Chapter 11 for more information on expansion bus architectures). The bus structure, which got its name from the fact that it resembles the lines on a city bus map, connects the controllers on the motherboard, the CPU, memory, I/O ports, and expansion slots.

The PC's bus architecture becomes very important when you add additional device controller cards to the motherboard's expansion slots. Most of the latest motherboard designs include expansion slots for multiple bus structures, including PCI (Peripheral Component Interconnect) and AT Bus, and possibly SCSI. Each of the bus architectures supported on a motherboard requires a bus controller chip.

While not technically a bus architecture, another interface type you will see listed as a major feature of some, especially the newer chipsets, is support for *AGP (Accelerated Graphics Port)*. AGP is a 66MHz bus that is usually combined with a 32-bit 33MHz PCI bus to provide advanced support and faster data transfers from main memory for video and graphics adapters.

AT Bus

The AT expansion bus is included on current PC motherboards primarily for backward compatibility to expansion cards from older systems, such as network adapters. The AT bus, which runs at 8MHz and uses a 16-bit data path, is commonly referred to as *ISA (Industry Standard Architecture)*. However, the ISA bus standard also includes the 8-bit PC XT bus, which is rarely used on any current PC.

Another bus related to the AT bus is the *Extended Industry Standard Architecture*, or *EISA*, bus. EISA bus expansion slots have been included on some motherboards since the time of the 386 processor. It is a 32-bit bus but is also backward compatible to the AT and ISA buses.

Local Bus

AT and ISA bus structures are unable to keep up with the speeds required for high-resolution graphics and faster processors, so many manufacturers have moved to what are called *local bus* architectures. A local bus architecture is more directly connected to the microprocessor than nonlocal buses by communicating directly to the processor through its dedicated controller and bypassing the standard bus controller. Although they provide for faster data movement, local buses do not support many devices, which is why most motherboards also include AT or ISA expansion slots as well.

The most common of the local bus architectures are the PCI and the VESA (Video Electronics Standards Association) local bus, or VL-bus. Of these two, the PCI, promoted by Intel, is becoming the de facto standard for virtually all Pentium class computers.

SCSI Bus

The Small Computer System Interface, or SCSI (pronounced "skuzzy") is a bus architecture that attaches peripheral devices to a PC through a dedicated controller card. SCSI supports very fast data transfer and multiple devices over the same I/O bus structure. Very few PCs, outside of the Macintosh, feature a SCSI interface as a standard, and if this bus is desired, it must be added to the PC through an expansion slot, typically a PCI slot.

USB

The *Universal Serial Bus*, or *USB*, is an emerging standard for device connectors and interface. USB is a plug-and-play architecture that allows users to add a wide range of peripheral devices to the PC without the need of an expansion card. It is considered a low-speed interface and works best for a keyboard, mouse, scanner, or printer.

Keyboard Controller

The keyboard controller's name describes what it does—it controls the keyboard. More specifically though, it controls the transfer of data from the keyboard to the PC. The keyboard controller on the motherboard interacts with a controller located inside the keyboard over a serial link built into the connecting cable and connector. When the keyboard controller receives data from the keyboard, it checks the data's parity, translates the scan code, places the data in its output buffer, and notifies the processor that the data is in its buffer. The keyboard controller is quite common on most older PCs, but newer PCs either include this control function in the chipset or in the Super I/O chip.

The functions performed by the keyboard controller, or its equivalent, are as follows:

- **Keyboard control and translation** When a key is pressed on the keyboard, a scan code is sent from the controller inside the keyboard to PC's keyboard controller, which then signals the processor through IRQ1 (interrupt request 1). The keyboard controller then translates the scan code into the character it represents and places it on the bus to move it to the appropriate location in memory.
- **Support for the PS/2 mouse** On those systems that have an integrated PS/2 connector on the motherboard, the keyboard controller supports its functions. This port is most commonly used to connect a PS/2-style mouse.
- **Access to the HMA** Although the support for the High Memory Area of system memory (RAM) is now incorporated into the system chipset on most newer PCs, access to this part of memory is controlled through the keyboard controller. See Chapter 7 for more information on the High Memory Area.

Super I/O Controller

The Super I/O (input/output) controller chip includes many controller functions that were previously performed by many separate chips. Combining these functions provides an economy of scale for similar activities and minimizes the space required on the motherboard and the cost of the chips used to support these activities.

The "super" in its name refers to the fact that the Super I/O controller combines many other chips and not what or how it carries out its functions. This chip controls the standard input/output peripheral devices and ports found on virtually every system. These functions can be combined onto a single chip because they control mature standardized devices that are virtually the same on every PC. Combining them on a single I/O chip frees the motherboard and system chipset to control other high-priority functions.

On some older PCs, many of the functions of the Super I/O controller were provided through I/O controller expansion cards, such as control for serial and parallel ports and the hard disk drive. Because these functions are common to every PC, incorporating them into a single chip placed on the motherboard has also freed up an expansion slot.

The major functions of the Super I/O controller chip are as follows:

- **Serial ports** The UART (universal asynchronous receiver-transmitter) is used to drive the serial ports and the control functions of data transfer are included in the Super I/O chip.
- **Parallel ports** The functions that drive the parallel ports, including the various parallel port standards, EPP (Enhanced Parallel Port) and ECP (Enhanced Capabilities Port), are included in the Super I/O controller.
- **Floppy disk drives** Support for the floppy disk drive and floppy-disk type tape drives are included on the Super I/O chip.
- **Miscellaneous functions** Newer versions of the Super I/O controller may also incorporate the keyboard controller's functions, the real-time clock, and perhaps the IDE hard disk controller, although this is more commonly found in the system chipset.

Other Device Controllers

Each device added to the PC that wishes to interact with the data bus requires a controller. In general, peripheral devices have their controller chips either on an adapter card (expansion card) or built into their electronics. On older, pre-Pentium PCs, every device generally had their own or shared a controller card. For example, it was common for the floppy disk and hard disk drives to share an I/O controller card.

Each device controller must be matched to the bus interface with which it is to interact. An IDE (Integrated Drive Electronics) disk drive requires an IDE controller and a SCSI controller is needed to connect a device with a SCSI interface.

Most peripheral devices installed inside the system case of a current PC interface through an IDE controller. For the most part, an IDE controller is included in either the PC's main chipset or the Super I/O controller. Most systems have the *floppy disk controller (FDC)* and the *hard disk controller (HDC)* built into the motherboard and, provided it is not a SCSI device, any tape drives, CD-ROM, or DVD devices added will share these controllers.

CHIPSETS

One of the fundamental design facts of a PC is that its microprocessor is always faster than the peripheral devices to which it must communicate. This fact has forced designers to develop interfaces that serve as buffers between the slower devices and the faster CPU to match up their speeds and help with the timing of the operations. The very first PCs had an individual chip to control each of the various operations.

It was common for an early PC to have the following separate chips:

- **Math coprocessor interface** This chip controls the flow of data between the processor and math coprocessor.
- **Clock generator** This chip controls the timing of the PC's operations.
- **Bus controller chip** This chip controls the flow of data on the motherboard's buses.
- **DMA controller** This chip controls the processes that allowed peripheral devices to interact with memory without involving the processor.
- **Programmable peripheral interface (PPI)** This chip supervises some of the simpler peripheral devices.
- **Floppy disk controller (FDC)** This chip controls the PC's diskette and tape drives.
- **CRT controller** This chip facilitates the PC's display.
- **UART (universal asynchronous receiver transmitter)** This chip is used to send and receive synchronous serial data.

These functions are explained more in the next section.

With the major design changes introduced with the 486 processor, many of these functions were combined for the first time onto a smaller group of chips that required less board space, which was in line with the shrinking size of the PC, and cost less to produce.

Every major component attached to a PC's motherboard depends on the system chipset for its ability to interact with the other components of the PC. The chipset of a PC is designed to support the functions of a particular CPU and, in some cases, a specific motherboard design. The design and function of the chipset is tied very closely to the designs of the CPU, motherboard, BIOS, and memory, the devices with which it directly interacts and supports. On a PC, you can upgrade the memory, the CPU, and even upgrade the hard disk, but to change the chipset, you have to change the motherboard. It is integral to the functions of the motherboard.

A number of a PC's characteristics are dictated by its chipset, including the memory type, the L2 cache type and size, the CPU, the data bus speed, and whether the PC supports one or more processors. Which interfaces are supported on the PC, such as AGP, IrDA, USB, and which IDE/EIDE features, are determined by the motherboard's chipset.

Intel is the largest chipset manufacturer, in terms of the number of chipsets produced and in use. Intel originally developed their first chipset to help promote the PCI bus for the Pentium processor platforms. There are other chipset manufacturers, listed later in this section, but Intel, since they produce the Pentium microprocessor, is usually the chipset of choice for motherboard manufacturers. More than likely Intel manufactured the chipset in your PC. The Windows Device Manager's listing for system devices (see Figure 5-4) should list the processor to PCI and PCI to ISA bridge controllers and the manufacturer. If these are Intel chips, then you can be sure you have an Intel chipset.

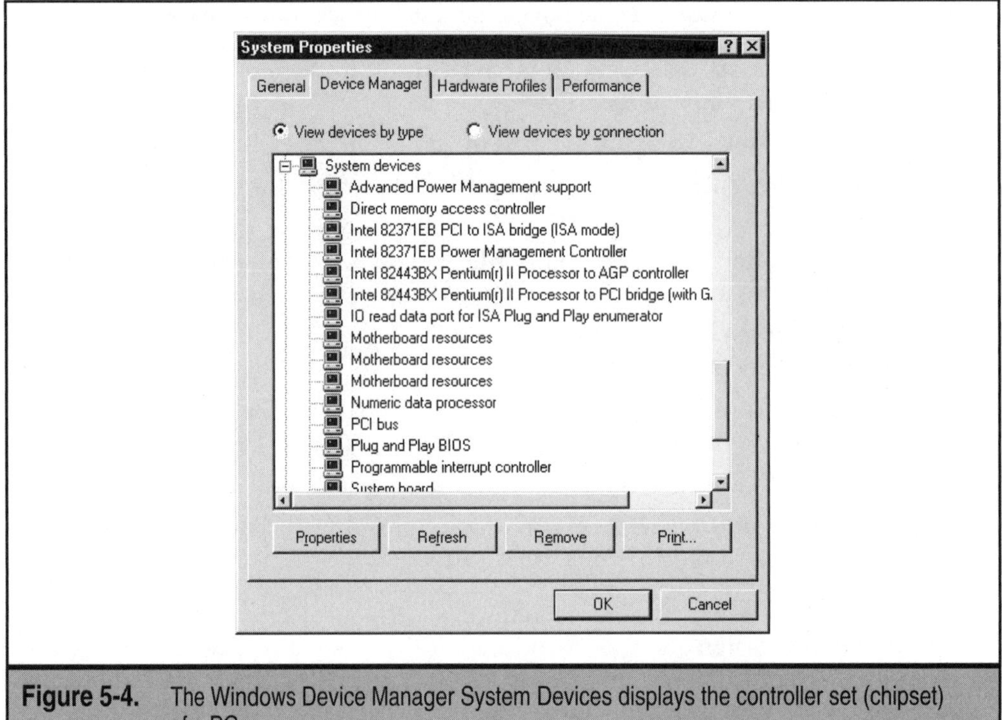

Figure 5-4. The Windows Device Manager System Devices displays the controller set (chipset) of a PC

Another way to check out the chipset on your PC is to open the system unit and find the large square chips, which are usually bigger than most everything else on the motherboard except the microprocessor. A chipset can have only one chip or as many as four separate chips.

Chipset Functions

A chipset integrates a number of *VLSI* (very large scale integration) chips that provide much of the PC's functionality. Each of the chips integrated into the chipset at one time could have easily been a stand-alone chip, but by combining them together into a single chip, the controllers and devices combined into the chipset can share common actions, reduce the physical space required on the motherboard, and reduce cost—all very important considerations in today's PC market.

Chipset Characteristics

The characteristics of a chipset can be broken down into six categories: host, memory, interfaces, arbitration, south bridge support, and power management. Each of these categories defines and differentiates one chipset from another. The characteristics defined in each of these categories are as follows:

- **Host** This category defines the host processor to which the chipset is matched along with its bus voltage, usually *GTL+ (Gunning Transceiver Logic Plus)* or *AGTL+ (Advanced Gunning Transceiver Logic Plus)*, and the number of processors the chipset will support.
- **Memory** This category defines the characteristics of the DRAM support included in the chipset, including the DRAM refresh technique supported, the amount of memory support (in megabits usually), the type of memory supported, and whether memory interleave, ECC (error-correcting code), or parity is supported.
- **Interfaces** This category defines the type of PCI interface implemented and whether the chipset is AGP-compliant, supports integrated graphics, PIPE (pipelining), or *SBA (side band addressing)*.
- **Arbitration** This category defines the method used by the chipset to arbitrate between different bus speeds and interfaces. The two most common arbitration methods are *MTT (Multi-Transaction Timer)* and *DIA (Dynamic Intelligent Arbiter)*.
- **South bridge support** All Intel chipsets and most of the chipsets for all other manufacturers are two processor sets. In these sets, the north bridge is the main chip and handles CPU and memory interfaces among other tasks, while the south bridge (or the second chip) handles such things as the USB and IDE interfaces, the *RTC (real-time clock)*, and support for serial and parallel ports.
- **Power management** All Intel chipsets support both the *SMM (System Management Mode)* and *ACPI (Advanced Configuration and Power Interface)* power management standards.

Chipset Built-in Controllers

The controllers and devices included in a chipset are typically those that are common to virtually every PC of the type the chipset is designed to support. The controllers and devices usually included in a chipset are as follows:

- **Memory controller** This is the logic circuit that controls the reading and writing of data to and from system memory (RAM). Other devices on the PC wishing to access memory must interface with the memory controller. This feature also usually includes error handling to provide for parity checking and *ECC (error-correcting code)* for every memory word.
- **EIDE controller** Nearly all mid- to upper-range motherboards now include at least one EIDE connector for hard disks, floppy disks, CD-ROMs, DVDs, or other types of internal storage drives. The EIDE controller typically supports

devices with ISA, ATA, and perhaps an ATA-33 or Ultra-DMA (UDMA) interface.

- **PCI bridge** Like a network bridge that connects two dissimilar networks, this device logically connects the PCI expansion bus on the motherboard to the processor and other non-PCI devices.
- **Real-time clock (RTC)** This clock holds the date and time on your PC; this is the date and time that is displayed to you on the monitor and is used to date-stamp file activities. This should not be confused with the system clock that provides the timing signal for the processor and other devices.
- **DMA (Direct Memory Access) controllers** The DMA controller manages the seven DMA channels available for use by ISA/ATA devices on most PCs. DMA channels are used by certain devices, such as floppy disk drives, sound cards, SCSI adapters, and some network adapters, to move data into memory without the assistance of the CPU.
- **IrDA controller** IrDA (Infrared Data Association) is the international organization that has created the standards for short-range, line-of-sight, point-to-point infrared devices, such as a keyboard, mouse, and network adapters. The IrDA port on your system is that small red window on the front or side of notebook and some desktop computers.
- **Keyboard controller** A chipset may include the keyboard controller, and many of the newer ones do. The keyboard controller is the interface between the keyboard and the processor. See the previous section for more information on this device.
- **PS/2 mouse controller** When IBM introduced the PS/2 system, the controller for the mouse was included in the keyboard controller. This design has persisted and usually wherever the keyboard controller is, so is the PS/2 mouse controller. This device provides the interface between the PS/2 mouse and the processor.
- **Secondary (Level 2, or L2) cache controller** Secondary (L2) cache is located on the motherboard, a daughterboard, or as on the Pentium Pro, in the processor package, and caches the primary memory (RAM), the hard disk, and the CD-ROM drives. The secondary cache controller controls the movement of data to and from the L2 cache and the processor.
- **CMOS SRAM** The PC's configuration settings are stored in what is called the CMOS memory. The chipset contains the controller used to access and modify this special SRAM area.

Intel Chipsets

Intel literally invented the chipset and has continued to dominate the market, giving ground on any level only when they decide to abandon it to move upward and onward to newer developments. Intel began making chipsets back in the days of the 486 and continues to dominate the market. The primary reason for this dominance is simple—chipsets support processors and motherboards. Since Intel dominates the processor market and because they know the processor so intimately, it is easy for them to design chipsets that efficiently and effectively support the processor.

486 Chipsets

Because there were several styles of 486 systems, there were many different chipsets for them. The two most common chipsets for 486 systems (called *fourth-generation* chipsets) were

- **420EX (Aries)** This chipset provided support on motherboards that combined the PCI and VL buses.
- **420TX (Saturn)** This chipset family was designed for 80486 systems up to the 486 DX4 systems; it supported most of the 486 overdrive processors and provided for power management. It was released in three revision levels numbered 1, 2, and 4. Revision 4 is known as the Saturn II chipset.

Chipsets for the Pentium and Beyond

Pentium chipsets (referred to as *fifth-generation* chipsets) were more closely tied to the design of the processor than were the 486 chipsets. When Intel created the Pentium processor, it also developed the PCI bus and a chipset to support and integrate the capabilities of these two developments. This PCIset, as it became known, was developed as an exact match for the Pentium processor.

Intel chipsets are designated in numbered series: the 420 for 486 chipsets, the 430 for Pentium chipsets, the 440 series for Pentium II, and the 450 series for Pentium Pro chipsets (along with the 440FX). The newer 460 and 800 series chipsets just being announced are designed to support the IA-64 (Intel Architecture—64 bits) processors, such as the Itanium, now emerging.

Here are some of the more common Intel Pentium and above chipsets:

- **430LX (Mercury)** The 430LX was the first Pentium chipset developed to support the 60MHz and 66MHz 5V processors. The Mercury chipset included the PCI bus and supported up to 128MB of RAM. This chipset was made obsolete by the chipsets that supported the 90MHz and 100MHz 3.3V processors.
- **430NX (Neptune)** The 430NX was developed to support Intel's second-generation Pentium chips. It supported Pentium processors running at 90MHz to 133MHz. Some of the improvements offered over the 430LX chipset are support for dual processors, 512MB of RAM, and 512 KB of L2 cache.
- **430FX (Triton I)** This was the first of the Triton chipsets. It featured support for EDO RAM, pipelined burst and synchronous cache, Plug-and-Play, and PCI level 2.0 compliance. However, it only supported 128MB of RAM (down from

the 512MB supported by the Neptune chipset) and did not have dual processor capabilities.

- **430MX (Mobile Triton)** This is a version of the 430FX designed for laptop, notebook, and other portable PCs.
- **430HX (Triton II)** This chipset supported EDO RAM and concurrent PCI buses and was designed for use in business-level servers. It was the next generation of the 430NX and included support for 512MB of RAM and L2 cache.
- **430VX (Triton III)** This chipset was developed to support the home PC market. It featured support for USB, SDRAM, and PCI interfaces.
- **430TX** With this chipset, Intel dropped the Triton label for its chipsets. The 430TX was adaptable for both desktop and mobile use and provided PCI, USB, DMA, and other interfaces.
- **440LX** Designed for the Pentium II, this AGPset chipset provides support for the LS-120 "superdisk," Ultra DMA, AGP, USB, SDRAM, ECC RAM, and the PC97 power management specification. Figure 5-5 shows this chipset.
- **440LXR** A low-end version of the 440LX chipset.
- **440BX** Another Pentium II chipset that supports 100MHz bus, dual processors, FireWire, and up to 1GB of RAM.

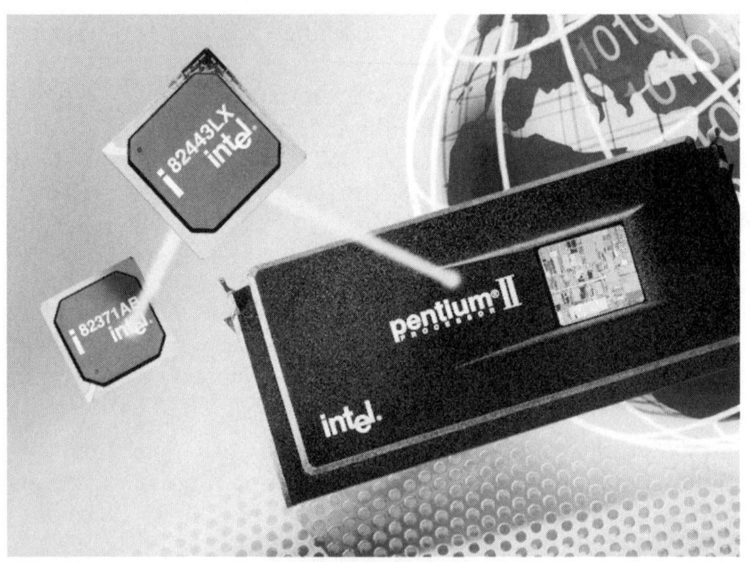

Figure 5-5. The Intel 440LX AGPset and the Pentium II processor. Photo courtesy of Intel Corporation

- **440GX** This chipset, shown in Figure 5-6, is designed for midrange workstations and supports dual CPUs and up to 2GB of SDRAM, along with dual AGP interfaces. This is an AGPset.
- **440FX (Natoma)** This chipset supported both the Pentium II and the Pentium Pro processors with USB, EDO RAM, ECC memory, dual processors, and PCI.
- **450GX (Orion server)** The 450GX chipset and the 450KX share the same basic design. However, the GX version is optimized for the Pentium Pro and supports four processors and 8GB of RAM but FPM memory only.
- **450KX (Orion workstation)** The workstation version of the Orion chipset supports dual processors and 1GB of RAM.
- **450NX** This is a high-powered chipset designed for Xeon workstations and servers. It supports up to four CPUs, 2MB of L2 cache, 8GB of EDO memory, and two 32-bit or one 64-bit PCI interface. Figure 5-7 shows the group of chips that make up this chipset.
- **460GX (Merced)** This chipset supports very high-end servers and workstations with supports for four CPUs and other high-performance features. You will see this chipset linked to the new high-powered Itanium processor.
- **810** This chipset is designed for value-priced PCs. It includes support for integrated 3-D graphics (AGP) with MPEG-2, 100MHz system bus, two USB

Figure 5-6. The Intel 440GX AGPset. Photo courtesy of Intel Corporation

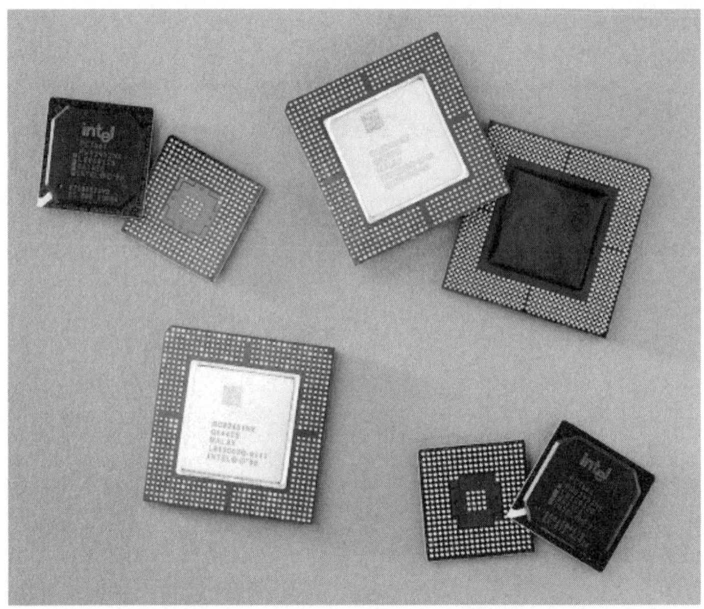

Figure 5-7. The Intel 450NX chipset. Photo courtesy of Intel Corporation

ports, and the Intel Accelerated Hub, which features a 266MB per second bus speed between memory and peripherals.

- **810e** This chipset, shown in Figure 5-8, is an extended version of the 810 chipset based on the 440BX chipset and intended for home market and office PCs. Its features are the same as the 810 chipset, with added support for 133MHz system bus and the ATA-66 interface.
- **815** The Intel 815 chipset is specifically designed to work with the Pentium III processor, but it also provides backward compatibility to other Intel processors.
- **820** Another extension of the 810 chipset designed to support high-end desktops and workstations.
- **850** The Intel 850 chipset was designed in tandem with the Pentium 4 processor and supports, among many high-performance innovations and features, a 400 MHz system bus that provides over 3 times the bandwidth of previous chipset and processor technologies.

Figure 5-8. The Intel 810e chipset. Photo courtesy of Intel Corporation

Non-Intel Chipsets

Besides Intel, ALi (Acer Labs), Via Technologies, and Silicon Integrated Systems (SiS) manufacture Pentium-class chipsets.

ALi (Acer Laboratories, Inc.)

Acer Laboratories is a small part of Acer (the PC manufacturer) that manufacturers chipsets for the Acer AcerOpen motherboards. The Aladdin III and Aladdin IV chipsets are comparable to the Intel 430VX and 430TX chipsets. The Aladdin V, also known as the M1541 chipset, supports higher CPU bus frequency (up to 100MHz), internal tag bits and tag RAM, high performance RAM controller, 64-bit ECC/parity memory bus interface, an AGP interface, and it includes device controllers for IDE, USB, and PS/2, as well as a Super I/O controller.

SiS

SiS (Silicon Integrated Systems Corporation) manufactures chipsets that combine the functions of the north bridge and south bridge into a single chip. SiS chipsets are available for nearly all sockets since the Socket 7 and feature a shared memory architecture and *UMA (Unified Memory Architecture)* type of video adapter.

Popular SiS chipsets are as follows:

- **730S** This single-chip chipset, shown in Figure 5-9, is designed to support the AMD Athlon Slot A/Socket A CPU.
- **630/630E/630S** These single chipsets are designed for Slot 1 and Socket 370 CPUs that integrate the north bridge, an advanced 2D/3D GUI engine, and a Super-South bridge.
- **600/620** These two-chip chipsets integrate a high-performance host bus interface, a DRAM controller, an IDE controller, a PCI interface, a 2D/3D graphics accelerator, and a video playback accelerator for Slot 1 and Socket 370 processor-based systems.
- **540** This single chipset is designed to support AMD K6 CPU based systems with Super Socket 7 sockets with highly integrated PCI devices.

VIA

VIA Technologies, Inc. is perhaps the third-largest chipset manufacturer, after Intel and SiS. VIA produces chipsets for Slot 1, Socket 7, and Socket 370 legacy systems. However,

Figure 5-9. The SiS 730S single-chip chipset. Photo courtesy of Silicon Integrated Systems Corporation

their more recent chipsets concentrate on the Cyrix and AMD processors. VIA now produces the Cyrix processor, having purchased that company a few years back.

A few of the VIA chipsets are as follows:

- **Apollo KT266** This two chip chipset is designed for use with the AMD Athlong processor and features a 266MHz bus and a new high-bandwidth architecture Socket A motherboards.
- **Apollo KX133/KT133** These single chipsets (the KX133 is shown in Figure 5-10) are designed to provide support to the AMD Duron, Thunderbird, and Athlon processors and feature a AGP4X graphics bus, up to 2GB of RAM, a 200MHz processor bus, and an ATA-66 IDE hard disk interface.
- **Apollo PM601** This single chipset provides support for the latest Intel Pentium III processors and the Cyrix III processor. It features advanced 2D/3D (two-dimensional/three-dimensional) graphics, a scalable processor bus, and a full set of integrated controllers and other features (see Figure 5-11).
- **Apollo MVP3** This Super Socket 7 chipset provides support for the AMD K-6 and Cyrix MII processors with speeds of up to 533MHz and features a flexible processor bus that scales from 66 to 100MHz along with advanced AGP graphics, power managements, and other integrated features. This is a high

Figure 5-10. The VIA Apollo KX133 chipset. Photo courtesy of VIA Technologies, Inc.

Figure 5-11. The VIA Apollo PM601 chipset. Photo courtesy of VIA Technologies, Inc.

performance, energy efficient chipset that supports AGP, PCI, and ISA bus on desktop and notebook PCs ranging from 66MHz to 100MHz. It features support for EIDE, USB, and keyboard/PS2-mouse interfaces, a 64-bit CPU and system memory, 32-bit PCI and AGP interfaces, 3.3V and sub-3.3V power.

- **Apollo MVP4** This Super Socket 7 chipset, shown in Figure 5-12, combines the Apollo MVP3 chipset with a high-end Trident Blade3D graphics engine for value PCs, Internet appliances, and notebook PCs.
- **Pro Savage PM133** This two-chip chipset supports Intel Pentium III and Celeron processors as well as the VIA Cyrix processor. It features high-performance graphics support, an integrated 10/100 Ethernet adapter, audio support, a built-in modem, Super I/O controller, flat panel monitor support, advanced power management, and support for four USB ports.

NEW DEVELOPMENTS

Intel now includes a bus architecture, called *Intel Hub Architecture*, to enhance the interface between the elements of the chipset. Before this, chipsets used the PCI bus as the interface between the north bridge (host, memory, and AGP) and the south bridge (PCI and

Figure 5-12. The VIA Apollo MVP4 chipset. Photo courtesy of VIA Technologies, Inc.

IDE controllers). Because the south bridge was a PCI device and the PCI controller at the same time, some efficiency (and one PCI slot) was lost. Its latest chipset, the 850 series, is built on IHA technology.

The hub architecture dedicates a high-speed data bus between redesigned north and south bridges, now designated as the Memory Controller Hub (MCH) and the I/O Controller Hub (ICH). The ICH is not a PCI device and a PCI slot is freed up. The dedicated link allows these two hubs to transfer data much faster, as much as 266MBps over 8 bits.

Acer Labs has recently announced its ALiMAGiK 1 chipset to support the AMD Slot A/Socket A processor family. A parallel chipset family, the AladdinPro 5, supports the Intel Slot 1/Socket 370 processor family. What is remarkable about these chipset families is that they are designed to handle DDR (Double Data Rate DRAM) and SDR (Single Data Rate) memory architectures on desktop and mobile platforms, both of which were not previously supported together. DDR has a relatively small market share at present, but many experts expect it to grow to about half of the motherboard market in the next five years. In fact, VIA has also committed to using only DDR in its emerging chipsets and its newest chipset, the Apollo KT266, provides support for DDR SDRAM.

The Apollo KT266 also features a new architecture enhancement, similar to Intel's IHA, which it calls *V-Link Architecture*. The V-Link architecture has replaced the PCI link that is used to connect the north and south bridges of many chipsets.

CHAPTER 6

The BIOS and the Boot Process

When you flick, push, or pull on the power to your PC, there are absolutely no instructions in memory for the PC to execute. In fact, when the PC is first powered on, it is almost like it is being turned on for the very first time ever. Although it is easy to think of the computer as having a brain and the ability to manage itself, the truth is that it is merely an electrical appliance and must to told what to do at all times. This is especially true at startup when the power is switched on.

The importance of the PC's BIOS (Basic Input/Output System) is that it performs all of the functions the PC needs to get started. The BIOS contains that first instruction the computer needs to get started, programming that checks that computer's hardware is attached and ready, and other routines to help the computer get up and running.

Another of the activities of the BIOS is that it provides the interface that connects the CPU to the input and output devices attached to the PC. The BIOS relieves the PC from needing to know about how hardware devices are attached to the computer. As new hardware is added to the computer, the BIOS eliminates the need for every piece of software in the computer to be updated as to where the hardware and its drivers are located. Only the BIOS configuration data needs to be updated when new equipment is added to the PC, a process usually managed by the BIOS itself without outside intervention required. As illustrated in Figure 6-1, the BIOS services the needs of the CPU, the hardware devices, and the software on the computer. The BIOS and the other functions involved in getting the PC up and running are discussed in this chapter.

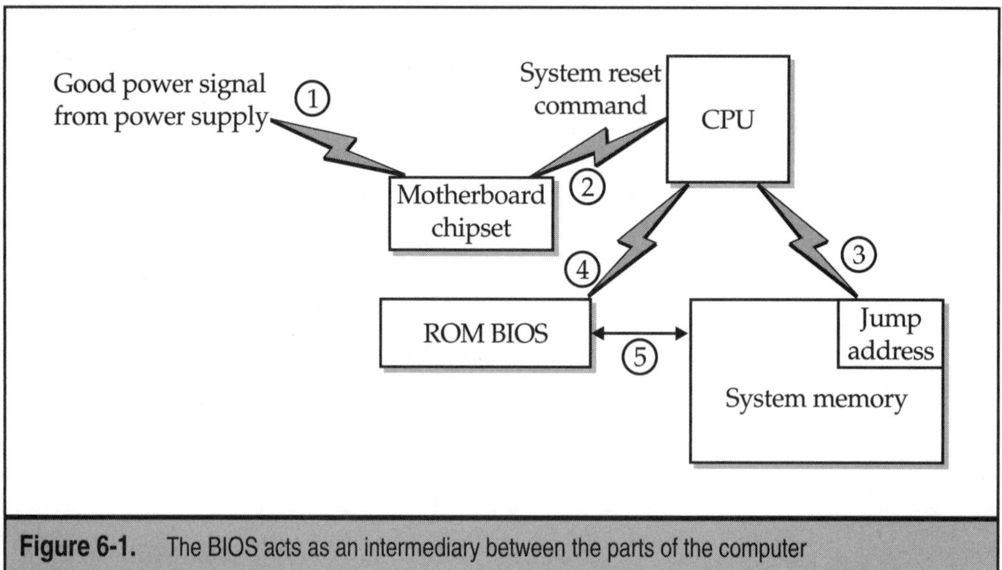

Figure 6-1. The BIOS acts as an intermediary between the parts of the computer

AN INTRODUCTION TO THE BIOS

A PC's BIOS (Basic Input/Output System) includes the programming to perform three vital and useful functions for the PC:

- It boots the computer.
- It validates the PC's configuration.
- It provides an interface between the hardware of the PC and its software.

The BIOS Utilities and Programs

In addition to starting up a PC, the BIOS also contains a collection of programs that are used by an operating system and application software to interact with the hardware, both internal and external, connected to the PC. While operating systems are beginning to include device drivers and utilities of their own to improve performance, most BIOSs contain software for accessing, reading, writing, and moving data between virtually every type of hardware device.

BIOS Manufacturers

The most well-known BIOS manufacturers are Award, AMI (American Megatrends, Inc.), and Phoenix. Like most BIOS manufacturers, these three license their BIOS ROM to motherboard manufacturers who install them on their motherboards and assume the support of the BIOS as well. AMI was once the sole BIOS provider to Intel, the leading motherboard producer. Today, over 80 percent of all motherboards are Intel boards that include a Phoenix BIOS. In 1998, Phoenix purchased Award and now markets the Award BIOS brand under the Phoenix name.

BOOTING THE COMPUTER

The process used to start up a PC each time it is powered on is called the *boot process*. While it sounds like it could refer to kick-starting, this term is actually derived from the saying, "Pulling one's self up by one's own bootstraps," which is a long-winded way of saying you are a self-starter. PCs are self-starters in the respect that when you flick on the power switch, the PC verifies its hardware configuration, runs a few function tests, and then gets its operating system loaded into memory and running on the CPU. It's almost like magic...well, not quite.

The boot process is performed under the guidance of the BIOS. The BIOS contains the instructions needed to verify, test, and start the PC—in other words, boot the computer. When the computer boots up, the BIOS is behind the scenes causing and managing the actions that are taking place. The PC's hardware cannot perform independent actions. It must have instructions to do anything at all. These instructions are in the form of the PC's software, which are blocks of instructions that guide the hardware to perform specific activities.

System Boot Sequence

The most important action of the BIOS is to boot the PC. The process used to do this is actually a fairly complex sequence of steps that verifies the configuration, checks the hardware, and loads the software. The actual steps included in a particular BIOS' boot sequence can vary by manufacturer, but the following are typical of the steps normally performed during the system boot sequence (reference Figure 6-2 as you go through the boot sequence steps):

1. When you turn on the PC's power switch, the internal power supply initializes itself. As I will discuss in Chapter 14, the power supply does not provide power to the rest of the PC immediately. As soon as the power supply is able to supply reliable power to the motherboard, it transmits a "good power" signal to the motherboard's chipset (see Figure 6-2), which sends a system reset command to the processor (step 2 in Figure 6-2). At this point, from all outward appearances, the PC looks as if it is still powered off.
2. The system reset command sent by the motherboard's chipset causes the CPU to read its first instruction from what is called the jump address (step 3 in Figure 6-2). The *jump address* is always located in a fixed preset location, typically address FFFF0h in system memory. The jump address contains the physical address of the BIOS' boot program on the ROM BIOS chip (see "ROMs, PROMs, and EPROMs: BIOS Chips" later in the chapter for more information on the ROM BIOS).
3. The CPU executes the first instruction, which copies the BIOS programs into system memory (steps 4 and 5 on Figure 6-2) and starts the BIOS running.
4. The BIOS next performs the *POST (Power-On Self-Test)* process (see "The POST Process" later in this section). The POST verifies and tests the hardware configuration stored in the BIOS configuration information. Should the POST detect any problems, it sounds *beep codes*, one or more beeps through the system speaker to indicate the nature of the problem, or displays an error message (see "BIOS Beep Codes" later in this section), and the boot process stops.
5. If the POST finds no problems, the boot process continues. At this point, the system BIOS (the one booting the PC) looks for the video adapter's BIOS and starts it. Virtually all peripheral devices on the PC have their own BIOS. This is the first time, aside from the noises of the disk drives and a single beep indicating all is well, that you will know the PC is booting. Information about the video card is displayed on the monitor's screen.
6. The display of the video adapter's information is followed by information about the system BIOS itself. This usually includes information on the manufacturer and version of the BIOS program.

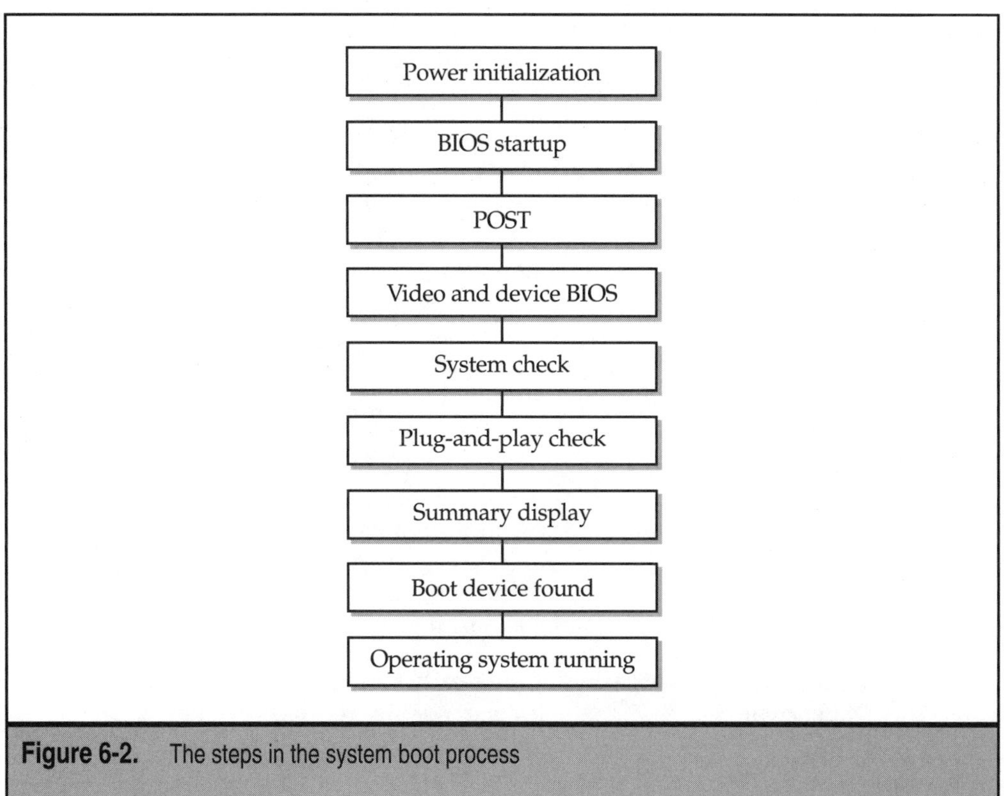

Figure 6-2. The steps in the system boot process

7. Any device BIOS routines are started. The video card's BIOS starts first to turn on the display, then information about the system BIOS and the other BIOSs is displayed as they are started.
8. Next, the BIOS begins a series of tests on the system, including the amount of memory detected on the system. This test is usually displayed on the screen as a run-up counter showing the amount of memory detected and tested. Because the BIOS now has use of the monitor, it displays error messages for any problems detected instead of the beep codes that it had to use prior to the display being available.
9. With the device BIOSs loaded, the system BIOS checks if the devices listed in the CMOS configuration data (see "Complementary Metal-Oxide Semiconductor (CMOS)" later in the chapter) are present and functioning, including their speeds, access modes, and other parameters. In this sequence, the serial and parallel ports are assigned their identities (COM1, COM2, LPT1, etc.). As each device is passed, a message is displayed that it was found, configured, and tested.

10. If the BIOS supports Plug and Play (PnP) technology, any PnP devices detected are configured. Information on each PnP device is displayed on the screen, although it typically goes by much too fast to read.
11. At the end of the test and configuration sequence, the BIOS should display a summary data screen that details the PC as the BIOS sees it and indicating that the system is verified and ready for use. Only one thing is missing…
12. To start the operating system running, the BIOS must first find it. Included in the CMOS data is a parameter that indicates the disk drives (floppy, hard, or CD-ROM) and the order in which they should be accessed to find the operating system. In most cases, the boot sequence parameters will be set to look for the operating system on first the floppy disk drive, then the hard disk drive, and perhaps, if all else fails, the CD-ROM drive. This sequence can be changed to reflect the sequence desired. If the first boot device is the hard disk, the BIOS looks for the master boot record (MBR) to use to start the operating system. If the boot disk is a floppy disk, the BIOS looks at the first sector of the disk for the OS boot program. If the boot program is not found on the first device listed, then the next device is searched and so on until the boot program is found. If no boot device is found, the boot sequence stops and an error message ("No boot device available") is displayed.

The PC should now be up and running and ready for use. Next time you boot up a PC, watch this sequence more closely to see if you recognize the actions taking place.

Cold Boots versus Warm Boots

The boot sequence used when a PC is powered on from a powered off condition is called a *cold boot*. A cold boot is done when the computer is started from a cold (or completely powered off) status. A *warm boot* happens when the PC is already powered on. Pressing the key combination CTRL-ALT-DEL or pressing the reset button. A cold boot causes the complete boot and POST sequence to run. However, the POST process does not run after a warm boot.

The POST Process

Immediately after the BIOS programs are loaded to memory, the *POST* (*Power-On Self-Test*) starts. The POST performs a check of the system components and hardware listed in the system setup (CMOS) data are present and tests to see that they are functioning properly. The POST process is done before the BIOS begins its startup procedures.

The POST process is fast and is typically unnoticed provided there are no problems. If the POST finds problems, it signals with beep codes (beeps emitted though the system speaker) indicating the source of the problem. At the time the POST runs, it has no other means of signaling problems because none of the hardware I/O functions have been loaded. The display and printer are not available, so the system speaker, which is technically a part of the motherboard, is the only means the POST has of signaling what is going wrong.

Depending on the cause of the error, the POST routine uses an established beep pattern to signal the type of problem encountered. The beep codes are similar to a POST Morse code. The pattern and meaning of the combinations of short and long beeps is unique to the BIOS' manufacturer. However, nearly all POST problems are fatal errors because the POST is testing only essential system components.

BIOS Beep Codes

Not all beep codes mean something bad. Nearly all BIOS programs will sound a single beep code to indicate that all is well and then continue the boot process. However, if the boot process does not continue, the single beep has a different meaning or there were additional codes you didn't hear. You may need to cold boot the PC at least once to hear all of the beeps. Often the beep codes catch you by surprise the first time they are sounded. Once you are sure you have heard all of the beeps, the next step is to figure out what they mean.

Each BIOS producer has its own collection of POST error beep codes, but the four primary beep code sets are IBM standard, AMI, Award, and Phoenix. As is illustrated in Tables 6-1 through 6-4, there is no standard beep code set. Each set of beep codes has a different sound pattern to indicate different problems. The different beep code sets involve short beeps, long beeps, and a varying number of beeps in a three- or four-beep series.

Actually, the codes listed in Table 6-3 are only possible examples of Award BIOS' beep codes. Award relies on motherboard manufacturers to generate the beep codes used with its BIOS. So, if you have an Award BIOS on your PC, you'll need to check with its manufacturer or the manufacturer of its motherboard to get a list of the beep codes in use.

Beeps	Meaning
No beep	Power supply failure
Repeating short beeps	Power supply or system board failure
1 short	POST is complete
2 short	POST error
1 long, 1 short	System board error
1 long, 2 short	Video display adapter failure
1 long, 3 short	Video display adapter error
3 long	Keyboard error

Table 6-1. A Sample of the Standard IBM Beep Code Set

Beeps	Meaning
1 short	POST is complete
2 short	Memory failure
3 short	Memory/parity failure
4 short	System timer failure
5 short	Motherboard failure
6 short	Keyboard controller failure
7 short	CPU failure
8 short	Video adapter failure
9 short	ROM BIOS checksum error
10 short	CMOS read/write error
11 short	Cache memory error
1 long, 3 short	Memory failure
1 long, 8 short	Video adapter failure

Table 6-2. A Sample of the AMI BIOS Beep Code Set

The Phoenix BIOS POST error beep codes, listed in Table 6-4, are more complicated than most other beep code sets. When an error is detected, the first set of beeps is sounded followed by a slight pause before the next set of beeps, and so on. For example, the beep code pattern that indicates that the BIOS itself may be corrupt is 1-1-4. This would sound something like beep, pause, beep, pause, beep, beep, beep, beep.

Beep Codes	Meaning
1 long	Memory error
1 long, 2 short	Video error
1 long, 3 short	Video failure
Continuous beeps	Memory or video failure

Table 6-3. A Sample of the Award BIOS' Beep Code Set

Beep Codes	Meaning
1-1-3	CMOS memory error
1-1-4	BIOS failed
1-2-1	System timer error
1-2-2	Motherboard error
1-2-3	Motherboard error
1-3-1	Motherboard error
1-4-1	Motherboard error
1-4-2	Memory error
2-_	Memory failure (2 beeps, followed by any beep combinations)
3-1-_	Chipset error (3 beeps, followed by 1 beep, followed by any beep combination)
3-2-4	Keyboard controller error
3-3-4	Video adapter failure
4-2-4	Expansion card failure
4-3-4	Time of day clock failure
4-4-1	Serial port error
4-4-2	Parallel port error
4-4-3	Math coprocessor error

Table 6-4. Phoenix BIOS Beep Codes

BIOS Startup Screen

If the POST completes successfully, the BIOS loads the video adapter's BIOS, which makes the PC display available. The BIOS then displays its startup screen (see Figure 6-3). This display, which varies slightly from one manufacturer to the next, generally contains the following information:

- The name, and possibly the logo, of the manufacturer or supplier of the BIOS, the serial and version numbers of the BIOS, and its release or version date, which is the key indicator of the feature set included in the BIOS version.
- The BIOS' serial number, which indicates the motherboard, chipset, and BIOS version combination the BIOS was designed to support. The serial number is

the key to upgrading the BIOS. The BIOS manufacturer should have information on its Web site to help you find the configuration associated with a particular serial number. For example, AMI (American Megatrends, Inc.) has downloadable utility software that you can use to decode the serial number of its BIOS versions. For more information on BIOS version and serial numbers, visit **www.ping.be/bios/**.

- The keyboard key that is pressed to gain access to the BIOS' setup program. The DELETE (DEL) key or a function (F1 or F2) key are the most commonly used, but a key combination such as CTRL-ESC is also used in some cases.
- The Energy Star logo. Nearly all PCs purchased today display this logo that indicates that the PC and its BIOS support the Green or Energy Star standard, which specifies power management and consumption guidelines. On older PCs, only those with an upgraded BIOS display this logo.

System Configuration Summary

To indicate that it has completed its task and is about to load the operating system and turn control of the PC over to it, the BIOS displays a summary of the PC's configuration.

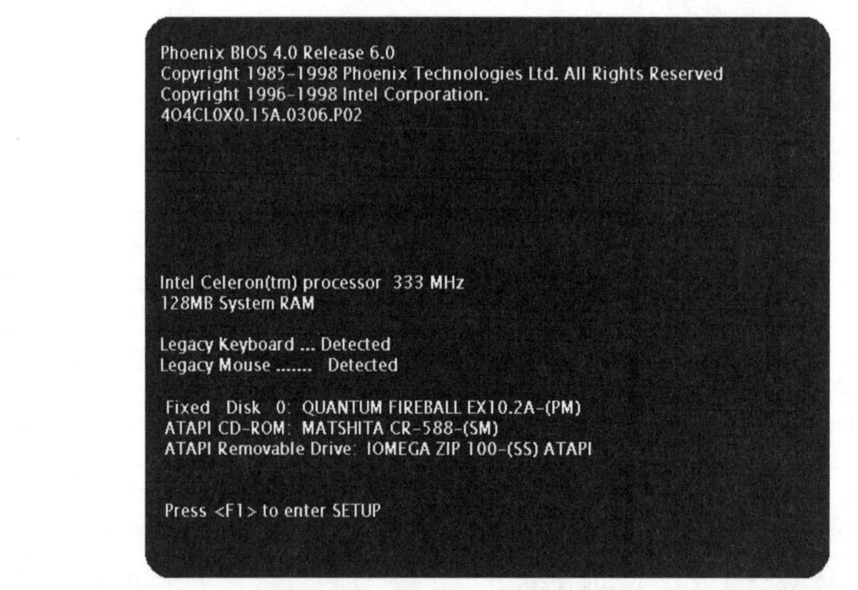

Figure 6-3. A sample of the start up screen for a BIOS

Like all other BIOS displays, the information included depends on the manufacturer and version of the BIOS. The following lists what is typically included:

- **Processor** The microprocessor, such as Pentium, Pentium II, K6, Athlon, etc., in the PC. The newer BIOS versions recognize all Intel, Cyrix, and AMD processors, but some older versions will sometimes indicate a 5x86 processor from one of the other manufacturers as a Pentium. This is a display problem and shouldn't affect the performance of the system. Those processors that incorporate the SMM (System Management Mode) power management standard may be listed as a Pentium-S processor.
- **Coprocessor** Virtually every microprocessor since the 386DX (with the exception of SX models of the 386 and 486 processors) has had an FPU (floating point unit) integrated into the processor chip. The BIOS should indicate these as Integrated. However, if a separate math coprocessor or FPU chip is installed on the system, the coprocessor is indicated as Installed.
- **Clock speed** The clock speed of the processor is its MHz (megahertz) rating, which indicates how may cycles per second the processor runs. This information is sometimes displayed with the processor type.
- **Floppy disk drives** If one or more floppy drives is detected on the system, its size (3.5″ or 5.25″) and capacity (in kilobytes or megabytes) are displayed.
- **Hard disk and CD-ROM drives** The following information is displayed for each IDE/ATA disk drive or ATAPI CD-ROM drive detected: whether it is the primary or secondary master or slave, the name of the manufacturer, the drive's capacity, and the access mode of the drive. The drive designation (C:, D:, E:, etc.) assigned to the drive by the BIOS is also displayed.
- **Memory size** System memory is divided into base, extended, and cache. The BIOS displays the amount of memory allocated to each type. *Base memory* (a.k.a. *conventional memory*) is always 640KB. *Extended memory* represents the remaining amount of memory on the system. The amount of *cache memory* is displayed as a separate number.
- **Memory type** This information regards the physical components making up the system memory and should not be confused with base, extended, or cache types of memory. The information displayed includes the number and technology of the memory banks or modules installed on the system. For example, the display may indicate "EDO DRAM at Bank 1" or "FP: 0 was detected."
- **Video type** If your computer is relatively new (not more than 10 years old), the BIOS will display your video type as VGA/EGA. However, if your PC has a CGA (Color Graphics Adapter) or MGA (Monochrome Graphics Adapter) card in it, the display should reflect that.
- **Serial ports** Each serial port detected on the PC is assigned certain system resources, including IRQ (interrupt request) and I/O (Input/Output) port

addresses (see Chapter 13 for more information on system resources). The display shows the resources assigned to each serial port by the BIOS.

- **Parallel ports** The system resources assigned to parallel ports by the BIOS is displayed.
- **Plug and Play devices** If any Plug and Play (PnP) adapter cards are detected by the BIOS, their information is displayed.

ROMS, PROMS, AND EPROMS: BIOS CHIPS

The BIOS programs and utilities are permanently stored on an electronic chip during manufacturing. The program code is literally programmed into the chip, a process commonly described as *burning in*, when it is manufactured. The reasons for burning the BIOS onto the chip are to prevent tampering or inadvertent changes to this vital program. The BIOS must be able to run, or the PC is just a large paperweight sitting on a desk. The following sections provide an overview of the electronic chips used to store the BIOS.

Read-Only Memory (ROM)

As its name implies, data stored on a *ROM (Read-Only Memory)* cannot be altered. Since the chip is read-only, it cannot be written to, which means it can only be read. Another benefit of using ROM to store the BIOS is that it is nonvolatile. *Nonvolatile memory* retains its contents safely even after its power source is removed, which makes it an ideal media to store system startup instructions. The most commonly used chip for BIOS programs is ROM. In fact, BIOS is commonly referred to as ROM BIOS. Figure 6-4 shows a ROM BIOS chip.

Programmable Read-Only Memory (PROM)

A *PROM* (Programmable Read-Only Memory) is a kind of do-it-yourself ROM chip ready to be programmed with data or programming. Using a ROM burner (a.k.a. ROM programmer), a PROM can be programmed with whatever data or programs you desire. The PROM is programmed with the ROM burner by inducing a higher voltage (12 volts of direct current [VDC]) than is normally used for PROM operations (5 VDC). The higher voltage burns a memory location and, where needed, turns a pre-existing binary 1 into a 0. Once this process is done, it cannot be undone. The 0s cannot be made back into 1s. This is why PROM memory chips are also referred to as *OTP* (One-Time Programmable) *memory*.

Erasable Programmable Read-Only Memory (EPROM)

A variation on the PROM chip is the *EPROM* (pronounced "e-prom" and meaning Erasable Programmable Read-Only Memory). The EPROM adds two important features to the PROM; it is erasable and can be reprogrammed. EPROM chips can be reused and don't have to be discarded when its contents are obsolete. The one drawback is that to reprogram the chip, it must be removed from the PC.

Figure 6-4. A ROM chip on a computer motherboard

As shown in Figure 6-5, the EPROM chip has a quartz crystal window on the face of the chip. This erasing window allows ultraviolet (UV) light to access the chip's interior circuitry. The UV light causes a chemical reaction that turns the 0s back into 1s, thereby erasing the EPROM. There is normally a label or piece of dark tape placed over the erasing window to prevent accidental erasures.

Electronically Erasable Programmable Read-Only Memory (EEPROM)

Newer PCs feature a newer type of ROM BIOS chip. The EEPROM (pronounced "e-e-prom" and meaning Electronically Erasable Programmable Read-Only Memory) can be reprogrammed like the EPROM, but the EEPROM does not need to be removed from the motherboard to be reprogrammed. An EEPROM is reprogrammed or updated with specialized software usually supplied by the BIOS or chip manufacturer. The process that updates an EEPROM under software control is called *flashing*, which is why an EEPROM is also referred to as *flash ROM*.

Because they are easily upgraded, EEPROM chips are used in a variety of applications, such as cars, modems, cameras, and telephones. Flashing allows you to easily apply bug fixes or add new features to your system that may not have been available at the time your system was manufactured, such as booting to a CD-ROM drive. Improving the BIOS can also add new routines that improve your system's boot or overall performance.

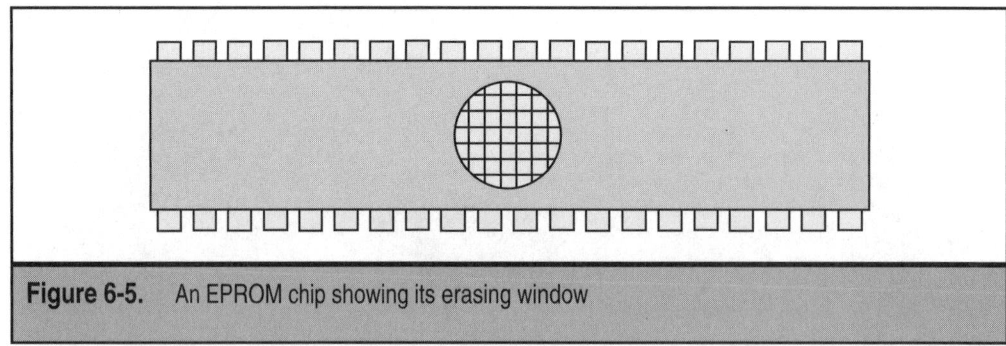

Figure 6-5. An EPROM chip showing its erasing window

Complementary Metal-Oxide Semiconductor (CMOS)

The configuration data for a PC is stored by the BIOS in what is called *CMOS* (pronounced sea-moss, meaning *Complementary Metal-Oxide Semiconductor*). CMOS is also known as NVRAM (nonvolatile RAM). CMOS is a type of memory that requires very little power (about one-millionth of an amp) to retain any data stored on it. CMOS can store a PC's configuration data for many years with power from low voltage dry cell or lithium batteries. Actually, CMOS is the technology that is used to manufacture the transistors used in memory and IC chips. However, the name CMOS, because it was used early on for storing the system configuration, has become synonymous with the BIOS configuration data.

The BIOS CMOS memory stores the system configuration, including any modifications made to the system, its hard drives, peripheral settings, or other settings. The system and RTC (real-time clock) settings are also stored in the CMOS.

The information on the computer's hardware is stored in the computer's CMOS memory. Originally, CMOS technology was used only for storing the system setup information. Although most circuits on the computer are now made using this technology, the name CMOS usually refers to the storage of the computer's hardware configuration data. When the computer is started up, the CMOS data is read and used as a checklist to verify that the devices indicated are in fact present and operating. Once the hardware check is completed, the BIOS loads the operating system and passes control of the computer to it. From that point on, the BIOS is available to accept requests from device drivers and application programs for hardware assistance.

ROM BIOS

Because the BIOS programs must be available to the processor each time it starts up, the BIOS is stored on a ROM chip located on the motherboard. From this ROM chip, the BIOS program is loaded into a reserved area of system memory, normally the last 64KB (memory addresses F000h to FFFFh) of the first 1MB in system memory. Microprocessor and BIOS producers have set this location in memory as a de facto standard, which means that processors always look for the start of the BIOS to be in this location in memory. After the processor loads the BIOS programs from this location, the system boot sequence starts.

As I've discussed earlier, there are several BIOS programs in a PC. In addition to the system BIOS, there are BIOSs to control the peripheral devices that have been added to the computer. For example, most video cards, hard disks, and SCSI adapters have a BIOS that controls parts of their interaction with the processor and other motherboard components.

Older 16-bit computers use a technique called *ROM shadowing* to speed up the boot process. Because ROM chips have a very slow access speed (150 nanoseconds), the BIOS stored on the ROM is copied into the system memory and the ROM's address is adjusted to point to the BIOS's new location. This allows the computer to work with the faster RAM and bypass the slower ROM. Newer 32-bit or higher PC systems load special 32-bit device drivers into RAM during system startup, which allows them to bypass the slower 16-bit ROM code.

THE BIOS CONFIGURATION

Most computers purchased today are shipped directly from the factory already set up and configured. When you buy a PC online, over the phone, or at the local computer reseller, it has all of its components installed and the system configuration and setup is already completed. There is usually very little need for you to ever change your BIOS or configuration data settings. It is reasonable to expect that a computer user would never press the DEL key during the boot sequence to open their system setup and change the PC's configuration.

However, it is also possible that at some point you may need to review or modify your PC's setup and configuration information. When that time comes, you will need an understanding of the information and configuration data stored by the BIOS setup program in its configuration data. This section covers the information you'll need if you ever have to run the setup program and change the configuration data.

System Configuration Data

The hardware configuration of the computer is stored in the computer's CMOS memory. This data is managed through the BIOS' setup program. This section discusses how to access the setup program and each of the menu types it displays.

Setup Program

Each BIOS program will tell you how to gain access to its setup program. Right after it finishes the POST, the BIOS displays the key you press to start the BIOS setup program and gain access to the configuration information. An example of this display is shown in Figure 6-3. The keystrokes used to access the setup program for most of the popular BIOS are listed in Table 6-5.

The BIOS setup program stores the hardware configuration of a PC in CMOS memory. What configuration data is included depends on the processor and BIOS in use.

BIOS	Keystroke
AMI BIOS	DEL
Award BIOS	DELETE OR CTRL-ALT-ESC
IBM Aptiva	F1
Compaq	F10
Phoenix BIOS	F2

Table 6-5. BIOS Setup Program Access Keys

To review or modify the system setup data, a.k.a. the BIOS or CMOS configuration, press the key indicated by the BIOS (usually DEL or a function key such as F1 or F2), which will open the setup program and display its configuration menu.

Standard Settings

Most Pentium or newer computers have two levels of setup configuration settings: standard settings and advanced features. The standard settings include most of the basic setup information, including the system clock, hard disk drives, floppy drives, and the video adapter, plus the processor type, memory type and speed, and the amount and type of memory.

Advanced Features

The advanced features, which are very specific to the combination of motherboard, processor, and chipset on a PC, are accessed through the BIOS setup program. There is no standard set of advanced configuration features and settings. However, the following list contains a sample of advanced feature configuration settings commonly found on most BIOSs:

- **System BIOS Cacheable** Sets whether the system BIOS is to be cached to memory address F0000–FFFFFh, which usually results in faster performance.
- **Video BIOS Cacheable** Sets whether the video adapter's BIOS is to be cached to memory address C0000–7FFFh to speed video operations.
- **Video RAM Cacheable** Enables the caching of video RAM to memory address A0000–AFFFFh.
- **Auto Configuration** If enabled, the configuration is based on the default values of the motherboard chipset.

- **DRAM Integrity Mode** Indicates whether the computer has error-correcting code (ECC) memory.
- **EDO DRAM Speed Selection** Sets the access speed of EDO DRAM.
- **SDRAM CAS (Column Access Strobe) Latency Time** Sets the cycle count controlling the access of SDRAM (synchronous DRAM).
- **SDRAM RAS (Row Access Strobe) Precharge Time** Used with the previous feature, this option sets the cycle count used to refresh DRAM.
- **SDRAM RAS-to-CAS Delay** Controls the number of cycles between SDRAM I/O operations.
- **Memory Hole at 15M-16M** Enables a 1MB block of empty RAM between the fifteenth and sixteenth MB of system RAM, allowing legacy software to run on systems with more than 16MB of RAM.
- **AGP Aperture Size** Enables and sets the size of an AGP (Accelerated Graphics Port) port.
- **CPU Waning Temperature** Sets the temperature ranges (high and low) at which CPU temperature warnings are triggered.
- **Current CPU Temperature** Enables the display of the CPU's temperature.
- **Shutdown Temperature** Enables the system to shutdown if either of the high and low CPU Warning Temperatures is reached.
- **CPU FAN Turn On Speed** Displays the speeds of the internal fan(s).
- **IN0-IN6 (V)** Displays the voltage of up to seven lines (IN0 through IN7).

NOTE: If you are just beginning to learn about computer hardware, you shouldn't attempt to change any of the advanced features in your PC. Seek help from an experienced, A+ Certified PC hardware technician before modifying any of the advanced settings on your PC.

Plug and Play

Most newer processors, BIOSs, and operating systems support Plug and Play (PnP) hardware options and include a special menu in the system setup program. If the operating system does not support PnP options, but the BIOS does, or vice versa, the advanced settings for PnP may need to be set off or on to match the capabilities of the BIOS and operating system.

Here are a few of the more common PnP options included on the Advanced Features menu:

- **Used Memory Length** Defines how much high memory is to be allocated.
- **Used Memory Base Address** Sets a base memory address for peripheral devices that require the use of high memory.
- **Assign IRQ for USB** If your computer has USB ports, this should be enabled.

- **PCI IRQ Activated By** If your computer includes the PCI bus and support, some devices may require this option be set to allow edge-triggered interrupts.

Extended System Configuration Data

If a PC's BIOS supports PnP, then the CMOS also stores *extended system configuration data (ESCD)*. This data includes the system resource assignments of PnP devices and serves as a communications link between the BIOS and the operating system.

Power Management

Another menu in the advanced features of the BIOS setup program is the Power Management menu. This menu contains options that are used to control when the PC automatically powers down based on a series of power conservation settings. Since 1998, the Advanced Configuration and Power Interface (ACPI) has provided the power conservation standards used on most PCs.

Integrated Peripherals

Many newer motherboard designs (see Chapter 4) integrate peripheral device controllers into the motherboard itself. The Integrated Peripherals menu in some BIOS Advanced Features menus is used to adjust the settings.

The more common settings found on this menu are as follows:

- **Base I/O Address** Sets the base port address for serial and parallel ports.
- **Interrupt** Assigns default IRQs to serial and parallel ports.
- **Mode** Sets the interface modes for serial, parallel, and infrared ports.
- **Serial Port A and B** Controls the assignment of port IDs to serial ports. An automatic assignment option allows the system to assign the first available COM port or the assignments can be made manually.
- **Parallel Port** Controls the assignment of LPT ports to parallel ports. This option works like the serial port setting.
- **Audio** Turns the audio system built into the motherboard on or off.

IDE Device Setup and Auto-detection

Another possible menu in the Advanced Features area of the BIOS setup program is the IDE Configuration menu. This menu is used to set the configuration of any IDE devices on the PC. IDE devices include hard disk drives, CD-ROM drives, tape drives, and so on.

Here are many of the options that can be configured on the IDE Configuration menu:

- **Auto Detect** This option is used to enable the system to automatically configure all IDE devices each time the PC is booted. It is not available on all BIOSs.
- **IDE Controller** Sets which IDE controllers are to be enabled.

- **Hard Disk Predelay** Allows disk predelays from 3 to 30 seconds to be set. Typically, this option is disabled.

IDE Configuration Submenus

The IDE Configuration menu contains submenus for configuring the Primary and Slave IDE drives. The options found on these submenus are as follows:

- **Type** Sets the IDE device types installed.
- **Maximum Capacity** Sets the capacity of the hard disk.
- **Multisector Transfers** Controls the sectors per block size for hard disk data transfers to system memory.
- **LBA (Logical Block Addressing) Mode Control** Enables the use of LBA mode for hard disk drives larger than 528MB.
- **Transfer Mode** Designates the mode to be used when moving data from one disk to another.

Security and Passwords

The Advanced Features menu also includes the Security menu. This menu is used to set two passwords:

- **User password** The user password controls the boot process of the PC. If the user password has been set, the PC will not boot until the proper password is entered and verified.
- **Supervisor password** The purpose of the supervisor password is to protect the BIOS configuration settings. After the supervisor password is set, if you access the setup program the configuration settings require the correct password. The system will boot, provided the user password is provided or not set, but access to the CMOS data is prohibited without the supervisor password.

There is one very strict rule that must be observed if either, or both, of these two passwords is set: you absolutely must remember the passwords. If you ever forget the user password, you will not be able to boot the system. Forgetting the supervisor password restricts you from the BIOS setup.

If you forget both passwords, your only recourse is to open the computer and reset the default values with the password-clear jumper (see Figure 6-6), which is located on the motherboard. On most motherboards, this jumper is near either the CMOS battery or the BIOS ROM chip. Another option is to clear all of the CMOS settings, including advanced settings and the passwords, by removing the CMOS battery for a few seconds (see Figure 6-7).

Your best bet is to keep a written copy of the system setup in a safe place and update it as changes are made. I don't recommend writing down passwords, but if you have a very

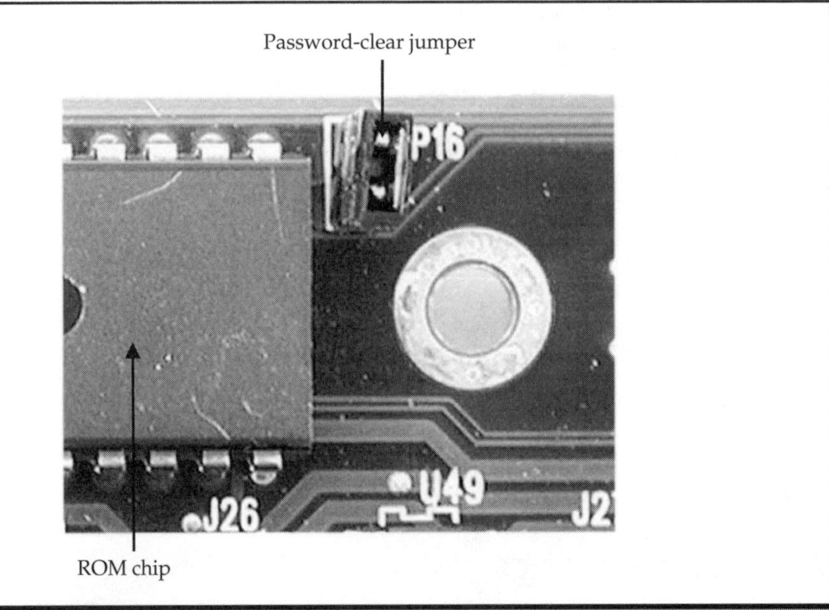

Figure 6-6. The Password-clear jumper on a PC motherboard

Figure 6-7. The BIOS ROM battery on a PC motherboard

safe place for them, you may want to try it. That is, of course, if you feel it is absolutely necessary to set the user and supervisor passwords in the first place.

BIOS UPDATES AND FLASH BIOS

On most older systems, if you wanted to upgrade the BIOS, you had to replace the ROM BIOS chip. This involved physically removing the old BIOS ROM chip and replacing it with a new ROM chip, containing the new BIOS version. The potential for errors and adding new problems into the PC, including ESD (electrostatic discharge), bent pins, damage to the motherboard, and more, was very high. The danger was so great that to avoid the stress and the problems, many people simply upgraded to a new computer.

The EEPROM (flash ROM), flash BIOS, and *flashing* soon replaced the PROM and EPROM as the primary container for BIOS programs. Some motherboards still require the physical replacement of the BIOS PROM, but most newer platforms support flash BIOS and flashing. Flashing is the process used to upgrade your BIOS under the control of specialized flashing software. Any BIOS provider that supports a flash BIOS version has flashing software and update files available either by disk (CD-ROM or diskette) or as a downloadable module from its Web site.

There are really only four things you need to update your PC's BIOS by flashing: a flash BIOS; the right serial number and version information, which is used to find the right upgrade files; the flashing software; and the appropriate flash upgrade files.

Flashing Dangers

Flashing a BIOS is an excellent way to upgrade your PC to add new features and correct old problems, provided there are no problems while you are doing it. Once you begin flashing your BIOS ROM, you must complete the process, without exception. Otherwise, the result will be a corrupted and unusable BIOS. If for any reason the flashing process is interrupted, such as somebody trips over the PC's power cord or there is a power failure at that exact moment, the probability of a corrupted BIOS chip is high.

Loading the wrong BIOS version is another way to corrupt your BIOS. Not all manufacturers include safety features to prevent this from happening in their flashing software. However, flashing software from the larger BIOS companies, the ones you are most likely to be using, such as Award and AMI, include features to double-check the flash file's version against the motherboard model, processor, and chipset and warn you of any mismatches.

Dealing with a Corrupt BIOS

Corrupting your BIOS may put you in the proverbial Catch-22. Your PC will not boot without a clean BIOS and you have to boot the PC to reflash the BIOS. In spite of the potential dangers, the process of flashing your BIOS usually involves just a few seconds during which the risk of catastrophic disaster striking are pretty slim.

These hints may seem obvious, but you can never be too safe:

- Avoid flashing your BIOS in an electrical storm.
- Protect your computer against power surges or brownouts with a UPS (uninterruptible power supply).
- Don't let anyone walk over the power cord during the flashing operation.
- Check twice that you are flashing your BIOS with the current version, and then check again.

Flashing Security

Another potential risk of flash BIOS is the danger of accidentally flashing the BIOS. As long as an accidental operation completes and uses the same complete BIOS version, there is no harm done. However, if an accidental flashing operation is interrupted or for some reason uses an older or incompatible version, the result is the same, accident or not.

To prevent an accidental flashing, some security features are available to block the flashing operation. On motherboards that support flash BIOS, a jumper can be set to disallow flash updates. With this jumper set, the case must be opened and the flashing security jumper removed before the BIOS can be flashed. If this jumper is used, there is no way an accidental flashing can occur. A side benefit to the flash security jumper is that it also prevents attacks from the new breed of computer viruses that attempt to change the code of a flash BIOS.

The Boot Block

The boot block does not block the boot. In fact, it does just the opposite. The *boot block* feature, which is showing up on the newest motherboards, recognizes the risk of a flashing operation corrupting the BIOS. The boot block works very much like the switch now included in newer cars to start a car when its battery goes dead. It is a 4KB program block that is included on the BIOS ROM that recovers a corrupted BIOS by restoring it from a special disk supplied by the BIOS provider. If a motherboard supports this feature, it may need to be enabled through a jumper. If you are planning to upgrade your BIOS with flashing, you may want to check your motherboard's documentation for this feature first.

CHAPTER 7

Computer Memory

In spite of all appearances to the contrary, computers, including personal computers, cannot think and cannot remember. This may seem contradictory when you consider that a computer's memory is one of its most important components. Everything a computer does and all of the data it processes are stored in its memory before and after they are passed to the CPU.

A PC's memory is made up of electronic components in which the PC temporarily stores data and instructions. Technically, any device that stores data or instructions on the PC can be called memory, including the hard disk, floppy disks, ROM, CMOS, RAM, and cache. However, what is commonly referred to as *memory* on the PC is its primary storage, which is also known as system memory, temporary storage, or RAM. With the exception of ROM, which is discussed in this chapter and in Chapter 6, the other forms of storage (hard disk, floppy disk, CD-ROM, and the like) are known as *secondary storage* (see Chapter 9 for more information on secondary storage devices).

A BRIEF OVERVIEW OF ROM

In order to change data stored on the computer, you must be able to write to it. If you cannot write to a memory, you cannot change it. It's logical then that data stored on *read-only memory (ROM)* cannot be changed, as its name implies. ROM also has the added feature of being *non-volatile*, which means that it can keep its contents even without a power source. This makes it ideal for storing the PC's startup instructions and system BIOS (Basic Input/Output System) (see Chapter 4). Figure 7-1 shows a ROM chip. While virtually all ROM chips are packaged in a DIP (dual inline packaging) form, there are three types of ROM used in a PC:

- **PROM (programmable read-only memory)** This type of ROM chip is programmed using a special type of programming device called a *PROM burner* (a.k.a. PROM programmer), which permanently stores machine language (binary instructions) code on the PROM chip. A PROM chip is also referred to as *OTP* (One Time Programmable) *memory*.
- **EPROM (erasable programmable read-only memory)** This type of ROM, pronounced "e-prom," is erasable and can be reprogrammed. Unlike a PROM chip that cannot be reused and can only be thrown out when it becomes obsolete, an EPROM chip can be reprogrammed and reused. As shown in Figure 7-2, an EPROM has a quartz window on the face of the chip that exposes the chip's interior circuits. When ultraviolet (UV) light is shined through this window, it causes a chemical reaction that erases the EPROM. In order to reprogram an EPROM, it must be removed from the computer, erased with UV light, and then reprogrammed on a PROM programmer.
- **EEPROM (electronically erasable programmable read-only memory)** Most newer PCs now include an EEPROM (pronounced "e-e-prom") that can be re-programmed like an EPROM, but, unlike the EPROM, doesn't need to be removed

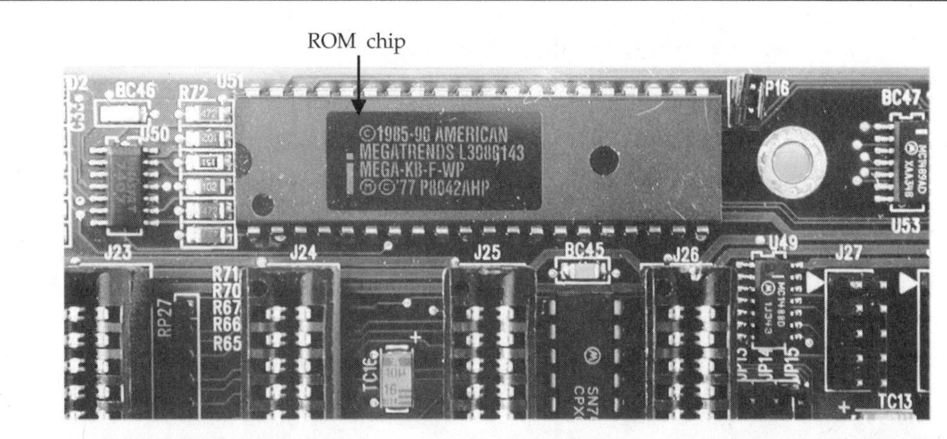

Figure 7-1. A ROM chip on a computer motherboard

from the PC to be reprogrammed. An EEPROM can be reprogrammed, a process called *flashing*, using specialized software that runs on your PC. An EEPROM is also referred to as *flash ROM*. Flashing lets you upgrade your computer's BIOS easily without removing and replacing the ROM chip. Chapter 4 discusses the pros and cons of flashing your system ROM.

One thing that all DIP chips suffer from (see "DIP Packaging" later in the chapter), including removable and replaceable PROMs and EPROMs, is a condition called *chip creep*. DIP chips are inserted into what are called *through-hole sockets* and can and do squirm out

Figure 7-2. An EPROM chip showing its erasing window

of their sockets. Should a ROM chip creep out of its socket, it can cause startup problems. If you have an older motherboard that includes removable DIP ROM or memory chips, you should check them occasionally for creep.

CMOS

Because of the initial cost of Complementary Metal Oxide Semiconductor (CMOS) technology, memory, transistors, and large parts of most microprocessors were once reserved for storing the startup configuration of the PC. With technology advances and lower costs, however, CMOS (pronounced "sea-moss") technology is now used throughout the PC. CMOS memory requires only about one-millionth of an amp to hold any data stored on it. Using only a lithium battery, CMOS memory is able to store the startup configuration of a PC for many years. The term CMOS is still synonymous with the PC's startup configuration data.

RAM

RAM, or *random access memory*, is used in the PC for its primary memory. RAM is where all active programs and data are stored so that they are readily available and easily accessed by the CPU and other components of the PC. When you execute a program on your PC, a copy of the program is copied into RAM from whatever secondary storage it is on, usually the hard disk. Once it is in RAM, the instructions that make up the program are passed one at a time to the CPU for execution. Any data the program accepts or reads from a disk is also stored in RAM.

There are several reasons that RAM is used in a PC, but perhaps the most important is that RAM can transfer data to and from the CPU much faster than all secondary storage devices. Without RAM, all programs instructions and data would be read from the disk drive, slowing the computer to a crawl. With RAM speeds as fast, if not faster, than the speed of the CPU, the entire PC operates much more efficiently.

RAM is a group of integrated circuits (*ICs* or *chips*) that contain small electronic components (called *capacitors*) that store binary 1s and 0s (see Chapter 2). A variety of memory chips can be used for RAM, but some are better suited to storing large amounts of data, fit better in the space available in the PC, and are less expensive. However, not all memory applications in the PC need to store a large amount of data, so most PCs use three different layers of memory: primary memory, level 1 (L1) cache, and level 2 (L2) cache. RAM, in its common usage, refers to the primary memory layer of the PC's memory. See Chapter 8 for more information on cache memory.

Random Access

Random access refers to the ability to access a single storage location in RAM without touching the locations that neighbor it. A good illustration is the difference between a cassette tape and a music CD. If you wish to listen to the third song on a cassette tape, you must fast forward over the first two songs on the tape. This is called *sequential* or *serial access*. Everything is accessed in its physical sequence or in series. To listen to the third song on a music CD, however, you merely indicate that you wish to move to track 3, and bingo—there you are. This is called *direct* or *random access*. You pick where you'd like to go randomly and then go directly there. Accessing something, a program or data, in RAM is very much like the music CD, except that your choices are millions of individual storage locations (bytes), each of which can be addressed directly by your programs.

Volatile versus Nonvolatile

ROM was described earlier as being *nonvolatile*, meaning that it holds its contents without a power source. The opposite of nonvolatile is *volatile*. Volatile memory cannot hold its contents, the data, or programs placed on it without an active power source, such as a wall socket or battery. RAM is a volatile form or memory and when it loses its power, it loses its contents. If you have ever lost everything you were working on when a power failure hit, someone tripped over the power cord, or you had to reboot the PC, then you've experienced the downside of volatile memory.

So, why is volatile memory used in the PC? Why not just use nonvolatile memory? If you were to use EEPROMs or any of the newer types of SRAM (see the section "RAM Types" later in this section), the cost for the amount of memory you need to run the high-graphic and feature-rich software of today would exceed that of the entire rest of the PC, including all of the options and bells and whistles you could add. Volatile RAM is inexpensive, readily available, easily expanded, and, as long as you protect your system against power problems (see Chapter 14), it is error- and trouble-free for the most part.

Bits, Bytes, and Words

Nearly everything the PC connects to is measured in bits these days, especially modems and Internet connections, but RAM is still measured in bytes—actually, kilobytes, megabytes, or gigabytes. Table 7-1 lists the various data units commonly associated with RAM.

Memory Speeds

RAM is much faster than a hard disk, floppy disk, CD-ROM, or any other form of secondary storage. On the average, accessing data from a hard disk drive takes from 8 to 16 *milliseconds* (ms). Accessing the same data from RAM takes from 50 to 80 nanoseconds (ns). There are 1,000ms and 1 billion nanoseconds in a second. What this works out to is that RAM at 50ns is over a million times faster than a hard disk. Other secondary storage devices, such as the CD-ROM or floppy disk, are even slower.

Clock Speeds

Most, but not all, of the actions taking place inside the PC are synchronized to one or more "clocks." These clocks provide electronic timings to which the components of the PC can synchronize their actions to those of the CPU and other devices. For example, the processor's *internal clock speed* provides the tempo at which electronic signals and data are sent around the PC.

Unit	Size	Description
Bit	One binary digit	Stores either a binary 0 or 1
Byte	Eight bits	One character
Word	16 to 64 bits	Numeric values and addresses
Kilobyte (KB)	1 thousand bytes	About one page of double-spaced text
Megabyte (MB)	1 million bytes	About the size of a short book
Gigabyte (GB)	1 billion bytes	1,000 short books
Terabyte (TB)	1 trillion bytes	An entire library
Petabyte (PB)	1 quadrillion bytes	Just about all the libraries in the U.S.

Table 7-1. RAM Units of Measure

The CPU's clock isn't really a "clock" like the cuckoo clock on the wall. The system clock sets the length and number of electronic cycles available in one second. These cycles, which are the timing mechanism used to synchronize the movement of data and execution of instructions, are measured in megahertz (MHz). A *hertz* is one shift of the clock's electronic signal from high to low (or low to high). A *megahertz* is one million hertz in one second. A CPU with a clock speed of 600MHz operates on 600 million cycles per second. To put this in terms of instructions, a single computer instruction, such as adding two binary numbers that are already in the CPU's registers, generally takes one CPU cycle. So, theoretically, a 600MHz computer is capable of completing 600 million of these instructions per second. Many processors are rated in *MIPS (million of instructions per second)*. Unfortunately, most processors cannot translate their megahertz ratings directly into MIPS. Data must be moved in and out of the CPU's registers to RAM, the hard disk, and other destinations, and these actions also require clock cycles to complete.

CPU Wait States

It should also be noted that RAM, which operates in nanoseconds, is faster than most CPUs. This suggests a problem, but the CPU works through *wait states*, which are intervals of a set number of cycles between CPU actions, such as data requests, reads, writes, moves, etc., to allow the requests to be carried out. To read data from memory, the CPU may use three wait states, as illustrated in Figure 7-3. The CPU issues the request for data along with an address. Receiving the address and transferring it to the memory controller uses about one wait state. Finding the data in memory also takes about one wait state. Transferring the data to the CPU's storage areas (called *registers*) uses a third wait state. Even if each wait state only took about 1/400 millionth of a second (based on a 400MHz

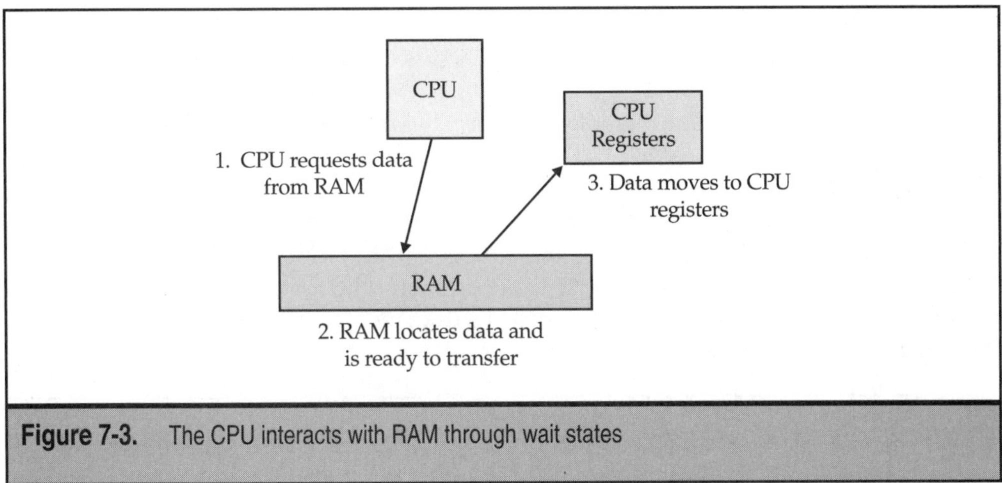

Figure 7-3. The CPU interacts with RAM through wait states

CPU), RAM only requires perhaps 50 to 60ns to do its part. The significance here is that the closer the RAM's speed is matched to that of the data bus and CPU clock, more data will be transferred from RAM to the CPU and other components of the PC on each cycle.

Another speed in the PC that must be considered is the speed of the data and address buses. Like the CPU, the bus transfer speed is in megahertz, which represents the speed used to move data and instructions between structures, such as the CPU and memory. Most RAM manufacturers include online guides on their Web sites to help match RAM and RAM speeds to bus and CPU speeds. Table 7-2 contains a sampling of RAM speeds and matching bus speeds.

Data Bus	RAM
20MHz	50ns
25MHz	40ns
33MHz	30ns
50MHz	20ns
66MHz	15ns
100MHz	10ns
133MHz	6ns

Table 7-2. RAM/Bus Speeds

Having more RAM in the PC does not improve the overall speed of the processor, but it does improve how much data the processor can access without the need to go to the slower hard disk drive. You may have heard that adding RAM to a slow PC will speed it up. Yes, but only because the processor was able to perform faster input/output (I/O) operations.

Memory Speeds

On older, pre-Pentium PCs, RAM speeds were in the range of 80 to 120ns (the higher number is the lower speed). Pentium and equivalent PCs have RAM speeds of 60ns or lower (faster). For the best results, RAM speeds should be matched to the speed of the motherboard's bus. Typically, a motherboard's documentation contains information on the RAM speed it requires and supports.

NOTE: When it comes to memory speeds, higher means slower, so 120ns is slower than 60ns.

Memory Latency and Burst Mode

Memory is arranged in rows and columns much like millions of cubbyholes, each of which stores a single byte of data. When the processor asks for data, it specifies the row and column of the location it wishes to start fetching or storing data. First the row is found, then the column, and finally, the required number of data cells is transferred. The amount of delay in the process required to locate the row, the column, and then the starting cell is called *memory latency.*

To minimize the effect of memory latency on the efficiency of the PC, memory accesses are done in sets (bursts) of multiple data segments, using what is called *burst mode access.* Because of the latency, it takes longer to read the first set of data than it does the next one, two, or three cells (four is a fairly common number of data segments in a burst operation). Burst mode access reads the four segments, the size of which is determined by the data bus, in series. This avoids repeating the latency for each segment. Burst mode operations are measured in the number of clock cycles required for each segment. For example, an 8-2-2-2 burst notation indicates that the first segment requires eight clock cycles to complete because of memory latency, but each of the remaining three segments requires only two cycles. The benefit of burst mode access is in the numbers. In the example, a total of 14 clock cycles were required to complete the access. Without burst mode operations, each access would require the full 8 clock cycles, which results in a total of 32 clock cycles for all four segments.

Burst mode access works with L2 cache, which is sized to receive and buffer as many of the burst segments as possible. For example, on a PC with a 32-bit data bus, the L2 cache of 256 bits would receive and buffer as many as two burst sets (or eight segments) from memory.

RAM Types

The two basic RAM types used in a PC are DRAM (Dynamic RAM) and SRAM (Static RAM). DRAM and SRAM are quite different beyond the similarity that they both store data and are random access memory. Table 7-3 lists some of the more commonly used types of RAM.

Name	Usage
SRAM (static RAM)	Also called Flash RAM, used in cache memory and in PCMCIA memory cards
DRAM (dynamic RAM)	Personal computers
PRAM (parameter RAM)	The equivalent of CMOS on a Macintosh computer
PSRAM (pseudo-static RAM)	Notebooks and other portable PCs
VRAM (video RAM)	Frame buffer for video and color graphics support

Table 7-3. RAM Types

Each of the different types of RAM has a specific purpose to which it is best suited:

- **Static RAM (SRAM)**, a.k.a. *Flash RAM* Used for cache memory and PCMCIA (Portable Computer Memory Card Industry Association) memory cards.
- **Dynamic RAM (DRAM)** Most commonly used for primary or main memory on a PC. It is commonly referred to as simply RAM.
- **Parameter RAM (PRAM)** Used on Macintosh computers to store internal information, such as the computer's date and time and other configuration data that must remain in memory after the computer powers down.
- **Pseudo-Static RAM (PSRAM)** Specifically made for use in portable computers.
- **Video RAM (VRAM)** Used on video adapter cards for buffering between the PC system and the video display.

To download an excellent tutorial on memory systems, visit Kingston Technologies' Web site at **www.kingston.com/tools/umg/** and download their "Ultimate Memory Guide."

Static RAM

The primary difference between SRAM and DRAM is that SRAM (pronounced "ess-ram") does not require the constant refreshing required of DRAM (pronounced "dee-ram"). DRAM must be electrically refreshed about every two milliseconds, but SRAM is only refreshed when data is written to it. SRAM is also faster than DRAM, but it is much more expensive and requires a much larger physical space to store the same amount of data as DRAM. Because of these characteristic differences, SRAM is most commonly used for cache memory (see Chapter 8) and DRAM for common system memory, a.k.a. RAM.

DRAM

The most commonly referenced form of RAM is *dynamic RAM* or *DRAM*. Compared to the other RAM technologies, DRAM is inexpensive and stores the largest number of bits in the smallest amount of physical space.

A DRAM cell, which stores one bit, is made up of a single capacitor. A *capacitor* stores either a positive or negative voltage value that is used to represent 1 or 0 binary values. DRAM must be refreshed every two milliseconds. This is done when the contents of every single DRAM cell (capacitor) is read and then rewritten by a refresh logic circuit. This constant refreshing contributes to the fact that DRAM is the slowest type of RAM. It averages transfer speeds of 50ns or higher.

DIP Packaging

On PCs with a 386 or earlier processor, DRAM chips were mounted on the motherboard as individual memory chips in sockets arranged in a group, called a *memory bank*. On newer systems (386DX and later), DRAM chips are installed as a part of integrated memory modules that mount in a special slot on the motherboard (see the following section).

Single DRAM chips are packaged in a DIP (dual inline package), a sample of which is shown in Figure 7-4. DRAM chips in a DIP packaging were mounted into individual sockets directly on the motherboard in banks of four or more chips. DIP memories are rare, except on older systems.

Single Inline Memory Modules

With the 386DX, DRAM began to be packaged in modules that mounted to the motherboard in a single long slot. This single-edge connector package incorporates several DIP memories into an integrated memory module.

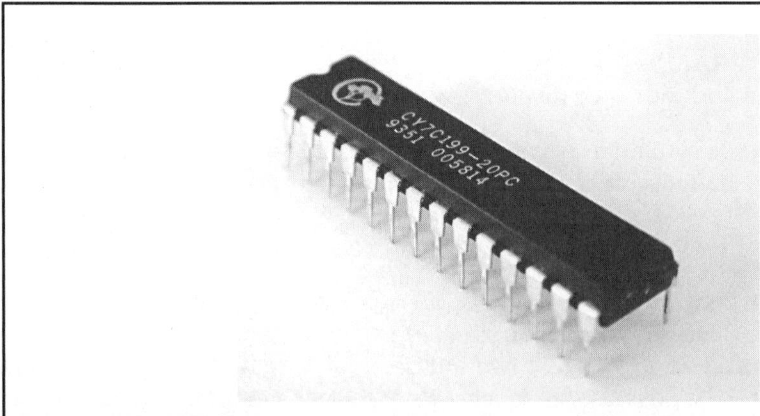

Figure 7-4. A DIP chip

The earliest type of memory module was the single inline memory module (SIMM). A SIMM consists of DRAM chips soldered to a small circuit board with either a 30- or 72-pin connector. A SIMM has a storage capacity that ranges from 1MB to 128MB. At the upper end of this range, SIMMs have DRAM chips mounted on two sides of the circuit board. Matching a SIMM to a motherboard and its memory slots involves only matching the number of pins in the mounting slot to that of the memory module. As illustrated in Figure 7-5, a SIMM is installed on a motherboard in a way that increases the number of modules and the amount of memory in a relatively smaller area than was required by DIP memories.

Dual Inline Memory Modules

Newer PCs, especially those with 64-bit systems, use an adaptation of the SIMM, the dual inline memory module (DIMM). This 168-pin module includes DRAM memory on both sides of the module and supports larger amounts of memory capacity. Matching a DIMM (see Figure 7-6) to a PC is more complicated than just matching the number of pins. DIMM modules are available in different voltages (3.3v and 5.0v) and are either buffered or unbuffered to match up with motherboards and chipset combinations.

A smaller DIMM version is the small outline DIMM (SODIMM), which is used primarily in portable computers.

Figure 7-5. A SIMM memory module on a motherboard

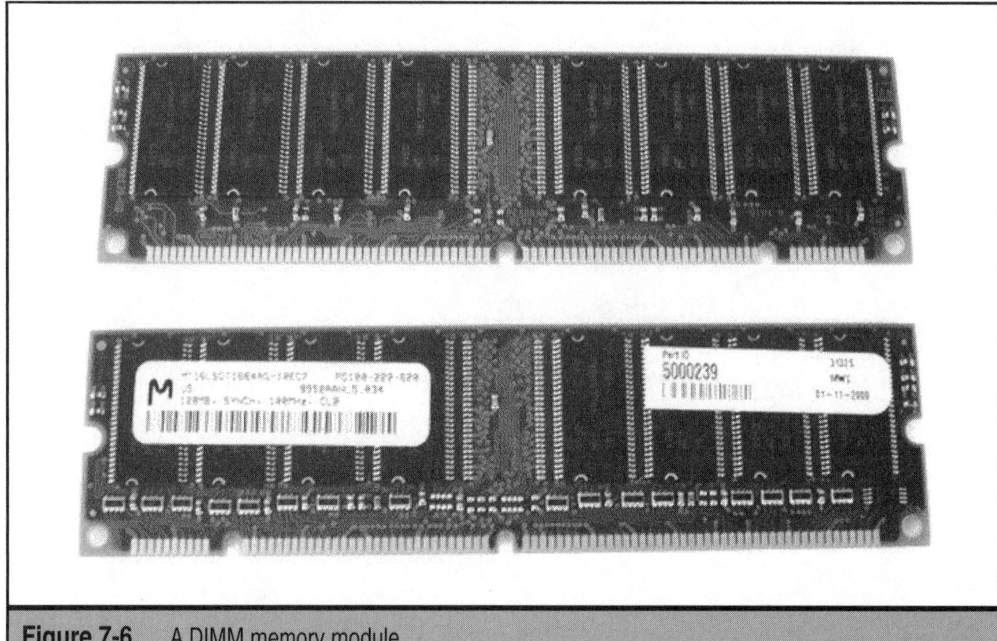

Figure 7-6. A DIMM memory module

Module Connectors

Over the years, the connectors on the edge of SIMM and DIMM modules and the connectors inside their mounting sockets have been made from either gold or tin. The connectors on a SIMM and its socket are available in either gold or tin and DIMMs use only gold for both. Older SIMMs also used gold, but most newer SIMMs now use tin. These two metals should not be mixed, which means that a tin SIMM connector should not be inserted into a gold SIMM socket, and vice versa. Mixing these metals can cause a chemical reaction that causes tin oxide to grow on the gold and possibly create an unreliable, and difficult to diagnose, electrical connection.

Matching Memory to the Motherboard

The memory added to a system, whatever its packaging, must be matched to the width of the data bus of the motherboard. Any data transferred to the CPU, to cache memory, or to the peripheral devices on a PC, moves over the data bus. The width of the data bus (also referred to as its capacity) is measured in bits. The data bus width also represents the amount of data that can flow over it in one clock cycle. The primary reason for memory banks on a motherboard is to arrange the memory in sets that take advantage of the bus width to transfer data. A memory bank holds enough memory so that the width of the memory matches that of the data bus.

Filling Up Memory Banks

It is entirely possible that a PC with installed memory chips or modules will fail during the boot process because it can detect no memory on the system. This is because, unless the first memory bank is completely filled with memory chips or modules, as the case may be, the PC simply ignores it. If the first memory bank (usually designated as Bank 0) is not completely filled, the PC will not boot because it does not detect any memory at all. Virtually all motherboards (see Chapter 1) include one or more memory banks that are numbered beginning with either 0 or 1.

Every memory module is marked with its *memory bit width*, or the number of bits it transfers to the data bus at one time. A module's memory bit width is used to determine how many modules must be installed in a memory bank to match the system's bus width. A 30-pin SIMM has an 8-bit width; a 72-pin SIMM has a 32-bit width; and a 168-pin DIMM has a 64-bit width. On a system with a 32-bit bus, the memory banks must have four of the 30-pin SIMMs (4 times 8 bits equals 32 bits) or one 72-pin SIMM (32 bits). A 32-bit system cannot install even one DIMM because its 64-bit memory bit width is too wide for the data bus. Table 7-4 lists the combinations of SIMMs and DIMMs that can be used for different data bus widths. Theoretically, eight 30-pin SIMMs could be used to fill a 64-bit memory bank. However, because of the physical space this would require, most newer systems do not support the 8-bit SIMM.

There are special adapter cards, called SIMM converters, that can be used to install 30-pin SIMMs on a motherboard with only 72-pin sockets. A SIMM converter plugs into a 72-pin socket and features two or more sockets into which 30-pin sockets can be installed. However, even with a SIMM converter, you still have to get enough memory installed to match the data bus width.

Those memory modules that support parity or error-correcting code (ECC), expand the memory bus by one additional bit. In general, parity and ECC systems add 1 extra bit for each 8-bits in the bus width, which increases an 8-bit SIMM's width to 9 bits and a 32-bit SIMM with parity to a data width of 36 bits. These bits do not affect the system data bus because they are not sent out.

Bus Width	8-bit Bus	16-bit Bus	32-bit Bus	64-bit Bus
30-pin SIMM	1	2	4	-
72-pin SIMM	-	-	1	2
168-pin DIMM	-	-	-	1

Table 7-4. Matching Data Bus Widths to Memory Modules

Deep, Wide, and Fast Memories

SIMMs and DIMMs and memory chips have special markings to indicate their bus width and data capacities. If these markings are not directly on the module or chip, you can definitely find this information in the technical specifications for your memory on its manufacturer's Web site.

The information marked on the memory is the *DWS* (depth, width, and speed) notation. The DWS, which looks something like 16x64-60, indicates the overall size of the memory on the module, but you do have to calculate it. For example, the marking of 16x64-60 does not mean 16 times 64 minus 60. This is the DWS notation for a DIMM that has 16 million bits on each of its 64 bits of width and has a data speed of 60ns. The "x" means *by*, which is another way to say *times*, as in 16 megabits *by* 64 bits. Think of it like a big matrix with rows and columns, which is how memory is organized anyway. The module in the example has 64 rows of 16 million bits each.

Memory depths on SIMMs and DIMMs range from 1 to 32 million bits (Mb). There are exceptions, especially in older and smaller SIMMs, which have 256 and 512 kilobits (Kb) depths, but these are the exception.

A memory module's width is always in bits and is usually 8 or 9 bits on 30-pin SIMMs, 32 bits on 256 or 512Kb SIMMs, 32 or 36 bits on 72-pin SIMMs, and 64 or 72 bits on 168-pin DIMMs. The different widths, such as the 32 or 36 bits on a 72-pin SIMM, reflect memory modules without parity (6, 32, or 64 bits) and those with parity systems (9, 36, or 72 bits).

The number of bits available to store data on a memory module is calculated as the memory depth times the memory width. For example, a DIMM with a 16x64-60 notation has just over 1 billion bits (1,024,000,000) of memory or 128 million bytes, calculated by dividing the number of bits by 8 (there are 8 bits to a byte). Table 7-5 shows the memory size for many SIMM and DIMM modules.

Memory Module	D x W	Memory Size (MB)
30-pin SIMM (without parity)	1 x 2	1
	1 x 8	1
	2 x 8	2
	4 x 8	4
	16 x 8	16
30-pin SIMM (parity)	1 x 3	1

Table 7-5. Storage Capacities for Common SIMM and DIMM Modules

Memory Module	D x W	Memory Size (MB)
	1 x 9	1
	2 x 9	2
	4 x 9	4
	16 x 9	16
72-pin SIMM (without parity)	1 x 32	4
	2 x 32	8
	4 x 32	16
	8 x 32	32
	16 x 32	64
72-pin SIMM (parity)	256K x 36	1
	512K x 36	2
	1 x 36	4
	2 x 36	8
	4 x 36	16
	8 x 36	32
	16 x 36	64
168-pin DIMM (without parity)	8 x 32	32
	4 x 64	32
	16 x 32	64
	8 x 64	64
	16 x 64	128
168-pin DIMM (parity)	4 x 72	32
	8 x 72	64
	16 x 72	128

Table 7-5. Storage Capacities for Common SIMM and DIMM Modules *(continued)*

Parity Memory

DRAM memory can include a mechanism used to verify and maintain the integrity of the data it holds. The two methods used most often are parity and error-correcting code (ECC). Parity and ECC memories are more expensive than nonparity memory, and as a result, nonparity memory is much more common. Nonparity memory is what most people think of as regular memory. Parity and ECC memories are less common and are the exception.

Even and Odd Parity

Parity has been around about as long as PCs themselves. Of course, there is really no way for a bit to know exactly what should be stored in it individually or in any part of its memory, for that matter. But, there must be some way to help prevent and detect bit errors in data being moved about as fast as memory does. To do so, parity systems add an additional bit to every eight bits of data—in other words, every byte gets an extra bit. The extra bit is used by the system to verify that the right amount of bits with the value one was sent, received, and stored.

There are two types of parity protocols: odd parity and even parity. Odd parity checks that the number of 1 bits (bits with the value of 1 stored in them) in a byte is an odd number. Even parity performs the same check on an even number of 1 bits. The parity bit is toggled on or off to make sure the number of 1 bits remains even or odd as required. Parity is achieved when the number of 1 bits in a byte plus the parity bit adds up to an odd number or even number, depending on the protocol in use. Table 7-6 shows the impact of the parity bit on the data width of SIMM and DIMM modules.

When a byte (and its parity bit) does not have the right number of bits, either even or odd, the result is a *parity error*. On most systems, a parity error is enough to halt the system with a blue screen of death. Memory parity errors can be an indication of a one-time memory fault or a seriously faulty memory module. Repeated parity errors are a fairly good indicator that your PC has a bad memory module.

One of the shortcomings of parity checking systems is that they only detect errors and not large ones, at that. Since they only check for errors in even- or odd-bit counts, parity systems cannot specifically identify where a parity error has occurred. All it knows is that

Memory Module	Nonparity Width	Parity Width
30-pin SIMM	8 bits	9 bits
72-pin SIMM	32 bits	36 bits
168-pin DIMM	64 bits	72 bits

Table 7-6. Memory Module Nonparity and Parity Bit Widths

an error was detected, but that is not all bad. If a byte starts out with six 1 bits but ends up with only five or gains one and has seven, there is definitely a condition in memory of which you should be aware.

Parity memory systems are able to detect only a 1-bit error and cannot fix the error. When a parity error is detected, normally an error message is displayed to the monitor and the system halts.

ECC Memory

Error-correcting code (ECC) goes beyond simple parity systems to detect errors of up to four bits and correct all 1-bit errors in memory. Four-bit errors in memory are extremely rare and when detected are an indication of a serious memory problem. However, 1-bit errors are quite common and ECC memory is able to correct them without reporting errors and keep the system running. Errors detected of two, three, or four bits are reported as parity errors and the system halts.

DRAM Technologies

As microprocessors and chipsets evolve, so do memory technologies. Since DRAM is still the primary type of memory used in the PC, it has had to adapt to keep pace. The result is that new DRAM technologies are created that improve on the previous DRAM technology in a sort of memory one-upmanship. Each new DRAM technology is based at least in part on a preceding DRAM technology, usually improving its organization, speed, and access method.

Some of the more common DRAM technologies are:

- **Fast Page Mode (FPM)** FPM DRAM, which is also known as non-EDO DRAM, is compatible with virtually all motherboards with bus speeds under 66MHz.
- **Extended Data Out (EDO)** EDO, the most common technology of DRAM, is slightly faster than FPM DRAM and is very common in Pentium and later PCs with bus speeds under 75MHz.
- **Synchronous DRAM (SDRAM)** SDRAM (pronounced "ess-dee-ram") is synchronized to the system clock to read and write memory in burst mode. This type of DRAM is more common on systems with higher bus speeds.
- **Burst Extended Data Out (BEDO) DRAM** BEDO (pronounced "beado") is EDO memory with pipelining technology added. *Pipelining* allows BEDO DRAM to transfer data and accept the next request from the CPU at the same time. BEDO DRAM is common on PCs with clock speeds of up to 66MHz.
- **Enhanced DRAM (EDRAM)** EDRAM (pronounced "ee-dee-ram") is a combination of SRAM and DRAM used for Level 2 cache (see Chapter 8).
- **Double Data Rate (DDR) SDRAM** A special form of SDRAM that is designed for systems with bus speeds over 200MHz.

- **Enhanced SDRAM (ESDRAM)** ESDRAM (pronounced "ehs-dee-ram") is actually SDRAM with a small built-in SRAM cache that is used to increase memory transfer times. It works with data bus speeds of up to 200MHz.
- **Direct Rambus DRAM (DRDRAM)** DRDRAM (pronounced "dee-are-dee-ram" or "Doctor DRAM") is a proprietary DRAM technology developed by Rambus, Inc. (**www.rambus.com**) and Intel. DRDRAM, along with a similar approach, SLDRAM (SyncLink DRAM), is capable of supporting memory speeds of up to 800MHz.
- **FRAM (ferroelectric RAM)** FRAM (pronounced "fram") has features of both DRAM and SRAM, which means it can store data even after its power source is removed.

Video RAM

Back when PC monitors were all monochrome (black and white), the PC could easily set aside 2K of memory to support the needs of the display. However, today's multicolor monitors require significantly more memory to generate their graphical displays. The monochrome monitor was fine using primary memory for its support, but today's monitors need a memory source much closer and faster than standard RAM. To provide the video system with the RAM it needs, memory has been added to the video adapter card, which places it much closer to the video controller and the monitor itself. This memory is called *video memory* or *video RAM (VRAM).*

DRAM as Video RAM

The first type of video memory used was standard DRAM. This didn't work out, primarily because it had to be continually refreshed, which meant that while it was being refreshed it couldn't be accessed by the video system. In addition, DRAM was unable to support the extremely fast clock speeds of video systems. DRAM is a *single-ported* memory. This means that it can only support access from one source at a time. In a video system situation, only the CPU or video controller could be accessing it, not both. These problems and others lead to the development of memory technologies specifically designed for the video system.

VRAM

To provide the support and speeds required by the video system, VRAM must be *dual-ported*, which allows it to accept data from the CPU at the same time it is providing data to the video controller. This means that while it is receiving data about new displays, it can be supplying the video system with the data it needs to refresh the display's image.

When an image is displayed on the monitor, the image data is transferred from primary RAM to the video RAM. The *RAM digital-to-analog converter (RAMDAC)* reads the data from VRAM and converts it into analog signals, which are used by the monitor's display device, such as a CRT (cathode ray tube), to create the image desired. More information is available on the RAMDAC and the video system in Chapter 12.

Some of the video memory technologies in use are:

- **Video RAM (VRAM)** The most commonly used form of VRAM ("vee-ram") is also called video RAM (VRAM). VRAM is a dual-ported DRAM that acts as a buffer between the CPU and the video display.
- **Windows RAM (WRAM)** Although its name (it is normally referred to as "Windows RAM," not "wram") suggests otherwise, this type of video memory has nothing at all to do with the operating system with a similar name. Its name comes from the fact that this type of video memory is accessed in blocks or windows, which makes it slightly faster than VRAM. Windows RAM is a high-performance video RAM that is better than standard VRAM for high-resolution images.
- **Synchronous Graphics RAM (SGRAM)** SGRAM ("ess-gee-ram") is a single-ported DRAM technology improved to run almost four times faster than normal DRAM. It is a single-ported clock-synchronized video RAM that uses specialized instructions to perform in a few instructions what would be a series of instructions for other forms of VRAM.

Parameter RAM

Macintosh computers store their internal configuration data, such as the system date and time and other system parameters that must be stored between system boots, in what is called *parameter RAM (PRAM)*. PRAM is the Macintosh computer equivalent of the PC's CMOS. In fact, the process called "zapping the pram" on a Macintosh is about the same operation as removing the CMOS battery on a PC to reset its configuration parameters back to their default values. See Chapter 6 for more information on PC CMOS.

LOGICAL MEMORY CONFIGURATION

Prior to Windows NT and Windows 2000, operating systems such as MS-DOS, PC-DOS, or Windows 3.*x* or 9*x*, organized the physical primary memory into a logical organization that fit its processing needs. DOS and Windows operating systems define memory into four basic divisions, as shown in Figure 7-7.

Conventional Memory

Conventional memory is the first 640KB of system memory (RAM). Two things came together in the early days of PCs to fix its size to 640KB. The early processors could not address more than 1MB of RAM and IBM reserved the upper 384KB of that space for its BIOS and utilities, which left the lower 640KB for the operating system and programs. In use, conventional memory usually contains the kernel of the operating system, user application programs, routines that terminate-and-stay-resident (TSR), and system-level device drivers.

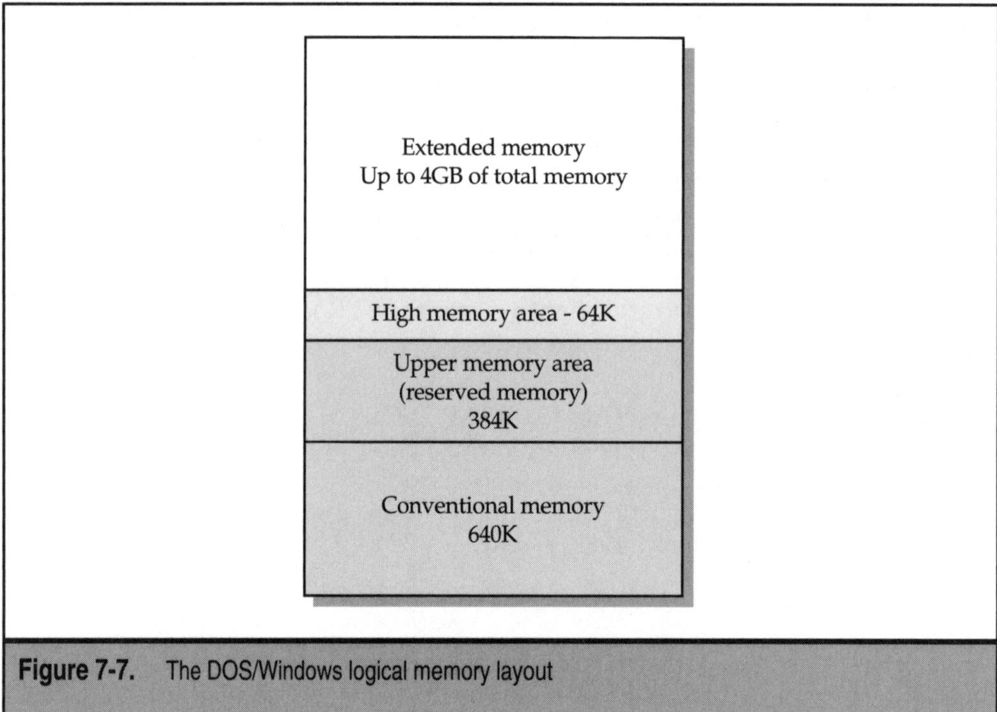

Figure 7-7. The DOS/Windows logical memory layout

The Upper Memory Area

The *upper memory area* was originally designated by IBM for use by the system BIOS and video RAM, the 384KB that remains in the first 1MB of RAM after conventional memory. As the need for more than the 640KB available grew, this area was designated as *expanded memory* and special device drivers were developed, such as EMM386.EXE, to facilitate its general use. The use of this area frees up space in conventional memory by relocating device drivers and TSR programs into unused space in the upper memory area.

Extended Memory and the High Memory Area

All of a PC's memory beyond the first 1MB of RAM is called *extended memory*. Every PC has a limit of how much total memory it can support. The limit is induced by a combination of the processor, motherboard, and operating system. The width of the data and address bus is usually the basis of the limit of how much memory the PC can address. The memory maximum usually ranges from 16MB to 4GB, with some newer PCs now able to accept and process even more RAM. Regardless of the amount of RAM a PC can support, anything above 1MB is extended memory.

Extended memory is often confused with expanded memory. Expanded memory (the upper memory area) expands conventional memory to fill up the first 1MB of RAM. Extended memory extends RAM all the way to its limit.

The first 64KB of extended memory is reserved for use during the startup processes of the PC. This area is called the *high memory area*.

DEALING WITH MEMORY ERRORS

Memory errors are a common occurrence on most PCs, although they shouldn't be so common that they are an everyday occurrence. There are two general types of memory errors—*hard errors* and *soft errors*. There isn't really a lot of difference between these two types of errors. The biggest difference is that hard errors can be repeated because something is definitely broken, and soft errors are transient or intermittent and may or may not be a one-time fluke.

A hard memory error happens when a memory module or chip, its mounting, or the motherboard is defective. Because this type of error is usually the result of a physical defect, the same error can be repeated consistently. For example, if a bit in the conventional memory area is damaged by ESD (electrostatic discharge), it could cause a consistently reported parity error. Another example is a SIMM module that is improperly seated, causing the memory not to be detected during the boot cycles. Hard memory errors are commonly the result of loose memory modules, system board defects, or defective memory modules. Typically, hard errors are fairly easy to find and repair because they are easily diagnosed and located. Because they can be repeated, you have a very good chance of isolating the problem.

Soft errors are transient in nature. A single bit can give the wrong data value one-time ever, or it can operate normally most of the time but malfunction intermittently. Soft errors can be difficult to diagnose because they are moving targets. A PC that develops a history of soft memory errors most likely has poor quality memory. However, the problem could also be with the motherboard or another component seemingly unrelated to the memory. Diagnosing a soft error can be an exercise in patience. Soft errors are usually not consistent, but they will eventually repeat if there is anything to worry about.

Common Memory Errors

Fortunately, most hard memory errors will show up during the boot process and are the result of a physical defect, system configuration, or component installation problem. Your built-in hardware diagnostic package, the POST (Power-On Self-Test), should find and report any hard errors it detects with either a beep code or a text message. See Chapter 6 for more information on the POST and its error modes.

However, if a memory error occurs after the system has booted, the operating system will usually display an error message. Here are a few of the more common error messages you will see for memory errors on a PC:

- **Divide by zero error** This error usually means that an operation has returned a bad value, a running program has a very serious code flaw, or some operation is working with a value that is too large to fit into one of the CPU's registers. This is likely a soft error, but attention should be given to any future errors of this type.
- **General protection fault** A running program has attempted to address memory outside of its allotted space. This type of error can be either a hard or soft error. A program may have a code flaw or there may be a bad patch of memory on the PC. Typically, the offending program is terminated or the whole system halts. If this error occurs more than once in a short timeframe, it is time to use a memory testing tool to test the system.
- **Fatal exception error** The operating system, a running program, or a device driver has passed an invalid instruction to the CPU, or a bad memory location was accessed. This error is usually caused by faulty memory and should be checked out.

Software Diagnostic Tools

Because memory errors can be intermittent and very difficult to isolate and diagnose, it is always a good idea to have a memory diagnostic program. As mentioned earlier, one of the most popular programs of this type is the POST (Power-On Self-Test) program that is included in your PC's BIOS startup utilities. The POST does a number of memory tests each time the system boots. It performs read and write tests to all of the memory it detects and then compares its memory test results to previous POST results. Any difference in the memory tests is dealt with like a memory error and it is signaled with a beep code or a text message.

However, the POST is not able to test for future failures or performance problems in memory. These tests are performed by memory diagnostic software, such as DocMemory from SimmTester (**www.simmtester.com**), Memory+ from TFI Technology (**www.tfi-technology.com**), or Gold Memory from Goldware CZ (**www.goldmemory.cz**). These programs are good tools for tracking down soft errors, because they can run continuously for hours or even days to find the source of a transient memory problem. A great site with an array of software diagnostic and troubleshooting tools is TweakFiles.Com (**www.tweakfiles.com**).

Memory Testing Tools

SIMM and DIMM memory testers thoroughly test a memory module at different speeds, voltages, and timings to determine if all of the memory cells (bits) on the module are good. These specially designed devices can also test for any indication that the memory may fail in the future. A SIMM/DIMM tester is fairly expensive and may be beyond the practical needs of the average users. However, if you support, maintain, or repair a large group of PCs on a regular basis, it would be a good idea to have one on hand.

INSTALLING MEMORY MODULES IN A PC

Before you open the system case and begin installing new memory modules in your PC, regardless of whether you are replacing existing modules or inserting additional memory, there are a few precautions you should take:

- **Back up the system** Anytime you open the system case to add, remove, or replace components such as the processor, memory, the power supply, or a disk drive, you should create a backup of the hard disk drive, especially if you are working on the hard disk drive itself. You never know what can happen, and it's better to be safe than to lose everything on the hard disk. If you have a large hard disk, you should use a tape drive, writable CD-ROM, back up across a network (perhaps the Internet), or use lots and lots of diskettes.
- **Protect against ESD** Always protect the PC against ESD (electrostatic discharge), the static electricity that can build up in the PC and you. It doesn't take much in the way of an ESD charge to damage a memory module. Work in an antistatic environment and wear an antistatic wrist or ankle strap.
- **Work in a well-lighted area** Most of the components in the PC are small, especially the screws. Anytime you open the system case, you should do so in a work area with plenty of direct light. If this is not possible, then have a reliable flashlight on hand to help you see what you are doing and to help you find all of the screws you drop inside the case.
- **Protect the memory module** Most memory modules, SIMMs and DIMMs, come packaged in an antistatic sleeve (see Figure 7-8). Keep all memory modules in their protective packaging right up to the moment you are ready to install them. Also, place any removed modules into a protective sleeve immediately after removing them from the PC, and never stack unprotected memory modules on top of each other.
- **Handle modules only by their edges** Avoid touching the module's connectors and components. It really doesn't take much in the way of ESD to damage the module. In fact, ESD you can feel is ten times more powerful than a charge that will damage an electronic circuit, such as a memory module.

Figure 7-8. A SIMM in its protective and antistatic packaging

Installing a SIMM in a PC

Before you begin installing a SIMM module, be sure that you have the right SIMM for your system. There aren't a lot of choices, but the ones you have are significant to your PC's acceptance of the new memory:

- **Match the number of pins** The number of pins on the SIMM must match that of the motherboard socket. A 72-pin module will not fit into a 30-pin socket. However, using a SIMM converter add-in board, 30-pin modules can be adapted into a 72-pin socket.
- **Parity versus nonparity** Verify whether your system uses parity or nonparity memory and avoid mixing and matching. A nonparity system will take a parity memory module and simply ignore the parity bits, but it is always better to match like components together. A parity system will take ECC memory.
- **Match the metal** Avoid mixing gold connectors with tin sockets and vice versa. Doing so could lead to intermittent memory problems or a failed memory module.

One end of a SIMM is notched, or slightly cut away, as shown in Figure 7-9. The socket on the motherboard has a similar notch or cut on one end. Before inserting a SIMM into the mounting socket, match up the notched ends. This will ensure that you have the SIMM oriented correctly for installation.

The SIMM is placed into the mounting socket at about a 45-degree angle with the module angled away from the back of the socket, as shown in Figure 7-10. Before setting

Figure 7-9. A SIMM module. Photo courtesy of Kingston Technology Company, Inc.

the module all of the way down into the socket, line up the edge-connector pins on the SIMM with those in the socket. Set the SIMM down into the socket and seat it in the slot connector using gentle but firm force. With the module seated in place, pull up on the module lifting it towards the back of the socket. Remember to only handle the SIMM by

Figure 7-10. A SIMM is first inserted into the socket at an angle

its edges and avoid touching the components on the board. The SIMM should click into place and stand vertically in the socket.

Installing a DIMM on a PC

Compared to a SIMM, a DIMM module presents a few additional challenges and choices. First, a DIMM is installed straight down into its socket on the motherboard. The module has alignment notches like a SIMM, but it is inserted vertically into its socket and pressed into place. The DIMM mounting socket has locking tabs that should snap into place when the module is correctly installed, as shown in Figure 7-11.

All DIMMs have 168 pins, with the exception of the SODIMM used inside portable computers. So that worry is removed, but a DIMM has a few other options that must be matched to your system:

- **Voltage** DIMMs are available with 3.3v or 5v to match the voltage used on a motherboard.
- **Buffering** DIMM modules are available either as buffered or nonbuffered. Buffering adds a small amount of logic to a DIMM to increase its output flow. For a glossary of memory terms, visit **www.memory.com/glossary.html**.
- **Notching** DIMM modules have different alignment notches based on the combination of its voltage and buffering options. So, if a DIMM module will not fit into the socket on your motherboard, it is likely the wrong type and combination for your PC.

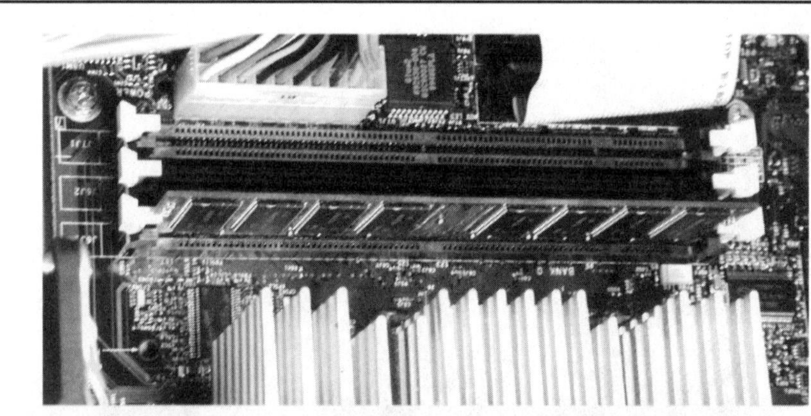

Figure 7-11. A DIMM module installed on a motherboard

Unlike a SIMM, a DIMM must be specifically compatible to your motherboard. You should never need to force a DIMM into a socket. If it doesn't align or seat with gentle force or a slight end-to-end rocking pressure, then double-check the motherboard's specifications and make sure you have the correct DIMM. If the key of the socket doesn't match the DIMM, it is likely you have the wrong voltage or buffer type and must exchange it. The most commonly used type of DIMM is an unbuffered memory with 3.3 volts.

Configuring the PC for Memory

Most newer PC systems will automatically recognize new memory added to the motherboard and make any necessary configuration adjustments. However, there are those that require that you configure the new memory by changing the BIOS configuration before they will recognize any new memory. Check your motherboard documentation to be sure that you don't also need to adjust jumpers or DIP switches on the motherboard to configure the memory. Some older PCs require these settings as well.

Removing a Memory Module

To remove a DIMM, simply release the locking tabs at each end of the socket and pull the module straight up and out of the socket. Refer to the precautions listed above and carefully handle and protect the module during this operation.

A SIMM is installed at an angle and then locked into its vertical position. To remove it, you must perform the installation steps in reverse. After releasing the locking tabs, snap the SIMM forward (away from the back of the socket) to a 45-degree angle and lift it up and out of the socket.

Immediately place the SIMM or DIMM in a protective antistatic sleeve for storage, regardless of how long it will be stored.

CHAPTER 8

Cache Memory

For some unexplainable reason, the major components of the PC—the microprocessor, the memory, motherboard data bus, the hard disk drive, and so on—all operate at different speeds. One would think that they would all be coordinated to operate together. Well, to a certain extent they do, but by and large they are all developed by different companies who are in competition to develop the fastest, biggest, and best computer component.

The two components that must work together closely and constantly are the CPU (microprocessor) and primary memory (RAM). Unfortunately, RAM is faster than the CPU. It is also the design goal of every PC to have the CPU idle as little as possible. If the CPU requests data from RAM, the data must be located and then transferred over the data bus to the CPU. Regardless of how fast RAM is, the CPU must wait while these actions are carried out. This is where caching comes in.

CACHE ON THE PC

Cache memory is very fast computer memory that is used to hold frequently requested data and instructions. As you will see later, it is a little more complicated than that, but cache exists to hold at the ready data and instructions from a slower device (or a process that requires more time) for a faster device. On today's PCs, you will commonly find cache between RAM and the CPU and perhaps between the hard disk and RAM. A *cache* is any buffer storage used to improve computer performance by reducing its access times. A cache holds instructions and data likely to be requested by the CPU for its next operation.

Caching is used in two ways on the PC:

- **Cache memory** A small and very fast memory storage located between the PC's primary memory (RAM) and its processor. Cache memory holds copies of instructions and data that it gets from RAM to provide high-speed access by the processor.
- **Disk cache** To speed up the transfer of data and programs from the hard disk drive to RAM, a section of primary memory or some additional memory placed on the disk controller card is used to hold large blocks of frequently accessed data.

SRAM and Cache Memory

Cache memory is usually a small amount of static random access memory or SRAM (see Chapter 7 for more information on SRAM). SRAM is made up of transistors that don't need to be frequently refreshed (unlike DRAM, which is made up of capacitors and must be constantly refreshed).

SRAM has access speeds of 2ns (nanoseconds) or faster; this is much faster than DRAM, which has access speeds of around 50ns. Data and instructions stored in SRAM-based cache memory are transferred to the CPU many times faster than if the data were transferred from the PC's main memory. In case you're wondering why SRAM isn't also used for primary memory, which could eliminate the need for cache memory all together, there are some very good practical and economic reasons. SRAM costs as much as six times more than DRAM and to store the same amount of data as DRAM would require a lot more space on the motherboard.

Caching in Operation

The CPU operates internally faster than RAM is able to supply data and instructions to it. In turn, RAM operates faster than the hard disk. Caching solves the speed issues between these devices by serving as a buffer between faster devices (the processor or RAM) and slower devices (RAM or the hard disk).

As discussed in Chapters 3 and 7, the CPU interacts with RAM through a series of wait states. During a wait state, the CPU pauses to allow a certain number of clock cycles for the data it has requested to be located and transferred from RAM to its registers. If the data is not in RAM already and must be fetched from the hard disk, additional wait states are invoked and the CPU waits even longer for its data. One of the primary purposes of the cache memory is to eliminate the cycles burned in CPU wait states. Eliminating any CPU idleness should make the entire system more productive and efficient.

Locality of Reference

The principle of *locality of reference* is a design philosophy in computing that is based on the assumption that the next data or instructions to be requested is very likely to be located immediately following the last data or instructions requested by the CPU. Using this principle, caching copies data or instructions just beyond the data requested into the cache memory in anticipation of the CPU asking for it. How successful the caching system is at making its assumptions determines the effectiveness of the caching operation.

As iffy as this may sound, PC caching systems surprisingly get a *cache hit* about 90 to 95 percent of the time. The cache memory's *hit ratio* determines its effectiveness. Each time the caching system is correct in anticipating which data or instructions the CPU will want and has it in cache, it is tallied as a hit. The number of hits divided by the total requests for data by the CPU is how the hit ratio is calculated. Of course, if the CPU asks for data that is not in cache, the data must be requested from RAM and a *cache miss*, a definite caching no-no, is tallied.

Saving Trips

If your PC did not have cache memory, all requests for data and instructions by the CPU would be served from RAM. Only the data requested would be supplied, and there would be no anticipation of what the CPU would be asking for next. This would be something like if every time you wanted a cold one, you had to run to the store for just one can, bottle, or cup of your favorite drink. If the CPU is very busy, it could get bogged down in memory requests, just like if you were very thirsty, you would spend all of your time running to and from the store.

Adding cache memory to a system is like adding a refrigerator to your situation. If you were able to purchase a six-pack or a case of your favorite drink, it would save you a lot of sneaker wear and tear. Caching anticipates what the CPU may next ask for and copies the equivalent of a case of data or instructions to cache memory. As long as the CPU requests the data stored in cache memory, the whole system speeds up. Since, the caching system guesses correctly about 90 to 95 percent of the time, caching saves a tremendous amount of wait cycles for the CPU.

In order to increase the amount of level 1 (L1) cache on a PC, you have to replace the CPU with a processor that is compatible with the motherboard and chipset that includes additional internal L1 cache. On the other hand, level 2 (L2) cache can be upgraded. L2 cache modules are plugged into special cache module mounts or cache memory expansion sockets located on the motherboard (more on this later).

Internal, External, and Levels of Cache

There are two types of cache memory:

- ▼ **Internal cache** Also called *primary cache*; placed inside the CPU chip
- ▲ **External cache** Also called *secondary cache*; located on the motherboard

As briefly touched upon already, cache is also designated by its level, which is an indication of how close to the CPU it is. Cache is designated into two levels, with the highest level of cache being the closest to the CPU (it is usually a part of the CPU, in fact):

- ▼ **Level 1 (L1) cache** Level 1 cache is often referred to interchangeably with internal cache, and rightly so. L1 cache is placed internally on the processor chip and is, of course, the cache memory closest to the CPU.
- ▲ **Level 2 (L2) cache** Level 2 cache is normally placed on the motherboard very near the CPU, but because it is further away than L1 cache, it is designated as the second level of cache. Commonly, L2 cache is considered the same as external cache, but L2 cache can also be included on the CPU chip. If there is a level 3 to cache, it is RAM.

L1 and L2 cache, as well as internal and external cache, are not exactly levels in the sense that L1 is higher in ranking than L2. The different levels of cache work together, and data is located in either level based on the rules and policies associated with the caching system—more on these later.

In contrast to these definitions of cache memory's placement and levels, older PCs, notably those with 286 or 386 processors, do not include cache memory on the CPU. Any cache memory on these PCs must be located on the motherboard and is designated primary (L1) cache. Yes, this external cache is L1 cache. Not to worry; this is the exception and it is dying as fast as these PCs.

Sizing Your Cache

As you may have guessed: when it comes to cache memory, more is better. However, you may have also guessed that there are limits and exceptions to how much cache a system will support. Adding cache or more cache to a PC can increase its overall speed. On the other hand, adding cache or more cache to a PC can decrease its performance, too. You can add so much cache to a system that simply keeping the cache filled from RAM begins eating up all of the CPU cycles that you were hoping to save.

If one refrigerator provides enough caching storage to eliminate some trips to the store for drinks, then it seems to make sense that two refrigerators could save twice as many trips. There is some logic to this, but your savings are dependent on your ability to carry two refrigerator's worth of drinks on each trip. If you are unable to carry enough to fill both refrigerators on a single trip, then you will need to make a second trip that seriously eats into your time savings.

Adding too much external (L2) cache to some PCs can affect the system's performance in this same way. Where adding a first 256K of cache improves the performance of a PC, adding an additional 256K may in fact reduce its performance.

Too Much RAM

Most Pentium-class PCs included enough cache memory to cache 64MB of RAM. This has emerged as the standard sizing for L2 cache on most newer systems. However, the PC's chipset determines how much main memory (RAM) is cached, and many of the more popular chipsets do not cache more than 64MB of RAM. What this means is that regardless of how much RAM you add to the system, it will not cache more that 64MB. This can be an issue if you wish to add more memory to your PC than it is capable of caching. Doing so will likely degrade the performance of the PC and leave you wondering why adding more RAM caused the PC to operate slower.

When there is memory installed on a PC in excess of its caching limit, all of the extra memory is *uncached*. This means that all of the requests for data or instructions stored in the uncached portion of RAM take longer to be served. The CPU must wait for the data to be located in RAM and then transferred over the data bus, in addition to the overhead of first determining that the data was indeed in the uncached memory. If 256MB of RAM is added to a PC that only caches 64MB of that RAM, nearly three-fourths of the RAM is uncached, and the system is a lot slower than it was with only 64MB of RAM.

Caching Impacts on Memory

Everyone knows that adding more and faster memory to your PC will make it perform better and faster. Right? Well, not so. In fact, the size of a PC's cache can neutralize, or at least seriously reduce, the benefit of adding more and faster memory. A PC with a large L1 and L2 cache very likely serves nearly all data and instruction requests from cache. Since the cache system is able to accurately predict the CPU's next request about 90 to 95 percent of the time, only 5 to 10 percent of these requests are ever served from RAM. Adding additional or faster memory will only impact the performance of 5 to 10 percent of all data requests. Therefore, replacing your memory with new memory that is 100 percent faster would gain you about a 5 to 10 percent gain in performance.

If you increase the size of your RAM with a faster memory, remember that the speed of the memory in Bank 0 is the speed the BIOS will set as your memory speed. There are also dangers associated with mixing memory of different speeds. See Chapter 7 for more information.

Tag RAM

As previously discussed, cache memory can be internal or external, level 1 or level 2. In addition, level 2 cache is divided into two parts:

- **Data store** The area of L2 cache where the data being cached is stored. The data store's size (256K is very common) sets the capacity of the cache.
- **Tag RAM** The number of bits of tag RAM (eight bits is typical) directly determines how much of primary memory can be cached and if a cache search will result in a hit or a miss.

A PC with 256K of data store in its L2 cache and eight bits of tag RAM is capable of caching 64MB of RAM. In order for your PC to cache more primary memory, the number of bits of tag RAM must be increased. The amount of data store on a PC does not determine how much RAM is cached, as is commonly assumed. It is the number of tag RAM bits that controls the caching capacity. Tag RAM is included in the chipset of most systems (see Chapter 5 for more information on chipsets), and upgrading a PC's chipset is one way to increase the number of tag RAM bits. The chipsets on some PCs, such as the Pentium Pro, are configured to support caching of up to 4GB of RAM. Some motherboards include an expansion socket for a tag RAM chip to be installed to add additional bits. Check the documentation of your PC's motherboard to determine its tag RAM size and whether it can be upgraded. Adding more data store without the tag RAM to support it is a waste of your time and money.

Moving Data in and out of the Cache

The data store (L2 cache) is organized into a series of *cache lines*, which are 32-byte blocks of data. Data is moved in and out of the data store 32 bytes (256 bits) at a time. Since the width of the data bus of most newer PCs is 64 bits, moving data to or from the CPU requires the cache line to be broken up into four 64-bit blocks and transmitted separately.

The sum of the data sent in the four blocks is called a *burst*. When data is requested from cache by the CPU, assuming the data is in cache, the first 64 bits of data take longer to send since they must locate the data in cache and send it out over the bus. Once the location of the remaining three blocks of 64 bits each is known, no time is lost looking for them and they are each sent along their way. For example, if the first 64-bit block takes four clock cycles, and each of the other three blocks takes one clock cycle, the timing for the burst is 4-1-1-1. This notation, which shows the number of clock cycles required to address, look up, and send each block in the burst, is the burst timing of the cache. Most cache systems include a burst timing in their specifications. None of the numbers in the burst timing are as important than their total value, which in this case is seven, meaning it takes seven clock cycles to complete the delivery of the requested data.

The Impact of a Cache Miss

As indicated in the previous section, there is a delay involved while the cache checks to see if the data requested is in the data store. If the data is not in cache (a cache miss), clock cycles are used looking for it. At this point, the data is requested from RAM. The impact of this is that the clock cycles used looking for the data in cache must be added to the time required to find and transfer the data from main memory. If 10 total clock cycles are normally required to transfer a data burst from RAM and a cache miss takes 2 clock cycles, each cache miss results in 12 clock cycles being required to get the requested data to the CPU. So a cache miss has a direct impact on the PC's performance.

A PC with not enough L2 cache can result in too many cache misses. A small data store translates into a low cache hit ratio and too much data served from RAM. If the PC is capable of supporting it, increasing the size of the external cache also increases the chances of cache hits, which also means it decreases the chances of a cache miss. The size of the data store has no impact on the time used to see if requested data is in cache. Therefore, adding more L2 cache increases the chance of finding the data in cache without an increase in the overhead used to find it.

Cache Memory Types

Functionally, there are three types of cache memory used on PC systems: asynchronous, synchronous, and pipelined burst. Their primary differences are in their timing and the level of support they require from the PC's chipset. In fact, the chipset and motherboard have the most to do with which type of cache memory is used on a PC.

- **Asynchronous cache** *Asynchronous* means that data is transferred without regard to the system clock's cycles. This type of cache memory is the slowest of the three, primarily because it transfers data without using system clock cycles. Asynchronous cache is common on 486 PCs, but because it requires nearly twice the cycles to transfer data at speeds of 66MHz or higher, it wasn't used on systems with speeds higher than 33MHz.
- **Synchronous cache** Synchronous cache, also known as *synchronous burst cache*, ties its activities to the system clock's cycles. In order to avoid problems such as system crashes or lockups, the speed of the SRAM used to implement this cache must match the system's bus speeds. However, like asynchronous cache, synchronous cache has problems at higher bus speeds and is being replaced by pipeline burst cache.
- **Pipelined burst** This improvement on synchronous cache memory transfers uses *pipelining* technology to send its data. Pipelining overlaps the blocks of a data burst, which allows it to be partially transferred at the same time. The

second block of the burst begins transferring before the first block is completed, and so on for the third and fourth blocks. In terms of speed, pipelined burst (PLB) cache is slower on its first block than standard synchronous cache because of the time required to set up the "pipe," averaging bursts of 3-1-1-1 on systems with bus speeds of up to 100MHz. This is the caching technology used on most Pentium-class motherboards.

Caching Write Policies

The data in cache is passed to and received back from the CPU. It is safe to assume that the data the CPU passes back has been updated or changed in some form. If the data in cache has been changed, it is also a safe assumption that the user wants to save the data back to the hard disk. There is no direct logical connection between cache memory and the hard disk. Therefore, some policy must be in effect on how data gets updated in RAM, so it can be eventually written back to the hard disk. There is also a need to keep the data in RAM and its mirror in cache synchronized to avoid passing a bad version of the data to the CPU or hard disk. *Caching write policies* govern these actions to ensure that the data mirrored in cache and RAM stays in sync.

There are two basic cache write policies used to control when data in cache is written back to main memory:

- **Write-back cache** If any of the data mirrored in cache is updated in RAM, only the line affected is updated in cache. When data that has been updated in cache by the CPU is cleared, the changed portion of the data is then written back to RAM. This policy saves write cycles to memory, which are time and cycle consuming. Write-back is better than write-through, in most cases, which is why it is the most common.
- **Write-through cache** Anytime data held in cache is modified, it is immediately written to both cache and main memory. This caching policy is simpler to implement and ensures that the cache is never out of sync with main memory. However, because it competes for clock cycles, it can contribute to slower system performance on a very active PC.

Nonblocking Cache

Another characteristic of caching systems is that they can be blocking or nonblocking. A *blocking cache* system handles only one request at a time. This can create performance problems, especially in the event of a cache miss. While the requested data is transferred from main memory, the cache is blocked and must wait for the transfer from RAM to finish. A *nonblocking* cache, also called *transactional cache*, sets aside requests for data not in cache and works on other transactions while the uncached data is transferred from main memory.

Most high-end Pentium processors use a nonblocking cache for L2 data store. For example, the Pentium Pro and Pentium II microprocessors support up to four nonblocking requests simultaneously on the Intel DIB (dual independent bus) architecture.

Cache Mapping

Some Pentium systems split the L1 cache and store data and instructions separately in their own cache partitions. This requires a *mapping technique,* which defines how the cache contents are stored and referenced. A mapping technique sets the functional features of the cache, including its hit ratio and transfer speed.

The three mapping techniques used with L1 caching are:

- **Direct mapped cache** Most motherboard mounted caches are of this type. This mapping technique uses a simple 4-byte index to track which RAM addresses are stored in the cache. This approach is the least complex of the mapping techniques. It has drawbacks stemming from the method used for indexing which can create duplicate references.
- **Fully associative cache** The name of this mapping technique refers to the fact that all data stored in cache is associated with its address in RAM, which is also called its *tag*. Fully associative caching uses additional memory to hold the tags associated with the data stored in cache. Complicated search algorithms are used to locate the cached data. It can be slow, but it provides the best hit ratios.
- **N-way set associative cache** The cache is divided into sets, which have *n* cache lines each, typically 2, 4, 8, and more. This mapping technique, which is a combination of the other two mapping techniques, provides better hit ratios than direct mapped cache without the speed impact of a complicated search. Processor-based L1 caches commonly apply either a 2-way or 4-way set associative cache.

Cache Mounts

Older PCs, namely 486s and early Pentiums, install SRAM chips directly on the motherboard in individual sockets, which means the cache can be added, replaced, or upgraded. Newer systems install external cache as fixed chips, usually soldered, directly on the motherboard. If your PC mounts its cache in sockets, you may be able to add additional SRAM to increase the size of the cache.

There are some motherboard types available that, although they have soldered SRAM on the board, also allow cache modules to be added to at least one open socket, usually with a jumper setting or two. If you can add SRAM to your system, its size and type will be set by the motherboard and chipset. Check your motherboard's documentation or visit its manufacturer's Web site to learn the specification of the cache you can add, if any.

A commonly used packaging form is the *COAST*, which stands for *cache on a stick*. A COAST module looks something like the SIMM (single inline memory module) memory module and an Intel module is 4.35 inches wide and 1.14 inches high. However, this is not the standard for COAST modules. Different manufacturers vary their size, especially the height and makeup. For example, Motorola's standard for a COAST module is between 4.33 and 4.36 inches wide and 1.12 and 1.16 inches high.

COAST modules are mounted on motherboards using a special socket called a *CELP* (card edge low profile). Some motherboards include only a CELP socket without other external cache on the board. More common are motherboards that allow COAST modules to be added to supplement soldered cache chips on the board. Since there are no clear standards for COAST modules, it stands to reason that there are no standards for CELP mounts. Check your motherboard's documentation for compatibility before purchasing a COAST module for your system. Typically, COAST modules are only compatible within the same manufacturer, but some motherboards do support modules from other manufacturers. The problem is in how they mount to the board. Check with the manufacturer of the motherboard for cache module compatibilities.

INSTALLING A CACHE MODULE

Your best bet is to take your PC to a certified PC technician and have that person install or add cache for you. This process involves matching the cache module to the motherboard and chipset, removing the motherboard, inserting the module, and then reinstalling the motherboard, reconnecting everything you disconnected when you took out the motherboard. If you aren't scared off yet, then here are some tips on what you'll need to know.

Review the motherboard's documentation or check with the PC manufacturer to determine if you can expand the L2 cache on your PC. If cache memory is already installed, you may be able to use the existing chips as a guide to the specification for compatible chips. If no cache memory is installed, use the motherboard's specifications to select the correct SRAM chips or COAST module.

Determine the type of mounting available on the motherboard. It will be a cache slot, cache sockets, or CELP socket. This is also valuable information to have when purchasing the cache module.

General Tips for Working on a Motherboard

After removing the motherboard from the PC, always place it on a flat, clean, and static-free work surface. It is important to place the motherboard so it won't flex or bend downward when you are pressing memory or cache modules or chips into their sockets. Always wear an antistatic wrist strap when working with electronic components. Keep antistatic materials available for storing components temporarily or longer, if necessary.

Installing a COAST Module

COAST modules are keyed, which means they have a guide pin or notch on the leading edge of the module that is matched to a related feature on the CELP socket that prevents it from being inserted into the socket incorrectly. Before installing the module into the socket, line the module along side of the socket, properly oriented, and visually match the pins of the module's edge-connector to the socket's connectors. If there are any problems, this is the time to spot them.

Place the module into the socket slot and press down with gentle but firm pressure until the module seats into the slot. The module is properly seated when only a little of the edge connectors are showing at the top of the socket.

Installation Problems

If your PC fails to boot after you've installed a cache module, you were warned. However, any new problem that arises immediately after installing a cache module is more than likely caused by the installation of the wrong type of cache module in the PC, if all else is fine.

Here are some other things to check out:

- Make sure the cache module is correctly installed.
- Touch the cache module with your finger after the PC has been powered on for a few minutes. If it is too hot to touch, you may have a bad cache module or it may be a motherboard problem associated with the cache module's socket.
- Disable the cache options in the BIOS. If after the cache is disabled, the problem goes away, the problem is not with the cache module. Oh boy, right?
- Check all drive and power supply connectors to see if you accidentally unseated or dislodged one when installing the cache.
- If you still cannot locate the problem, take the PC to a certified technician like you should have in the beginning.

Enabling the Internal Cache

The PC's internal cache is enabled or disabled through the BIOS' setup program. Other than during troubleshooting what could be a cache-related problem, there is no reason to disable your internal cache. However, if you must, enter the BIOS setup area using the key indicated during the boot process. Check your BIOS' advanced settings to make sure the internal cache is enabled and functioning. If for any reason the internal cache is disabled and you cannot enable it, there is a problem with hardware configuration. Be aware that if you disable the internal cache, the performance of the PC will degrade.

Enabling the External Cache

If your PC has L2 cache installed, it should be enabled. Like the internal cache, external cache is enabled through the BIOS settings. If you cannot enable the external cache, there is a conflict in the configuration or specification of the motherboard, chipset, processor, and possibly the external cache itself.

CHAPTER 9

Hard Disks and Floppy Disks

Virtually every PC sold today has at least one hard disk drive installed inside its system case. At one time, this was also true of floppy disk drives, but PCs with floppy disk drives are beginning to disappear, giving way to Zip disks, Super disks, and other forms of removable mass storage.

The hard disk and floppy disk are types of *secondary storage*, with the PC's RAM providing its primary storage (see Chapter 7). Where *primary storage* stores data temporarily while it's in use, secondary storage holds data, programs, and other digital objects permanently. In fact, RAM is referred to as *temporary storage*, and the hard disk and floppy disk are considered *permanent storage*. The data is not permanent in the sense that it is etched in stone, but compared to the volatility of RAM, it is far more enduring. Permanent storage on a disk drive means that the data is still available even after the primary power source is removed.

HARD DISK DRIVES

The hard disk is hardly a personal computer invention. The first hard disks, which first showed up in the 1950s on mainframe computers, were 20 inches in diameter and held only a few megabytes of data. Hard disks were originally called "fixed disks" and "Winchester drives" and became known as hard disks later to differentiate them from floppy disks. However, the basic technology used in the earliest hard disks has not changed all that much over the years, although the size and capacity of the drives has.

Hard Disk Construction

There are many different types and styles of hard disks on the market, all of which have roughly the same physical components. The differences among the different drive styles and types are usually in the components—the materials used and the way they are put together. But essentially one disk drive operates like all others. The major components in a typical hard disk drive are as follows (see Figure 9-1):

- Disk platters
- Spindle and spindle motor
- Read/write heads
- Head actuators
- Air filter
- Logic board
- Connectors and jumpers
- Bezel

Of this list, only the connectors and jumpers are accessible outside of the enclosure that houses all of the other components of the disk drive. The metal case and the components

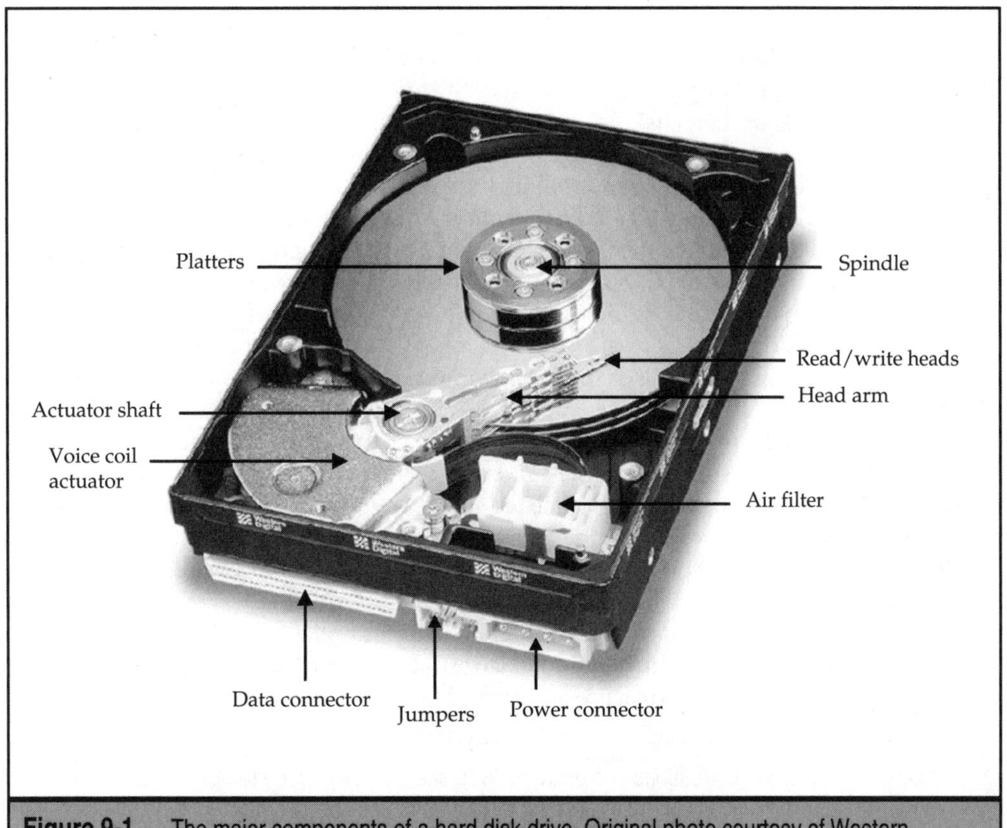

Figure 9-1. The major components of a hard disk drive. Original photo courtesy of Western Digital Corporation

it encloses form what is called the *Head Disk Assembly (HDA)*. The HDA is a sealed unit that is never opened.

The following sections provide an overview of each of the hard disk's components.

Disk Platters

Whether you call them *platters* or *disks,* as they are more commonly called, the primary unit of a hard disk drive is its disks. The disks are the storage media for the disk drive and it is on them that the data is actually recorded. Disks are made from a number of different materials, each with its own performance and storage characteristics. The primary two materials used in disks are aluminum alloys and glass.

The traditional material for platters was an aluminum alloy, which provided strength yet was lightweight. However, because aluminum disks tend to flex by expanding under heat, many disk drives now use a glass-ceramic composite material for disk platters. The platters of the disk drive, whether aluminum or glass are rigid (the source of the name *hard* disk), unlike the flexible disk in a floppy disk.

The glass platters are more rigid and as such can be less than half as thick as the aluminum disks. A glass disk does not expand or contract with changes in temperature, which results in a more stable hard disk drive. Most of the top hard disk manufacturers use glass composite materials in their disk drives, including Seagate, Toshiba, and Maxtor. As the disk drives continue to get smaller, storing more data, and operating at higher speeds, glass materials are likely to be used in all disk drives.

Most PC hard drives generally have two platters. There are those with more (as many as 10) and many have less (1 platter), especially smaller form factor drives. The number of platters included in a disk drive is a function of design and capacity, which is controlled somewhat by the overall size of the disk drive. Like the case, motherboard, and power supply, a hard disk drive has a *form factor*. The form factor of a disk is essentially the size of its platters, although it has also come to mean the size of the drive bay into which the drive can be installed.

The more common form factors and their actual platter sizes are listed in Table 9-1.

There are disk drives in mainframes and other systems that have 8-inch, 14-inch, or even larger platters. Of the form factors listed in Table 9-1, the 3.5-inch drive is currently the most popular, having replaced the 5.25-inch drive, in desktop and tower-type PCs. The 2.5-inch drive and 1.8-inch drives are popular in notebook computers.

Each platter is mounted on the disk spindle so that each side of the disk can be accessed with a read/write head. The surface of each disk platter is polished and then covered with a layer of magnetic material, which is used to store data. The disk spindle, read/write head, and how data is stored on the disk are all covered later in the chapter in more detail.

NOTE: In different publications and on some Web sites, you will see *disk* spelled as *disc*. The two spellings have become interchangeable, but there are those who still insist that the round platters inside the disk drive are individually called *discs*. Others, largely the CD-ROM and DVD folks, insist that the term *disc* is reserved to refer to optical disks. Either is fine—a disk is a disc is a disk—but you will find the *disk* spelling used most often.

Form Factor	Platter Size
5.25 inches	5.12 inches (130 millimeters [mm])
2.5 inches	2.5 inches (63.5 mm)
3.5 inches	3.74 inches (95 mm)
1.8 inches	1.8 inches (45.7 mm)

Table 9-1. Disk Form Factors

The Spindle Motor

The disk platters are mounted to a *spindle* separated by *disk spacers* that keep the platters evenly spaced, as illustrated in Figure 9-2. The spacers provide a consistent spacing that is needed for the read/write heads to have access to the top of one disk and the bottom of the one above it. In operation, the spindle rotates the platters in unison at speeds of 3,600 rpm (revolutions per minute), 4800, 5400, 7200, and—on newer devices—10,000 and 15,000 rpm. A direct-drive motor that is mounted directly below it rotates the spindle.

The motor that rotates the spindle and the disks mounted to it is called the spindle motor. The spindle motor, shown in Figure 9-3, is always connected directly to the spindle without using belts or gears so that the drive mechanism is free of noise and vibration, which could, if transferred to the platters, cause data read and write problems. The spindle motor is a vital part of the disk drive's operation. In fact, most hard disk failures are really spindle motor failures.

The spindle motor is a brushless and sensorless DC motor that is attached directly to the disk spindle. There are two types of spindle motors in use: *in-hub motors* that are placed inside the HDA and *bottom-mount motors* that are attached to the spindle outside of

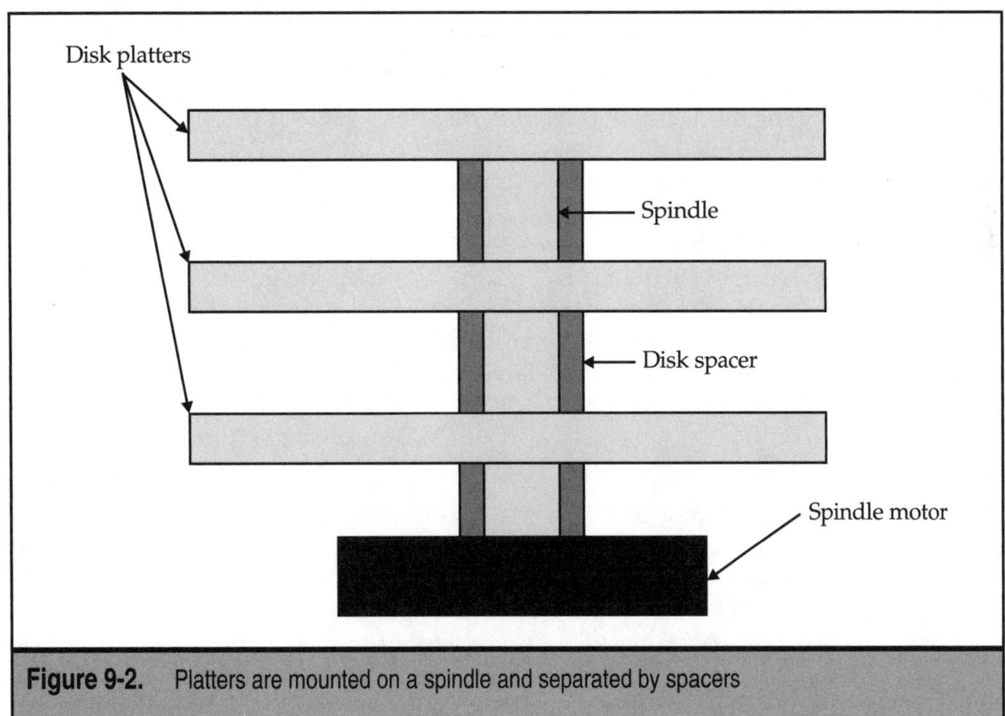

Figure 9-2. Platters are mounted on a spindle and separated by spacers

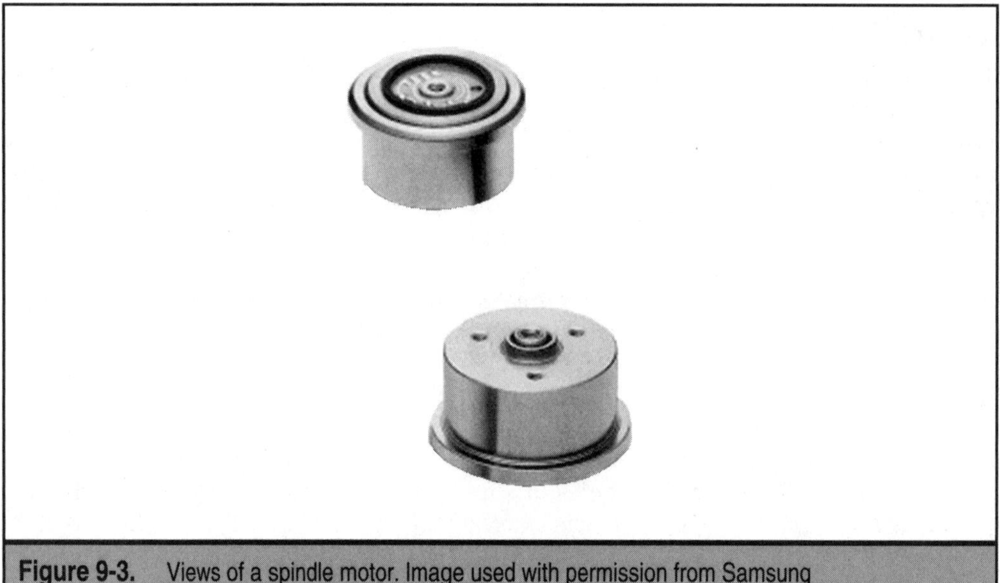

Figure 9-3. Views of a spindle motor. Image used with permission from Samsung Electro-Mechanics of Korea

the HDA case. The spindle disk motor is designed to prevent oil or dust from contaminating the components to the sealed dust-free environment inside the HDA. At the spindle and spindle motor's high rotation rates, the lubricating oil in spindle and motor assembly can be turned into a mist. Special seals are placed in the spindle motor to prevent oil leaks.

On the bottom of most hard disk drives is the *spindle ground strap,* which is a small flat and angled piece of copper with a piece of carbon or graphite (some older drives may have a Teflon pad) that is mounted so that it is in contact with the spindle. The purpose of the ground strap is to discharge any static electricity created as the spindle turns preventing it from being discharged inside the HDA and damaging the disk drive or corrupting stored data.

Storage Media

Although not listed as a major component in the list at the beginning of this section, the material on which data is actually stored is nonetheless a very important part of the disk drive. The *storage media*, or the magnetic material that holds data on the platters, is a very thin layer of magnetic substance in which electromagnetic data is stored.

Data is stored on a hard or floppy disk using electromagnetic principles. A magnetic field is generated from a magnetic core wrapped or surrounded by an electrical wire through which an electrical current is passed to control the polarity of a magnetic field. As this magnetic field is passed over the disk, it influences the magnetic polarity of a certain area of the recording media. Reversing the direction of the flow of the electrical current reverses the polarity of the magnetic field, which reverses the influence it has on the recording media.

There are two types of media used on hard disk platters:

- Oxide media
- Thin film media

Oxide Media

Oxide media is less popular on newer disk drives. A relatively soft material, it can be damaged by a head crash should it be jostled while it is operating. Oxide media was very popular on older low-end disk drive models because it was easily applied and inexpensive.

The primary ingredient in an *oxide media* is iron oxide (a.k.a. rust). This media is applied to the center of the platter in a syrupy liquid form. The disk is then spun at very high speed, which causes the media to flow out to the edges of the disk, coating it evenly. After the liquid media is cured, the disk is polished to even out its surface. It is extremely important that the surface of the disk be smooth and free of bumps or blemishes, as will be discussed in the section on read/write heads. Finally, a layer of material that protects and lubricates the surface is added and polished smooth. Although it may sound like a lot of material is being added to the disk, the thickness of the finished material is around 30 millionths of an inch.

Thin Film Media

Virtually all disk drives manufactured today use *thin film media*, which is an extremely thin layer of metals placed on the disk's surface. The thin metal film is put on the disk as a plating, like the chrome on your car, or by a process called *sputtering*. Despite its unusual name, sputtering is a very complicated way of plating a platter that electrically binds the metal media to the disk in a vacuum. Thin film media is also called *plated media* and *sputtered media* because of how it is applied to the disk. Sputtering is the method most commonly used to place the recording media on disk platters.

Thin film media is harder and thinner than oxide media, and it allows stronger magnetic fields to be stored in smaller areas. All of which combine to allow higher density of data and smaller disk sizes. Thin film is hard and if the disk is jostled during operation, the read/write head just bounces off without damaging the media. It is extremely thin and is very smooth, which allows the read/write heads to float closer over the media.

Read/Write Heads

Each side of a disk platter has media applied to it that allows it to store data. Accordingly, each side of a disk platter also has at least one read/write head, as illustrated in Figure 9-4. As shown, a disk drive that has two disk platters has four read/write heads. There are exceptions to this rule, but generally a disk drive has two heads for each platter, one to read and write data to the top side and one for the bottom side.

The read/write heads are all connected to the same actuator mechanism, as illustrated in Figure 9-4, which moves the heads in unison in and out, from the spindle to the edge of the platter. Remember that the disk itself is spinning rapidly by. This means that when the read/write head for the top platter, usually referred to as disk 0, is over track 29,

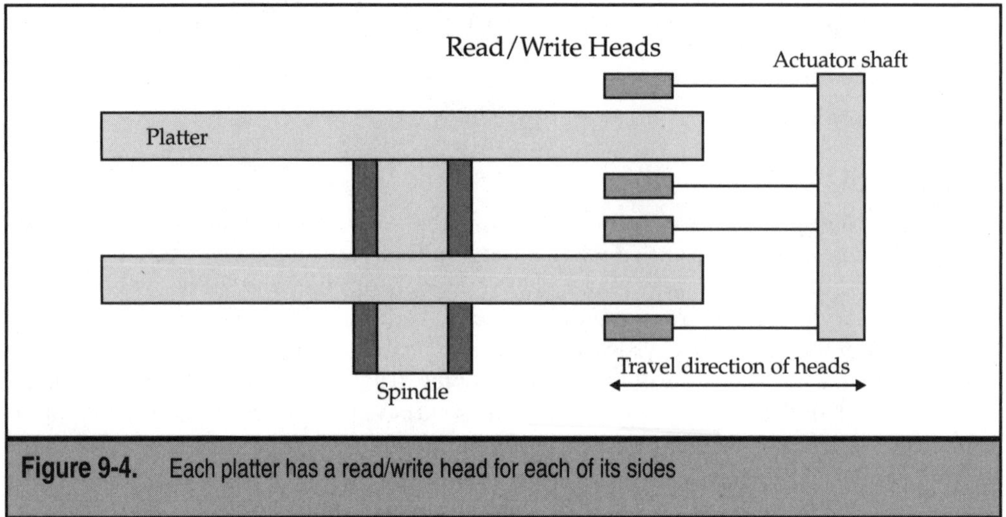

Figure 9-4. Each platter has a read/write head for each of its sides

all of the other read/write heads are over track 29 on each respective disk. Disk organization and tracks are discussed later in the chapter. In most disk drive designs, only one read/write head is active at a time.

Floating Heads

The read/write heads float over the surface of the platters on a cushion of air pressure. When the disk drive is off and the platters are not turning, the springs in the head arms actually force the read/write heads onto the surface of the disk. But when the drive is operating, the high-speed rotation of the disk platters creates air pressure that pushes the read/write head away from the disk surface. The springs in the head arms provide resistance so that the read/write head floats above the disk's surface at a constant height, which is around three to five microinches (millionths of an inch).

The gap between the platter and the read/write head is so small that serious damage can happen to the read/write head if it bangs into any foreign obstacle on the disk. Particles like dust or smoke, which are like the Himalayas to the read/write head, can cause the read/write head to crash on the disk's surface. Smoke particles and the oil of a human fingerprint are well over a thousand microinches in height. The HDA is a sealed unit and it is very unlikely that this will happen, but this is a very good reason for you not to open the HDA for any reason, unless you just happen to have a class-100 environment. Disk drives are manufactured in this type of environment, which doesn't allow more than 100 tiny foreign particles airborne in the facility. Just for reference, humans exhale more than 500 such particles each time they breathe.

When the power is turned off, the disk stops spinning. This eliminates the air pressure cushion on which the read/write head was riding. Although this sounds like a disk head crash in the making, disk drives have a *landing zone*, beyond the inside edge of the recording area of the platters, where the read/write head can safely "crash" when the disk is powered off. Virtually all disk drives made in the past 20 years have included automatic head parking, which moves the read/write heads to the landing zone. Some even include a locking feature that holds the heads in the landing zone until power is turned on.

Read/Write Head Operation

The space between the spinning disk platter and the read/write head is called its *floating height* or its *head gap*. The size or distance of the head gap is a function of the disk drive's design and the type of read/write head technology in use. The size of the gap is very important, because the head must be exactly the right height to properly sense flux transitions on the disk without banging into the disk surface. Most disk drives have a head gap of five millionths of an inch or shorter.

The read/write heads in a disk drive are U-shaped and made from electrically conductive materials. Wire through which an electric current can flow is coiled around each of the heads—the U-shaped objects. By running a DC current through the wire in one direction or the other, a magnetic field with one of two polarities is created. These two polarities, if you haven't already guessed, are used to store electrical values representing binary 1s and 0s.

There are four types of read/write heads used in hard disk drives:

- **Ferrite heads** This is the oldest of the magnetic head designs, and as such, they are bigger and heavier than any of the thin film heads and use a larger floating height to guard against contact with the disk. Ferrite heads use an iron-oxide core that is wrapped with electromagnetic coils. The coils are energized to create a magnetic field. During the 1980s, a composite ferrite head was popular that incorporated glass to reduce its weight and size and improve its operation. Ferrite heads have largely been replaced by TF and MIG head technologies.
- **Metal-in-Gap (MIG)** A MIG head is an enhanced version of the composite ferrite head. Metal is added to the trailing edge of the head gap to help it ignore nearby magnetic fields and focus on the cells beneath the head. *Single-sided MIG heads* have a layer of magnetic alloy on the trailing edge of the gap. A *double-sided MIG head* adds a layer of metal alloy to both the leading and trailing sides of the gap. For a while, MIG heads were the most popular type in use, but demands for higher capacity disks have resulted in the TF head becoming more popular.
- **Thin film (TF)** TF heads, which are manufactured much like a semiconductor (see Chapter 3), are used in small form factor high-capacity drives. TF heads are the most common type of disk drive head in use. They are light and much more accurate than the ferrite heads and operate much closer to the disk surface.
- **Magneto-resistive (MR)** MR heads are found in most 3.5-inch disk drives that have 1GB or higher capacity. Instead of signaling a flux transition, an MR head merely changes the resistance on an electrical line. MR heads are power-read heads only. Disk drives with MR heads typically also have a TF head for writing.

When the energized head passes over the recording media of the platter, the magnetic field's polarity is used to change the orientation of the magnetic particles in the media to represent an electrical value. If the polarity of the head is changed, then the data stored on the media will have a different electrical value. Reversing the electrical flow in the wire wrapped around the U-shaped head changes the polarity of the magnetic field, which is used to change the value of the platter's media, and presto, data is written to the disk.

As discussed earlier, the material used to coat the disk platter is made of iron oxide. On a new or erased disk, the magnetic field of each particle is randomly assigned, which has the same effect of cumulatively canceling out the magnetic fields of its neighboring particles. To the read/write heads, the disk has no recognizable patterns and looks blank. As the read/write head passes over the disk, if the particles in one particular area are aligned in the same direction, their cumulative magnetic fields will create a recognizable pattern that the head will detect as a binary digit.

Flux

The read/write head uses magnetic flux to record data on the disk media. *Flux* refers to a magnetic field that has a single and specific direction. As the disk surface rotates under it, the read/write head uses a reversal in its polarity, called a *flux reversal*, to change the alignment of magnetic particles on the disk surface. This is how data is recorded on the disk. Simply put, the read/write head creates a series of flux reversals in an area called a *bit cell*, which is a cluster of magnetic particles used to represent a single binary digit (bit).

As illustrated in Figure 9-5, as the disk and bit cells rotate under or over the read/write head, the head acts as a flux voltage detector. Each time it detects a flux transition, a change from positive to negative, or the reverse, it sends out a voltage pulse. If no transition—that is, no change in the polarity of the bit cell—is detected, then no pulse is sent. Notice how these two activities can be matched to the 1s and 0s of binary data.

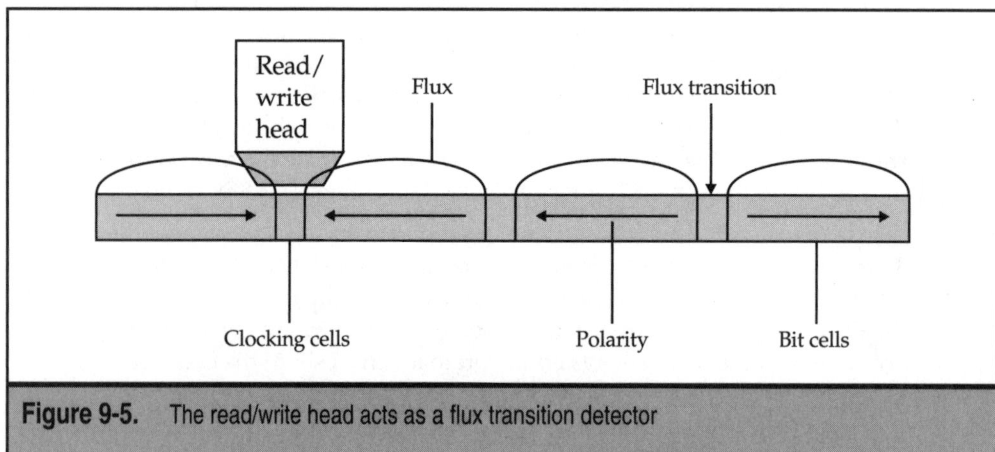

Figure 9-5. The read/write head acts as a flux transition detector

Because the read/write head only sends a signal on a flux transition, a device called an *encoder/decoder,* or *endec,* is used to convert these signals to actual binary data and to convert binary data into flux transitions. During a write operation, the endec focuses on creating a signal pattern for the read/write head. In a read operation, the endec interprets the read/write head signals converting them into binary data. To ensure that all of the electronic devices involved in this process remain in sync, each data signal is preceded with a clock signal that is used by the sending and receiving devices (the read/write head and the endec) to make sure they are both working on the same signal. If one gets ahead of the other, the clock signal is used to resynchronize them. Clock cells are actually placed on the disk media between bit cells.

Encoding Methods

The different disk media and head technologies used on disk drives directly control how much data can be placed on a disk. Because of this, there are a number of different ways to encode data, called *encoding methods,* so it requires a minimum number of flux transitions, including clocking cells, to maximize the data storage capacity of the disk drive. Each encoding method defines a particular scheme for how magnetic particles are arranged in a bit cell.

There are three primary encoding methods in use:

- **FM (frequency modulation)** This was one of the earliest methods used for encoding data on disk storage. This scheme simply recorded a 1 or a 0 as different polarities on the recording media. Although quite popular into the late 1970s, FM is no longer used today.
- **MFM (modified frequency modulation)** This is the encoding method still used on all floppy disks, as well as many hard disks. It was developed to optimize FM and to reduce the number of flux transitions used to store data. MFM uses a minimum of clock cells, using them only to separate 0 bits only. This resulted in twice as much data being stored with the same number of flux transitions as the FM encoding method.
- **RLL (run length limited)** RLL has emerged as the most commonly used hard disk storage encoding method. It yields higher data density by spacing 1 bits farther apart and specially encoding groups of bits to be accessed together. RLL introduced data compression techniques, and most current disk drives (IDE, SCSI, and so on) use a form of RLL encoding.

Head Actuators

The read/write heads of the hard disk drive are moved into position by the *head actuator*. This mechanism is used to extend and retract the heads so that data can be read from or written to the disk platters. There are a number of actuator types, but they can generally be categorized into two groups: stepper motor actuators and voice coil actuators. There are large differences in performance and reliability between these two actuator categories. Stepper motor actuators are slow, very sensitive to temperature changes, and less reliable.

On the other hand, voice coil actuators are fast, not affected by temperature changes, and extremely reliable. The type of actuator used in a disk drive tells you a lot about the drive's overall performance and reliability.

Stepper Motor Actuators

A *stepper motor* is an electrical motor that moves in a series of steps. The motor cannot stop between steps and must advance from one step to the next to operate. On a disk drive that uses a stepper motor actuator to move the read/write heads, the stepper motor is located outside of the HDA and connects to the head arm gang through a sealed hole in the HDA case.

The actual mechanism that connects the stepper motor to the heads is either a flexible steel band that is wrapped around the motor's spindle or through a rack-and-pinion gearing arrangement. Each step of the motor typically represents one track on the disk surface. So, in order to move 30 tracks, in or out, the stepper motor must move to the 31 step in the appropriate direction. A big problem with this approach is that over the life of the disk drive, the heads, head arms, and other mechanical parts of the disk drive may drift slightly from their original positions. A disk drive using a stepper motor actuator positions the heads over the disk with a *blind location system* because the heads are at the mercy of the stepper motor to place them over the correct part of the disk.

Voice Coil Actuators

A *voice coil actuator* is used in many disk drives with capacities above 40MB, nearly all disk drives with 80MB of capacity or more, and virtually all high-end hard disk drives. It gets its name from the construction of its core mechanism, which is very similar to that used in the voice coil of a typical audio speaker. Audio speakers use a large magnet enclosed by a voice coil that is directly connected to the paper speaker cone. By energizing the coil, it interacts with the magnet to produce sound from the speaker cone.

On a hard disk drive, the electromagnetic coil is placed on the end of the head gang, and then positioned near a stationary magnet. The coil and the magnet never touch, but as the coil is energized with positive or negative polarity, the head gang is attracted to or pushed away from the stationary magnet. Because there are no real moving parts in the actuator itself, voice coil actuators are fast and very quiet.

Unlike the stepper motor actuator, a voice coil system does not have predetermined steps to use to position the heads. Instead, it uses a guidance system that is able to position a head above a particular track on the disk. This system, called a *servo*, tells the actuator exactly where the heads are in relation to the tracks and cylinders on the disk and when the heads are over the target locations. Unlike the blind system used by the stepper motor, voice coil actuators receive feedback signals from the hard disk drive find head positions.

Nearly all voice coil servo systems use a *rotary voice coil actuator*. At one time, another type was used, the *linear voice coil actuator*, but it was too heavy and slow for today's faster, higher-density disk drives. Rotary actuators attach their coil to the end of an actuator arm that is mounted like a pivot. As the stationary magnet moves the coil, the head arm swings in and out moving the heads over the surface of the disk. The advantage of this system is that it is lightweight and very fast. The disadvantage of this system is that the further into the disk area, that is, the closer to the inside of the platter, the heads are tilted slightly, which creates an azimuth problem. *Azimuth* measures the alignment of the heads to the disk and cylinders. This is overcome on most systems by limiting how much of the disk near the center can be used for data.

Servo systems enable the head to be positioned precisely above a specific track on a disk, using information called *gray code,* which was written to the disk when it was manufactured. Gray code is a special binary notation code that identifies each track (cylinder) and, in some systems, each sector on the disk. Through the gray code, the head positioning system on the disk drive has the ability to place the heads directly over the cylinder it desires. The gray code written to the disk during manufacturing cannot be overwritten in normal use, as the area of the physical disk that it occupies is set aside.

Air Filters

It may seem odd that a sealed device like the HDA would have air filters, but it does. In fact, most drives have two air filters, a *recirculating filter* and a *barometric* or *breather filter*. These filters are permanently sealed inside the HDA and never have to be changed. They are designed to last the life of the drive. PC hard disk drives do not bring outside air into the HDA and circulate it (see Figure 9-6). The purpose of the recirculating filter is to trap any particles of media that may be scraped off the disks by the read/write heads or any small particles that may have been trapped in the HDA during manufacturing. How

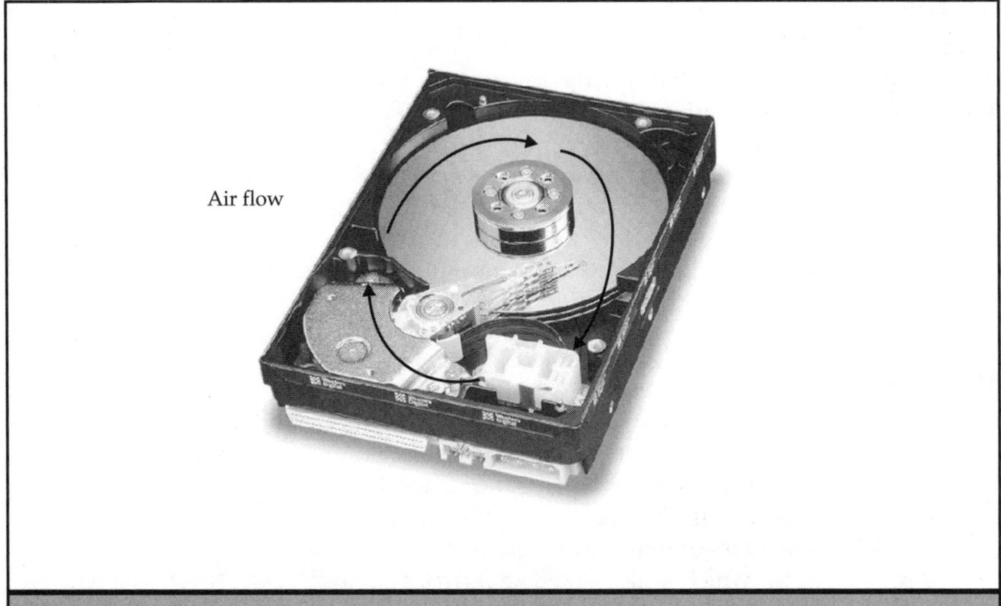

Figure 9-6. The recirculating airflow inside the HDA. Original photo courtesy of Western Digital Corporation

clean the outside air is may have an effect on the PC, but it won't have any impact on the hard disk at all.

While the HDA is sealed, it is not airtight (or watertight, for that matter). This doesn't mean that outside air can get in and gum up the works, though. The HDA has a vent that allows it to equalize the air pressure through a breather filter. This vent and filter adjust for barometric pressure changes that the PC may experience—between its manufacturing plant in Taiwan at near sea level and an office in Denver one mile above sea level, for example. As the altitude changes, air is sucked in or vented out through the breather filter until the internal air pressure equals the outside air pressure. Most manufacturers rate an altitude range for their hard drive's operation, typically between 1,000 feet below sea level and around 10,000 feet above sea level. This covers nearly all scuba divers and mountain climbers. The problem of operating the disk drive outside of its altitude range is that there may not be enough air pressure to float the heads.

While not directly related to the air filters, there is one other environmental consideration for hard disks—adapting to temperature changes. When the ambient operating temperature of a PC changes significantly, the hard disk must be allowed time to acclimate itself before it is powered on. For example, if a hard disk is shipped during the winter and sits for some time at temperatures less than 50 degrees Fahrenheit, it should be allowed to acclimate to normal room temperatures for at least 13–15 hours before it is powered up. Check with your hard disk's manufacturer for information on its environmental and operating condition requirements.

Logic Boards

Hard disk drives include logic boards that control the functions of the drive's spindle and head actuator and interact with the device controller to pass data to and from the disk. Some disk drives also include the hard disk controller on the drive. Along with the spindle motor, logic boards account for a large share of disk drive failures. In fact, many disk failures are really logic board failures and not problems with the mechanical parts of the disk.

The logic board of a disk drive can be easily replaced, but most people tend to replace the entire drive. The logic board is usually mounted to the disk drive through a plug connector and one or two screws. Replacing the logic board is also an easy way to troubleshoot a drive you suspect of logic rather than mechanical problems.

Connectors and Jumpers

Figure 9-7 shows two of the three general types of connectors found on most disk systems: data and power. The third type, an optional connector on most drives, is not shown; it is usually a tab with a single screw hole used to connect the disk drive to the chassis for grounding purposes. Your disk drive's documentation should have information on whether your drive offers or requires the grounding connection.

The *data connector*, which is also called an *interface connector*, carries both the data and command signals from the controller and CPU to and from the disk drive. Some drives use

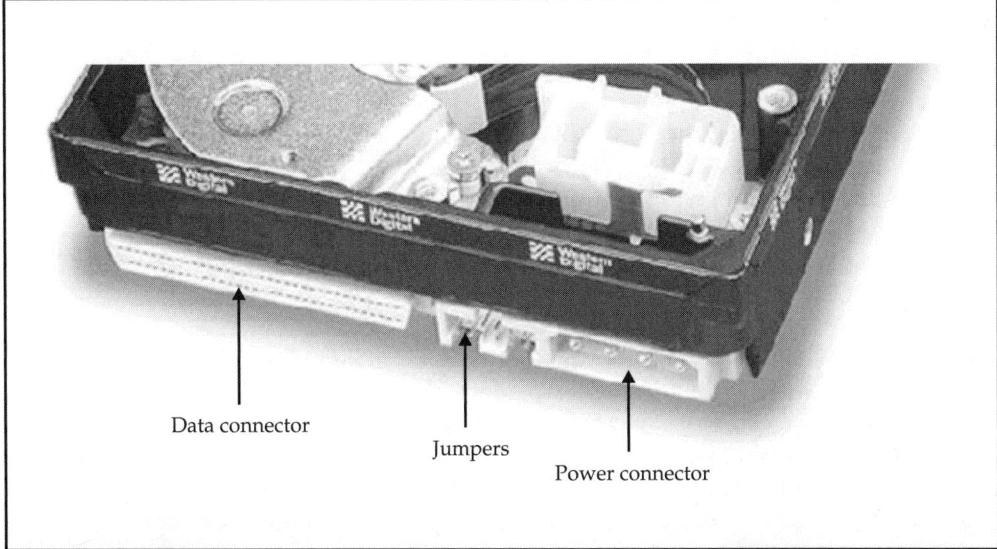

Figure 9-7. The connectors on a standard EIDE/IDE type disk drive. Original photo courtesy of Western Digital Corporation

only a single cable for data and control signals, such as SCSIs (Small Computer System Interface) and IDE/EIDEs (Integrated Drive Electronics/Enhanced IDE). These systems also allow more than one drive to be connected to the cable. The IDE interface supports two disk drives on the cable, and the SCSI interface allows up to seven drives on the same interface cable. There are special adapters and controllers available to extend the number of drives that can share an interface. For example, a special EIDE controller is available that allows eight EIDE devices to share an IDE controller.

The *power connector* is the standard power connector available from the PC's power supply that supplies the disk with 5V and 12V DC power. The logic power and other circuitry of the disk drive uses 5V, and the spindle motor and head actuator use 12V power. How much power the drive consumes in watts is something you should know about your drive to avoid overloading the power supply. This is more important on older systems than it is on newer ones with 3.5-inch or smaller form factor disk drives. The 3.5-inch drives use only a fraction of the power that the older 5.25-inch drives require.

If your system has a *grounding tab*, you may want to use it to create a positive ground to the PC's chassis. If the disk drive is mounted directly to the chassis in a drive bay, this connection is probably not needed. However, if the hard disk is mounted in a plastic or fiberglass mounting, it's an excellent idea to connect the grounding tab. Without the grounding connection, the disk drive may have read, write, or remembering problems.

The *jumpers* on the disk drive are used to configure the drive as a master or slave on a shared interface, as well as other configuration settings. See your disk drive documentation for the correct position for the jumpers, as they differ among manufacturers and even models.

Bezel

Many older hard disk drives included a faceplate, or *bezel*, with the drive. Older form factor cases, such as the early AT cases, did not have LEDs on the front of the case for the hard disk. On these cases, the hard disk bezel was allowed to show. The bezel included LEDs for activity and power. As the front panel of the system case now provides this function, hard disk drives typically do not offer a bezel as a standard feature, but one can be obtained as an optional item.

INTERFACES

The mechanism that controls the transmission of data between the CPU and other devices on the PC is an interface. Disk storage devices, such as hard disk drives, floppy disk drives, tape drives, CD-ROM drives, DVD-ROM drives, all use a transfer interface to move data to and from themselves and the rest of the PC. The form and function of an interface is defined in the device controller and other drive electronics. Because hard disks and other storage devices are manufactured to work with a wide range of PC systems, a variety of interface protocol standards have been adopted to ensure compatibility.

The interface standards that have been used with hard disk drives are:

- ST506
- ESDI
- IDE
- SCSI
- FC-AL

The first two are largely obsolete now, along with the PC AT, the PC on which they were used. Most of the hard disks in use today use either an IDE or a SCSI hard disk drive interface. FC-AL is found on very high-end disk array products associated with large network servers.

ST506/412 Interface

Seagate Technology developed the ST506/412 drive interface for its 5MB (ST506) and 10MB (ST412) disk drives in the early 1980s. Nearly all manufacturers making hard disk drives for PCs used the ST506/412 standard, which made it virtually the standard for PC hard disk interfaces at the time. It was essentially universal in that no custom cables were needed to connect ST506/412 drives from any manufacturer to any ST506/412 controller. This interface is obsolete for all new systems. It lacks the capacity, speed, and expandability needed to survive in today's market.

ESDI

The *Enhanced Small Disk Interface (ESDI)*, pronounced "ez-dee," was the hard disk interface standard that replaced the ST506/412 standard. It introduced a number of innovations, such as adding the endec into the drive. ESDI drives were used on high-end systems from brand-name manufacturers in the late 1980s, but soon the lower-cost, higher performing IDE drives made it largely obsolete, except on some high-end proprietary systems.

IDE

The *IDE (Integrated Drive Electronics)* interface, one of the more popular interface technologies in use today, was originally developed as an alternative to the expensive SCSI technology. As its name implies, IDE technology integrates the disk controller as a part of the disk drive. IDE is also known as AT Attachment (ATA) interface. Since the drive controller is a part of the disk drive, IDE devices can usually be connected directly to the motherboard or by using a pass-through board. IDE interface cards are usually multifunction cards that not only support the hard disk, but a floppy drive, a game port, perhaps a serial port, and more.

An ATA IDE drive should never be low-level formatted. A low-level format, which scans the disk media for defects and sets aside any sectors with defects, is performed at the factory during manufacturing and should never be performed by a user or a technician. Only a high-level format (such as that performed by the Windows formatting function) is necessary to prepare the disk partitions for the operating system and data.

The standard IDE interface supports up to two 528MB drives. EIDE (Enhanced IDE), also called ATA-2, is a newer version of IDE that increases the capacity of the interface to four multigigabyte drives. Recent developments have extended the EIDE interface to eight drives.

Another standard closely related to the EIDE interface standard is the *ATAPI (ATA Packet Interface)*, an interface standard for CD-ROMs and tape drives that connect to common ATA (IDE) connectors.

SCSI Interface

The *Small Computer Systems Interface (SCSI)*, pronounced "scuzzy," is not an interface standard in the way that IDE is. It is a system standard that is made up of a collection of interface standards covering a range of peripheral devices, including hard disks, tape drives, optical drives, CD-ROMs, and disk arrays. Up to eight SCSI devices can connect to a single SCSI controller by sharing the common interface, called a SCSI bus or SCSI chain.

Like IDE devices, SCSI controllers are built into the devices. As SCSI devices are added to the SCSI bus, each device is assigned a unique device number to differentiate it from the other devices. The SCSI controller communicates with the devices on the bus by sending a message encoded with the unit's device number, which is also included in any replay sent by the device. A SCSI bus must be terminated to prevent unclaimed or misdirected messages from bouncing back onto the bus.

FC-AL Interface

The *FC-AL (Fiber Channel-Arbitrated Loop)*, or fiber channel for short, is used with very large systems or networks that incorporate high bandwidth and high-end disk arrays. It is a very high-availability type of system, which means that it has built-in data recovery and fault-tolerant components. As you might guess, fiber channel disks are much more expensive than disks using other interfaces, including SCSI devices.

FC-AL uses fiber optic cables to connect the disk drives to the controller and the PC. It transfers data at the rate of over 100MB per second. Fiber channel can support up to 127 devices, and because it uses fiber optic cabling, the devices can be as far as 10 kilometers apart. FC-AL devices can be hot-swapped, which means that they can be inserted and removed without interfering with the operation of the system.

System Bus Interface

Hard disk interfaces also interface with the rest of the PC system on one of the system's I/O bus architectures. Commonly, the available buses are *PCI (Peripheral Component Interconnect*), VLB (VESA Local Bus), or the *ISA (Industry Standard Architecture)* bus.

IDE/ATA and SCSI require faster transfer modes over a local bus, which means they use either the PCI or VLB buses. Where most older PCs and hard disks (ST506/412 and ESDI) used a dedicated hard disk controller mounted into a system bus slot, newer PCs use the PCI bus on motherboards that typically have two IDE/ATA channels and possibly one EIDE channel built into the motherboard itself.

See Chapter 11 for more information on the system bus structures.

Transfer Protocols

Data is transferred from the disk drive to system memory using one of two transfer modes:

- **Programmed I/O (PIO)** PIO is the data transfer protocol used on most older disk drives. The PC's CPU executes all of the instructions used to move data from the disk to the PC.
- **Direct Memory Access (DMA)** DMA transfers data directly to or from memory, without involving the CPU in the transfer, which frees the CPU to perform other tasks. The device's built-in controller handles the transfer without help from the CPU. Nearly all new IDE/ATA hard disks support DMA, which is commonly used in floppy disks, tape drives, and sound cards.

Data Addressing

Data is addressed on the disk using two methods:

- **CHS (cylinder-head-sector)** This is the data addressing method used on most IDE drives. It locates data on the disk by its cylinder (track), head (meaning platter side), and sector on the track. For example, a file could begin on cylinder 250, head 4, and sector 33. The number of cylinders, heads, and sectors on your hard disk can be found in the BIOS setup configuration data.
- **LBA (logical block address)** In this method of data addressing, each sector on the disk is assigned a sequential logical block number. LBA addressing simply lists a single logical location for each file. LBA is used on SCSI and EIDE drives.

DATA ORGANIZATION

Both hard disks and floppy disks set organization schemes that allow them to store data, and more importantly, find it again later. The disk is organized into cylinders, tracks, sectors, and clusters. Remember that this organization is over and above the servo and gray code systems that were placed on the disk when it was manufactured.

Each disk is organized into the following organization building blocks:

- **Tracks** As illustrated in Figure 9-8, *tracks* are concentric areas on the disk that complete one circumference of the disk. On a hard disk, there can be 1,000 tracks or more. The first track, which is where data is usually written first, is along the outermost edge of the disk. Tracks of the same number on all platters of the drive form a *cylinder*.
- **Sectors** *Sectors* divide the disk into a number of cross-sections that intersect all of the tracks on the disk. Sectors break tracks into addressable pieces, as illustrated in Figure 9-8. A sector is typically 512 bytes in length, and disk drives have from 100 to 300 sectors per track. Without a sector division, a track could only be addressed at its beginning, wherever that would be. Sectors provide segment beginning points on the tracks as well as the disk as a whole.
- **Cylinders** *Cylinders* reflect how the read/write heads move in and out of the disk platters in unison. This grouping technique is unique to hard disks. A cylinder is the logical grouping of the same track on each disk surface. For example, if a hard disk drive has three platters, as illustrated in Figure 9-9, it has six disk surfaces and six track 52s. All six track 52s combine logically to create cylinder 52. Data is written vertically between disks following the track and cylinder path, which eliminates the need to move the read/write heads.
- **Clusters** A *cluster* is formed from groups of sectors. This logical grouping is used by operating systems to track data on the disk. There are normally around 64 sectors to a cluster, but the size of the disk drive and the operating system in use determine the actual number of sectors in a cluster. A cluster transfer is also called a *block mode* transfer.
- **Multiple Zone Recording** This is a technique used on some disk drives to eliminate the effect of the shape of the disk in recording sectors. More sectors are placed on tracks closer to the outer edge of the disk and fewer sectors are placed on the tracks closer to the inside edge. On drives without zoned recording capabilities, the size of the sector and the number of sectors per track are fixed numbers, which means that at the point on the physical media where the fixed track size can no longer be accommodated, there can be no additional tracks. Zoned recording allows more of the disk, the part closer to the inside edge of the disk, to be put to use. The disk is divided into zones, each with its own sizing and spacing criteria. Virtually all IDE and SCSI drives use zone recording methods.

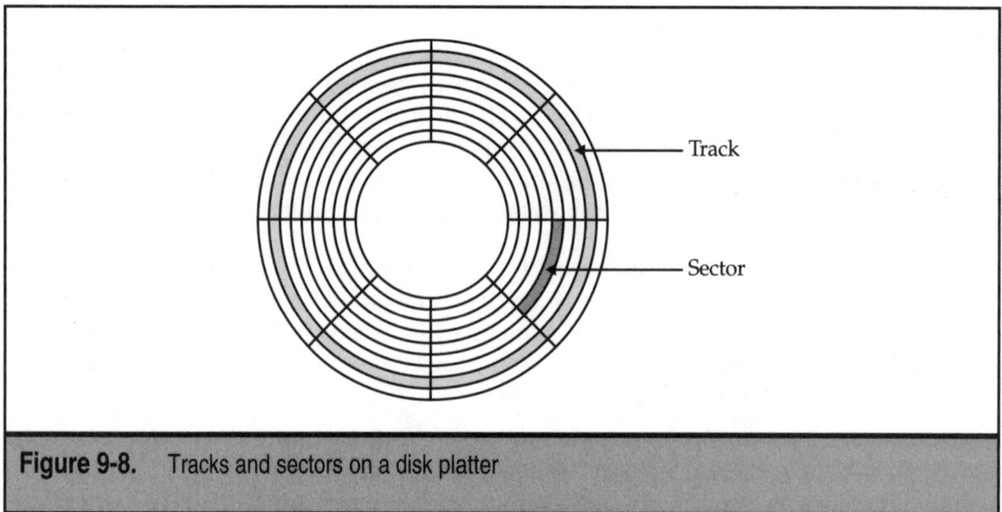

Figure 9-8. Tracks and sectors on a disk platter

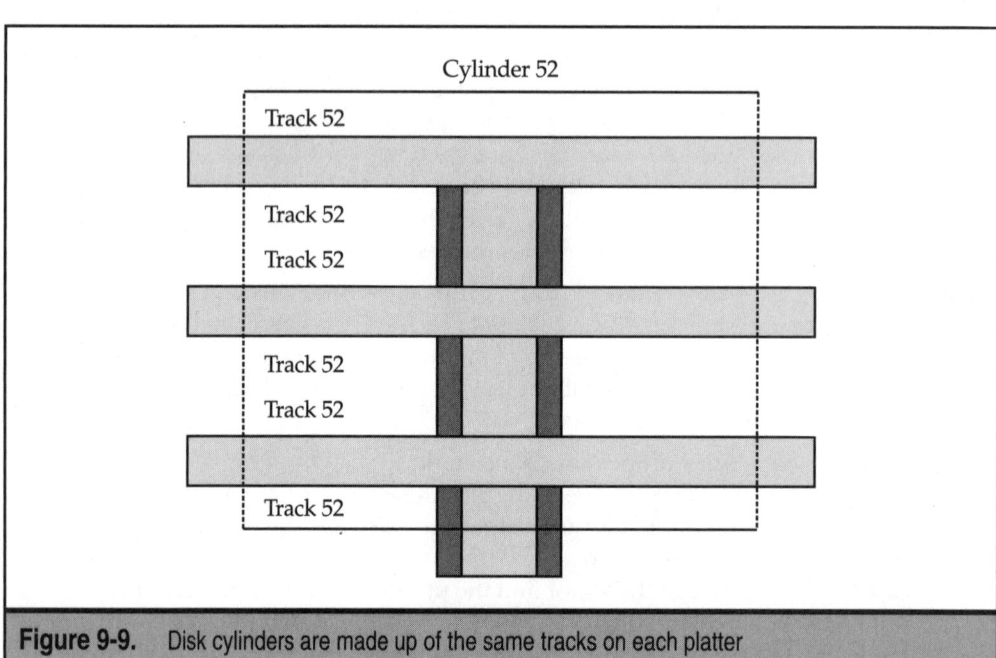

Figure 9-9. Disk cylinders are made up of the same tracks on each platter

Disk Capacities

Disk drive capacities are generally stated in megabytes and gigabytes, but drives with terabyte capacity are beginning to appear. Table 9-2 lists the more common data capacity units used with disk drives and their abbreviations. Just in case you're curious, the next two units after an exabyte are the zettabyte (1,000 exabytes) and the yottabyte (1,000 zettabytes). However, it will likely be a year or two before those capacities show up on disk drives for PCs.

A typical hard disk drive purchased with a system today would likely be in the 4 to 30GB range, depending on the PC and how much you spend. To get more disk storage space, you'd either have to add a second drive or switch the interface from IDE to SCSI.

HARD DISK PERFORMANCE

A number of performance metrics and indicators are available that you can use to choose the best disk drive for your PC or your particular requirements. Most people never worry about the detail performance criteria of their hard disk, provided it is doing the job. However, if a hard disk hasn't been doing the job, the performance specifications published by every hard disk system manufacturer can help you find just the disk for your particular need.

Unit	Abbreviation	Capacity
Kilobit	Kb	One thousand bits
Kilobyte	KB	One thousand bytes
Megabit	Mb	One million bits
Megabyte	MB	One million bytes
Gigabit	Gb	One billion bits
Gigabyte	GB	One billion bytes
Terabit	Tb	One trillion bits
Terabyte	TB	One trillion bytes
Petabit	Pb	One quadrillion bits
Petabyte	PB	One quadrillion bytes
Exabit	Eb	One quintillion bits
Exabyte	EB	One quintillion bytes

Table 9-2. Common Data Capacity Units

Performance Indicators

The most common of the performance specifications are

- **Seek Time** This is one of the more important performance indicators of the speed of a hard disk. Manufacturers like to dazzle you with their rotation speed, which is an important element of the disk's access time, but *seek time*, which is measured in milliseconds (ms), is the time it takes the head actuator to move the head arm and read/write heads from one track to the next. Seek time does not include the time required to move to a specific data location. *Average seek time* is a commonly used benchmark for comparing drive performance. Average seek time is calculated from the drive's performance over a number of randomly located requests. Most current disk drives have average seek times of 8 to 14 ms.
- **Access Time** This time includes seek time and measures the time required to position the read/write heads on a particular track and to find the sector containing a particular disk location. Access time involves latency, or rotational delay, which is the time required for the disk to rotate the sector being accessed under the read/write head. Latency is also measured in milliseconds and is generally around one-half the time required for the disk to make a single revolution. At 7,200 rpm (revolutions per minute), a very common disk rotational speed today, the latency is around 4 ms. As the rotational speed of the drive increases, the latency time decreases proportionately.
- **Data Transfer Rate** This is the amount of data that can be moved between the disk and RAM in one second. The data transfer rate is normally given as a number of megabytes (MB) per second. The higher the data transfer rate, the less time a user will wait for software to load or data to be retrieved. Data transfer rates of 5 to 40 MBps are common on today's hard disk drives.
- **Data Access Time (QBench)** This measurement combines the data access time and the data transfer rate to provide a rating of a disk drive's overall performance. This specification was developed by a hard disk manufacturer, Quantam (**www.quantum.com**), who also developed a benchmarking tool called Qbench, which has become a widely used standard for drive performance measurement and comparison.
- **Disk Capacity** A very important criteria for disk performance is how much data it can actually store. Disk drives typically have two capacity ratings: unformatted and formatted. The formatted capacity is usually the most important metric for most people, since it is the one that states the usable disk space on the drive. Nearly all drives being sold today are in the range of 500MB to 30GB.
- **Areal Density** While not technically a performance measurement, the areal density of a disk is an indication of a disk drive's storage capacity. The *areal density* of a disk is calculated by multiplying the number of *bits per inch (bpi)* (the number of bits in the total length of a track) by the number or tracks on the

disk. The result is the number of bits (expressed as megabits and gigabits) per square inch on the disk. An area density of around 1.5Gb per square inch is common on newer disk drives.

Interleaving

Although most newer drives no longer need it, *interleaving* was applied to older disk drives, such as the ST506/412, to offset the impact of latency and to all slow disk controllers to keep up with data transfer rates without missing sectors.

Interleaving allows the read/write head to use the rotation of the disk to its advantage. A disk drive with an interleave ratio of 3:1 (which stands for 3 to 1, but really means 3 minus 1) writes one sector and then skips two before writing the next. Likewise, an interleave of 2:1 means that it writes to every other sector (2 minus 1 equals 1). An interleave of 1:1 is the same has having no interleaving at all.

As the disk rotates under the read/write head, the disk controller may need the amount of time it takes to skip over one or two sectors to get ready for its next read or write action. By interleaving "empty" sectors into the process, the disk controller is better synchronized to the speed of the disk's rotation. However, the "empty" sectors skipped over in the interleave action do not remain empty and will be used by other read/write actions. Applying interleaving by changing the controller card to one that supported it enabled some older drives to double or triple their transfer rates.

FORMATTING THE DISK

Hard disk drives must be formatted before data can be stored on them. Two formatting levels are performed on a disk media to prepare it for use: low-level and high-level formatting. On most new PCs, the hard disk media is low-level formatted at the factory and pre-formatted diskettes are commonly available, so formatting is used largely to prepare a hard disk for the operating system or to erase it for reuse. Here is more detail on the two formatting types:

- **Low-level formatting** A low-level format permanently erases the disk and is not reversible because it performs a destructive scan of the disk to find any defects in the recording media. The location of any defect found is recorded as unusable to avoid data problems.
- **High-level formatting** High-level formatting is done after low-level formatting and after the disk has been partitioned (see next section). The high-level format prepares the disk's partitions by creating a root directory and the File Allocation Table (FAT). The FAT is used to record the location and relationships of files and directories on the disk.

A low-level format should not be done on an IDE or SCSI hard disk. This is performed during manufacturing and should not ever be needed again. Because the low-level format erases the disk at the media level (physical erase), in most cases should the disk need to be cleaned off, a high-level format (logical erase) is usually enough. The high-level format erases the FAT, which erases all references to the files stored on the disk, which in effect, erases the disk.

Partitioning the Hard Disk

As described in the previous section, a disk must be physically formatted (low-level format), partitioned, and logically formatted (high-level format) before it can store data. The partitioning phase creates physical divisions of the disk that can be used to segment the disk and allow for two or more operating systems or the creation of multiple file systems.

Partitioning the hard disk allows you to:

- Divide the disk into logical "subdrives" that can be addressed separately with a drive letter assigned to each, such as C:, D:, and E:
- Create separate areas on the disk for multiple operating systems, such as storing Windows and Linux on the same hard disk, each in its own partition
- Separate program files from data files on separate disk partitions to facilitate faster and easier data backups

Partitioning a hard disk can improve the disk's efficiency. For example, Windows assigns disk clusters (logical collections of sectors) that are sized in proportion to partition size. Bigger clusters may sound like a good thing, but just the opposite is true. Large disk drives or bigger partitions result in bigger clusters, which unfortunately result in small unused spaces on the disk. By reducing the size of the disk or more smaller partitions, the result is reduced cluster sizes.

If you wish to have only one partition on your disk, that's perfectly all right. However, you should know that on some systems, if you wish to use the entire disk, you will have to create smaller partitions. For example, on DOS, Windows 3.*x*, or an early release of Windows 95, partition sizes must be smaller than 2GB, which means that a disk larger than 2GB must be divided into two or more partitions if you wish to use the entire disk. Windows 98 and Windows 2000 allow you to create partitions of up to 4TB (terabytes).

A hard disk can be divided into two types of partitions:

- **Primary partitions** The primary partition contains the operating system and is usually the one from which the PC is booted. A hard disk can be divided into a maximum of four primary partitions, but on most operating systems, only one primary partition may be active at a time.
- **Extended partitions** This type of partition can be divided into as many as 23 logical partitions, each of which can be assigned its own drive identity. Extended partitions can be used for any purpose.

File Systems

Operating systems use a file system to manage the allocation and utilization of the disk storage. The high-level format process creates the operating system's file system, copies the operating system to the primary partition, and builds the management tables and files, such as the File Allocation Table (FAT). Each operating system uses a *file system*, like the FAT, to track the usage of the disk and the placement of files. Table 9-3 lists the names of the file systems used by some of the more popular operating systems.

Here is a brief description on the file systems referenced in Table 9-3:

- **FAT (File Allocation Table)** This file system, also called FAT16, is used by DOS and Windows 3.*x* to place and locate files and the pieces of fragmented files on the hard disk.
- **HPFS (High-Performance File System)** Many later file systems, such as NTFS, evolved from HPFS, which features better security, reliability, speed, and efficiency than FAT.
- **UNIX File System/Linux File System** The Unix and Linux file systems use a branching-tree file structure that emanates from a root directory, which can have an unlimited number of subdirectories and sub-subdirectories, and so on.
- **VFAT (Virtual File Allocation Table)** VFAT is available in Windows for Workgroups and Windows 95. It actually serves as an interface between applications and the physical FAT. Its most outstanding feature is that it was the first Windows file system to allow long filenames.
- **FAT32 (32-bit FAT)** This is the file system in later releases of Windows 95 and in Windows 98. It supports larger disk capacities (up to two terabytes) and uses a smaller cluster size to produce more efficient storage utilization.
- **NTFS (NT File System)** NTFS is one of the two file systems used by the Windows NT operating system (the other is the standard FAT file system for backward compatibility purposes). NTFS uses transaction logs to help recover from disk failures; it has the ability to set permissions at the directory or individual file level and allows files to span several disks or partitions.

DISK SPACE REQUIREMENTS

In today's world of downloadable music, graphics, interactive media, and disk-consuming software, it can be hard to know just how much disk space is enough on a system. Table 9-4 lists the disk space requirements for some of the more popular graphics programs.

Operating Systems	File System
DOS	FAT
OS/2	HPFS
UNIX/Linux	UNIX File System/Linux File System
Windows 3.*x*	FAT/VFAT
Windows 95	VFAT and FAT32
Windows NT	NTFS
Windows 2000	NTFS

Table 9-3. File Systems

Application	Disk Space Needed	Recommended Extra Space
Audio (WAV)	1 minute–10MB	
	1 hour–600MB	
MP3 music	1 hour–120MB	
	3 hours–360MB	
Business/financial software	30–70MB	60–80MB
Interactive graphics/games	100–350MB	250–300MB
Multimedia e-mail	2–5MB	
MPEG video	100MB–10GB	
Streaming video	2MB–1GB	
MS Office	500MB–640MB	200MB

Table 9-4. Disk Space Requirements for Common Applications

Disk Compression

Since hard disks have become large enough for most users, disk compression has passed out of vogue. But on older systems with 1GB or smaller hard disks, disk compression extends the capacity of a hard disk drive. *Disk compression* uses data compression techniques to reduce the amount of disk space a file uses. The effect is that more files fit into the same space. Understand that nothing is really happening to the disk; the data is actually being compressed and stored in a special file. The compressed data must be translated in and out of the compressed data store.

A disk compression utility must reside in memory and work between the operating system and the disk controller. The compression utility intercepts any file read and write actions sent to the disk. When the operating system saves a file to disk, the compression utility intercepts the file and compresses it before it's written to the compressed data store. When the operating system reads a file, the compression utility intercepts the file, decompresses it, and then passes the data on to the system memory. This utility does add some overhead to the process and slows down all file access from the compressed disk.

A number of third-party disk compression utilities are available, all of which work essentially the same. Windows has included disk compression software in nearly all of its versions. Windows 3.*x* featured a routine called DBLSpace. Windows 95 included DriveSpace, which could compress and uncompress data on floppy disks, removable media, or hard disk drives. DriveSpace works by creating a new uncompressed logical drive, called the host drive, where it stores the CVF (Compressed Volume File), a form of VFAT for the compressed drive. The uncompressed drive also contains files that should not or cannot be compressed, such as system files. Any unused space is available to the user. The Windows 95 version of DriveSpace creates compressed drives of up to 512MB. Large disk drives usually can't be compressed as a single volume. The version available in Microsoft Plus! and Windows 98 can compress drives up to 2GB.

RAID

A *Redundant Array of Independent (or Inexpensive) Disks (RAID)* is a technique applied to disk drives as part of a high availability or fault tolerant program to protect the integrity of the data stored on the disks. RAID employs two or more drives in combination to store more than one copy of data or to spread the data over several disk drives to lessen the impact of a disk drive failure. RAID technology is used frequently on network file servers but isn't generally used on PCs.

A fundamental concept in RAID systems is *data striping*, in which data files are written across several disks. Data striping retrieves and stores more data than a single disk can supply or accept. As the first block of data is being written to or retrieved from the first disk drive, the second block is being set up by the second disk drive, and so on. Another feature of a RAID system is *data mirroring*, which involves writing duplicate data segments or files to more than one disk to guard against a device failure.

Ten different RAID levels exist—0 through 7, 10, and 53, and each one is more complicated than its predecessor. In general usage, there are only four RAID levels—0, 1, 3, and 5—used on most systems. Here is a brief overview of these RAID levels:

- **RAID 0 (Striped disk array without fault tolerance)** This level provides data striping but does not include any mirroring or other redundancy. If a disk drive is lost, the portion of the data stored on it is also lost.
- **RAID 1 (Mirroring and duplexing)** A very common RAID level on high-volume disk systems. It features complete data redundancy and does not require the data to be rebuilt. Should a disk failure occur, a copy of the data only needs to be loaded to the replacement disk (usually a hot-swap disk).
- **RAID 3 (Parallel transfer with parity)** This level is very much like Level 0, except that it sets aside a dedicated disk for storing parity and error-correcting code (ECC) data that can be used to reconstruct the data should a hard disk fail.
- **RAID 5 (Data striping with parity)** On systems requiring a high-degree of data protection and availability, this RAID level is popular. RAID 5 provides for data striping at the character level and implements error correction at the stripe level. The error correction data is stored on a separate disk from the data it represents. RAID 5 requires at least three disk drives to implement.

FLOPPY DISK DRIVES

Although manufacturers have been trying for years to replace the floppy disk, a.k.a. *diskette*, with a device that holds more data, the 3.5-inch floppy disk drive is still very common on most PCs sold today. The floppy disk has survived well beyond what anyone expected. It has changed in size over the years and is available in drives that fit inside the system case as well as outside. The floppy disk has come in a variety of sizes over its lifetime, but for about the past ten years the most popular size has been the 3.5-inch diskette. Figure 9-10 contrasts the older 5.25-inch diskette to the 3.5-inch disk.

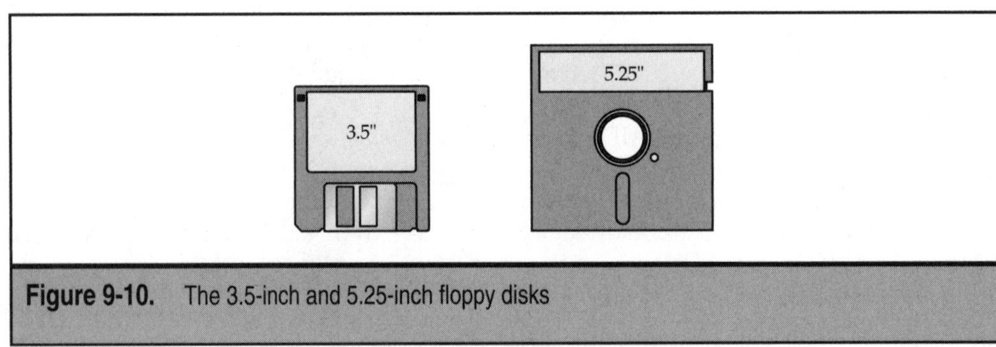

Figure 9-10. The 3.5-inch and 5.25-inch floppy disks

At one time, the *floppy disk* was the primary data storage device on the PC, but it has lately been relegated to a role of removable media for single files or small collections of files. As file sizes grow, the floppy disk is less able to serve in the role it once did. Where it once was the media on which new software was released, CD-ROMs or Internet downloads are now used. The floppy disk still has a role for transferring data from one PC to another (aptly called a *sneaker net*), backing up small files and compressed files (zips, tars, and archives), and device driver distribution, although this is also moving to CD-ROM or downloading.

Floppy Disk Construction

The floppy disk drive is an internal device that is mounted into an open drive bay of the system case. While it is an internal device, its bezel extends through the drive bay opening and should be visible through a removable bay cover on the case, as well.

A 3.5-inch floppy disk drive is about the same size as most newer hard disk drives. Newer cases mount the diskette in either a smaller drive bay or require an adapter kit to mount it into a full-size drive bay. If your system is old enough to have a 5.25-inch drive, it is most likely a half-height drive (about 1.75-inches in height) and fits into a full-sized drive bay.

The floppy disk, as shown in Figures 9-11 and 9-12, is made up of a number of components that are very similar in name and function to those of a hard disk drive. The primary components of the floppy disk drive are:

- Read/write heads
- Head actuator
- Spindle motor
- Connectors and jumpers
- Media

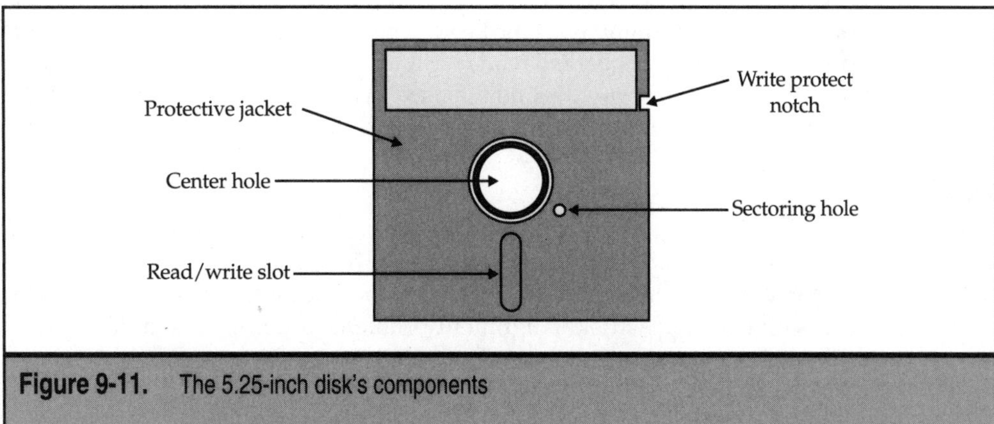

Figure 9-11. The 5.25-inch disk's components

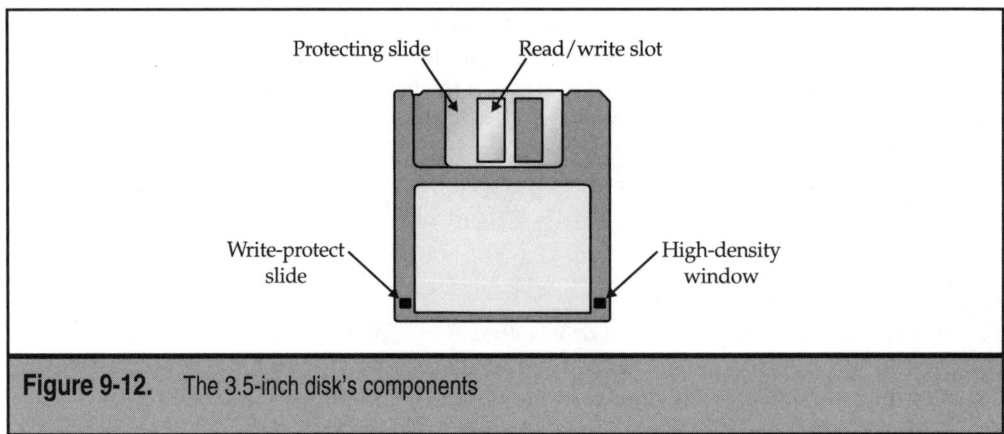

Figure 9-12. The 3.5-inch disk's components

Read/Write Heads

Like the heads on the hard disk, the read/write heads on the floppy disk use an electromagnetic field to store binary data on the floppy disk media. However, there are some differences between the read/write heads on these two media. The primary difference is in the density of the media. The floppy disk's media is made to hold much less data on a much lower areal density. While the size of the media is similar in most cases, because the floppy disk media is portable, it is designed with less data density. There are fewer tracks on a floppy disk. Where a hard disk can have thousands of tracks, a floppy disk may have only 70 to 150 tracks. Because of these factors, the read/write heads on the floppy disk are larger and more primitive in their design.

Another difference is that floppy disks record data through direct contact with the media, much like a tape recorder. The read/write heads directly contact the media to transfer data to the media. Although the floppy disk turns about 10 to 20 times slower than the hard disk, there is still some wear as the recording media's magnetic oxide material and any dirt or debris from the air gets on the head, which is why floppy disk drive heads should be cleaned occasionally. There is a read/write head for each recordable surface on the floppy disk. On nearly all floppy disk media used over the past ten years, there have been two recording surfaces, one on each side of the disk.

Head Actuator

The head actuator positions the read/write heads over a specific track on the floppy disk. In most cases, a floppy disk has 80 tracks per side and the head actuator, which is powered by a stepper motor, moves from track to track. The stepper motor has detents or stops for each of the tracks on the floppy disk. Alignment problems are minor on a floppy disk because should the drive get out of alignment, the $25–$30 it costs to replace the drive is much less expensive than realigning the read/write heads.

Seek times on a floppy disk are relatively slower than on a hard disk. It is common that the seek time associated with moving the read/write head from the innermost track to the outermost track on the disk requires 200 or more milliseconds.

Spindle Motor

When the floppy disk is inserted into the drive, clamps attached to the spindle motor clamp the disk into place. The spindle motor then rotates the disk so that the media moves under the read/write heads. The speed of the spindle motor is tied to the physical size of the disk, but for the 3.5-inch disk, the spindle motor rotates the disk at 300 rpm. This very slow rotation speed adds to the latency and data transfer speeds of the disk, but it also keeps the contact heads from wearing out the disk.

Connectors

A floppy disk drive connects to the system through two connectors. The data connector is used to connect the floppy disk to the floppy disk controller. Typically, the data cable connects either one or two floppy disk drives. On systems that connect two floppy disk drives (extremely rare on newer systems), the cable is used to connect one drive as the A drive and another as the B drive.

The other floppy disk connector is used to connect the disk drive to the power supply. This connector will be either a very similar connector to the one on the hard disk drive or a much smaller connector that should have a mate coming from the power supply on nearly all power supply form factors.

Media

The first floppy disks were eight inches, but the first ones to gain widespread use on the PC were 5.25 inches, still large when compared with today's popular 3.5-inch size. A 5.25-inch disk, shown in Figure 9-11, has primary components: the flexible round piece of magnetic oxide coated plastic media and the outside somewhat rigid plastic jacket. The 5.25-inch disk has a large center hole used to clamp the disk to the spindle so it can be rotated. The outside jacket does not turn; the disk is rotated inside of it. The read/write head contacts the disk through the read/write slot that is long enough to allow the head to reach all of the tracks on the disk. In an effort to prevent the disk from being written to accidentally and overwriting some important data, the write-protection notch can be covered to disable the write function.

The 3.5-inch disk was developed to overcome the fragility of the 5.25-inch disk and to provide a smaller, more protected disk. The 3.5-inch diskette added a sturdier packaging, a metal slide to protect the read/write slot and a sliding switch for write-protection of the disk.

Both the 5.25-inch and the 3.5-inch disks have had different data density standards over the years. Usually the density was given a name that generally described how dense the disk actually was. The density standards have gotten increasingly higher, from the original single-density disks, which had a bit density of around 2,500 bpi and 24 tracks per inch (tpi), to the extra-high density specification for 3.5-inch disks that have just under 35,000 bpi and 135 tpi. The higher the density standard of the disk, the more data it will hold, and the more it will cost. Most disks proudly display their density and their storage abilities on their packaging.

Formatting

A floppy disk, regardless of its size or density, must be formatted before it can receive and store data. *Formatting* performs two tasks, in two separate steps of the same process:

- **Low-level formatting** This level of formatting creates the organization structures on the disk, including the tracks and the beginning points for each sector on the track.
- **High-level formatting** This format level adds the logical structures, including the file allocation table (FAT) and the disk's root directory.

You can pay a little more and buy preformatted disks just about anywhere, including the supermarket. However, not all PCs will work with these diskettes and you may need to reformat them on your PC.

The low-level and high-level formatting processes together create the storage characteristics of the floppy disk, which summarizes the overall storage structure for the disk. Table 9-5 lists the characteristics for the two most popular diskette sizes in use.

Disk Size	Capacity	Tracks	Sectors/Track	Total Sectors/Disk	Bytes/Sector
5.25″	1.2MB	80	15	2,400	512
3.5″	1.44MB	80	18	2,880	512

Table 9-5. Typical Diskette Storage Characteristics

CHAPTER 10

CD-ROMs and DVDs

The *CD-ROM (Compact Disc-Read Only Memory)* wasn't developed specifically for the PC. It was designed initially for use as an audio storage device to replace the cassette tape. It hasn't been totally successful in that mission—cassettes are still around—but it has gained acceptance and proven to be very popular. However, the CD-ROM did discover a ready and willing market of personal computer users. The CD-ROM and its comparatively huge storage capacity (over floppy disks) was very attractive to software and multimedia producers and soon virtually all software, including databases, books, encyclopedias, and other materials not available to the PC in the past suddenly became very available and accessible for the PC.

Because the majority of software titles are available only on CD-ROM, today's PCs have a CD-ROM drive. A CD-ROM drive is as common on PCs today as floppy drives were only a few years ago. In fact, some manufacturers now replace the floppy disk drive with a single CD-ROM on their latest PC models. The CD-ROM is by far the most common method of software distribution and data storage due to their combination of high capacity and easy, inexpensive manufacturing.

When CD-ROMs were first introduced to the market, most software distributors included floppy disks along with the CD-ROM version of the program or provided a coupon that could be mailed in for a CD-ROM version of the software. In the past few years, this was reversed, and the coupon became the means of getting a diskette version of a software package. Today, the coupon has disappeared altogether and the CD-ROM is now the only option available. A PC without a CD-ROM drive simply is not able to install the vast majority of PC software available on the market today. Some CD-ROM software even requires that your PC's drive meet a specific minimum requirement. For example, if you have an older CD-ROM drive, such as a 4X, in your system, it may need to be replaced before it can run some newer CD-ROM titles that require at least a 12X drive.

THE TECHNOLOGY OF THE CD AND CD-ROM

The CD-ROM uses compact disc (CD) technology, the same technology used to record the music on your favorite audio CDs. The physical media used for recording data, programs, music, and multimedia on a CD-ROM is the same as that used to record music. In fact, the physical disc (see Figure 10-1) is the same for both.

CD-ROM Formats

There are a number of different formats and applications of the CD technology, not all of which are for the computer. The two that most people are familiar with are the formats used for music CDs and data CD-ROMs, but there are a few others. The *format* of the CD is the pattern and method used to record its contents. The CD is often compared to the old vinyl record because they are produced in a similar fashion and their contents is recorded in a spiraling pattern, as opposed to data arranged in tracks, as on a music cassette or a disk drive.

Figure 10-1. A compact disc can be used for data or music

CD-Digital Audio (CD-DA)

The first standard CD format was the one used to produce audio CDs that could play in all regular CD players: *CD-Digital Audio,* or *CD-DA*. The CD-DA standard was defined in what is called the Red Book, a specification developed by the two originators of the CD technology, the Royal Philips Electronics Company and the Sony Corporation. The Red Book standard, issued in 1980, defines the technical specification for CD-DA (audio CD), including sampling and transfer rates, the data format for the digital audio, and the physical specifications for compact discs, including the media's size and the spacing of tracks. The Red Book defined the standard for the structure of the media and how a CD is read that is still used today.

The technical details of the Red Book standard include:

- 16-bit sample.
- Sampling is at 44.1kHz (kilohertz), which is about twice the highest frequency that humans can hear.
- Sampling is done in stereo.
- Each one second of sound stored on the CD requires 176,400 bytes.

Compact Disc-Read-Only Memory (CD-ROM)

The large capacity of the CD was attractive to nonmusic producers as well, including software publishers, database producers, and multimedia developers. The CD-ROM holds about 640 million bytes of data. The CD-ROM technology had approximately the same speed as the CD-DA, which was designated as 1X (one times) the relative speed of a music CD at about 150KB per second.

In order to store data, the CD-DA standard had to be modified. In 1984, Philips and Sony issued the Yellow Book standard that defined the CD-ROM for storing computer data. The Yellow Book defined two new kinds of content sectors: Mode 1 and Mode 2. Mode 1 sectors store computer data and Mode 2 sectors are used to store compressed audio or video and graphic data. This new standard recognized the need for the CD-ROM to store data more precisely than the audio CD.

Audio CD (CD-DA) has 99 accessible tracks on which music is stored. The Yellow Book defined the CD-ROM with what amounted to a file system. Both Mode 1 and Mode 2 sector formats have a few bytes at the front of each sector. Table 10-1 lists the contents of a Mode 1 sector, showing the space used for the header and error detection and correction.

The size of CD-DA and CD-ROM Mode 1 and Mode 2 sectors are the same, but the amount of user data varies because of sync bytes, header bytes, and error correction and detection. The CD-DA format uses all 2,352 bytes of a sector for user data (music). CD-ROM Mode 1 blocks have 2,048 of user data and Mode 2 blocks provide 2,336 user bytes. Because of the amount of data they transfer, the two modes have different transfer speeds (about 1.22Mbps for Mode 1 and 1.4Mbps for Mode 2).

In the Mode 1 sector, the first 12 bytes of the header are sync bytes that are used for sector separation. The sync bytes at the beginning of a sector are intended to identify the sector mode, but since the value of the sync bytes could coincidentally appear in the user bytes, the length of the sector is also used to identify the mode type. The next four bytes are the header bytes, three of which are used for addressing. The fourth byte indicates the mode used to record the contents of the sector. The address stored in the header bytes contains the length of any blocks in the sector in minutes and seconds, plus other identifying information.

The header byte mode indicator contains the *CIRC (Cross Interleaved Reed-Solomon Code)*, which is the standard error detection and correction method used by CD-DA and

Bytes	Use	Purpose
12	Sync bytes	Sector separator
3	Header bytes	Addressing (minutes, seconds, and tracks)
1	Header byte	Mode indicator (CIRC)
2048	User bytes	Data
4	EDC bytes	Error detection
8	Unused	
276	ECC bytes	Error correction

Table 10-1. CD-ROM Mode 1 Sector Format

CD-ROM formats. On CD-ROM Mode 1 discs, the CIRC method used is called *Layered EDC/ECC (error-detection code/error-correcting code)*, which determines if an error has occurred in a data block and corrects it. This error detection and correction method requires the use of additional bytes at the end of the sector. EDC uses 4 bytes, ECC uses 276 bytes, and between them are 8 bytes of unused space.

A Mode 1 sector provides 2,048 bytes of user data. This area can be divided into blocks of 512, 1024, and 2048 bytes each, but a CD-ROM typically has the same block length throughout. A block cannot be bigger than a sector, which is also the smallest addressable unit on the CD-ROM. CD-ROM Mode 2 sectors do not use additional error detection and correction, which leaves the bytes behind the sync and header bytes (2,336 bytes) as user bytes.

CD-ROM Extended Architecture (CD-ROM XA)

The Red Book CD-DA and the Yellow Book CD-ROM formats soon proved too restricting to producers, so Philips, Sony, and the Microsoft Corporation combined to develop the CD-ROM Extended Architecture, or CD-ROM XA format. The CD-ROM XA format is an extension of the Yellow Book format standard.

CD-ROM XA discs can mix CD-ROM Mode 1 and Mode 2 formats to store computer data, compressed audio, graphics, and video content. CD-ROM XA does not use additional EDC/ECC capabilities, so the user gains the 288 bytes used in CD-ROM Mode 1 formats for this purpose. This format *interleaves*, meaning that it mixes different types of data together in different mode formats on the same CD, allowing music, data, programming, and graphics to share a single CD.

CD-ROM XA discs require a drive certified for the CD-ROM XA format. Because they usually contain compressed audio and video, these devices include hardware decoders that decompress the data as it is read.

CD-Interactive (CD-I)

In 1986, the demand and rapid growth of multimedia were the catalysts leading to the creation of the CD-Interactive or CD-I format. CD-I discs contained text, graphics, audio, and video on a single disc format. Special hardware was used to connect CD-I players to television screens for output. CD-I, like the CD-ROM XA, is a derivative of the Yellow Book, but the CD-I used a proprietary and unique formatting.

Bridge CD

The term bridge CD refers to discs that support extensions of the CD-ROM XA format, defined in what is known as the White Book. These discs are called bridge CDs because they bridge the CD-ROM XA and the CD-I formats and can be used for either. Using the White Book specification, CD-I discs will work in CD-ROM XA drives, and CD-ROM XA discs will work in CD-I drives. Examples of a bridge CD is the Kodak Photo CD and the Video CD format.

Video CD (VCD)

The *video CD (VCD)* is used to store compressed video information using a standard also defined in the White Book. VCDs use MPEG (Motion Picture Experts Group) compression to store 74 minutes of full-motion video in the same space used by CD-DA audio. To play a video CD requires a CD-ROM drive or video CD player that is video CD-compatible. The compression algorithm used for VCD does not produce a high quality video; this format will likely give way to the DVD.

Photo CD

The Photo CD standard, another standard developed by Philips—this time with Kodak—is adapted from the CD-ROM XA standard to hold photographs in digital form. This standard is defined in the Orange Book that also defined the CD-Recordable. A photo CD uses CD-ROM Mode 2 formatting to store photographic images. Normal camera film is first developed into photo prints, which are then scanned and converted into digital images. The digitized photographs are then converted to photo CD formatting and written to the CD, using essentially the CD-R process (this is covered later in the chapter). A photo CD is a type of bridge CD, which means a CD-I player can read it.

CD-PROM

A CD-PROM (Compact Disc-Programmable Read-Only Memory) is a combination of the manufactured CD-ROM and the CD-R disc developed by Kodak. Part of the disc can contain mastered data and another part of the disc can be recorded in a CD-R drive.

CD-Recordable

Each of the CD types covered to this point have been CD-ROMs, or read-only discs, which means that except for during their manufacturing processes, data cannot be stored to them and they cannot be modified, other than to be destroyed. To take advantage of its large storage space, methods have been developed, along with special CD media that allow data to be written to a CD.

A CD Recordable (CD-R) disc is manufactured essentially the same as a CD-ROM disc, with some slight variations. In place of the substrate is a layer of organic dye, over which is placed a reflective gold-colored metallic coating. Over this is the protective lacquer layer, just like on a CD-ROM.

Two general types of CDs that can be modified in a special CD-R are:

- **WORM (Write Once/Read Many)** A special CD disc type to which data or music can be written to one time in a CD-R drive, after which the data is permanent and cannot be changed.
- **Magneto Optical (MO) discs** These versatile discs can be written to, read, and then modified. These are also referred to as CD-RW (read, write) discs.

Compact Disc Media

Like other computer storage media, such as hard disks and floppy disks, a CD stores data in digital form, which means that it actually stores only two values: 1s and 0s. However, where the hard disk and diskette store data in magnetic form, data on a CD is recorded in a physical recording technique. A CD starts out as a round piece of polycarbonate substrate about 4.75 inches in diameter and 1.2 millimeters (approximately 1/20th of an inch) thick. A metal stamp, made from a master of a finished disc, is then used to stamp indentations into the substrate, a process called *mastering*. A CD-ROM produced this way is said to have been *mastered*. The indentations are referred to as *pits*, and the flat, unpitted surfaces are referred to as *lands*, as shown in Figure 10-2. The substrate surface and its pits are then covered with a shiny, reflective silver or aluminum coating, which plays a very important part in reading and playing the contents of the CD. A clear plastic cover is then placed over the silver coating on which a paper or silk-screened label is applied. A disc manufactured in this way is called a *single-session* disc.

Reading the CD

When a CD is loaded into a player or CD-ROM drive, it spins and a laser moves over the lands and pits, sensing thousands of them per second. When the laser hits a land, its light reflects off the metallic coating to a sensor. A pit on the CD surface does not reflect the laser back to the sensor. When it hits a pit, the light does not reflect back to the sensor. Whether the sensor sees a reflection or not is how it knows if the bit on the CD is a 1 or a 0. Unlike a floppy or hard disk, a CD is recorded on a single long (about three miles long, in fact) spiral, rather than in discrete tracks. The spiral is wound onto the disc in a pattern that is the equivalent of about 16,000 tracks per inch on a hard disk drive.

The top of the CD is its data surface, and the data is placed on substrate core directly beneath the CD's label. The laser is focused on the bottom of the CD directly through the CD's substrate, which is about 1 millimeter thick. Scratches on a CD shouldn't interfere with the CD's ability to be read because the laser shines through them. As long as the substrate remains intact and undamaged, the disc should be readable. However, should the scratches be deep enough to remove any of the reflective coating, the disc would be unreadable.

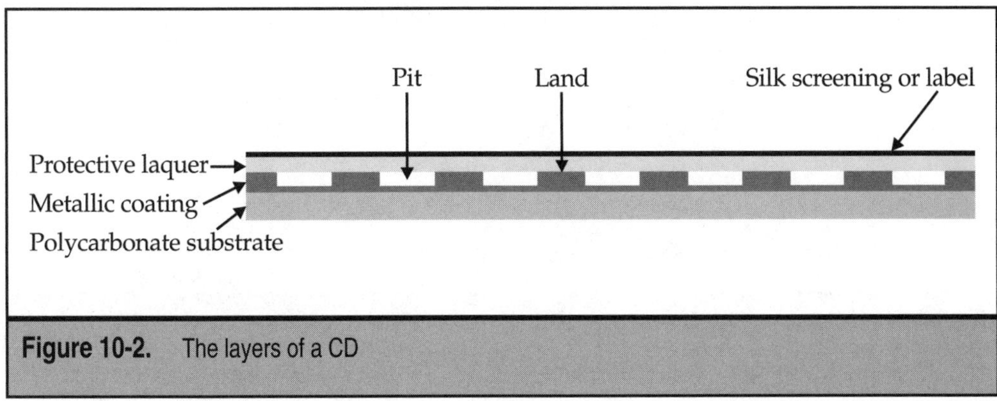

Figure 10-2. The layers of a CD

The first sector on the CD is located at two minutes, no seconds, and no hundredths of seconds (00:02:00), or 600 blocks. On a CD-ROM using 512-byte blocks, a minute of data contains 18,000 blocks, which means that there are 300 in a second and 600 in the first two seconds. This also means that Logical Block 0 is at 00:02:00 as well.

Writing to a CD

The CD-R WORM disc contains a layer of organic dye. The laser changes the light absorbing or reflecting properties of this dye to store digital data to the CD. The CD-RW (CD-MO) disc has an internal layer of a special metal alloy. The laser changes the light-reflecting characteristics of this metal alloy, and the read laser is reflected differently depending on the data value stored in each bit.

A new type of CD is now emerging called CD-Erasable (CD-E) that uses a phase-change technology that erases the contents of the CD so it can be rerecorded. The CD-E has a data layer of silver alloy that is recorded using a higher energy laser than is used to read the disc. The high-energy laser crystallizes part of the metal alloy to change its reflective states. Different laser temperatures are used to record and erase the disc.

Any CD-ROM and most CD players can read a CD-R disc. However, to date, a CD-RW or a CD-E disc cannot be read by a standard CD-ROM drive or CD-player.

CD-ROM Drive Operation

A CD-ROM drive fits in a standard 5.25-inch drive bay on a PC. Its height of about 1.75 inches makes it a half-height device, which is the type of drive bay included with most PC cases (see Figure 10-3). The drive has a sheet metal enclosure that surrounds the drive and

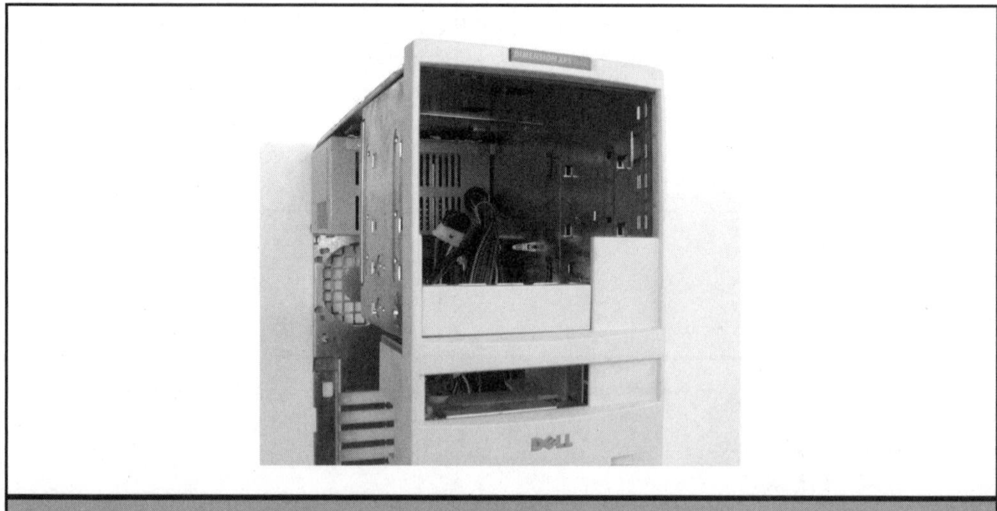

Figure 10-3. Empty drive bays on a PC case

screw holes are tapped into the sides of the enclosure that allow for mounting it directly into a standard drive bay, as shown in Figure 10-4. On some older PCs, a CD-ROM, as well as a hard or floppy disk drive, is mounted in the PC bay with mounting rails that attach to the sides of the drive and then slide into the drive bay.

The Laser and Head Assembly

The laser in a CD-ROM drive is a beam of light that is emitted from an *infrared laser diode*. The laser is aimed not directly on the CD but toward a reflecting mirror in the read head assembly. The read head moves along the spiraling track of the CD just above the surface of the disc. The light from the laser reflects off the mirror and then passes through a focusing lens that directs the light directly on a specific point on the disc. The light is reflected back from the shining metallic coating on the disc. The amount of light reflected depends on whether the laser is hitting a flat or a pit. The reflected light is passed through a series of collectors, mirrors, and lenses that are used to focus the reflected light and send it to a *photo detector*. The photo detector converts the light into an electrical signal, the strength of which is determined by the intensity of the reflected light. Figure 10-5 illustrates the components of the CD-ROM drive's head assembly.

Since the disc spins, most of the components used to "read" the CD are fixed in place, with only the read head assembly, which contains the mirror and read lens, actually moving. The CD-ROM is a single-sided media and data is recorded on one side. This means that the CD-ROM drive requires only one read head and head assembly, resulting in an overall design that is relatively simple.

Probably the biggest problem for the CD-ROM drive is that because it uses light, the laser must not be obstructed. Dust or other foreign material on the disc or on the focus lens in the read head can cause problems for a CD-ROM drive to the point of causing errors or even a drive failure.

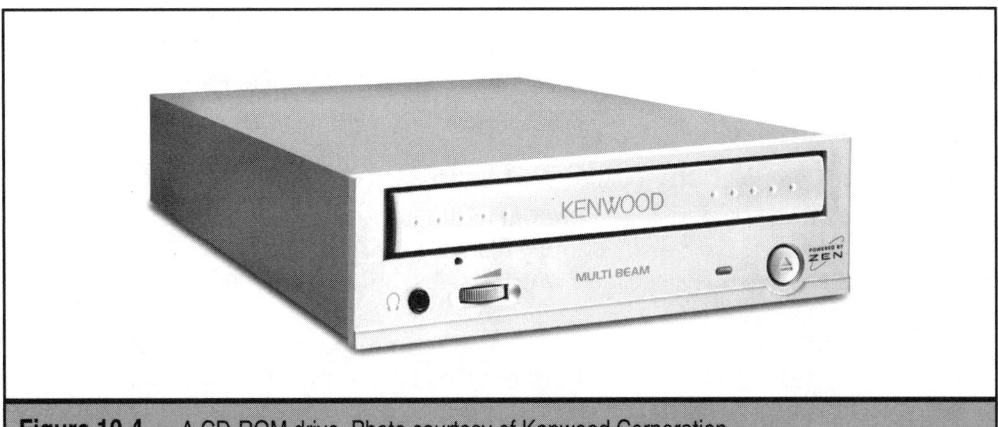

Figure 10-4. A CD-ROM drive. Photo courtesy of Kenwood Corporation

Figure 10-5. The head assembly, including the read head, of a CD-ROM drive

The Read Head

The part of the head assembly that moves across the CD-ROM is the *head actuator*, also called the *read head*, which consists of the read lens and a mirror. The technology used to move a CD-ROM drive's read head is much like that used for floppy disk and hard disk drives.

The read head is guided over the disc on a set of rails that, at one end, positions the head on the outermost edge of the disc and, on the other end, stops it near the CD's hub ring. The mechanism used to control the positioning of the CD read head over the disc is an integrated microcontroller and servo system (small motors used to move the head).

Constant Linear Velocity (CLV) and Constant Angular Velocity (CAV)

The CD-ROM drive uses a spindle motor to rotate the disc so that it can be read. Unlike the spinning media in a hard disk or floppy disk drive, a disc in a CD-ROM drive does not spin at a constant speed. The speed at which the disc spins varies depending on the part of the disc that is being read.

On a hard disk drive, the disk spins at the same speed regardless of where the read/write heads may be. Using a constant spin speed for the media is called *constant angular velocity (CAV)* because every spin of the media takes the same amount of time at all times. On the hard disk and floppy disk, the disk's inside tracks are much shorter than those on the outside of the disk. When the disk's heads are on the outside tracks, they travel over a much longer linear path than when they are over the inside tracks. Another speed measurement on a disk is its *linear velocity*, which on most disk drives is not constant. However, many of the latest hard disk designs now store more information on the outer tracks of the disk than they do on the inner tracks (a process called *zoned bit recording*) to take advantage of this condition.

A CD-ROM drive adjusts the speed of the spindle motor to keep the linear velocity of the disc constant. When the read head is near the outside of the CD, the motor runs slower; when the head moves near the inside edge of the disc, the motor runs faster. This ensures that the same amount of data goes past the read head in any amount of time. The process used by the CD-ROM is called *constant linear velocity (CLV)*.

Early CD-ROM drives operated at the same speeds as standard CD-DA players, which was about 210 to 539rpm (revolutions per minute), with a standard transfer rate of 150KB or 1X (times) the CD-DA transfer rate. Increasing the spindle motor's speed and beefing up the CD-ROM's electronics increased the transfer rate of the CD-ROM drive. This allowed the CD-ROM drive to transfer data fast enough to support multimedia software.

Up to transfer ratings of 12X (12 times the transfer rate of a CD-DA), the spindle motor speed is varied to maintain CLV. Newer CD-ROM drives now incorporate the CAV method and vary the transfer rate depending on where the read head is on the disc. On a CAV CD-RM, the "X" transfer speed rating is an indication of the best possible speed data (near the outside edge) can be transferred. For example, a CAV drive with a claim of 50X data transfers can't really transfer data at that rate over the entire CD.

As the spindle motor speeds of today's CD-ROM drives approach 13,000rpm, the change back to CAV is being made to avoid the difficulty of changing the motor speed from 5,000rpm to 13,000rpm and then back to 5,000rpm. In spite of these higher, faster speeds, the spin-up and spin-down of the CD-ROM drive is a factor of how slow a CD-ROM drive performs, especially when doing random accesses on data located at different edges of the CD.

The Disc Loading Mechanism

The *disc loading mechanism* is the mechanical or physical way that the CD is loaded into the CD-ROM drive so it can be accessed or played. There are three distinct ways used to load CD-ROM media into a CD-ROM drive:

- **Tray-loading** This is the most common loading mechanism in use on PCs. The tray-loading method uses a plastic horizontal tray (jokingly called a "cup holder") that is opened and closed by motorized gears in the drive (see Figure 10-6). Pressing the eject button on the front of the CD-ROM drive activates the gears and servos to extend the tray out of the drive. The CD is then placed in the fitted portion of the tray and either a gentle nudge or pressing the eject button pulls the tray and the CD back into the drive. To remove the CD, the tray is extended, the CD removed, and the tray returned inside the drive. On some PC cases, the CD-ROM drive is installed vertically; these CD-ROM drives use tabs that extend and retract to hold the disc in place until the drive is closed.

- **Caddy** This method was used in early CD-ROM drives and has reappeared on some higher-end drives manufactured today. A CD caddy is a small plastic case that looks much like the CD jewel case. The caddy is hinged on one side and opens so that a disc can be placed inside. The caddy has a sliding metal cover on its bottom that slides out of the way to allow the laser to access the disc when the caddy is inserted into the CD-ROM drive. In many ways the caddy method works very much like a 3.5-inch floppy disk.
- **Front-loading** This method is very common on car CD players, but it is not too common on PCs, although some Apple Macintosh computers use it.

Audio Output and Controls

Reflecting their relationship to the audio CD, many CD-ROM drives include the controls needed to play and listen to audio CDs. However, drives that include these controls are becoming increasingly rare, and these controls are moving to keyboards or software players. Figure 10-7 shows the placement and use of the controls commonly included:

- **Headphone Output** A mini headphone jack is provided that allows you to plug in headphones so you can listen to the CD.
- **Volume Control Dial** Most drives include a dial control that allows you to set the volume of the CD audio output on the headphone output.
- **Start and Stop** On some drives these may be the only controls on the front panel. These buttons are used to start and stop the playback of the CD.
- **Next Track and Previous Track** With these buttons included, the CD-ROM drive is the equivalent of a CD player. They are used to move forward and back to tracks on the CD.

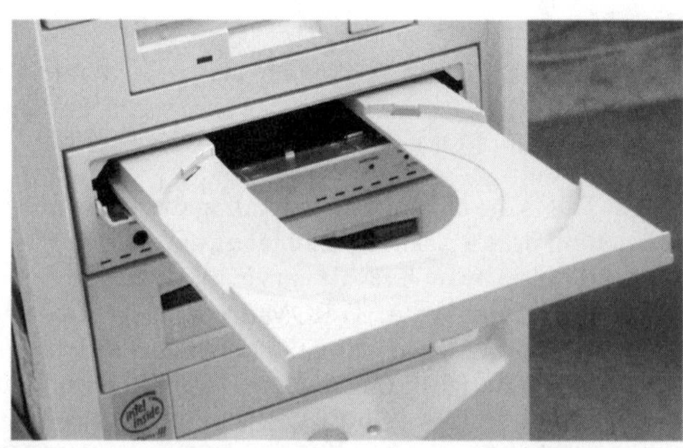

Figure 10-6. A CD-ROM drive with its tray extended

Figure 10-7. The Windows CD Player includes features to control the playback of a CD-ROM drive

Amplifier

If the CD-ROM drive includes audio playback controls, it will also include an amplifier. The amplifier is included to provide just enough power for the use of headphones. The amplifier doesn't improve the digital audio sound quality and you can get better quality by feeding the CD audio through a soundcard on your PC to desktop speakers or to a home stereo system with a built-in amplifier.

Connectors and Jumpers

The jumpers and cable connections on a CD-ROM drive are very similar to those found on a hard disk drive. CD-ROM drive manufacturers have standardized the location and use of the jumpers and connectors. The jumpers and connectors are always located at the back of the CD-ROM drive, as shown in Figure 10-8.

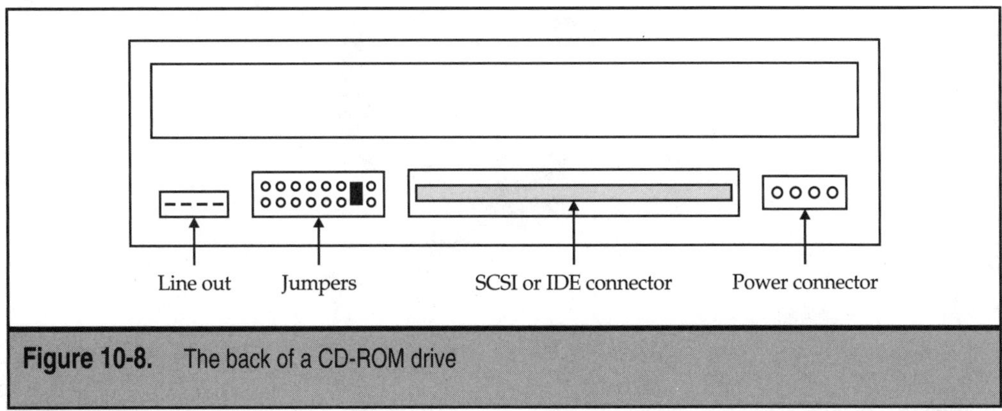

Figure 10-8. The back of a CD-ROM drive

The 4-pin power connector is the same type used on most internal peripherals, such as the hard disk drive or floppy drive. The other connections or jumpers on the drive are dependent on the type of interface in use. The two most popular types of interfaces are the IDE/ATAPI (Integrated Drive Electronics/AT Attachment Package Interface) and the SCSI (Small Computer System Interface). An ATAPI drive uses a standard 40-pin data connector and jumpers to set the drive as either the master or slave device. A SCSI drive uses a 50-pin connector and jumpers to set the device ID and termination, identities required in SCSI device chains (see Chapter 9 for more information on SCSI devices).

ATAPI is an interface between the PC and the CD-ROM drive. This interface is also used for tape drives. ATAPI adds some additional commands to the standard IDE interface that are needed to control a CD-ROM drive. SCSI is an interface type that allows the PC to communicate with peripheral hardware, including disk drives, tape drives, CD-ROM drives, and more.

A CD-ROM also has a thin audio connector that is used to connect it to a sound card (see Figure 10-9). The audio connector is either a three- or four-wire cable that sends the CD's audio output directly to the sound card so it can be recorded on the PC or played back on the PC's speakers.

Logic Board

Every CD-ROM drive contains a logic board that includes the circuitry and controllers used to control the drive and the interface to the PC, which is usually either IDE/ATAPI or SCSI.

Single and Multiple Drives

By far the most common CD-ROM drives can only load a single CD at a time. However, some drives can handle two, four, or even more discs at once. The primary benefit of a multidisc CD drive (see Figure 10-10) is it allows you to access multiple discs, although

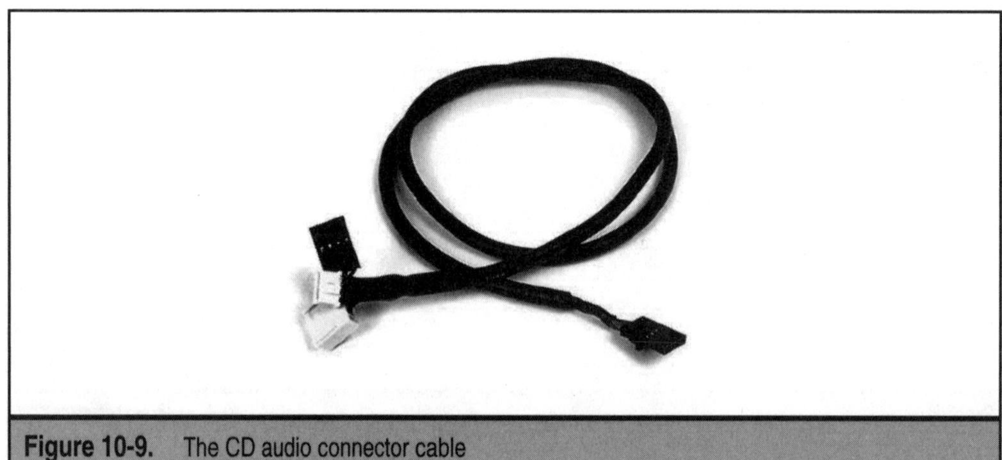

Figure 10-9. The CD audio connector cable

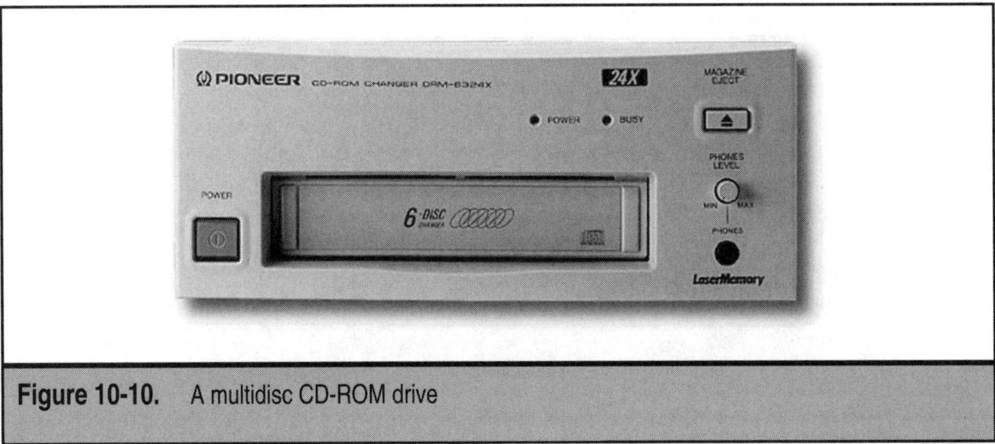

Figure 10-10. A multidisc CD-ROM drive

still only one at a time, without requiring you to physically remove and replace the discs in the drive. The discs that you use frequently can remain in the CD-ROM drive until they are needed.

A single disc CD-ROM drive is mapped to the PC with a single drive letter, usually E: or something close to that. However, a multidisc CD-ROM drive is mapped to the PC with a drive letter for each disc it is capable of loading. Multiple disc drives also require special software device drivers to give you access to each disc independently.

DIGITAL VERSATILE/VIDEO DISC (DVD)

In attempts to develop a standard for a new high-density disc format, two formats were proposed in the early 1990s: the Multimedia CD (MMCD), proposed by Philips and Sony, and the Super Density Disc (SDD), proposed by a consortium of Toshiba, Matsushita, and Time-Warner. In 1995, a high-density format was accepted, largely based on the SDD format—the *Digital Versatile Disc (DVD)*, also called the *Digital Video Disc*. Figure 10-11 shows a DVD and drive in a PC.

The reasons you would want to install a DVD drive in your PC are still a little vague beyond your desire to sit at your PC and watch movies. However, because a DVD drive also reads CDs, it may be a good hedge against future technologies should more DVD software or media become available. Many experts are saying that the DVD-RAM will be the CD-R of the future, but this is still open to debate and remains to be seen.

DVD Technology

A DVD can store the equivalent of 17 gigabytes (GB) or about 25 times more than a CD-ROM. Through the use of MPEG (Motion Pictures Experts Group) and Dolby compression technologies, a DVD can also store hours of high-quality audio-visual content,

Figure 10-11. A DVD loaded to a DVD drive

such as a full-length movie plus other supporting content. One layer of a DVD-Audio stores 4.7GB of data, which means that each second on a DVD-Audio stores more than 1,100 times more information than one second on an audio CD. One DVD-Audio can hold up to 400 minutes of 2-channel stereo sound or 74 minutes of 6-channel sound.

The DVD was designed to be backward compatible with an existing CD-ROM, which means DVD drives are able to read the CD formatting. The DVD uses a read mechanism that includes a dual focus pick-up to read the disc. The DVD is the same size as a CD-ROM, and the DVD drive uses the same form factor as the CD-ROM drive, but the formatting on the DVD is considerably different than that used on the CD. Table 10-2 shows a comparison of a DVD-Audio to a CD-DA.

Feature	DVD-Audio (single layer)	CD
Capacity	4.7GB	640MB
Recording time	200 minutes	74 minutes
Transfer rate	9.6Mbps	1.4Mbps
Max sampling rate	192kHz	44.1kHZ

Table 10-2. Comparison of DVD and CD

There are probably more types of DVDs available than you think. Here are the primary DVD types:

- **DVD-ROM** This is a read-only form of DVD that stores interactive media, data, audio, and video. This type of DVD is not compatible with DVD Video players (the kind connected to TVs), but they will play back DVD-Video movies. DVD-ROM drives are the type installed in PCs and notebook computers.
- **DVD-R (Recordable)** A WORM-type disc that can record up to 3.95GB. DVD-R is recorded using the same dye-layer technology as the CD-R.
- **DVD-RAM** This type of DVD, which looks more like a big diskette than a CD-ROM, is a rewritable form of DVD that uses essentially the same technology as a CD-R. A DVD-RAM has a capacity of 4.7GB per side and is available in both single-sided and double-sided versions. A DVD-RAM drive will read most DVD-Videos and DVD-ROMs, as well as all types of CD media.
- **DVD-RW (Read/Write)** A version of rewritable DVD that competes with the DVD-RAM, the DVD-RW also holds 4.7GB per side and is capable of being rewritten more than 1,000 times. A DVD-RW does not require a unique drive like the DVD-RAM and can be read in a DVD-ROM drive.

Installing a DVD Drive in Your PC

Installing a DVD drive in your PC requires a DVD kit. This kit will usually include an ATAPI/EIDE DVD drive, an MPEG II decoder card, the various cables required to connect the drive, and perhaps some software as well. The process of installing the DVD drive is the same as installing a CD-ROM or CD-R drive, with the possible exception of loading some DVD software. Some computers have DVD software already loaded, but using software decompression can really impact the performance of some PCs. It is recommended you use hardware decoding if it's available.

When installing the DVD drive, the MPEG decode card is installed in a PCI expansion bus slot, the DVD drive is connected to an EIDE connector, and an audio cable is used to connect the decoder card to the sound card. Some DVD kits install a cable to connect the decoder card to your video card as well. On Windows systems, the decoder card, because it is in a PCI slot, will be automatically detected and you will be prompted to load the device drivers, which usually come with the drive on a CD. After the DVD drive is installed in your PC, you will be able to read regular CDs and view DVD movies using the DVD controller software usually included in the kit.

To support a DVD drive, your PC should be at least a Pentium with at least a 200MHz clock speed, 32MB of RAM, a free PCI slot for the MPEG decoder, a PCI video card with at least 2MB of video RAM that supports DirectX and Direct Draw technologies, and a Sound Blaster–compatible sound card. Windows 98 and 2000 Pro have built-in DVD support and nearly all DVD software is written for Windows.

CHAPTER 11

Expansion Cards

In the early days of the PC, very little support was included in the motherboard for peripheral devices. The controllers and adapters used to drive and interface any peripheral devices, such as the monitor, hard disk, floppy disk, and so on, had to be added to the motherboard's circuitry through *expansion cards*, which are also known as expansion boards, adapters, add-in cards, and daughterboards. These days, much of the support for peripherals is built into the motherboard, but on older PCs, adding a new peripheral device usually means adding an expansion card.

Expansion cards are also added to the very latest PCs, often to upgrade the quality or speed of the PC's graphics and sound or to connect to nearby computers or printers or the outside world. Figure 11-1 shows a typical expansion card. Expansion cards can be used to improve the video performance, add or improve the sound system, add additional or new ports or connectors, provide a network connection, and many other functions. They can add a completely new function or capability or augment or replace an existing one.

It may sound obvious, but expansion cards are inserted into expansion slots. These slots are located on the PC's motherboard and are receptacles that provide an interconnection for

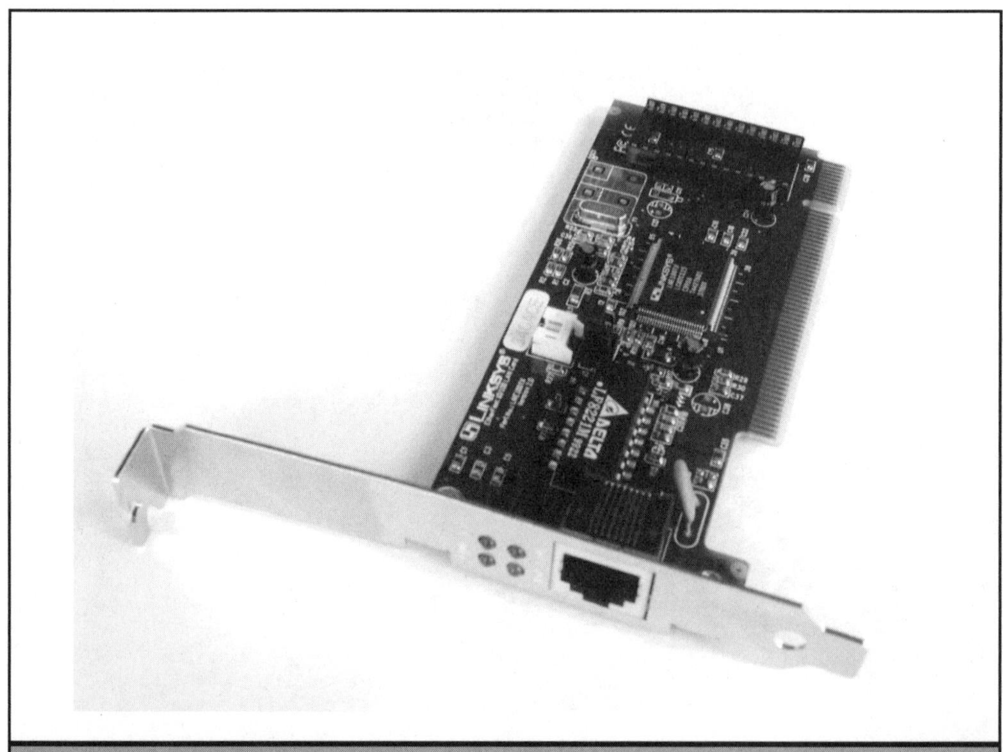

Figure 11-1. A network interface card is a type of expansion card used to connect a PC to a network

the card into the system bus structures. An expansion slot contains metallic, typically copper, springy fingers that clamp onto the expansion card's edge connectors when the card is inserted into the slot. The edge of an expansion card has metal connectors attached that will match up to the fingers of the slot and complete the connections that connect the card to the motherboard and its bus structure through the slot. As I will discuss later, the card and slot have to be the same type of interface. Figure 11-2 shows a card being inserted into a slot. Notice the card's edge connectors and how they match up to the expansion slot.

USING EXPANSION CARDS

Expansion cards were used to add basic functions to older PCs, including memory, hard disk and floppy disk controllers, video controllers, serial and parallel ports, modems, and even the clock and calendar functions. Today's PCs add only a few of these functions through expansion cards since most of these capabilities are built into the motherboard or chipset. Typically, expansion cards are now used to improve or add to the capabilities of a PC, such as controllers and adapters for special purpose hardware and network interfaces. Through expansion cards a PC can become a sound system, a graphics workstation, a movie theatre, or a member of a global network.

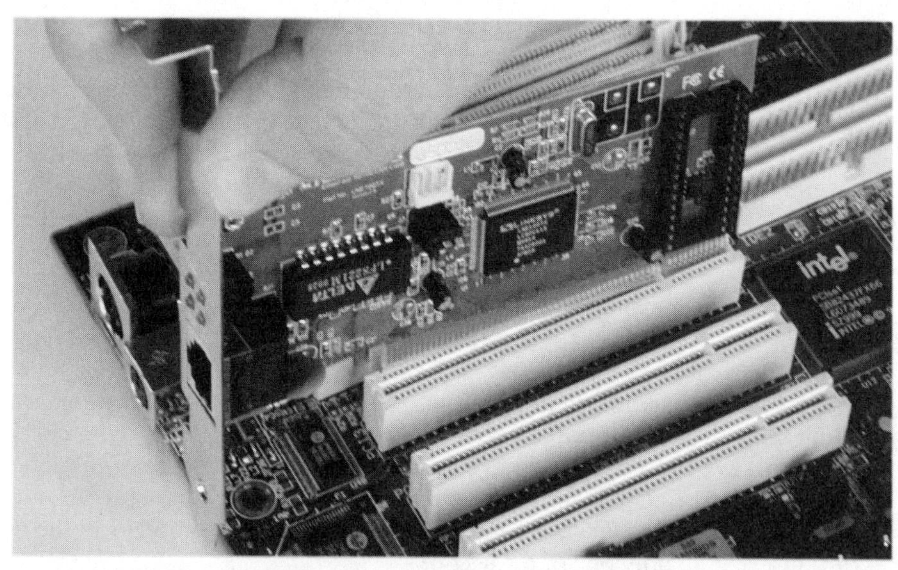

Figure 11-2. An expansion card and an expansion slot on a motherboard

The challenges of working with expansion cards, beyond choosing the right one, are installation, configuration, and operation, with the emphasis on the first two. A personal computer is configured and balanced to a pretty exact set of parameters when it is manufactured. The established hardware standards are for the most part generally accepted and supported, but standards are open to interpretation and not all devices work the same in different manufacturers' PCs. Adding new functions to the PC may create conflicts among the assignable resources and introduce problems in areas that were perfectly fine before the new device was added. Expansion cards exist in a world of system resources that is made up of IRQs, DIP switches, jumper blocks, and system resources. Understanding how the CPU interacts with an expansion card and the role of the system resources and their assignments is the key to success with expansion cards and PCs. However, before I get any further into that, let's review the fundamental components, concepts, and technology behind expansion cards and their use with PCs.

EXPANSION BUSES

Every expansion card, whether it is a video adapter, modem, or network interface card, is designed to communicate with the motherboard and CPU over a single communications and interface standard that is called a bus. A PC usually supports at least two different expansion buses and often more, and more is always better. An expansion bus, which is also called a bus architecture, defines a specific interface that consists of how much data it carries, how fast it transfers it, how it connects to the motherboard, and how it interacts with the CPU or RAM.

Since the beginning, the PC has not used all that many types of expansion buses. In fact, the standard used on the original PCs is still available on most motherboard designs. On the other hand, several that sought to improve on the original have passed into history, leaving essentially only a few. Here are the PC bus structures that have been the most popular over the years:

- **ISA (Industry Standard Architecture)** The ISA expansion bus (which is pronounced as the letters "eye-ess-aye," not "ice-a") is now generally obsolete, but most motherboards still have at least one ISA slot to provide backward compatibility for older hardware. You can still buy ISA expansion cards, but they are becoming hard to find. On most motherboards, the ISA bus slots are 16-bit that will also support 8-bit cards. Figure 11-3 shows a drawing of a 16-bit ISA card. An 8-bit card would have only the left-most half of the edge connector on the bottom edge of the card. The ISA slot, as illustrated in Figure 11-4, is divided into two sections. The 16-bit card occupies both sections and the 8-bit card inserts into only one of the sections.

  Some newer ISA cards are Plug-and-Play compatible, but for the most part they are not. This means that ISA devices require at least some manual configuration and setup. The ISA bus is also called the AT bus, for the IBM PC AT on which it

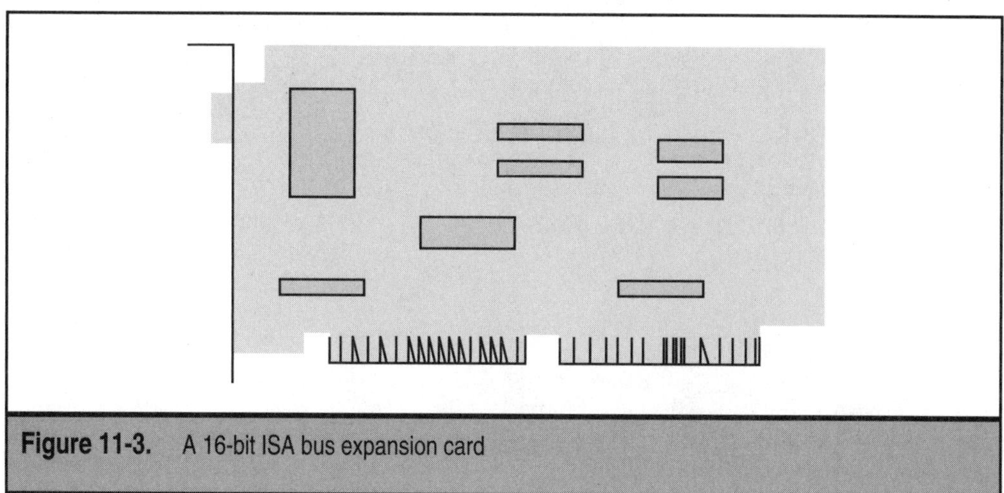

Figure 11-3. A 16-bit ISA bus expansion card

was originally featured. Compare its edge connectors to those of the expansion cards for the other expansion bus structures shown. On the motherboard, ISA slots are typically black.

- **EISA (Extended ISA)** The EISA (pronounced "ee-sa") bus extended the ISA bus to 32 bits and added bus mastering (see "Bus Mastering" later in the chapter). EISA expansion slots are also backward compatible to ISA cards, with a sectioned slot (shown in Figure 11-4) that support 8-bit and 16-bit ISA cards. EISA has been replaced by the PCI bus (described next), but it is still available on some motherboard designs. Like the ISA slots, EISA are black and are placed next to the ISA slots on those motherboards that include them.
- **VESA local bus (VL bus)** VL bus is a bus architecture developed by VESA (Video Electronics Standards Association) for use with the 486 processor. A local bus is one that is attached to the same bus structure used by the CPU. VL bus is a 32-bit bus that supported bus mastering. The PCI bus has essentially replaced the VL bus on modern PCs. If your PC has a VL bus expansion slot, it is the one next to the ISA and EISA slots that has the extra slot added to the end and is about four inches long in total. Figure 11-4 shows an illustrated view of the relative size of the most common expansion slots.
- **PCI (Peripheral Component Interconnect)** The PCI bus was introduced with the first Intel Pentium computers and has become the de facto standard for expansion cards on newer motherboards. The PCI bus is common on PCs, Macintoshes, and high-end computer workstations. The PCI bus, which is a local bus, typically supports devices mounted or connected directly to the motherboard as well as in the PCI expansion slots. Most motherboards include three or four of the white PCI expansion slots.

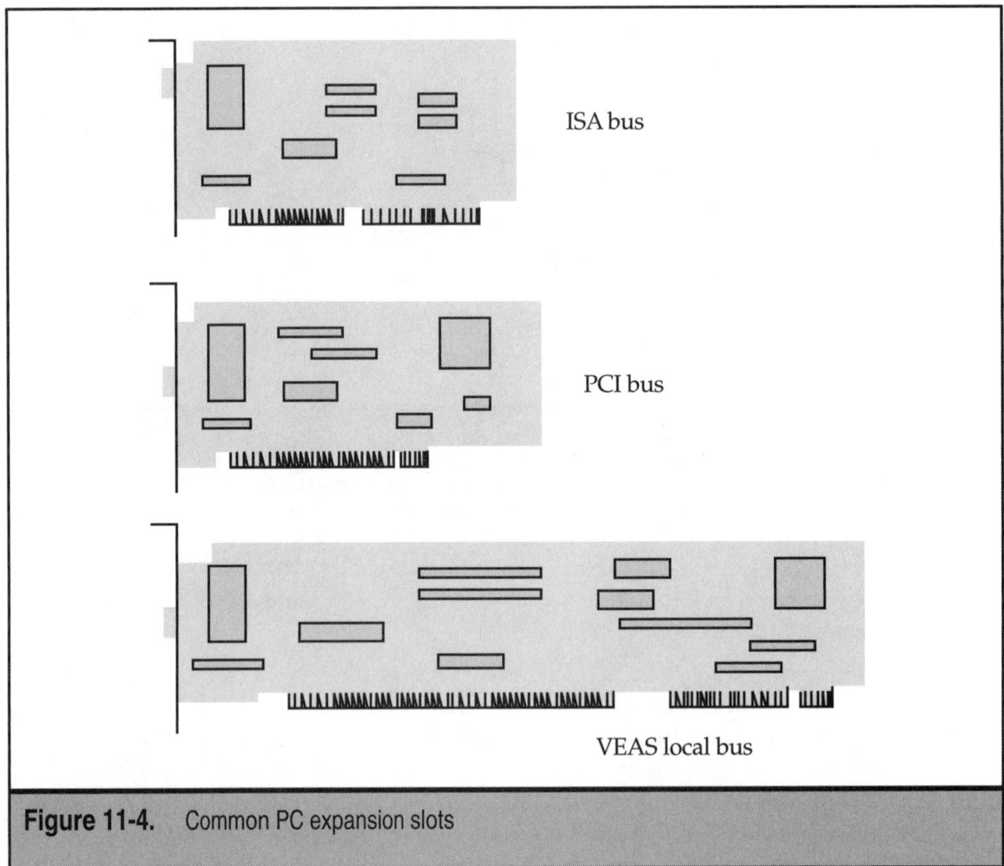

Figure 11-4. Common PC expansion slots

The PCI bus supports 32-bit and 64-bit interfaces and full Plug-and-Play capability, which provides nearly foolproof installations and configurations. Its shorter slot length helps keep motherboards small, one of the reasons for its popularity. Figure 11-5 shows an example of a PCI expansion card.

- **AGP (Accelerated Graphics Port)** While this expansion bus is an expansion bus like the ISA and PCI buses, it is used for only one type of expansion card—video cards. It was developed primarily to improve 3D graphics. Another objective of AGP was to make video cards less expensive by removing memory from the video card, but because memory became less expensive, its benefit is largely in 3D graphics performance. AGP runs at faster speeds than the PCI bus. There are different speed ratings for AGP video cards: 1xAGP, 2xAGP, and 4xAGP, which transfer video data at 264Mbps to 1Gbps. The brown AGP slot is just a little shorter than the white PCI slot and is usually nearby. Figure 11-6 shows the placement of the AGP slot on an AT form factor motherboard in relationship to the ISA and PCI slots.

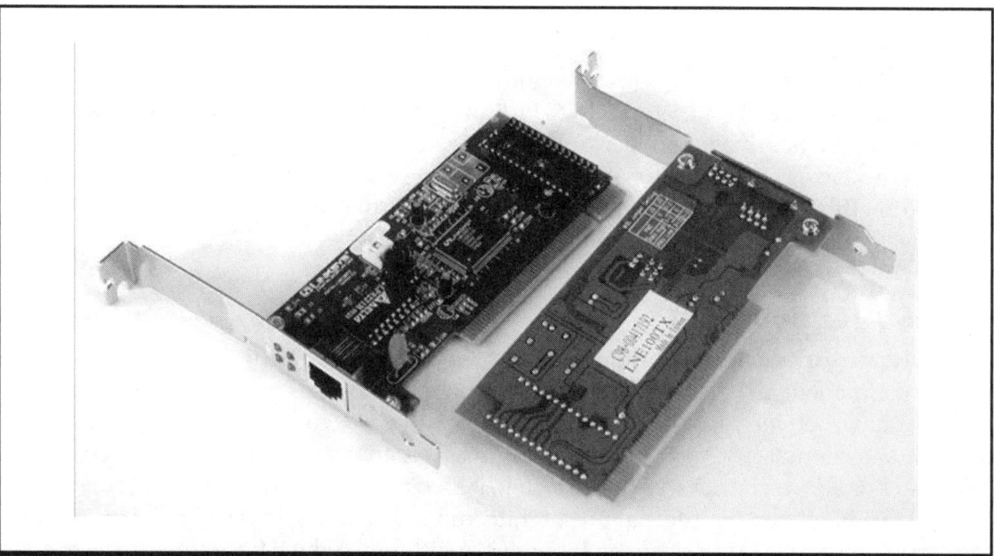

Figure 11-5. A PCI bus network interface card

Figure 11-6. The placement of the expansion slots on a motherboard. Original photo courtesy of AOpen America, Inc.

Bus Mastering

The PCI bus architecture includes a technology called bus mastering that allows an expansion card to directly transfer data to and from the PC's main memory (RAM) and to and from other bus mastered peripheral device controllers without the need to pass through the CPU. Bus mastering allows the PCI bus controller to transfer data from a PCI device directly to memory. This frees the CPU to perform other tasks, thereby making the entire system more efficient.

Local Bus Architectures

Typically, the expansion bus is independent of the system bus structures used by the core system components. The CPU, chipset, and main memory uses an internal or system bus to move data between themselves interacting with the expansion and I/O bus when needed. The internal system bus is said to be "local" to the CPU and other internal devices. The local bus allows the devices that attach to it the ability to operate and move data at the higher speeds offered by internal bus architectures. The bus speeds of the local bus and the expansion and I/O buses are no longer very different, which has reduced the need to use local bus architectures like the VESA local bus (VL-bus).

Portable PC Interface

Portable PCs, such as laptops, notebooks, palmtops, and other compact and portable computers, use a special expansion interface—the PC Card. The PC Card interface allows specially designed expansion cards to be inserted and used immediately, while the system is running and without the need to open the computer's case. This interface, formerly known as the PCMCIA (Personal Computer Memory Card International Association) interface after the standards body that developed it, uses a 68-pin socket that connects directly to the computer's system bus. PC Cards are inserted into the socket to add resources or devices to the computer. Figure 11-7 shows a notebook computer with a PC Card network adapter being inserted.

PC Card Characteristics

PC Cards are credit-card sized expansion cards that are used to add not only the adapter or controller for a peripheral device, but the entire device itself. PC Cards can be used to add more memory, a hard disk, a modem, a network adapter, a sound card, or more. The cards that fit into the PC Card slot are all a standard height and width of 85.6 millimeters (mm) by 54 mm, or approximately 3 1/3 inches by 2 ¼ inches. Where PC Cards differ is in their thickness, with thicker cards containing usually more function or capability.

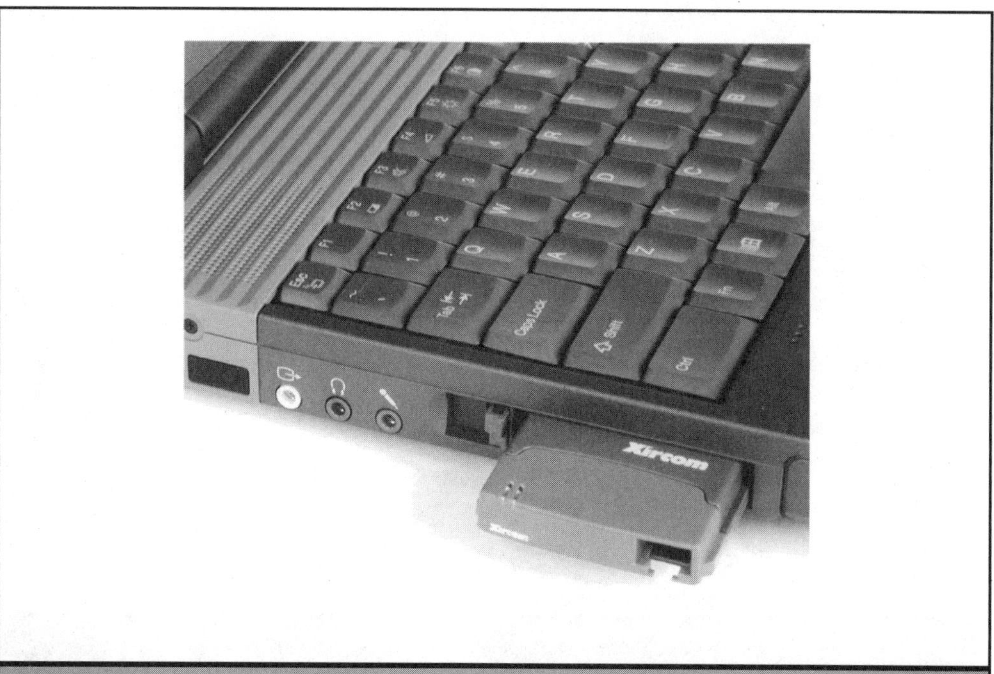

Figure 11-7. PC Cards provide expansion capabilities to portable computers

The PCMCIA has developed standards for three PC Card slot sizes (and the devices that fit them):

- **Type I** This slot and card is 3.3mm (about one-eighth of an inch) thick. It is used to add additional DRAM and flash memory. Type I slots are commonly used on very small computers, such as palmtops. PCMCIA has now developed a new smaller form factor called the Miniature Card that is 73 percent smaller than the Type I PC Card. The Miniature Card, which is just under 1.5 inches square, is being used in palmtop computers and the new smart phones, among other devices.
- **Type II** This slot is 5mm (about one-fifth of an inch) thick. Type II cards are mostly I/O cards, such as modems and network interface cards (NICs). Figure 11-8 shows a Type II PC Card network adapter with its dongle connector. The dongle connects into a slot port on the end of the card and serves as an adapter for the RJ-45 connector on the network cable.
- **Type III** Type III slots are 10.5mm (just under a half-inch) thick. They are used for adding hard drives, multifunction modems and NICs, and 802.11 wireless network transceivers (Figure 11-9).

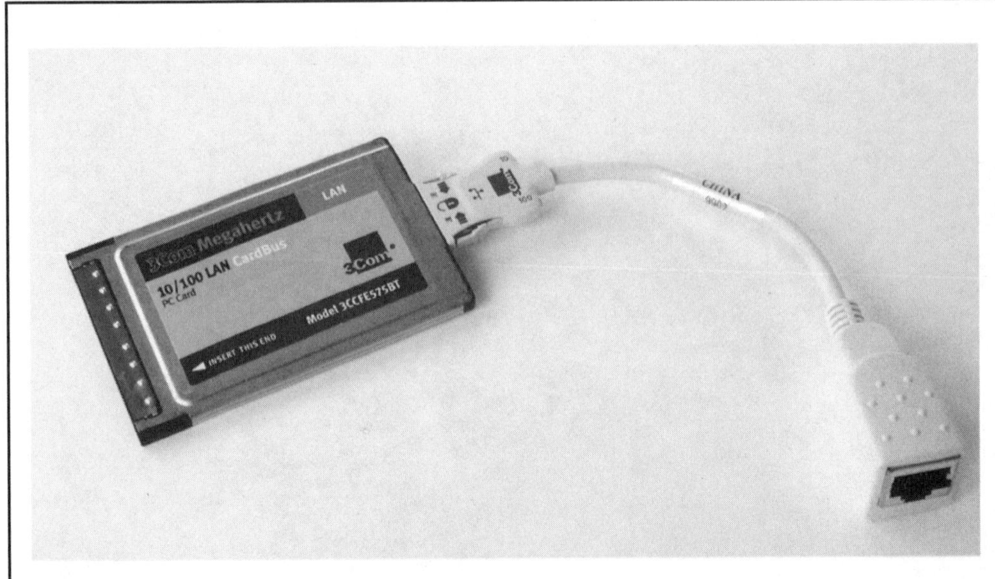

Figure 11-8. A Type II PC Card network interface and connection dongle

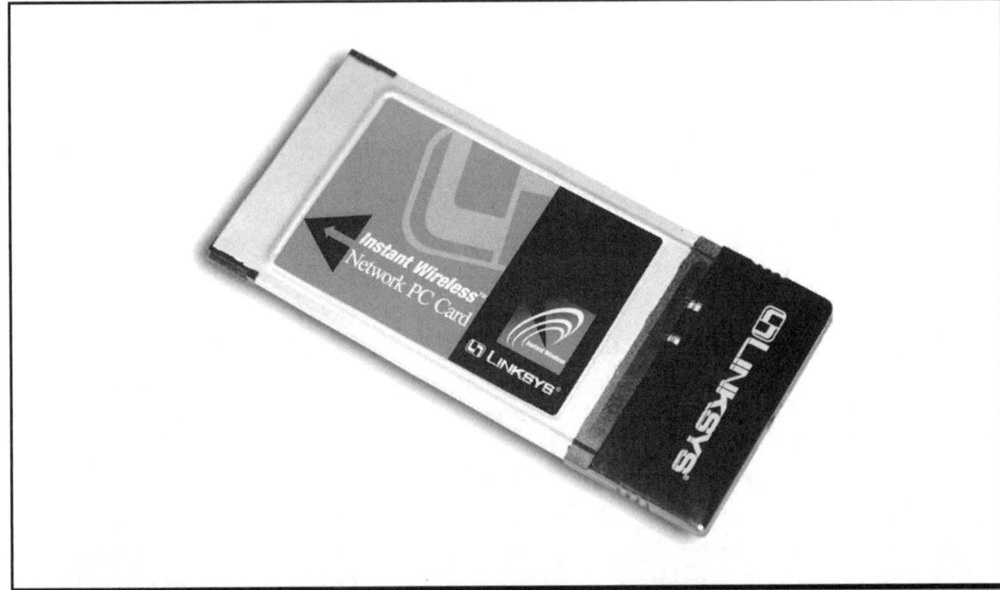

Figure 11-9. A Type III PC Card wireless networking transceiver. Photo courtesy of Linksys Corporation

Hot Swap

PC Cards are hot-swappable, which means they can be inserted and removed while the system is running and do not require the system to be restarted to recognize the card. Not all PC Card devices totally adhere to the PCMCIA specifications; these require a software driver before they are fully functional.

SCSI Interfaces

The SCSI (Small Computer System Interface) is not technically an expansion bus structure, but it can be used to add additional internal and external devices to a PC. Because they are more expensive than comparable ISA or PCI devices, SCSI (pronounced "skuzzy") devices are usually found on network servers and high-end workstations and not on home PCs.

SCSI adapters provide a very easy way to connect multiple (as many as 15) internal and external devices on a single interface. These devices can be either inside or outside the system case. SCSI, which is covered in detail in Chapter 9, has been around for some time and has a variation to fit just about every system, including both ISA- and PCI-compatible host adapter (expansion) cards.

Serial and Parallel Ports

Serial and parallel ports have been on PCs from the beginning. Serial ports are usually associated with communications and parallel ports with printing, but there are serial printers and many peer-to-peer networks are connected over parallel ports.

On older PCs, such as PC XTs through and including most 486s, serial and parallel ports were not included on the PC's motherboard but were added through expansion cards, which were inserted primarily into ISA slots. Commonly, a multifunction card was used that added one parallel port and a 25-pin serial port. Daughterboards, inserted into another slot and connected back to the main multifunction card by a twisted-pair cable, were used to add still more serial or parallel ports to the system.

On today's PCs, which rarely require more than one serial or parallel port, these ports are mounted directly on the motherboard. Additional ports can be added through an expansion card. See Chapter 19 for more information on these and other I/O ports and connectors.

USB and IEEE 1394 Interfaces

Two newer interface standards that are used to connect external peripheral devices to a PC are the USB (Universal Serial Bus) and the IEEE (International Electrical and Electronic Engineering) 1394 standards. The IEEE 1394 standard is more commonly known as FireWire or by its generic name, the High Performance Serial Bus (HPSB). Both device interfaces support low-speed devices like keyboards and mice as well as high-speed, high-performance devices like video cameras, scanners, and printers. These interfaces are hot-swappable and Plug-and-Play compatible, which means they can be added or removed from a PC without the need for rebooting or proprietary installation procedures. Windows 98/2000 directly supports USB and IEEE 1394.

The basic difference between these two interface standards is speed, with IEEE 1394 providing better data transfer speeds and protocols. A new USB standard, USB 2.0, has closed the gap somewhat, but FireWire is still a better interface for real-time devices and high-definition graphics.

USB devices can be connected to external USB hubs that can be daisy-chained together to the point of 127 devices on a single USB bus. This means 127 devices are sharing not only one bus, but one set of system resources as well. Figure 11-10 shows a USB port and connector on the back of a PC. The USB port shown in Figure 11-10 is mounted directly on the motherboard, but on many PCs, a USB or IEEE 1394 port must be added through an expansion card.

IEEE 1394 is a slightly faster interface designed to support the bandwidth and data transfer speeds of devices requiring an isochronous (real-time) interface. The 1394 interface supports up to 63 devices that can have different device transfer speeds on a single bus.

EXPANSION CARDS

As the PC advances, more and more of the devices, controllers, and adapters that used to be added to the PC via expansion cards are incorporated onto the motherboard. Many of the functions that once required a separate adapter or controller card are now built into the chipset or the Super I/O chip (see Chapter 5 for more information on chipsets). The following sections review the common expansion card types.

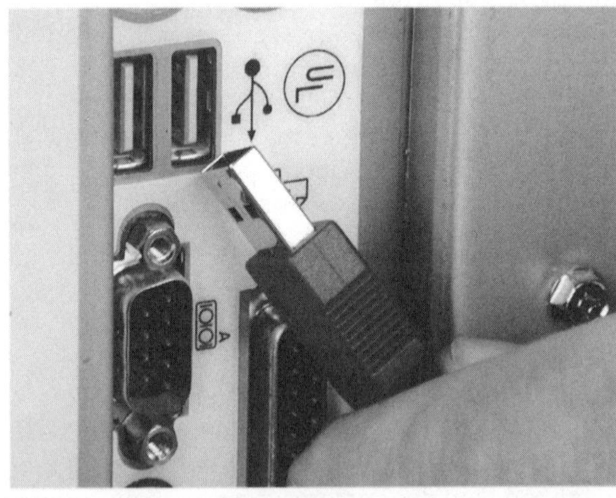

Figure 11-10. A USB port and connector on a PC

Controller Cards

A controller, a.k.a. adapter, card is a type of expansion card that contains the circuitry and components needed to control the operations of a peripheral device, such as a disk drive. Controller cards are less common on newer PCs since device controllers are now typically included in either the system chipset, the Super I/O chip (see Chapter 5 for more information on chipsets), or on the device itself.

Controller cards are easy to spot in the PC. They have flat 40-wire ribbon cables connecting them and the hard disk, CD-ROM, DVD, and floppy disk drives. In many older PCs, the disk controller card supports both the hard disk drive and the floppy disk drives. If a CD-ROM device was installed in an older PC, it typically had its own controller card, but it could also share the common (multipurpose) controller card. On most Pentium PCs and after, the device controllers are built into the motherboard and chipset. But there are still some devices, such as some scanners, that require their own controller card.

The SCSI host adapter, which is installed in either a PCI or ISA slot, is not a controller card, although it does control the SCSI interface chain of devices on the system. SCSI devices are like IDE (ATA) devices and have their device controllers integrated into the device itself (see Chapter 9 for more information on IDE and SCSI storage devices).

Input/Output (I/O) Cards

I/O expansion cards add I/O ports, such as serial and parallel ports, to a PC. This type of expansion cards was once commonly found in PCs, but because the ports they add are typically included in the PC as a part of the motherboard, they are inserted only to upgrade the existing ports. Both serial and parallel I/O expansion cards are available for either ISA or PCI buses (Figure 11-11).

You may want to add new parallel ports to a system to add IEEE 1284 capabilities like ECP (Enhanced Capabilities Port), EPP (Enhanced Parallel Port), and bi-directional data transfer support.

Cards that add serial and parallel ports are primarily 8-bit ISA cards, but there are also16-bit and 32-bit PCI cards available, as well as faster interfaces, like the USB or FireWire, that can be added with a PCI card.

It is possible to add additional serial and parallel ports by connecting a port block into a USB port. A quick, efficient, and up-to-date way to add additional serial ports is to add a USB expansion card, like the one shown in Figure 11-12, which typically adds two or four USB ports to the PC. Then plug a two serial port block into one of the USB ports.

Interface Cards

Interface cards are the most nondescript of the expansion cards. In fact, just about any expansion card can be and usually is classified as an interface card. In general, an interface card connects any external device, network, or gadget such as a mouse, an external CD-ROM, scanner, or camera to a PC. Interface cards are also the PC Cards used to connect external devices to notebook PCs.

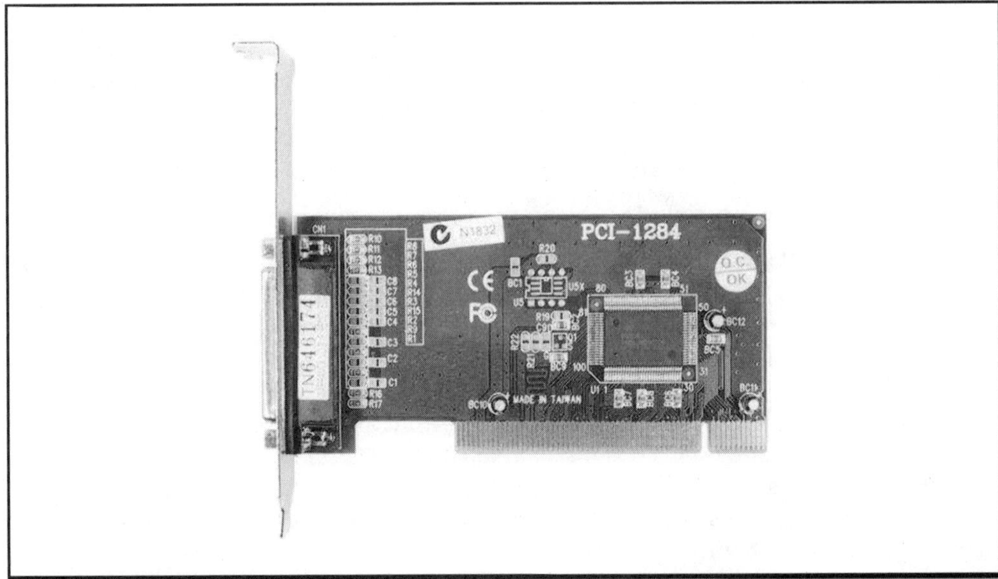

Figure 11-11. A PCI parallel port expansion card

Figure 11-12. A PCI expansion card that adds two USB ports to a PC. Photo courtesy of ADS Technologies

Memory Cards

Most PC technicians do not think of memory modules as expansion cards, but in the strictest interpretation of an expansion card, the memory modules used to add memory to a PC are just that. As discussed in detail in Chapter 7, memory modules are like little expansion cards that are mounted on the motherboard in slot sockets. The two general categories of memory modules used on PCs are SIMM (single inline memory modules) and DIMM (dual inline memory modules). Figure 11-13 shows a memory module installed on a motherboard.

Memory Expansion Card (MEC)

Higher-end microcomputers, such as those in use as network servers or engineering or graphics workstations, often need more memory even after they have already filled the memory module slots. In cases like these, the solution is to install a special expansion card, called a Memory Expansion Card (MEC). A MEC can add up to 16GB of additional RAM (usually SDRAM) to a computer. One slight drawback is that the MEC sits on the system bus and is therefore slower than the memory mounted in the SIMM or DIMM slots on the motherboard. However, when weighed against the benefit of additional memory, the advantages far outweigh the disadvantages. Figure 11-14 shows a drawing of a MEC module manufactured by Dell Computer for its workstation line of computers.

Figure 11-13. Memory modules are installed in slot sockets on the motherboard

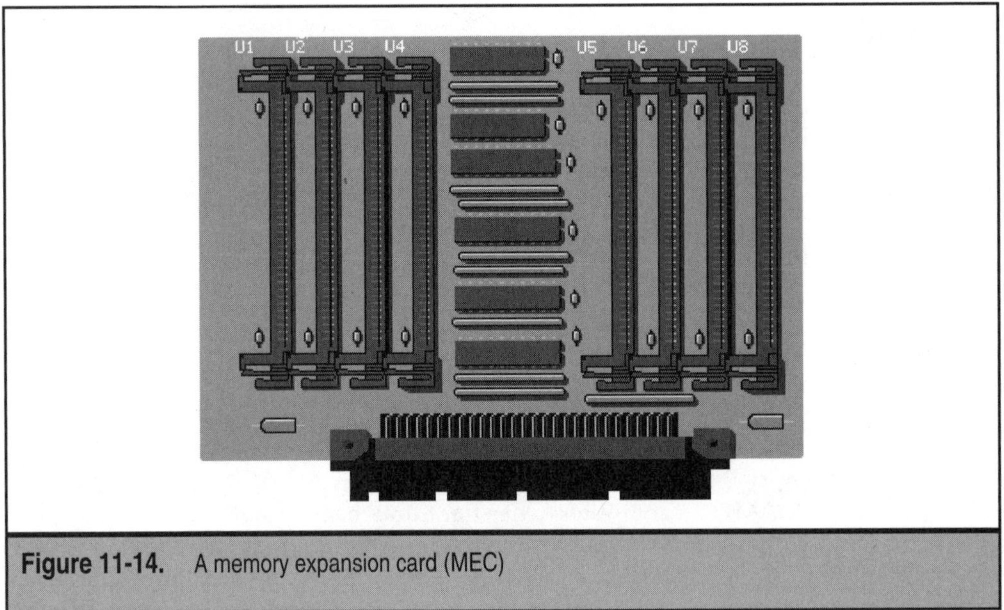

Figure 11-14. A memory expansion card (MEC)

As Figure 11-14 illustrates, a MEC is able to mount a number of memory modules (usually DIMMs). The card illustrated has 8 memory slots, and other MECs are available to handle as many as 16 modules.

PC Card Memory

Memory can be added to a portable PC, virtually on the fly, with a PC Card Type 1 memory card. Remember that the standards organization for PC Cards is named the Personal Computer Memory Card International Association (PCMCIA), with the emphasis on memory card.

PC Card memory cards are credit card–sized or smaller memory modules that incorporate flash memory (SRAM). Flash memory cards, like the one shown in Figure 11-15, are not substitutes for hard disks or other permanent storage devices, but they do instantly add additional working memory to the portable PC. PC Card memory modules are available with 8MB to 512MB of flash memory, with the promise of more as the technology advances.

Modem Cards

A modem (which is short for modulator/demodulator) allows you to connect to and communicate with other computers over the public telephone network. An internal modem is one that plugs into an expansion slot on the motherboard. External modems, which connect to the PC via a serial or USB port, have indicator lights that signal the

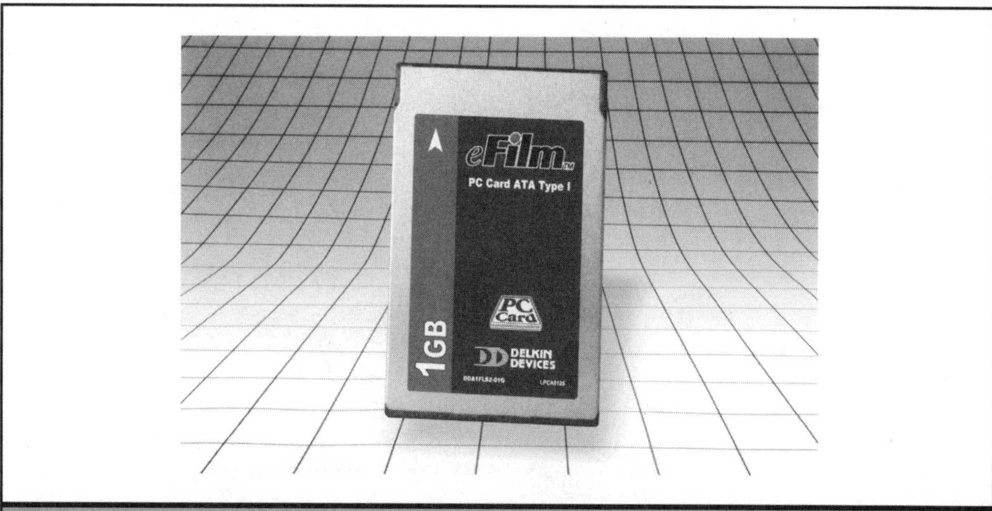

Figure 11-15. A PCMCIA (PC Card) flash memory card. Photo courtesy of Delkin Devices, Inc.

activity of the modem. However, when using an internal modem, because it is mounted inside the system case, the user must rely on a software interface to control the modem and view the status of a communications session.

Internal modem cards, like most other expansion cards, are available for either the ISA or PCI expansion buses. Figure 11-16 shows a PCI modem card. Installation of the modem card may require some COM (serial) port assignment, but typically the modem will have an installation disk that also includes its device driver. Any problems that are created with the installation of the modem usually involved system resource conflicts.

Just about all notebook computers and other portables have a modem built into the system. Should you wish to use an external modem, it would typically be added to the system in the form of a PC Card Type 2 card. The telephone cable is attached with what is called an X-jack, a connector that pops out of the end of the card to allow the phone cable's RJ-11 connector to plug in (see Figure 11-17).

See Chapter 20 for more information about the functions and configuration of modems, internal and external.

Sound Cards

Although sound (audio) processing is included on the motherboards of some newer PCs, it is usually added to a PC through an expansion card. Sound cards, which are covered in detail in Chapter 21 along with video cards, are fairly standard in their basic function, which is reproducing sound. There is a wide range of choices among sound cards, and you'll get what you pay for—prices of sound cards range from $20 to $400.

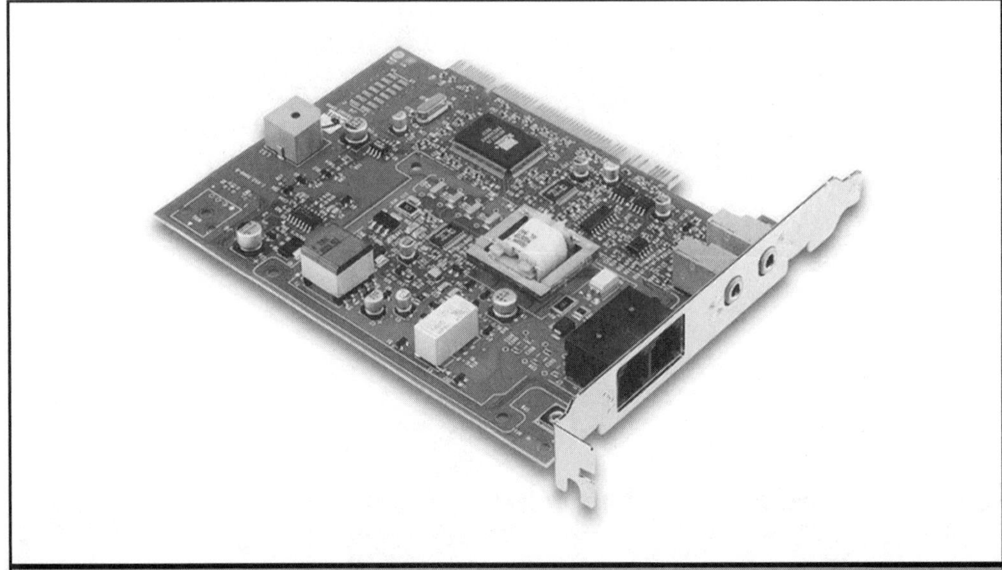

Figure 11-16. A PCI modem expansion card. Photo courtesy of 3Com/U.S. Robotics

Figure 11-17. A PC Card modem for a portable computer with an X-jack. Photo courtesy of 3Com/U.S. Robotics

You can find sound cards for both the ISA and PCI interfaces, but most sources recommend using the PCI interface. ISA cards are the least expensive and sound like it. If you want to watch DVD movies (assuming you have a DVD drive), play games, or listen to your Napster downloads on your PC, a PCI card is your best bet.

As with most expansion cards, about the only problem you'll run into when installing a sound card in a PC is system resource conflicts, especially IRQs. See the "Troubleshooting Expansion Cards" section of this chapter for more information on resolving resource conflicts for expansion cards. Chapter 21 goes into detail on the various features and components found on sound cards and just what they are and do.

Sound Card Voices

One rule of thumb you can use to judge how good the sound produced by a sound card will be is the number of voices it reproduces. A voice on a sound card is essentially one instrument. For example, a piano sound is one voice, a trumpet another, a drum, a third, and so on. The number in the sound card's model name, such as SoundBlaster 16, Soundwave 32, or a SoundBlaster AWE64, is the number of voices it can reproduce. Contrary to common belief, this number is not how many bits the sound card uses to decode sound samples. The resolution of the sound in bits describes the sound's amplitude and frequency. Nearly all PC sound cards use a 16-bit digital sound resolution, the same used on CD players and CD-ROM drives.

Speakers

Don't forget that the sound card is only half the puzzle; in order to hear the sound, the PC must have a set of speakers. Most sound cards have a full set of output jacks into which you can plug your speakers and connect to amplifiers and microphones. Just as with the sound card, you get what you pay for with speakers. Luckily, nearly all PCs now come with a sound card and a set of speakers as standard equipment. But, if you want to upgrade the sound, verify the capabilities of the sound card first. It could be that the speakers are just not robust enough to handle what may be a quality sound card. If the speakers are good quality, then upgrade the sound card.

Video Cards

Depending on how you look at it, your PC's video card may be the most important expansion card in your system. The video card provides your PC with its ability to display images, text, and graphics on the monitor. Some newer motherboards now integrate the video processing into the chipset or on the motherboard itself, but for the vast number of PCs in use, a video expansion card is used to drive the video signal.

To provide the best possible image, the video card must be matched to the monitor it drives (see Chapters 12 and 16 for information on video cards and monitors). These two components must be matched in their capabilities. The video card must be able to drive the monitor, and the monitor must be able to display the output of the video card.

When choosing a video card for a PC, you should look at three important features or components: its processor or chipset, its bus, and its memory.

Video Processors

Video cards all have some level of processing capability. The onboard processor generates some or all of the image to be displayed by the monitor. How much of the video load is carried by the video card's processor and chipset depends on the age of a video card and, typically, how much it cost.

Video cards use three different technologies to generate the image for the monitor:

- **Frame buffer** Older cards use the frame buffer technology that focuses on displaying one video frame at a time and leaving the CPU (the one inside the PC) to create the graphic image to be displayed.
- **Graphic acceleration** The video cards that use this technology are called (what else?) graphic accelerators. On this type of video card, the video processor performs all of the routine and common tasks associated with generating graphic images, and the CPU is used strictly for what needs to be done and when. This type of video card processing is the most common in PCs.
- **Graphics Processing Units (GPUs)** On newer, high-end video cards, the onboard processor and chipset have the complete responsibility for generating all displayed graphics, which leaves the CPU free to do other tasks.

Video processors are divided into two categories:

- **2D** This is normal everyday ordinary graphics, the kind used by most standard applications, such as word processing and spreadsheets, and many multimedia applications, such as PowerPoint and CorelDraw. In fact, this is the minimum level of graphics on a PC.
- **3D** This is the graphics type used by games and 3D rendering and drawing software. Unfortunately, 3D graphics and the processor commands used to generate them are not standardized. As a result, some 3D programs and games may not work with every video card.

Video Bus

Video cards use either the PCI or AGP bus architectures. The PCI bus is independent of the processor, which makes for fast video. The AGP bus offers a higher bandwidth and with it, higher frame rates. It has a direct line to RAM, which allows it to better prepare 3D images and textures.

Video RAM

Video RAM (VRAM) serves two purposes on the video card: one, it acts as a buffer between the CPU and data bus and the monitor, and two, it is the work area used by the video processor and chipset to perform the calculations used to formulate the graphic image as an analog signal for the monitor.

Most video cards are standard with at least 16MB of memory; some go all the way up to 64MB of VRAM. Much like the standard memory in most PCs, the type of memory on video cards is usually SDRAM. VRAM is usually either SDR (single data rate), which is less expensive, or DDR (double data rate). DDR memory increases the bandwidth and speed (and cost) of your video card. Video memory is usually dual-ported, which means it can be written to at the same time it is being read. This allows the CPU to write to VRAM while the monitor is reading it. A new type of video RAM that is becoming very popular on high-end graphics packages is RAMBUS memory, which operates much faster than other forms of VRAM.

A/V Outputs

Beyond the standard output port for the monitor, some video cards may also include additional output ports that can be used to connect the video card to a TV, VCR, or projector. Generally, these extra video output ports are either composite, which is the most common type of video output, or S-Video. Composite video supports good image quality and will interface directly to virtually all TVs and VCRs. S-Video is a high-quality display interface that produces better color and resolution than composite video.

Other Video Outputs

Some miscellaneous output ports and interfaces are included on some video cards. Here are a few of the most common:

- **VR (virtual reality) goggles** This port supports video formatted for VR goggles or can be used to enhance the depth perception of a standard monitor.
- **DVD** DVD (digital versatile disc) drives need special video interfaces; many of the newer high-end video cards come with ports to support DVD drive or MPEG-2 decoder card interfaces.
- **TV tuner** This port allows the computer to receive video streams from a TV, VCR, laserdisc, or a TV cable feed or antenna.
- **SLI (scan line interleaving)** Through this interface, two 3D acceleration cards can divide the monitor's display and share the load of generating the displayed image between the two cards.

EXPANSION CARD OPERATION

The CPU communicates with the expansion bus and the cards inserted into it to request data, give commands, or write data. This communication is conducted through the system resources of a PC, which consist of the IRQs (interrupt requests), I/O (input/output) addresses, and DMA channels of the PC. Chapter 13 discusses the elements of the system resources in detail.

Interrupt Requests (IRQs)

Let's say that it is your job to provide a service to a large number of people in an office setting. In your office, there is a desk with a single bare light bulb on it. If any of the people you are to take care of need your help, they flip a switch on their desk and it turns on your light. Each time the light lights up, you have to drop whatever you were doing to take care of whatever is needed for whomever lit it. As willing as you are to serve, the problem is that you don't know who turned on the light to request help. The solution to this problem is to place numbered individual lights on your desk, one for each person who can request your services. Now when a light lights up, you will be able to determine just whom you should be assisting.

As strange as this situation may seem, it is essentially the way that the CPU interfaces with the devices installed on the PC. Like the people in the office, each device is assigned an IRQ (interrupt request) that they can turn on to signal to the CPU that some kind of service is needed. The services needed might be to move data from RAM to a device, transfer data from a device to RAM, or the like. Whatever the need, the device requests service from the CPU by turning on its IRQ. The CPU interrupts whatever it is doing and services the request.

Chapter 13 discusses IRQs in more detail, but one issue that is common to nearly all expansion cards is IRQ conflicts. When two devices are assigned the same IRQ, the CPU cannot know which device requested the service. IRQ conflicts occur for a number of reasons, but the most common is proprietary installation software that preassigns the system resources, including the IRQ, rather than assigning available resources. Although there is no established standard for the assignment of IRQs, the list in Table 11-1 represents the default assignments used by the majority of processors and BIOS manufacturers.

The available IRQs listed in Table 11-1 are available to be used by any expansion card added to the system. IRQs 3 and 4 are shared among the COM (serial) ports because all four ports are rarely installed on a PC and, if they are, they are rarely in use at the same time. On the PC, two devices can be assigned to share an IRQ, but only in situations where just one of the devices is active at a time.

IRQ	Default Assignment
0	System timer
1	Keyboard
2	Video card
3	COM2, COM4

Table 11-1. Default IRQ Assignments on a PC

IRQ	Default Assignment
4	COM1, COM3
5	Sound card
6	Floppy Disk Controller (FDC)
7	LPT1
8	CMOS Clock
9	Reserved link to IRQs 0–7
10	Available
11	Available
12	Available
13	Math coprocessor
14	Hard disk controller
15	Available

Table 11-1. Default IRQ Assignments on a PC *(continued)*

I/O Addresses

After a device requests an action from the CPU using an IRQ, the CPU responds to the requesting device with a signal that indicates that either the task is completed or it couldn't be done, or the CPU has some data or value it needs to pass to the device. The CPU can't send the data to the device over the IRQ line, so a small amount of memory is set aside for each device to receive responses from the CPU. Sort of like one-way message boxes. Each of these boxes has an assigned address that represents where it is in memory and its size. This message box is more formally called the I/O address (or base memory address, I/O port, or port address). The address of the I/O area assigned to each device is represented as a hexadecimal address range in memory. Table 11-2 lists a few of the I/O addresses assigned on a PC. I haven't listed all 65,000+ addresses that are available to be assigned, only a few that deal with expansion cards.

Direct Memory Access

Direct memory access (DMA) allows a device to communicate directly with the PC's system memory without the assistance or intervention of the CPU. In a normal PIO (programmable input/output) data transfer (the normal kind of data transfer), the CPU controls the movement of the data into RAM. A DMA transfer moves data directly from its source to RAM.

Device	I/O Address Assignment
Primary IDE	1F0–1F7h
Games port	0200–0207h
Sound card	0220–022Fh
Plug and Play	0270–0273h
Parallel port	0278–027Ah
Network adapter	0300–031F
VGA adapter	03C0–03DF
PCMCIA port	03E0–03E7
Direct memory access (DMA)	

Table 11-2. Default I/O Address Assignments on a PC

DMA devices are assigned one of the eight DMA channels available, which cannot be shared by two devices. The expansion card that is typically assigned a DMA channel is the sound card, which may actually get two or more channels, if they are available. The most common assignments of DMA channels are listed in Table 11-3.

DMA Channel	Assignments
0	Reserved for system
1	Sound card (8-bit transfer)
2	Floppy disk controller (8-bit transfer)
3	Open (8-bit transfer)
4	Link to DMA channels 0-3
5	Sound card (16-bit transfer)
6	Open (16-bit transfer)
7	Open (16-bit transfer)

Table 11-3. Default DMA Channel Assignments on a PC

Setting System Resources

Every expansion card installed in a PC must be assigned some system resources, typically an IRQ and an I/O address. In most cases, the expansion card is configured to work with a certain set of system resources. However, most cards can be configured to work with other resources if their default resources are unavailable. System resources are configured on an expansion card in two ways: physically on the card through DIP switches or jumper blocks, or through software. The software used to assign a card to a set of system resources may be a dedicated installation program or a configuration interface, such as the BIOS setup program or an operating system feature, like the Windows Device Manager.

A DIP switch block has either four or eight slide switches that can be moved between two settings (representing on and off or 0 and 1). The documentation with the expansion card should specify the settings for a card's physical configuration for a particular PC type. The same is true of jumper blocks. The jumper is set to cover two pins (on), one pin (off), or no pins (neutral). A three-pin jumper can be set to represent eight values, each of which designates a different system resource setting for the card. The values for a card's switches or jumpers are typically in its documentation.

If the expansion card comes with installation software, the system resources will be automatically set. However, if system resource conflicts result, you can use the Windows Device Manager (assuming a Windows system) to check on the resource settings. These settings can also be modified in the BIOS setup program.

Plug and Play

Plug and Play (PnP) enables expansion boards to be automatically configured, including system resource settings, by the BIOS and operating system on a PC. Windows 98/2000 supports PnP out of the box, but Windows NT only supports some devices. Understand that PnP does not mean hot-swappable. If you remove or install a PnP device, you may need to reset the system before the PC will recognize it.

WORKING WITH EXPANSION CARDS

The rest of this chapter contains a number of procedures that can be used to install and troubleshoot expansion cards. As with any PC component, nothing is more valuable than the component's documentation for the process that should be used to install, configure, or troubleshoot it. The procedures included in this chapter are meant as general guidelines.

Installing an Expansion Card

Follow this general procedure to install an expansion card in a PC (assuming that you are strictly following the ESD protection guidelines outlined in Chapter 14):

1. Create a backup of the hard disk's contents. Typically, installing an expansion card should not have any effect on the hard disk, but you never know.

2. Turn off the computer's power and remove the AC power cord from the outlet.
3. Open or remove the system case, depending on the case design of the PC.
4. Identify an available slot of the appropriate expansion bus. Remember expansion cards are manufactured to fit the slot style of a certain bus structure. If the PC is fairly recent, as well as the card, more than likely either an ISA or PCI slot is what is needed. An older 8-bit card will fit into an ISA 16-bit slot. To make room for the card, you may need to rearrange the existing cards.
5. Remove the screw holding in the metal slot cover for the slot in which you will be inserting the new expansion card. Hang onto the screw; you'll need it to secure the expansion card.
6. Before inserting the card, read its documentation to verify its configuration and settings. It is very hard to set DIP switches and jumpers once the card is inserted into a slot and fastened down.
7. Handle expansion cards only by their edges and avoid touching their circuit side (the one with the electronic stuff on it), their pin side (the backside), or the edge connector. That doesn't leave much, I know, but the top and side edges do give you enough of the card to hold.
8. Insert the card by aligning it to the slot (refer to Figure 11-14) and then, with steady pressure, press the card into the slot. You may need to rock it very slightly, front to rear, to get it to settle into the slot. Don't force it. It should be snug, but you can also damage the slot or the card, or both, by forcing the card into the slot too fast and too hard. As you work, keep the card from rubbing or touching other cards already installed. Figure 11-18 shows how to align the card to the slot, but Figure 11-19 represents a more realistic situation.
9. When it is evenly and securely in the slot, fasten the card with the slot screw.
10. You may want to plug the PC in and test it for a very short while with the system case covers off. This way if there is a problem, it is a much shorter path back to where you are. When you are sure all is well, replace the system case cover.

Troubleshooting Expansion Cards

If you get an error relating to an expansion card, it will most likely be right after you've installed it, but errors can come at any time. Immediately after you install any new hardware, you run the risk of getting a boot or POST error that indicates a possible expansion card problem. If you don't get boot errors, the new device or card (or another device or card) may not perform as it should. If either of these situations should occur, there are three possible scenarios: a bad connection, system resource conflicts, or the new or old card is bad.

Figure 11-18. Align the expansion card to the slot before pushing it into the slot

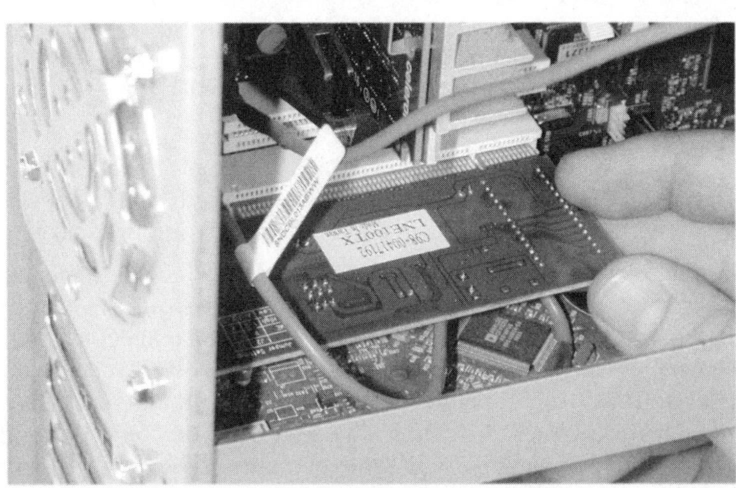

Figure 11-19. Installing an expansion card in a PC

Here is a troubleshooting procedure you can use to track down the problem:

1. If you can boot the system and the problem is that a new card or an existing device is not working correctly, use the operating system's device manager to verify that no system resource conflicts exist. On a Windows system, access the Device Manager through either My Computer's properties or the System icon on the Control Panel. Figure 11-20 shows the Computer Properties screen.

   To view the system resource assignments for an individual device: highlight the device in the installed device list (you may need to open a certain device type family by clicking on the "+" symbol by the name of the family); click the Properties button to display the device's properties; and click the View Resources tab. The display should be similar to that shown in Figure 11-21.

   A red X or a yellow exclamation point in front of the device or resource name indicates conflicts in the Device Manager. If any conflicts are identified, which are likely to be IRQs, reconfigure the newer device or the one used less frequently to an available resource setting. Retest the system.
2. If the problem cannot be fixed with software or requires a hardware solution, always begin by organizing a workspace around the PC as much as possible and preparing the workspace, the PC, and yourself against ESD as outlined in Chapter 14. This can't be emphasized too much. Even the smallest static discharge can inflict enough damage to have caused the problem you are now trying to track down.
3. Power down the PC and unplug it from the AC power source. Turn off all peripheral devices connected to the PC and remove their power cords from their AC outlets as well. It isn't enough to just switch off the plug strip. If there are any phone cables, network cables, or any other telecommunications lines connected to the PC, disconnect them as well.
4. Remove enough of the PC's case to allow unobstructed access to the expansion slots on the motherboard. On most new case designs, the top or one side of the case lifts off easily to provide access to the motherboard and internal components.
5. Verify that every expansion card, not just the last one you installed, is firmly seated in its slot. The heat-up and cool-down cycles that the electronics on the motherboard go through constantly can cause cards to creep (push) out of their slots over time. And as careful as you try to be, you can accidentally push a card out of its slot slightly when installing another. If any of the cards are loose or not seated completely, you may have found the problem. Without putting the case back on, power on the PC and test to see if the error is gone.
6. Check the connecting cables on each of the expansion cards to verify that each end of the cable is snuggly connected. Disconnect and reconnect the cable connector of each card one end at a time. Never force connectors, and pay attention to the keys on the connectors that are meant to prevent you from connecting it incorrectly. You have a choice now: you can power the PC up after reconnecting each card, or you can wait until you have completed checking all of the cards. If the error is gone when you reboot the system, the problem was obviously a loose connector.

Computer Properties

View Resources | Reserve Resources

Interrupt request (IRQ) | Direct memory access (DMA)
Input/output (I/O) | Memory

Setting	Hardware using the setting
00	System timer
01	Standard 101/102-Key or Microsoft Natural Keyboard
02	Programmable interrupt controller
04	Communications Port (COM1)
05	Promise Technology Inc. Ultra66 IDE Controller
05	IRQ Holder for PCI Steering
06	Standard Floppy Disk Controller
07	ECP Printer Port (LPT1)

OK | Cancel

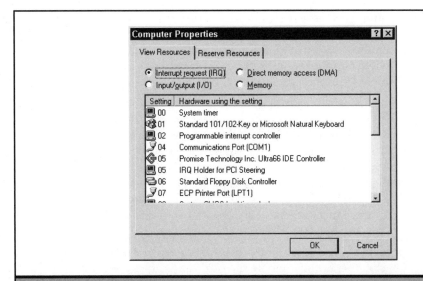

Figure 11-20. System resource conflicts will show up on the Computer Properties window of the Windows Device Manager

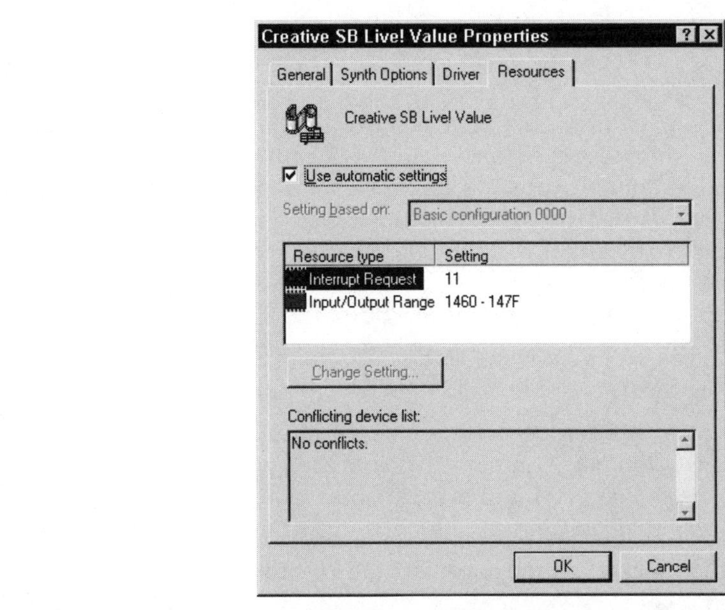

Figure 11-21. The system resources for an individual device are displayed on the Properties window for the device

7. If you have gotten this far and still haven't found the problem, it is not a generic one, such as loose cards or connectors. Beyond this point, you'll need some tools: a Phillips screwdriver, the documentation for all of your expansion cards, and possibly a probe or stylus or needle-nose pliers (if your cards use switches or jumpers for their configuration settings).
8. If you have just installed an expansion card, start with it. If you configured the card manually, verify the DIP switch or jumper settings against the card's documentation. A common error is that when you set the jumpers or switches, the card was backward to the orientation assumed by the documentation. For example, you (or the documentation) may have had the card upside-down. ISA cards have configuration settings for IRQs and I/O addresses, and in some cases, DMAs. Make sure you have set all three, as needed, to the recommended settings in the card's documentation. Retest the system after verifying each expansion card.
9. If the problem persists, it's all or nothing time. Write down the order and slot placement of each card in the PC and label each cable. You may want to sketch the expansion slot area to show where the cards and cables are connected. You should also enter the system BIOS configuration data and record all of the BIOS settings for the PC.

   Get a supply of antistatic bags or make lots of room on a clean static-free surface. Leaving only the hard disk controller card, if one is in use, remove all of the expansion cards from the PC. Place each card in an antistatic bag or where it will be safe (never stack expansion cards on top of each other, whether they are in antistatic bags or not).

   Install one expansion card at a time and test the system after each card. This procedure tries to isolate the card that is causing the problem. It's your call, but to test for the fault with this process, you really should put the case cover back after installing each card. The problem could actually be something like the card is grounding to the case. If you find the suspect card, retest it without the case on, just to be sure.

   You may need to change the system BIOS setup data to indicate that one or more of the cards has been removed and then reconfigure the BIOS data after it is installed using the data you recorded prior to starting this procedure.
10. Should you find an expansion card that causes the original problem (and not some new problem), you may want to verify that the slot is not causing the problem. Retest the slot with a different compatible card.
11. If the problem persists, it is likely that problem may be related to the motherboard. It could also be time to contact the PC or motherboard's technical support folks.

Dealing with Choke Points

A choke point is a point in the system hardware or configuration where too much data is trying to get through too small of a passageway or it is trying to move through a point too fast. One common cause for a choke point occurs when a completely functional but inappropriate expansion card is used. For example, using an ISA video card on a Pentium III PC will likely cause a choke point when the graphics attempt to run over the low-speed ISA bus. The system will work, but it may be very slow and not have the quality you'd expect.

If an expansion card is performing poorly or very slowly, the problem could very well be a choke point caused by too much traffic on a bus. This is rarely an issue with a PC purchased from a reputable dealer or manufacturer.

Some things you can do to prevent or eliminate a choke point for peripheral devices and expansion cards are

- Upgrade the motherboard to one with built-in controllers for the floppy disk, hard disk, and as many other devices as possible to eliminate controllers and adapter cards on the expansion bus.
- If one is not available on the motherboard, install a USB or IEEE 1394/FireWire port expansion card and use it to add future peripheral devices where possible.
- Try using one of the USB devices that provides additional serial and parallel ports; this can save expansion bus slots.

Resolving Resource Conflicts on Windows PCs

If a PC has system resource conflicts, it will let you know in one of the following ways:

- The system fails to boot and sounds or displays an error beep code or error message indicating an error on the motherboard or expansion bus.
- During the boot sequence, the system freezes up and will not complete the boot.
- The system halts or freezes up for no apparent reason during an I/O operation or when an application program is running.
- An I/O device performs erratically or intermittently.

The only cause for resource conflicts is a recent hardware (and in extremely rare cases, software) upgrade. If the answer to any one of the following questions is yes, then it is very likely that the PC's problem is a system resource conflict:

- Has a new internal device, expansion card, or device driver been recently added to the system?
- Did the error first appear after a new component was added to the PC?
- Was the PC operating okay before a new component was added?

If the answer to any of these questions is yes, you need to review and modify the system resource assignments to resolve the problem:

NOTE: If the new device is a sound card, you can just about count on the problem being a system resource conflict.

1. Write down the current resource settings and assignments, including those in the BIOS' configuration data (see Chapter 6 for information on how to access the BIOS configuration). It is also a very good idea to run a virus checker on the system before making any changes. Some viruses can cause damage that will show up much like a system resource problem (see Chapter 22 for more information on viruses).
2. Open the Windows Device Manager and select the device (expansion card) that was recently added to the PC. If the device has a yellow exclamation mark or red X symbol in front of its name, it is conflicting with another device or its configuration cannot be resolved by the BIOS or operating system.
3. Open the Properties window and display the Resources tab information. At the bottom of the display (refer to Figure 11-21), there should be information regarding the conflicting device.
4. At this point, you will need to change the conflicting resource (probably an IRQ—and definitely an IRQ if the device is a PCI card) to another available setting. If there are no IRQs available, you may need to share with another device, but make sure that the sharing device will not be in use at the same time as the new device. You may need to change the settings on the expansion card using jumpers or DIP switches using the card's documentation as your guide to the new values or positions. The system BIOS of the PC may support the reassignment of IRQs (for PCI slots) in the setup program. Most resource conflicts exist between expansion slots, and many can be resolved in the BIOS settings.

Resolving Resource Conflicts with Plug-and-Play Devices

Plug-and-Play (PnP) devices can cause IRQ conflicts because the PnP processes in the operating system and BIOS may not detect all other devices, or it may not correctly detect a new device. PnP devices are configured after all other devices are assigned resources during the boot cycle, so there is always the chance for a conflict.

To resolve a resource conflict on a PnP device:

1. Remove the new device from the Windows Device Manager and restart the PC to see if the problem was a one-time occurrence.
2. If the conflict is not resolved by rebooting the system, verify that the most current device drivers are installed. Visit the manufacturer's Web site to find the latest drivers and install them on your PC. The manufacturer may also have

a list of device compatibilities or usage bulletins. If so, read them—they may hold the answer to your problem.

3. If the new device is not being detected, use the Add New Hardware Wizard from the Control Panel to install it. If the Add New Hardware Wizard is not able to install the device, you will need to configure the system resources manually.
4. Open the Device Manager, highlight the selection for the device in question and click the Properties button. On the Properties window, choose the Resources tab. Clear the Use Automatic Settings check box.

   Now choose the system resources that are in conflict and use the Edit Resource function to reassign them to available or unassigned resources. The Device Manager will not let you assign values outside of the assignable range. If you assign a resource already in use, you will also get a warning. When all is well, click OK and close the Device Manager.
5. Restart the system. The problem should be solved. If not, repeat this process until you arrive at a workable set of system resources. If the manufacturer has technical support available, don't be too stubborn to call or e-mail them.

CHAPTER 12

Video Cards

Video output is a very important part of the PC, at least to the user. Without video displays, the output from the PC would be much slower and most likely limited to text only. The outputs on the PC are geared to the human senses of sight and sound. Think about doing any task on a PC without the use of the monitor; it would be virtually impossible. The PC's video system and monitor share the credit for the growth in popularity of the PC. It is doubtful that the PC would be nearly as popular if its output were printed on paper.

The heart of the PC's video system is the video card, or graphics card or graphics accelerator, as it is also called. From its beginning, when it could display only text to today's 3D and full motion video, the video card has essentially performed the same tasks. This chapter provides a look into the video card and how it generates the video display and the technology it uses to do it.

The video card does a lot more than just provide a connection for the monitor to the PC. It also controls the look, movement, color, brightness, and clarity of images displayed on the monitor. The video card processes every bit of the data sent to the monitor by any of the software running on the PC, turning digital data into text, graphics, and images on the monitor.

HOW A VIDEO CARD WORKS

The text and images displayed on the monitor are generated by software running on the PC. The software could be the operating system, as in the case of Windows, or in an application program, such as Microsoft Word, Adobe PhotoShop, or Paint Shop Pro. Regardless of its type, the software generates graphic data and instructions for a series of video frames that instruct the PC's CPU exactly how each frame of video output should look. The CPU and the video card then work together (more on this later) to create the image displayed on the monitor.

The instructions generated by the operating system or application software is sent to the CPU. The CPU sorts through the data and extracts the instructions it needs and sends the rest on to the video card. Depending on the type and capabilities of the video card, the CPU, the video card, or both create images by formatting pixels (picture elements—see Chapter 16) to form text or 2D images or tiny polygons and triangles for 3D graphics.

The text, images, shapes, and shadows formed by the pixels and triangles are generated in two phases: the transform and lighting phase and the setup phase.

Transform and Lighting Phase

The images displayed on the monitor rarely remain the same. As you type a letter or play a card game, each keystroke or mouse click causes a change in the display. Each of these changes, regardless of how bold or subtle they may be, are called transforms. In the transform phase, the graphic data is analyzed to determine just what has changed and the image data is constructed to change the displayed image accordingly.

Depending on the color scheme used on your monitor, as you type your letter or play your game, the text, cards, cars, or characters have contrast, colors, shapes, and shadows. These elements of the display are generated in the lighting phase. In the transform phase, the pixels and triangles are arranged to create the image desired by the application software. Then any lighting effects are applied to the tips of the triangles.

As is discussed later, the CPU, the video card, or both may perform the transform and lighting phases. In any case, the CPU sorts through the graphics instructions generated by the software and either acts on them or sends it onto the video card for processing. However, the final step, the setup phase, is always performed on the video card.

Setup Phase

The setup phase of the video generation process maps out the image to specific pixels or polygons on the screen. This very math-intensive process determines the vertical, horizontal, and 3D placement of each bit of the data created by the transform and lighting phases to describe the image. The graphic instructions are then mapped to specific locations on the screen in what is called the hardware triangle setup, which prepares the data for display.

Dividing Up the Work

If you are playing a video game on the PC and the scene shifts to the left, the software running the game sends instructions to the video system that details the color and brightness that each pixel in the display should be. These instructions are sent whether there is movement or not. The display information is updated around 70 times per second to eliminate screen flicker and to keep the animation on the screen from being choppy and flowing smoothly. The information and instructions for the video display are embedded in the data stream being sent to the CPU that may also include computation and data retrieval requests.

The CPU separates the video display data from the graphics software's data stream and, depending on the age and technology of the video system, acts on the video instructions or passes them onto the video card.

On older systems, the system CPU was used to perform the transform and lighting phases on the graphic instructions generated by software. Of course, this meant that any other tasks that needed the CPU, like moving data from a hard disk or performing a computation, had to wait until the graphic instructions were processed and sent on to the video card for the setup phase.

Newer video cards, such as graphics accelerators and 3D graphics cards, have the processing power to perform the transform and lighting phases, along with the setup phase. On a PC with a newer video card, the CPU is needed only to extract the transform and lighting data from the graphic data stream and route it to the video card. This frees the CPU to perform other tasks for the game, such as the physics or calculations related to a game's logic, or other applications running on the PC. The overall effect of the video card processing the graphic data is that the entire PC performs more efficiently.

2D and 3D Graphic Data

As you might guess, the transform and lighting processes used to generate 3D graphics are much more complex than those used to generate 2D graphics. 3D graphics also require and use considerably more computing resources as well.

To create a 2D image, the color, brightness, and placement (X and Y coordinates) of each pixel must be generated. The X and Y coordinates of the pixel are the 2 *D*s of the graphic data. The X coordinate specifies the horizontal (side to side) placement, and the Y coordinate places the pixel vertically (top to bottom) on the screen.

Of course, 3D images have a third *D*. In addition to horizontal and vertical placement, each pixel also has depth. In a 3D image, a pixel can be made to appear to be closer or further from the viewer with brightness and the attributes of surrounding pixels. To create this effect, the video card must address the X and Y placement of a pixel as well as the values that result in the pixel appearing to be in front or behind another pixel.

Converting Digital to Analog

Once the graphics data has gone through the setup phase, it is stored in the video card's memory. The video RAM is also called the frame buffer because it holds the instructions for each video frame as a buffer between the processing phases and the process that converts the digital data into the signal required by the monitor.

The RAMDAC (RAM digital to analogy converter) may well be the most important component in the entire process. In spite of the fact that it sounds like a character in a very bad science fiction movie, the RAMDAC converts the digital data stored in the video card's RAM into an analog signal that is used by the monitor to create images on the screen. The RAMDAC constantly reads from the video card's RAM, converts the data into an analog signal, and sends it on to the monitor. Remember that the graphic data is being refreshed about 70 times a second, so most of the data being sent to the monitor merely refreshes the display without changing it.

Pathways and Converters

Regardless of where the transform and lighting phase is performed, the CPU and video card must communicate with each other. On most PCs, this communication takes place over one of two interface bus structures: the Accelerated Graphics Port (AGP) bus or the Peripheral Component Interconnect (PCI) bus. More on these bus structures later in this chapter (as well as in Chapter 11).

VIDEO CARD STANDARDS

The video display capabilities of the very first PCs did not include graphics. The IBM PC and PC XT used the Monochrome Display Adapter (MDA) that displayed only text on a monochrome (one-color) monitor. Because text only was much too confining, the

Monochrome Graphics Adapter (MGA) that combined graphics and text on the monochrome monitor soon followed. A company named Hercules Computer Technology, who is given credit for beginning the evolution of PC graphics, developed the MGA standard.

After the MGA, IBM developed a string of graphics standards, each with more graphics capabilities than the last. The first was the CGA (Color Graphics Adapter) standard that included a range of colors (other than shades of one color). CGA had the capability of displaying up to 16 colors, but could only display 2 colors at its highest resolution setting of 640 × 200. Later in the chapter, the relationship between resolution, colors, and memory will be discussed.

The next graphics standard developed by IBM was EGA (Enhanced Graphics Adapter), which increased the screen resolution to 640 × 350 with up to 64 colors. Along with the MDA, MGA, and CGA standards, EGA is virtually extinct.

The next IBM video standard, VGA (Video Graphics Array), released in 1987, increased the number of colors available to the display to 256 on a resolution of 640 × 480. VGA has had an enduring quality. It was a standard adopted by many PC manufacturers, and it is still the default standard for many operating systems, including Windows, on today's PCs. Figure 12-1 demonstrates that VGA settings are still available. Figure 12-2 gives an example of the display after these settings are applied.

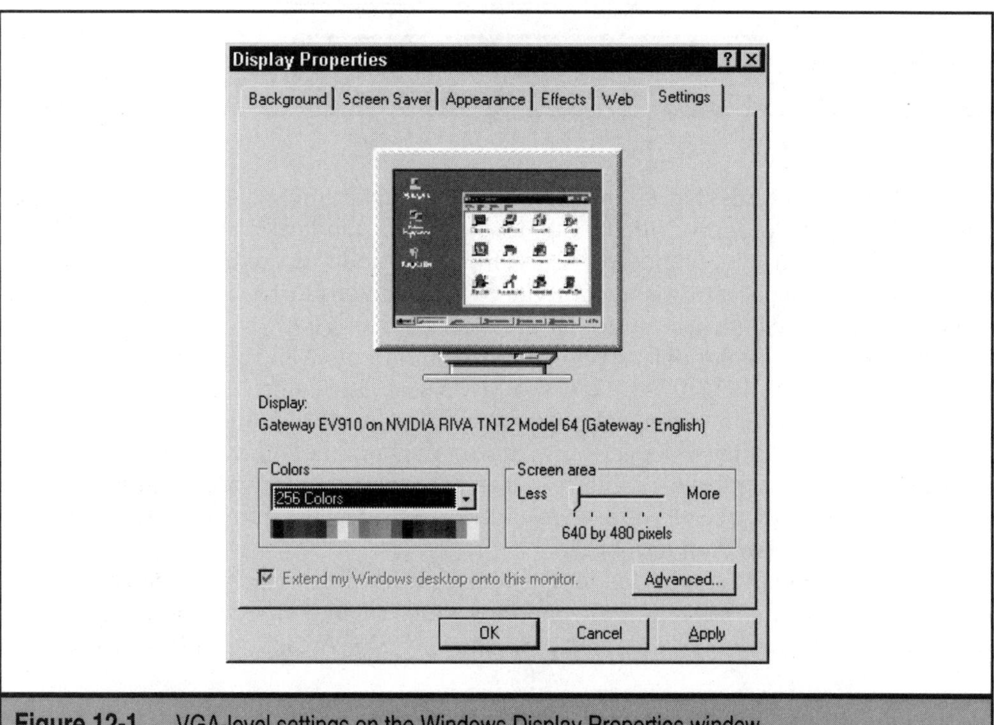

Figure 12-1. VGA-level settings on the Windows Display Properties window

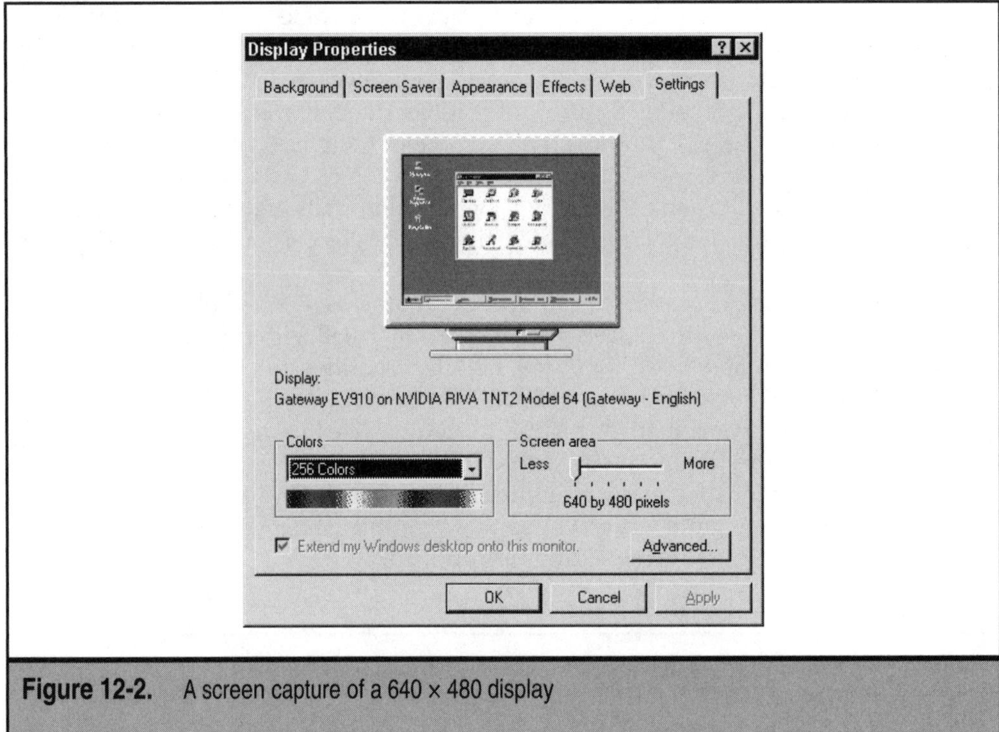

Figure 12-2. A screen capture of a 640 × 480 display

The video standards that followed VGA are grouped into a collection of standards based on the SVGA (Super Video Graphics Array), a standard that was developed by VESA (Video Electronics Standards Association), a standards organization made up of monitor and graphics card manufacturers. SVGA includes virtually all video graphics standards that have better resolution or more colors than VGA.

SVGA supports a color palette with over 16 million colors and a range of resolutions, including 800 × 600, 1024 × 768, 1280 × 1024, 1,600 × 1,200, and higher. Not all SVGA boards (nearly every video card sold today) will display all 16 million colors or support all of the SVGA resolutions. Depending on the manufacturer of the card, some or all of the SVGA standard is supported. Table 12-1 lists the more popular video graphic adapter standards in use today. Notice that as resolutions increase, the number of simultaneous colors that can be displayed decreases.

Because the SVGA standard is fairly broad and from the user's perspective is used mainly to match the video card to the monitor, video cards on the market today are less tied to video standards. For the most part, they are SVGA cards, but their focus is on

Video Standard	Resolution(s)	Colors
VGA (Video Graphics Array)	640 × 480	16
	320 × 200	256
SVGA (Super VGA)	800 × 600	16
	1,024 × 768	256
	1,280 × 1,024	256
	1,600 × 1,200	256
XGA (Extended Graphics Array)	640 × 480	65,536
	1,024 × 768	256

Table 12-1. PC Video Adapter Standards

increasing the video card's capabilities to process more of the graphic information and to produce better displayed images. Rather than the video standard, a card is typically chosen because of its price, its memory, and the graphics language or API (application program interface) it uses to produce 3D graphics.

Connector

One standard that has endured from the beginning is the connection used to connect the monitor to the video card. The monitor connects to the video card through a 15-pin HD15 (high-density 15-pin) DB-style connector, as shown here:

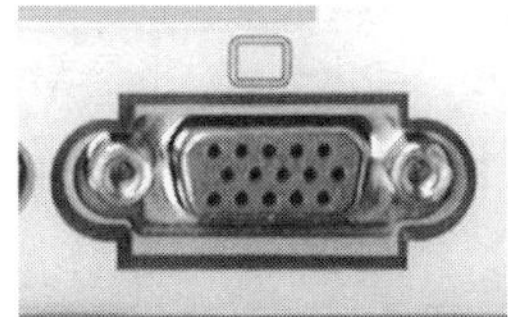

VIDEO CARD COMPONENTS

A video card is virtually a separate computing system that is mounted inside the PC to handle video graphics reproduction on the monitor. It has its own processor, BIOS, memory, chipset, and connectors, all of which are focused at processing graphic images for display.

Video Processor

On most older video cards, the PC's CPU is also the video processor and performs all of the geometric and mathematical calculations of the transform and lighting phases. The CPU sends the raw screen image to the video card's frame buffer (the video card's memory), from which the video card reads it, performs the setup phase, and writes it back for the RAMDAC to use.

On newer video cards, the transform and lighting phases are performed on the video card by its processor, which is also called the graphics processing unit, or GPU. The CPU extracts the graphics instructions from the application software's data stream and passes it to the GPU over the interface bus in use (either AGP or PCI). The GPU performs the calculations required to produce the data needed for the setup phase. Like the data processed on the CPU, this data is written to the video card's memory for use in the setup phase. Regardless of which processor performs the transform and lighting phases (the CPU or the GPU), there is much more information produced in these calculations than is received from the application. When the GPU performs this task, there is less data transmitted over the system bus, which further reduces the workload of the CPU. Because it has no other responsibilities, the GPU is able to process the graphics information about 10 times faster than the CPU.

Video Memory

A certain amount of memory is required to hold the graphics information being passed to the setup phase from the transform and lighting phases. The amount of memory needed is directly related to the amount of graphics information being passed, the resolution of the monitor, and the number of graphic dimensions being generated. For example, a monochrome text display on an MDA monitor required less than 2KB of space, but today's 3D high-resolution displays can use as much as 64MB of video RAM.

Like the video processor, the location of the memory used to store the graphics information has changed as well. The 2KB of memory used by an MDA display was carved out of the Upper Memory Area in the PC's RAM. This was appropriate at the time because the CPU did most of the processing for monochrome text graphics. Working out of system memory was convenient and, at the time, less expensive than putting RAM on the video card. However because the need for video memory increased from kilobytes to megabytes and there was a need for faster data transfers, video memory, more commonly called video RAM, is now located on the video card along with the GPU, which performs most of the processing.

In some less-expensive home PCs, some of the video processing functions are integrated into the motherboard, and the frame buffer is located in the system RAM. This approach to video RAM is called unified memory architecture, which means that the system RAM is being used to support video along with everything else running on the PC. This design eliminates the need for a separate video card, along with its cost. This approach produces a lower quality video compared to those supported directly by a video card with its own video RAM and processor. The other problem with this design approach is that if the video system fails, the entire motherboard must be replaced.

Resolution

The two factors that impact the amount of video RAM needed on the video card are resolution and color depth. Each pixel of the display requires a certain amount of data to encode exactly how it should appear. As the number of pixels used to create the display goes up, so does the total amount of data used to describe the display. For example, about 6MB of data are needed to generate a true color image for a display using 1600 × 1200 resolution.

Resolution is the number of pixels used to generate a display. While it's true that the size of the display (such as 15-inch, 17-inch, etc.) has some bearing on the number of pixels available, using more pixels to create an image will obviously increase the amount of detail in the picture and improve its quality. A monitor using 640 × 480 resolution (640 pixels on each horizontal line and 480 rows of pixels) uses 307,200 pixels to create its display. If the same monitor is set to a resolution of 1280 × 960, it uses 1,228,800 pixels, and in the same display space. As the pixel count increases on any monitor, the size of each pixel and the space around it must decrease in order to fit in the display space.

As the resolution increases, the detail in the display also increases, while its size decreases, as was illustrated earlier in Figures 12-1 and 12-2. Try using the Settings tab on the Display Properties of a Windows PC to change the display resolution. Here's how:

1. On the Windows Desktop, right-click an empty space to display the Desktop's shortcut menu, shown here:

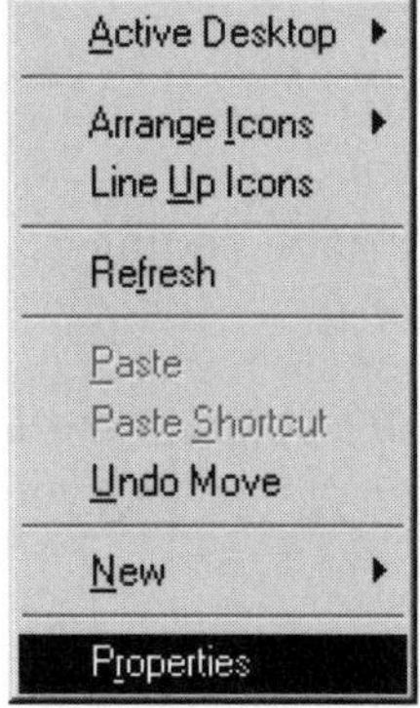

2. Select Properties to open the Display Properties window, shown in Figure 12-3.
3. Select the Settings tab (as shown in Figure 12-3) to display the resolution and color depth settings currently in use. Make a note of the current display settings in use.
4. Slide the pointer in the Screen Area setting to the left to select 640 × 480 and choose 256 colors from the Colors pull-down list.

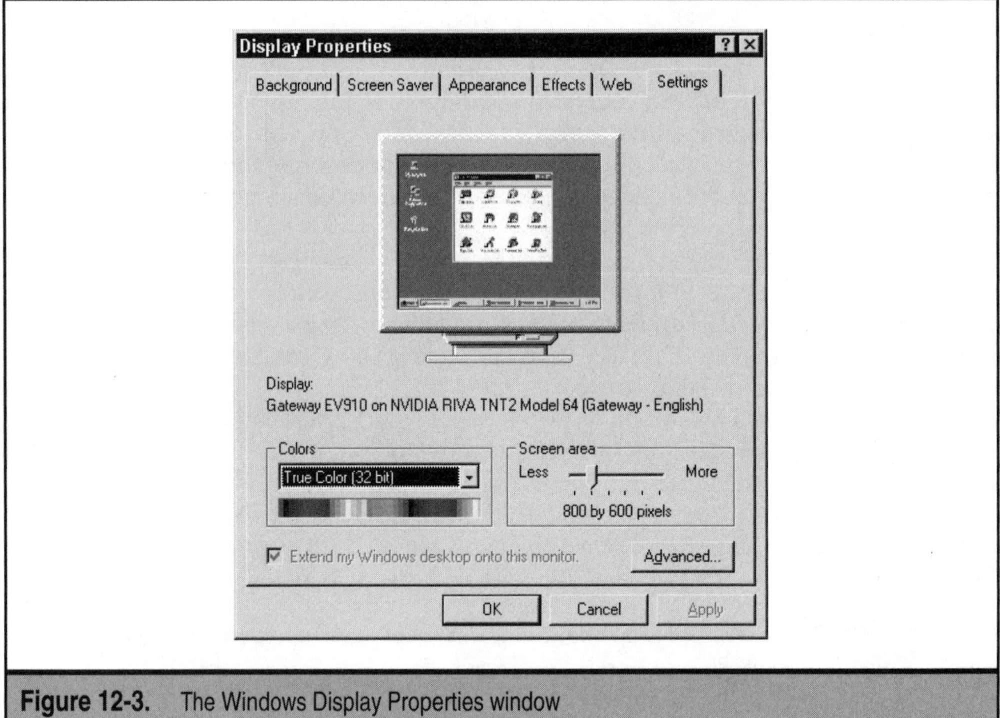

Figure 12-3. The Windows Display Properties window

5. Click Apply to change the display settings. A Compatibility Warning box, as shown in Figure 12-4, will display asking you if you wish to restart the PC with the new colors or apply them without a restart (which should be the default). Choose Apply the New Color Settings Without Restarting? and click OK. Another warning box will display telling you that it may take a few seconds to install the new settings. Click OK.
6. The screen will appear in its new settings. Now repeat this process, changing the display settings to the highest resolution and color depth settings available.
7. Reset the display settings to their original settings.

Color Depth

The other major factor in determining the amount of video RAM a system requires is the color depth, which is the number of individual colors that each pixel can display. The color depth is expressed as the number of bits used to describe each color in the color set. The common color depth settings are 8-bit, 16-bit, 24-bit, and 32-bit color. Figure 12-5 shows an example the color depth settings on a Windows PC.

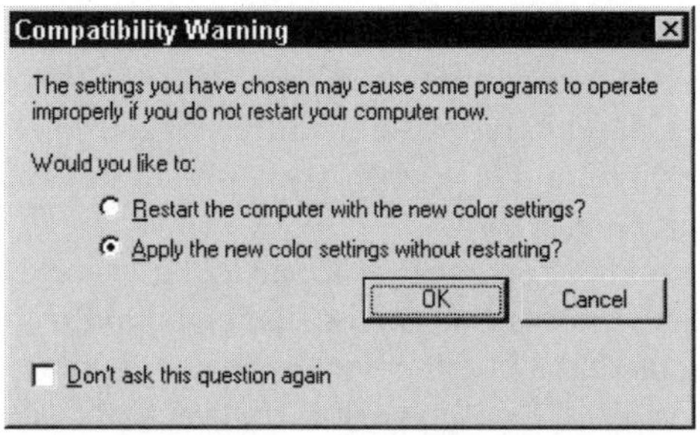

Compatibility Warning

The settings you have chosen may cause some programs to operate improperly if you do not restart your computer now.

Would you like to:

- Restart the computer with the new color settings?
- Apply the new color settings without restarting?

OK Cancel

Don't ask this question again

Figure 12-4. The Compatibility Warning box displays when you change the display settings

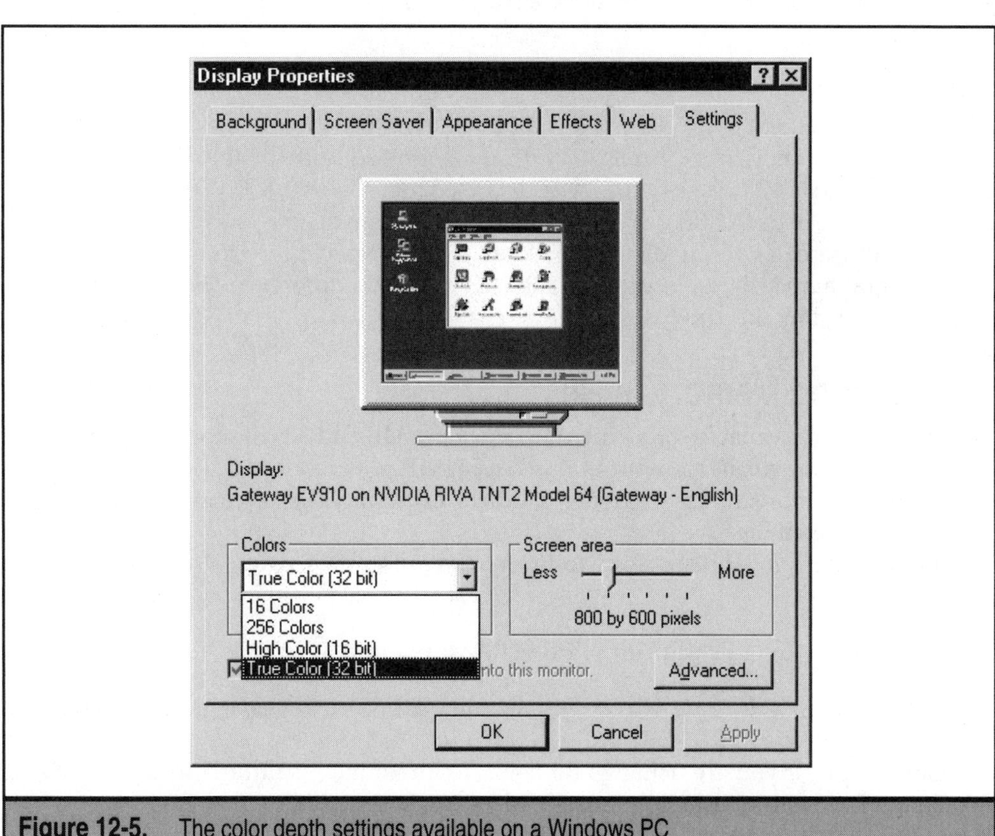

Figure 12-5. The color depth settings available on a Windows PC

The number of bits in the color depth determines the number of colors that can be displayed. For example, 8-bit color uses 8-bits to number each of the colors. In binary numbers, the range of numbers available in 8 bits is 00000000 to 11111111, or the range in decimal numbers of 0 to 255, which represents different 256 colors. The colors included in the color palette for a particular color depth are represented in the binary values stored in the number of bits available.

To determine the number of colors that a particular color depth includes, it's represented as the largest binary number that can be displayed in the number of bits of the color depth plus one. This means that a 16-bit color depth can display 65,536 colors (or $2^{15} + 1$), the 24-bit color depth has over 16.7 million colors that each pixel could conceivably display, and a 32-bit color depth supports over 4 *billion* colors. Depending on the PC, video card, and monitor, either 24-bit or 32-bit is typically designated as True Color setting.

NOTE: The human eye cannot distinguish beyond 16 million or so colors. Above that the eye may have difficulty discerning the colors of two adjacent pixels.

Aspect Ratio

Another measurement used to define the capabilities of the video display is its aspect ratio. This is the ratio of horizontal pixels to vertical pixels used to create the display. The standard aspect ratio is 4:3 (read as 4 to 3), which is used for 640 × 480, 800 × 600, and 1280 × 768 resolutions. The aspect ratio determines how well certain shapes, such as circles, can be drawn on the screen without distortion. As a user, the aspect ratio isn't a big thing, but if you are a graphics designer or programmer, it can make a difference on the quality of the image produced by the video card.

How Much Video Memory Is Needed?

Most video cards available today include between 8MB and 32MB of video RAM. Some high-end cards are available with as much as 64MB of video RAM. There are opinions that 64MB is far more than is needed, but others, especially the 3D crowd, think that this may soon not be enough.

The following formula is used to figure the amount of video RAM needed for a particular system:

Resolution * (Color Depth / 8) = Video RAM required

The color depth is divided by 8 to convert the calculation into bytes, which is the common measurement for video RAM.

For example, if you are using 24-bit color depth with a resolution of 1024 × 768, the calculation for the minimum amount of video RAM needed is:

1024 * 768 = 786,432 (pixels in the resolution)
24 / 8 = 3 (bytes in the color depth)
786,432 * 3 = 2,359,296 (bytes of video RAM needed)

So, for a 1024 × 768 resolution using 24-bit color depth, the video card must have at least 2.4MB of video RAM, and more is always better.

Another example: To display a 1600 × 1200 resolution with a 32-bit color depth, the graphics card needs about 8MB of video RAM:

1600 * 1200 = 1,920,000 (pixels of resolution)
32 / 8 = 4 (bytes of color depth)
1920000 * 4 = 7,680,000 (bytes of video RAM required)

Understand that the above calculations are figuring the video RAM requirements for 2D images. Table 12-2 shows the amounts of video RAM required by several common graphics settings.

3D Video Memory

Video cards that support 3D graphics require more video RAM than 2D cards even on the same resolution and color depth settings. This is because in addition to the 2D (down and across) a third dimension of depth is added.

Real 3D cards, video cards that truly support three dimensional displays, use three buffers to hold the graphics data: a front buffer, a back buffer, and a Z-buffer. The addition of the Z-buffer consumes enough of the available video RAM to typically require that the resolution be reduced. For example, a 2D video card with 4MB of video RAM can support display settings of 1600 × 1200 resolution and 16-bit color depth but can only support a 3D game using 800 × 600 resolution and a 16-bit color depth setting.

The front and back buffers are each the size required to hold the color data according to the color depth in use, such as 24 or 32 bits. The Z-buffer is usually 16 bits (or 2 bytes) in size.

Use this formula to calculate the amount of video RAM needed to support a 3D display:

Resolution * ((Color Depth (in bytes) * 2) + 2) = 3D video RAM requirements

Resolution	Color Depth	VRAM Required
640 × 480	8-bit	307KB
1,024 × 768	16-bit	1.57MB
1,024 × 768	24-bit	2.36MB
1,600 × 1,200	24-bit	5.76MB
1,600 × 1,200	32-bit	7.68MB

Table 12-2. Common 2D Video RAM Requirements

For a 1024 × 768 resolution using 16-bit color, the calculation is as follows:

1024 * 768 = 786,432 (pixels of resolution)
16 / 8 = 2 (color depth in bytes)
2 * 2 + 2 = 6 (buffers required in bytes)
786,432 * 6 = 4,718,592 (video RAM required for 3D graphics)

The result of this calculation is a video card with 4MB of video RAM (even if it is a 3D card) cannot support a 3D display setting of 1024 × 768 resolution using 16-bit color depth without adding additional video RAM.

Video RAM Technologies

The video card's memory is also called the frame buffer because it holds the graphic instructions that define each frame before it is processed by the setup phase and RAMDAC. The earliest video RAM was standard DRAM, which requires constant electrical refreshing to hold its contents. DRAM didn't work well for video RAM because it cannot be accessed while it is being refreshed, which meant video performance suffered.

A variety of memory technologies have been and are being used as video RAM on video cards. The most common RAM technologies used with video cards are the following:

- **Dynamic Random Access Memory (DRAM)** This is the same RAM used on early PCs. EDO DRAM has largely replaced DRAM on the PC, but other types of video RAM are in use.
- **Extended Data Output DRAM (EDO DRAM)** EDO DRAM provides a higher bandwidth than standard DRAM and manages read/write cycles more efficiently.
- **Video RAM (VRAM)** VRAM, not to be confused with the generic term *video RAM*, is dual-ported, which means it can be written to and read from at the same time. VRAM, which is a special type of DRAM, doesn't need to be refreshed as often as standard DRAM.
- **Windows RAM (WRAM)** The video RAM used on Matrox video cards. It is dual-ported and runs a bit faster than VRAM.
- **Synchronous DRAM (SDRAM)** SDRAM is very much like EDO DRAM, except that it is synchronized to the video card's GPU and chipset, which allows it to run faster. SDRAM is a single-ported memory technology that is very common on video cards.
- **Multibank DRAM (MDRAM)** MDRAM is a newer memory type that is divided into 32KB banks, which can be accessed independently. MDRAM also offers the advantages of interleaving, true memory sizing, and better memory performance. Interleaving allows memory accesses to overall memory banks. MDRAM can be sized exactly to the amount of video RAM needed to support a particular display type.

- **Double Data Rate SDRAM (DDR SDRAM)** DDR SDRAM doubles the data rate of standard SDRAM to produce faster data transfers. DDR memories are becoming more commonplace on video cards, especially 3D video accelerators.
- **Synchronous Graphics RAM (SGRAM)** An improvement on SDRAM that supports block writes and write-per-bit, which yield better graphics performance. Found only on video cards with chipsets that support these features, such as many Matrox video cards. SGRAM is a single-ported memory technology.
- **Double Data Rate SGRAM (DDR SGRAM)** DDR SGRAM is showing up on the very latest cards. It doubles the data rate of SGRAM and offers better performance.
- **Direct Rambus DRAM (RDRAM)** A newer general-purpose memory type, also being used on video cards, which includes bus mastering and a dedicated channel between memory devices. RDRAM runs about 20 times faster than conventional DRAM.

See Chapter 5 for more information on memory technologies.

Bus Mastering

Bus mastering allows the video card to control the PC's system bus and transfer data into and out of system RAM directly without the assistance of the CPU. This improves the performance of certain video operations that use RAM for calculations, such as 3D acceleration.

Video Chipsets

The logic circuits that control the video card's functions are grouped together as the video card's chipset, which is also called the graphics chip, the accelerator, or the video coprocessor. Much like the functions performed by the system chipset on the motherboard, the video chipset supports all of the functions performed by the GPU, as well as the interfaces, data transfers, and compatibility of the card.

Some video card manufacturers make their own video chipsets, such as Matrox and 3dfx, who design and build their cards from start to finish; others use chipsets manufactured by other companies, such as Diamond Multimedia. The video chipset is important because it holds the key to the card's performance, capabilities, and compatibility.

An important feature controlled by the video chipset is the video card's refresh rate. A higher refresh rate means less flicker on the screen, which translates to less eyestrain for the user. A good video chipset should provide a refresh rate of at least 75Hz. However, the refresh rate must be balanced to the resolution settings. Using a higher resolution setting should result in a lower refresh rate, and vice versa.

The Video BIOS

The function of the video BIOS (Basic Input/Output System) is very much like that of the system BIOS. It provides an interface between the system BIOS, the PC's operating system, and any application programs running on the PC to the video card and ultimately to the monitor. The issues that impact the video card at the BIOS level are video interfaces, system resource requirements, and video drivers.

Video System Interfaces

A large amount of data must be moved between the video card and the PC's CPU and RAM. The video system interface is the pathway over which this data travels. This pathway connects the GPU and video RAM to the PC. Because of the amount of data to be transferred, the video system interface requires more bandwidth than any other peripheral device on the PC.

One common mistake made by users is to assume that the number of bits used on the video card is also the number of bits required in the video system interface. But a 64-bit or 128-bit video card only uses this bandwidth internally between its onboard components. The width in bits of the interface to the CPU and memory will be either 16 bits (ISA/EISA cards) or 32 bits (VL-Bus, PCI, or AGP). There is a 64-bit PCI bus available on newer motherboards and video cards that use a 64-bit interface, but there is not a 128-bit interface—not yet, anyway.

The two most popular video system interfaces in use today are the PCI and AGP buses:

- **Peripheral Component Interconnect (PCI)** Support for the PCI interface bus is included in the system chipset on all Pentium-class computers. PCI is commonly used for 2D graphics cards, sound cards, network interface cards, and other expansion cards that attach directly to the motherboard. Of course, a PCI card slot is required. PCI is a bus structure and as such may support a number of different devices. PCI slots, shown in Figure 12-6, are found on virtually all Pentium-class motherboards boards.
- **AGP (Accelerated Graphics Port)** This interface was designed specifically for use as a video system interface. AGP, which runs twice as fast as the PCI interface, creates a high-speed link between the video card and the PC's processor. The AGP interface is also directly linked to the PC's system memory, which makes it possible for 3D images to be stored in main memory and for 2D systems to use system RAM for some calculations. All AGP video cards require the motherboard to have an AGP slot. AGP is a port and as such can support only a single device. There is usually only one AGP slot on a motherboard (see Figure 12-6), and it is reserved for the graphics card.

AGP is fast replacing PCI as the interface of choice for video cards because of its faster transfer rates. In fact, AGP has evolved into several standard versions, each noting its multiple of the original standard. For example, AGP 1X has a data transfer rate of 266MBps (compared to PCI's 133MBps), AGP 2X supports 533 MBps, and AGP 4X transfers data at 1.07GBps.

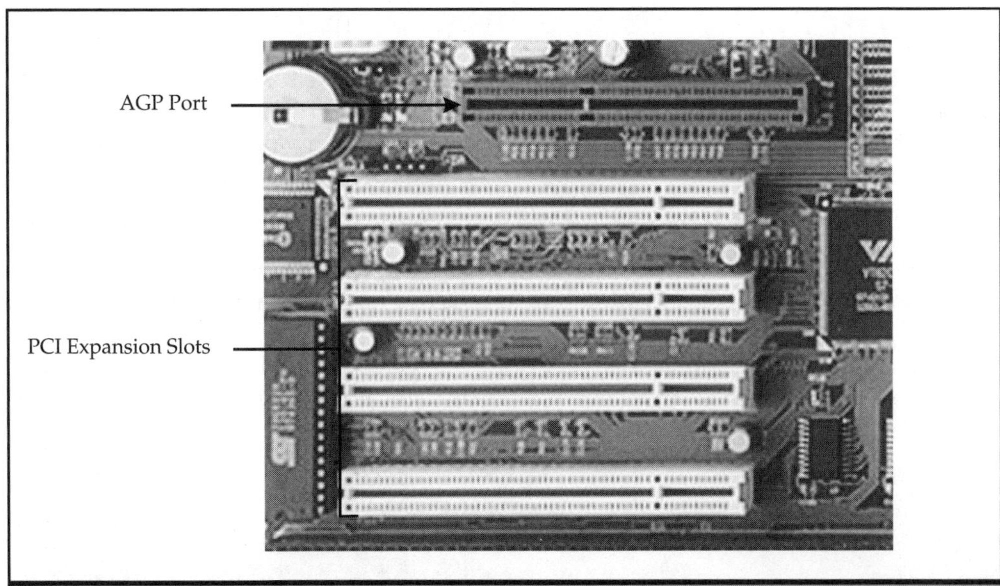

Figure 12-6. A motherboard with PCI and AGP interface slots

Video System Resources

Unlike other peripheral devices mounted inside the PC's case, video cards do not consume much in the way of system resources. Not all video cards use an IRQ. Those video cards that do use an IRQ use one of the pair set aside for PCI devices (IRQ 11 or IRQ 12). All VGA-compatible video cards, which are virtually all of them, use a standard pair of I/O port addresses (3B0–3BBh and 3C0–3DFh). Manufacturers of other types of expansion cards avoid these addresses, which eliminate possible conflicts during installation.

Video Device Drivers

The video card's device driver translates the images generated by an application program into instructions that the GPU can use. Where the software may consider the display as a collection of pixels, the GPU sees it as a series of line and shape drawings, and it's the job of the graphics driver software to convert between the application's vision and that of the graphics processor.

Typically, there are separate graphics drivers for each resolution and color depth combination the video card supports. Because it uses a separate piece of software for each unique combination of settings, the video system may not perform the same on different resolution and color depth settings. The same may be true of the different drivers used for each operating system for a particular video card. Video drivers are frequently updated, so if optimum video performance is your thing, check the manufacturer's Web site frequently.

The RAMDAC

The RAMDAC (RAM digital to analog converter) solves the simple problem that the PC and video card are digital and the monitor is an analog device. The information stored in the video memory is digital data that must be converted into an analog signal before it can be used by the monitor to create the display image.

The RAMDAC reads data from the video memory, converts it to an analog signal wave, and then sends it over the connecting cable (the one connected from the back of the PC to the monitor). The RAMDAC has a direct impact on the quality of the screen's image, how often the screen is refreshed, the color palette used, and the resolution and color depth used in the display.

There is a DAC (digital to analog converter) for each of the three RGB (red, green, and blue) colors that are used together to create the right color mix for each pixel. The speed of the RAMDAC has a lot to do with how well it is able to support the quality of the display. Today, a fast RAMDAC has a rating between 300MHz to 350MHz, but then in 1999, 150MHz was fast.

3D GRAPHICS

The video displayed on the monitor is actually a very fast moving set of still images. It is very much like an electronic flipbook—the more images that the PC can display in a second, the smoother the images or actions on the screen will appear. The higher the frame rate on the video card, the faster the card performs the transform and lighting processes.

3D applications, such as games and animations, generate data that reflect everything going on in a game. This data reflects the action of the software in terms of mathematical data, including camera (the user's viewpoint) movements, the movement of objects in relationship to other objects, the calculations of the physics engine (how objects move and interact), and any other factor affecting the display and the simulated action taking place. Typically, this data is filtered through the graphics language's API and then sent to the video RAM for processing through the transform, lighting, and setup phases. You may find references that refer to the entire process as the 3D pipeline, which also includes the rendering phase.

3D Graphics Accelerators

The 3D images displayed on a PC monitor are actually *surface modeling*, a process that creates the illusion of a three-dimensional scene on a 2D (flat) surface. Surface modeling represents 3D objects using a mesh of polygons, typically triangles, to create images with their outside edges. If enough triangles can be used to create an image, even the curved surfaces can be made to look smooth on the PC's display. A variety of geometric descriptions is used to define each triangle, including its vertices (corners), vertex normals (which side is pointing out and which is inside to create shading), reflection characteristics of its surface, the coordinates of the viewer's perspective, the location and intensity of a light source, the location and orientation of the display plane, and more.

With this information available, the GPU and graphics chipset render the 3D image onto the 2D screen. To create the 3D look, mathematical equations calculate the tracing through a scene, determine any light reflections and light sources, place some objects in view and obscure others, and make distant objects smaller and darker (called depth cueing). Obviously, the 3D rendering process is very complicated, involving a tremendous number of calculations regardless of the complexity of the scene displayed. If shading is added to the process, the number of computations required is doubled.

To speed up the process, all of the computations are made on the video card by the GPU and chipset and the graphics program; the one running on the PC is written in a standard 3D graphics language such as OpenGL. The graphics program may also use an API that provides a library of standard graphic commands that can be passed to the graphics processor. Graphics APIs allow the game or application to remain compatible to all versions of a 3D card.

Transform and Lighting

Creating the graphic images for 3D involves the transform, lighting, and setup. The transform phase compares the data of one frame to the next and decides what has changed and must be rendered (drawn) into each frame. Every object in the frame, including those that end up behind other objects in a frame, is transformed.

As you watch a 3D game or animated image, the objects on the screen move, rotate, and change in scale and perspective. When an item, such as a car, a plane, the focus of a camera, or an imaginary gun moves, it creates what is called movement or translation. Whenever your point of view on the screen changes, movement has occurred. When an object changes in size relative to other objects, the action is called scaling. If the object should turn or spin, the action is called rotation. Movement, translation, scaling, and rotation as a group are called transforms.

Lighting effects, such as shadows, spotlights, and indirect lighting sources are then applied to each transformed frame. Next, the setup phase builds the triangles (polygons) that make up the 3D objects in the frame. They are created through a floating-point engine, and the frame is ready to be rendered.

Setup

The third step in the process used to prepare graphic images for display is setup. This phase of the process is split into two steps: the geometry setup and the triangle setup. The geometry setup creates the data that describes how the triangles that make up the display are to be configured. The triangle setup translates this data to represent formatted polygons and triangles that essentially define the basic 3D image, its lighting, textures, and more that is to be converted for display on the 2D monitor screen.

Rendering

The final step in the preparation phases for a 3D display is the rendering phase. The previous phases have defined the image to be included in a video frame, how it is to be lighted, how this image is represented in terms of three-dimensional geometry, and finally, how it can be created as a series of triangles that construct the form of the image. The rendering phase finishes the process by assigning color, texture, lighting, transparency, fog, and other treatments to each row of pixels that makes up each triangle that has been rendered (drawn). After each row of pixels in each triangle of the image frame has been assigned its values, the image is fully rendered.

Fill Rate

The rendering process draws the frame using the instructions generated by each of the previous phases. How fast this happens is based on the video card's fill rate, or how many pixels or texels (the triangles used to create texture on the screen) can be rendered per second. The fill rate may be the most important performance indicator of a 3D video card. A card can have a fire-breathing 3D pipeline that is quenched by a slow fill rate.

Rendering Activities

The rendering process includes a variety of filtering and texturing processes that are used to create the effect desired in each frame:

- **Anisotropic Filtering** One of the more advanced texturing techniques, in which 16 texels are used to form the texture map of each polygon.
- **Antialiasing** A technique used to reduce the "noise" added to the image when all of the graphic information is not available. The information about an image should include its position, colors, size change, and more, but if it is not available, the missing factors are filled in with what is called noise. Antialiasing attempts to remove this noise.
- **Bilinear filtering** A standard texturing method on virtually all 3D graphic cards that reads four texels, calculates the averages of their positions, colors, and other properties, and displays the result as a single-screen texel. This technique is used to reduce blockiness in the display and has a blurring effect on objects as they approach the viewer.
- **Bump mapping** This technique is used in place of embossing to create the illusion of depth or height on a textured surface. This is the process used to create rough roads, bomb craters, and bullet holes on walls.
- **Filtering** This process smoothes the textures applied to blend, or slightly blur, the colors of adjacent pixels to eliminate a blocky look.
- **Mip mapping** This technique improves the appearance of textures by grouping pixels into mip-maps that cluster four texels together to remove jagged edges between pixels and texels. The term *mip* stands for the Latin phrase *multum in parvol,* which means multitude in a small place.

- **Point sampling** This texturing technique uses one texel to establish the texture of a triangle. While it is the easiest and fastest technique and uses the lowest bandwidth of the texturing techniques in use, it results in poor image quality with a lot of aliasing (jagged edges and missing texture) elements.
- **Texture mapping** This step applies a picture in 2D format over 3D objects to create levels of detail and texture, or to create a perspective change, such as an object moving closer or further away.
- **Z-buffering** As the pixels of a 3D image are rendered, the accelerator does not know which pixel is to be displayed first. Z-buffering encodes each pixel with a Z-value that is used to sequence the pixels.

Shading

After each triangle is rendered with its basic color, shading is applied to indicate the effect any light sources calculated during the setup phase have on it. The shading applied adds a bit of realism to the rendered polygon. Here are a few of the shading techniques applied:

- **Flat shading** This technique calculates a single light intensity and applies it to the entire triangle. The benefit of flat shading is that it requires very little resources from the processor. Its disadvantage is that it produces poor image quality with sudden changes of light intensity between triangles.
- **Gouraud shading** This is the most commonly used shading technique. It calculates a different light intensity for each point (vertex) of the triangle and then averages the light intensity between the points.
- **Phong shading** This shading technique is done completely with software and requires a great deal of processor time. A different light intensity may be calculated for each pixel in the triangle, resulting in an extremely realistic image. The name comes from its developer, Phong Bui-Tuong.

Fog

As a 3D object moves further away from the viewer, the 3D video card cannot draw it into infinity. If an object moves beyond the limit at which the video accelerator can no longer draw the object, it just disappears from view. How far away an object can move in relation to the viewer is dependent on the processing capabilities of the processor. This also means that objects will suddenly appear when moving towards the viewer once they reach the distance limit.

Fog is a trick to avoid the sudden appearance and disappearance of objects. An object moving away or toward the viewer at a distance is covered with fog, which blends the pixels of the object with a certain fog color when it is further away. As the object moves over the drawing limit, it is drawn but made invisible by a cover of fog. When it moves closer, the fog color fades away and the object comes into view without suddenly popping up. Fog is the 3D graphics version of a fade in and fade out.

Three very different types of fog are used in 3D graphics:

- **Linear fog** This is the easiest technique to apply. The fog color is increased linearly as an object moves away from the camera.
- **Lookup table fog** A fog lookup table lists how much of an influence the fog should make for each point of depth. As the object passes certain distances from the viewer, the distance is found in the table and the corresponding fog intensity is applied.
- **Exponential fog** This technique matches the effect of real fog and progressively fades an object in or out in relationship to its distance from the viewer.

INSTALLING A VIDEO CARD

To install a new video card in a PC, follow this process:

1. First, make sure you are following appropriate ESD safeguards (see Chapter 24) to protect your video card, the PC, and yourself. Remember that you shouldn't wear an ESD wrist strap or any form of body grounding when working with the monitor. Leave the new video card in its antistatic packaging until you are ready to install it.
2. Remove the old video card both physically and logically from the system. Completely uninstall the previous video card's drivers and switch over to the Standard VGA Display Driver for Windows. The display may be bad until a few more adjustments are made. Disconnect any cables attached to the card and remove it by grasping it by the upper corners and pulling firmly upward.

   OR

If you are replacing the PC's integrated video system, which means that the video system is built into the motherboard, it must be completely disabled before you can install the new video card. Check the documentation of the motherboard and chipset for instructions on how the integrated video adapter is disabled. Most likely you will need to change a jumper value or disable the port in the BIOS configuration data using the BIOS Startup program.

If you are unsure of the type of video card or adapter in use, you can use the DOS Debug command to display this information. Follow the instructions listed below in "Determining the Type of Video Card in a PC" on how to use the DOS Debug command.

1. Wth any luck, you determined the adapter interfaces available on your PC before you bought the card and made a choice. If you plan to use a PCI interface, be sure the card is a PCI card; if you plan to use an AGP slot, you should have an AGP card. Now is a very good time to verify this. The PCI slots are the long

white expansion slots on the motherboard, and the AGP is the short brown one typically to the right of the right-most PCI slot (see Figure 12-6 earlier in the chapter). Motherboards with a Pentium II processor or higher usually have an AGP port that can be used for video cards only. You must also be running Windows 95 OSR2 (the updated OEM version released in 1996), Windows 98, Windows NT, or Windows 2000. The fact that your PC has an AGP port most likely means you are able to install or upgrade to an AGP card.

2. Assuming the PC's case is open, remove the video card from its anti-static package. Hold it only by its ends and, avoiding contact with its components or edge connectors, align the card's edge connectors to the appropriate slot with the metal mounting bracket fitting into the open slot in the case. With your fingers spaced evenly across the top of the card, press down firmly to seat the card in the slot. Align the mounting bracket with the screw hole in the case and attach it with a screw.
3. Some video cards, especially AGP cards, have a power supply connector. Use an available connector to connect the card to the power supply. Check the card's documentation if you are unsure about which power supply connector to use, if any. Typically, it is the same type of power supply connector used for the hard disk drives.
4. The card is installed and ready to go as soon as the software is installed. If the PC's operating system, typically Windows, is installed, it's time to install the device drivers and utilities for the video card. Typically, the video card comes with a CD-ROM that will auto-start when you close the CD tray and open an installation wizard of one kind or another that will guide you through the installation of the device drivers.
5. After the video drivers and any other utility software for your video system are installed, restart the PC. If you have problems, review the next section.

TROUBLESHOOTING THE VIDEO CARD

If you are unsure about what is causing a problem on a video card, use the following general troubleshooting steps to determine the problem. Remember that when all else fails, most video card manufacturers have technical support available or at least a FAQ (Frequently Asked Question) list on their Web sites. The documentation that came with the video card may also have a troubleshooting guide in it.

1. Make sure the video card is firmly seated in the appropriate bus slot. There is actually little worry that you have a PCI card in an AGP slot or vice versa. One shouldn't fit in the other—if it was forced, the card is probably no longer good to use.

2. If the card requires it, verify that the card is properly connected to the power supply using one of the power supply's connectors. Most video cards that require power use the same type of power supply connector as a hard disk drive.
3. Verify that the video card has not been assigned system resources that had already been assigned to another conflicting device. Typically, video cards are not assigned IRQs, but check anyway; the card you are troubleshooting may just be one of the ones that do. Use the Windows Device Manager to check on this. If the video card has either a red *X* or a yellow exclamation mark by it, there is a problem with either a device driver or a system resource conflict.
4. Verify that the device drivers are installed. You may want to reinstall the device drivers before taking any other more drastic measures. Always use the device drivers that came with the video card or that you downloaded from the manufacturer's Web site. Avoid using the library drivers that come with Windows, as they are often out of date and can cause more problems.
5. Check the documentation of the video card. Many cards have specific requirements for the BIOS settings of the PC. If this is the case, reboot the PC and access the BIOS' configuration data by pressing the key (typically F1, F2, or DEL) during the boot sequence to enter the BIOS Startup program and the CMOS setup. Verify that the BIOS settings are correct for the video card. Often the Hidden Refresh, Byte Merge, Video BIOS shadow and cache RAM, VGA Palette Snoop, and DAC Snoop settings may need to be disabled. If you change any of the CMOS settings, be sure to save them before exiting.
6. If the above steps do not solve or isolate the problem, it's time to call technical support at the video card manufacturer or check with the reseller.

Determining the Type of Video Card in a PC

If you are in doubt about the type of video card installed or in use in a PC, use the DOS Debug utility, shown in Figure 12-7, which is included with virtually all versions of Windows. To use the DEBUG command to display the video card information on your PC, follow these steps:

1. Open a MS-DOS prompt or command line.
2. Type **debug** and press ENTER. A dash prompt is displayed.
3. Enter **d c000:0010** as shown in Figure 12-7.
4. After the first block of data is displayed, look at the text translation of binary data on the right side of the display. If the video card data is not shown, type **d** and press ENTER to display the next block of memory.
5. The video data should appear in either the first or second blocks.

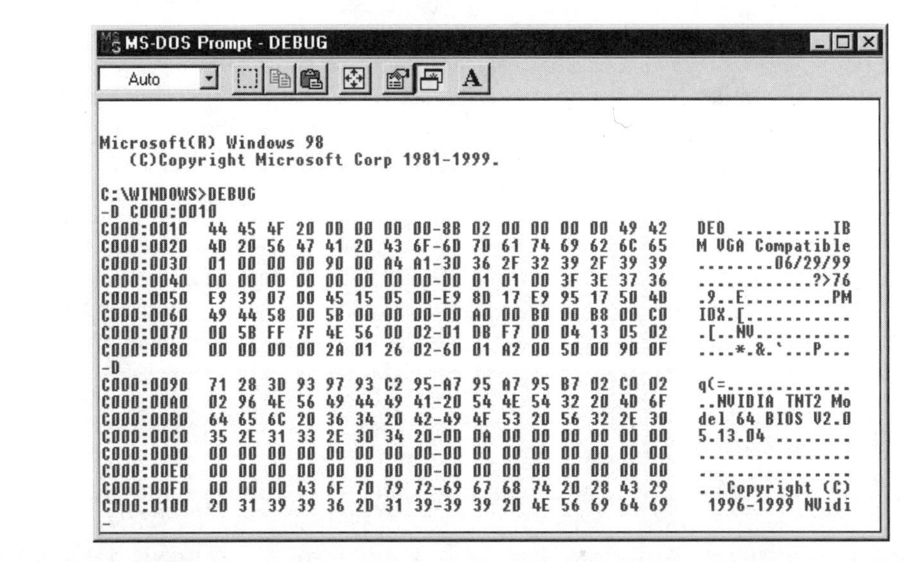

Figure 12-7. The DOS Debug command can be used to display the type of video adapter a PC is using

TROUBLESHOOTING VIDEO PROBLEMS

The following sections include some procedures you can use to troubleshoot specific video-related problems. If you are unsure of the problem, use the general steps listed in "Troubleshooting the Video Card."

Nothing Is Displayed on the Monitor

First thing, check the obvious:

- Is the monitor plugged into a power source?
- Is the monitor switched on?
- Is the monitor connected to the proper connection on the back of the PC?

If you really want to eliminate the monitor as a suspect (or confirm that it is the problem), try connecting another monitor (one that you know for sure works) to the PC. If it works, then the original monitor may be bad. If the second monitor does not work, then the problem is likely not the monitor.

If the above is as it should be, check the following:

1. When you boot the system, if you are getting three short beep tones or something similar (depending on your BIOS—see Chapter 6) and nothing is displaying on the monitor, your video card may be loose or defective.
2. Open up the system case and reseat the video card.
3. Reboot the system. If the problem persists, try the video card first in another slot on the same PC and if that fails, try it in another PC. If the card fails in the new system, it's time to get a new video card. If the video card works in either the new slot or PC, you may have a bad expansion slot on the motherboard. Hopefully, it is not the AGP slot, because that means you either need to switch to a PCI video card or get a new motherboard.

The Display Is Scrambled

If the display looks like the picture on a badly adjusted TV set, the problem is most likely that the refresh rate on the video card is set too high for your system. This is definitely the problem if the display is okay through the boot cycle and then fritzes out when Windows comes up. To fix this, do the following:

1. Boot into Windows Safe Mode by pressing the F8 key when Windows first starts up. When the Startup menu displays, select Safe Mode.
2. Windows will start up and load only the essential device drivers it needs to function. Once the Windows Desktop is displayed, right-click an empty part of the display on the Desktop shortcut menu (see the section "Resolution" earlier in the chapter). Select Properties to open the Display Properties window. Select the Settings tab and click on the Advanced button at the bottom of the display.
3. Select the Adapter tab and, as shown in Figure 12-8, a Refresh Rate setting is near the middle of the window. If it is not set to either Optimal or Adapter Default, you may want to check the documentation for the video card and monitor for the best rate. Typically, it will be around 70Hz or 72Hz. After clicking the OKs, restart the PC.

The Display Appears Fuzzy or Blurry

A blurry or snowy monitor could be a refresh rate problem (see "The Display is Scrambled" above). But if the refresh rate is set as it should be and you've had your eyes checked recently:

1. The problem is not likely the video card and is probably the settings on the monitor itself. Adjust the brightness and contrast settings on the monitor.
2. If the problem persists, the monitor may be defective.

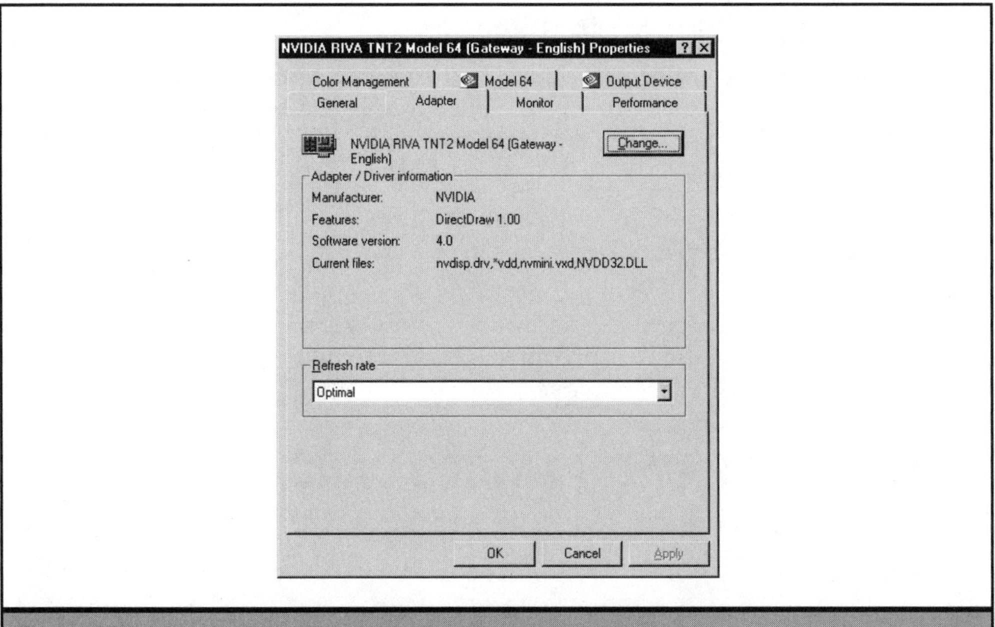

Figure 12-8. The Adapter tab on the Display Properties window

The Settings for the Video Card Are Not Listed in the Windows Display Settings

If you have tried to change the Desktop settings in Windows to reflect a new video card but only 640 × 480 and 16 colors are available, it is likely that the video card's software drivers are not installed or need to be reinstalled.

1. To check on which video device drivers are installed, open the Device Manager. To see which video driver you have currently installed, right-click on My Computer and select Properties.
2. Click on the Device Manager tab and find the video card entry. If the video card is a PCI card, you may need to drill down to it through the Plug and Play devices and the PCI bus entries. Once you have located it, if it is listed as Standard VGA, you need to install the device drivers for the video card.
3. To install the device drivers, use the disk or CD-ROM that came with your video card. If it doesn't start up by itself (which means, if it is a diskette), use the Add Hardware icon on the Control Panel to install the video card and its drivers. Be sure you click the Have Disk button when asked for the location of the drivers. If you can avoid it, never (repeat: never) use the driver from the Windows library when you have a disk.

Higher Resolutions Cannot Be Selected

If there is not enough RAM on the video card to support a higher resolution or color depth, it is likely that they are disabled on the Windows Display Settings window. In order to provide access to capabilities that the video card has within its specifications, you may need to add more memory.

1. Verify with the manufacturer how much additional video RAM can be added to the card and then follow the steps in "Upgrading the RAM on a Video Card" in the following section.
2. To calculate the amount of RAM needed to support the resolution and color depth you desire, use the calculations shown in "How Much Video Memory is Needed?" earlier in the chapter.

UPGRADING THE RAM ON A VIDEO CARD

The video RAM on many newer video cards can be upgraded to increase its speed, color palette, and the performance of its graphics.

1. Video RAM must be matched to the video card and to its bus structure (PCI, AGP, ISA). If you are unsure of the video card, see the "Determining the Type of Video Card in a PC" section.
2. Verify the amount of memory already installed on the card by the manufacturer and how much you can add. You should be able to get this from the card's documentation or from the manufacturer's Web site. You may need to call the technical support number of the manufacturer. If you really want to upgrade the video RAM on the video card, you need to know these facts. Typically, you should add memory in 2MB increments, but follow the advice of the manufacturer on this.
3. You must remove the video card from the PC to add video RAM to it. Be sure you are working on a flat surface that is ESD protected.
4. Follow the instructions in the video card's documentation on the manufacturer's Web site for how new memory chips are installed on the card. However, if none are available, use the following generic steps.
5. Locate the mounting on the card for the memory chip. The mounting should have four toothed edges that align with four dots on the corners of the memory chip. Align the edges and dots and push the memory chip into place, making sure the chip is firmly in place and will not fall off.
6. You can verify that the new video RAM is recognized by the system by checking the BIOS configuration data. Reboot the system (you need to anyway) and enter the BIOS setup utility. From the Startup menu, select Devices and I/O Ports and then choose Video Setup. The amount of video RAM recognized by the PC is listed. If the amount is not the new total, check the installation of the video RAM on the card and verify that the card is installed correctly.

CHAPTER 13

System Resources

The microprocessor, aka the processor or the CPU, controls either completely or in part the activities of all of the devices that are integrated into or attached to the motherboard of the PC. This control comes about from the CPU's ability to communicate its commands, requests, and data directly to each device over private communications vehicles that are created specifically for each device. In addition to the CPU needing to communicate with the PC's devices, the devices also need to be able to get the CPU's attention from time to time to request an action or service from the CPU, such as getting data from the keyboard, reading data from a disk drive, or printing information on the printer.

For the sake of explanation, let's say a PC has ten internal devices to which it must communicate commands, addresses, and data. (PCs typically have more than ten devices to control, but ten should be sufficient in this example to help you understand how the CPU communicates with the devices of the PC.) One way to ensure that the CPU is able to communicate to each device directly is to link it to each device with a dedicated bus line. However, this approach has two problems: it adds complexity to the motherboard's circuitry, and it limits the PC to only the number of devices for which dedicated buses are provided. The first problem adds too much cost and the second issue is much too limiting.

Getting the CPU's Attention

When a device needs the CPU to perform an operation for it, it must first get the CPU's attention. In our example of a PC with ten internal devices, the CPU may be busy taking care of another device's request when another device needs it. Think of an elementary school teacher with ten students all wanting his or her attention. As fast as everything inside the PC is happening, when the device needs the CPU, it needs it now. In much the same way that elementary students raise their hands to get noticed, each device must have a means of getting the CPU's attention.

If each device had control of a toggle switch that it could flip to turn a light on whenever it needed services from the CPU, the CPU could constantly scan for it, even if it was busy. When a particular device's light went on and the CPU got to a point where it could set aside whatever it was doing, it would take care of the new request. Each time a new light was switched on, the CPU would interrupt what it was doing to take care of the request. Remember that the CPU does a lot more than just handle device requests.

Communicating to Devices

As soon as the CPU completes the tasks it was requested to do, it communicates back to the requesting device that the task is completed. To do this, it must have a means—just switching off the request light would not be enough in most cases. For example, if a device asks the CPU to get some data from memory, it needs to know where the CPU put the data. It would be very difficult to convey the address of a data location through a toggle switch. So, each of the devices connected to the PC is assigned its own two-way mailbox.

These mailboxes work almost like a private mail system inside the PC. Devices get messages and data from their own mailboxes and they pass messages and data to other devices through their mailboxes. After the CPU completes the requested task, any data or instructions it needs to pass back to the requesting device is placed in the mailbox assigned to that device.

Taking Control

Some devices have the ability to serve themselves for some actions and don't need to bother the CPU at all. This allows the CPU to continue to serve other requests and not be interrupted or need to pass messages back to interrupting devices. Most of the actions requested of the CPU by devices center around moving data in and out of memory. A device that has the ability to directly access memory on its own without the need to interrupt the CPU helps the whole PC operate more efficiently.

The PC's System Resources

The system resources of a PC, described in general terms above, are a set of three mechanisms used by a PC's devices and the CPU to communicate.

- **Interrupt request (IRQ)** The mechanism used by devices to request services from the CPU. The IRQ is actually a wire on the motherboard bus over which a signal is sent by a device to get the CPU's attention. There are 16 IRQs on all newer (since the PC XT) PCs. However, only 10 of them are available for devices. The remaining 6 are reserved for system-level purposes.
- **Input/output (I/O) address** The message box used by the CPU to pass information to each of the devices on the PC. Every device attached to the PC has an I/O address.
- **Direct memory access (DMA)** A limited number of DMA channels are available to devices that need the speed of accessing memory directly without the assistance of the CPU.

INTERRUPT REQUEST (IRQ)

Peripheral devices communicate directly to the CPU through an interrupt request (IRQ). When a device needs services that only the CPU can perform, it sets an IRQ to get the CPU's attention. The CPU reacts to the IRQ by interrupting its activities to service the request. There are 16 IRQs available, and they are assigned to devices that require the CPU to handle data movement, data interpretation, error processing, and other tasks.

On the original PC design (the IBM PC and PC XT), only 8 IRQs were available. Today's PC has 16 IRQs that are made up of two sets of 8 IRQs linked together by an IRQ in one set that points to an IRQ in the other set.. Of the 16 IRQs, 5 are set aside for use by internal system-level devices and one is used as the link between the two IRQ sets, leaving 10 available for assignments to I/O devices. Table 13-1 lists the standard default assignments of IRQs.

IRQ	Assignment
0	System timer
1	Standard keyboard
2	Programmable interrupt controller (PIC)
3	Serial ports 2 and 4 (COM2 and COM4)
4	Serial ports 1 and 3 (COM1 and COM3)
5	Standard sound card
6	Floppy disk controller (FDC)
7	Parallel port (LPT1)
8	CMOS and real-time clock (RTC)
9	Hardware MPEG
10	Modem audio
11	VGA video card
12	PS/2 mouse
13	Math coprocessor/numeric data processor
14	Primary IDE controller
15	Secondary IDE controller

Table 13-1. Typical IRQ Assignments

Checking Out IRQ Settings

Not every PC has all of the devices listed in Table 13-1. In fact, on any PC, the IRQs can be assigned differently. To find what the IRQ settings are on a Windows PC, use the following steps:

1. From the Windows Desktop, right-click the My Computer icon. From the shortcut menu that appears, choose Properties to display the System Properties window, shown in Figure 13-1.
2. Select the Device Manager tab. Highlight the Computer entry and click the Properties button located at the bottom of the device window. This displays the Computer Properties window, shown in Figure 13-2.
3. Select the View Resources tab and click the Interrupt Request (IRQ) radio button to display the IRQ assignments on your PC.

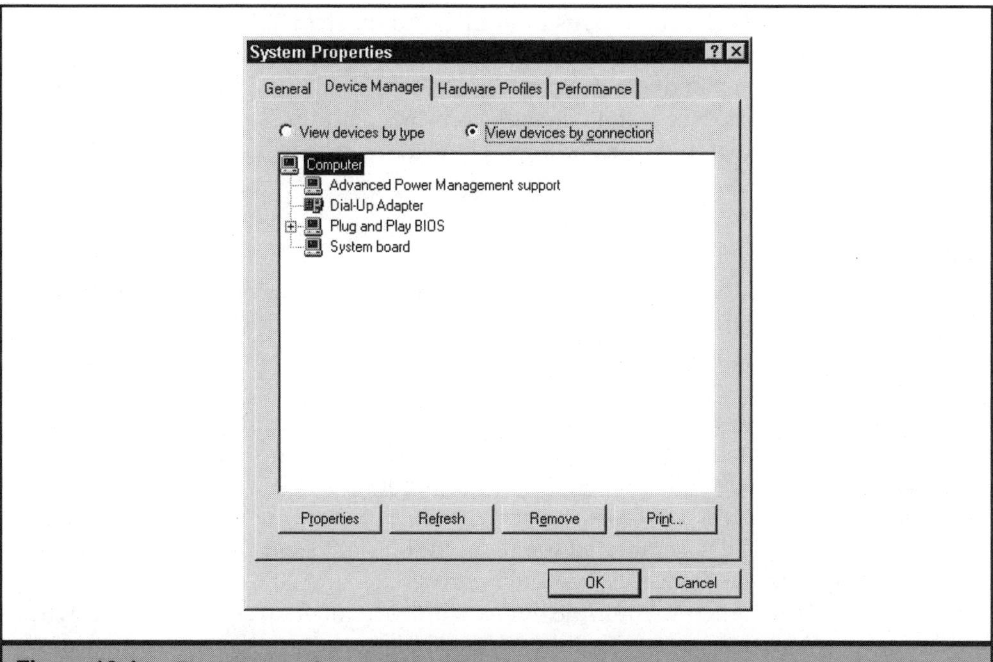

Figure 13-1. The Windows System Properties window

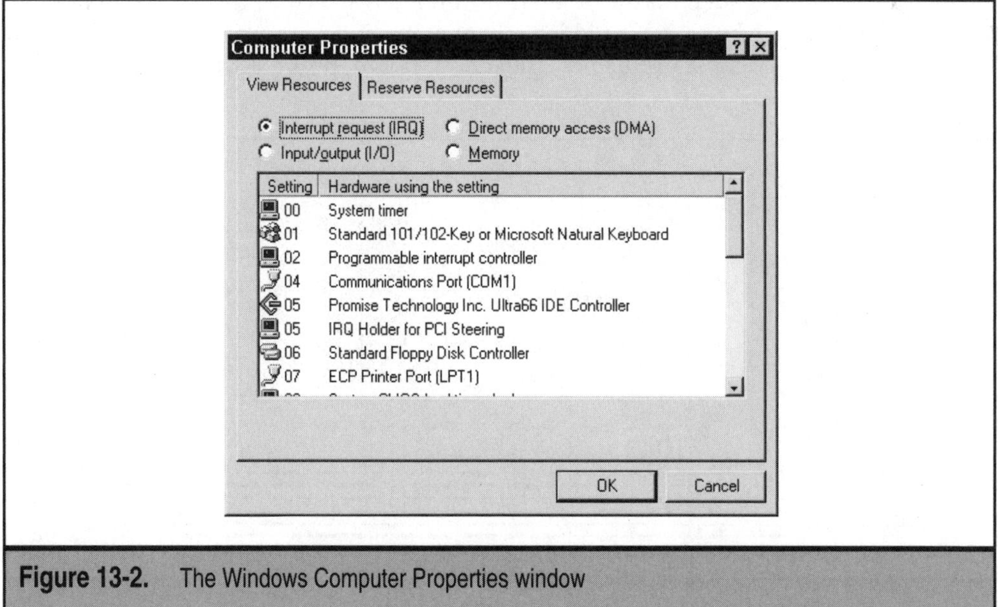

Figure 13-2. The Windows Computer Properties window

4. Compare the IRQ assignments of your PC to those in Table 13-1. They should match for the most part. Any exceptions are likely because of Plug-and-Play devices or adjustments that were made to avoid conflicts (more on that later). If there are differences, don't change your IRQ settings. Table 13-1 lists typical, or what are called default, settings. They are by no means the only settings that will work.

IRQ Connections

Interrupt requests are wires in the system bus on the motherboard. Each IRQ wire is connected to every one of the expansion slots on the motherboard. Regardless of which expansion slot an I/O adapter is placed in, it has access to the IRQs of the PC. As illustrated in Figure 13-3, each expansion slot can be assigned a particular IRQ line. The type of controller or adapter and its preset values determines which IRQ line it is assigned. Each device can have only one IRQ assignment. The number of the assigned IRQ is what identifies the device to the CPU when the device requests services.

When a device sends an IRQ signal over its bus line, the bus line number identifies the device. When the CPU has completed the requested task, it sends a clearing signal over the IRQ bus line and the device knows it may proceed.

An IRQ can be assigned to multiple devices, but you must do so carefully. If two active devices are sharing a single IRQ, the CPU will have no way of knowing which device sent the request. In fact, the CPU never knows if there is more than one device on an IRQ; it only knows that whatever is attached to the other end of the IRQ line has sent a request for services. If two devices are in contention for a single IRQ line, one device could be trying to process data intended for the other. In addition, there is the physical danger of two active devices sending bus signals (which means a certain number of volts on the line) at the same time. This could short the bus, the motherboard, or the device controller.

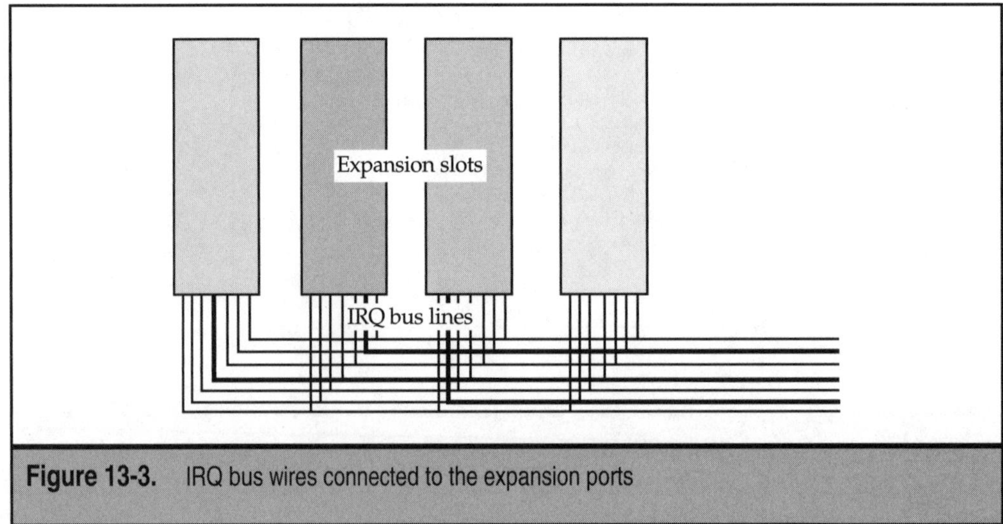

Figure 13-3. IRQ bus wires connected to the expansion ports

Typically, if two devices share an IRQ, like the COM ports listed in Table 13-1, only one can be active at a time. On early systems, it was a common problem for the mouse and the modem to end up on the same IRQ, since both devices were commonly connected to serial ports. There really wasn't a problem, until you needed to use the mouse while the modem was operating. On today's PCs, it is fairly common for a scanner or a Zip drive to share the parallel port and IRQ7 with a printer.

IRQs have priorities set by the system that determine which IRQ is to be handled if two or more requests come in at the same time. The programmable interrupt controller (PIC), discussed later in the chapter, manages priorities and other IRQ control issues.

IRQ Assignments

The IRQ assigned to a device is usually determined by common practice and any working standards currently in use in the computing industry. There has never been a set-in-stone standard for IRQ assignments. Manufacturers of processors, motherboards, chipsets, and I/O adapters have more or less created the default settings currently used in the industry.

Table 13-2 compares the IRQ settings of the three primary bus structures that are used in PCs. Notice that even Tables 13-1 and 13-2 differ slightly. Table 13-1 shows common IRQ settings used today and Table 13-2 shows the default settings that were or are used on different bus structures.

IRQ	Slot Size (bits)	PC XT Bus	PC AT Bus	Current (Pentium-class PCs)
0	n/a	System timer	System timer	System timer
1	n/a	Keyboard controller	Keyboard controller	Keyboard controller
2	n/a	8-bit Available	2nd IRQ Controller	2nd IRQ Controller
3	8-bit	COM2/COM4	COM2/COM4	COM2/COM4
4	8-bit	COM1/COM3	COM1/COM3	COM1/COM3
5	8-bit	Hard disk controller (HDC)	LPT2	Sound Card

Table 13-2. IRQ Assignments on Bus Structures

IRQ	Slot Size (bits)	PC XT Bus	PC AT Bus	Current (Pentium-class PCs)
6	8-bit	Floppy disk controller (FDC)	FDC	FDC
7	8-bit	LPT1	LPT1	LPT1
8	n/a	Real-time clock (RTC)	RTC	RTC
9	8-bit	n/a	Available	Available
10	16-bit	n/a	Available	Available
11	16-bit	n/a	Available	Available
12	16-bit	n/a	PS/2 mouse	PS/2 mouse
13	n/a	n/a	Math coprocessor	Math coprocessor
14	16-bit	n/a	HDC	Primary IDE controller
15	16-bit	n/a	Available	Secondary IDE controller

Table 13-2. IRQ Assignments on Bus Structures *(continued)*

Configuring IRQ Settings

There is a variety of ways to set an IRQ setting for a particular adapter or controller expansion cards. Most of today's expansion cards are PCI (Peripheral Component Interconnect) and are Plug-and-Play compatible (more on this later in this section). However, ISA (Industry Standard Architecture), EISA (Extended ISA), and VESA (Video Electronics Standards Association) local bus cards are still supported on most PC motherboards, and these cards require different amounts of physical setup to assign their IRQ (and other system resource settings).

Regardless of the method used to set the IRQ for a new device, the current IRQ settings should be reviewed before the new card is installed and configured. You should also review the documentation of the new device to determine the IRQ (and system resource) settings it wishes to use. If the default IRQ of the device is available on the system, there should not be any problems with the installation and operation of the device. However, if it is not available, you may need to reassign the IRQ or to reconfigure the new device to an available IRQ.

Jumper Settings

Older adapter cards, especially video or network interface cards, use jumper blocks to set their IRQ settings. The position of the jumper, like those shown in Figure 13-4 on a NIC card, determines which of usually two alternative IRQs the card will use. Cards that use jumpers to set their system resources are usually preset to a default setting but offer one or more alternative settings using different positions of the jumper block. A two-position jumper (one with two pins) can be set to four different values, and a three-position jumper can be set to eight different values.

DIP Switches

Another means used to configure the system resources of an expansion card is a DIP (dual inline packaging) switch. A DIP switch is a block of typically four or eight switches (as illustrated in Figure 13-5) that are used, like a jumper, to represent a binary value by moving the switches to on or off positions, also referred to as open or closed positions. A card that uses DIP switches to set its system resource settings should also have a manual or other documentation that specifies the switch settings to use for each resource value.

Proprietary Installation Software

Another common means of configuring the system resource settings for an expansion card is a proprietary installation program that comes with the card on a diskette or CD-ROM. Some diskettes may only include a startup program that downloads the installation software from the manufacturer's Web site. This ensures that the latest system resource setting values and device drivers are used to install the device.

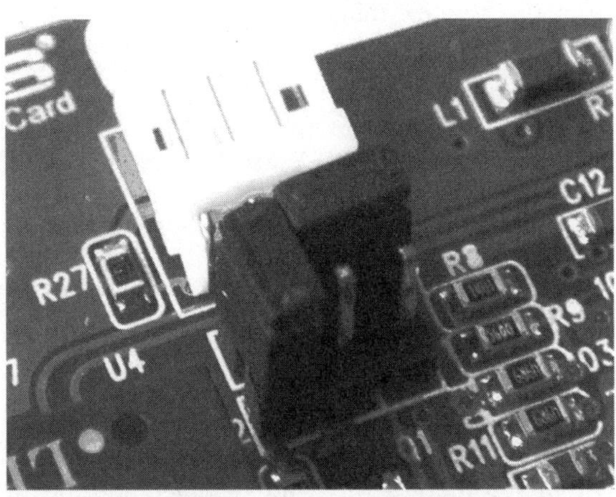

Figure 13-4. A set of jumper blocks on an expansion card

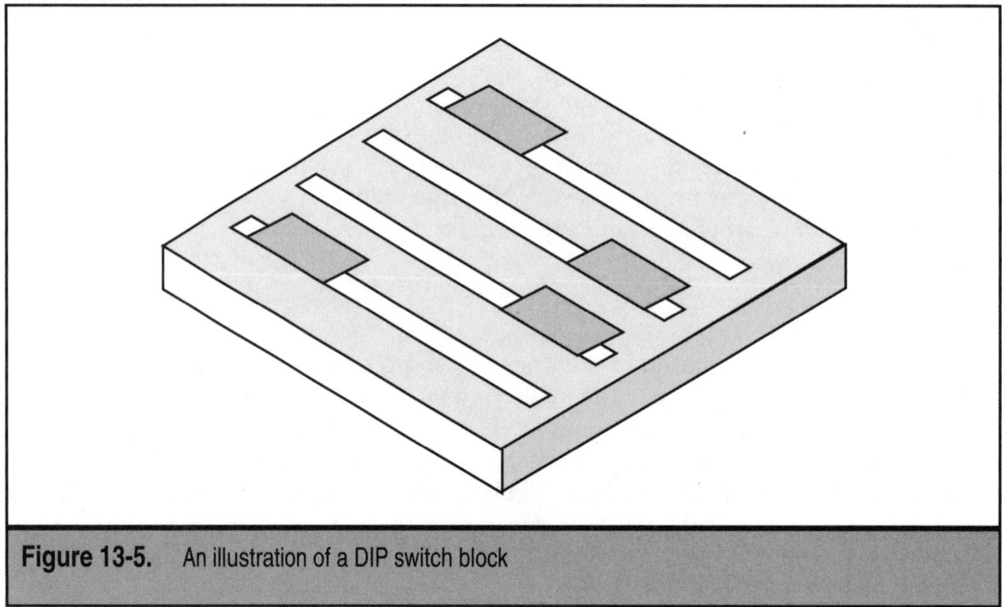

Figure 13-5. An illustration of a DIP switch block

Some installation software can read the IRQ settings and adjust the IRQ assignment for its device. However, this is rare, and you should always verify the system resources assigned by a manufacturer's installation software and check for resource conflicts.

Setting an IRQ with the Windows Device Manager

About the only time you use the Windows Device Manager to configure IRQs is after a Plug-and-Play device or proprietary installation program has created a conflict by assigning a new device to an IRQ already in use by another device.

When you open the Device Manager, its default view lists the PC's devices by type, which means the general category of each device, as shown earlier in Figure 13-1. By clicking the plus sign (+) next to each category, you can expand the device list to show the devices installed in a category.

If there are any problems with the device, it is indicated with one of three symbols:

- **A yellow circle with a black exclamation point** This symbol before a device name (see Figure 13-6) indicates a possible resource conflict.
- **A red *X*** This symbol before a device name indicates the device has been disabled, removed, or that Windows is unable to locate it.
- **A white circle with a blue lowercase *i*** This symbol before a device name indicates only that automatic settings are disabled and the device was configured manually, possibly under software control. There is no problem, necessarily; this symbol is just a reminder.

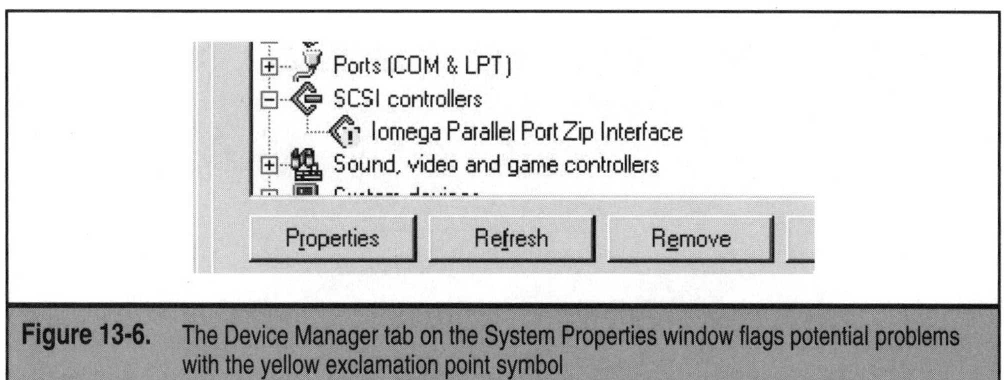

Figure 13-6. The Device Manager tab on the System Properties window flags potential problems with the yellow exclamation point symbol

Of course, your first clue that an IRQ conflict may exist is if a new device isn't working properly, if an existing device suddenly stops working, or if, when you begin using either a new or existing device, another device stops working. If a resource conflict is detected, Windows will mark it (as described in the preceding bullets) in the Windows System Properties Device Manager tab.

If there is a device conflict, the details of the problem are listed in the Properties window for the device itself in the Conflicting Device List box at the bottom of the window. Figure 13-7 shows a device with no device conflicts, so if this device is having problems it is more likely to be a device driver issue than an IRQ conflict.

If you encounter an IRQ or I/O address conflict with a device, it may be necessary to change its resource assignments. If required, follow these steps to change the resource settings for a hardware device on a Windows PC:

1. On the Device Manager Devices By Type list, locate the device for which you need to change the IRQ setting.
2. Highlight the device name and click the Properties button or double-click the device's name to display its Properties window.
3. Choose the Resources tab. The display should be very much like that in Figure 13-6.
4. Depending on the version of Windows running on the PC, you will have a check box labeled Use Automatic Settings or something similar. Deselect this box to leave it unchecked.
5. Highlight the IRQ setting and click the Change Resource button to open the display shown in Figure 13-8.

Linksys LNE100TX Fast Ethernet Adapter Propert...

General | Driver | Resources

Linksys LNE100TX Fast Ethernet Adapter

Use automatic settings

Setting based on: Basic configuration 0000

Resource type	Setting
Interrupt Request	10
Memory Range	F4020000 - F40200FF
Input/Output Range	1000 - 10FF

Change Setting...

Conflicting device list:

No conflicts.

OK Cancel

Figure 13-7. The Device Manager Properties window showing no resource conflicts

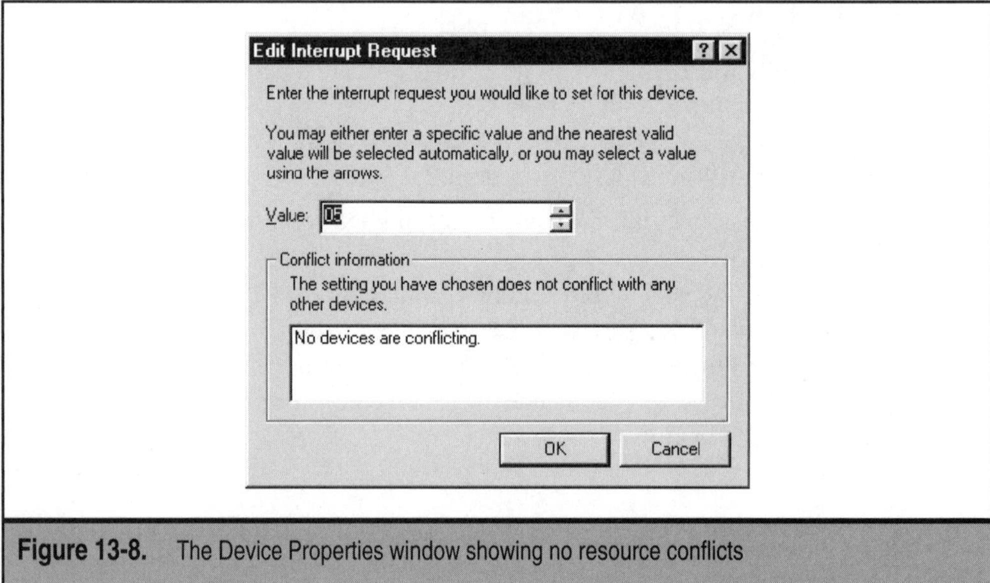

Figure 13-8. The Device Properties window showing no resource conflicts

You may find that very few of your system resources can actually be changed and when you attempt to change a resource an error message box pops up telling you that you cannot change the values of a resource. The primary reasons for this condition are:

- The device is a legacy device and its resource settings are configured with jumpers or DIP switches on the adapter card.
- The device is integrated into the motherboard or chipset or mounted to the motherboard through a riser (daughter) board and has a preset resource setting.
- The device cannot be configured to any of the available resources, and resources must be freed up.

Resource Error Codes in the Windows Device Manager

If a resource conflict exists and you are unsure of the source of the problem, you should look on the General tab of the device's Properties window. Figure 13-9 shows a device with no problems; if a problem did exist related to the device's system resource settings, an error code and message would be included in the Device Status box. Windows 98/2000 PCs include a Solutions button that suggests possible solutions.

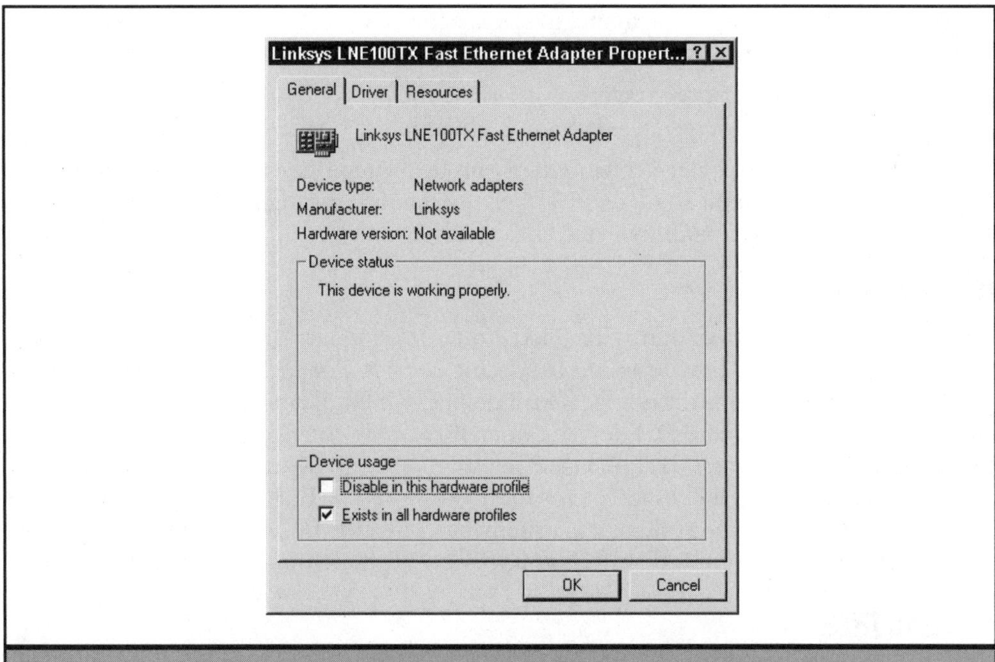

Figure 13-9. The Device Status box on the General tab of a Device Properties window

There are many (about 35 and growing) Device Manager error codes, most of which deal with device driver issues, but here are the codes that relate to resource conflicts:

- **Code 6** Another device is already assigned the resources needed by the device. The solution is to change the new device's resource settings.
- **Code 9** The BIOS is reporting the device's system resources incorrectly. It could be that you only need to remove the device from the Device Manager and let the system detect and install it, or you may need to upgrade the BIOS on the PC.
- **Code 12** No free resources of at least one type are available to assign to the device. Another device must be removed or disabled, or its resources must be shared before the new device can be installed successfully.
- **Code 15** The device is causing a resource conflict and must be reconfigured.
- **Code 16** Windows cannot identify the resource needed by the device. You may need to fill in some missing resources on the device's Properties window. Follow the device documentation for the values you should use.
- **Code 17** A child device has been assigned a resource not assigned to the parent. Either use automatic settings or configure the device to be compatible to its parent.
- **Code 27** Windows is unable to specify the resources for the device as configured. Check the documentation and make any necessary adjustments.
- **Code 29** No resources were assigned to the device by the PC's BIOS. Most likely the device needs to be enabled in the CMOS setup data.
- **Code 30** The device is trying to use an IRQ already assigned to another device that cannot share its IRQ. Change the IRQ setting for the device or find a more compatible device with which to share.

BIOS Settings

If automatic resource allocation is disabled, you can designate the IRQs and DMA channels you want Plug and Play to assign to specific devices. For each IRQ or DMA channel, you can designate whether it is a PCI/PnP device, which means it is available to be assigned to Plug and Play and PCI devices, or an ISA Legacy device, which is not available for automatic assignment. PCI/PnP is the default type on all Pentium-class or later PCs.

You can typically set the resource type for IRQs 3, 4, 5, 7, 9, 10, 11, 12, 14, and 15, with the rest reserved for use by the system. It is usually best to let the IRQs default to PCI/PnP unless there are one or two particular IRQs you wish to specifically reserve for legacy devices.

PCI and IRQs

PCI devices can share a single IRQ because it has a group of interrupts that are internal to the PCI bus. The internal PCI interrupts are mapped to the single system IRQ, typically IRQ 9, 10, 11, or 12, through a process called *IRQ steering*.

Each PCI expansion slot has four interrupts of its own, which are designated PIRQs (PCI interrupt requests) A through D. The PCI expansion card determines which of the four it will use, normally PIRQ A. Without IRQ steering, the system BIOS would assign each slot to a different IRQ and potentially cause conflicts or a lack of resources for other devices. IRQ steering is available on Windows versions beginning with Windows 95 OSR2 (OEM). For IRQ steering to work correctly, the BIOS, chipset, PCI cards, and the software drivers must all support it.

However, if there are IRQ conflicts between PCI devices, you may need to disable PCI bus IRQ steering to determine where the conflicts occur.

To check if IRQ steering is enabled on your system, follow these steps:

1. Open the Windows Device Manager. Click the plus sign (+) to expand the System Devices device type.
2. Highlight the selection for PCI Bus and click Properties.
3. Select the IRQ Steering tab to display the window shown in Figure 13-10.

In order for IRQ steering to be activated, the Use IRQ Steering check box must be checked. The other check boxes on this window tell IRQ steering where it should look for its IRQ routing information:

- **ACPI (advanced configuration and power interface) BIOS** This setting indicates that this is the first IRQ routing table Windows should use to program IRQ steering. ACPI is a power management specification that provides hardware status information to the operating system.
- **MS specification table** This setting indicates that the MS (Microsoft) specification table is the second IRQ routing table that Windows should use to program IRQ steering.
- **PCI BIOS 2.1 real mode** This selection is not checked by default and should be selected only if a PCI device is not working properly. When checked, it specifies that this is the third IRQ routing table that Windows should use to program IRQ steering.
- **PCI BIOS 2.1 protected mode** This setting indicates that this routing table is also to be used by Windows to program IRQ steering.

If the BIOS is struggling with a PCI device, you may want to try a different combination of options, including selecting the PCI BIOS 2.1 real mode. But, in most cases, if the default selections do not work, it is more likely that you need to update the BIOS. One surefire way to tell that you may need a BIOS update is that IRQ steering is causing the system to lock up or kernal32.dll error messages.

To deselect IRQ steering, merely click the Use IRQ Steering check box and reboot the system.

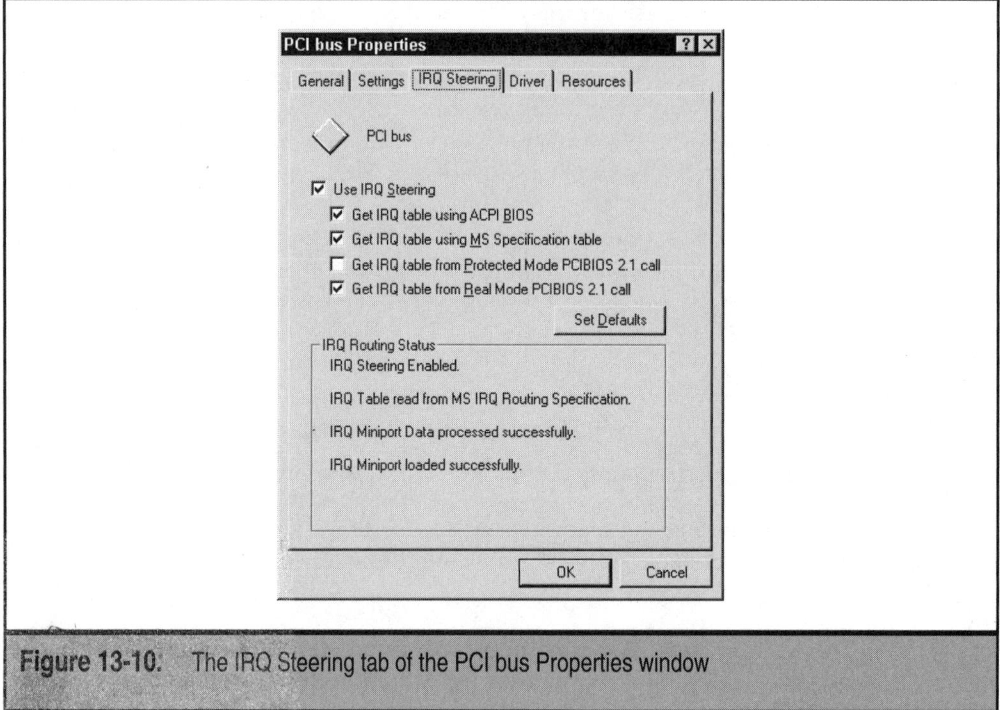

Figure 13-10. The IRQ Steering tab of the PCI bus Properties window

Plug and Play Resource Assignments

Plug and Play (PnP) is a device configuration feature that must be supported by the operating system, chipset, and BIOS on the PC. With this support, a new hardware device that is attached to a port or an expansion slot connected directly to the motherboard can be automatically detected and configured for system resource assignments.

However, PnP is not without its problems, not the least of which are IRQ conflicts. PnP is limited to those IRQs that have been designated for PCI/PnP use. The system is limited to PCI/PnP and legacy ISA devices. PnP does not work on legacy ISA devices. By the way, all PCI devices are PnP devices, but not all PnP devices are PCI. Should a new device require a certain IRQ, or should the system run out of available IRQs to assign, PnP cannot itself overcome the problem. In these cases, the device will be added to the system (and listed on the Device Manager) but will be flagged with a symbol (either a yellow exclamation point or a red *X*) to indicate a problem exists.

Programmable Interrupt Controllers

Interrupt requests (IRQs) are handled by two special integrated circuits called programmable interrupt controllers (PICs) that are integrated in the PC's chipset, along with many other devices (see Chapter 5 for more information on chipsets). Each PIC contains the circuits and logic required to control eight IRQ lines. Figure 13-11 illustrates the general design of a PIC. It is called a *programmable controller* because chipset, processor, and motherboard manufacturers can program the chip and address each of its registers to fit a particular purpose or function.

Figure 13-11 shows how the PIC works in general. The individual IRQ lines have one interrupt mask register (IMR) and two interrupt status registers, which are named PIC1 and PIC2. The IRQ enters the PIC through its IMR, which determines if the IRQ is masked (disabled) and if it is, the request is ignored. If the IRQ is not masked, the request is recorded in the interrupt request register (IRR). The IRR holds the IRQ requests until after they have been processed or acknowledged, depending on the service or action requested. The priority resolver (PR) acts as a sort of traffic cop to ensure that the highest priority request is handled first. IRQ priority is essentially the lowest number first. Once the IRQs are prepared for processing, the CPU is notified on its INT (interrupt) line that requests are pending and, as soon as it completes its current task, the CPU responds with an interrupt acknowledgment (INTA).

After the CPU acknowledges the INT query, the active IRQ is placed in the in-service register (ISR) that holds the IRQ currently being processed. The fact that this IRQ is being serviced is also updated in the IRR and the applicable ISR. The address of the IRQ is sent to the CPU, and the IRQ is serviced. When the requested activity is completed, the ISR

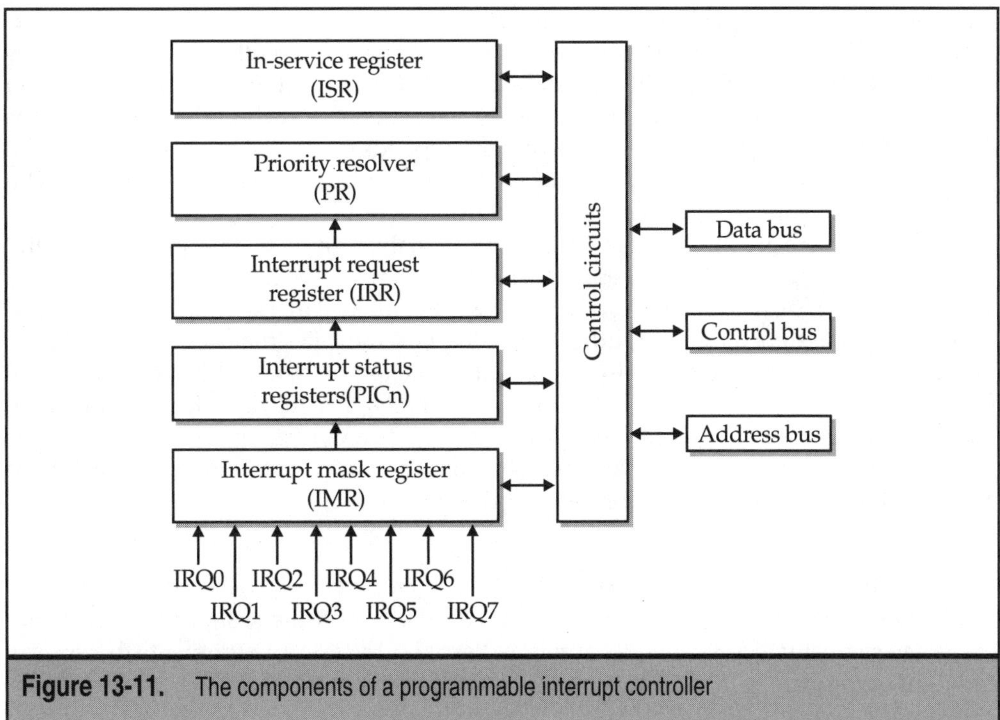

Figure 13-11. The components of a programmable interrupt controller

tells the PIC that the IRQ has ended and the ISR is cleared. The highest priority IRQ pending in the IRR is then placed in the ISR, and the process repeats.

I/O ADDRESSES

As I explained earlier in the chapter, the CPU and peripheral devices must have a way to communicate with each other and a place to store messages and data they need to pass to other devices. To that end, each device is assigned a small space in memory where it can place and receive data. This area is called by many names: the I/O address, the I/O port, the I/O base address, and a few others. It is most commonly referred to as an I/O address or the address through which a device performs its input and output operations.

For example, when a network adapter gets information from the CPU to send over the network, the data is placed in the NIC's I/O address. When the NIC gets data from the network to pass to the CPU, the data is placed in the NIC's I/O address. Each device has an I/O buffer assigned to it that should be large enough for the tasks it performs and the data it handles.

This approach to how devices communicate is called Memory-Mapped I/O. Each device is mapped to a specific location in memory (hence the name). After a device has placed data in its I/O address area, it contacts the CPU to let it know the data is ready, perhaps with an IRQ. If the CPU knows which device it is servicing, it knows where in memory that device's I/O buffer is located.

Not every device processes the same amount of data; as a result, I/O addresses vary in size. A NIC must handle much more data than a keyboard and therefore needs a bigger I/O area to buffer its incoming and outgoing data than the keyboard ever needs. The amount of space assigned to a particular device depends on its design and the bus architecture it uses. Most devices use 4, 8, or 16 bytes, but there are some devices that use as little as 1 byte and some that use as much as 64 bytes.

Although there are thousands of I/O areas available, conflicts do occur when multiple devices try to use the I/O address, which represents only the first byte of a device's assigned I/O area, or when devices have overlapping areas. For example, network cards are commonly assigned the I/O address of 360h (the *h* indicates that the I/O address is a hexadecimal number and is usually expressed as such). The default I/O address for the first parallel port (LPT1) is 378h. If the NIC requires 32 bytes of I/O space, its ending address would be 37Fh. As you can see, this would create an overlapping conflict with the parallel port. If there are no parallel devices in use, this isn't a problem, but if a printer is attached to the LPT1 port, a different location needs to be assigned to the NIC.

Common I/O Address Assignments

While there are no hard and fast rules or standards that set the assignment of I/O addresses in stone, there is a generally accepted list of I/O address assignments that is used throughout the computing industry. Table 13-3 lists the most common or default I/O address assignments used on PCs.

I/O Address (hexadecimal)	Size in Bytes	Assigned To
0000 – 000F	16	Slave DMA controller chip
0010 – 001F	16	System
0060 – 0063	4	Keyboard
0064 – 0067	4	PS/2 port
00C0 – 00DE	32	Master DMA controller
0130 – 014F	32	SCSI host adapter
01F0 – 01F7	8	Primary IDE channel
0200 – 0207	8	Game port
0220 – 022F	16	Sound card
0270 – 0273	4	Plug-and-Play hardware
0278 – 027A	2	Parallel port (LPT2)
0280 – 028F	16	LCD Display
02E8 – 02EF	8	Serial Port—COM4
02F8 – 02FF	8	Serial Port—COM2
0300 – 031F	32	Network interface cards
0320 – 032F	16	Legacy hard disk controllers
0330 – 0331	2	MIDI interface
0360 – 036F	16	Network interface cards (alternate)
0378 – 037A	2	Parallel port (LPT1)
03C0 – 03DF	32	VGA video display adaptor
03E0 – 03E7	8	PC Card (PCMCIA) port controller
03E8 – 03EF	8	Serial Port—COM3
03F0 – 03F6	8	Floppy disk drive interface
03F8 – 03FF	8	Serial Port—COM1
0533 – 0537	4	Windows sound system
0678 – 067F	8	EPP parallel port
0CF8 – 0CFB	4	PCI data registers
FF00 – FF07	8	IDE bus mastering

Table 13-3. Commonly Used I/O Address Assignments

There are 65,536 bytes available between 0000h and FFFFh. Table 13-3 does not list every possible I/O address assignment, but because they are uniform in size or layout, there are on occasion not enough I/O ports to go around. In addition to those listed in Table 13-3, there are several other I/O address assignments that are commonly used for supplemental space for some devices, such as IDE bus mastering, serial ports, parallel ports, and IDE controllers, which further complicates their assignments.

I/O addresses are intended to be assigned to a single device. Multiple devices sharing an I/O port would have the same disastrous results as multiple active devices sharing an IRQ. There would be no way for the CPU or the devices to know the device a message was intended for or from which data was being sent. There are some legacy situations, such as on parallel ports and ISA adapters, where it is necessary on occasion to double up on a particular address, but they are disappearing. ISA adapter cards typically can be configured to only one or two I/O addresses on the card with a jumper or DIP switch setting. This limitation can create an I/O address collision with another legacy device.

I/O Addresses in Windows

Like IRQs, I/O address assignments can be viewed on a Windows PC through the Device Manager. Figure 13-12 shows the Computer Properties window with the I/O addresses resources displayed. As you scroll down the list, you will see the PC's devices assigned to various I/O addresses. You may also see entries that are listed as In Use by an Unknown Device or listed as Alias To entries for devices requiring additional space.

As with IRQs, you can access an individual device (see Figure 13-13) to view its specific I/O address assignment. You can also resolve any conflicts listed by assigning the

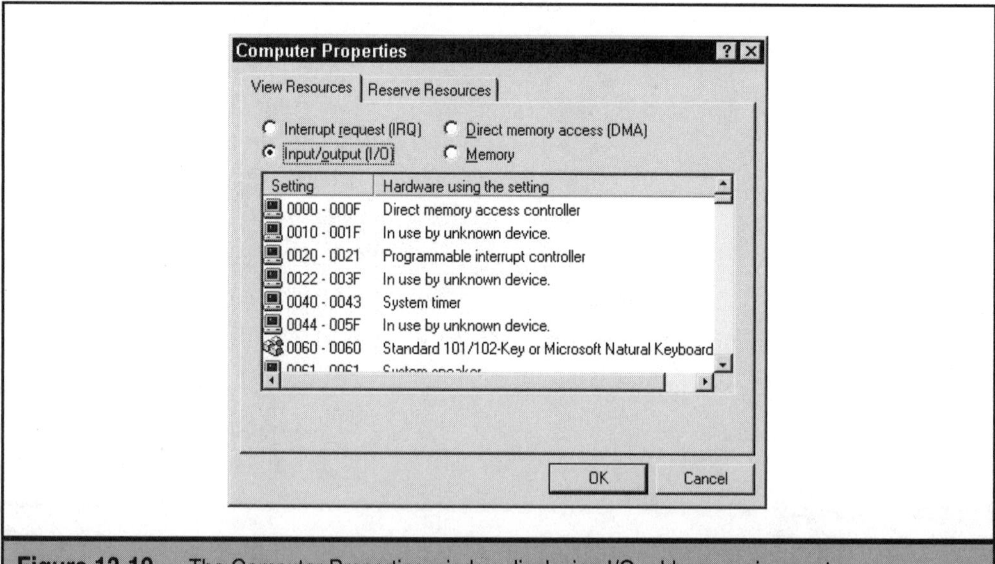

Figure 13-12. The Computer Properties window displaying I/O address assignments

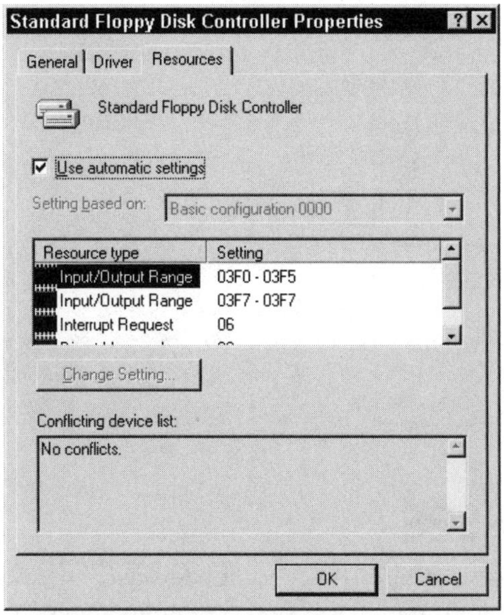

Figure 13-13. The Properties window of a specific device showing its I/O address assignments

device to a different I/O address. Remember that it is unusual for a PC to have even two serial ports or parallel ports. The I/O addresses for the second serial port or the second parallel port are set aside and are usually available for use, if needed.

Logical Devices

In computing, physical and logical have opposite meanings, although they can be used to describe the same input/output or storage devices. A physical device is the actual hardware and its support circuitry, such as a serial or a parallel port. A logical device is a serial or parallel port and disk drive, devices that are assigned a name that can be used in lieu of its actual (and physical) address. For example, the first serial port on a PC may have a 32-bit address that would be very awkward for general reference use. A logical name like COM1 is much more practical for referencing the PC's first serial port. Likewise, LPT1 is the logical name of the first parallel port and A: and C: are the logical device names for the floppy disk drive and the hard disk drive, respectively.

The POST (Power-On Self-Test) process assigns logical device names during the system boot sequence. The BIOS locates each physical device using a predefined order of I/O addresses of each device and assigns it an appropriate logical name. The serial ports become COM ports; the parallel ports are assigned the logical name of LPT; and the disk drives are identified as A:, B:, C:, etc. Table 13-4 lists the logical device names assigned to the COM and LPT ports.

Logical Device	I/O Address	IRQ
COM1	3F8 – 3FFh	4
COM2	2F8 – 2FFh	3
COM3	3E8 – 3Efh	4
COM4	2E8 – 2Efh	3
LPT1	378 – 37Fh	7
LPT2	278 – 27Fh	5

Table 13-4. Logical Device Names for Serial and Parallel Ports

MEMORY ADDRESSES

In addition to or in place of I/O addresses, many devices require a block of memory in the upper memory area for their own use. This block of memory, referred to in conjunction with the system resources used by the device, is primarily for mapping a device BIOS into memory or as a temporary holding area for data it is using or both. Memory address blocks are assigned during the system boot process.

These memory blocks are not system resources in the sense of IRQs, I/O addresses, and DMA channels, but Windows lists them along with the system resources on the Computer Properties window (see Figure 13-14). Like the system resources, memory addresses can create problems or conflicts should two devices overlap their memory blocks.

As illustrated in Figure 13-13, the devices that commonly use the memory address blocks are Plug-and-Play device BIOS, bus architectures, CPU to bus bridges, and other chipset and add-in card bus-related device controllers—in other words, devices that require their own device BIOS running in memory. A SCSI host adapter is another common device that uses a dedicated memory address for its own BIOS. Network cards that feature Wake-on-LAN technology that allow a PC to be booted across a network also use a memory address block to hold its boot BIOS.

DIRECT MEMORY ACCESS (DMA)

Direct memory access (DMA) is a technology that provides non-PCI bus adapters and devices with the ability to access memory directly to move data in and out of RAM without the need for assistance from the CPU. Normally, the CPU controls all activities on the bus, but on most newer systems, the DMA controller, which is a device that is integrated into the motherboard, is permitted to move data into and out of RAM while the CPU takes care of other tasks. ISA expansion cards and slots and IDE/ATA bus devices have access to the DMA channels on the system. The PCI and AGP buses do not support DMA.

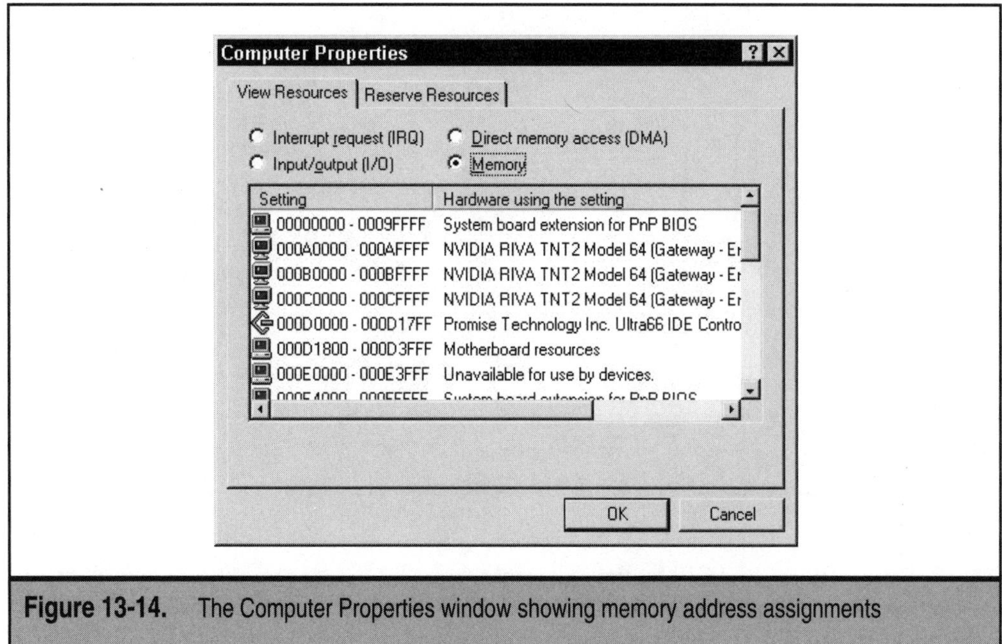

Figure 13-14. The Computer Properties window showing memory address assignments

DMA Operation

Without DMA, data is transferred from a peripheral device, such as a modem, through the IRQ process using two separate data transfers. The modem issues an IRQ to the CPU, and the CPU stops what it is doing to process the transfer of data first to the CPU's internal registers and then to RAM.

A DMA data transfer does not involve the CPU. When a DMA peripheral, such as the floppy disk drive, needs to transfer data, it requests assistance from the DMA controller that takes control of the system bus and acts as a pass-through between the DMA device and RAM, as illustrated in Figure 13-15. While the DMA controller controls the system bus, it transfers data from the DMA peripheral directly to memory. When the data transfer is complete, control of the bus is transferred back to the CPU and the DMA controller waits for the next DMA data transfer request.

DMA data transfers are more efficient, involving fewer steps than are required to have the CPU move the data. In addition, the overhead of the interrupt processing is eliminated. Whenever the CPU is interrupted, it must save its current state (what it was doing), process the interrupt, restore its state, and then resume what it was doing. Saving and restoring its state requires quite a few CPU cycles and, on some operating systems, interrupt processing requires that the state of the operating system must also be saved and restored. Eliminating the interrupt through a DMA transfer makes the entire PC more efficient.

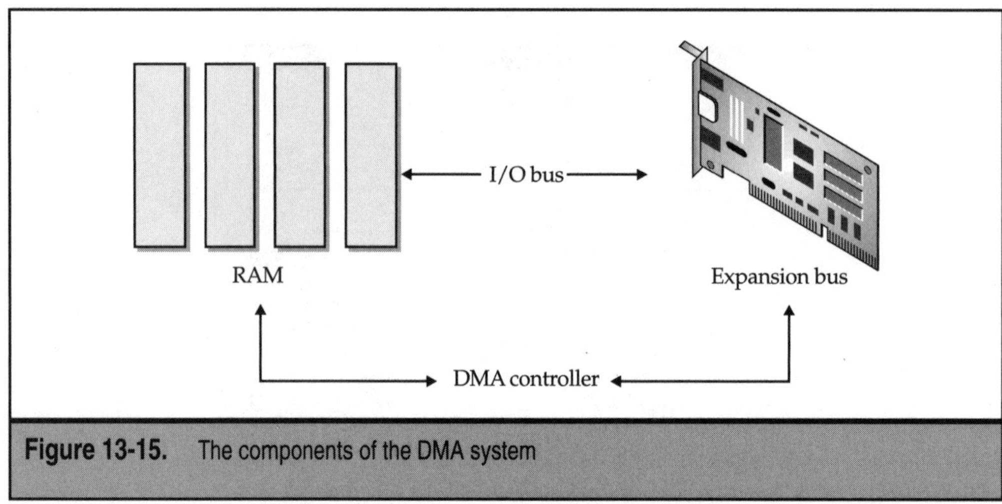

Figure 13-15. The components of the DMA system

On some systems, the CPU must still wait for the DMA data transfer to complete and the system bus to be released. However, on most systems, this is not the case and the CPU operates from its cache while the bus is in use.

DMA Channels

A DMA device is assigned to a DMA channel, which is a single-device system resource. Like two devices sharing any system resource, two devices cannot typically share a single DMA channel. There are very limited instances where two devices can share a DMA channel, but like an IRQ, they cannot use the channel at the same time.

There are eight DMA channels, but of these, channels 0 and 4 are reserved by the system, and channel 2 is typically assigned to the floppy disk drive; only five channels are available for assignment to ISA devices. Another DMA channel will be used (either DMA channel 1 or 3) if the PC includes an ECP (enhanced capabilities port) parallel port.

Table 13-5 lists the DMA channels and the devices most commonly assigned to each.

Figure 13-16 shows the Device Manager's Computer Properties window showing the DMA channel assignments on a typical PC.

DMA Modes

IDE/ATA devices, such as a floppy disk drive, use several different DMA modes to transfer data. These modes are grouped into two sets that are differentiated by how much data is moved . The first group is called single-word DMA modes. A single-word

DMA Channel	Common Device	Other Uses
0	Memory refresh	None
1	Sound card	SCSI host adapter, ECP port, NIC, voice modem
2	Floppy disk drive	Tape drive
3	Open	SCSI host adapter, ECP port, NIC, voice modem
4	Cascade to DMA 0 – 3	None
5	Sound card	SCSI host adapter, NIC
6	Open	Sound card, NIC
7	Open	Sound card, NIC

Table 13-5. DMA Channel Assignments

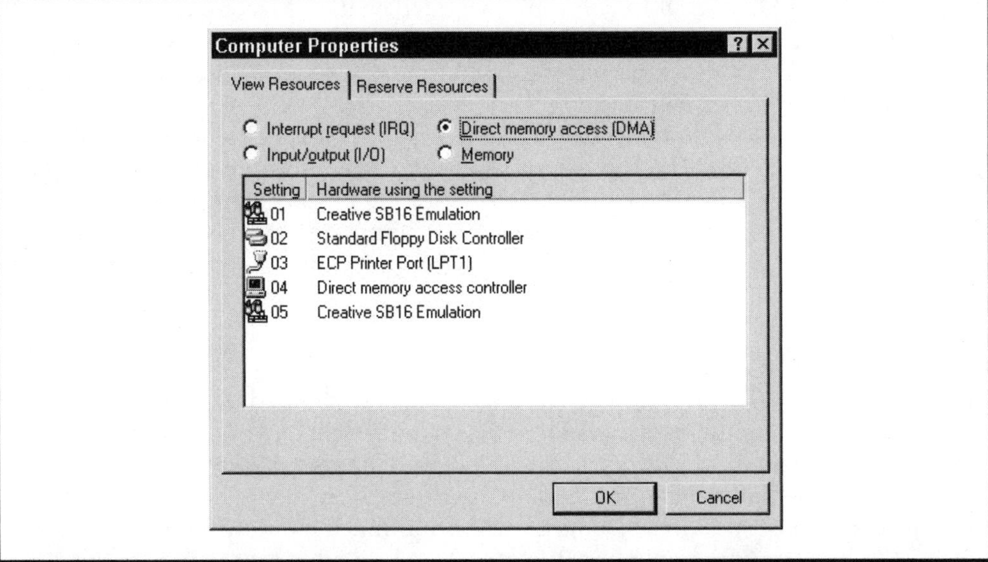

Figure 13-16. DMA Channel assignments shown in the Computer Properties window of the Windows Device Manager

DMA mode moves one word (2 bytes or 16 bits) of data in each transfer. There have been three single-word DMA modes, differing in their transfer speeds that range from as much as 960 nanoseconds to as fast as 240 nanoseconds to move 2.1 MBps to 8.3 MBps of data, respectively.

Single-word DMA transfers require the entire DMA transfer process to be repeated for each two bytes of data being transferred. This is why single-word DMA modes have largely been replaced by multiword DMA modes. A multiword DMA transfer does basically what its name implies—it transfers data in burst or a string of multiple words. This eliminates the overhead involved with transferring only two bytes at a time. Multiword DMA modes range from 480 nanosecond cycle times and 4.2 MBps (Mode 0) to a 120 nanosecond cycle time that transfers 16.7 MBps of data (Mode 3). All DMA modes used on today's PCs are multiword.

DMA Parties

Normal DMA is also called third-party DMA because the DMA controller on the motherboard controls the transfer of data between the DMA device and RAM (the first two parties in the transfer). Third-party DMA is also called conventional DMA and is considered old and slow in comparison to what is called first-party DMA. ISA devices use conventional DMA.

In first-party DMA, the DMA controller is located on the DMA device itself, which allows the device to control the DMA data transfer directly. First-party DMA does not require assistance from the motherboard's DMA controller and uses what is called bus mastering to control the data transfer.

Bus mastering means that the DMA device takes over the bus, becoming the bus master, which allows the device and memory to transfer data without either of the CPU or the DMA controller. For an IDE/ATA device to implement bus mastering, its adapter must be installed in a PCI bus slot. The main benefit of bus mastering DMA is that it frees the CPU to work on other tasks. Bus mastering is an integral feature of what is now called Ultra DMA or UDMA (see below).

Programmed I/O

In the past, IDE/ATA devices transferred data using programmed I/O (PIO), which uses the CPU to directly control data transfers between the system and the hard disk. Five PIO modes have been used over the years for disk drive data transfers, with the fastest supporting 16.7 MBps data transfers. PIO works great for slow devices like keyboards and modems, but for faster devices like the hard disk it is much too slow for advancing technology. PIO transfers depend on the IRQ process, which adds processing overhead and wastes valuable CPU cycles.

Ultra DMA

PIO data transfers are no longer used on newer systems, having been replaced by DMA and more recently, Ultra DMA (UDMA), which supports data transfers between a device and RAM of up to 100 MBps. Most of today's PCs support at least UDMA/33 (33 MBps transfers) and many support UDMA/66. UDMA mode 5, the newest version, supports data transfers of 100 MBps and is known as UDMA/100 and Ultra ATA/100.

DMA versus UDMA

Understand that UDMA is a transfer mode that is used almost exclusively by ATA (AT Attachment) and ATAPI (ATA Packet Interface) devices, like hard disk drives, CD-ROMs, or DVDs. UDMA is not normally considered a system resource and was included primarily to contrast it to DMA, which is a system resource that is assigned to and used by many devices.

RESOLVING RESOURCE CONFLICTS

As has been mentioned more than once in this chapter, the Windows Device Manager is a good place to start when you think you may have a system resource conflict. How do you know you have such a conflict? Typically, if you've installed a new device and any of the following symptoms show up, you most likely have a resource conflict:

- The PC locks up frequently for no apparent reason.
- The mouse operates erratically or not at all.
- The PC boots into Windows Safe Mode.
- You cannot format a floppy disk in the floppy disk drive.
- Anything printed on the printer is gibberish.
- The monitor displays distorted or strange images.
- The sound card either doesn't work or doesn't sound just right.
- Any existing device that was working before suddenly stops working.
- You have updated your antivirus program and scanned the PC, so a virus is not causing the problem.

Once you've determined you might have a system resource conflict, look at the Device Manager to see if any of the installed devices have one of the three get-your-attention symbols: the blue *i*, the red X, or the yellow exclamation point. If they do, determine if it may be related to the problem. It isn't always easy to tell if a particular device is causing problems with another; if a device has a red or yellow symbol, your best bet is to resolve that issue before proceeding.

Plug and Pray

A common problem with PCs is that users assume that everything is Plug and Play (PnP) and that PnP is an infallible system—wrong on both counts. In order for a PC to support PnP at all, it must have PnP support from the motherboard, the chipset, the processor, the operating system, and the device itself. Virtually all PCI cards are PnP compatible, but only if the other components of the PC are also PnP compatible. The second problem with PnP is that it can cause resource conflicts if the resources the device is expecting to use are already in use.

One Step at a Time

When installing new devices in the PC that require system resources (that is, virtually every device), install one device at a time and then test the system. Don't install several new devices and then try to figure out which one may be causing a resource conflict. It is much easier to debug if you add each device in a completely separate installation process.

Read the Fantastic Manual (RTFM)

I am a firm believer in reading the documentation that comes with a device or component, especially the parts that deal with installation or troubleshooting. Often there is a ready remedy available to the problem caused by the device. In the worst case, the telephone number of their technical support desk is usually included in the documentation.

Troubleshooting IRQs

In the beginning, PCs had only 8 IRQs. When the second group of 8 IRQs was added, the two groups were linked through IRQs 2 (on the lower group) and 9 (on the upper group). Video cards and other devices are sometimes assigned to IRQ 2, which means that they will conflict with anything installed on IRQ 9.

If two devices are installed to the same IRQ and they will not be used at the same time, such as a modem and a NIC (although that is a really strange pair of devices to share an IRQ), there should be no problem. However, more commonly you may find that you have installed devices on both COM2 (like a modem) and COM4 (like a serial mouse) and they cannot operate at the same time. This is especially common on legacy systems on which a device is installed using proprietary installation software.

About the only problem you can experience with IRQs is that two devices have been assigned to the same IRQ. The solution is to reassign one of the devices to a new IRQ using the Device Manager, the BIOS settings, or by changing the card's jumper or DIP switch values.

Troubleshooting DMA Channels

DMA channels are fairly straightforward to troubleshoot. A DMA device will use whatever channel is available to it, so what may look like a DMA channel problem (meaning it is not an IRQ problem) may actually be either an I/O address or memory address issue.

First, try choosing another I/O address or memory address for the device, if the device lists alternatives. If that fails, try using the Windows Troubleshooting utility before calling the manufacturer's technical support.

Running Windows Troubleshooting

Boot the PC into Windows Safe Mode by pressing the F8 key when you see the first Windows screen and choosing Safe Mode from the menu. From the Safe Mode Desktop, do the following:

1. Open the Control Panel and double-click the System icon.
2. Choose the Performance tab and choose the File System button from the Advanced Settings near the bottom of the window.
3. The File System Properties window displays, as shown in Figure 13-17. Choose the Troubleshooting tab.
4. Check every option in the Settings area and attempt to reboot the PC into normal mode.
5. If the PC does boot into normal mode, uncheck one item and restart the PC. Keep repeating this step, unchecking another item and restarting the PC until it fails. You should have isolated the problem device.

However, if the PC will not reboot into normal mode, reboot into Safe Mode. Use the Device Manager to disable every device (except those under System Devices) and then attempt to reboot into normal mode. If you can, more than likely the issue is a bad or out-of-date device driver. Re-enable devices by type and restart the PC. You should eventually isolate the device group that has the problem device.

The really bad news comes when you cannot get the PC to boot into Safe Mode. In this case, you need to physically remove devices from the PC and restart until the PC will boot and you have isolated the device causing the problem. Just to be sure, try putting the other devices back into the PC and rebooting. More than one or a combination of devices may be causing the problem.

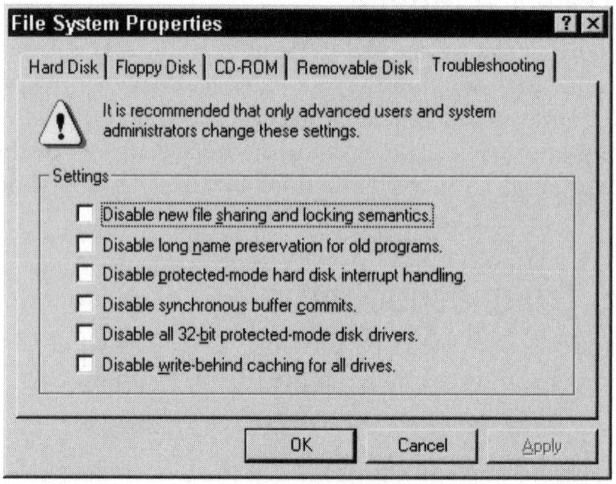

Figure 13-17. The File System Properties dialog box

CHAPTER 14

Power Supply and Electrical Issues

Everything in a computer runs on electricity. Even the data is just positive or negative electrical values stored in transistors and capacitors. Without electricity, there would be no computer, or at least as it is known today. It would probably look more like an abacus. Fortunately, there is electricity and there are computers—but there is a catch.

Electricity as it exists in the everyday world, running appliances, lighting lights, enter taining the masses, cooking, cooling, and much more, isn't the kind of electricity that a computer is designed to use. The computer must convert the electricity that comes for the wall socket and turn it into the type of electricity it can use. The PC's power supply is charged (pardon the pun) with the task of converting electricity for the PC. This chapter is about how the computer uses electricity and how it gets into the form the computer can use.

UNDERSTANDING ELECTRICITY

Electricity flowing through a circuit is like water flowing through a hose. When the water faucet is opened, the pressure in the water line forces the water to flow into the hose at some gallons-per-minute rate. Friction reduces the force and rate of the water before it exits the hose. When electricity flows into a wire from a source such as a battery or the wall outlet, some of its pressure is lost to resistance in the wire.

The water in the hose can be measured in terms of its gallons-per-minute and water pressure. The forces involved with the flow of electricity through a wire or circuit is measured in volts, amps, and ohms. Table 14-1 compares the measures used in the water hose to their electrical equivalents.

Counting Electrons

As indicated in Table 14-1, electricity can be measured, and this extends to the electricity inside the computer. Each type of measurement tells you something different about the circuits in the computer. Here is a brief overview of each of these electrical measures and how each is used:

- **Amps** An amp is a measure of the strength in a circuit or its rate of flow. The amp rating on a device indicates the amount of current needed to operate the device. For example, a hard disk drive needs about 2.0 amps to start up, but only 0.35 amps for its normal operation.
- **Ohms** An ohm measures a conductor's resistance to electricity. Conductors are covered later, but for now a conductor is a wire that carries an electrical flow. For example, if the resistance in a circuit is less than 20 ohms resistance, then current can flow through it.

Water Measure	Electrical Measure
Water pressure	Voltage
Rate of flow	Amps
Friction in the hose	Ohms

Table 14-1. Comparison of Water and Electricity Measures

- **Volts** A volt measures the electrical pressure in a circuit. Most PC's operate on several different voltage levels: +3.3V (V is the abbreviation for volts), +5V, –5V, +12V, and –12V.
- **Watts** A watt measures the electrical power in a circuit. PC power supplies are rated in the range of 200 to 600 watts.
- **Continuity** Continuity is an indicator of the existence of a complete circuit or a continuous connection. Electricity cannot flow if a complete circuit is not present. For example, if you attempt to measure the volts in one pin of a device's connector, it won't register anything until it is grounded to another of the connector's pins, completing a circuit.

Measuring Current

The measurements you are most concerned with on a PC are volts and amps. *Volts* measure pressure and *amps* measure current. Although it may sound contradictory, you don't need current to have voltage. When a water faucet is turned off, there is no current but there is definitely water pressure. When an electrical circuit is open (which means it can't flow), voltage (pressure) is still in the line despite the fact that no current is flowing. An open circuit, like two separated pieces of a hose, will not allow electricity to flow. A closed circuit, like the two pieces of hose connected together, allows the electricity to flow.

As illustrated in the top part of Figure 14-1, when two wires are both attached to a terminal of a battery but are not connected together, the circuit is open and no current flows through the wires. If the two wires are connected together, the circuit is closed and the current begins to flow. If you were to hold one of the wires in each hand, you would close the circuit and feel its pressure (volts) as a shock.

A variety of devices can be used to read the power and fury of an electrical current. Such devices as ammeters, ohmmeters, and voltmeters can measure specific properties of

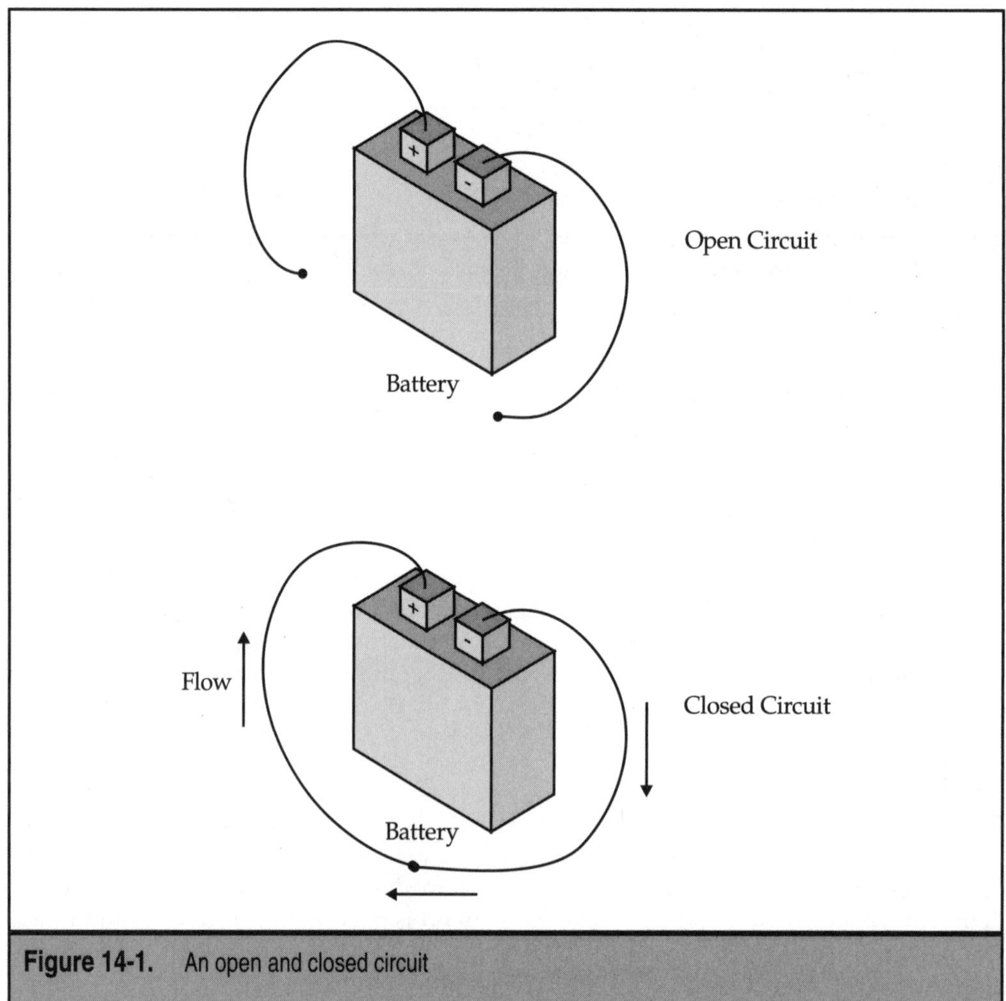

Figure 14-1. An open and closed circuit

electricity, but for most technicians, a multimeter, like the one shown in Figure 14-2, also called a digital multimeter (DMM) or a digital voltage meter (DVM), is the best choice because it combines several measuring tools into a single device.

A digital multimeter is typically a rugged, handheld electronic device that measures volts and amps and checks diodes. They are usually battery operated and come in a rubberized case to protect them from inevitable drops. There are usually two probes attached to the meter, a red and a black, that are used to make contact with the items being tested.

Figure 14-2. A digital multimeter combines several electricity measurement tools

Switching AC to DC

Electricity has two current types: AC (alternating current) and DC (direct current):

- **AC electricity** This is the type of electricity available from the electrical outlets in a home or business in North America. AC current changes directions about 60 times per second, moving first one way, then the other. This causes the current to switch its flow direction in the wire as well. AC power has advantages for the power company and your household electrical appliances, but these advantages are of little value on a low-voltage system like a PC.
- **DC electricity** This is the type of electricity used inside the PC. Direct current electricity flows in only one direction at a constant level. In a DC circuit, negatively charged particles seek out and flow toward positively charged particles, creating a direct electrical current flow. DC current has a constant level. For example, if you were to wire a light bulb to a battery, the current flows from the negative terminal to the positive terminal through the light bulb, where the electrical current causes heat and light and the light bulb glows.

Has it been mentioned that the computer runs on DC power? The PC's power supply converts AC power from the wall socket to DC power for the computer. Even the devices outside the computer case use DC power. Peripheral devices, such as printers, external modems, and disk drives, use AC power converters to convert AC power to DC power.

ELEMENTARY ELECTRONICS

Now that you know something about electricity, you can move onto some basic electronics. This section contains a series of definitions and concepts that provide you with some background on electronics. Don't worry, this discussion is basic and is intended to act only as an orientation.

Digital Circuit

An electronic circuit that accepts and processes binary data using the rules of Boolean algebra (AND, OR, XOR, and NOT) is a *digital circuit*. A digital circuit is made up of one or more electronic components that are placed in a series and work cooperatively to realize the circuit's logical objective. The objective of the circuit might be to compare one data value to another, to move data from one location to another, or to add two numbers together. Whatever the objective, the components designed into the circuit determine exactly what the circuit is capable of doing. Remember that the circuit is actually dealing with low-voltage electrical values the entire time.

Semiconductors, Conductors, and Insulators

A *conductor,* such as copper and gold, carries, or conducts, an electrical current. An *insulator,* such as rubber, doesn't carry an electrical current, which is why a copper wire conductor is usually wrapped with a rubber insulator. In between a conductor and an insulator is a *semiconductor*. A semiconductor is neither a conductor or an insulator but can be altered electrically to be one or the other. Charging a semiconductor with electricity or high-intensity light will toggle it to either a conductor or a semiconductor—whatever it is not at the time it is zapped. Think of a semiconductor as an electronic component that has a switch on it that selects how it behaves.

Electronic Building Blocks

Nearly all electronic circuits in a PC are built from just four basic electronic components, including a fifth basic electronic component made from these four components. Each of the four components has a specific function and makes a different contribution to a circuit. These components are as follows:

- **Resistor** A resistor slows down the flow of electrical current in a circuit, much like a funnel slows down a flow of water.
- **Capacitor** A capacitor stores an electrical charge. A PC has some very large capacitors, each of which has enough of an electrical charge to seriously injure you or worse, such as the capacitors in the monitor and power supply. However, there are also several levels of smaller capacitors used in the circuits on the PC.

- **Diode** A diode, despite its two-way sounding name, is a one-way electronic valve that directs the current to flow in only one direction.
- **Transistor** A transistor, which is the workhorse of a computer, is a semiconductor capable of storing a single binary value.
- **Logic gates** A logic gate is produced from a combination of a transistor, resistor, capacitor, and diode. Circuits are made up of logic gates, and circuits make up electronic systems, like that on the PC's processor.

There really isn't any reason for you to understand the function of these components much deeper than this. In fact, if you are reading this book front to back, you have already run into these terms in several earlier chapters.

STATIC ELECTRICITY AND ESD

Static electricity has its good and bad sides in and around a PC. Unfortunately, you, as the user or technician, never really encounter the good side of static electricity, but you absolutely will or have already experienced the bad side. The bad side of static electricity (electrostatic charge) on a PC is ESD, or electrostatic discharge.

If you have ever rubbed a balloon or a piece of wool cloth on your hair (something I'm sure you do everyday), you have experienced an electrostatic charge—it was what made your hair stand on end. There isn't much you can do about static electricity; it is a part of nature and it's all around you. Static electricity itself is not the problem. The problem occurs when it comes into contact with a positively charged entity and rapidly discharges. Just like it did on the battery earlier in the chapter, negatively charged particles (like static electricity) will always flow to a positively charged source (like you when you touch the door knob). There is a great deal of danger and potential for damage in an ESD. You know how when you reach for the door knob and, zap! a blue spark jumps from your finger to the metal? Well, the snap of the discharge and the tingle in your finger are only minor events, but in that harmless spark is the potential for a lot of damage to a PC. To put EDS in a kind of perspective for you: lightning is ESD.

You can feel an ESD that carries around 3,000 volts, but only about 30 volts are needed to fry circuits and parts on a PC's motherboard. This means that even if you can't feel an ESD, it's not harmless to an electronic component. ESD is by far the greatest threat for damage to a PC from its environment.

One way to avoid ESD damage to your PC is to always wear a grounded wrist strap, like the one shown in Figure 14-3. The wrist strap should be connected to either a grounding mat or the PC chassis whenever you are working inside the PC or handling any part of the computer, except the monitor and power supply. For more information on why you don't want to wear a wrist strap when working on a monitor, see Chapter 16.

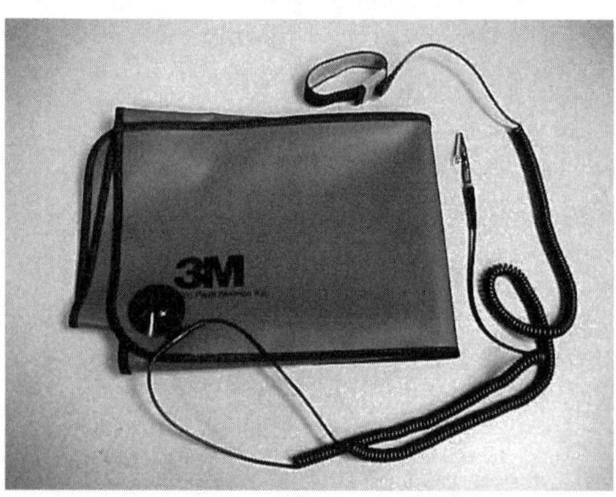

Figure 14-3. An antistatic wrist strap and antistatic mat

ESD

Nearly all cases now produced are designed to provide some level of ESD protection, as long as the case is intact and properly closed and fastened. Many case covers are chemically treated on their undersides or have copper fittings or strips designed to channel any electrostatic charge on the case away from the components inside the case.

The real danger from ESD is created when the case is opened and components inside the case are exposed. A static discharge can travel along the wires that interconnect the various components on the motherboard. The wires on the motherboard generally lead to one or more components. When a discharge on a circuit encounters a metallic part with an opposing charge, the internal wires could explode or weld together, and that's not a good thing.

Here are some ESD facts:

- A majority of a PC's electronic components use only from 3V to 5V of electricity.
- An ESD of 30V can destroy a computer circuit.
- You can only feel an ESD that has more than 2,500V.
- You can only see an ESD that carries more than 20,000V.

Unfortunately, ESD damage is not that obvious. With the really big pops, such as when an entire chip or circuit is destroyed, it is obvious that you must replace the piece. However, when a component has been damaged but is not the point of failure, it may take days, weeks, or even months for the component to fail completely. In the meantime, it drives you crazy with intermittent failures that cannot be diagnosed.

Dealing with Static Electricity

Static discharge can be avoided through good preventive measures that help to eliminate, or at least reduce, static electricity. Here are a few ways to prevent static discharge problems:

- **Treated carpeting** A major source of static electricity is the carpeting in an office or home. The carpet can be treated fairly inexpensively with antistatic chemicals that help to reduce static buildup in the carpet.
- **Antistatic bags** When not in use, electrical components should be stored in antistatic bags. Never stack up electronic boards whether they're in antistatic bags or not.
- **Grounding pads** Placing a grounding pad under a PC provides a place to ground you or the PC before it is worked on. If you touch the pad before you touch the computer, all built-up static electricity will be discharged.
- **Environmental** Dry air can cause static electricity. The humidity around a PC should be kept above 50 percent to minimize the amount of static electricity generated. Installing humidifiers to add moisture to the air can raise the humidity in an area or room.

The best and most effective way you can avoid the threat of ESD damage to a PC is by always wearing an ESD grounding strap on your wrist or ankle when you are working inside its case. The strap should be connected to either the chassis of the PC or to a grounding mat.

Using Antistatic Bags

Replacement components are generally shipped in plastic or foam bags or wrapping that has been treated to be antistatic. Understand that this means that they are treated so that they are conductive. An antistatic bag *absorbs* static electricity from the components placed in or on it. This is a commonly misunderstood fact. Most people believe that antistatic bags are insulators. However, just the opposite is true; they are conductors.

Antistatic Hazards

Never, ever dismount the motherboard, or any other electronic circuit board, and place it on antistatic material while still connected to the PC or peripherals, and then turn on the PC's power. The conductive antistatic material will short every pin and component on the part of the circuit board in contact with the antistatic material. Count on every 5V component that is connected to a 12V component to be destroyed.

THE POWER SUPPLY

The primary job of a PC's power supply is to convert AC power to DC power. In making this conversion, the functions the power supply performs are voltage conversion, rectification, filtering, regulation, isolation, cooling, and power management. Here is an explanation of each of these functions:

- **Rectification** A rectifier converts AC power to DC power. The primary task of the power supply is to rectify the AC power of the power source into the DC power used by the computer.
- **Filtering** When electricity is rectified, electrical ripples are occasionally introduced in the DC voltage. These ripples are smoothed out through electrical filtering.
- **Voltage conversion** The PC uses only a small range of voltages, including +/–5V, +/–12V, and +3.3V. The 110V AC primary power source must be converted into the +12V and +5V DC used by many older PCs and the +3.3V DC used by most newer PCs.
- **Regulation** Voltage regulation, along with filtering, removes any line or load variations in the DC power produced by the power supply.
- **Isolation** The AC power must be kept separate, insulated, and isolated from the DC power.
- **Cooling** The main system cooling fan that controls the airflow into or out of the system case is typically located inside the power supply. Some systems also have auxiliary fans located outside of the power supply.
- **Power Management** Nearly all newer PCs have energy efficiency tools and power management functions to help reduce the amount of electrical power consumed by the PC.

Outside of North America, where the primary power source is already DC, the power supply performs all of the same tasks, except rectification. Most power supplies have the ability to take 110V AC or 220V DC and have a two-position slide switch on back of the power supply near the fan grill that is used to select the power source voltage. If this switch is on 220V, it will not harm the system to plug it into a 110V source. The power supply will not be getting as much power as it believes it should be and will not function at all. So, if a PC seems to not have power the first time you plug it in, the first thing to check is the voltage selector. If it is on the wrong setting, it is likely that the factory, which is probably not in North America, tested the system on 220V and forgot to change the switch before shipment.

Good Power Signal

After rectification, one of the power supply's most important functions is sending the POWER_GOOD (or PWR_OK) signal to the motherboard. The POWER_GOOD signal tells the motherboard that the power supply has completed its cycle-up process and is now able to provide clean power in the voltages needed by the PC. Should there be a problem with the power or with the power supply, no signal is sent and the boot process never completes.

The power supply performs a self-test when the power is switched on that checks the incoming power for the required voltages. If all is well, the POWER_GOOD signal wire is set high (turned on) to indicate that the power supply is able to supply a good power stream in the right voltages. If there are any problems with the power source or the power supply's ability to produce a certain voltage stream, the POWER_GOOD signal is not set. The POWER_GOOD wire is attached to the microprocessor's timing chip, and if it does not get the POWER_GOOD signal in the right amount of time, the processor resets the startup process, which may or may not result in a loop that is continually resetting the startup process. When this happens, the PC appears to have stopped somewhere in the boot process.

Soft Switches

Beginning with the ATX form factor and including most of the form factors that followed, the motherboard is able to power the PC on or off using what is called a *soft switch*. The motherboard uses the PS_ON (power supply on) signal over one of the wires connecting it to the power supply. How do you know if your PC has this feature? If your PC powers off—or attempts to—when you shut down Windows 98 (or later), you have it.

On some newer PCs, the power-on switch on the front panel is directly connected to the motherboard and not the power supply. This creates *momentary-on* or *always-on* soft switches that jump-start the boot process when pressed. When the soft switch is used, the voltage lines (see Figure 14-4) connecting the power supply to the motherboard are activated. Each of the

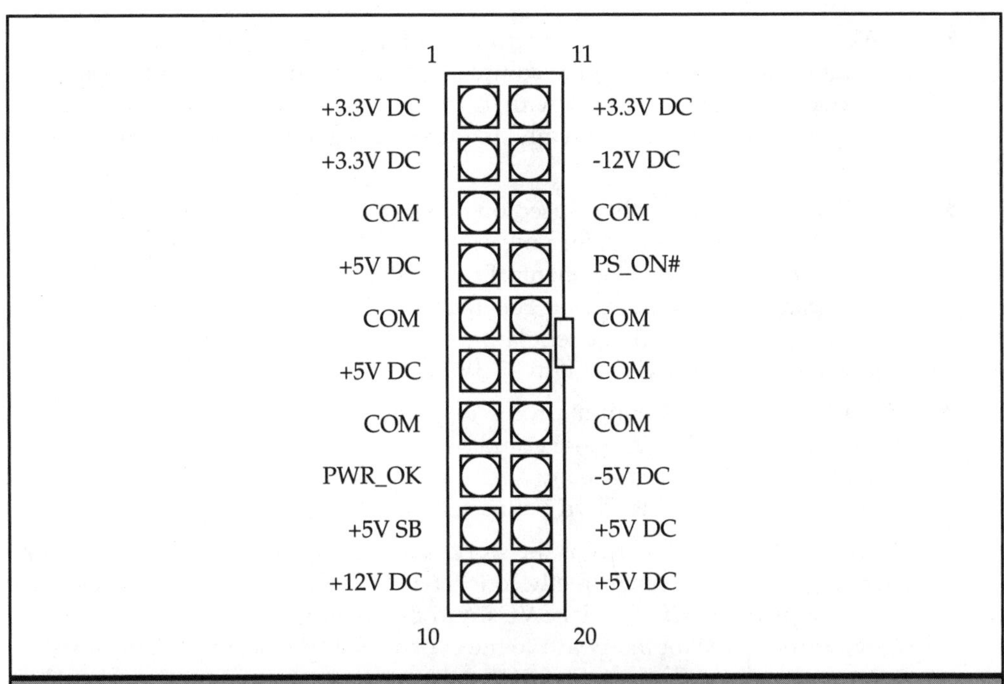

Figure 14-4. ATX/NLX power supply to motherboard connector and pinouts

wires attached to the connector represented in Figure 14-4 has a specific purpose and voltage. When the soft switch is activated, the power supply is signaled to provide each wire with its voltage.

One word of caution about always-on or momentary-on motherboards: unplug the PC before working inside the PC. This may seem like common sense, but many earlier PC models advised you to leave the power cord in the wall socket for grounding purposes. However, your best bet these days is to turn it off and unplug it before opening the system case.

Voltages

As indicated on numerous occasions in this chapter, the devices inside the PC are designed for a specific voltage level. This is why the PC's power supply generates multiple voltage levels. Here are the voltages required from the power supply in a typical PC:

- **–12V** This is a holdover from earlier systems. It was used primarily for serial ports. This voltage is still common on nearly all power supplies for backward compatibility to older hardware.
- **–5VDC** This voltage level is no longer used. It was used on some of the earliest PCs for floppy disk controllers and ISA bus cards. It was available on many power supplies strictly for backward compatibility purposes, but it is generally not used.
- **+/–0VDC** A circuit that carries zero volts of direct current (DC) is a grounding circuit that is used to complete circuits with other circuits using another voltage level. A circuit with 0VDC is also called a common or earth *ground circuit.* (By the way, it really doesn't matter if the circuit measures out at plus or minus zero volts.)
- **+3.3VDC** This is the voltage used on most newer PCs, especially those on the ATX and NLX form factors, for powering the CPU, memory, AGP ports, and the other motherboard components. Prior to the ATX form factor (on the Baby AT, for example) and the second generation of Pentium processors (Pentium Pro, Pentium II, etc.), voltage regulators were located on the motherboard and used to reduce a +5VDC circuit to +3.3VDC.
- **+5VDC** Prior to the Pentium processor, +5 volts was the primary voltage on motherboards for CPUs, memory, and nearly all devices attached or connected to the motherboard. For the Baby AT form factor and the power supplies that preceded it, this is the standard voltage.
- **+12VDC** After +3.3V, +12V is the workhorse voltage on the PC. It is used for powering the devices that directly connect to the power supply, including hard disks, floppy disks, CD-ROMs, DVDs, and the cooling fan. This voltage is passed through the motherboard to the expansion bus slots to provide power to any expansion and adapter cards installed.

Power Supply Form Factors

Nearly all form factors also specify a power supply that is compatible with the other parts of the PC they define. A power supply must conform to one or more form factors to fit and function with certain case styles and motherboard specifications.

The Power Supply and the Case

The *form factor* of a power supply defines its physical shape, how it fits into a case, and the amount of power it produces. In most situations, the power supply's form factor is the same as that of the system case and the motherboard. Since the power supply is normally bought already installed in the case, there are rarely any matching issues. It is only when you need to replace a power supply, or when you buy a case without a power supply, that form factor issues ever arise. There are newer power supplies that are compatible with several form factors, and there are cases that can fit several different power supply form factors. However, the most important part of matching the power supply to the system is to match the motherboard's power requirements to the capabilities of the power supply. Most AT class power supplies, which include the AT, Baby AT, ATX, and a few others, differ only in their size and mounting requirements; their power capabilities are roughly the same.

The capabilities of the power supply are directly related to the size and shape of it case. Mid- and full-sized tower cases are typically larger (in both height and width) and use more power for cooling its interior components. Because of its size, a mid- or full-size tower case usually has more components installed inside the case. On the other hand, a desktop or a smaller tower case typically has fewer interior components, which means they need less power from the power supply. The more demand on the power supply, the larger the power supply needs to be. Therefore, the power supplies defined by smaller form factors, such as the microATX and the LPX, are much smaller than those used for a full AT or ATX form factor PC. See Chapter 15 for more information on system cases and their form factors.

Form Factors

Here is a quick overview of the most common power supply form factors:

- **PC XT** The IBM PC and its successor, the IBM PC XT, created the first form factor for PC power supplies (see Figure 14-5). The power supply was placed in the rear right corner of these desktop cases. The power switch was an up-and-down toggle switch mounted directly on the power supply.
- **AT** The power supply of the IBM PC AT (see Figure 14-6) was larger, had a different shape, and produced about three times more power than the PC XT. The AT standard quickly became the form factor of choice among clone manufacturers, who built a wide variety of AT-compatible systems. The AT form factor was the foundation of several form factors that followed.

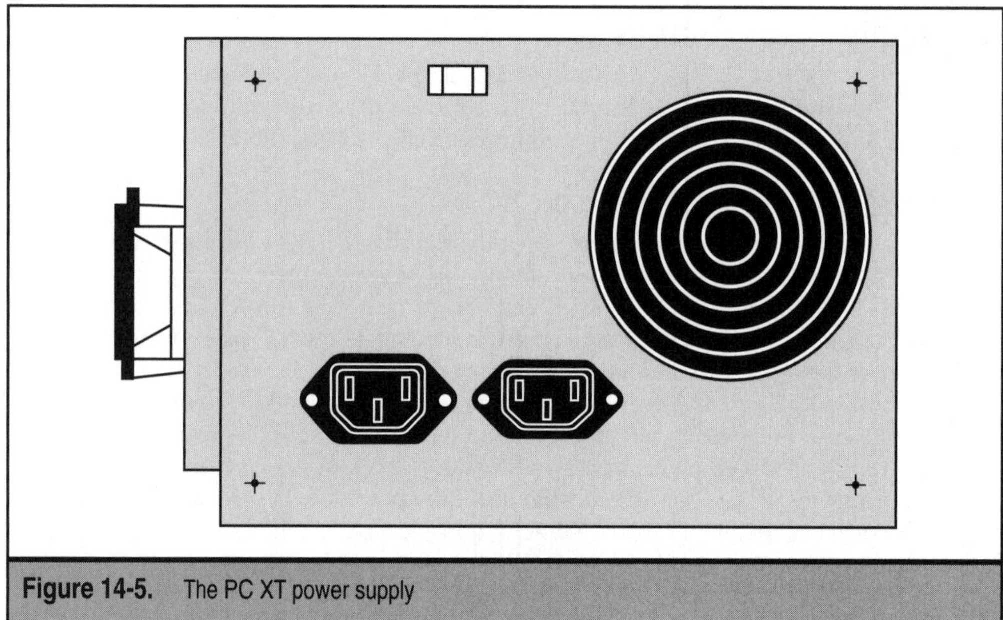

Figure 14-5. The PC XT power supply

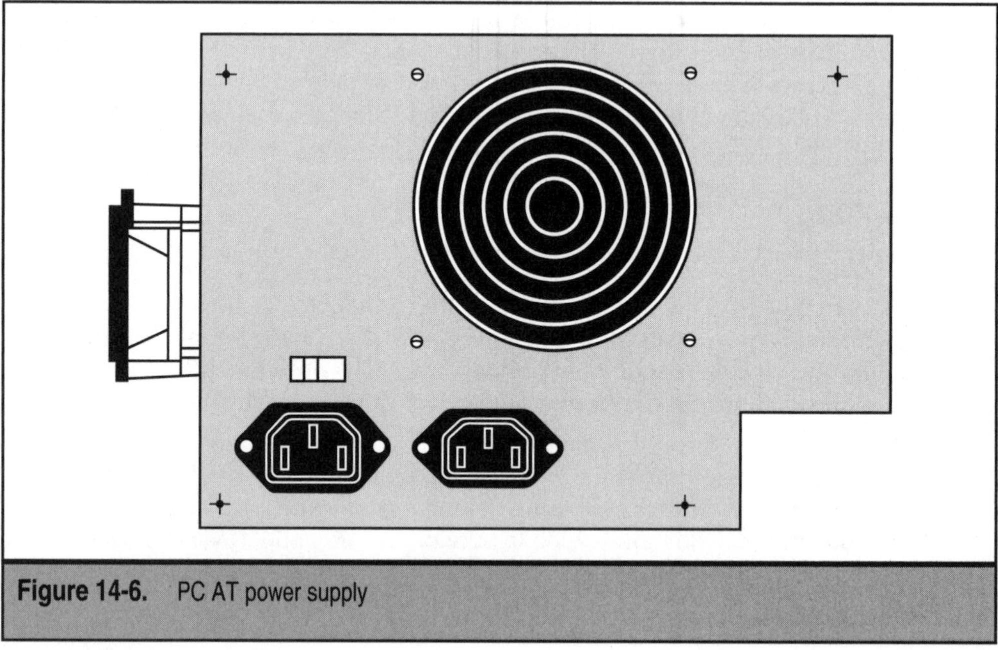

Figure 14-6. PC AT power supply

- **Baby AT** This is a smaller version of the AT form factor; it has the same height and depth but is two inches narrower than the AT form factor. The Baby AT power supply (see Figure 14-7) was very popular during the late 1980s and early 1990s.
- **LPX** This form factor is also known as the Slimline or PS/2 form factor. The LPX (low profile) power supply (see Figure 14-8) is shorter and smaller in general, but it produces the same power and cooling ability as the Baby AT and AT. The LPX form factor has generally replaced the Baby AT.
- **ATX** The ATX form factor was a major change from the form factors based on the PC XT and PC AT. The ATX is considered the de facto form factor standard for all PCs, whether desktop or tower. On the outside, the ATX power supply (see Figure 14-9) looks the same as the LPX in size and has its cables in about the same place. The AC power pass-through outlet, which was used for PC monitors on early form factors, was removed from the ATX power supply.
- **NLX** The NLX form factor does not define a power supply and uses the same power supply as the ATX. As a result, the ATX form factor is also called the ATX/NLX form factor.
- **SFX** This is a power supply–only form factor. Intel developed it for use in the microATX and FlexATX form factors. *SF* refers to its *small form*.

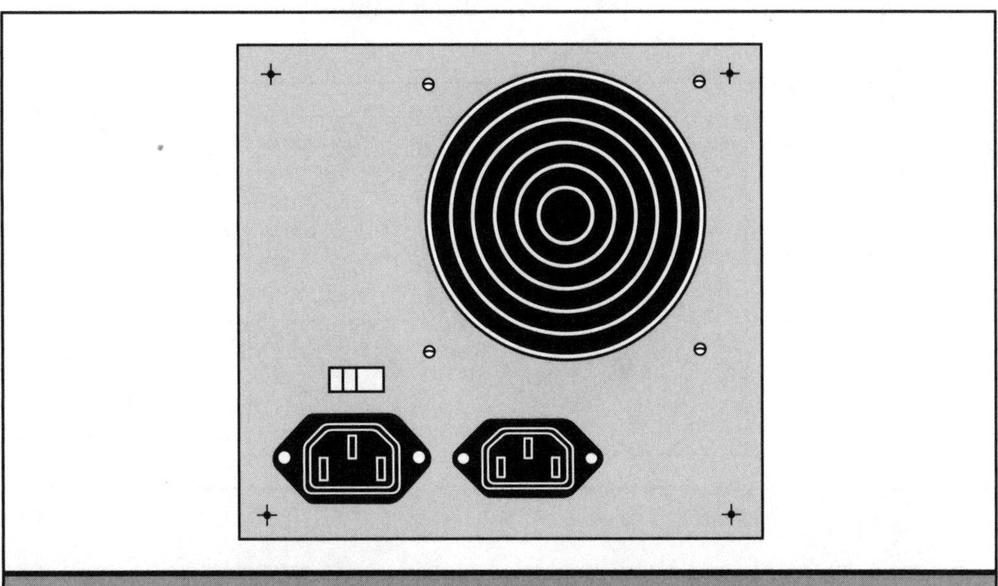

Figure 14-7. Baby AT power supply

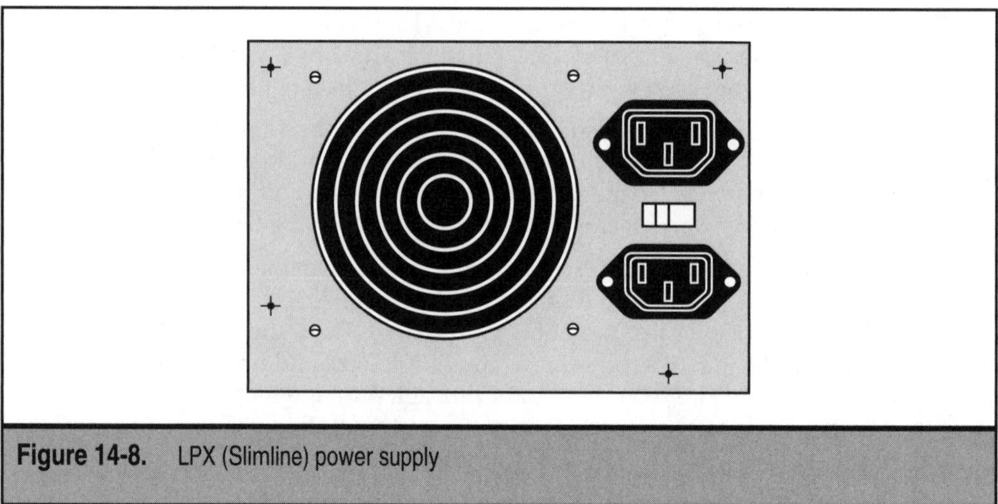

Figure 14-8. LPX (Slimline) power supply

- **WTX** This form factor is designed for use in large workstations (the *W* stands for workstation) and servers. The WTX power supply, illustrated in Figure 14-10, is bigger and more powerful than the power supplies in most other form factors. One feature that sets the WTX apart is that it features two system cooling fans.

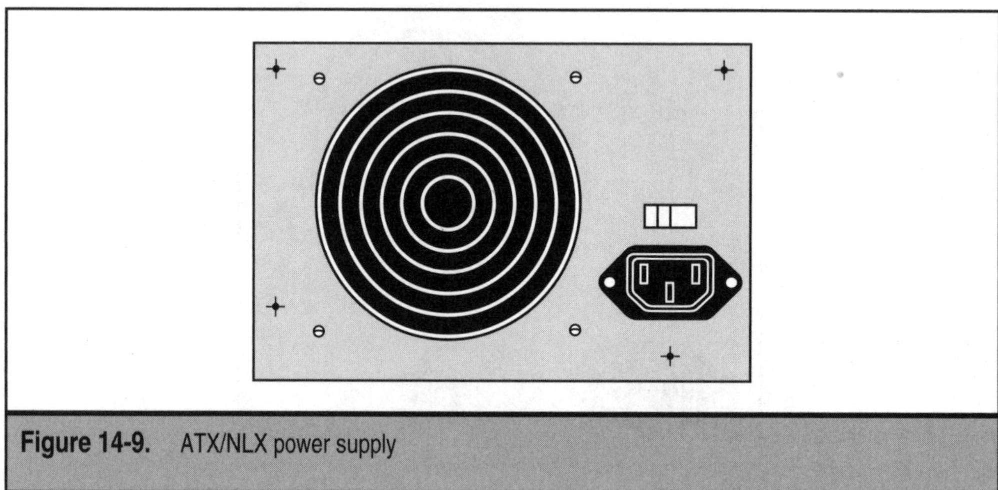

Figure 14-9. ATX/NLX power supply

Figure 14-10. WTX power supply

The features of these form factors are compared in the following table:

Form Factor	Dimensions (WxDxH) in inches	Case Style
PC XT	8.8 x 5.7 x 4.8	Desktop PC XT
AT	8.5 x 6 x 6	Desktop or Tower
Baby AT	6.6 x 6 x 6	Desktop or Tower
LPX	6 x 5.6 x 3.4	Desktop
ATX/NLX	6 x 5.6 x 3.4	Desktop or Tower
SFX	4 x 5 x 2.5	Desktop or Tower
WTX	6 x 9.2 x 3.4 (single fan) 9 x 9.2 x 3.4 (double fan)	Tower

The voltages supported by each of the form factors are listed here:

Form Factor	Output Voltage
PC XT	+/–12V, +/–5V
AT	+/–12V, +/–5V
Baby AT	+/–12V, +/–5V
LPX	+/–12V, +/–5V
ATX/NLX	+/–12V, +/–5V, +3.3V
SFX	+/–12V, +5V, +3.3V
WTX	+12V, +5V, +3.3V

Operational Ratings

Manufacturers list a number of operational ratings in the specification lists of their power supplies. These items are very technical, but they help you to determine if a power supply is compatible with the form factor and operational ratings of your PC's case, motherboard, processor, and chipset. The ratings you should find in most operational rating specifications include its operating range, frequency, efficiency, EMI, output current, regulation, ripple percent, hold time, PG delay, agency approval, noise, and mean time before failure. The list should also include the voltage outputs the power supply produces and any testing laboratory safety approvals (such as UL or TUV) it has been awarded or conformities to FCC (Federal Communications Commission) or other regulatory agency radio frequency (RF) emission standards.

Here is a brief explanation of the more common items you may find in a manufacturer's specification list:

- **Operating range** States the minimum and maximum of its input and output voltages. This is the least and most input voltage a power supply can take and be able to produce its designated output values. An operating range that is wide indicates that the power supply is able to produce reliable output voltages from even a fluctuating, unreliable power source.
- **Efficiency** The amount of output power that is produced from its input power source. This number is usually stated as a percentage.
- **EMI (electromagnetic interference)** All power supplies produce some electromagnetic noise, but the FCC limits the amount of EMI noise a power supply can produce. Most power supplies on the market today meet or exceed the FCC requirements.
- **Output current** The maximum volts that the power supply can consistently produce and supply to the motherboard and the disk drives.
- **Line regulation** Measures the amount of change passed through to the output voltage from fluctuations in the input voltage.
- **Load regulation** Measures the voltage change caused by increases in voltage demands on the power supply.
- **Ripple percent** A certain amount of variance, called a *ripple*, occurs in the output voltage as the result of incomplete conversion of the AC power source. The ripple percent indicates the percentage of output voltage affected.
- **Hold-up time** The amount of time the power supply will continue to provide operating levels of power after its input power source is lost. This time should be matched to the cutover time of the PCs UPS.
- **PG delay** The amount of time needed by the power supply to cycle up before it can send the POWER_GOOD signal.

- **Noise** The amount of sound measured in decibels (dB), such as electrical buzz and fan noise, that the power supply and its fan produce.
- **Mean time before failure** The manufacturer's best estimate of how long it should be before the power supply should fail or develop problems.
- **Safety certifications** It is important to know what safety testing and certifications the power supply has been awarded. Some companies and buildings have strict requirements on the electrical equipment that can be purchased and operated on its premises. Included in the power supply's specifications should be a list of test and certification agencies that have tested and approved it. These certifications indicate which safety, environmental, and regulatory requirements the power supply has been tested against and passed, including design, RF and EMI emissions, environment issues, and product safety. The most common of these certifications are UL (Underwriters' Laboratory), CSA (CSA International), TUV (Technischer Uberwachungs-Verein), and FCC (Federal Communications Commission).

ELECTRICAL POWER ISSUES

A PC's power supply is the source and cause of more component failures than any other component of the PC. It is the cause of at least a third of PC failures, and many other problems that show up in other components are actually caused or aggravated by the power supply. A faulty power supply can burn out or weaken the electrically fragile electronics on the motherboard and peripheral devices.

The power supply is like the guardian at the gate for the PC when it comes to its power. AC power tends to be a fluctuating, noisy, and unreliable power source, and the power supply has the job of smoothing out the problems in the AC line to produce steady, reliable DC power. Some of the more common electrical problems encountered by the power supply are as follows:

- **Spikes** AC power fluctuates within a range of from 90 to 130V. Nearly all power supplies are built to handle AC fluctuations within this range. However, there are occasional unexpectedly high voltage fluctuations that last only a short period time that can pose problems for PC power supplies and any other electrical equipment. An electrical spike is caused by such things as lightning, switching from one generator to another, or even electrical motors on the same power source as the PC.
- **Blackouts** A blackout is just what it sounds like: a total loss of the AC power source. Blackouts can last only a split second or several days. If you have no other power source, then your hope is that the Hold Up Time on your power supply is longer than the blackout. Typically, the Hold Up Time is about $1/20^{th}$ of a second, and if the blackout lasts any longer than that, most likely your PC will reboot or shutdown.

- **Power Surge** A power surge, which is also called an over-voltage event, increases the voltage outside normal levels like a spike, but for longer periods of time. A power surge can begin as a spike, but instead of dropping off as suddenly as it came, it slowly drifts back to normal levels. Power surges are usually caused by sudden increases in line voltage on the AC power system. For instance, should a large nearby electrical user suddenly drop its power, it would cause a surge over the system.
- **Brownouts** A brownout is a drop in the voltage in the incoming AC power that lasts for some time. A brownout is the opposite of a surge, except where the spike is quickly over, the brownout can last for several seconds or longer. If the voltage drops too far or lasts too long, its effect on the PC can be the same as a blackout.
- **Noise** Electrical noise on the AC power line can be caused by electromagnetic interference (EMI) and radio frequency interference (RFI). The exposed AC power lines act like antennas to pick up EMI and RF signals emitted by computer monitors, fluorescent lighting, electrical motors, radio transmitters, and lightning.

Protecting the Power Supply

There are a number of devices you can use to protect your PC and its power supply from the problems associated with AC power. The range of these devices is from essentially one-time surge protection to full-battery backup with line conditioning.

Surge Suppressors

Most plug strips advertised for computer use also include some capability to protect the devices plugged into them against a power spike or surge. These devices are interchangeably called *surge suppressors* and *surge* protectors (Figure 14-11). A surge suppressor is rated in Joules, which is a measurement of the amount of electrical surge the device can absorb.

Surge suppression devices have a built-in component, a metallic oxide varistor (MOV), to divert the over-voltage power to a grounding circuit. An MOV is a one-time device. Once the MOV has been hit with a power surge, it is essentially not there and will have no effect on any future surges. However, there are some surge suppressors with advanced technologies, such as gas discharge tubes and pellet arrestors, that can handle more than one event.

UPS Devices

A UPS (uninterruptible power supply) is also referred to as a battery backup and standby power device. However, UPS devices can also provide, depending on the model and how much you pay for it, surge suppression and even line conditioning. The UPS is essentially a large battery and a battery charger. It provides a PC protection against short-term power outages, surges, spikes, and brownouts.

A UPS helps provide a constant, reliable, and nonfluctuating stream of AC power by monitoring the AC power line and providing voltage from its battery whenever the voltage of the AC line is below a certain level. The UPS also help buffer spikes and surges by storing off any voltage above a certain level as well.

Figure 14-11. A plug strip that includes a surge suppressor

The power stored in the UPS' battery is passed through an inverter that creates an AC supply for the PC to convert to DC power. Figure 14-12 shows an example of the type of UPS commonly found in an office setting. Better UPS devices supply AC power to a PC that is usually better than the AC power from the wall. A less expensive UPS may not provide a smooth power wave and may actually damage equipment plugged into it.

UPS Device Types

There are two general types of UPS devices, which are differentiated by how they store and supply power to a PC. The two categories are:

- **Standby** This type of UPS is nothing more than a battery backup that acts as a safeguard against a blackout or brownout. As long as the UPS is in standby mode, it uses a small amount of power to charge its battery but passes the remaining unfiltered AC power to the PC. Should there be a need for power, the UPS continues to provide the PC with AC power. One of the downsides to standby type UPS units is that it will typically pass any large surges or spikes through to the PC.
- **Online** An online (a.k.a. inline) UPS provides AC power from its battery and a power inverter that converts the battery's DC power to AC power. The UPS' battery is constantly being recharged from an AC power source through an input inverter. The UPS absorbs all high and low-voltage events, such as spikes, blackouts, and brownouts, on the AC power line. Extended brownouts and blackouts are restored from the UPS' battery, which begins discharging immediately and will eventually fail without the AC power being restored. With this type of UPS, the PC gets its power from the UPS' battery with the battery constantly being from the AC power source. Figure 14-13 shows a large online UPS that would be used to protect one or more servers on a network.

Figure 14-12. An uninterruptible power supply (UPS). Photo courtesy of American Power Conversion, Inc.

Figure 14-13. A rack mounted UPS used for network servers

UPS Device Characteristics

Here are some of the features commonly found on a UPS:

- **Information displays** All UPS devices will issue a warning before its battery is completely discharged, but the better devices have information displays to provide information on the charge level of the battery, the amount of power being demanded by the PC, and other information you need to decide how much time you have before the battery is dead.
- **Monitoring systems** Many UPS devices include a serial cable that is attached to a serial (COM) port on the PC, which is used by software running on the PC to monitor the "heartbeat" of the UPS. The UPS sends a signal at regular intervals over the serial cable. These signals are monitored by a software program running in background on the PC. If the UPS fails to send too many signals, the software assumes that the UPS is gone and begins to shut down the PC. The software program that monitors the UPS is usually supplied by the manufacturer of the UPS. There are advanced monitoring systems that can display console messages, send e-mail, or dial a pager to notify the system administrator.
- **Line conditioners** A line conditioner, also commonly called a power conditioner, eliminates line noise from the incoming power and keeps voltage within normal levels. Line conditioners don't protect against blackouts, but they do smooth out any low or high-voltage conditions on the incoming power line.
- **Alarm systems** Most UPS and line conditioning devices sound an alarm when the input power source drops below a certain level or if the power becomes unreliable.

Watts and Volt-amps Ratings

Most UPS devices are rated in volt-amps, but the power requirements of most PC devices, including that of the power supply, are generally stated in watts. To determine the right-sized UPS device for your system, you need to understand the difference (and similarities) of these two electrical measures:

- **Watts** The real power used by an electrical device. It is the power actually taken from the AC input source.
- **Volt-amps (VA)** The VA rating of a device is computed as the volts it uses times the amount of current in amps it draws from the circuit. The volt-amps rating is used for determining the size of wiring, circuit breakers, and UPS devices.

The watts and volt-amps ratings for PCs are usually different values. In most cases, the VA rating is never less than the watt rating and is generally larger. In fact, many devices have what is called a "power factor" that indicates the percentage their watts rating is to their VA rating. The power factor is a ratio that is expressed either as a fractional number, like 0.8, or as a percentage, like 80 percent. The industry standard for UPS device power factors is around 0.6 or 60 percent. Typically, a UPS device will list only its VA rating, but you can count on its watts rating being somewhere around 60 to 80 percent of the VA rating. The general rule of thumb for UPS sizing is that the total demand in watts should be only 60 percent of its VA rating. The worst thing that could happen if you oversize your UPS is that it will last longer than its load ratings.

A UPS' VA rating indicates roughly the amount of volt-amps it can supply for about a five-minute period. A UPS with a 300VA rating can provide 300VA for about five minutes with a full load of around 180 watts (60 percent of 300VA). If the load is less, the UPS can last longer. If the load is only 120 watts, the UPS may be able to provide power for 15 minutes or more.

Sizing a UPS

You can size a PC by using either the amount of watts you need or the number of volt-amps you need, whichever number you happen to have. The capacity of the UPS should be enough to power your system for 15 minutes. This is ample time for you to shut down the system without losing data or programs. One thing to bear in mind is that the higher the VA rating, the more the UPS will cost. You can most definitely find a UPS that will power your PC for an hour or more, but expect the cost to be prohibitive.

Here is a formula you can use to calculate the amount of time a UPS will support your system:

```
(Max. Load (Amps) x 120) + (Power (Watts) x 1.4) = Volt Amps Required
Total Volt Amps Required / Full Draw = Minimum Supply
Total Volt Amps Required / Half Draw = Nominal Supply
```

- **Maximum load in amps** The total draw in amps of the PC and any other devices to be powered by the UPS. The "120" multiplier is the volts on the AC power source.
- **Power supply (in watts)** The watts demand of the power supply on the PC. The 1.4 factor converts it to a VA rating.
- **Full draw** Dividing the Total VA Required number calculated above by the Total VA rating of the UPS should be greater than 5 minutes. However, you never want to load a UPS this heavily.
- **Half draw** Using a loading factor of 50 to 60 percent, the result will be a UPS on which you can relay to supply the emergency power you need, buy typically at least 15 to 20 minutes of standby power.

To calculate the VA requirements for your system, you can gather most of the information you need from your system's documentation or its manufacturer's Web site. The VA requirements for some of the components in the PC you should consider when determining this value are:

- **Power supply** 110 to 180VA (180 to 300 watts)
- **Pentium processor** 40VA (50 watts)
- **Hard disk drive** 15VA (24 watts)
- **Motherboard** 20 to 35VA (30 to 50 watts)
- **CD-ROM** 20 to 25VA (30 to 35 watts)
- **Expansion cards** 5 to 15VA (7 to 20 watts)
- **Floppy disk drive** 5VA (10 watts)

A very handy tool available for sizing a UPS to your particular need is the UPS Selector on the American Power Conversion (APC) Corporation Web site at **www.apcc.com**.

PART III

External Components

CHAPTER 15

The System Case

Your PC's system case is probably high on the list of components you think about the least. However, in spite of the fact that the system case has only one or two components that are active, namely the power supply and the front panel, the PC's case plays a major role in the PC's operation.

The system case consists of six major components, as shown in Figure 15-1:

- Power supply
- Cover
- Chassis
- Front panel
- Switches
- Drive bays

Each of these components of the system case and their respective components are detailed in the sections that follow.

Another aspect of the system case that is discussed in this chapter is the form factor of the system case. The *form factor* of the case is its shape, the way its components fit together, and most of all, its size. Typically, the form factor of a PC includes its case, power

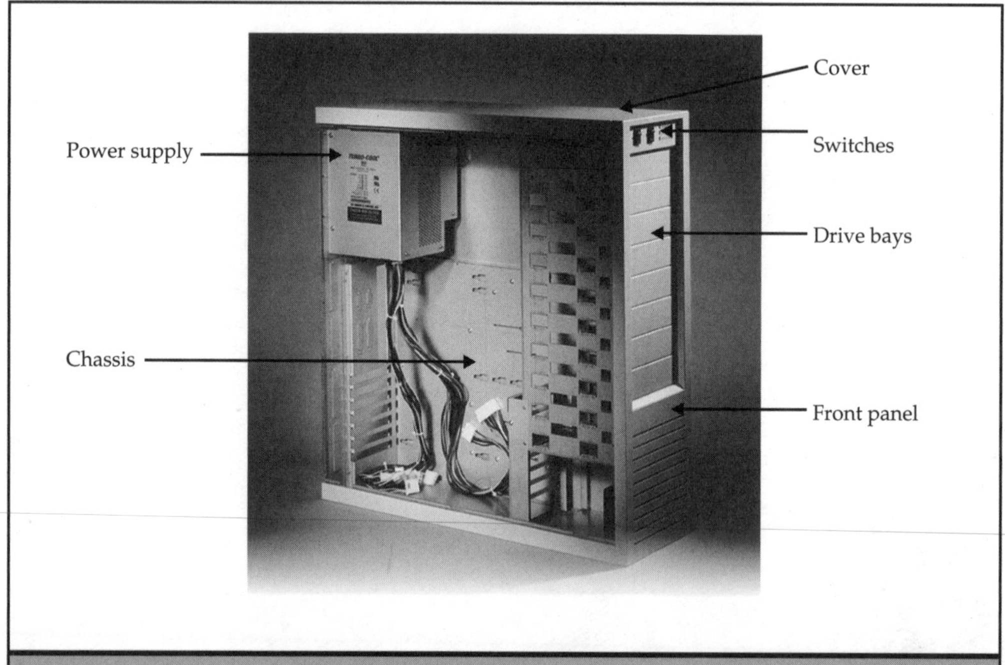

Figure 15-1. The major components of the system case. Photo courtesy of PC Power and Cooling, Inc.

supply, and motherboard, because these components must fit together to supply protection, power, and safety. You may be surprised at how many form factors there are and how specifically they are defined.

THE CASE FOR THE CASE

In spite of the fact that the PC's case just seems to sit there, it does perform a number of very valuable functions. Most people take the functions listed below for granted, but they are important nonetheless. In addition to providing the aesthetics of the system, the case also provides the PC with its structure, and it provides protection and cooling for the electronics and other devices mounted inside the case. So you see, the PC's case is not just another pretty face; it also has a very important role to play in the overall function of the PC.

PC cases come in all sizes, shapes, colors, and animals (see Figure 15-2). These variances in size and shape are driven by the case's form factor, but more and more case designers are adding color, new plastic and metal materials, and even faces to the case design in attempt to make them less boring. The cases shown in Figure 15-2 represent a wide variety of case types and form factors.

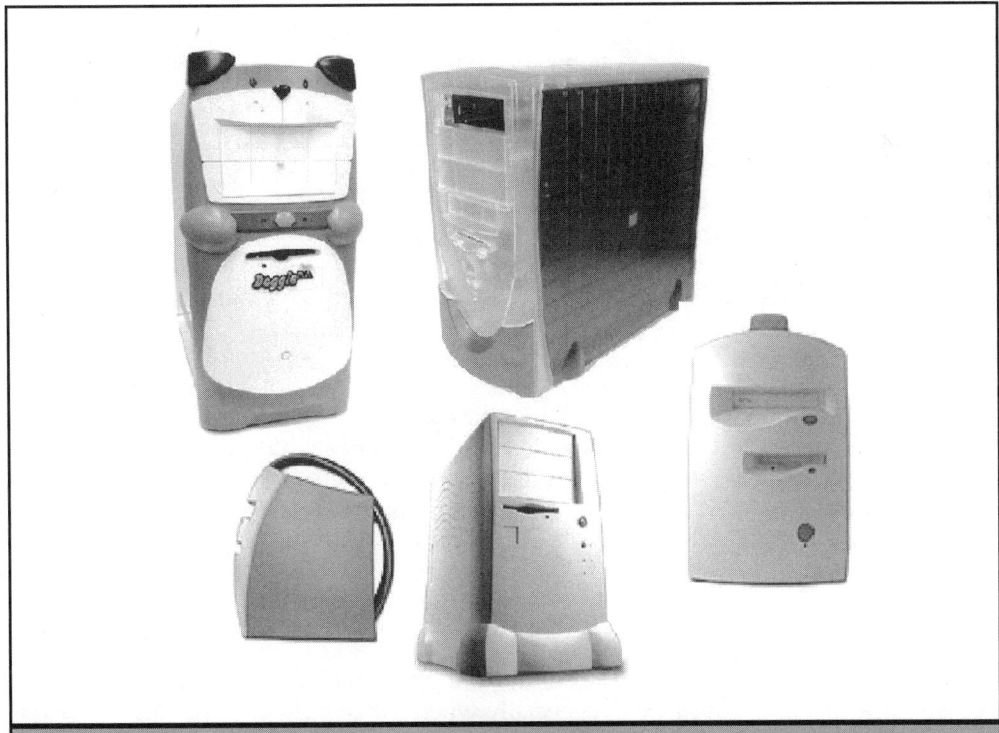

Figure 15-2. An assortment of PC case shapes and faces

Case Components

As shown in Figure 15-2, not all system cases are identical in size or shape, but most contain components and parts common to all PC cases. Here is a list of the most common system components found in PC cases:

- **Chassis** The skeletal framework that provides the structure, rigidity, and strength of the case.
- **Cover** Plays an important role in the cooling, protection, and structure of the PC.
- **Power supply** A very important component, not only to the case assembly, but to the PC and its other components. The primary tasks of the power supply are to rectify (convert) AC power into DC power for use by the PC's internal components and to house and power the mail system cooling fan. Power supplies are not discussed in detail in this chapter, other than to discuss their conformity to the various form factors and their fit into the different case styles. See Chapter 14 for more information on power supplies.
- **Front panel** In addition to providing the PC with its looks and color, the front panel also provides information on the PC's status, allows the user to physically secure the PC, and, on some case types, is the starting point for removing the case cover.
- **Switches** Most newer systems now have their two main switches, the power switch and the reset switch, on the front panel. If the power switch is not on the front panel, it is likely either on the right rear corner or near a corner on the back of the PC.
- **Drive bays** Beginning with the PC XT, disk drives with removable media have been mounted in the system case so that they can be accessed from the front panel. Typically, the drive bays are used for 5.25-inch and 3.5-inch disk drives, such as floppy disks, CD-ROMs, DVDs, and removable hard drives.

The Chassis

Beneath the sheet metal or plastic exterior of the case is a metal framework that provides the structural framework for the PC. Just like the interior of a building or the human skeleton—to stretch the point—the PC's chassis (pronounced "chass-ee") provides the frame on which all other parts of the PC mount, attach, or hang. As shown in Figure 15-3, the sheet metal of the chassis gives the PC its shape, size, rigidity, strength, and the location of its components.

Construction

The frame of the PC must be a rigid structure. Many of the components and devices in the PC cannot withstand being flexed, especially when the devices are operating. The one component of the PC that strength of the frame protects most is the motherboard. If the

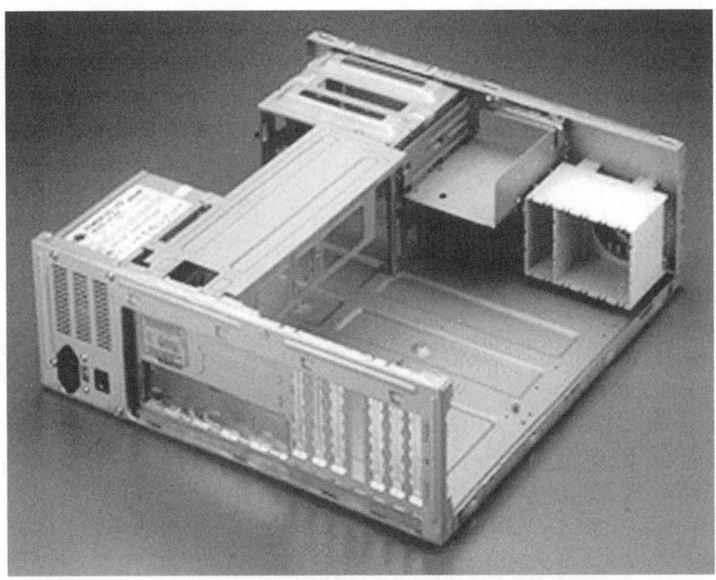

Figure 15-3. The chassis of a desktop PC. Photo courtesy of Enlight Corporation

frame can twist and bend, especially when the PC is on, the fragile electronic traces on the motherboard could break, or the motherboard's mountings could slip or break, grounding the board to the case. For these reasons and many others, the rigidity and strength of the case's chassis is one of its key requirements. When evaluating a system case, assure yourself that the chassis' structural framework is constructed to protect the components mounted to it.

The frame should be constructed from at least 18-gauge steel (16-gauge is even better). Less expensive cases may use lighter gauge steel or even aluminum. There is nothing wrong with a lighter metal or aluminum case, if the case is reinforced in key locations with heavier gauge steel, but be wary of bargain cases made of lightweight aluminum. They are much too pliable and can flex too much when being moved or lifted and may cause problems inside of the case. The few pounds you save by buying a lightweight case made of lighter gauge metals are not worth the potential for problems that a bendable case can cause.

Another consideration and key attribute of the case chassis is its design and layout. Where the crossbeams are located in relationship to where the chassis mounts the motherboard, power supply, disk drives, and other components could later pose a problem when you are trying to repair or upgrade the PC.

The Cover

Speaking of mounting things to the chassis, there are many ways to attach the cover to the chassis. Most systems use a few screws to attach the cover to the chassis, but there are screw-less or tool-less systems where the case hangs on the chassis using keyholes or slide-and-lock features. However the cover attaches to the chassis, how snugly and securely it fits is very important.

The case's cover is designed into the airflow dynamics of the case as well as its RFI (radio frequency interference) and EMI (electromagnetic interference) engineering. If your PC is FCC- (Federal Communications Commission) certified, then the case was designed as part of the RF emissions control of the PC. One of the risks of having a cover that doesn't fit tightly and securely without gaps or loose parts is that it could emit RF signals and affect other devices near it. Another is that the loose parts of the cover may rattle in the breeze of the escaping airflow, which would be a nuisance of the first order.

There is a wide variety of ways in which the outer cover of the case mounts to the chassis. The most common way is to attach the cover with screws that bind the cover pieces to the front, sides, and rear of the chassis. It is very rare that you need to completely remove the cover from the chassis. Normally, only the side (tower) or top (desktop) is removed to provide access to the inside of the case. The following sections discuss the various types of covers and how they are attached and removed from the chassis.

Legacy Desktops

Until recently, the desktop PC has been the most common of the case designs. There are desktop models for nearly every form factor (discussed later in the chapter), including the earliest PCs, such as the PC XT and the PC AT systems; the more common PCs, such as the Baby AT and ATX systems; and the newer LPX slimline systems. For the most part, older systems have a U-shaped piece that incorporates the covers for the top and sides of the PC. This piece is attached to the chassis with four or five screws to the rear panel and is removed by sliding it all the way back or forward off the PC or by sliding it back a bit and then lifting it straight up. The benefit of this cover design is its simplicity, but you must be careful when removing or replacing it that you don't snag power and data cables, expansion cards, or disk drives and dislodge or damage them.

Legacy Towers

There are many different types of tower cases, but the oldest of the tower designs is typically a full-sized AT, Baby AT, or ATX case. On these cases, the cover is a U-shaped piece with very long sides that fit down and over the frame of the tower's case. This cover is attached to the rear of the case with four to six screws. To remove this cover, the screws are removed and the cover is lifted straight up and off, or it slides back a bit and then is lifted up and off.

Single-Screw Cases

Many name brand PCs feature a case that has a single large knobby screw on the back of the case (see Figure 15-4). This type of case is called "tool-less" because you should be able to remove or replace the screw with your fingers. The cover pieces are held firm by spring clips inside the case to apply pressure and hold the cover pieces in place. Like the legacy cases described earlier, the cover lifts off or slides back and off.

Screwless Cases

On this type of case cover, there are several individual cover pieces, generally one piece to a side. Typically, the front panel is attached by a spring clip and is pulled up and lifted off one or more hook-like tabs built into the chassis. After the front panel is removed, the top is removed, typically by lifting it straight up, and then the sides are removed, one at a time.

Figure 15-4. A single screw holds on the cover on a single screw case design

Some screwless cases have an indentation at the bottom of the front panel so you can grasp the edge to pull it up. On others, where no such handhold is provided, you may need to use a small screwdriver or pry bar to pull the front panel up enough to gain a grasp of its edge. A minor drawback to a screwless case is that you will have several case parts to keep track of instead of just the one-piece legacy type case.

Release-Button Desktops

This type of case, which is used by Compaq for its desktop models, is removed by pressing release buttons located on the front (on Compaq desktops) or rear of the PC. After pressing the release buttons, the cover, which includes the front, rear, top, and sides of the cover, lift straight off the case.

Another case in this group is the flip-top case. This case also uses release buttons to unlock the cover, but instead of the entire top lifting off, the top cover lifts up like a top-loading washer or CD player. If for some reason you need to remove the entire case, strategically placed screws can be removed to do this.

Front-Screw Cases

On this case style, the screws that hold the cover on the PC are located on the front panel, usually hidden behind sliding tabs or a snap-on panel. Removing these front-panel screws (and possibly some on the rear panel as well) allows the case to be pulled forward and off the case.

The form factors (AT, ATX, LPX, etc.) mentioned in this section and the various case styles (desktop, tower, and others) are looked at in a little more detail later in the chapter.

The Front Panel

The primary purpose of the *front panel*, or *bezel*, as it is also called, is to cover up the front end of the chassis, but since it is the part that the user looks at most of the time, efforts have been made to make it useful and appealing (see Figure 15-5).

Some PCs now also feature doors and snap-on panels to mask disk drives, the power and reset switches, and even the LEDs on the front of the PC. Typically, doors on the front panel are a characteristic of larger PCs and network servers. Figure 15-6 shows a server with two doors, one for the removable drives and the other to cover the normal parts of the front panel. This computer also features a key lock for the doors to provide a small amount of security.

Status LEDs

Most PCs have LEDs (light emitting diodes) on the front panel to show the status and activity of certain parts of the system. Typically, there are two LEDs: one that is lighted when the power is on and one that indicates when the hard disk is being accessed. There are other LEDs visible on the front of the PC, but they are generally a part of a disk drive installed in a drive bay. Very old PCs also have a Turbo LED that indicates the system is in turbo mode, which raises the processor speed of the PC. These systems are generally obsolete now.

Figure 15-5. A unique front-panel design by ColorCase that should appeal to cat lovers. Photo courtesy of Rainer Company

Figure 15-6. A WTX form factor computer with two front-panel doors. Photo courtesy of Super Micro Computer

Here is a quick overview of the front panel's LEDs:

- **Power LED** Typically green in color and illuminated when the PC's power is on.
- **Hard drive LED** When the disk drive is seeking, reading, or writing data, this red, orange, or amber LED is lit and flashes. The speed with which the hard drive LED flashes is a good indicator of how busy your PC might be. Typically, this LED is wired to the motherboard or the disk controller card so that it reflects the activity of all disk drives on the PC.
- **Turbo LED** If present, this yellow LED indicates that the PC is in turbo mode. The turbo button was used on very early systems as part of a backward compatibility strategy. There wasn't a lot of software available to begin with, and when the 8MHz systems were released, many people had a fair investment in software that would run only in the older 4.77MHz, or PC XT mode. Normal mode on these systems, 286 and 386 processors, was turbo mode. However, when the turbo button was released, two things happened: the PC processor was slowed to 4.77MHz and the turbo LED was turned off.

Front-Panel Switches

Nearly all PCs now have at least one main switch, and many have two, on the front panel of the PC. If there is only one switch, it is the main power switch. If there is another switch on the front panel, it is the reset switch. Figure 15-7 shows a PC front panel with two switches.

Figure 15-7. The power and reset switches on a PC front panel

Power Button

On older PCs, the power switch was a part of the power supply and extended through the case wall on the right rear corner of the PC. Nowadays, the power switch is located on the front panel.

On Baby AT and earlier systems, the power switch located on the front panel is not a switch in the sense of a physical on/off switch. It is actually a proxy switch; pressing the front-panel switch activates the actual power supply switch, which is located on the back of the front panel and wired directly to the power supply.

Newer systems such as the ATX, NLX, and LPX form factors have an actual power switch on the front panel, but instead of being wired to the power supply, the switch is now electronic and connected to the motherboard. On these systems, you don't turn the computer on or off with the power switch; you request that the motherboard do it for you.

Reset Button

The *reset switch*, also referred to as the *reset button*, performs a hardware reset when pressed. This provides the user with a means of restarting the PC should it halt and not respond to normal shutdown or restart commands. Using the reset button is better than powering the PC off and back on, which can sometimes result in POST or BIOS errors.

On some older PCs, the reset button was placed on the front panel and easily accessed, which caused more than one unexpected system reset. Newer cases now recess the reset switch to prevent inadvertent resets from taking place. A few manufacturers have moved the reset button to the back of the PC, which is safer yet.

Some manufacturers, such as Gateway, do not include a reset button on their systems. Resetting the PC must be done via the keyboard (CTRL-ALT-DEL) or using the operating system's restart process.

Turbo Button

As explained earlier (see "Status LEDs" earlier in this section), the turbo button and its functions are now obsolete except on 286 and early 386 computers. If your front panel has a turbo button, chances are it is not connected to anything; to avoid possible problems, you should never press it.

Keylocks

Although not technically a switch, some cases have keylocks on their front panels. There are two types of keylocks available on PC front panels:

- **Keyboard lockout** When locked, this type of keylock locks out the keyboard for the system, preventing anyone from using the PC. When someone attempts to use the PC while this keylock is locked, an error message is displayed on the monitor that says, in effect, that the system is not available for use. While this keylock is locked, the PC will not boot. The keyboard lockout keylock was intended to be a first-level of security for PCs in large offices and work areas. The keys for a PC keylock are usually a round key, and many manufacturers use the same key for all of their systems, so the security it provides is limited. Anyone with a screwdriver can open the case and disable the lock and, for some cases, they don't even need the screwdriver.

▲ **Front-panel door lock** If the front panel of your PC has one or more doors, it may also have a door lock either on the door or on the front panel. When the doors are closed and locked, curiosity seekers are prevented from accessing the drives behind the doors. However, since the doors are made of plastic and can be easily pried open, this feature should not be used as a means to secure the system.

If your case has a keylock or a front-panel door lock, be sure that it also has keylock keys. Typically, you will get two of each key. If you plan to use them, store one of the keys in a safe place so that you will be able to unlock your PC after you lose the other one.

Drive Bays

Since the PC AT, users have been able to decide the number and type of disk drives in their computers. As long as the power supply and cooling system support them, you can add floppy disk drives, hard disk drives, CD-ROM drives, tape drives, and more to your PC.

Generally, drives are installed in the drive bays provided on virtually all PC case designs and form factors. Figure 15-8 shows a desktop computer with its drive bays exposed. This system, an ATX case from Enlight Corporation, provides three 5.25-inch "half-height" drive bays, two 3.5-inch one-inch high drive bays, and two 3.5-inch drive bays hidden inside the case.

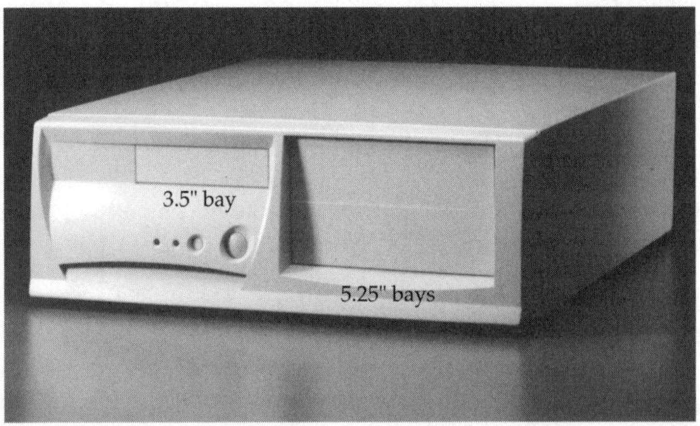

Figure 15-8. The drive bays of an ATX desktop chassis. Photo courtesy of Enlight Corporation

Originally, disk drives required a drive bay that was 3.5-inches in height. As technology was able to reduce the size of the overall drive, that height was cut in half and now most of the drive bays available for 5.25-inch devices are less than 2 inches in height and are called *half-height*.

Internal versus External Bays

As indicated in the previous paragraph, there are two types of drive bays:

- **External drive bays** These drive bays are actually internal to the case and chassis, but they can be accessed externally. External drive bays are typically used for drives that have removable media, such as floppy disks, CD-ROMs, DVDs, tape drives, and the like.
- **Internal drive bays** These drive bays are completely inside the system case and are not accessible from outside the chassis, as shown in Figure 15-9. These bays are designed for devices with no need for external exposure, primarily hard disk drives.

Internal devices can be installed in external bays. Before internal bays were common, hard disk drives were installed in the external bays, the only kind available, and a solid face plate was put over the external opening of the bay to hide the drive.

Figure 15-9. Internal drive bays inside a chassis. Photo courtesy of Enlight Corporation

Mounting Rails

There are two methods to mount a device in a drive bay, internal or external. One is the use of drive rails and the other is mounting the device directly to the walls of the drive bay.

- **Drive rails** These are just about what they sound like: two strips of metal that are mounted to the sides of the disk drive. With the drive rails attached, a device is placed into the drive bay with the rails sliding into notches or facets on the sidewalls of the bay. The device is suspended from the rails, which are now secured to the walls of the bay.
- **Sidewall mounting** This is now a common feature of most newer cases. It involves attaching the disk drive to the sidewalls of the drive bay. Screws are placed through holes in the sidewall that match the standard placement and spacing of prethreaded holes on the sides of the disk drive. The drive is solidly attached to the chassis.

A newer feature on system cases is snap-in cages for internal drive bays, like those shown previously in Figure 15-8. To install a hard disk in an internal cage, you remove the cage, install the drive, and snap the cage and drive assembly back into place. If you use a cage to install an internal drive, think ahead to the cables and connectors that may be added later and the process that will be needed to remove the drive for servicing.

SYSTEM CASE STYLES

The two basic styles of PC cases are the *tower case* and the *desktop case*. Figure 15-10 shows a family of PC cases from Enlight Corporation that includes both tower and desktop styles. The tall, thin cases are the tower style, and the flat, boxy one is the desktop case style. At one time, the two styles were very much alike and, in fact, the tower came about when people trying to save space turned their desktop PCs on their sides. Today, these case styles are very distinctive because of their internal designs, the way the case is attached, and the features each supports.

Tower versus Desktop

Which case style is right for a particular setting really depends on how it is to be used and the setting itself. Tower cases are designed to sit on the floor or large shelves. Desktops are designed to sit on desks, which is why they are called desktops. A tower case does free up desktop space, but if the space on the floor is limited, it can be in the way, get kicked, or worse. Desktop cases are a lot smaller then they were when the demand for nondesktop units first grew.

The two case styles really aren't interchangeable, despite the claims of the vendors selling conversion kits. Turning a desktop PC on its side changes the orientation of the removable media drives, namely the CD-ROM, DVD, and other such drives. If you wish to move from a desktop to a tower, or vice versa, it is recommended that you purchase the appropriate case and convert the PC into the new case.

Figure 15-10. A family of PC cases. Photo courtesy of Enlight Corporation

Desktop Cases

Although this case style is not as popular in recent years as it once was, desktop cases are still generally available from most PC manufacturers and resellers. Because it also doubles as the base for the PC's monitor, the desktop case is actually more space efficient than the mid-sized tower models. Some tower styles are small enough to sit on a desktop but cannot hold the monitor and end up using more space than a desktop unit would. There are still situations in which the desktop PC is better suited than a tower PC, primarily in situations where floor space is limited.

Until about the last year or so, the desktop case style was the unofficial standard for PC cases. The first PCs, the PC XT and PC AT, were desktop units. The desktop cases of today are smaller than those of the original PC AT and its clones. The common desktop form factor is the Baby AT and now the LPX low profile case, which is also known as the pizza box case. Newer slimline cases, such as the NLX, which was designed to replace the LPX, are becoming more popular.

Tower Cases

In today's market, the tower case style is by far more popular than the desktop case style. This is largely because a tower case can sit under a user's desk to free up workspace, and it provides more internal space inside the case for expanded or upgrading the PC than the desktop case. Three of the more popular tower case sizes are the minitower, midtower, and full tower.

There are variations on these sizes between manufacturers, as there are no standard sizes associated with these three case sizes. Figure 15-11 shows a tower case family from one vendor, HungTech Industrial; Figure 15-10 showed the tower cases of Enlight Corporation. What one vendor calls a minitower, another may call a mini-midtower. After you pick the brand of computer you wish to purchase, look to the sizes and styles of cases available. Among the tower style cases, the primary difference is usually the number of external drive bays and the size of the power supply included in the case design. As more external bays are included, the tower case gets taller and, typically, the power supply gets more powerful.

Here is a brief overview of the popular variations of the tower case style:

- **Full tower** Full tower cases are the largest standard PC cases available. They offer the most of any case style in the way of expandability, typically having three to five external drive bays and a few internal bays as well (see Figure 15-12). A full tower case will normally have a high-end power supply under the assumption that the case will be filled with devices. This style of case is popular among high-end users and for servers.
- **Midtower** A midtower case is a slightly shorter version of the full tower case. This particular size seems to vary the most among manufacturers, but within a single manufacturer's line it represents a good compromise of size

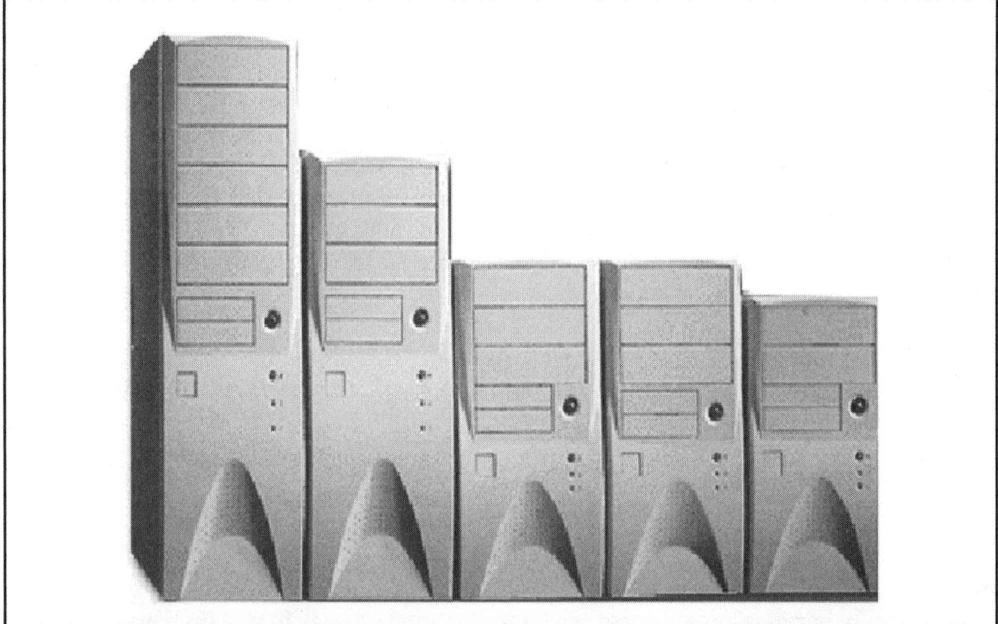

Figure 15-11. A family of computer cases showing a full AT Tower on the left down to an ATX minitower on the right. Photo courtesy of Hungtech Industrial Co.

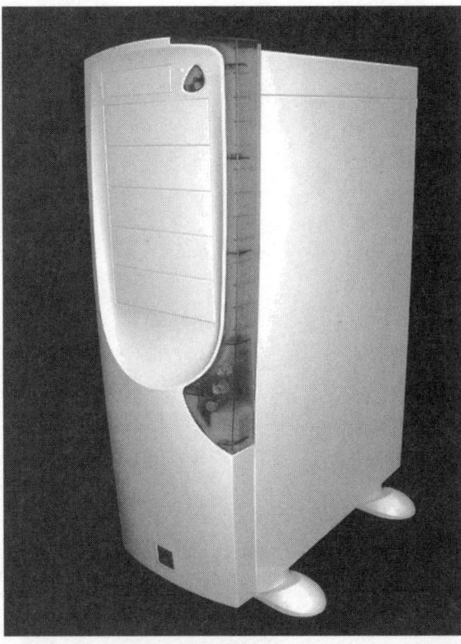

Figure 15-12. A full tower case featuring six external drive bays. Photo courtesy of AOpen America, Inc.

and price. For example, the midtower case shown in Figure 15-13, from In-Win Development (**www.inwin.com**), provides five external drive bays and can accommodate either ATX or full AT form factor system boards, which should be room enough for most applications.

- **Miditower** This case exists somewhere between the midtower and the minitower cases. By definition, a miditower is smaller than a midtower and larger than a minitower. However, typically what you will find advertised as a miditower is either a small midtower or a large minitower or, as is available from one manufacturer, a mini-midtower. Regardless of the case's style name, if it fits your needs, it's the right one.
- **Minitower** This case size is probably currently the most popular. It provides slightly more expansion capacity than desktop cases and is small enough to sit on a desktop next to the monitor. If you are considering converting a desktop case to a tower, this would be an excellent and economical (they run around $25 or less) choice. Figure 15-14 shows a minitower case.

Figure 15-13. A midtower case. Photo courtesy of In-Win Development, Inc.

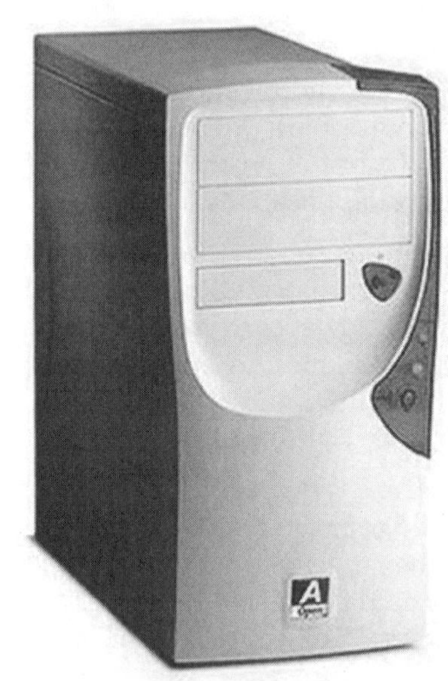

Figure 15-14. A minitower case. Photo courtesy of AOpen America, Inc.

System Case Form Factors

The *form factor* of a PC case defines its style, size, shape, internal organization, and the components that are compatible with cases of that form factor. Computer form factors define a general standard for compatibility for the system case, the motherboard, the power supply, the placement of I/O (input/output) ports and connectors, and other factors.

The three most popular types of case form factors are:

- **Baby AT** Though virtually obsolete by today's standards, the Baby AT form factor is still considered popular because of its very large installed base stemming from its popularity in past years. The Baby AT is a smaller version of the AT form factor that is narrower in width, but otherwise shares the AT form factor's dimensions. Baby AT power supplies and motherboards are backward-compatible with AT cases, but the reverse is not true. AT power supplies and motherboards will not fit into Baby AT cases. Because of its smaller footprint, the Baby AT soon became preferred over the AT form factor. The Baby AT form factor is used for desktop and tower configurations.
- **ATX** Intel developed this form factor in the mid-1990s and it has become the de facto form factor for motherboards and system cases. All Pentium-based systems require motherboards and chipsets that use the ATX form factor specification. This, and the fact that most new systems are using ATX, accounts for why the ATX form factor is so popular. ATX is actually a family of form factors and has replaced the Baby AT form factor as the de facto standard for PC cases, motherboards, and especially power supplies (many form factors, such as NLX, do not define a power supply). Because ATX is generally compatible with Baby AT, many users are now upgrading to this form factor. Other form factors in the ATX family are the slightly smaller MiniATX motherboard specification, the slightly larger Extended ATX motherboard specification, and other smaller specifications, such as the MicroATX and the FlexATX
- **NLX** The NLX form factor, which is also called Slimline form factor, is quickly becoming the new standard for mass-produced desktop systems because it offers manufacturers more flexibility and room for future advancement. The NLX has been established as a true form factor standard. Many experts are predicting the NLX, which is used for both desktop and tower PCs, will become the most popular form factor in the future.

Here are some of the other form factors that have been or are in use for system cases:

- **PC XT** This form factor was used for both the original IBM PC and its successor the PC XT. When the IBM PC AT was released in 1984, it generally replaced the PC XT form factor, but PC XT and its clones survived for a few years. The PC and the PC XT were only available as desktops. The U-shaped case was made of heavy-gauge steel and was fastened on the rear of the PC and removed over the front of the case. The power supply had 130 watts (only 63.5 watts on the PC) and was located at the rear of the case with a power switch that protruded through a cutout on the case.

- **AT** The IBM PC AT, while not much different on the outside, was quite different on the inside. The AT had a larger power supply, and the motherboard and power supply were repositioned inside the case. Because of IBM's policy of open systems, the AT quickly became the form factor of choice among manufacturers. The AT established the form factor on which all subsequent form factors, desktop and tower, have been based, one way or another.
- **LPX** Although never officially accepted as a standard form factor, LPX is the oldest of the "low profile" form factors. It has been around since the late 1980s and over the past ten years or so has been one of the most popular slimline form factors sold. Slimline cases are a little shorter than the cases used with a Baby AT or ATX form factors. This is achieved by moving expansion cards to a riser board that mounts them horizontally in the case instead of vertically, thereby saving inches of height.
- **MicroATX and FlexATX** These two ATX-based form factors define specifications for motherboards smaller than the MiniATX and the NLX. Technically, MicroATX and FlexATX do not define a case form factor, but manufacturers are designing proprietary cases to take advantage of the smaller size (9 inches by 7.5 inches) of these motherboards. These form factors are intended for PCs targeted to the mass market and home users. Figure 15-15 shows In-Win's FlexATX PC case, which is designed for mass-market appeal.
- **WTX** This form factor goes in the opposite direction of the MicroATX and FlexATX standards. Its *W* stands for workstation, and it is a form factor intended for high-performance workstations and servers. This form factor defines a modular case that features a larger motherboard footprint that is twice the size of an ATX motherboard. A WTX case features space for high-capacity, redundant power supplies, removable panels for easy access to components, a large number of hard drive bays, and support for multiple cooling fans. See Figure 15-6 (shown previously) for an example of a WTX form factor computer.

For more information on PC form factors as they relate to motherboards and power supplies, see Chapters 3 and 14, respectively.

SYSTEM CASE FEATURES

Depending on its form factor and from whom you purchased it, your system case will probably include some preinstalled components and features (see Figure 15-16). These components and features, which are explained in the following sections, are usually the optional pieces that conform a generic case to fit a particular form factor and your particular requirements. As several of the form factors are very close in their size and component placement, manufacturers make cases that can be used with a number of form factors. Applying such items as an I/O template, the appropriate power supply, and motherboard mounts turns a generic case into a custom case that's just right for your needs.

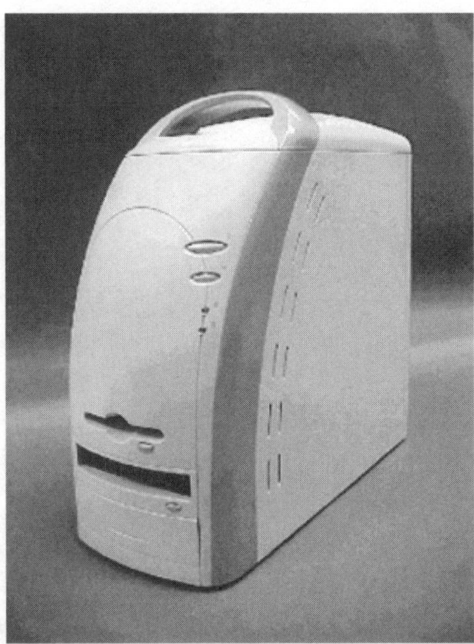

Figure 15-15. In-Win's FlexATX case. Photo courtesy of In-Win Development, Inc.

I/O Templates

Each motherboard form factor also defines the location and placement of the ports used for such input/output devices as the keyboard, mouse, printer, and others. For the most part, these ports are connected either directly or indirectly to the motherboard. Directly connected ports are physically mounted on the motherboard. The case must accommodate these ports with a hole in the right shape so the PC user can access the port. Indirectly connected ports usually mount to the case and are attached to the motherboard with a cable; the case has to either be manufactured with the portholes already in place or provide an adapter for this purpose.

Older form factor cases, such as the PC XT, AT, Baby AT, and the LPX, were manufactured with holes cut into the rear panel of the case to match a particular form factor. However, to make cases more flexible and allow them to service more than a single form factor, manufacturers devised I/O templates, which can be snapped into a case to provide the I/O port pattern desired. Figure 15-16 shows where on the case an I/O template is located; Figure 15-17 shows what the templates look like out of the box.

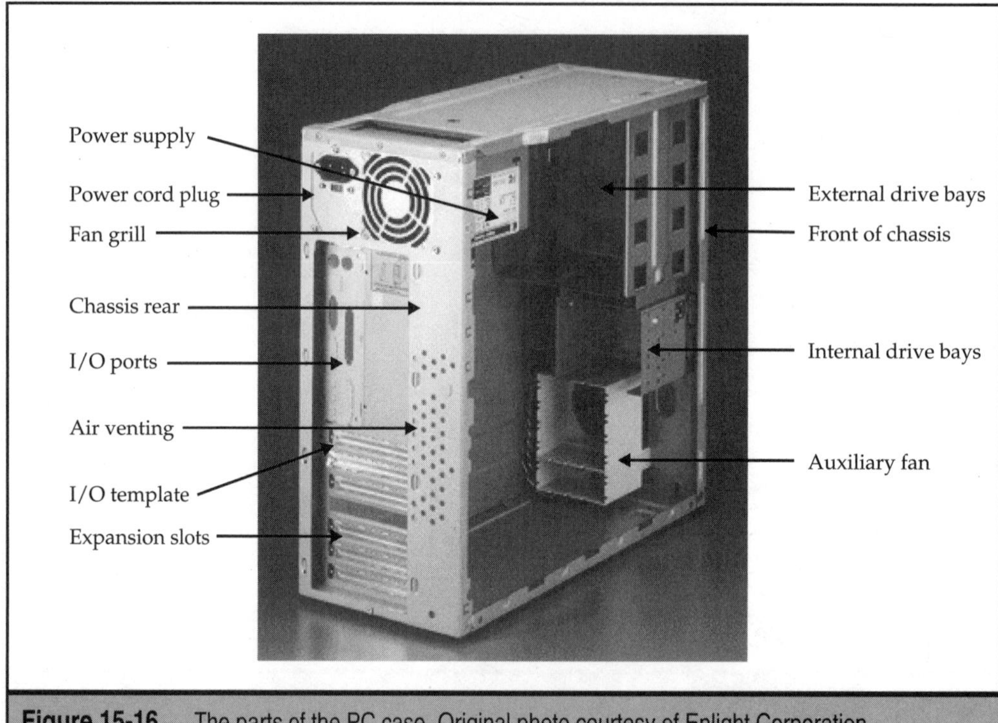

Figure 15-16. The parts of the PC case. Original photo courtesy of Enlight Corporation

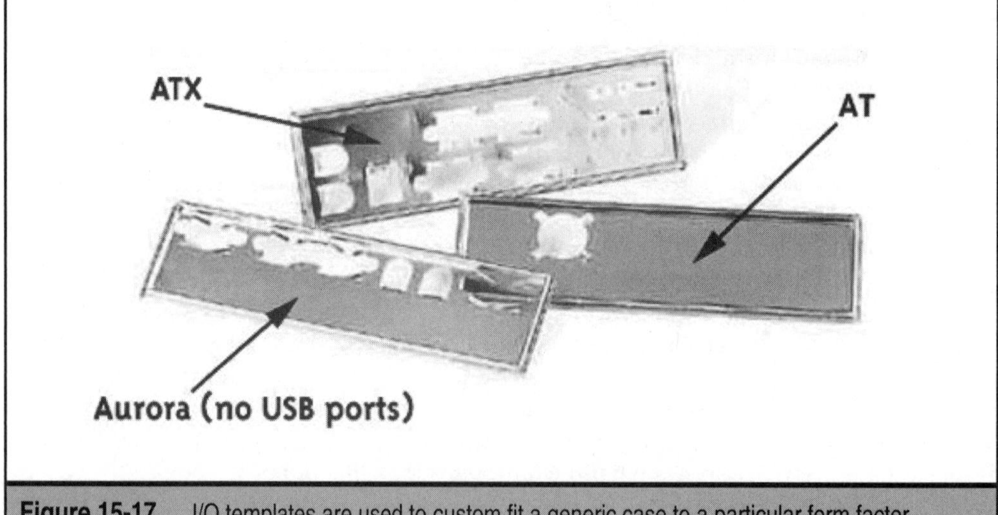

Figure 15-17. I/O templates are used to custom fit a generic case to a particular form factor. Photo courtesy PC Power and Cooling, Inc.

Since the earliest form factors, computer cases have included a number of expansion slots (see Figure 15-18) that can be used to add ports or functions such as sound cards, video cards, video capture cards, scanner controller cards to the PC. The ports for these types of devices are not included in the form factor definition because it is very difficult to predict how each user wants to configure their PC in terms of its peripheral devices. The number of open expansion slots varies by form factor. When choosing a case for your project, be sure to examine the specifications to determine which best meets your needs.

When you wish to use an expansion slot and extend its port through the case, the slot cover is removed to expose the case slot. However, when an expansion slot is not in use, it should be covered. Many cases do not come with slot covers to close their unused expansion slots, so be sure you ask for them or have some on hand.

A current trend among case manufacturers is to leave a punch-out or knockout slug in the I/O ports on the I/O template and the expansion slots (see Figure 15-19). If you are not using a port or slot, you can leave the slug in place. However, be sure you understand how this affects the case cooling before assuming it is a part of the overall case design.

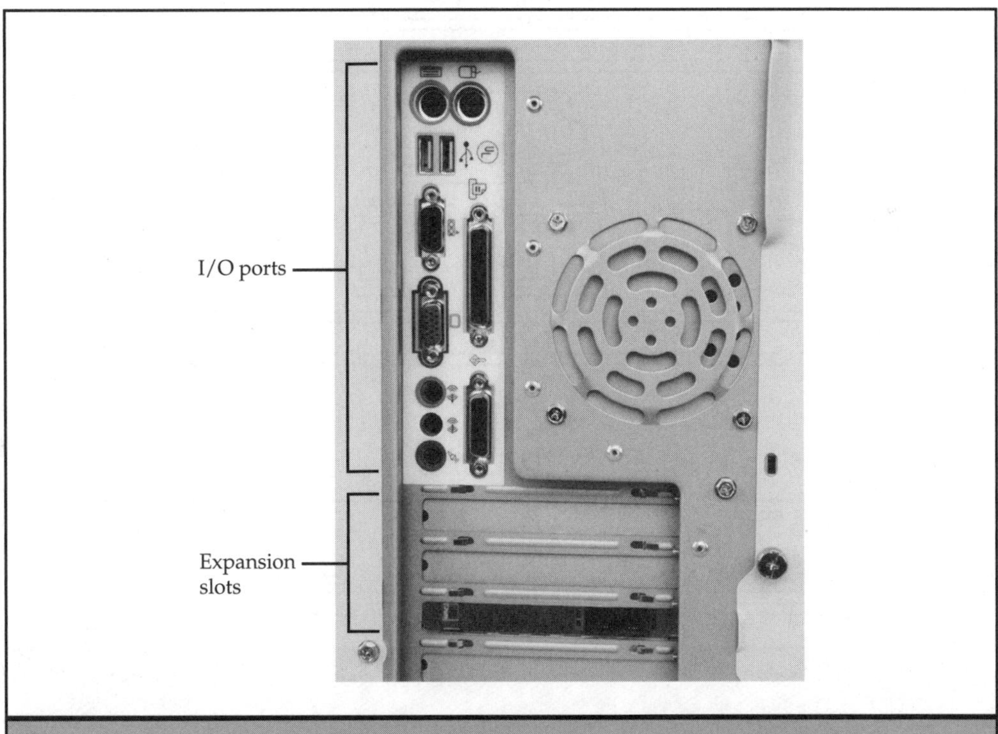

Figure 15-18. The location of I/O ports and expansion slots on an ATX mid-tower chassis

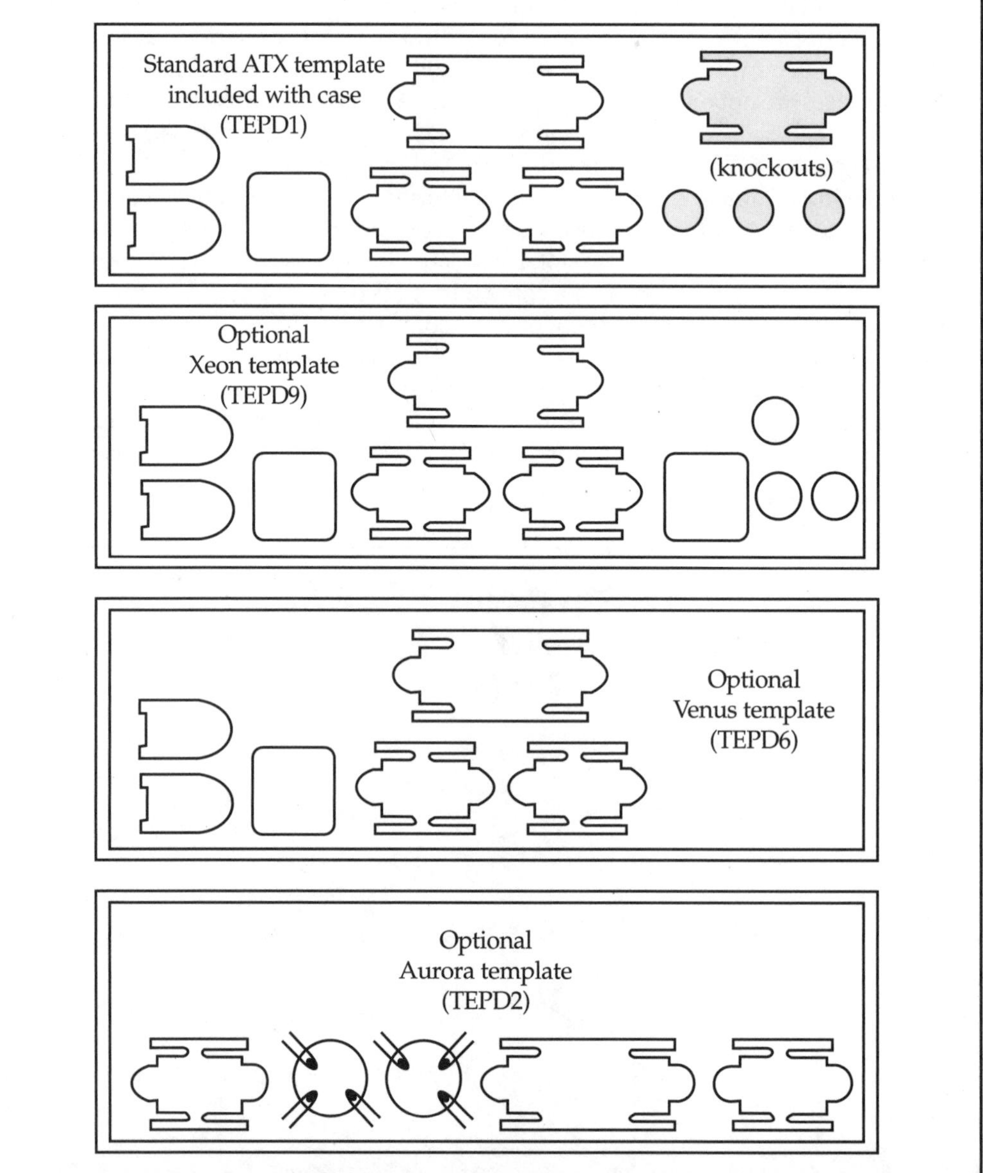

Figure 15-19. Illustrations of I/O templates showing the port slugs in place. Photo courtesy of PC Power and Cooling, Inc.

Power Supply

Most system cases come with a power supply (see Figure 15-20) matched to its form factor. However, the power supply is not a part of the case, even though they are generally sold together as one assembly. When buying a PC case, be sure that a power supply that is appropriate for your application is included or, if you prefer, that a power supply is not included. Many case manufacturers allow you to customize their cases to meet your needs.

See Chapter 14 for more information on power supplies.

Auxiliary Fans

The main cooling fan in the PC is in the power supply. This is one of the very important reasons that you should match the power supply to the form factor of the motherboard and case, in that order. Many newer case form factors provide a location for an auxiliary or supplemental fan to help cool the inside of the PC. Typically, the location of the auxiliary fan, if available, will be on the opposite front or back panel from the main cooling fan, as shown in Figure 15-21.

Figure 15-20. A power supply may be purchased separate from the system case. Photo courtesy of AOpen America, Inc.

Figure 15-21. The locations of the main cooling fan and an auxiliary fan on an NLX case. Photo courtesy of Enlight Corporation

LEDs, the Speaker, and Some Connecting Wires

Under the heading of miscellaneous stuff that a PC case must include are LEDs (see "Status LEDs" earlier in the chapter), the system speaker, and the wiring that connects these two items and others to the power supply and motherboard.

- **Speaker** The system speaker is not intended for stereo sound or to play your audio CDs. It is meant to act as a basic means of communication between the motherboard, BIOS, chipset, processor, and other system components and the user. At best, it sounds beep codes during the boot and other monotone sounds while using the PC. The speaker is normally mounted inside the case near the front panel (so it can be heard by the user), but it may come unattached in some cases so that you can decide where inside the case to mount the speaker.
- **Front-panel wiring** On the back of the front panel near the system speaker, the LEDs, and the keylock, there is a small bundle of multicolored wires that connect these items to the motherboard and perhaps each other. The LEDs

have two wires, one that is either black or white and one that is some other color, which have to be precisely connected to the motherboard. Normally, the colored wire is positive and the black or white is the ground. If they are connected backward, the LEDs simply don't work—no harm, no foul.

The speaker also has two wires that connect to the motherboard with either a four-pin connector or two single-pin connectors. Once again, if it is wrong, it just doesn't work.

Cooling Vents

Although it may seem obvious, air must have a means to get into or out of the system case. Usually, the case has a grouping of small vent holes, cuts, louvers, or the like. A bigger case cools the internal components better than a smaller case because of its larger airflow, but both must still have a way to vent the case. You can assume that any case you buy from a reputable manufacturer (such as those that have been kind enough to supply figures for this chapter) have engineered their cases to properly cool them.

When assembling a system case and its components, be aware of where the vents are and take care not to block them.

Mounting Hardware

If you are buying a new case, it should come with mounting hardware. These pieces normally come with the case, *not* the motherboard. Make sure you have the appropriate mounting hardware, or your system assembly will stall in pretty short order! The exact hardware included varies greatly and depends on what the manufacturer decided to include in the case, but you will generally find some combination of the following (since most cases will use a combination of mounting holes):

- **Plastic standoffs** These small plastic parts are also called "spacers," "risers," and "sliders." The standoffs used inside the system case to mount the motherboard are typically small plastic legs (see Figure 15-22) that snap into the mounting holes on the motherboard and then slide into the mounting slots on the case. In addition to anchoring the motherboard in place, the standoffs keep the motherboard from contacting the system case and grounding or shorting itself.
- **Metal standoffs** Metal standoffs are largely obsolete now for two reasons: they are a bother to work with, and they cost more than the plastic type. However, if you have a case that has threaded holes in place of mounting slots, these brass hexagon spacers need to be used. The standoff has screw threads on one end and a threaded screw hole on the other end. The screw end is screwed into the case; the motherboard, along with some insulating Teflon, Delran, or paper washers, is attached to the other end with a screw. The

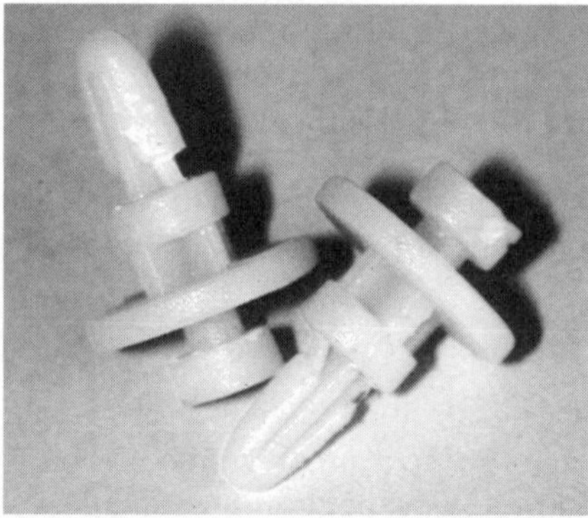

Figure 15-22. The type of plastic standoffs used to mount a motherboard in the case

washers are placed between the standoff and the motherboard and between the motherboard and the screw. This keeps the metal-edged mounting hole from contacting the screw and standoff and prevents it from shorting the board.

▲ **Fixed mounting hardware** There are cases that already have their mounting hardware fixed in place—that is, soldered or welded—to match the mounting holes of a motherboard of the same form factor as the case. This is intended to save you time, but if you ever want to move to another form factor motherboard, you'll need a new case.

CHAPTER 16

Monitors and Displays

There would be no What You See Is What You Get (WYSIWYG) on PCs if there were no monitors or displays on which to see what you get. The PC must produce outputs that can be handled by the senses of humans, and so far, technology is limited to sight and sound. Given a choice, most of us still prefer sight over sound. You can accomplish a lot on a PC without sound, but not much would get done without the ability to see what you are working on.

CRTs VERSUS FLAT-PANELS

The two general categories of PC visual presentation are the monitor and the display. As I define it, a monitor has a CRT (cathode ray tube) and looks something like a traditional television set (without the controls, of course). On the other hand, a display is a flat-panel device that can be attached to a portable PC or hung on the wall. A monitor (see Figure 16-1) is largely desk or table-bound, but a display (see Figure 16-2) can get up and move about.

A flat-panel display is really an adaptation of the monitor, but because it uses different technology, they are treated as two different components. In the following sections, both are discussed in some detail.

Figure 16-1. A PC desktop monitor. Photo courtesy of ViewSonic Corporation

Figure 16-2. A flat-panel PC display. Photo courtesy of ViewSonic Corporation

The PC Monitor

With personal computer technology advancing as fast as it is, it is hard to believe that any part of a PC could be considered an investment. However, the PC monitor is the only part of the personal computer that actually holds its value and has some durability. A good quality monitor will last for years through several generations of PC systems. When making a decision about investing in a PC monitor, a number of things should be considered. Although this entire chapter is about the technologies used in PC displays, here is a quick overview of the decisions you must make:

- **Type** Although there are variations within each type of monitor, such as color versus monochrome, resolutions, dot pitch, etc., the basic choice is between the more traditional CRT display and the state-of-the-art digital flat-panel LCD (liquid crystal display) display.
- **Size** Size has a lot to do with the monitor's capability, but more importantly, it impacts your comfort in working with it. As is true in many things, bigger is better when it comes to monitors. Many experts recommend that with technology where it is today that you should never use a CRT monitor smaller than 17 inches or an LCD monitor with a resolution lower than 1024 × 768 (more on this later).

- ▲ **Cost** Your budget is a very important consideration when shopping for a new monitor. If you cannot spend more than around $400, you can probably forget LCD displays until their prices come down a bit more. If you have a relatively unlimited budget, your choices and comparisons are many.

CRT Displays

Until very recently, standard PC system packages only featured CRT displays. Lately, more and more PCs are being offered with flat-panel displays. As prices continue to drop, many experts believe the CRT will soon be replaced by the flat-panel display on all standard PC packages and be available only as an option. But then, the floppy disk was supposed to have been obsolete over five years ago.

A CRT display has some advantages over the LCD displays. It is bright, well-lit, economical, and produces excellent color and graphic qualities. A CRT display uses the same technology common to the television set. The CRT (cathode ray tube) is a funnel-shaped glass tube that uses electron guns to light up (or as it is technically known, *excite*) phosphor elements on the back of the display glass. The lighted phosphors blend to form images and movements that show through the display of the CRT for the user to view. The user views the phosphors through a single pane of glass, which is why the display is so bright and why it is easily viewed from an angle. There is a lot more to how the phosphor is used to create an image, and it is discussed a little later in the chapter.

Flat-Panel Displays

If you have limited space on a desk or worktable and need to have a PC monitor available, a flat-panel display is probably best for your situation. The major selling point of LCD displays is their size, meaning their depth. A typical CRT display, especially the larger displays in use today, are at least 12 inches or more from front to back, which can take up a considerable amount of workspace on a desk. Flat-panel LCD displays are typically only a few inches deep including its foot, which makes them perfect for small desks, cubicles, or places where a large CRT monitor would negatively impact the aesthetics or decor. Even the new PCs that are integrated into the same package as a flat-panel display are only inches in depth.

Flat-panel displays are backlit, which means the light source of the display shines through several layers of filters and glass before you see it. This is why LCD displays appear to be less bright than a CRT-style display and less legible from an angle. However, LCD displays are digital, which means they are able to reproduce images more accurately, especially colors.

Flat-Screen versus Flat-Panel

Many people are confused by the terms flat-screen and flat-panel. As I discussed above, flat-panel displays are displays that use LCD technology to reproduce images on a screen. On the other hand, a flat-screen display is a type of CRT that has a flat, square screen as opposed to the more standard type of display that has a curved glass screen on the CRT.

The front glass panel on a standard CRT is like a section out of a ball—curved both horizontally and vertically. This places each phosphor element the same distance from the electron beams, which eliminates the distortion along the edges of the display that can be common in flat-screen CRT displays. The electrons on a flat-screen display have further to travel. As a result, they are less focused and arrive slightly later than those in the middle portion of the screen, making them appear slightly distorted.

Some displays, such as the Sony Trinitron CRT, compromise with a CRT that is like a section out of a cylinder—curved horizontally, yet vertically flatter. This allows the screen to be flatter, but the image can look concave at times. Many newer CRTs have screens that are curved like a section from a much bigger ball, which makes the screen appear to be flat to the viewer. These CRTs also have improved the focus of the electron-beam focus that allows it to travel longer distances. Still other CRTs now have a special glass plate over the CRT to optically remove the distortion that appears near the edge of the screen of the flat-screen display.

The flat-panel display avoids all of this by illuminating each pixel equally from behind, which eliminates the need for a curved screen or any optical effects. Flat-panel monitors really are flat.

Viewable Size

As I mentioned earlier, when it comes to PC monitors, bigger is better. As I will discuss in more detail later, a bigger monitor provides higher resolutions and better graphics modes. However, the downside can be that a bigger monitor will also take more room on your desk, unless you can afford a bigger flat-panel monitor.

CRT Display Sizes

CRT monitor sizes are given in what are called nominal sizes. The most popular monitor sizes are 15-inch, 17-inch, 19-inch, and 21-inch. However, this is the size of the CRT measured diagonally from a top corner to an opposite bottom corner, case and all (in the same way a television set is measured and marketed). On a CRT monitor, the case of the monitor includes a front bezel (the plastic around the edge of the display) that covers up a small portion of the display in order to hold it in place. The bezel cuts down the area of the CRT that can be viewed by as much as a full-inch all of the way around the edge of the monitor. Most CRT monitor manufacturers are upfront about this and will usually list the viewable size of the monitor along with the nominal size.

The viewable size of a 17-inch CRT display is actually a bit less than 16 inches. When comparing monitors, it is good idea to compare the viewable image size rather than the nominal screen size. You may be surprised that a smaller monitor may be a better value for your money when you compare the price-per-inch of viewable screen. Table 16-1 illustrates this point by listing the average nominal and viewable screen sizes for CRT monitors.

Nominal Size	CRT Viewable Size	LCD Viewable Size
14"	13.2"	14"
15"	13.8"	15"
17"	15.9"	17"
19"	18"	19"
21"	19.8"	21"

Table 16-1. Display Nominal versus Viewable Screen Sizes

LCD Display Sizes

As illustrated in Table 16-1, LCD flat-panel displays may provide a better bargain on a price per viewable inch basis. The nominal size of an LCD display is its viewable area as opposed to the one-inch margin of error used by CRT manufacturers.

Dots and Pixels

The images displayed on a PC's monitor are created from a pattern of dots in much the same way as the photographs in a newspaper. Dots are shaded lighter or darker so that your eyes can form a visual image from them. The CRT creates these dots from the phosphor on the back of its screen using masking methods that isolate each dot so that it can be illuminated by an electron gun. (I'll go into exactly how the dots are created a little later in the chapter.)

A monochrome, or single color, monitor has phosphor of only one color, so that when the phosphor dots are illuminated, the text and graphic image is a single color on a contrasting background. Typically, the background is black and the display color is green, amber, or white.

The image produced on a color monitor is created by illuminated small triangles of phosphor dots called picture elements, or pixels for short. In the CRT, one-third of the dots are red dots, one-third are green dots, and one-third are blue dots. These different colored dots are interspersed evenly on the screen so that a dot of each color can be grouped with a dot of each of the other colors to form a triangle or pixel.

A color CRT has three electron guns that are used to light up the phosphors in each pixel. The combinations and intensities used to illuminate the phosphors define the image produced on the screen. The electron guns sweep over the pixels from side to side, one row at a time, to create or refresh the displayed image.

LCD displays are of two different types: passive matrix and active matrix. A passive matrix display has a layer of LCD elements on a grid (matrix) of wires. When current is applied to the wire intersections, the diodes (pixels) are lighted. A passive matrix refreshes the display by applying current to the pixels at a fixed refresh rate. Active matrix displays control each LCD element (diode) individually with one or more transistors that continually refresh each element of the display.

Resolution

The number of pixels on a monitor, whether CRT or LCD, determine the amount of detail that can be used to create and image. As the number of pixels increases, the better the image resolution a monitor can produce. The number of pixels on a monitor is its resolution, which is expressed in the number of pixels on each row of the display and the number of rows of pixels on the display. For example, the VGA standard resolution is 640 × 480, which is read as 640 by 480. This means that the monitor has 640 pixels arranged horizontally on each row of pixels and 480 vertical rows of pixels. A monitor with 640 × 480 resolution uses 307,200 (640 times 480) pixels to create displayed images. Table 16-2 shows the resolutions most commonly supported by today's monitors.

Larger size monitors, such as 19- or 21-inch, have trouble displaying smaller resolutions and on most smaller monitors, such as a 14- or 15-inch monitor, higher resolutions don't have the image quality you desire. It is always best to match the monitor and its resolution to your needs.

Resolution is mostly a real estate issue. Most of the larger monitors that natively support higher resolutions can also support lower resolutions, though not well, by using fewer pixels to produce the display. LCD displays have fixed resolutions for the most part and if you use another resolution higher or lower, the image quality will suffer. Where the CRT can enlarge or reduce an image, based on the resolution in use, LCD panels have some trouble doing so.

Because of their construction, LCD displays have natural resolutions that are set by the number of pixels on each line of the display. This is why an LCD display must often reduce the size of the display area to reproduce images in resolutions lower than its natural one. For example, a 12.1-inch LCD monitor (800 × 600 resolution) has 800 pixels

Resolution	Total Pixels Used
640 × 480	307,200
800 × 600	480,000
1024 × 768	786,432
1280 × 1024	1,310,720
1600 × 1200	1,920,000

Table 16-2. Monitor Resolutions

on each row of its display. If the resolution is changed to 640 × 480, it is not possible to evenly represent 640 pixels with 800 pixels and produce clear text or images. So, the display image area is reduced to 10.4 inches for the 640 × 480 image. However, as the natural resolution and the size of the display get larger, reproducing lower resolutions become much easier in the standard screen area. Table 16-3 illustrates how LCD displays adjust for resolutions other than their natural resolution. In the table, *small* means the display is reduced, *full* means it is the natural resolution, and *linear* means that the user must scroll up and down and left and right to see all of the displayed image.

Listed LCD screen sizes generally are accurate, so a 15-inch LCD is closer in viewable image size to a 17-inch CRT than a 15-inch CRT.

Aspect Ratio

The aspect ratio of a monitor is the relationship of its height (in pixels) to its width (in pixels). On most of the commonly used CRT resolutions, the aspect ratio is 4:3, which is by far the most common. The aspect ratio helps software determine how to place images on the screen in relationship to each other and to help shapes like circles look round and not elliptical and squares look square and not like rectangles.

Monitor Size and Resolution

As explained earlier, resolution is a real estate issue. As the space available to hold more pixels increases, so does the monitor's ability to handle higher resolutions. This is not a hard and fast rule, but in general it holds true. Another factor in this equation is the age of the monitor. Most newer monitors can display higher resolutions than many older and larger monitors.

Higher resolutions use smaller pixels and, when applied on a smaller monitor, may require a magnifying glass to read the screen. A 15-inch monitor may support 1280 × 1024 resolution, but you may never actually use it. In fact, you may never actually use the highest resolution available on any monitor smaller than a 19-inch monitor. On the other hand, lower resolutions look better on smaller monitors. Larger monitors display lower resolutions in pixel blocks that can really detract from the image on the screen.

Natural Resolution	640 × 480	800 × 600	1024 × 768
640 × 480	Full	Linear	Linear
800 × 600	Small	Full	Linear
1024 × 768	Small	Small	Full

Table 16-3. LCD Resolutions

Color Depth

In addition to its resolution, the color depth of a monitor is another very important characteristic, depending on your needs. The color depth of a monitor is the maximum number of colors that it can display. The color depth is represented as the number of bits required to hold the number of colors in the color depth. For example, an 8-bit color depth has a maximum of 256 colors, because that is the highest value that can be written in 8-bits. In binary numbers, the range of numbers available in 8 bits is 00000000 to 11111111, or the range in decimal numbers of 0 to 255, which represents different 256 colors. The colors included in the color palette for a particular color depth are represented in the binary values stored in the number of bits available. Table 16-4 lists the number of colors associated with each of the color depths, which are also called bit depths, supported on current monitors.

Depending on the PC, video card, and monitor, either 24-bit or 32-bit is typically designated as True Color setting. The number of colors that 32-bit color, which is popular with 3D video accelerator systems, can develop is perhaps overkill. The human eye cannot distinguish beyond 16 million or so colors. Above that the eye may have difficulty discerning the color distinction of two adjacent pixels.

Checking Out the Color Depth and Resolution

The following is an exercise you can do to check the resolution and color depth on your own Windows PC or notebook computer.

1. At the Windows Desktop, right-click in an empty space to display the Desktop menu shown here:

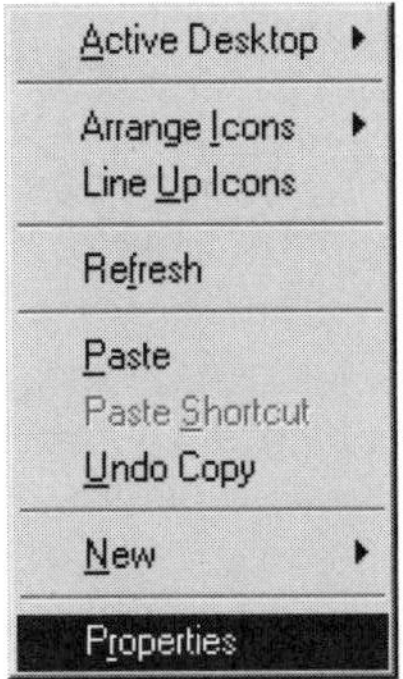

2. Choose Properties to open the Display Properties window shown in Figure 16-3.
3. Select the Settings tab.
4. Towards the bottom of the Settings tab are two side-by-side settings that control the color depth (Colors) and the screen resolution (Screen Area), as shown in the next illustration.

5. Change the Screen Area setting to its lowest (the slide all of the way to the left) value. It should be 640 × 480. Now change the color depth (Colors) to 256 (8-bit) color. These settings are the VGA standard settings. Click Apply. Do not restart the system when asked and apply the new settings without restarting the PC.
6. Unless these settings were what your monitor was set on to begin with, the displayed image should be constructed of much larger elements and may not fit onto the display.
7. Reopen the Display Properties window and change the resolution (Screen Area) and color depth (Colors) to the highest settings available. Once again, accept the settings without restarting your PC. The display should be much more detailed, and all of the elements should be much smaller than under VGA standard settings.
8. Reset the Display Properties to their original settings, unless you prefer their new values.

Refresh Rate

Another key setting on a video system is its refresh rate, or the number of times per second that the screen is entirely redrawn. The refresh rate is actually a function of the video card and indicates how many times per second the data used by the monitor to refresh the displayed image is sent.

The phosphor on the CRT's screen begins to dim almost immediately, so the electron gun must sweep back over each pixel a number of times per second to keep the display sharp and bright. A low refresh rate can make the CRT screen flicker and can cause eye fatigue and headaches. You definitely want a monitor that supports a refresh rate of 75Hz (Hertz) or faster, especially at higher resolutions and color depths. LCD displays do not have refresh rate issues. Because of the way LCD technology works, it can provide stable images at 60Hz and sometimes less.

To set the refresh rate on your monitor, or to check to see what it is set at, follow the steps used above to display the Display Properties Settings window. Click on the Advanced button to display the Properties window for the video adapter in your PC. Select the Adapter tab. The Refresh Rate is selected from a list box that is located about in the middle of the window. On most Windows 9*x* or Windows 2000 systems, the refresh rate is likely set to Optimal.

If you change the refresh rate and the result is a distorted or blurry image, reboot your PC into Windows Safe Mode and reset the refresh rate.

Color Depth (in bits)	Colors Available	Common Name
1	2	Monochrome
4	16	VGA standard
8	256	256-color
16	65,536	High color
18	262,144	LCD color
24	16,777,216	True Color (24-bit)
32	4,294,967,296	True Color (32-bit)

Table 16-4. Color Depths

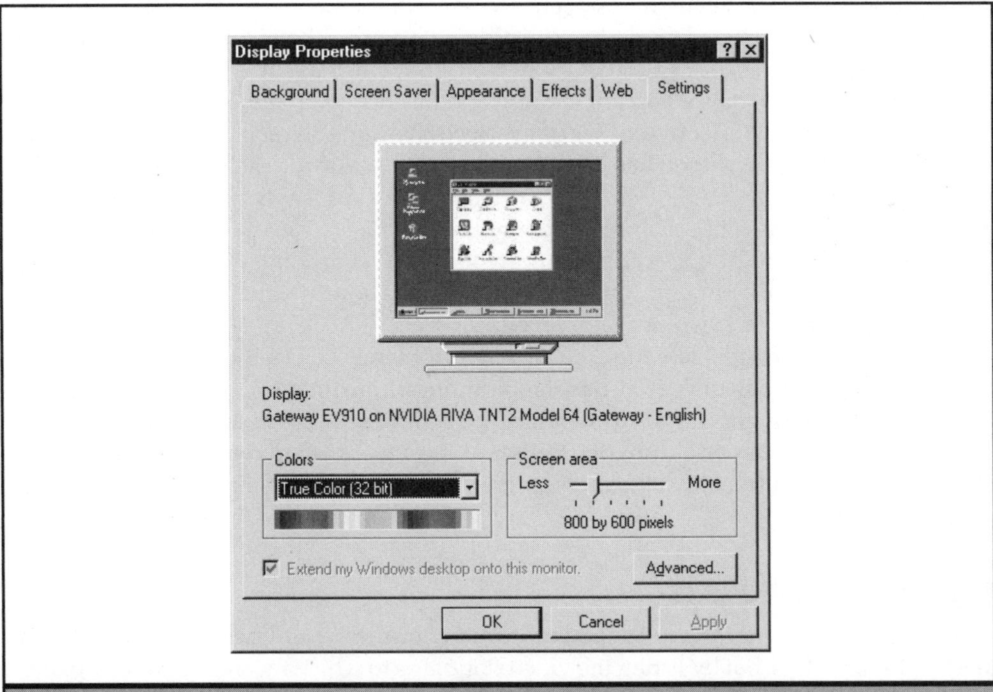

Figure 16-3. The Windows Display Properties window

Signals and Connectors

Another major difference between CRT and LCD displays is that a CRT is an analog device that uses an electrical wave to create the display, and an LCD is a digital device. CRTs, even those with a digital connection, must convert the PC's digital signal into an analog signal. This is done either on the video card or in the monitor by a device called a digital-to-analog converter (DAC). The video card sends the digital information generated by an application program to its DAC, which converts the signal into an analog wave and sends it over the connecting cable to the monitor. Even if the CRT has a digital interface, the signal must still be converted to analog.

A flat-panel LCD monitor connected to a standard DAC video card must reprocess the analog signal through its analog-to-digital converter (ADC), which can lead to image degradation. Analog and digital flat-panel monitors are available. If you wish to use a digital flat-panel LCD monitor, make sure your video card is capable of producing digital output.

Monitor Controls

Most CRT style monitors have a control panel on the front or side that allow you to adjust the brightness, contrast, focus, and screen size or shape. Some use separate knobs for each feature that can be adjusted, and others use a single control knob or wheel. Virtually all new monitors, whether LCD and CRT, have onscreen displays (OSD) that allow you to see exactly what adjustment you are making and its effect on the display. Focus controls on a CRT really adjust the convergence of the electron beams on each pixel. As is discussed in more detail later, each pixel has three electron beams (one for each phosphor dot) that can become misconverged, which is a techie way of saying out of alignment. Misconverged beams cause a blurry or fuzzy image.

The CRT's size and shape adjustments are used to fix barreling (when the sides of the display bow outward), pin-cushioning (when the sides bow inward), and rotation (when the top or bottom of the display is not level).

Although they do not have misconvergence problems, LCD panel monitors can have display and focus problems. A flat-panel monitor has adjustments to synchronize it to the video card. LCD monitors are set to standard VGA timings at the factory, and a particular PC and video card may use a slightly different timing. This can result in a distorted or blurry display. To correct this, the monitor has adjustments for its Frequency/Clock and Focus/Phase settings.

Video Display Standards

Video display standards are developed more to define the capabilities of video cards than they are for monitors, but by listing the video standards to which the monitor is compatible, its capabilities in terms of color depth and resolution are automatically defined.

What differentiates one video display standard from another is the resolutions it supports, how it creates text characters, whether it is color or monochrome, and its color depth, color palette, refresh rate, scan rates, and bandwidth. Table 16-5 lists the resolutions

Standard	Name	Resolution(s)	Color Depth
VGA	Video Graphics Array	640 × 480	16
		320 × 200	256
SVGA	Super VGA	800 × 600	16
		1024 × 768	256
		1280 × 1024	256
		1600 × 1200	256

Table 16-5. Video Standards

and color depths of the VGA and SVGA video standards, the two most commonly used standards today.

Over the years, several video display standards have been used. Here are a few of the more popular ones:

- **Monochrome Display Adapter (MDA)** This standard displayed only text data in only one color on a solid contrasting background.
- **Color Graphics Adapter (CGA)** This standard provided the first color graphics support. CGA supports 2 or 4 colors out of a 16-color palette on a 640 × 200 resolution.
- **Monochrome Graphics Adapter (MGA) (a.k.a. Hercules Graphics)** Developed by Hercules Graphics Corporation, this standard incorporated graphics into the monochrome display. It supported a 720 × 350 resolution for text and a 720 × 348 resolution for graphics, both in monochrome.
- **Enhanced Graphics Adapter (EGA)** This standard improved the text and graphics display capabilities of the CGA standard. EGA supported graphics with a 640 × 350 resolution and up to 16 colors from a 64-color palette.
- **Video Graphics Array (VGA)** VGA is now the de facto graphics standard for all monitors, video cards, and software. It supports a range of resolutions and color depths, as shown in Table 16-5, including 640 × 480, which is commonly known as VGA standard resolution.
- **Super VGA (SVGA)** SVGA is a collection of standards that defines graphics above the VGA standard. SVGA is commonly linked to the 800 × 600 resolution and 256 colors. Most manufacturers consider SVGA the current standard.

Of the video display standards listed above, only VGA and SVGA are in common use today. The others were part of the video standards evolution, and each new standard was an improvement on the last. You may encounter other video display standards, such as XGA (Extended Graphics Array) or UVGA (Ultra VGA), which are loosely defined standards that vary from manufacturer to manufacturer.

The VGA (Video Graphics Array) display standard is considered the base standard for video display systems today. Virtually all current monitors and video cards support the VGA standard. It is the default standard for Windows and almost all other operating systems and device drivers that interact directly with the video system.

Most monitors on the market today claim to be at least SVGA-compatible. What this actually means is that they have some capabilities that are higher than the VGA standard, including resolution and color depth. The same holds true for UVGA and XGA, which are more marketing identities than they are video standards. The Video Electronics Standards Association (VESA) has recently defined the VESA SVGA standard in an attempt to standardize the standards above VGA.

Video Cards

In general, the video card processes the graphics data produced by software running on the PC and prepares it for use by the monitor by converting it from digital data to an analog signal. The video card also sends out the data needed by the monitor to refresh the image or renew it as it changes.

Video cards, graphics cards, and accelerator cards are all names for the adapter card inside the PC that is responsible for generating the signals that tell the monitor what to display. The relationship between the video card and the monitor should be carefully matched. These two devices must be compatible in terms of the signal used to communicate to the monitor, the type of connector used to connect them together, the video display standards they support, and their speed.

For more information on video cards, see Chapter 12.

THE CATHODE RAY TUBE (CRT)

The biggest and most expensive part of a conventional PC monitor is the cathode ray tube (CRT). The CRT applies the same basic technology used in picture tube–based television sets to display the video output of a personal computer.

Painting the Screen

The primary element of the CRT, as illustrated in Figure 16-4, is the electron gun that shoots a beam of electrons on the back of the display screen, which is lined with millions of tiny dots of a phosphorous material. The phosphor dots glow when struck by the electrons. If you look very closely at the monitor's screen, you can see these dots.

Three of the phosphor dots are grouped together to form a pixel (picture element), which is also called a triad. In each pixel (see Figure 16-5), one dot is red, one is green, and one is blue in color. How much intensity is used to light each dot of the pixel determines the color your

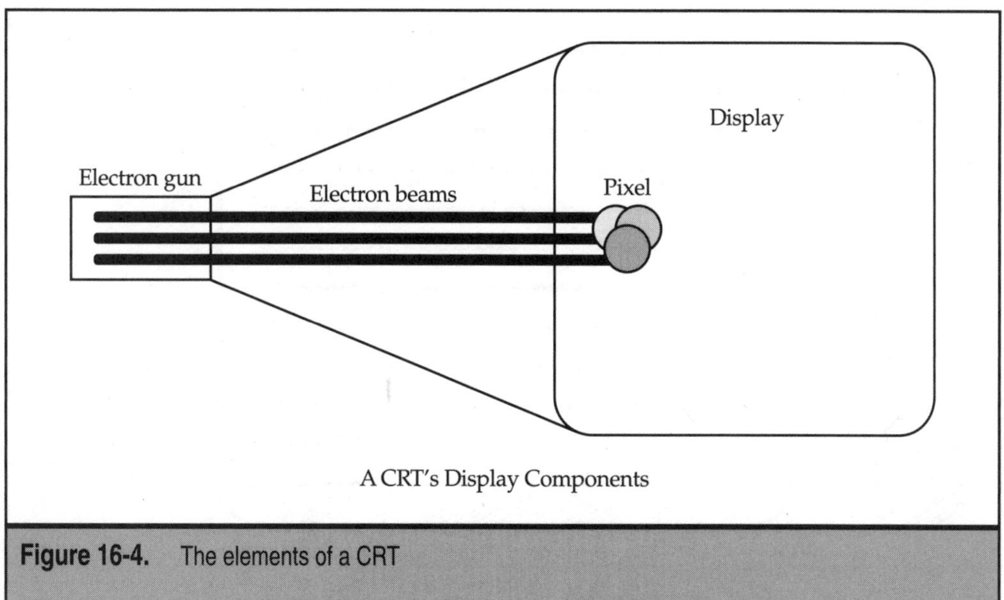

Figure 16-4. The elements of a CRT

eye sees in the pixel. The blending of these three colors is the basis of what is called RGB (red/green/blue) color, which is the color display standard used in all monitors.

As the monitor receives an analog wave from the video card's DAC with instructions for the image to be displayed, it is translated into the color and intensity of each dot in every pixel and illuminates (or as the videoheads say, "excites") them accordingly. As illustrated in Figure 16-6, the electron beams sweep across and down the CRT's display area, illuminating the pixels to produce or refresh the displayed image. The electron beams

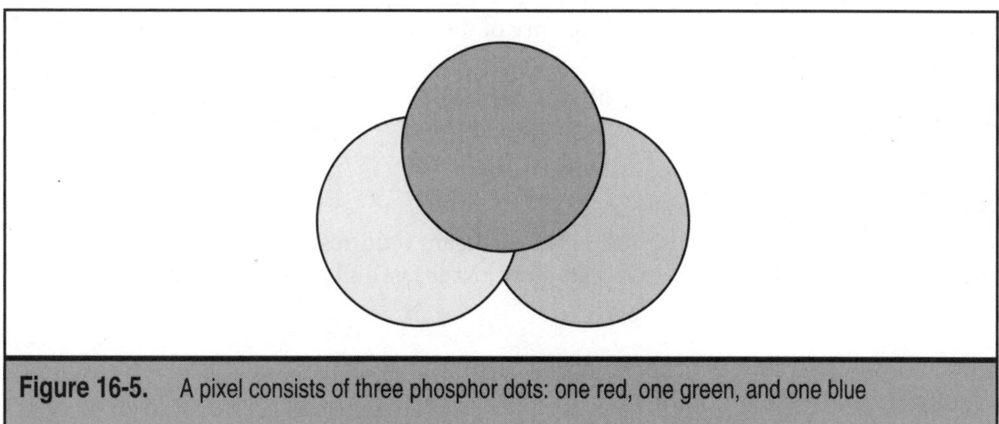

Figure 16-5. A pixel consists of three phosphor dots: one red, one green, and one blue

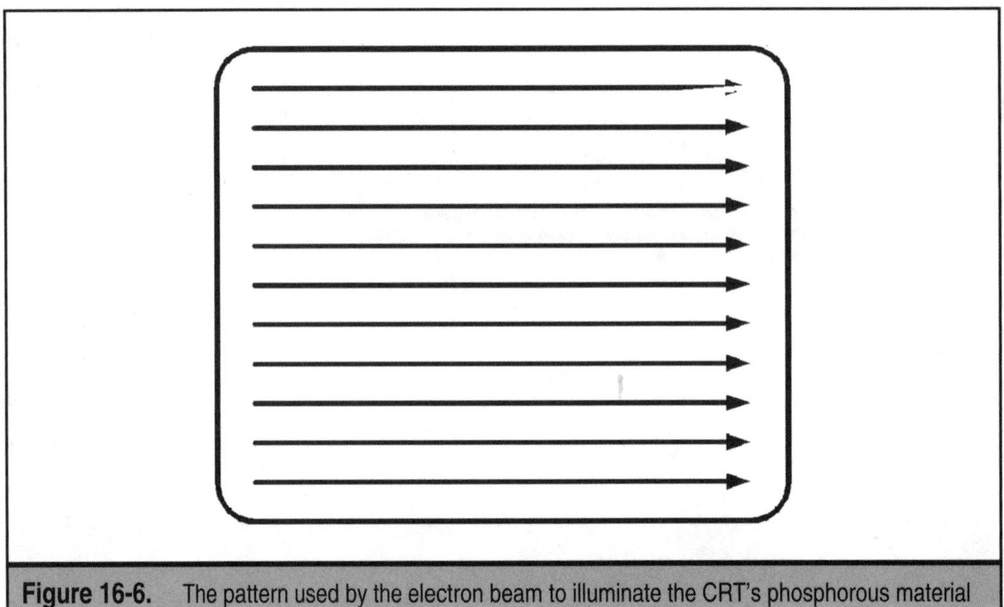

Figure 16-6. The pattern used by the electron beam to illuminate the CRT's phosphorous material

follow a pattern that moves left to right over the top row of pixels and at the end of that row returns to the beginning of the next row and so forth. At the bottom of the screen, the sweep moves back to the beginning of the top row and begins again. The intensity of electron beam, which controls the color and brightness of each pixel on the screen, is adjusted as it moves across the screen to "paint" the display's image.

On a color monitor, the electron beam is made up of three electron streams that come from three separate electron guns. There is one stream for each of the red, green, and blue dots on the display. The streams are arranged to match the standard arrangement of the dots in the pixels. By changing the intensity of the streams, the closely grouped dots will appear to the human eye to produce a certain color. Its color depth sets the number of colors the monitor can produce, but the VGA standard is 256 colors. Most of today's monitors are SVGA (see below) and are capable of displaying over 16 million colors.

Refreshing the Display

One pass of the entire display by the electron beam requires only a fraction of a second. However, the phosphor begins to lose its glow just as fast and must be refreshed constantly.

Most monitors refresh the display between 60 and 75 times per second. A CRT's refresh rate is expressed in Hertz (which means per cycles per second) and common refresh rates for CRT monitors (and video cards) is 60 to 75Hz.

If the refresh rate of the CRT is set too low, the screen will flicker, which can cause eye strain or headaches for the viewer. The refresh rate can be set higher to avoid flicker. Some monitors also use a technique used on televisions to cut down on screen flicker. Televisions use a 50Hz refresh rate. On a PC monitor this rate would likely cause the screen to flicker, but because the television uses interleaving, the flicker is largely eliminated.

Interleaving divides the screen into two (or more) passes by refreshing every other row as it sweeps down the display. On one pass it refreshes the odd numbered rows, and on its second pass it refreshes the even numbered rows. When you consider that most CRTs have at least 600 rows of pixels and 300 of the rows are refreshed in each pass, the screen has an even balance of refreshed pixels. Without interleaving, the top of the screen fades when the bottom is being refreshed, which causes the image to appear to flicker.

Masking the Display

As fast as the electron beam is moving, it is hard for it to be precise. A CRT will include one of two different types of guides to prevent the beam from lighting up the wrong phosphor materials and producing the wrong colors: a shadow mask or an aperture grill.

Shadow Mask

The shadow mask (see Figure 16-7) is a very fine screen that is mounted between the electron gun and the pixels and has openings that permit each beam to hit only where it should. Any phosphor material in its shadow is masked and will not be illuminated, hence its name. The holes in the mask are aligned perfectly with the pixels on the screen.

Aperture Grill

The alternative to the shadow mask method is the aperture grill (see Figure 16-8). On an aperture grill display, pixels are masked into vertical stripes between fine metal wires, which are held in place by thin wires that run horizontally across the display. The vertical wires perform the same function as the shadow mask and keep the electron beam from illuminating the wrong parts of the phosphor. Two popular types of CRTs that use this method are the Sony Trinitron and the Mitsubishi Diamondtron, which are used in many of the more popular monitor brands.

Aperture grill monitors have some advantages over those that use shadow mask CRTs. The advantages include a brighter picture, a sharper image, and because the front of the tube is vertically flat, less glare and less distortion. However, because the vertical

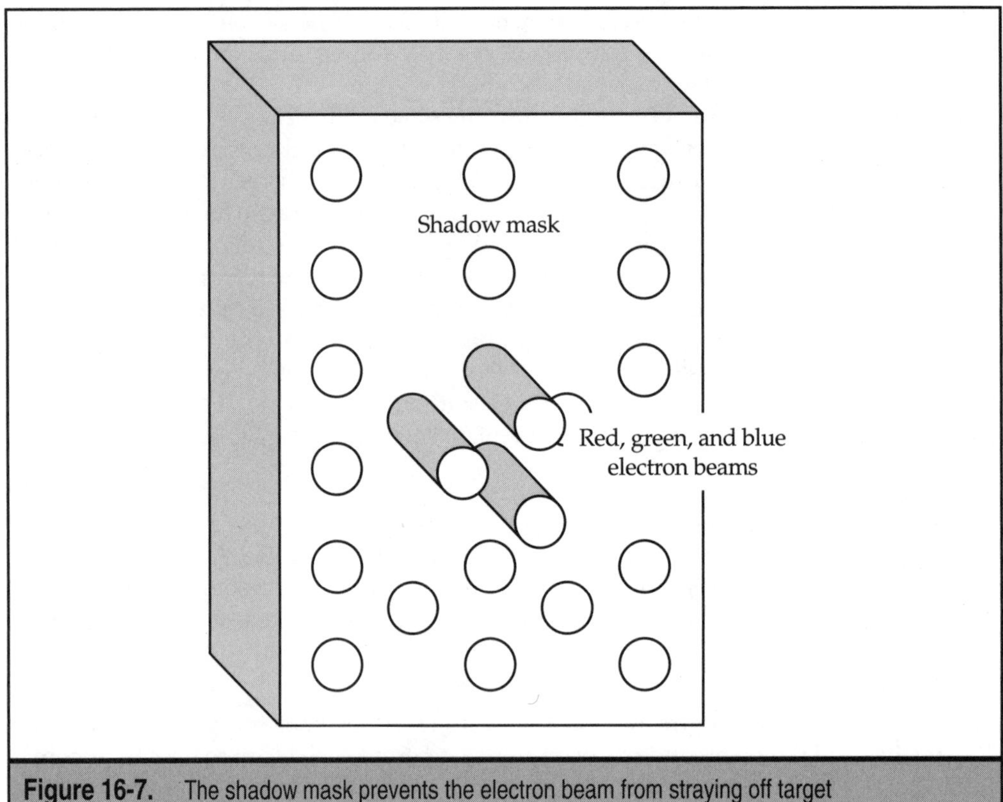

Figure 16-7. The shadow mask prevents the electron beam from straying off target

wires used to mask the phosphor tend to vibrate, especially in larger monitors, thin wires are placed horizontally across them to hold them in place and dampen the vibrations. This results in very faint lines across the screen where the horizontal wires run.

Dot Pitch and Stripe Pitch

The distance between two phosphor dots of the same color is a monitor's dot pitch. The dot pitch (see Figure 16-9) is a measurement in millimeters of how far apart pixels are placed on the screen. A monitor with a lower dot pitch will produce better images than one with a higher dot pitch. Although there isn't a great deal of difference among all of the monitors on the market, even the smallest difference will show up on the screen, especially on a larger monitor. On current monitors, dot pitch distances are in the range of .24 millimeters (mm) to .31 mm, with .28 mm probably the most common.

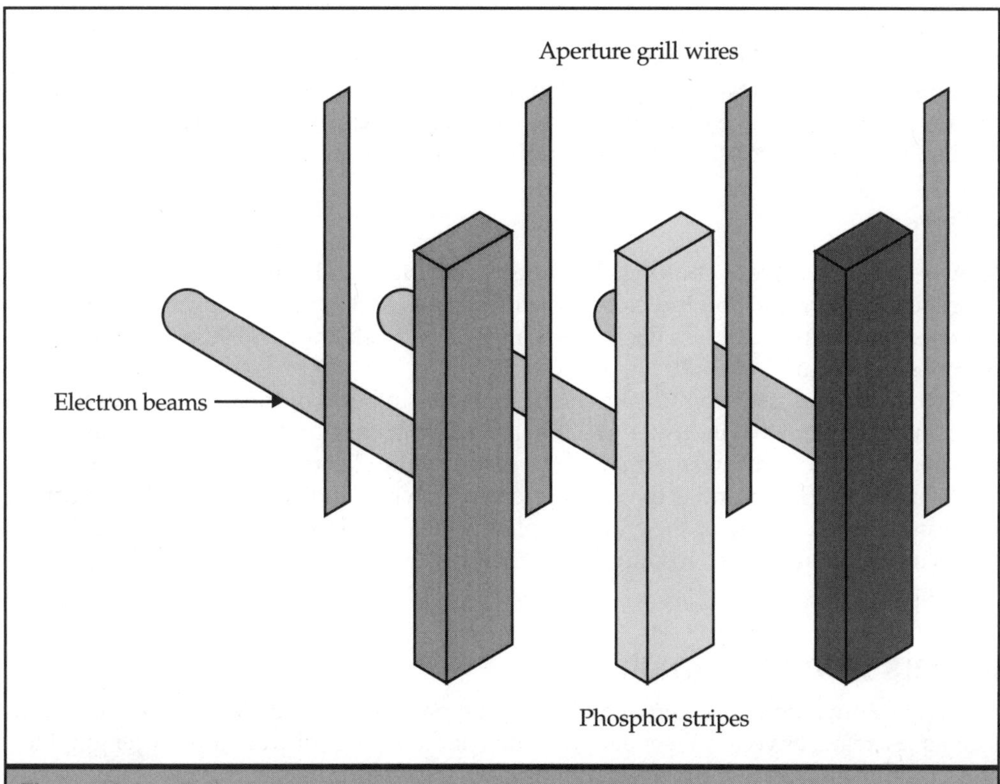

Figure 16-8. The aperture grill divides the display into vertical stripes

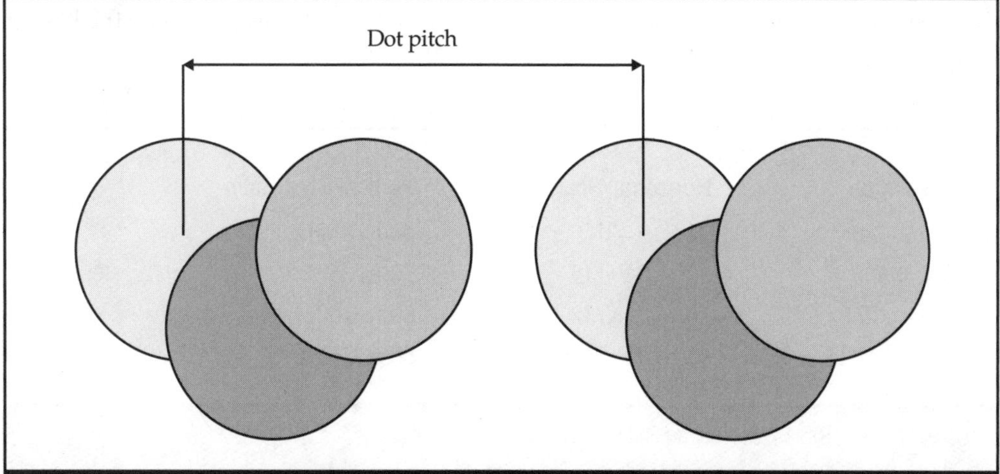

Figure 16-9. Dot pitch measures the distance between two dots of the same color

Aperture grill monitors use stripe pitch instead of dot pitch to indicate the distances between two stripes of the same color. Common stripe pitch distances are about the same as current dot pitch distances—from .24 mm to .32 mm. However, the two measurements cannot be compared to each other. Stripe pitch distances compare only to other stripe pitches. Like a dot pitch though, smaller is definitely better.

Scan Rates

How fast a CRT is able to complete its sweep left to right and complete the refresh of the entire screen of pixels is an indicator of its brightness and image sharpness. The quicker the screen can refresh, the less likely it is that parts of the display will fade before they can be refreshed again.

Two scan rates used to indicate the frequencies in hertz of the CRT. The first is the horizontal scan rate that indicates in kilohertz (KHz) or the number (in increments of one hundred) of left to right sweeps that can be made by the electron gun to refresh the pixels on a single row. The second is the vertical scan rate, which indicates how fast the electron gun can complete a scan of the entire display area. Table 16-6 lists the scan rates for the more commonly used CRT resolutions. Remember that it takes one hundred kilohertz to make one hertz.

Raster versus Vector Graphics

An image drawn on the screen of a CRT can be produced using two different drawing techniques: raster or vector. Essentially, all paint and imaging software uses raster graphics, and virtually all freehand drawing and animation software uses vector graphics. Nearly all graphic output devices, including monitors and printers, are raster devices. In fact, vector graphics must be translated before they can be printed. Most printers include a special processor, called a raster image processor, to perform this conversion. On the PC, metafile formats, such as the Windows Metafile format (.wmf files), combine the best of bitmapped (raster) and vector graphics into a single file.

Resolution	Horizontal Scan Rate	Vertical Scan Rate
640 × 480	31.5 to 43KHz	60 to 85Hz
800 × 600	32 to 54KHz	50 to 85Hz
1024 × 768	48 to 80KHz	60 to 100Hz
1280 × 1024	52 to 80KHz	50 to 75Hz

Table 16-6. Typical CRT Scan Rates

Raster Graphics

A raster graphic, which is also known as a bit-mapped graphic, is a two-dimensional array of pixels that is drawn by assigning a value to each *x* (horizontal) and *y* (vertical) pixel position on the screen. This is the most common technique used to create the image on the CRT display. Colors used in raster graphics can be found in a Color Lookup Table (CLUT), which contains the supported color depth subset of the entire color palette of the video graphic standard in use.

Raster graphics are formed by patterns of pixels on the monitor's screen. A raster graphic is made up of a matrix of on and off pixels. For example, to draw the letter *H* on the screen, a pattern of pixels must be illuminated, as is illustrated in Figure 16-10. As shown, raster graphics are by nature blocky images.

This is even more apparent in images that have curved or sloping edges, like the diagonal line shown in Figure 16-11. A diagonal line drawn on a raster display is a problem because of the row and column orientation of the pixels. Diagonals often have a jagged look resembling a staircase, such as the exaggerated example in Figure 16-11. This effect is minimized as the resolution of the display increases. Another technique used to minimize the jaggedness of the image is antialiasing, which shades the pixels along the edge of the image to minimize the sharp contrast of the image to the background.

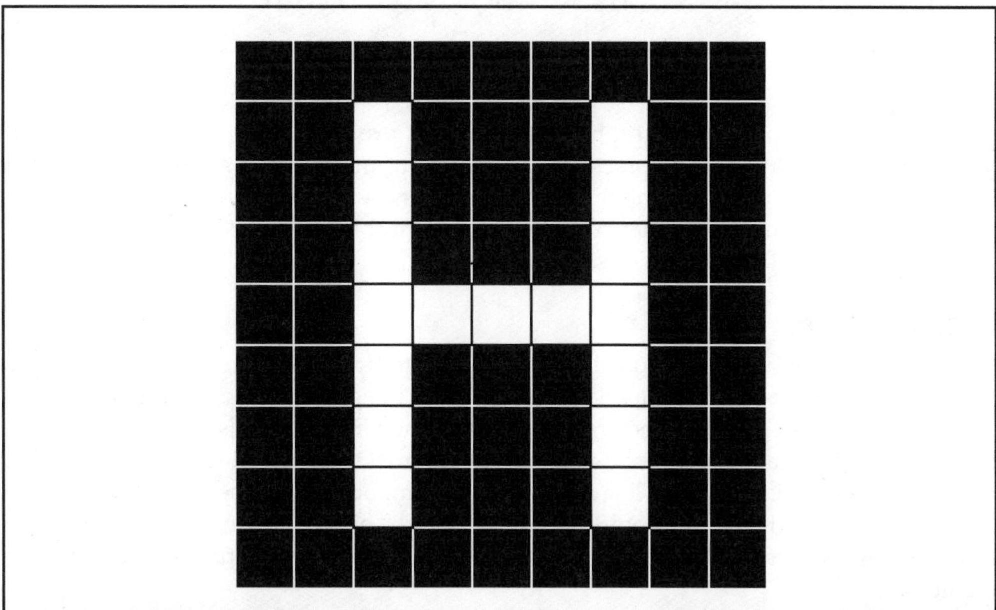

Figure 16-10. A text character created using raster graphics

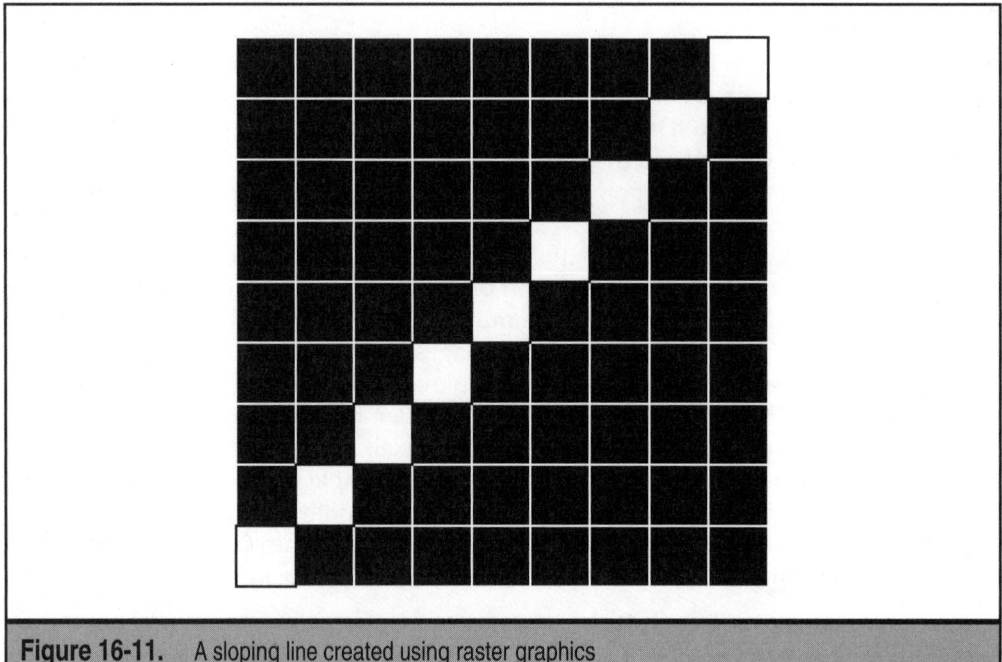

Figure 16-11. A sloping line created using raster graphics

The advantage of a raster graphic CRT is that it provides fixed-rate refreshing and does not differentiate one graphic image type from another. However, as illustrated above, its graphic images can have jagged edges, and every pixel must be redrawn in every refresh cycle. In spite of these relatively minor problems, raster graphics is the most popular type of CRT used with PCs.

Vector Graphics

Vector graphics, which are also called object-oriented graphics, are based on vectors, mathematical information that defines how a graphic image is to be drawn on the display. For example, a line created in vector graphics is defined in terms of its length, width, and the direction it is drawn from a source point. In contrast to the bit-mapped diagonal line in Figure 16-11, a vector graphic line is straight with smooth edges. The vector information to create a circle on the screen would contain the *x* and *y* pixel location of its center, its line thickness, line structure (whether it is solid or dashed), and any texturing or coloring of the line or fill.

The advantages of vector graphics, besides smooth lines and edges, are that they are easily resized, repositioned, or stretched without degrading the original image, and they require less video memory than a raster graphic. However, they can use more memory if used to display a photograph, a particular image type for which a vector graphic is not well-suited.

Vector graphic monitors are very expensive and are typically reserved for use on engineering workstations and other high-end applications, such as GIS (geographic information systems).

Analog versus Digital CRTs

In contrast to the rest of the PC, the monitor has evolved from digital to analog, which does seem to go against the grain a bit. PCs are digital devices and for a while monitors were digital devices, too, but when the demand grew for more than 64 colors about the time of the VGA standard, monitors became analog. Using an analog signal allows the CRT to develop more shades of red, green, and blue.

Theoretically, an analog signal can represent an unlimited number of colors and shades. However, standard analog color is limited to 256 color variations of each of 65,536 colors (16-bit color), which means that over 16 million different colors are encoded in the analog signal. Virtually all monitors in use today are analog monitors.

FLAT-PANEL DISPLAYS

The technologies used in flat-panel displays are completely different from those used in CRTs. For one thing, there is the obvious: a flat-panel display may be only 1 inch deep as opposed to the CRT that may be as much as 18 inches deep. However, the primary difference is in how the displayed image is formed on the screen.

Liquid Crystal Display (LCD)

Liquid crystal displays (LCD) are used in many products, including wristwatches, microwave ovens, CD players, and even PC monitor displays. In fact, virtually all PC flat-panel monitors sold today have an LCD screen. LCD is popular because it is thinner, lighter, and requires less power than other types of displays, especially the CRT.

LCD monitors are more expensive than CRT monitors simply because they cost more to produce. To increase the size of a LCD screen, more transistors must be added. As the number of transistors in a display increases, so does the potential for bad transistors. Manufacturers reject as much as 40 percent of LCDs on the production line, which has a direct impact on the retail price.

Liquid Crystal

Although the name is seemingly an oxymoron, liquid crystal is a material that exists somewhere between a solid and a liquid. Crystals are normally rock-hard, slightly opaque solids, but liquid crystal is not really that kind of crystal. Liquid crystal is created by applying heat to a suitable substance to change it from a solid into a liquid crystal form. Not much more heat is needed to turn the liquid crystal into a complete liquid, which is why liquid crystals are sensitive to temperature changes; this is what makes them perfect for thermometers and mood rings. This is also why notebook computer displays do not work exactly right after being exposed to cold or heat for very long.

More than one type of liquid crystal exists, but computer displays are what are called *twisted nematic* (TN) crystals, which are rod-shaped crystals that are twisted lengthwise. When a current of electricity is applied to a TN crystal, it begins untwisting in a predictable way. With enough electricity applied, the TN crystal will completely untwist. These are the crystals used in LCD flat-panel monitors.

Without getting too technical, TN crystals are placed on layers of polarized glass filters. Without electricity applied to the liquid crystal, light passes through the first glass filter to the last one. When electricity is applied to an area of a filter, the TN crystals in that area begin untwisting, which blocks the path of the light and creates a darkened area on the display.

The Liquid Crystal Display

The display is constructed from layers of different materials, all of which are designed to play a part in using light to create an image on the display. As shown in Figure 16-12, the layers in the LCD are (bottom to top):

- **Mirror** The back of the LCD is a mirror for reflecting light.
- **Polarizing film** A piece of glass coated with a polarizing film on its back.

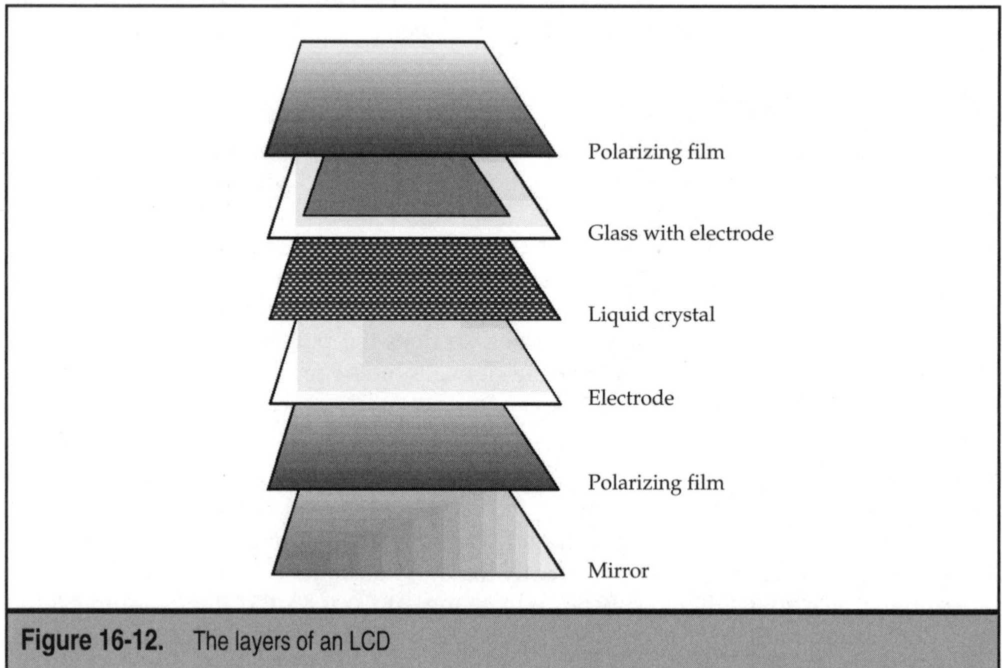

Figure 16-12. The layers of an LCD

- **Electrode** The common electrode plane for the assembly. The electrodes in an LCD are transparent.
- **Liquid crystal** A layer of TN liquid crystal.
- **Electrode** A layer of glass with one or more smaller electrodes attached.
- **Polarizing film** Another layer of polarizing film at a right angle to the other layer of polarizing film.

With no current flowing through the LCD assembly, any light entering the front (or the top in Figure 16-12) will pass through to the mirror and be reflected back out of the assembly. However, when electricity is applied to the electrodes, the liquid crystals between them untwist and block the light from passing through it. The result is that the areas where power was applied now show through the front of the LCD as darkened or black areas.

In a simple LCD, like that on a wristwatch, a top layer of electrodes forms all of the sections used to create the numbers to be displayed. When the electrodes are energized in a certain pattern, the liquid crystal darkens and the viewer sees it as the time. Figure 16-13 illustrates the pattern or electrodes that would be used to display numbers. As the electrode sections are energized, that portion of the display turns black and numbers form, as in Figure 16-14.

LCD Light Sources

Liquid crystals do not produce light, so any light source must come from outside. There are two types of LCD light sources: reflective and transmissive. A reflective LCD reflects the light entering through its polarized filters using only the light available from its environment. A transmissive LCD, which is the type used in portable computers and

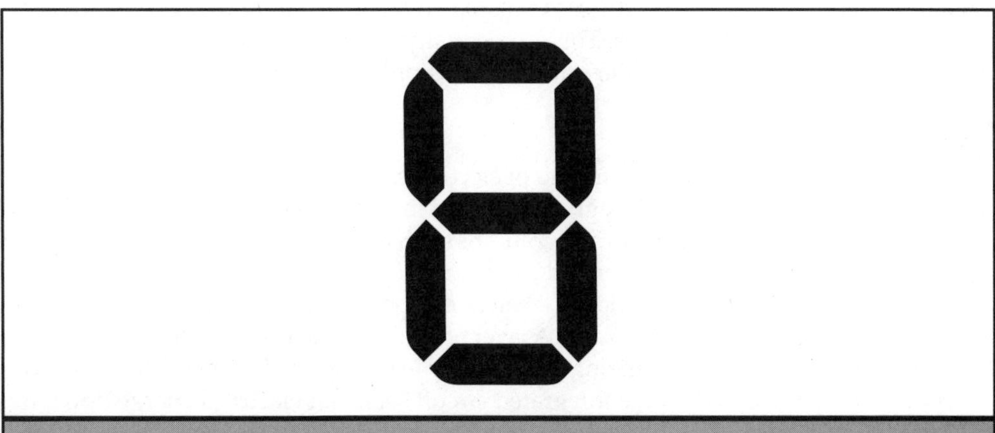

Figure 16-13. The pattern of electrodes used to produce a number on an LCD

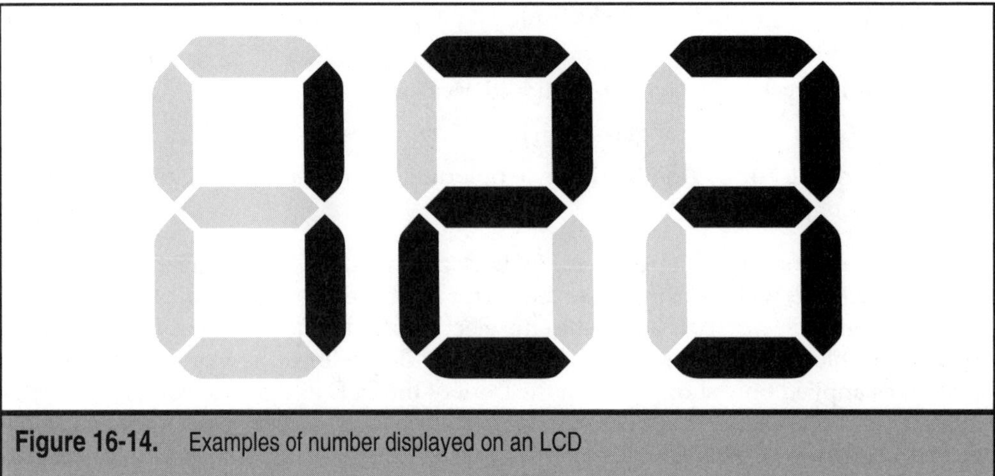

Figure 16-14. Examples of number displayed on an LCD

flat-panel monitors, incorporates back lighting elements. Most computer displays are lighted with built-in fluorescent tubes around the edges and sometimes behind the LCD.

LCD Types

There are three different types of LCD used in various devices: common-plane, passive matrix, and active matrix.

Common-Plane LCD

Common-plane LCD is not used for PC displays, but it is the type used on watches, handheld games, and microwaves. This is essentially the type of display discussed above that is very good for displaying the same information repeatedly.

Passive Matrix LCD

A passive matrix LCD uses pixels instead of electrodes, but the principles are the same as used in the common-plane LCD. A grid organized in rows is used to energize the pixels. Integrated circuits control the rows and columns to ensure that a charge sent over the grid gets to the specific pixel it was intended to activate.

The rows and columns of the grid are created on separate layers of a transparent conductive substrate, typically indium tin oxide. A layer of liquid crystal is sandwiched between the two substrates, and a layer of polarizing film is added to the top and bottom of the sandwich.

A pixel is energized when the integrated circuit sends an electrical charge down the appropriate column (on one of the substrates) and a grounding charge over the appropriate row (on the other substrate). The two charges converge at the pixel located at the intersection of the row and column. The charge untwists the liquid crystals of the pixel and the area darkens.

Unfortunately, in spite of its simplicity or because of it, a passive matrix LCD has its disadvantages. The major disadvantage is its refresh speed or response time, as it is called on LCDs. Another is that the grid system delivers electricity imprecisely. The charge sent to open (untwist) a liquid crystal pixel may also affect the pixels around it, which partially untwist, causing a fuzzy display and image contrast problems.

Passive Matrix Liquid Crystal Types There are three types of liquid crystals used in passive matrix displays:

- **Twisted nematic (TN)** This type of liquid crystal has a 90-degree twist. It is used in low-cost displays and provides a black on gray or silver background. Not too common on recent computer products but still used on consumer electronics and appliances.
- **Supertwisted nematic (STN)** Despite its ominous name, this is the type of liquid crystal used in most portable PCs and personal digital assistants (PDAs). It has 180-degree or 270-degree twists, which means it has more tolerance against the electricity radiating from nearby pixels and provide more degrees of color shading. It is used for both monochrome and color displays.
- **Dual-Scan STN (DSTN)** This type of LCD divides the display into two halves, which are scanned individually and simultaneously, which doubles the number of lines refreshed and cuts in half the time to refresh the display.

Active Matrix LCD

Active matrix LCDs use thin film transistors (TFT), which are switching transistors and capacitors, arranged in a matrix on a glass substrate. Three transistors are used to support each liquid crystal pixel in the display, one for each of the RGB colors. For example, a color VGA 640 × 480 display uses 921,600 transistors, and a 1024 × 768 display uses 2,359,296 transistors, which are etched into the substrate glass. If a transistor has a problem, it creates a bad pixel that may not be able to display one or more colors. It is common for TFT displays to have some bad pixels.

A pixel is addressed somewhat like the process used in a passive matrix, with the exception that when a certain row is addressed on an active matrix display, the other rows are switched off and the signal is then sent down the appropriate column. Since only the addressed row is active, there is no danger of energizing any pixel besides the one addressed. The capacitor in the TFT is able to hold the charge until the next refresh cycle recharges it. By controlling the amount of electricity that flows to the pixel, the amount that the liquid crystal untwists is also controlled, along with the amount of light that is allowed to pass. In fact, most active matrix screens are able to display 256 levels of brightness per pixel.

The active matrix display produces a sharp, clear image with good contrast. However, active matrix displays are more expensive than passive matrix displays due to their higher manufacturing costs.

Color Displays

LCDs that display colors have three subpixels at each pixel location that have red, green, and blue filters over them to produce a color on the screen. By controlling the voltage applied to each subpixel, each of which has its own transistor, it can display 256 shades of its color. Combining all of the possible shades for all three of the subpixels yields over 16 million colors that can be displayed.

Viewing Angles

The viewing angle of a display measures how far above, below, or to the side of the display the user can be and still be able to accurately view its image. Table 16-7 compares the viewing angles of the two LCD displays to a CRT. Figure 16-15 illustrates the relative differences of the viewing angles of these displays.

What impacts the viewing angle as much as the shape of the screen is the amount of image contrast the display produces. An active matrix (TFT) display has deeper color, clarity, and contrast than a passive matrix display. LCD displays begin to lose their picture quality as the angle of view increases because less of the display's light (image) is able to reach the viewer.

INTEGRATED PC AND MONITORS

New systems are being introduced almost on a weekly basis that integrate the PC into a flat-panel monitor. These PCs are the ultimate in desktop space efficiency, making the keyboard the largest single piece of the PC. The PC's footprint is literally the space taken by the foot on the monitor's stand. PCs integrated with flat-panel monitors have been a mainstay in many industrial applications for a few years, but now the technology is transferring to the desktop.

These systems vary in features and pricing and generally offer a fair to good configuration in terms of RAM and disk space. However, because of their tight packaging, there isn't much room for expansion cards, disk drives, or other internal devices. Any additional peripheral devices that the user wishes to add must be done through either a USB or an IEEE 1394 (FireWire) connector.

Display Type	Viewing Angle
Passive Matrix LCD	49–100 degrees
Active Matrix LCD	90–120 degrees
CRT	120–180 degrees

Table 16-7. Display Viewing Angles

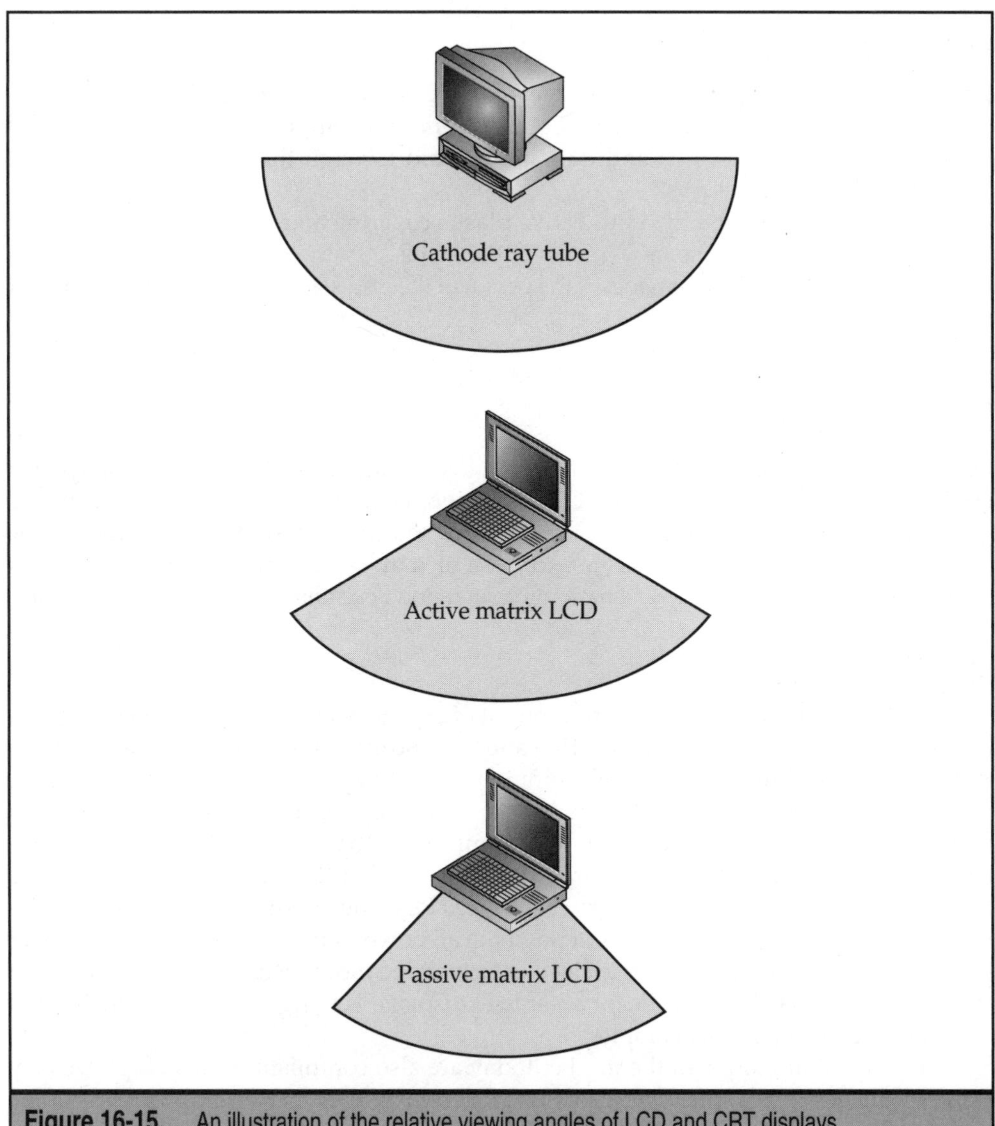

Figure 16-15. An illustration of the relative viewing angles of LCD and CRT displays

This special PC configuration, which is also referred to as Web or Net station, integrates the motherboard, disk drive, CD-ROM, and perhaps a floppy disk drive into the housing of a flat-panel monitor. In effect, this configuration is the equivalent of a notebook computer with a very large flat-panel display.

PEN-BASED SYSTEMS

An application of passive matrix LCD technology is the portable pen-based computer, a.k.a. the personal digital assistant (PDA) or palmtop computer. Although it may also have a keyboard, commands and data are entered through the screen with a special nonwriting pen or stylus.

The display is covered by a protective plastic covering and beneath the display is a mechanism to recognize the movements of the stylus. A wire grid is placed beneath the display that records the movements of the pen over the grid's intersections, which is similar to the technology behind touch-screens.

MONITOR POWER

Monitors do not run off the PC's power supply. Even in the days when the monitor's power cord could plug into the back of the PC's power supply, the plug it used was an AC power pass-through plug. A PC monitor uses more power than all of the other components of the PC added together, with the possible exception of some laser printers. Because of how it works, several power issues exist on monitors that don't exist on a PC or its power supply.

Power Management

In an effort to reduce the tremendous amount of energy being consumed by monitors in active mode, one government initiative and one industry initiative emerged to try to reduce the power consumption of PC monitors when they are idle.

The U.S. Environmental Protection Agency (EPA) developed a program called Energy Star that certifies monitor (and personal computers) that meet the guidelines for reduced energy consumption. This program is also called the Green Standard and the computers that meet the standard are called *green PCs*. The Energy Star program certifies monitors that use less than 30 watts of power in all power modes and reduce their power consumption by 99 percent when in sleep or suspended mode. Most PCs sold today meet this standard; you will see the Energy Star logo displayed on the monitor during the boot sequence on those PCs that comply.

Virtually all monitors on the market today are also compliant with VESA's Display Power Management System (DPMS) protocol. DPMS is used to power down parts of the monitor and PC after they have been idle for a certain period of time. DPMS is a BIOS-supported protocol that can be enabled in the CMOS settings of the PC.

Degaussing

Over time, the internal components of a CRT become magnetized and can have a negative impact on the image quality of the monitor. If the CRT becomes overly magnetized, the display can develop color blotches near the edges and especially in the corners. There are lots of ways that the CRT can be magnetized, including having a set of stereo speakers or another form of magnet sitting too close to the monitor, bumping the monitor very hard, or sitting on top of the PC's system unit over the power supply.

The remedy to magnetization of the CRT is a process called degaussing, which is a term derived from gauss—a measure of magnetic force. Most better monitors have a built-in degaussing circuit that neutralizes the CRT's magnetization with a coil of wire inside the monitor. The degaussing circuit is activated by either a manual switch or automatically through the monitor's controls.

On monitors with a manual degauss switch, pressing the switch will neutralize the magnetization problems of the monitor. Over degaussing a monitor can hurt it; so don't just keep pushing the degauss button to solve what may be display problems. The degauss process involves some clicking and buzzing and takes only a few minutes to complete.

Most newer monitors perform an automatic degauss process when they are powered up. The static buzz and click you hear when the monitor is powered on is the degaussing circuit neutralizing any magnetization build up. If the built-in degaussing circuits of the CRT do not clear up the magnetization problem, I recommend taking the monitor to a repair shop for manual degaussing with a special degaussing tool.

Screen Savers

When monochrome monitors were the standard, screen saver software became necessary to keep the electron beam on a monitor from burning a static image into the phosphor. If the monitor screen became idle with an image on it, the CRT would continually refresh it until the phosphor burned the image into the surface of the CRT screen. This was called ghosting and was a real threat on monitors that were idle with a static display for long periods of time. Take a look at the monochrome displays at the airport some time.

Screen saver software kept the screen changing and did not let the same image remain on the screen long enough to burn into the glass. On modern color monitors, a screen saver really does nothing to help the monitor as there is little chance of the pixels burning their image into the CRT display. Screen savers are primarily entertainment these days. However, a screen saver can be a first-line security device to keep prying eyes from viewing your work. Most screen saver systems can be assigned a password that controls who can deactivate the screen saver and access the PC. On a Windows system, the screen saver password is set on the Display Properties window, as shown in Figure 16-16.

MONITOR MAINTENANCE

The life span of a PC monitor, assuming the user wishes to keep using it, should be between five and eight years. In fact, the monitor is the one part of the PC that holds its value over the life the PC. Monitors cost about the same as they did three to four years ago, and as long as the monitor is still doing its job, there is little sense in replacing it. In most situations, the monitor is purchased along with the PC and stays with it as long as both are working.

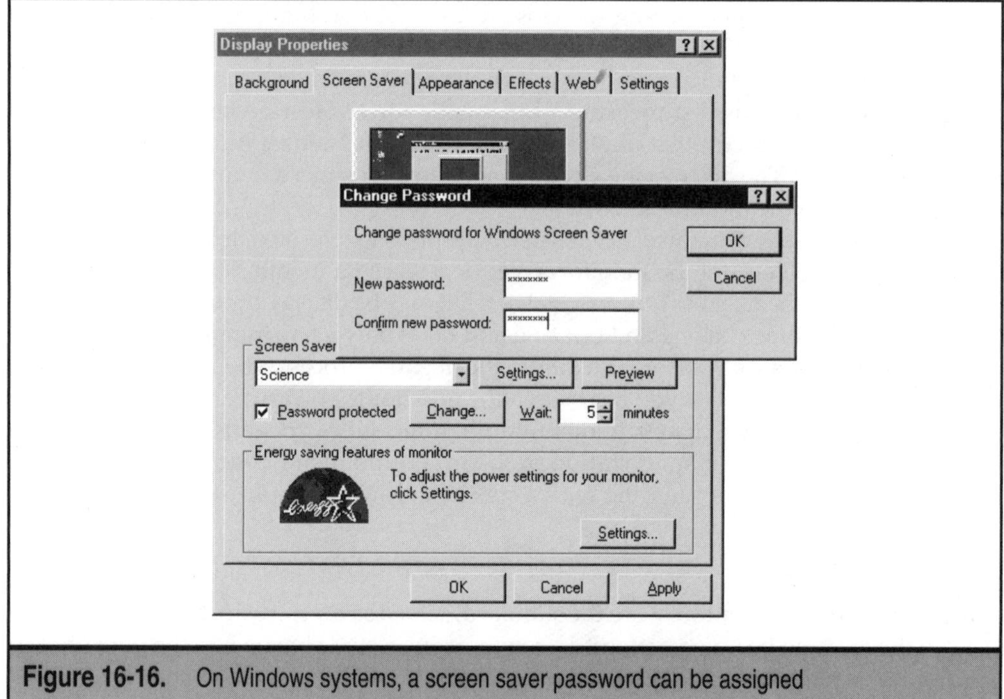

Figure 16-16. On Windows systems, a screen saver password can be assigned

Should a monitor, regardless of whether it is a CRT or a flat-panel LCD, need repair, it should be repaired only by the manufacturer or an authorized repair shop. However, before having repairs done, compare the cost estimate to the cost of a new monitor. Most of the time, the cost to repair a monitor is relatively inexpensive as the problem is typically common and can be easily and quickly repaired.

Caring for the Monitor

Here are some tips you should use for extending the life of a monitor. Most of them apply to CRT monitors, for obvious reasons, but common sense should be your guide with any monitor.

- A CRT monitor should always have plenty of free space and airflow around it to allow its cooling system to work efficiently.
- Never stack anything on top of the monitor or around it. If you do, you may shorten the life of the CRT by causing it to overheat. The CRT is the most expensive part of the monitor to replace.

- You should never place heavy items of any type on top of the monitor. This can cause the case to crack or at least flex and perhaps cause something inside the case to short. In particular, never put tapes, disks, or other magnetic media on top of a monitor. A very large magnet lives inside the case and another magnet could easily erase the data on the media.
- Keep the monitor (and PC) at a distance from heat sources, damp environments, magnets (including those in standard PC or stereo speakers), motors, or areas in which static electricity is a problem.
- Use the power cord supplied with the monitor. Typically, this cord is specially designed to handle your monitor's voltage. If it is misplaced, obtain a replacement from the manufacturer or a dealer for that brand of monitor. Don't confuse the PC's power cord with the monitors when moving the system.
- The monitor's case should only be cleaned with a damp lint-free cloth. Always unplug the monitor before cleaning it or using any water-based cleaning solution on it. The monitor's screen can be cleaned with the same cloth or with a little glass cleaner. Don't spray any liquids on the screen. Instead spray it on the cloth, wipe the screen, and then wipe the screen completely dry. Avoid strong degreasers or ammonia-based cleaners because they can impact the screen's glass and even affect the colors of the display (they leave a residue).
- The stand that shipped with the monitor is actually engineered as a part of the cooling system. If you remove it and sit the monitor on its case bottom, you run the risk of blocking the air vents on the bottom of the case. The monitor needs to be sitting up to allow proper airflow for the cooling system.
- Avoid touching the screen with your hands. Oil and dirt from your hands are very hard to remove from the screen.

MONITOR SAFETY

Rule number one when working with a CRT monitor is that you never—repeat, *never*—open the monitor's case. Any and all repairs that must be done to the monitor are invariably inside the case and should be performed at a repair shop that is set up to work on monitors.

Personal Safety

The reason for all of this caution is that inside the monitor is a very large capacitor, which is an electronic device that holds power and uses it to regulate the power stream it receives. Remember that the monitor is not powered by the PC's power supply; it is plugged directly into an AC outlet. The monitor has a power supply much like that in the PC, and it holds power to absorb power spikes and fill in under voltage events. Inside the monitor case is a 1000-microfarad capacitor, which holds more than enough electricity to seriously harm you or worse, even when the monitor is off and unplugged.

Another safety tip that could save your life is that if you ignore these warnings and insist on opening the monitor case to work on it, absolutely do *not* wear an ESD wrist strap. If you do, you will become the grounding circuit for all of that stored electricity.

Environmental Issues

There are two primary environmental issues involving PC monitors, specifically CRT monitors. The first issue is radiation emissions and the other is disposing of a CRT properly.

Electromagnetic Emissions

There is no debate as to whether a CRT emits small amounts of electromagnetic radiation in what are called the Very Low Frequency (VLF) and Extremely Low Frequency (ELF) ranges. The debate concerns whether this radiation is harmful.

Most VLF and ELF radiation, which is not a lethal variety like an X-ray or gamma ray, is emitted from the back and sides of the monitor and through the screen. This radiation does not carry far and is virtually nonexistent only a few feet from the monitor. The general rule of thumb is that users sit an arm's length from the monitor's screen to protect their eyes. If you impose this limit on the back and sides, everyone should be safe.

None of the research performed to date has found any real danger, although many experts believe there is still some danger, in being exposed to these radiations for extended periods. The belief is that extended exposure at close range may increase a user's risk for cancer, leukemia, or abnormal pregnancies, miscarriages, or birth defects. The Swedish government through its TCO environmental standards organization has instituted very tough CRT emission standards, first in its MPR-II standards and with its latest series of standards—TCO '92, TCO '95, and TCO '99. Although many manufacturers believe these standards to be overly strict, they have complied. If you wish to buy a monitor that meets the TCO standards, expect to pay a bit more for it. For more information on the TCO personal computer standards, visit **www.tco-info.com**.

CHAPTER 17

Printers

Once considered an expensive luxury for any PC, especially for home or small office systems, a printer is now virtually a necessity on any PC system. Technology has advanced to the point that good quality, color printers are available for less than $200, and it is common for PC sale bundles to include one.

When software was still fairly unsophisticated and applications that produced output worth saving were few, the printer was a true luxury. Electronic spreadsheet and word processing applications allowed the user to prepare budgets, reports, letters, and other documents prepared for the sole purpose of being physically shared. Even in today's networked environments, where documents can be shared and collaborated on electronically, the need to produce a printed paper copy of a document is still a necessity for a significant portion of documents produced on the PC. The printer has definitely become a necessity for today's PC user.

It is certainly a toss-up whether the modem or the printer is the next most important peripheral device (after the monitor, of course). However, it is safe to say that these three peripherals are the must-haves of most PCs. The printer provides a means of permanently saving what the monitor can only display temporarily. For visual content, the monitor is capable of only temporarily holding its contents and only until the next visual image comes along. On the other hand, a printer's output is a permanent record of a visual image, drawing, chart, or document.

This chapter looks at the various types of printers commonly used with PC systems, their best uses, how they work, and a bit of minor troubleshooting.

PRINTER TYPES AND TECHNOLOGIES

Today, a wide variety of printing mechanisms have been adapted for use with a personal computer. However, that wasn't always the case. Here is an overview of how the printers used today evolved.

The Evolution of the PC Printer

Over the years, the printing mechanisms used to print words and graphics on paper have dramatically changed. Before the printer was paper and pen, the printing press, and then the typewriter. Remington Rand developed the first dedicated computer printer in 1953 for use on the UNIVAC computer. Many of the earliest computers and much of the punch card equipment used in the 1950s and 1960s used specially adapted electric typewriters as printers.

Teletype Terminals

The next advancement was the Teletype terminal, or the TTY printer. It was used very much like a keyboard and monitor are used today. The operator entered data and commands through the keyboard, and the system (in this case, a mainframe computer) responded to the printing mechanism built into the TTY terminal (see Figure 17-1).

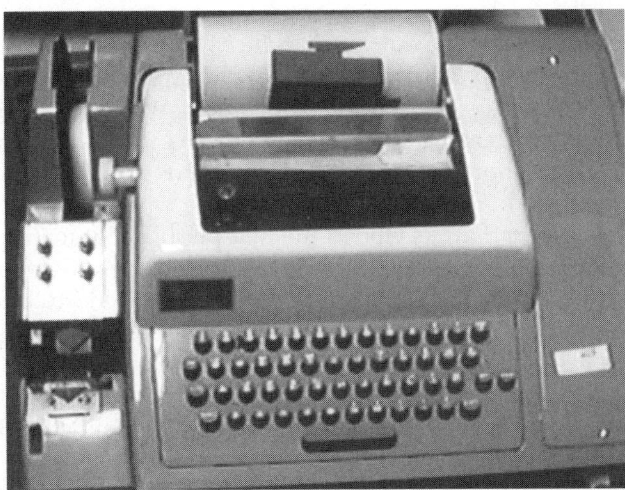

Figure 17-1. A teletype incorporated a keyboard and a printer into a single terminal

Eventually, as the personal computer became popular, a need for PC printers was recognized by a number of manufacturers who had been making printers for mainframe and minicomputer systems. As opposed to the large, high-speed line printers used on the larger systems, PC printers needed to be low in cost and simple to operate.

Daisy Wheel Printers

The earliest printers were daisy wheel printers, an easy adaptation from typewriters that used the same mechanism. The print mechanism is a plastic or metal wheel that rotates to position the letter to be printed into position in front of a print hammer that strikes the letter into an inked ribbon and onto the paper. The raised letters and special characters are located on to a flexible arm emanating from the center ring of the wheel. The arms of the daisy wheel are like the petals of a daisy, which is where it gets its name.

Daisy wheel printers, which are largely obsolete today, are the standard for what is called letter-quality (letter meaning character and not document) printing. Since the print mechanism is virtually a typewriter that prints one character at a time, the daisy wheel was an excellent printer for high-quality documents and multipart forms. These printers could only produce the characters on the daisy wheel and could not produce graphics at all. In spite of their print quality, daisy wheel printers are very slow and quite noisy. These two problems, along with the limitation of printing text characters only, quickly lead to the virtual disappearance of daisy wheel printers.

Dot Matrix Printers

The next printer to emerge was the dot matrix printer, which, as discussed in more detail later in the chapter, creates a pattern of dots that are arranged to produce alphabetic, numeric, and graphical characters on the printed document. While still somewhat noisy, the dot matrix printer was much faster and much quieter than the daisy wheel. In addition, the dot matrix printer incorporated a mechanism that feeds continuous-form paper while keeping it properly aligned.

The Centronics Corporation developed the first popular dot matrix printers for the early Apple computers. These printers were very simple to operate through a front panel menu pad that included only choices for online/offline, line feed (to advance the paper a single line), and form feed (to advance the paper one page). When the printer was online, it received printing instructions from the computer indicating whether the characters to be printed were letters, numbers, or punctuation. The connector used on the printer's end of the cable that attached the printer to the computer was a distinctive 36-pin connector that featured pins arranged on a center bar (see Figure 17-2).

The dot matrix printer has been largely replaced by inkjet and laser printers in the home and small office. However, because it is an impact printer (it prints with a mechanical device that physically strikes the paper) and because it can accurately feed multipart continuous forms, the dot matrix printer continues to have a market. Many printer manufacturers, including IBM, Epson, and Lexmark, still offer full lines of dot matrix printers.

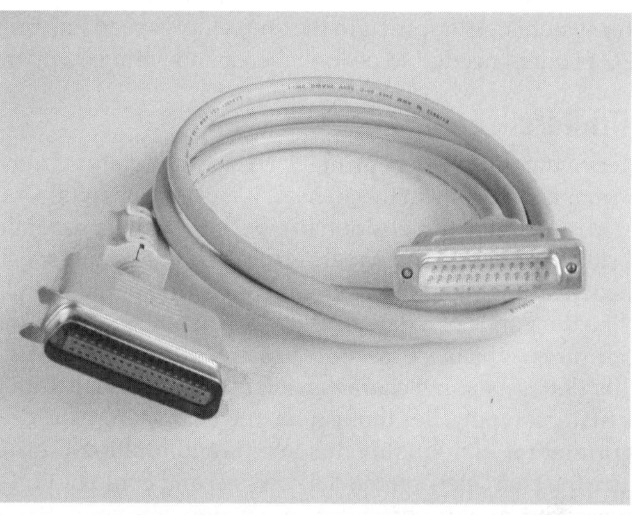

Figure 17-2. A printer cable with a 36-pin Centronics head on one end and a DB-25 connector on the other

Inkjet Printers

The inkjet printer, which is also known as the bubble jet, was first introduced in 1976, but it took until the late 1980s before it became popular with home users, largely because of its printing problems and its cost. Inkjet printers like the one shown in Figure 17-3 create a printed image by spraying small droplets of very quick-drying ink through tiny nozzles (jets) onto the paper. As I will explain later, the print quality of the inkjet, like that of the dot matrix and—in a similar way—the image quality on a monitor, is measured in dots per inch (dpi). The greater the number of dots of ink used in a square inch of paper, the higher the print quality will be.

For the most part, inkjet printers produce a better quality print than a dot matrix printer at roughly the same cost. Inkjets are also less expensive and usually physically smaller than most laser printers, which appeals to most home and small office users. Unfortunately, inkjets are somewhat slower than laser printers and have the reputation for occasionally smearing, bleeding, or running the ink on the printed page, as well as frequent page feed problems. In spite of its problems, the inkjet printer offers good quality printing at a reasonable price and is very popular today with home users.

Laser Printer

The barrier to the laser printer to this point has been cost—not only the cost of the printer itself, but the cost of its supplies. The laser printer was born out of the technology used in the copy machine. In fact, its original concepts were developed at the Xerox Palo Alto Research Center (PARC), where a laser was added to Xerox copier technology to create a printer. The processes used in a laser printer to create a printed document are discussed later in this chapter.

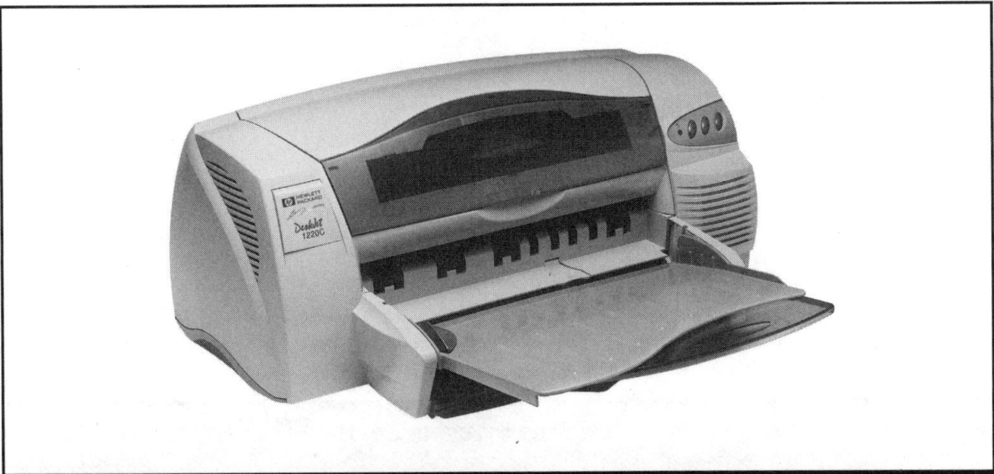

Figure 17-3. An inkjet printer. Photo courtesy of Hewlett Packard Corporation

The laser printer, like the Epson printer shown in Figure 17-4, is just beginning to capture the home and small office markets. Manufacturers like Epson, Hewlett Packard, and Brother are producing lower-end, good quality laser printers and multifunction printers (combining a copier, scanner, fax, and printer into a single box) that are priced for the home market.

Although this group of printers is collectively referred to as laser printers, other light sources, such as liquid crystal displays (LCD) and light-emitting diodes (LED), are sometimes used in place of a laser. In general, LCD and LED printers produce the same print quality as the laser printer but at a typically much lower price.

Line Printers

Larger systems, such as mainframes, that print thousands of pages of reports, checks, or billing statements daily, are called line printers. The name indicates that an entire line of text is printed in one strike. These printers are usually capable of printing 132 to 168 characters per line. At each character position is a print chain that contains each of the characters in the printer's font set. As each line is formed, the chain at each character position is rotated to the proper character and the line is struck through the ribbon to the paper. The character positions are then reset and the next line is printed.

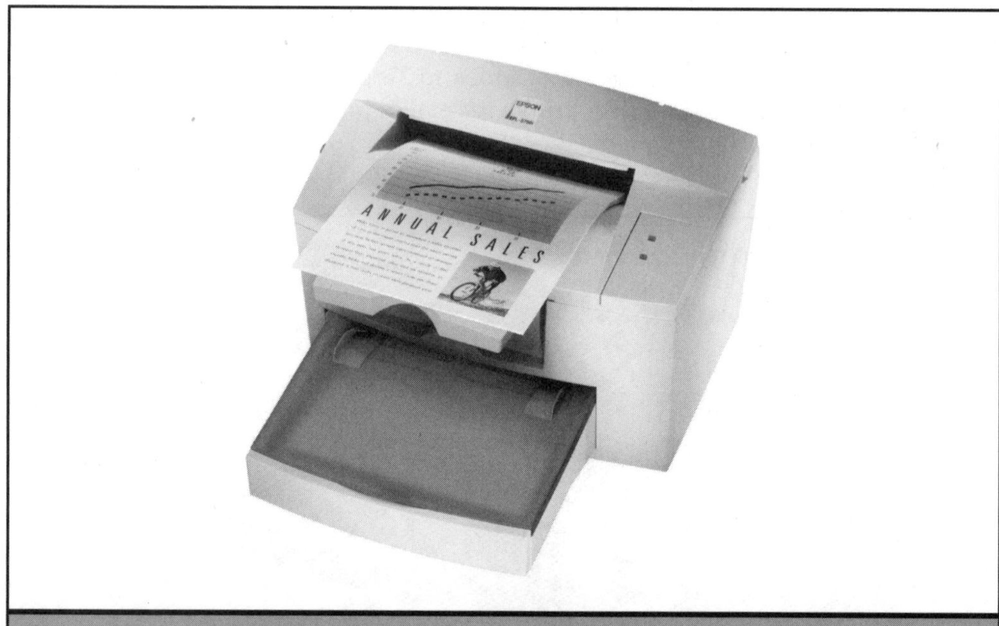

Figure 17-4. A laser printer is excellent for printing graphics and text in the same document. Photo courtesy of Epson America, Inc.

A Quick Look at Printer Characteristics

The terms used to describe the characteristics of a printer are essentially the same for all printer types. The following sections describe each of the major characteristics used to define and describe the capabilities of a printer.

Type Quality

Printers are compared to the standard of the typewriter and daisy wheel printer that create a printed character by striking a solid character form through a ribbon onto the paper. The type quality issue was first developed to describe the range of capabilities of dot matrix printers, which varied depending on the number and pattern of pins used to form characters.

The type qualities most commonly used to describe a printer are as follows:

- **Draft quality** A printer with a draft type quality rating produces low quality print in which the dots or print elements used to form the characters are individually visible on the page. Figure 17-5 illustrates a draft quality character in comparison to the other type qualities. Low-end inkjet and dot matrix printers produce draft quality type.
- **Near letter quality (NLQ)** This type quality is somewhere between letter and draft. NLQ is considered good enough not to be draft quality, but because the dots or elements used to form the characters are partially visible, it cannot be considered letter quality type. Printing the character twice with the second pass slightly offset from the first produces an NLQ character. The results look something like the example in Figure 17-5. Inkjets and dot matrix printers that print at 150dpi use NLQ as their type quality default.
- **Letter quality (LQ)** The best type quality a printer can produce. A printer with a letter quality rating is able to produce characters that appear to have been created by a typewriter or a solid character form. Daisy wheel, high-end inkjet, dot matrix, and laser printers produce letter quality type. Letter quality print requires a printer capable of producing 300 dots per inch (dpi), which is a print quality measurement used on inkjets and dot matrix printers. Letter quality characters appear to be solid without any gaps appearing, like the example shown in Figure 17-5.

Print Speed

The print speed of a printer is measured in characters or pages. The print speed rating used for printers that form characters one at a time, such as daisy wheel and dot matrix printers, is characters per second (cps). The rating used for inkjet and laser printers is pages per minute (ppm). Large printers, such as the printers used with mainframe computers (line printers), that print an entire line at once, use lines per minute as their print speed rating.

Daisy wheel printers are by far the slowest, with a top print speed of around 30 characters per second. Line printers are the fastest at around 3,000 print lines per minute,

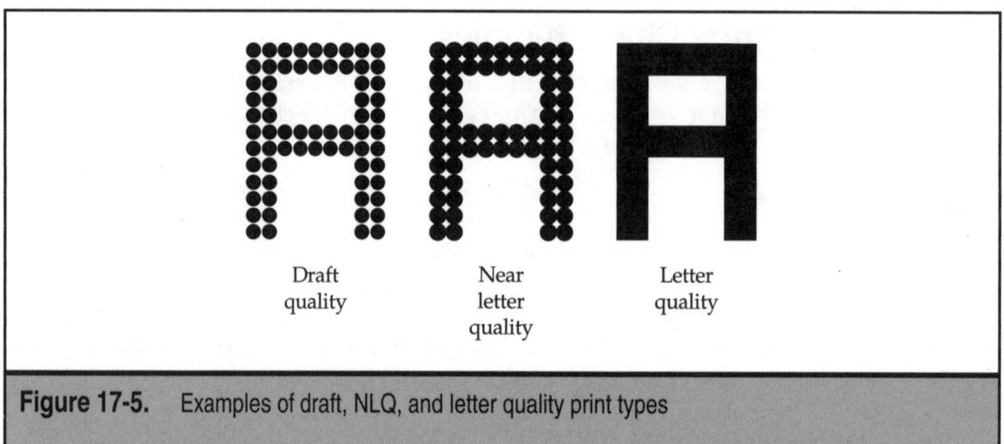

Figure 17-5. Examples of draft, NLQ, and letter quality print types

which would roughly translate to 6,600 characters per second. Dot matrix printers can print up to 500cps, inkjet printers print from 2 to 10ppm, and laser printers range between 4 to 20ppm. To draw some correlation between these different ratings, a laser printer that has a print speed of 6ppm prints at the equivalent speed of around 40cps—but at letter quality, remember.

Impact versus Nonimpact

Dot matrix, daisy wheel, and line printers actually make contact with the paper when they print. Each of these printers uses some form of a striking mechanism to bang an inked ribbon into the paper to create all or a portion of a character or graphic (the daisy wheel printer can only produce text and special characters). These printers are classified as impact printers. Impact printers are typically slower and noisier but are better for continuous and multipart forms.

The opposite of an impact printer is a nonimpact printer, which by definition does not use a striking mechanism to create the printed document. Nonimpact printers, such as inkjet, thermal, and laser printers, use other methods to produce a document.

Text and Graphics

Some printers, particularly daisy wheel and line printers, can only print letters, numbers, and special characters. Because their character sets are cast on the arms of the daisy wheel or the print chains of the line printer, they do not have the flexibility to produce the vectors needed to create a graphic.

Special printers, called plotters, use a combination of inkjet technology and the *x-y* coordinates of the drawing elements to create drawings for use in engineering and other technical areas. Laser printers, inkjets, and many dot matrix printers are capable of merging text and graphics into a single document.

Fonts and Typefaces

The style and design of a printer's character set, that is, block, script, or another style, is its *font* or typeface. Figure 17-6 shows a sampling of some of the more common fonts. Word processing and graphics software now offer literally thousands of font styles and typefaces, but not every printer can handle every font. For example, a daisy wheel printer has only one font per wheel and to change the font, the wheel must be changed. Early dot matrix printers offered between 2 to 16 fonts depending on the number of pins in the print head. Most dot matrix printers either have a set of fonts built in or have them loaded by installation software. Laser and inkjet printers are able to produce just about any font the PC can generate because they treat the document as a graphic image. How many fonts these printers can handle is often more dependent on how much memory is available rather than how many fonts are available.

Print Styles Fonts can be modified with print styles. A print style is applied to emphasize a character, word, title, etc. Figure 17-7 shows samples of the four standard print styles. The styles used with most fonts are as follows:

- **Normal** The natural typeface of the font.
- **Boldface** This print style darkens the type. (The word *boldface* at the beginning of this item is in bold style.)
- **Italics** This print style normally tilts the typeface slightly to the right.
- **Underline** This print style places a horizontal line beneath the type.
- **Strikeout** Often called strikethrough in word processors, this font style places a horizontal line in the middle of the character.

Print Size Another feature of a font is its scalability, which is its ability to be printed in different character sizes. Font size is measured in points. A point is 1/72nd of an inch;

This is Times New Roman font
This is Courier font
This is Bookman font
This is Lucinda font
This is Garamond font
This is Arial font
This is Script font

Figure 17-6. Samples of common fonts

This is the natural typeface
This is the bold typeface
This is the italic typeface
This is the underlined typeface
~~This is the strikeout typeface~~

Figure 17-7. Common print styles used to modify text

there are 72 points (abbreviated as pts) to an inch. Figure 17-8 shows a comparison of different point sizes for the Times New Roman font.

Fonts fall into one of two classifications:

- **Bitmapped** A bitmapped font forms its characters from patterns of dots and specifies the pattern used for each letter, number, and special character for a particular typeface (Times Roman, Courier, etc.), print style (bold, italic, etc.), and type size (10 pts, 12 pts, etc.). Bitmapped fonts are stored as a file that contains the predefined patterns of a font for particular point sizes. If more point sizes are added to the bit-mapped font, more disk space is needed to store the character formats.
- **Scalable** Scalable fonts are generated from a base font as required. Whenever a certain point size of a character is needed, it is generated from a base font, which outlines the basic font typeface and design and contains a mathematical formula that is used to generate the character in the requested point size. TrueType and PostScript fonts are scalable fonts.

Typewriters, which of course could only use one font at a time, could also use only one font size at a time, typically either 10 or 12 points. These two font sizes remain the defaults for most fonts, although it is software and not the printer that now usually controls the font size to be printed.

Daisy wheel and line printers have only one print size available, but dot matrix printers commonly support two print sizes for each of their fonts. Print size is typically not a problem for laser printers and inkjet printers, but some inkjets do struggle a bit when the font size exceeds 300 points. You could change a daisy wheel printer's font and type size by changing the daisy wheel, but in one document, unless you were very fast, you were stuck with the font and type size on the installed wheel.

This is 8 point font size

This is 10 point font size

This is 12 point font size

This is 18 point font size

This is 24 point font size

This is 36 point font size

Figure 17-8. A comparison of font point sizes

DOT MATRIX PRINTERS

It may be premature to say that dot matrix printers are obsolete, but they have been replaced by the inkjet printer as the printer of choice for home and small office systems. Not so long ago, the dot matrix printer, like the one in Figure 17-9, was by far the most popular printer for PC systems. Compared to its predecessors, daisy wheel printers and adapted electric typewriters, it was faster, relatively quieter, included more fonts and print sizes, and offered flexibility for cut-sheet paper or continuous-feed paper and forms. For these same reasons, dot matrix printers are still in use in many offices.

Dot matrix printers for PCs have two standard sizes: narrow and wide. A narrow width printer is usually limited to 80 columns and is typically used only for correspondence or forms. A wider dot matrix printer has a 132-column width and can be used as a general printer. However, dot matrix print heads have been adapted into several special-purpose printers as well.

Compared to inkjet and laser printers, dot matrix printers are slow and noisy. However, in environments where printing on multipart or continuous-feed preprinted forms is more important than the printer's noise or speed, dot matrix printers continue to thrive. For this reason, you will commonly see dot matrix printers in pharmacies, receiving docks, warehouses, and other administrative offices. Other common uses for dot matrix printers include mailing labels, cash registers, and automatic teller machines (ATM).

Printing on a Dot Matrix Printer

After the user chooses an application to print a document, the application communicates with the operating system to create a data file that contains the print commands and

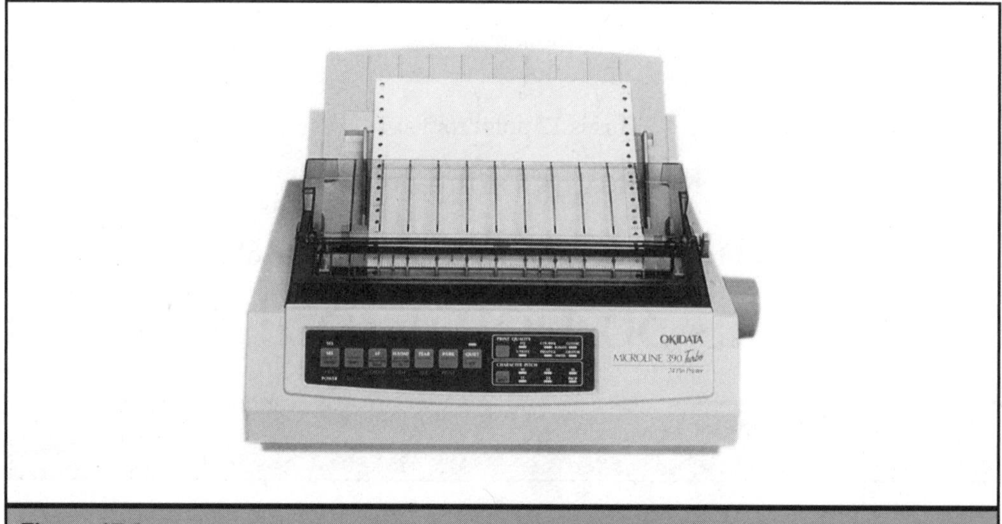

Figure 17-9. A dot matrix printer. Photo courtesy of OkiData Americas, Inc.

codes used to create the letters, numbers, special characters, graphics, print styles, and other document effects, such as tabs, line feeds, page (form) feeds, etc. This data file is stored in the operating system's print queue. The print queue is the buffer that holds the print data files waiting to be sent to the printer. If the printer is not in use, the file is sent to the printer immediately. However, if the printer is in use, the print data file will be held until the printer is available and no other print jobs are in the queue ahead of it.

Print Buffer

When the printer is available, the print data file is transferred to the dot matrix printer and is stored in its buffer. The printer's buffer is needed because it takes much longer to print a document than it does to transfer it from the computer to the printer. By storing the print data file in the printer's buffer, the computer is released to perform other tasks. Early printers did not have print buffers and the printer had to ask the computer for each print command, which tied up both the computer and the printer until the document was completed.

Print buffers on dot matrix printers typically hold between 8 to 60 kilobytes (KB) of data, depending on the age, manufacturer, and model of the printer. Dot matrix printers with enhanced graphics or extended font capabilities tend to have larger print buffers. The size of a dot matrix printer's print buffer is commonly listed right along with its print speed as one of its major features. More is always better.

When the entire file has been transferred into the print buffer or if the print buffer fills up, the printer tells the computer to quit sending the data until the buffer has space. While this is going on, the data in the buffer is fed to the printer's processor that interprets the codes and commands for printing. As the processor reads off the data in the buffer, more of the print data file can be sent from the computer to the printer. This continues until the entire file is transferred. After the file is completely transferred to the printer, the computer disengages and moves on to other tasks.

The printer's processor reads the instructions for one line of print from the buffer and translates it into the dot patterns needed to form each character on the print line. The processor also decides the travel direction of the printhead to print the line, which means whether the line will be printed when the head is traveling left to right or right to left, or both. The processor must also control the movement of the paper, advancing it a single line, to the top of the next page, or feeding an entire page.

Forming a Dot Matrix Character

The key to understanding how a dot matrix printer works is to understand how it forms its characters. As described earlier and illustrated in Figure 17-5, a dot matrix printer forms its characters with a pattern of dots. Characters are formed in stages by the pins; there are typically 9, 18, or 24 pins in the printhead. A 9-pin printhead, in which the pins are arranged in a single column, as shown in Figure 17-9, forms characters by printing the appropriate dots in a series of connecting columns to complete the character. Dot matrix printers with 9-pins are capable of producing only draft quality print and are usually used for forms. Eighteen-pin printers have largely disappeared, and 24-pin printers are used in high-end dot matrix applications.

The Printhead

As with all printers, the printhead is the most important part of the dot matrix printer. It forms the characters and prints them on the page. The major components in the printhead, as illustrated in Figure 17-10, are the solenoids and pins, along with a permanent magnet and wire coils and springs on each pin.

Inside the printhead is a large permanent magnet that exerts a magnetic force on the pins that draws them back and away from the printhead. Each pin is attached to a wire that is wrapped with a coil of wire and a spring that pushes against the pull of the magnet. When power is put on the coil of wire, its electromagnetic force neutralizes that of the permanent magnet and the spring forces the pin forward to strike the ribbon. When the power is removed from the wire coil, the magnet retracts the pin.

The speed at which the pins are moving and the constant energizing and de-energizing of the coil electromagnets, along with the friction of the moving parts, creates heat. The printhead of a dot matrix printer gets very hot when it is printing, which is why most have a heat sink attached or designed into the housing of the printhead. The heat sink provides cooling to the printhead.

Dot Matrix Print Speeds and Resolutions

Dot matrix printer speeds have dramatically increased over the past few years to the point that their speeds range from 200cps to 1200 and 1400cps. These printers that originally featured only 10dpi (dots per inch) now boast resolutions of 150dpi and higher. Dot matrix printers that are capable of producing high-resolution graphics offer Super High

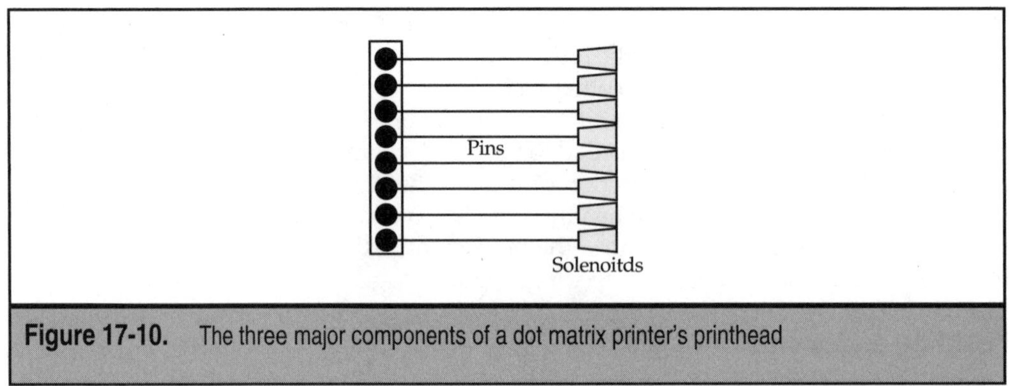

Figure 17-10. The three major components of a dot matrix printer's printhead

Resolution graphics in the range of 240 × 216 to 360 × 360dpi. A typical dot matrix printer is more likely to support around 75dpi printing for NLQ print.

Color Dot Matrix Printers

There are such things as color dot matrix printers. Some require the addition of a color kit to the printer, but for the most part, the color capability, if available, is built-in. In order to print color, a dot matrix printer must have this capability included in its firmware because a character's color must be blended from multiple colors that are included on the printer ribbon. Changing a color-enabled dot matrix printer from a single color to multiple colors usually only entails changing the ribbon. The printer's device drivers and internal firmware take care of translating the color coding of the print image into a printed color image.

The ribbon of a color dot matrix is divided horizontally with two to eight color ribbons. The print mechanism shifts the ribbon up and down to place the correct color in front of the print head as needed. As you can probably guess, a dot matrix printer is not the most efficient way to produce color documents, such as charts, graphs, and desktop publishing documents. Inkjet printers are far better for this purpose and typically cost less.

INKJET PRINTERS

Like most of the really great technology discovery stories, inkjet technology was discovered by accident when a researcher at Canon, Inc. heated a syringe filled with printer ink with a soldering iron. The heat caused a bubble of air to form in the shaft of the syringe. Eventually, the bubble grew and forced ink out of the syringe. This discovery led to the development of what Canon called the bubble jet printer. Although Canon still refers to their printers as bubble jets, the industry has adopted the term inkjet for these printers.

Inkjet technology has advanced over the years to the point where it is now used in applications that range from simple text-only documents to complex graphic designs. The inkjet printer is now virtually everywhere, in classrooms, small businesses, corporate offices, and especially in homes. It provides a low-cost, high-quality printing solution with a printer model to fit just about every need.

Inkjet printers appear to be slow, but when you consider that each of its dozens of printhead nozzles is firing thousands of times every second to print a document or reproduce an image as the printhead moves back and forth across the paper, it is actually working very fast.

However, inkjets do tend to be a bit slow when printing in color, not to mention that their ink cartridges are a bit pricey, especially if a lot of color printing is being produced. But, all in all, the inkjet printer is, for the majority of PC users, the low-cost alternative to laser printers, particularly color laser printers. Today's inkjet printers are a high-quality color printing alternative at a price less than $300.

Inkjet Technologies

Inkjet printing uses small drops of ink to print text and graphics on paper. An inkjet printhead has a number of nozzles through which ink is jetted onto the paper. What differs from one technology to the next is what causes the ink to jettison from the nozzle onto the page.

There are two general types of inkjet technology: continuous flow and drop-on-demand. Drop-on-demand inkjet printing has two forms: Piezoelectric and thermal. Here is a brief overview of the three major inkjet technologies in use:

- **Piezoelectric** One of two inkjet technologies included under drop-on-demand inkjet approaches. In this approach to inkjet printing, a series of ink nozzles that are connected to the printer's ink supply are lined up vertically on the printhead. As the printhead moves over the paper, Piezoelectric crystals in each nozzle are charged with electricity, which makes the crystal expand. The expansion of the crystal forces a droplet of ink out of the nozzle with enough force to strike the paper. This process involves literally thousands of drops squeezed through a nozzle smaller than a human hair hundreds of times a second.
- **Thermal** The other drop-on-demand inkjet technology. It is very much like the Piezoelectric but, as its name implies, heat is involved. The ink droplet is about 10 picoliters in volume (a picoliters is about one-trillionth of a liter). Between the ink supply (called the reservoir) and the nozzle there are ink channels through which the ink travels to the nozzle. As the ink moves down the channel, it is heated and forms a bubble. When the bubble pops, a droplet of ink is forced out of the nozzle onto the page. As one droplet is spraying onto the page, the next droplet is being drawn into the channel and the process repeats as demanded.
- **Continuous flow** As its name implies, the ink flows continuously through the printhead. However, not all of the ink is put on the paper. Ink droplets are passed through a variable charge chamber where they are selectively given an electrical

charge. Not all of the droplets are charged, only the ones that are selected by the timing mechanisms for use in printing on paper. After the droplets are charged they flow over a deflector plate that sends the charged droplets onto the paper and the uncharged droplets back into the ink supply to be reused. The uncharged droplets represent white space or unprinted areas of the printed page. Continuous flow inkjet printers have another major difference to drop-on-demand printers: the nozzle remains fixed in place and the paper is moved back and forth under the print head. This prevents the ink from being splashed about, which would happen if the head were to move.

Piezoelectric Inkjet Technology

Piezoelectric inkjet printers can change the size of the droplet put on the paper by changing the amount of electricity, which alters the amount of expansion or contraction of the Piezo crystal. A larger electrical charge causes more expansion in the crystal and forces more ink from the nozzle.

The advantages of the Piezoelectric approach to inkjet printing are speed and a better on-page ink quality. A thermal inkjet must cool the ink channel between each droplet, and the Piezo crystal reacts faster to the electrical charge than the channel can cool. Although the time savings are very small fractions of a second, they can add up over a large print job. Another advantage is that because the ink is not heated, special ink that can withstand high temperatures is not required, which results in lower prices. Not heating the ink can also result in truer colors from print to print or even within the same print, a problem common to the thermal inkjet. Probably the biggest drawback to Piezo technology–based inkjet printers is the cost of the printhead, which can drive up the cost of the printer itself.

A limited number of manufacturers produce Piezoelectric inkjet printers, including Epson, Xerox, Mutoh, and a few others.

Thermal Inkjet Technology

The thermal type of inkjet printer has its advantages over the Piezoelectric type. First, thermal inkjets are the most common type in use and its supplies are readily available—some supermarkets even sell ink cartridges and paper.

The thermal process involves heating the ink in the ink channel between the ink reservoir and the printhead's nozzles. It may sound as if all of the ink in the channel is being heated. Actually, only about a third of the ink is actually heated and at full speed, the temperature gain is only around 30 degrees Celsius.

Thermal inkjet printers are primarily produced by Hewlett Packard, Lexmark, and Canon, the companies that hold nearly all of the thermal inkjet patents.

The Inkjet Printing Process

The printing process for any type of printer always begins with the PC and its software. Typically, an application program (such as a word processor like Microsoft Word or Corel

WordPerfect, a graphics package like Adobe Illustrator or Photoshop, or a desktop publishing package like Microsoft Publisher or Adobe PageMaker) generates a print-image file, which can be anything from a plain text document to a complex full-color photograph. The application communicates to the operating system that it would like to send its file to the printer. The operating system places the print file in the system print queue, where it awaits the availability of the printer.

When the printer is available, the operating system and the printer's device driver begin transferring the print file to the printer, which involves translating the print file into commands and information that the printer can interpret into a printed document or image. The following sections describe the process used to convert the application's print file into a printed document or image on an inkjet printer.

Halftoning

The first step of the inkjet print process is called halftoning. You may not know it, but you are most likely very familiar with this technique of producing a graphic image—or at least the outputs of this process, anyway. Halftoning is the technique used to produce graphics and photographs in most newspapers. If you look very closely at a newspaper picture, you will see thousands of small dots of various shades of gray, black, and white that your eye and brain blend to form a picture. The image's halftones are created by the arrangement of the dots on the page.

To print an image in halftones requires that the page be divided into a number of cells. Each cell is a rectangular matrix of dots (a.k.a. pixels), as shown in Figure 17-11. A solid black cell has all of its dots printed black and a white cell has no printed dots. Printing only some of the dots in the cell black produces shades of gray. Lighter grays have fewer printed dots; darker grays have more printed dots. For example, a 10 percent grayscale has one-tenth of the dots in a cell printed black, and a 50 percent grayscale has half of its dots printed. The number of dots in a cell determines the number of grayscale shades available. A cell made up of 4 dots by 4 dots can produce 17 (4 x 4 + 1) shades of gray. An 8 x 8 cell is capable of 65 shades of gray. The cells are then used like tiles across and down the page to create an image.

Compression and Decompression

The output from the halftoning process is a bitmapped version of the image to be printed. In addition to the bitmap image, the file now also contains some additional bits that indicate which of the four CMYK (cyan, magenta, yellow, black) colors are on or off for each dot. The bitmap image file is compressed to minimize its space and the amount of data that is transmitted from the computer to the printer. The printer's device drivers perform the compression of the file. The compressed file is sent to the printer one line at a time, which means one pass of the printhead across the page. Since an inkjet printer does not print an entire line of text in one pass, it can take many passes to complete one line of 12-point text. The computer can send the data to the printer much faster than the printer can print each line. Therefore, the print data is received into a print buffer that the printer uses as

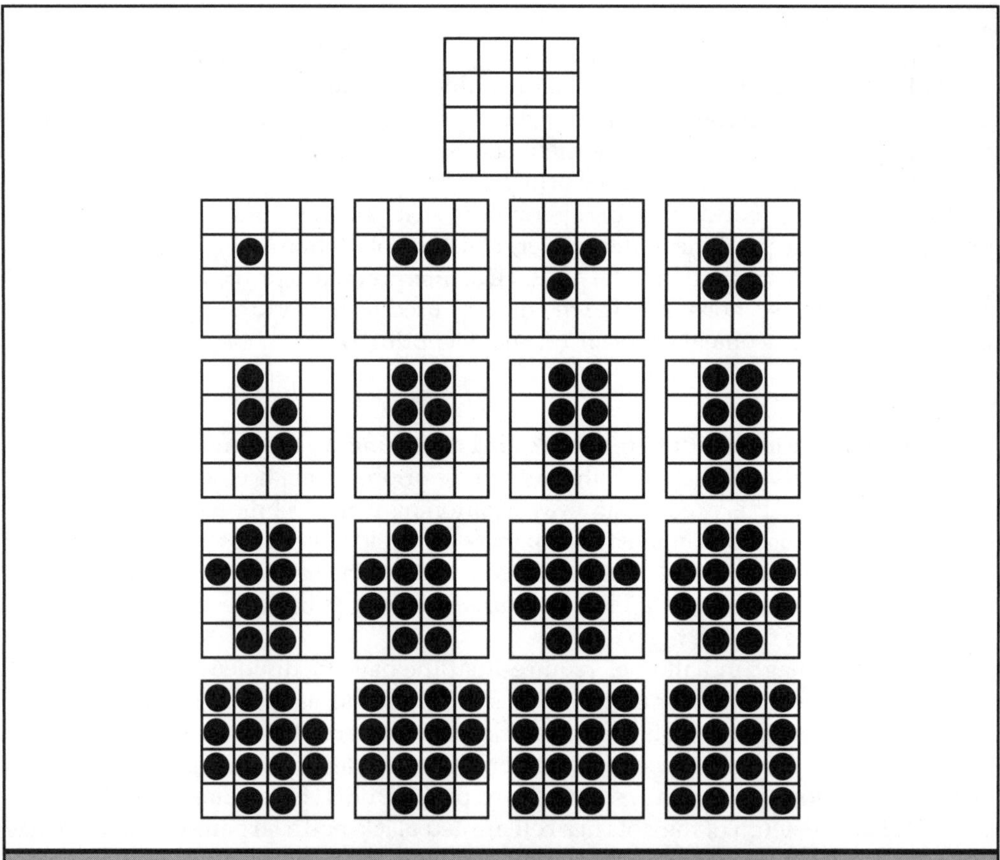

Figure 17-11. The 17 halftone dot possibilities using a 4 x 4 halftone cell

the source of its instructions. If the buffer fills up, the printer tells the computer to stop sending data; when space is once again available in the buffer, the computer is sent the signal to resume transmitting data. The printer reading data and sending instructions to the printhead creates space in the buffer.

As the printer reads data from the print buffer, the data is decompressed and passed to the printer's controller. The controller interprets the print data and sends instructions to the printhead and the inkjet nozzles as to when to print and which colors to use.

The nozzles on the printhead are very small. In fact, there is a block with dozens of nozzles for each of the CMYK colors. Some printers use more nozzles per color. The Epson Stylus Pro 5000, for example, uses 64 nozzles for each of the CMYK colors.

The controller interprets the data from the bitmap file for one pass of the printhead. When a certain color is called for, a signal is sent to the printhead to fire that color's nozzle block when it passes over the correct spot on the printed line. As the printhead passes over the exact spot on the print line that calls for a certain color, either the nozzles for that color heat up or the Piezo crystals fire for precisely the right amount of time and place precisely the amount of ink called for in the image file sent from the application program. Remember that this process involves spraying drops of ink that are about one million times smaller than a small drop of water out of nozzles thinner than a strand of human hair.

Color Conversion

The challenge with printing an application-generated or scanned color image on a color inkjet printer is in the conversion of the colors from the RGB (red, green, blue) color scheme used inside the computer to the CMYK color scheme of the printer. Colors are actually combined wavelengths of light. As color wavelengths are added or subtracted, different colors are created.

The page or image displayed on the monitor in RGB color must be converted to CMYK colors before it can be printed. The computer's internal color schemes are designed for the monitor, which is a radiant device. The RGB color scheme, which uses up to 24 bits to specify each pixel of an image, depends on the radiance (the wavelengths) of the RGB dots within each pixel to blend and create its colors. This additive approach to color creates a spectrum that ranges from black (the absence of color wavelengths) to white (the presence of all color wavelengths).

Paper is a reflective device that produces color through a subtractive process. An unprinted sheet of paper appears white because it includes light from all color wavelengths. To print a color on a sheet of paper, wavelengths are absorbed from the paper to create colors. The colors of the CMYK model absorb different color wavelengths. When used in combination, they absorb enough color wavelengths to create a wide array of colors. For example, cyan (blue) ink absorbs red wavelengths and produces greenish-blue colors. Magenta (red) ink absorbs green wavelengths and creates reddish-blue colors. Yellow absorbs blue wavelengths to create yellowish-red colors. Black ink absorbs all color wavelengths.

To convert the color scheme, a color lookup table (CLUT) is used. The binary RGB code for each pixel is looked up in the CLUT, and its corresponding CMYK binary code is recorded for the corresponding dot on the page. While this sounds straightforward, it is not. It is impossible to exactly match RGB colors with CMYK colors. This is why a printed version of a color document may often look slightly different than it did on the monitor.

Color Halftoning

After RGB colors are converted to CMYK colors, the printer's driver software generates instructions for each of the printhead nozzles. The printhead's nozzles are either on or off, so binary data is added to the color instructions that indicates when the nozzles of a particular color are to be turned on and off. Remember that colors are mixed to form other colors, so the nozzles of one, two, three, or all four colors may be on or off for any given dot in the image. Leaving a color's nozzles open for a longer time results in more of that color being used in producing the color of the dot on the page. The on and off commands to the nozzles control how much of a color is sprayed. Four bits are used for each dot to indicate which of the four colors are on or off. In contrast, a monochrome (black-ink only) printer requires a single bit for each dot.

Where monochrome halftoning creates an image to be printed using cells that produce shades of gray, color halftoning is able to produce a wide range of colors with only four ink colors. Color halftoning works very much like monochrome halftoning except that four halftone layers are created: one for each color with a dot anywhere that color is used. When the layers are logically superimposed on the printed page, the actual colors of the image emerge.

The challenge of the halftone process is to hide the dots used to create an image and present a smooth blending of colors that creates a realistic looking image to the viewer. This requires very sophisticated software, which is why color qualities vary by manufacturer, and a process that allows the viewer's eye to smooth the dot patterns on the page. This is accomplished using one of two halftoning methods: ordered dithering or image diffusion.

Most inkjet printers use image diffusion as their halftoning method because it creates more uniform dot patterns. However, some manufacturers, most notably Lexmark, offer both halftone methods and allow the user to choose which to use on a given project.

Ordered Dithering Ordered dithering creates the transition from one color to another by evenly spacing pixels of each color along the common edge of the two colors (see Figure 17-12). This high-end method is used on professional-level graphics that require more accurate color representations. Ordered dithering is also faster to create than image diffusion.

Like monochrome halftoning, ordered dithering divides each color plane into cells. Each cell uses a separate pattern of dots, depending on the size of the cell. The number of pixels in a cell is a function of the print resolution of the printer, but the more dots in the cells, the more shades of a color that can be represented.

A separate threshold screen or matrix is used for each layer to determine the cells that are to be printed. The threshold matrix allows only the cells in certain locations to be printed and blocks any other cells from being printed to create the dithering (or transition) for each color. Remember that each layer of the color halftone represents only a single color. The other color involved with the ordered dithering is handled on that color's layer.

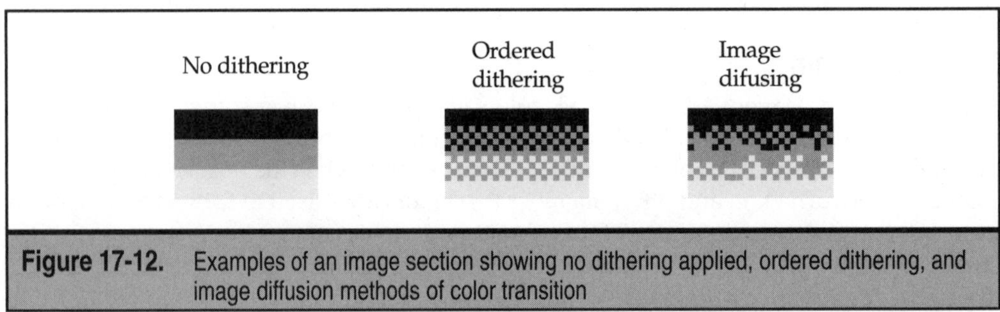

Figure 17-12. Examples of an image section showing no dithering applied, ordered dithering, and image diffusion methods of color transition

The determination of whether a color is to print or not is actually a mathematical activity. Each cell has a binary value associated with it that indicates which of its dot locations are in use. The threshold matrix has a binary value for each cell location. Each cell is compared to the threshold, and if the value in the halftone cell is greater than that in the screen, the cell's dots are printed. Otherwise, if the screen's value is equal to or greater than the halftone cell, the dots are not printed.

Image Diffusion Image diffusion, also called diffuse dithering and error diffusion, is the technique used by virtually all inkjet printers. It is preferred because it creates realistic images without distinguishable patterns.

This process treats each dot in the image as if it could be printed in one of 255 shades of a color or grayscale. An inkjet printer is only capable of printing the dot in one of its four colors. For discussion purposes, let's assume the color being printed is black, which has a value of 255 (no dot, or white space, has a value of 0). The image diffusion process determines a color (grayscale) value for each dot in the image. It then calculates an error value that represents the difference of what will actually be printed at the dot's location (either a black dot or no dot) and the grayscale value it determined for that location.

For example, if the drivers determined that a dot should have a grayscale value of 128 and no dot is to be printed, the error for that dot would be 128 minus 0, or 128. If a dot were to be printed at that location, the error would be 128 minus 255, or an error of negative 127. The error values are used to diffuse the color of the adjacent dots. If the error is a negative number, then black dots are less likely to be printed in adjacent pixels. If the error is positive, black dots are more likely to be printed in the adjacent cells. The final determination depends on the error diffusion applied to the neighboring dots.

Inkjet Ink

The ink used in an inkjet printer is chosen very carefully, especially in thermal drop-on-demand inkjet printers. The research into inkjet inks has been ongoing since the first inkjet printer was introduced. The ink used impacts the design of the entire printhead, including the ink reservoir, the nozzles, the ink channels, and particularly the heaters. Ink is an integral part of the printer's overall design. Should the ink clog the nozzles, change color when heated, or not dry fast enough, the page produced by the printer will not be usable and will most likely not be readable.

Inkjet printer ink has a number of very important characteristics:

- **Quick drying** The ink, particularly color ink, must dry very quickly after it hits the paper. If it doesn't, it can overlap neighboring ink droplets and cause degradation of both the image's resolution and the color quality.
- **Water resistance** Water-resistant ink stays on the paper even after it gets wet. This is an important characteristic because printed documents will be handled and smudged by sweat or body oils as fingers move over the ink.
- **Light-fast** Light-fast ink doesn't fade when exposed to sunlight.
- **Thickness** The ink must be thick enough to produce quality images on the paper but not so thick that it clogs the nozzles, even when heated.

Inkjet Cartridges

Monochrome inkjet printers have only a single ink cartridge. Color inkjet printers typically have two cartridges, one black and one tricolor (CMY). (The black cartridge is separate because the vast majority of printing done on an inkjet is text or line drawings that only use black.) One of the downsides to having cyan, magenta, and yellow in the same cartridge is that when one color runs out, regardless of how much ink remains of the other colors, the cartridge needs to be replaced. Newer color inkjet printers feature ink cartridges with a replaceable ink tank for each of the CMY colors, which addresses this problem.

Virtually all inkjet cartridges have a built-in printhead, which guarantees a fresh printhead each time a new cartridge is installed. The printhead has 64 to 128 microjets through which the ink is fired to the paper. The printhead also contains built-in resistors on the flexible circuits located on the front on the cartridge. These resistors do wear out in time and can cause slanted or wavy print. When this happens, the cartridge should be replaced. Also located on the cartridge is the ink reservoir that contains a sponge.

The jury is still out on whether or not refilling ink cartridges is a good idea. It certainly is less expensive than buying new cartridges, but at least with a new cartridge you know what you are getting and it should have some warranty. The worst things that can happen with a refilled ink cartridge, beyond the mess you might make refilling it, are that it doesn't print because the ink is too thick for the printer or that it may smudge or smear because it is too thin. Most manufacturers do not recommend using refilled ink cartridges, especially color cartridges, but then, most of them also manufacture ink cartridges.

Inkjet Paper

The challenge for inkjet manufacturers has been producing good print quality on standard, plain bond paper. Inkjet printers have always been able to produce outstanding print quality on special papers. Inkjet inks are more absorbent than the toner used in laser printers or sold inks, like those on the ribbon of a dot matrix printer. Because of this, inkjets typically work better with paper that has been treated for inkjet inks. This has been especially true with high-resolution images, such as photographic reproductions.

Inkjet ink performs better on paper that has been primed to bond the ink to the paper. Canon has developed a process that primes the paper immediately before the ink is applied. Other manufacturers, such as Hewlett Packard and Epson, have concentrated their efforts on improving the quality of print on plain paper.

Paper Flow

The paper feed mechanism of the inkjet printer is controlled by the commands sent to the printer from the computer and its application software. The paper control commands are included at the beginning of the entire bitmap file, at the end of each line (printhead pass), and at the end of the file.

At the beginning of the file, the printer's device drivers place a command to load the first sheet of paper and position it for the first printhead pass. As the printhead completes each pass across the page, the controller sends a signal to the paper feed motors to advance the paper rollers that pull the paper forward into position for the next printhead pass. At the end of the bitmap file, a command ejects the paper. If another page is to be printed, a sheet of paper is loaded and the process starts over.

The paper flow controls are provided in the bitmapped data file used to print the document. However, the printer controls some parts of the paper flow process, including when the printer is out of paper, when a paper jam occurs, and when the printhead is not moving. In these cases and a few more, the printer's controller signals the computer, which in turn signals the application or printer drivers to cease sending the bitmapped data file and to display an error message to the user.

Printer Drivers

The workhorse of the inkjet printing process is the software device drivers that perform the graphics conversions from RGB to CMYK, perform the calculations used in halftoning operations, and manage the flow of the bitmapped data file from the computer to the printer. The printer driver controls the applications and hardware with which the printer will work and manages the communications between the printer and the computer to keep the printing process flowing smoothly.

A printer's device driver is usually included with the printer on a diskette or CD-ROM, but newer versions of device drivers are constantly being made available, along with updated BIOS systems and firmware for the printer. Most manufacturers now have an alert system that will announce via e-mail or fax when new drivers are available for a particular printer model.

LASER PRINTERS

A laser printer, like the one shown in Figure 17-13, is an electrophotographic (EP) printer that uses the same basic technology found in a photocopier. In general, the laser printer has become popular as an office printer, but as prices come down, it is also becoming popular as a home system printer. Laser printers produce clean documents quietly, two of the major reasons for its popularity, but its print quality is the primary reason why laser printers are chosen over other forms of printers.

A laser printer produces a printed document using a focused beam of laser light and a rotating mirror to reproduce the image of a document as an electrostatic charge on a photosensitive drum. Toner, the "ink" of the laser printer, is added, and the charge on the drum attracts and holds it in the image of the document. A sheet of paper is fed from the paper supply and electrostatically charged. The paper is rolled over the drum and picks up the toner. Heat is then applied to the toner, it fuses with the paper, and the document is completed and placed on the output rack of the printer. To provide an overview of how the laser printer works, this process has been overly simplified, but in essence this is what happens when a document is printed on a laser printer. It is also the same process used when a document is copied on a photocopier.

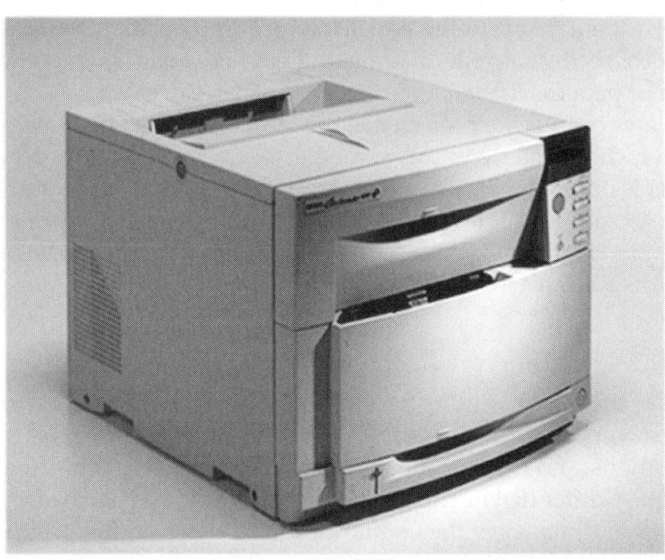

Figure 17-13. A laser printer. Photo courtesy of Lexmark International, Inc.

A laser printer is a page printer. It produces a finished page on each cycle. This is in contrast to the other types of printers that print single characters (daisy wheel, dot matrix) or all or part of a line of print (line printer, inkjet) on each cycle. A laser printer produces all the text and graphics of one full page at one time. It is a cut-sheet printer; its paper supply is a stack of individual sheets of paper. It cannot handle multipart forms or any type of continuous forms. However, it can produce the pages of a completed multipart form on separate sheets with the right software.

The processes used to form the page to be printed are essentially the same as used for the inkjet printer, with some minor differences that are explained later.

Laser Printer Technologies

Laser printers use three different printing processes to produce a printed page. Each of the technologies in use is directly attributable to one or more laser printer or photocopier manufacturer(s):

- **Electrophotographic (EP) process** The EP process, developed by Xerox and Canon, was the first laser printer technology used. It is the print process used by virtually all laser printers in one form or another. Its characteristics are the use of a laser beam to produce an electrostatic charge and a dry toner to create the printed image. *EP* is also used to represent electrostatic photocopying, which is another name for this same process.

- **Hewlett-Packard (HP) process** The HP process is essentially the same as the EP process; it differs from the EP process only in some minor operating procedures. It's similar enough to be considered the same process, yet different enough to get its own name.
- **Light-Emitting Diode (LED) process** LED printers are not technically laser printers, but outwardly you can't really tell an LED printer from a laser printer. An LED printer uses an array of around 2,500 light-emitting diodes (like very small light bulbs) in place of a laser as the light source used to condition the photosensitive drum.
- **Liquid Crystal Display (LCD) process** LCD printers use light shone through an LCD panel in place of the laser to condition the photosensitive drum. See Chapter 16 for more information on how liquid crystal works, but in general, liquid crystals are used to block and permit light to pass through onto the drum creating a pattern of pixels or dots on the drum. LCD printers are also called LCD shutter printers.

Electrophotographic Process (EP)

The electrophotographic process (EP) used in the laser printer has its roots in the dry photocopy method called xerography. There are actually two methods used in photocopiers, wet and dry. The wet method uses liquid inks and the dry method uses a dry, granular ink powder, more commonly known as toner.

Closely aligned with the Xerox Corporation, xerography roughly translates to dry writing and is the name for a photocopying process used in nearly all laser printers and all dry photocopiers. Xerography is ideal for the laser printer because it requires no liquid inks or special paper (e.g., those used with a thermal copier). This process relies on the fact that some substances become electrically charged when exposed to a light source.

In the EP process, as xerography is called when applied to a laser printer, the printer's drum, which is made from selenium or another photosensitive (light sensitive) material, is charged. The print image file generated on the computer by an application is used to create a logical image of the document to be printed. This image is then used to guide the laser and mirrors to shine light on the drum in the areas where no part of the image, whether text or graphic, is to appear on the finished document. Where light strikes the drum, it loses its charge.

Next, negatively charged toner is sprayed on the drum and adheres to the parts of the drum that still has a positive charge. This creates a mirror image of the document on the drum. A sheet of paper is fed from the paper supply, positively charged, and fed closely past the drum and toner. The positive charge on the paper attracts the toner onto the paper, and with only the positive charge holding the toner in place, the sheet is fed through a set of heated rollers that literally melt the toner onto the paper to create a permanent document. If multiple copies of the same document are being printed, then additional toner is added to the drum and another sheet of paper is charged, passed by the drum, and fused. If only one copy is being printed of the page, any remaining toner is removed from the drum, the drum is recharged, and the process begins again.

A quick word about the toner used in a laser printer before I go into more detail about the EP process. Laser printer toner is made up of plastic-coated iron particles. Toner is a dry powder that consists of iron particles coated with a plastic resin. The toner is applied to the drum as it rotates and attaches to the dot row just completed by the laser immediately after it scans a row.

The EP laser printing process can be organized into six separate phases, as follows:

1. **Charging** The entire drum is uniformly charged to –600V by the primary corona wire (also known as the main corona) located inside the toner cartridge.
2. **Exposing** The laser printer's controller uses a laser beam and one or more mirrors to create the image of the page on the drum. The laser beam is turned on and off to create a series of small dots on the drum to match the document to be printed. Where the light of the laser contacts the photosensitive drum, the charge at that spot is reduced to about –100V. After the entire image of the document has been transferred to the drum, the controller starts a sheet feeding through the printer, stopping it at the registration rollers.
3. **Developing** Inside the developing roller, which is also located inside the toner cartridge, is a magnet that attracts the iron particles in the toner. As the developing roller rotates by the drum, the toner is attracted to the areas of the drum that have been exposed by the laser, creating a mirror image of the document on the drum.
4. **Transferring** The back of the paper sheet is given a positive charge. As the paper passes the drum, the negatively charged toner is attracted from the drum onto the paper. The paper now has the image of the document on it, but the toner, held in place by simple magnetism, is not bonded to it.
5. **Fusing** The fusing rollers apply heat and pressure to the toner, melting and pressing it into the paper to create a permanent bond. The fusing rollers are covered with Teflon and a light silicon oil to keep the paper and toner from sticking to them.
6. **Cleaning** Before the next page is started, the drum is swept free of any lingering toner with a rubber blade and a fluorescent lamp removes any electrical charge remaining on the drum. Any toner removed in this step is not reused but is put into a used-toner compartment on the cartridge.

Hewlett Packard (HP) Process

The Hewlett Packard laser printing process is the same as the EP process except in the first two phases. The charging phase of the EP process is adjusted to become a conditioning phase, and the exposing phase is replaced with the writing phase. The HP process more closely represents the specific process performed in a laser printer, as opposed to those carried out in photocopiers.

The HP print process also consists of six stages:

1. **Conditioning** The drum is conditioned with a uniform negative charge by a charge roller.
2. **Writing** The laser and mirrors are used to reduce the charge on the areas of the drum that form the document to be printed. In the HP process, the drum is discharged to ground in selected areas. In the EP process, the drum is discharged to only –100 VDC.
3. **Developing** The drum rotates past the developing roller and toner is attracted to its discharged areas. The drum now has toner stuck to it where the laser has created the mirror image of the document to be printed.
4. **Transfer** A strong positive charge is applied to the corona wire and the toner is pulled onto a sheet of paper.
5. **Fusing** The fusing rollers melt the toner onto the paper using a high temperature (350 degrees Fahrenheit) halogen lamp and a pressure roller.
6. **Cleaning** A rubber blade inside the toner cartridge removes any toner left on the drum into a used toner receptacle inside the cartridge. A bank of LEDs are used to clear the drum, and the cycle starts over.

LED Printing

An LED printer replaces the laser and mirrors used to discharge the print drum with a bank of light-emitting diodes (LEDs). The number of LEDs used is directly related to the dots-per-inch capability of the printer. LEDs are physically very small and produce a very bright light, which allows the printer to use one LED for each of the dots to be discharged on the drum to form the image of the document. A printer rated at 600 dots per inch (dpi) has 600 LEDs in each inch of its light source. As the drum rotates past the light source, the LEDs are used to discharge the dots that form a single line of the image.

LCD Printing

The phases used in LCD printing are the same as the HP process except that in the Developing phase light passing through an LCD (liquid crystal display) panel is used to discharge the drum to receive toner. These printers are also called LCD shutter printers because of the way liquid crystal elements work.

Liquid crystal is neither a liquid or a solid; it exists somewhere between those two states. Each piece of the crystal is a long, thin shaft that has a twist between 90 to 270 degrees. When electricity is applied to the crystal, it untwists in a predictable way. In its uncharged state, liquid crystals do not block any light passing through its panel. However, after electricity is applied and the crystal untwists, the crystal will not block the light. The amount of electricity applied determines the amount of light it blocks.

There is a liquid crystal pixel for each of the tiny dots on the drum that can be discharged to create a document. So, if the printer is rated for 1200dpi, 1200 liquid crystals are used in each inch of the light source. As the drum rotates past the light source, the crystals are opened and closed to create the dots on the drum for each line of pixels in the document's image.

Inside the Laser Printer

Laser printers use toner to create the image on the printed page. Toner is supplied to the printer in a removable cartridge that typically also contains many of the most important components of the printing process (see Figure 17-14). Located inside the toner cartridge are the photosensitive drum, a charging mechanism, typically a corona wire, used to condition the drum, a developing roller used to deposit toner on the drum, and, of course, the toner. Including these parts of the process in the toner cartridges provides the printer with a fresh drum each time the toner cartridge is changed, preventing drum imaging problems common to older photocopiers, which includes scratches or grooves being etched into the drum by paper bits, staples, or other foreign bodies that fall into the print drum area. These types of problems are avoided when the drum is new and sealed inside the cartridge.

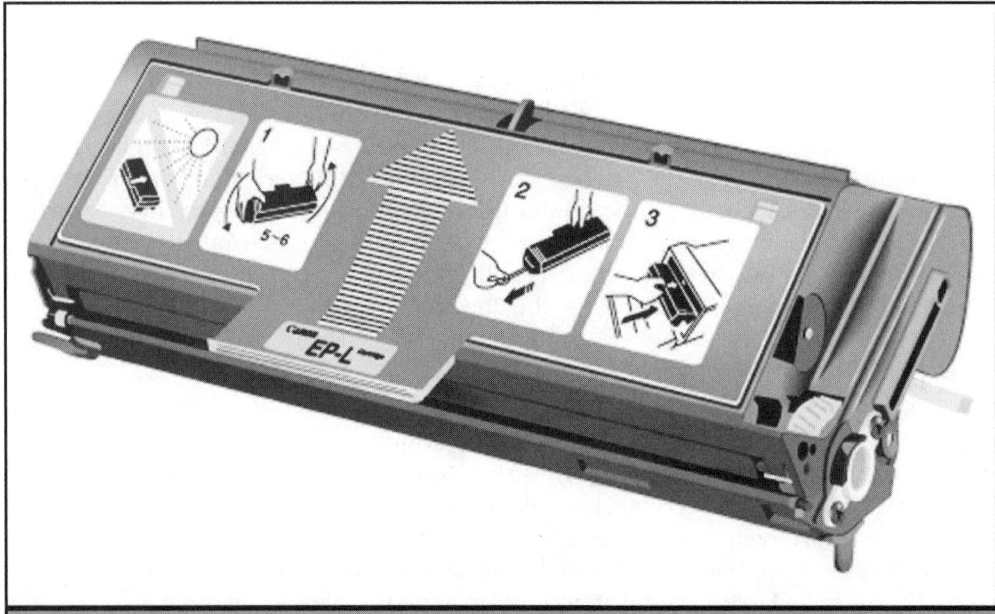

Figure 17-14. A laser printer toner cartridge

Including the toner cartridge, an additional eight standard assemblies exist in a laser printer. As illustrated in Figure 17-15, these assemblies are as follows:

- **Drum** The drum inside the toner cartridge is photosensitive, which means it reacts to light. The drum holds an electrostatic charge except where it is exposed to light. The light source, usually a laser, is reflected onto the surface of the drum to create a pattern of charged and not-charged dots that form the image of the page to be printed.
- **High-voltage power supply** The electrophotographic process used in laser printers applies very high voltage to charge the drum and to transfer and hold the toner on the paper. The high-voltage power supply converts AC current into the higher voltages used in the printer.
- **DC power supply** The electronic components of a laser printer use direct current (DC) power. For example, logic circuits use +/–5 VDC (volts direct current), and the paper transport motors use +24 VDC. Like a PC's power supply, the laser printer's DC power supply also houses its cooling fan.
- **Paper transport** Inside the laser printer are four sets of rubberized rollers used to move the paper through the printer, each driven by its own motor. The four roller sets of the paper transport system are the feed roller or the paper pickup rollers, the registration rollers, the fuser rollers, and the exit rollers. The rollers are very much like the platen roller in a typewriter, daisy wheel printer, or dot matrix printer. They are rubberized to grip the paper and adjusted to grip only as much as is needed to move the paper along to the next station. The paper transport system, and particularly the paper feed rollers, is where most paper jams happen in a laser printer.

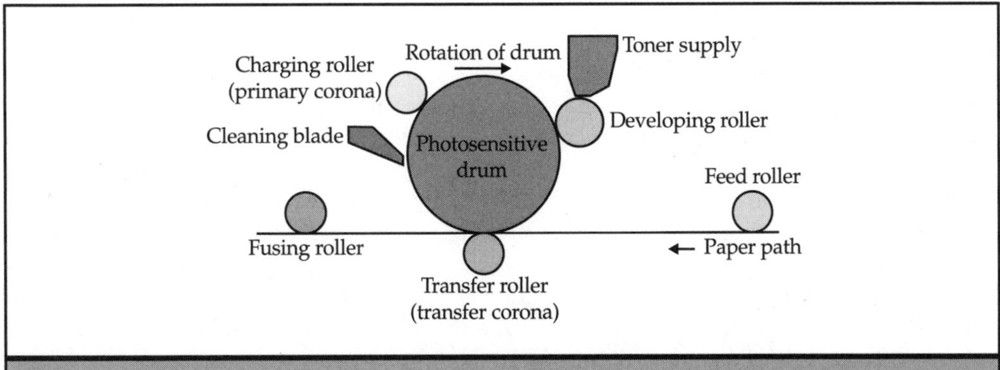

Figure 17-15. The internal components of the laser printing process

- **Primary corona** Also called the main corona or the primary grid, this device forms an electrical field that uniformly charges the photosensitive drum to a negative 600V prior to the image of the document being placed on the drum by the light source.
- **Transfer corona** This mechanism causes the page image to move from the drum to the paper. The transfer corona charges the back of the paper, and the charge pulls the toner from the drum onto the front of the paper. As the paper exits the transfer corona, a static charge eliminator strip reduces the charge on the paper so that it won't stick to the drum. Not all printers use a transfer corona; some use a transfer roller instead.
- **Fusing rollers** The toner is melted permanently to the page by the fusing rollers through pressure and heat, usually between 165 and 180 degrees Celsius. The fuser, and not the laser, is why the pages coming out of a laser printer are hot.
- **Controller** The controller is effectively the motherboard of the laser printer. It communicates with the PC, houses the memory in the printer, and forms the image printed on the page. The controller board also holds the memory of the printer. The memory on a laser printer can be expanded and adding memory allows the printer to reproduce larger documents or graphics in higher resolutions or to support additional soft fonts.

Color Laser Printers

Monochrome laser printers use the same halftoning techniques as the monochrome inkjet printer (see "The Inkjet Printing Process" earlier in the chapter). The difference, of course, is that the image of the document to be printed is detailed onto the print drum all at once instead of as a series of printhead passes. However, before this can be done, the print commands and image data must be converted into the pattern of dots that will produce the document.

Printing Color Documents

The Raster Image Processor (RIP), which is part of the internal control circuitry of the laser printer, translates the string of characters and printing commands sent to the printer by the computer into the dots that make up the image the printer will transfer to paper. The RIP computes the position of each dot on the page and creates an image of the document in the printer's memory, where one bit of memory corresponds to each dot position of the image.

The controller than directs the use of the laser (or LED or LCD) light source to create the dot pattern on the drum. In a laser printer, the laser beam is focused on a multisided mirror that directs the beam onto the drum. Each place the beam touches represents a dot in the image. LED and LCD printers turn their light sources on and off for each of the dot positions on the drum.

The number of dots in use to create printed pages varies with price and manufacturer. Laser printers commonly offer resolutions of 400 to 1200dpi (dots per inch), with 600dpi very common. Heavy-duty workgroup laser printers can offer up to 2400dpi, but these are normally outside the price range of most home or small office users. A 600dpi laser printer offering standard paper widths (8.5 inches) uses over 5,000 dots in each row on the drum.

A color laser printer must image each of its colors separately. This is why color laser printers have two page-per-minute (ppm) ratings: one for monochrome and one for color. The color ppm rating will always be the slower of the two. A laser printer may have a 16ppm rating for monochrome but only 3ppm for printing color documents.

Most color printers use the four CMYK colors (cyan, magenta, yellow, and black) to create its color palette, and for each color used in a document, a complete print cycle must be completed. That is, for each color, the drum is written, the controller directs the correct color toner to be applied, the partial image is transferred to the paper, and the excess toner is removed. The paper actually makes as many as four passes around the drum to collect each color layer of the image. The fusing process is performed only once on the page, after all of the colors have been applied.

Hewlett Packard uses what it calls a *one-pass* system. In this system, each layer of toner is applied to the drum before the full-color buildup is transferred to the paper. For each color in the image, the drum completes a complete cycle (except that there is only one conditioning phase). After all of the colors to be used are added to the drum, the paper passes the drum for a single transfer phase. *One-transfer* would be a much more descriptive name for this technique.

The advantage of the HP one-pass process is that color registration issues are virtually eliminated. As each layer of the color is applied, the paper must be kept in exact registration to the drum for each pass so that the dots that must be adjacent to one another actually are. Should the paper become even slightly misaligned as it is passed around the drum multiple times, the color layers may be overlaid, produce the wrong color or shade, or distort the image.

High-end color laser printers use a belt to which the toner from each color layer is transferred. After all of the colors are on the belt, the toner is transferred to the paper and fused. The use of a belt ensures that any paper registration problems are eliminated.

Building Up the Image

The light source (whether laser, LED, or LCD) of a "laser" printer can create millions of dots on the print drum. These dots are then coated with toner, and the toner is transferred and fused to a sheet of paper. The challenge of color laser printing is creating millions of colors and shades using only four CMYK colors.

Two main color printing technologies are used in color laser printing:

- **Bi-level** This basic color technology provides no control of the intensity of a color. Each color dot is either on or off. The color is either there or it's not; there is no in-between shading. Dithering, explained earlier in the chapter, extends the bi-level process to create transitions between colors and place color in adjacent or neighboring dots to create color visuals. (See the "Color Halftoning" discussion in the "Inkjet Printing Process" section of this chapter.)

- **Multilevel** This is a more advanced method of managing the four primary colors of the laser printer to create multicolored images. Multilevel color printers have the ability to adjust the intensity of each color to produce 256 shades of each color (256 shades of cyan, 256 shades of magenta, etc.) and then mix the 256 shades of each color to produce a total of over 16 millions colors that can be printed on the page. This ability eliminates the need for dithering to produce a solid color. Another name for this process is continuous-tone printing.

Continuous-tone printing mixes colors at the same spot and varies their intensity (and therefore the resulting color) by controlling the amount of each color placed on the dot. The range in laser printers is from bi-level four-color printers to full continuous-tone printers. The common application is to use just enough multilevel processing to reduce the amount of dithering required on an image. For example, a printer may use halftoning with some multilevel processing by creating the halftone image in 2 x 2 cells and then using different dot color combinations in the cell to create the illusion of additional colors.

Nearly all printers place one color dot on top of another color dot and then use the fusing process to blend the dots into the final color. Some printers are able to control how much toner is placed on a dot by controlling the size of the dot. For those printers that can create larger or smaller dots, the amount of toner of a particular color that is used in a "dot-stack" also controls the color that results from the dots. How long the laser is allowed to strike the drum at a particular dot determines the size of the dot. A bigger dot will collect more toner during developing. Shortening the time the laser beam contacts the drum produces a smaller dot. A smaller dot collects less toner.

Toner

Toner is the dry granulated ink used in laser printers (and copy machines as well). It is made from a variety of ingredients, but in general, toner is made from the following ingredients:

- **Plastic** The outer shell of each toner particle is made from styrene or a blend of styrene and acrylic plastics. This part of the toner melts in the fusing phase to adhere to the paper.
- **Iron** As much as 40 percent of a toner particle is ferrous oxide, which is akin to iron rust, that has very specific magnetic properties. Toner particles are held to the drum and paper prior to fusing strictly with simple magnetism. The toner particles are given a negative charge that attracts it to the drum and paper where it is needed to form the image of a document.
- **Sand** Silica (very fine sand) prevents the toner from clumping.
- **Charge dye** This is added to control the electrostatic charge that can be applied to the toner.
- **Wax** The wax helps flow the toner when it melts during the fusing phase.
- **Carbon black** This is added to black toner to deepen its color.

As you can see from this list, toner is a lot more than just dried ink. These ingredients make toner work in the laser printer, but they are extremely difficult to work with outside of the printer. If you've ever spilled toner on the floor, you know how tough it can be to clean up. One tip is that you never want to vacuum up toner with a standard vacuum cleaner. Typically, the airflow in a conventional vacuum cleaner passes over or through the motor, which can be hot. As the toner is heated by the vacuum cleaner's motor, it melts and clogs up the motor and all else it strikes.

Toners are usually matched to the capabilities of particular printers. Some printers have hotter or cooler fusing rollers that can affect how well the toner adheres to the page. Newer printers use what is called "micro-fine" toner, which has smaller particles and produces sharper text and graphic images.

LED PRINTERS

LED printers use light-emitting diodes (a semiconductor that illuminates when an electrical charge is applied to it) instead of a laser. The LED printhead uses a micro-miniature battery of LEDs in two staggered parallel rows that have tiny spaces between them. Each LED, which is about the size of a human hair, is attached to an IC (integrated circuit or chip) that controls the on and off of the LED.

The LED rows are positioned behind two rows of precision-ground optical lenses that are positioned to create one continuous line of LEDs that stretches across the width of the drum. The light emitted from the LEDs is a special wavelength near the infrared range that is invisible to the human eye but easily detected by the photosensitive drum. The LEDs are used to discharge dots on the drum; after that, the print process is the same as on a laser printer.

One advantage the LED printer has over the laser printer is the elimination of moving parts in the light source mechanism. The laser and the rotating mirrors can get out of adjustment and impact the quality of the printed document. Another advantage is price. LED printers are available for less than two hundred dollars.

THERMAL PRINTERS

Essentially, a thermal printer uses a heating element to cause a thermal change in a chemically treated paper to print information on the paper.

Two types of thermal printers are available:

- **Direct thermal** This type of thermal printer uses heat to change the chemical coating that has been directly applied to the thermal printer paper. The thermal paper used in this printer can be expensive.
- **Thermal transfer** This type of thermal printer includes a ribbon or carrier that is used to apply the thermally reactive chemicals to the paper. This process allows the printer to use less expensive paper.

Thermal printers use a resistance tip that heats up when electricity flows through it. The resistance in the printhead of the thermal printer is very small and heats up and cools down in a fraction of a second. Using the heated resistance as a stylus, the thermal printer moves over the thermal paper to create text through a series of dots.

The thermal paper is treated with a chemical that reacts to a moderate temperature by changing color. The color varies by the type of paper, but generally the paper turns a dark gray (white paper) or white (dark paper). In contrast to the dot matrix or inkjet printers, the thermal printer's printhead doesn't have any moving parts, so only the printhead moves side to side to print. Because a thermal printer requires very little power to heat the resistance element, they are lightweight, portable, and can even run on batteries. A real advantage to a thermal printer is that they are virtually silent in operation.

Thermal printers are typically used in specialized applications, such as server stations in restaurants, where their lack of noise is a plus. They are also used on a great many cash registers, and have been popular for portable printers for notebooks and other portable PCs. However, the inkjet printer is quickly becoming a more practical device for the latter.

The paper is the real drawback to a thermal printer. To the paper, heat is heat without regard to its source. Any heat source can discolor the paper, which tends to make a thermal printout less than permanent.

CONNECTING THE PRINTER TO THE PC

Most PC printers connect through a parallel port, which is usually designated as LPT1. A PC may have more than one parallel port, but on most systems there is usually only one. The most commonly used connectors used to connect printers directly to a PC are as follows:

- **25-pin DB (data bus) female connector** The LPT/parallel port on the back of a PC is usually a 25-pin female connector into which the male connector on the printer cable is connected. Most PCs only have a single LPT port that is mounted on the motherboard or an expansion card.
- **36-pin Centronics** This is the common connector on the printer end of the cable. The PC end of the cable is normally a 25-pin male connector, as described in the previous bullet. The 36-pin Centronics connector is so named because Centronics Corporation produced a large share of the early printers. The connector design was actually developed by Ampenol Corporation. The Centronics connector is also the standard connector for the HP-IB (Hewlett Packard Interface Bus) used on all HP printers.
- **USB (Universal Serial Bus)** Some of the latest printers feature a USB connection in addition to the standard parallel connector. If the parallel port is already in use by a scanner or Zip drive, the USB port allows the printer to be connected to the PC without using the parallel port or any additional system resources. Older printers can be connected via a USB connection using a

USB-to-parallel adapter cable that has a Centronics connector on the printer end and a USB connector on the PC end.

- **IR (infrared) or IrDA (Infrared Data Association)** There are adapters available that can be used to connect a parallel printer to a PC through its IrDA connection, like the one made by Extended Systems (**www.extendedsystems.com**). This frees the parallel port on the PC for other uses. A number of handheld-size printers are available for use with notebooks and PDAs with an IrDA connection.

Parallel cables have distance limitations. Older Centronics cables should not be more than 15 feet in length; between 9 feet and 12 feet is best. Newer IEEE-1284 cables can extend up to 30 feet in length, and there are some 50-foot high-end cables available as well. Typically, if you need to be more than 10 feet away from a printer, you would connect into a network.

Using a Switchbox

You can use a switchbox, either manual or automatic, to connect more than one nonlaser printer or any other parallel device or devices to a single parallel port. You can also use them to allow multiple PCs to share a single printer. A dial designates which PC or device is to be connected to the primary device of the switchbox. Switchboxes are also called A/B switches because the devices attached are labeled as A, B, C, and so on. An automatic switchbox senses activity on a line and automatically switches to that line.

In general, a laser printer should not be connected to a switchbox, especially newer laser printers. Laser printers are highly interactive with the printer and have very high voltage requirements. There is also the issue of electrical noise. Taking the laser printer on- and offline by changing the active location, either manually or automatically, can interrupt device driver commands and create electrical noise spikes that could possibly damage the laser printer or the PC's parallel port.

Printer Standards

In 1984, the IEEE (Institute of Electrical and Electronics Engineers) standardized parallel port protocols. The standard has a very long name but is commonly known as IEEE 1284. This standard incorporates the two legacy parallel port standards with a new protocol. The standards included in IEEE 1284 are as follows:

- **Standard parallel port (SPP)** This parallel standard allows data to travel in only one direction—from the computer to the printer.
- **Enhanced Parallel Port (EPP)** This parallel standard allows data to flow in both directions, but only one way at a time. An EPP connection allows the printer to communicate with the processor to signal out of paper, open cover, and other conditions.

- **Enhanced Capabilities Port (ECP)** This is the newest of the parallel protocols. It allows bi-directional simultaneous (full-duplex) communications over special IEEE 1284–compliant cables. Many bi-directional cables exist, but they may be EPP cables, which do not support ECP communications.

IEEE 1284 established the standard for bi-directional communications on the parallel port, and the ECP protocol allows for full-duplex (simultaneous communications in two directions) parallel communications.

Connecting to a Network

With the cost of a high-quality, high-volume laser printer, it is wise to share it among several PCs by placing the printer on the local area network (LAN). Printers to be shared over a network can be purchased network-ready or can be easily adapted for connecting to a network.

Printers that are network-ready have an installed network adapter into which an RJ-45 network connector can be inserted. A printer that is not network-ready can be attached to a network through a network printer interface like Hewlett Packard's JetDirect. These devices can be used to connect one or more printers to the network. A printer connects to a network interface device through its parallel port. The network interface device provides the network adapter that interfaces the printer to the network. Figure 17-16 illustrates both a network-ready printer connected directly to the network and another printer that is not network ready connected with a network interface device.

PRINTER SAFEGUARDS

Here are a number of common-sense procedures and a few more technical ones that you can use to keep a printer working and reliable:

- **Power protection** Plug inkjet, dot matrix, and other nonlaser printers into a surge protector or UPS (uninterruptible power supply). However, you should never plug a laser printer into a conventional UPS. Laser printers draw a tremendous amount of power at startup, and few UPS units have enough power to handle the demand. If you use a UPS for your laser printer, be sure the UPS can handle the peak loading (peak power requirements) of the laser printer.
- **Paper** Always use the type and weights of paper recommended by the manufacturer for the printer, and never use paper heavier than the recommended maximum weight. This will help avoid print feed and paper path jams. Some printers prefer laser printer paper that is finished on one side; check your printer's documentation.
- **Cleaning** Clean dot-matrix printers regularly with a vacuum or blow them out with compressed air. If you wish to vacuum out a laser printer, be sure you use only a vacuum and dust bag specially made for that task. The toner can really gum up the works of a regular vacuum cleaner.

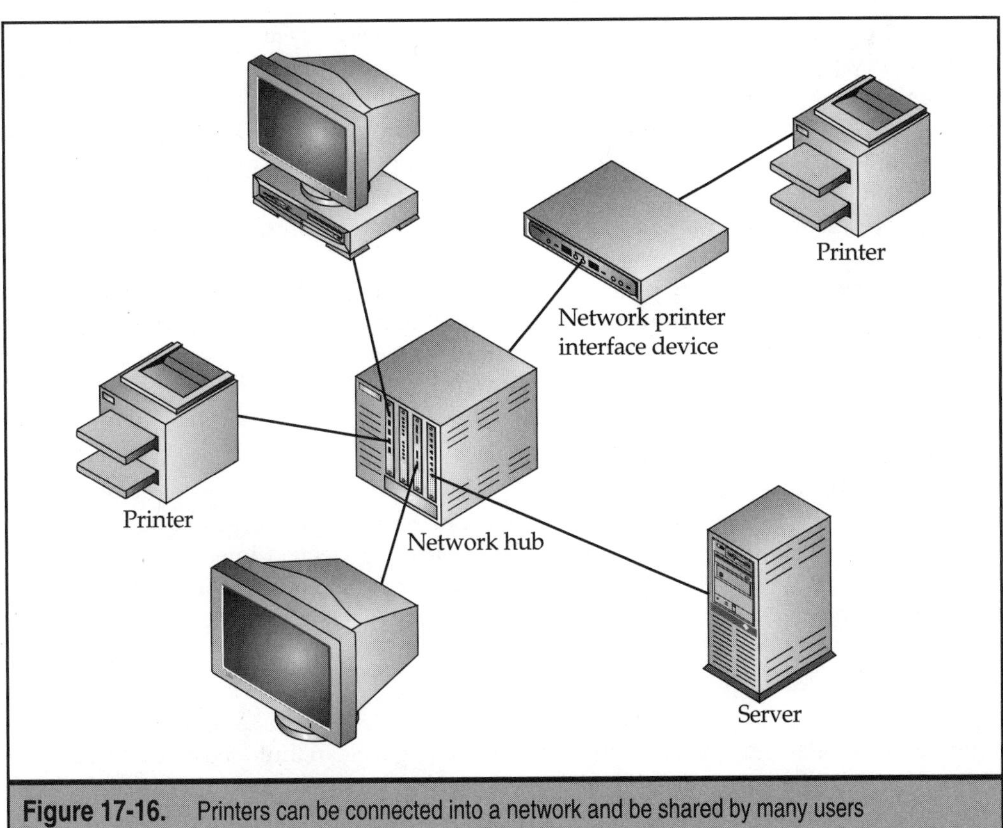

Figure 17-16. Printers can be connected into a network and be shared by many users

- **Conditioning** Use a flexible wire brush or rubber-conditioning product to clean and maintain the paper transport of an inkjet or laser printer. Never put anything inside a laser printer while it's running to try to clear the paper path, and always wait until the fusing area has cooled down before working in that area of a laser printer. The fusing area uses high heat to melt the toner and stays hot for some time afterward.

Laser Printer Care

Laser printers have special needs when it comes to maintenance. The following sections contain tips to help you care for a laser printer.

Toner

Toner cartridges are typically sealed units that require you to remove a strip, tape, or tab. It is rare to have a toner incident, but should you ever have spill toner or see toner spilled inside the printer, don't use a standard vacuum cleaner to clean it up. Remember that toner is very fine particles of iron and plastic. The particles are so fine that they seep through the walls of most vacuum bags and get into the motor, where the plastic melts. Special types of vacuums and vacuum cleaner bags are made for working with toner.

Should you get toner on your skin, never rinse it off with warm or hot water. Hot water may cause the toner to fuse to your skin. It's best to first wipe off as much of the toner with a dry paper towel or soft cloth. Then rinse with cold water, and finish by washing with soap and cold water.

A cleaning brush or large plastic swab with a cotton pad is usually packed with the toner cartridge to clean the transfer corona wire. You can clean the primary corona wire with an ordinary cotton swab as well, but make sure the laser printer has had time to cool down. While cleaning these wires, be very careful not to break them.

Ozone and Exhaust

During the print process, the laser produces a gas called *ozone*, and the toner emits an exhaust when it is heated. Most laser printers have an ozone filter that also captures toner dust and exhaust and paper dust. This filter should be replaced or cleaned in accordance with the manufacturer's instructions in the printer's manual. Spare filters are usually shipped with the printer. If not, contact the manufacturer or vendor to get spare filters, if needed.

Cleaning the Mirrors

Inside the laser printer are two or more multisided mirrors that are used to reflect the laser onto the drum. Periodically clean these mirrors using a clean, lint-free cloth. Be sure the power is off and the unit is unplugged. Never, ever, repeat, never look directly at the laser. Along this same line, never operate the printer with its covers off. Most printers will not power up with its cover open, anyway.

Fuser Pads and Rollers

The fuser cleaning pad (that cleans the fusing roller after it presses the melted toner onto the paper) and the fusing roller can become dirty and begin to leave unwanted toner blobs on the paper. Check the fuser cleaning pad and the fuser rollers regularly and clean them as necessary.

SETTING UP A PRINTER IN WINDOWS

Setting up a printer on a Windows system is the same for virtually every printer. However, you should always follow the setup instructions that come with the printer.

Windows 9*x*, Windows NT, and Windows 2000 each carry a remarkable number of printer drivers with them. However, to be absolutely certain that you have the very latest driver for the PC's operating system, visit the manufacturer's Web site. Some printers come with a separate printer driver included on a diskette or a CD-ROM.

Add new printers through the Printers function found on the Control Panel or on the Settings option of the Start menu. In either case, the Printers dialog box displays the Add Printer Wizard icon (see Figure 17-17). The following steps detail the process used to add a printer to a Windows computer.

1. From the Windows desktop, click the Start button to display the Start menu. Access the Settings menu and choose the Printers option. Or double-click the My Computer icon to display the My Computer folder. Open the Control Panel and choose the Printers icon.
2. With the Printer folder open, choose the Add Printer icon to start the Add Printer Wizard.
3. If the printer being added is not listed in the supported printers list, use the diskette or CD-ROM that came with the printer to supply the device driver by clicking the Have Disk button when appropriate. In fact, even if the printer is listed and you have a disk, use the disk.
4. After the printer driver loads, an icon for the new printer will display in the Printers folder. You many want to open the Properties window for this printer and make any print control adjustments you desire or set the new printer as the system default.

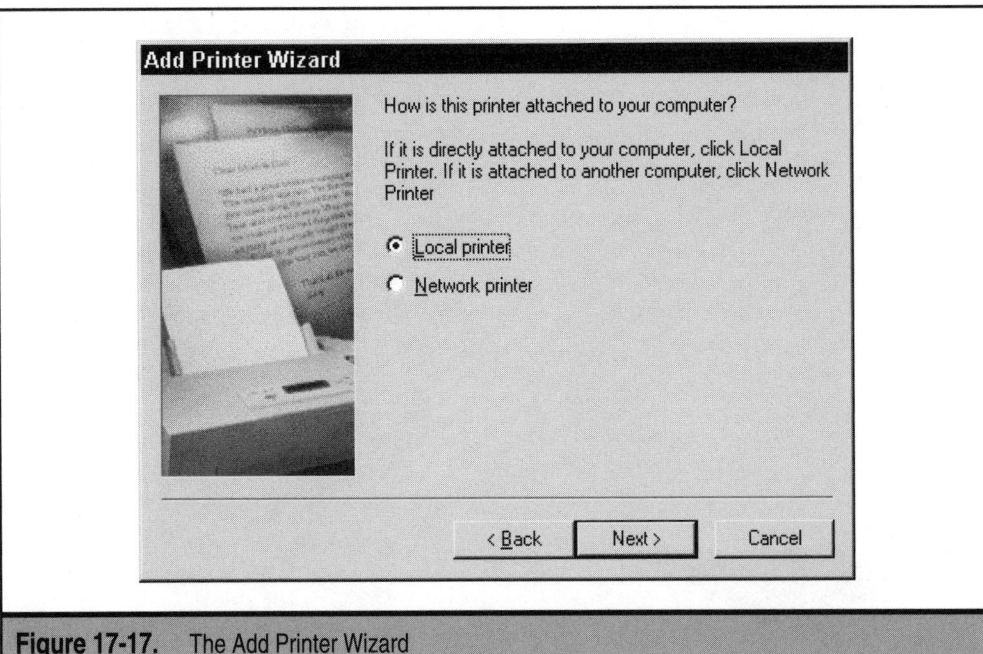

Figure 17-17. The Add Printer Wizard

CHAPTER 18

Keyboards, Mice, and Pointing Devices

Input devices serve two distinct purposes on a PC. First, they allow the user to command and control the activities of the PC; second, input devices allow the user to capture and enter data into the PC. The most important thing to know about an input device is how to operate it. The input and output devices of the PC exist to allow the human operator and the PC to communicate with one another.

Output devices are adapted to human senses of sight and sound, but input devices are adapted to gather data from a number of sources. For example, the operator can manipulate the keys on a keyboard using a combination of sight and touch to enter text and numeric data. A mouse captures the movement of the user's hand to point, select, and execute objects displayed on the PC's monitor. Scanners convert captured images and text into computer-readable forms for manipulation by the user. Video capture cards convert analog video into digital data that can be viewed on the PC. There are also devices to capture sound as well as devices that capture data so that the PC can control the temperature in a building. The options for output devices are limited to sight and sound (so far), but the options for input devices are virtually limitless as more devices are adapted to capture data in its natural form, such as thermometers, timing devices, pressure pads, and a wide variety of other types.

Unlike many of the PC's components, it really isn't necessary to know all of the technical parts and operational details of most input devices. In today's technology, the primary input devices—the keyboard and mouse—are considered disposable devices. Should they stop working or become broken, it is usually far easier and often less expensive to simply replace them than it is to repair them. However, these input devices and other nondisposable input devices must be cared for to keep them operating properly.

This chapter does provide some technical details on most of the current classes of input devices. This is done primarily to acquaint you with the technologies in use and not to teach you how to dissect and repair internal technical problems with these devices.

KEYBOARDS

The most common input device is the keyboard. The keyboard allows a user to communicate with the PC through keystrokes that represent character data and commands. Virtually every PC sold has a keyboard included as a part of its standard package. In fact, most people take their keyboard for granted and rarely even think about it. As long as the keys work and the user is able to enter data, the keyboard is just fine.

The keyboard, despite its many variations and ergonomic (human engineering) styles is very much a standardized device. Virtually all keyboards, like the one shown in Figure 18-1, have a standard keyboard layout, connect to a PC with primarily one connector, and are for the most part interchangeable between manufacturers.

Figure 18-1. A typical PC keyboard

Keyboard Elements

Most keyboard layouts are still a variation on the key layout of a typewriter, at least for the alphabetic, numerical, and special character keys. All keyboards have a core component of keys founded on the keyboards of a particular continent (North America, Europe, etc.), country (France), or language (Chinese). However, keyboards also include a variety of other keys that are dedicated to specific functions or are assigned functions by the software running on the PC, such as a keyboard's function keys.

A keyboard's keys can be grouped into functional groups, as illustrated in Figure 18-2:

- **Alphabetic keys** The alphabetic keys along with the row numbers and special characters. These keys match those on a typewriter.
- **Cursor control keys** Located to the right of the alphabetic keys, this group of keys has two smaller groups of keys: the cursor function keys and the cursor arrow keys.
- **Function keys** Typically located across the top of a keyboard today, they were once located on either side of a keyboard. Current keyboards have 12 function keys, while most older keyboards have 8.
- **Number pad keys** The number pad, which is located on the extreme right side of nearly all modern keyboards, contains keys for ten numbers, as well as the four arithmetic functions. The number pad can also be used as a cursor control pad by toggling the NUM LOCK key.

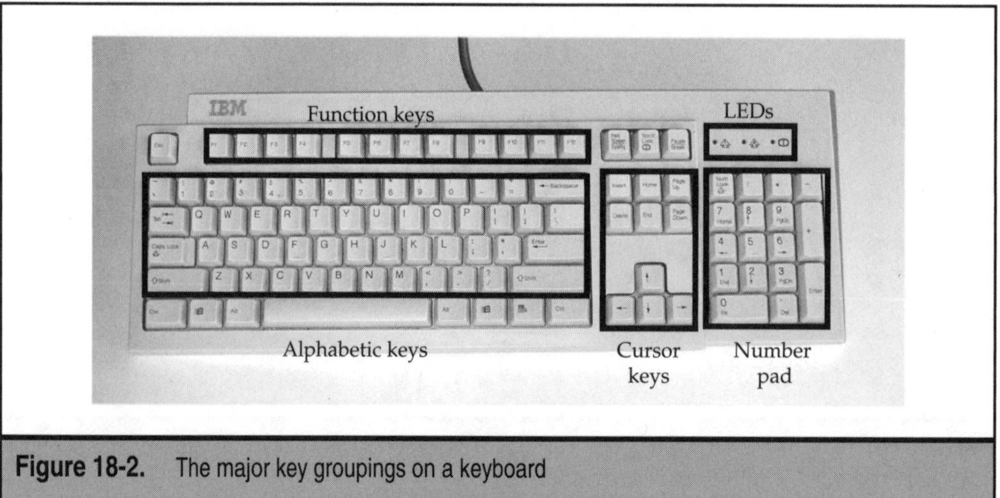

Figure 18-2. The major key groupings on a keyboard

Alphabetic Keys

These keys make up the main area of the keyboard, as illustrated in Figure 18-3, and are the keys used for most keyboard input by the user. This group of keys includes:

- **Alphabetic keys** The English language alphabet characters of A through Z. These keys default to a lowercase character and produce an uppercase letter through either the SHIFT key or the CAPS LOCK key.
- **Punctuation and special characters** This group of keys is embedded in the alphabetic keyboard. These keys are located on the left-edge of the alphabetic keyboard and include this group of punctuation and special characters: \ (backslash), | (vertical bar), / (forward slash), ? (question mark), . (period/dot), > (greater than), , (comma), < (less than), ; (semi-colon), : (colon), ' (single quote/apostrophe), " (double-quote), [(open/left bracket), { (open/left brace),] (close/right bracket), } (close/right bracket). Most of these keys have lowercase characters and uppercase characters that are accessed through the SHIFT key.
- **Action keys** The keys in this group can be divided into two subgroups: the character selection keys and the command action keys. The character selection keys include the SHIFT keys, the CAPS LOCK key, and the BACKSPACE key. The command action keys are the CTRL key, the ESC key, and the ALT key.
- **Enter key** This may be the most used key on the keyboard; it is certainly the largest. The ENTER key performs a variety of functions from ending the line or entry in application software to serving as a weapon trigger in a shooting game. In word processors, the ENTER key simulates the action of the carriage return button on an electric typewriter.

Figure 18-3. The alphabetic keys on the standard keyboard

- **Character selection keys** The SHIFT key is used to toggle a key between its lowercase and uppercase characters. The CAPS LOCK key locks the alphabetic keys into uppercase characters (the SHIFT key is used to toggle to the lower case letters when the CAPS LOCK key is engaged). The BACKSPACE key erases a character by replacing it with the character or white space that follows it.
- **Command control keys** The Control (CTRL) and ALT (short for alternate control keys) keys are used in combination with the alphabetic, numeric, and function keys to designate or control actions or commands to software programs.
- **White space keys** The SPACEBAR and the TAB keys are commonly referred to as the white space keys. The SPACEBAR produces one character of white space and the TAB key defaults to half an inch of white space.
- **Number/special character keys** Across the top of the alphabetic keys is a row of 12 or 13 keys that contain 26 different numbers and special characters. The number keys (1 through 9 and 0) are standard on all keyboards, but the special characters that are located on these same keys can vary depending on the region. The special character keys, which are accessed through the SHIFT key, are ~ (tilde), ` (single quote), ! (exclamation point), @ (at sign), # (pound or number sign), $ (dollar sign), % (percent sign), ^ (carat), & (ampersand), * (asterisk), ((opening/left parenthesis),) (closing/right parenthesis), - (hyphen), _ (underscore), = (equal sign), + (plus sign).

Toggles and Locks

Some keys, such as the SHIFT, CTRL, and ALT keys are toggle keys. Toggle keys have two values that can be selected, a default value when the key is not pressed and an alternate value when pressed. For example, the SHIFT key's default is lowercase, which is what you get if you do not press the SHIFT key and press an alphabetic key. Pressing the SHIFT key toggles any pressed alphabetic character to its uppercase value. The toggle value is only in effect while the toggle key is being pressed. When the key is released, the value reverts to its default.

Locking keys, which are the CAPS LOCK, NUM LOCK, and SCROLL LOCK keys, also toggle between two actions or values, but unlike the SHIFT, CTRL, and ALT keys, they remain toggled when released. These keys are like the on/off button on a monitor. When the button is pressed, the monitor is powered on and stays on until the button is pressed again to reverse its state. When the CAPS LOCK key is pressed, it has the same effect as pressing the SHIFT key permanently. The alphabetic characters only are shifted to uppercase as their default values. In fact, if you use the SHIFT key after the CAPS LOCK is pressed, the shifted value will be a lowercase character. The NUM LOCK key toggles the number pad on and off alternating to a cursor control pad. The SCROLL LOCK key enables and disables software scrolling control of the display.

Key Repeats

Many new keyboards and operating systems allow you to repeat a key virtually forever by merely holding it down. The rate of the repeating key is controlled through the Windows Control Panel's Keyboard icon, which opens the Keyboard Properties window shown in Figure 18-4.

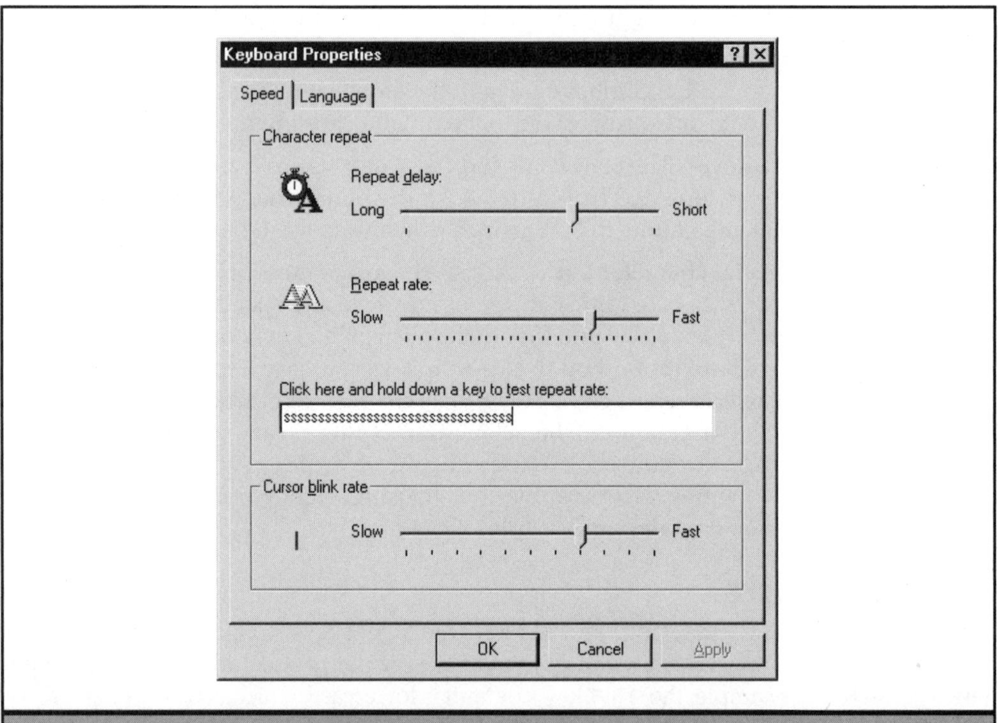

Figure 18-4. The Keyboard Properties window is used to control the repeat of repeating keys

Cursor Control Keys

The 101-key design of the keyboard included a separate group of cursor control keys. Prior to this design, the number pad had to serve double-duty as cursor control keys. The NUM LOCK key was used to toggle and lock the number pad between these two functions. On the 101-key design and those that followed, a set of four dedicated cursor control (arrow) keys and a six-key set of cursor action (a.k.a. navigation) keys were added between the alphabetic keys and the number pad, as illustrated in Figure 18-5.

This group of keys includes:

- **Cursor control (arrow) keys** This group of four directional keys is used to move the cursor left, up, down, and right. Virtually all software supports the use of these keys. Game software relies on these keys to move characters through scenes using points of the compass represented by these four keys where up is north, down is south, left is east, and right is west. Some keyboards add four diagonal direction keys that move the cursor (or the action) in directions between the standard four keys.
- **Cursor command/navigation keys** A group of six keys located to the right of the alphabetic keys and above the cursor control keys, these keys, shown in Figure 18-6, duplicate the six control functions originally included in the number pad's cursor control keys. The keys included are INSERT, DELETE, HOME, END, and PAGE UP and PAGE DOWN. The function of each of these keys is as follows:
- **INSERT** This is a locking key that toggles software between insert and replace modes. Insert mode, which is the default mode for most word processing systems, inserts characters at the point indicated by the cursor. Replace mode, which is also called typeover mode, replaces any existing characters with the characters being entered.

Figure 18-5. The cursor control keys on a standard keyboard

Figure 18-6. The cursor command and navigation keys on a standard keyboard

- **DELETE** The function of this key is controlled by the software application running on the PC, but it is essentially used to remove a single character to the right of the cursor or a selected object.
- **HOME and END** In most applications, the HOME key positions the cursor at the beginning of a text line. The END key does the opposite and moves the cursor to the end of a text line. When used in combination with other keys, such as the CTRL key, the HOME key moves the cursor to the beginning of a document, and the END key moves the cursor to the end or bottom of a document.
- **PAGE UP and PAGE DOWN** These keys are used primarily in document-based software to scroll one entire screen up or down. On many keyboards they are labeled PG UP and PG DN.

The Number Pad

Every one of the keys on the number pad can be found elsewhere on the keyboard. This set of keys, shown in Figure 18-7, was originally added to the keyboard to facilitate the entry of numeric data. It replicates the key placement used on a ten-key calculator or cardpunch machine. Most users simply ignore it, but for those users who must enter large volumes of numeric data, the numeric keypad is an absolute necessity.

The keys included in the number pad are as follows:

- **NUM LOCK** This key is used to toggle and lock the number keypad between its function as a number pad and its cursor control function. The default setting (on or off) for the NUM LOCK is set in the PC's BIOS settings. Virtually all systems set the NUM LOCK on during the boot and leave it on, ignoring the cursor control functions of the number pad.
- **Arithmetic operators** The number pad includes keys for the four standard arithmetic operators, / (divide), * (multiply), - (subtract), and + (add).

Figure 18-7. The number pad on a standard keyboard

- **Number/cursor keys** When the NUM LOCK is toggled on (and the NUM LOCK LED is lighted), the ten number keys type the digits 0 to 9. When the NUM LOCK is toggled off (the LED is off), these keys become cursor control keys. Most keyboards with 101 keys or higher include keys for diagonal movement, which are typically the 1, 7, 9, and 3 keys (without the NUM LOCK key on) that move down-left, up-left, up-right, and down-right, respectively.
- **INSERT/DELETE** These two keys are the zero and period of the number pad when it is in number mode; in cursor control mode, they duplicate the actions of the INSERT key and the DELETE keys.
- **ENTER** This is a second ENTER key that remains an ENTER key regardless of the number pad's mode.

Function Keys

The 12 keys on the top row of the keyboard are the function keys, shown in Figure 18-8. These keys have no default functions and are completely controlled by software, whether it is the operating system or an application. Some software applications make extensive use of the function keys, such as WordPerfect (a word processing system from Corel). For example, on the DOS and Windows command line, the F3 key (all function keys are designated with an *F* to differentiate them from the number keys) is used to repeat the last line entered, and in virtually all Windows applications, the F1 key is used to open the Help system.

The earliest PCs had ten function keys that were arranged to the left side of the keyboard is two columns of five keys. When the enhanced keyboards were introduced, the keys were expanded to twelve keys and placed along the top edge of the keyboard.

Figure 18-8. The function keys on a standard keyboard

Special-Purpose Keys

A few other keys on the keyboard are used only for very special purposes, if at all. Some users rarely or never use these keys because not all applications support them or their functions just do not come up in most data processing situations. These special-purpose keys are:

- **ESC** The Escape key is typically enabled as an exit key by most software applications. It is used to cancel out of a command or to exit an application. It is also used in combination with other keys to create special key values and to indicate other actions. For example, in Windows the ESC key can be used to close a context menu.
- **PRINT SCREEN/SYSRQ** The PRINT SCREEN mode of this key got its name back in the MS-DOS days, when pressing it sent the image of the display to the printer. On a Windows system, the image of the monitor's display is sent to the Windows Clipboard. Figure 18-9 illustrates the contents of the Windows Clipboard Viewer after the PRINT SCREEN key was pressed with a Web browser on the screen. The alternate mode of this key is a system request action. This key has no real function on most PCs unless the PC is emulating an IBM terminal connected to a mainframe computer.
- **PAUSE/BREAK** In its default mode (PAUSE), this key will, if enabled by software, pause the display or the action of an application program. If used in combination with the CTRL key, the alternate mode of this key interrupts or halts some software programs, primarily MS-DOS commands and applications. Using the CTRL and BREAK keys together is the same using the CTRL and C keys to break an action.

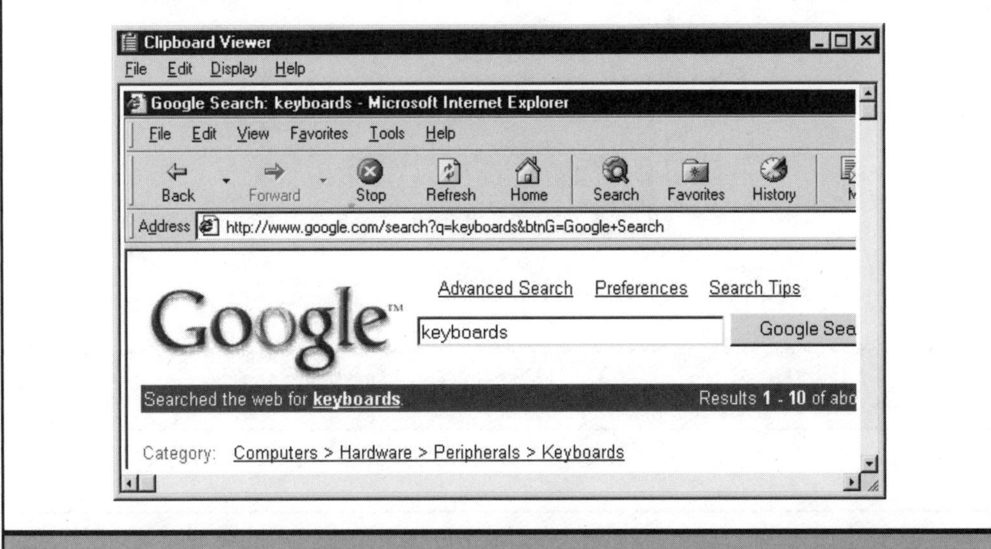

Figure 18-9. The Windows Clipboard Viewer showing a screen captured by the PRINT SCREEN key

Windows Keys

Most newer keyboards have added three Windows-specific keys on either side of the SPACEBAR that serve as shortcuts to the Windows menus. Figure 18-10 shows the two keys on the right of the SPACEBAR.

- **Windows key** This key (there are two, one on each side of the SPACEBAR next to the ALT keys) with the flying Window on it will, if used by itself, pop up the Windows Start menu, as illustrated in Figure 18-11. However, if used in combination with other keys, the Windows key will start or open several other actions or applets, as listed in Table 18-1.
- **Context menu key** This key is located on the right side of the SPACEBAR between the Windows key and CTRL. Pressing the context menu key performs the same action as right-clicking anywhere on the display—it pops up the context menu (also called the shortcut menu) for the current application (illustrated in Figure 18-12).

Figure 18-10. The two Windows-specific keys to the right of the SPACEBAR are used to display the Windows Start menu and the current context menu

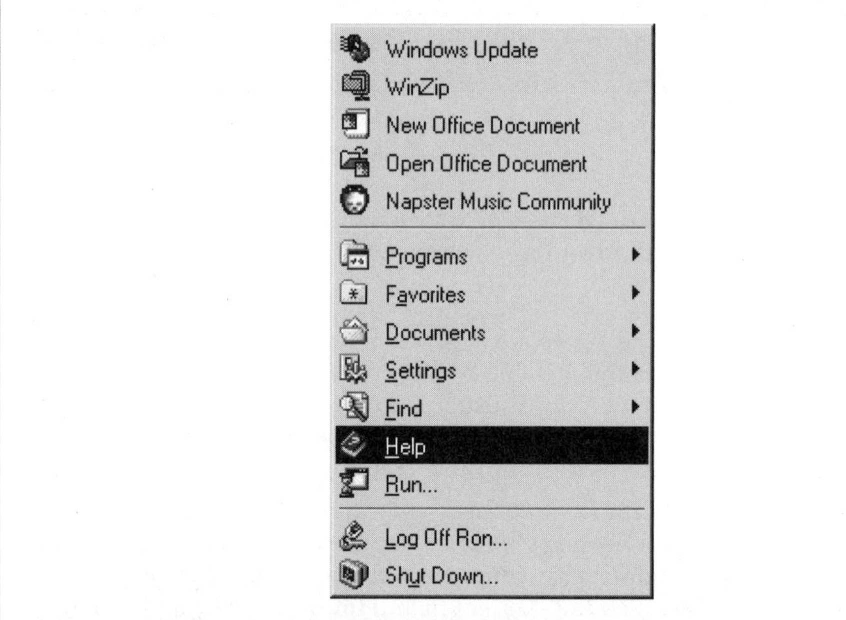

Figure 18-11. The Windows key pops up the Windows Start menu

Key Combination	Action	Equivalent Actions
Windows-TAB	Cycle through the Taskbar applications	ALT-TAB
Windows-BREAK	Open the System Properties window	Right-click My Computer icon
Windows-F1	Start Windows Help	Click Start, choose Help
Windows-E	Open Windows Explorer	Right-click Start, choose Explore
Windows-F	Open the Find Files or Folders dialog box	Click Start, choose Find, choose Files and Folders
Windows-CTRL-F	Open the Find Computer dialog box	Click Start, choose Find, choose Computer
Windows-M	Minimize all open windows	Click the Desktop icon on the Taskbar tray
Windows-SHIFT-M	Restore all current windows	Click each application on the Taskbar
Windows-R	Open the Run dialog box	Click Start, choose Run

Table 18-1. Windows Key Actions

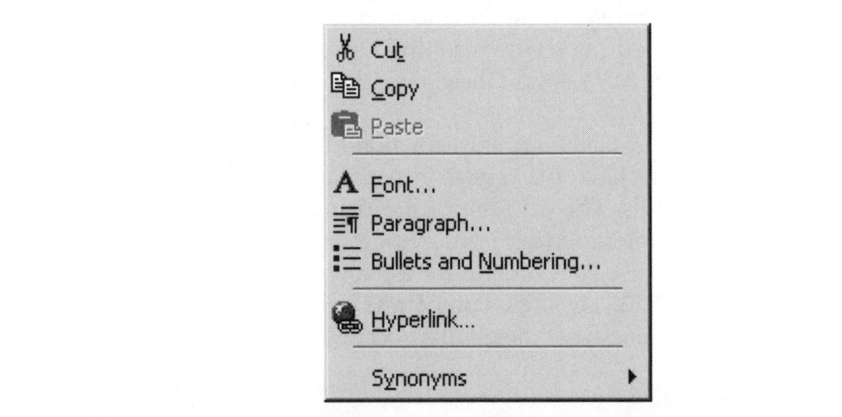

Figure 18-12. The context menu for an application can be displayed by pressing the Context menu key

Keyboard Layouts and Styles

Keyboards, regardless of which region of the world they are from, tend to follow some fairly basic layout patterns. The style and layout of a keyboard is a direct function of the number of keys it has. It is logical that a keyboard with only 83 keys can be much smaller and more simply laid out than one with 108 keys.

Early Keyboards

The very first PC keyboards were those of the IBM PC and PC XT. These keyboards had 83 keys. Judged by today's keyboards, this keyboard design does have its faults, but it did establish the design basis for all keyboards that followed. Some of its more enduring characteristics were that it was a separate unit from the PC, had ten function keys, and included a ten-key number/cursor control pad.

The 84-key keyboard of the IBM PC AT added one additional key, the SYSTEM REQUEST key, and made several other adjustments, including better spacing of the keys, enlarging the SHIFT and ENTER keys, and adding three LED indicators to the keyboard for the locking keys (CAPS LOCK, NUM LOCK, and SCROLL LOCK).

Enhanced Keyboards

The last version of the IBM PC AT (Model 339), which was introduced in 1986, included an enhanced keyboard (as IBM called it) that had 101 keys. This keyboard, with some minor variations and not too many added keys, continues to endure as the de facto standard for all keyboards. Actually, there isn't much you can do to revolutionize keyboards beyond adding special keys and functions. Over the years, keyboards have remained true to the basic design of the Enhanced 101 keyboard. Even the newest emerging keyboard standard, the 104-key Windows keyboard (see below) is virtually identical to the 101-key design.

The primary differences between the enhanced keyboard and the 84-key AT keyboard are the addition of the dedicated cursor control keys, new multiply and divide keys on the number pad, CTRL and ALT keys on the right side of the SPACEBAR, and two more function keys.

Variations of the enhanced keyboard exist for non-English speaking regions of the world. Most of these variations have 102 keys to incorporate additional special characters and language-specific symbols. The differences are primarily in the keys, with many special characters moved or replaced (different money symbols are common), but some arrangement differences also exist. For example, the top row of keys on an English-language keyboard starts with QWERTY keys. In France and other countries, these keys are AZERTY because of the frequency that these letters occur in other languages.

Windows Keyboards

The current standard for keyboard layout is the Windows keyboard that features 104 keys. The three keys added to the 101-key design are the Windows and Context menu keys discussed earlier in the chapter. Figure 18-13 shows the Windows keyboard.

Natural and Ergonomic Keyboards

Flat keyboards are easy to manufacture and package, but they can be hard on the user, particularly if the user is entering data for extended periods. In an attempt to help relieve some of the stress caused by the position a user's hands and wrists must be in to use the standard keyboard, and to prevent repetitive stress injuries such as carpal tunnel syndrome, newer keyboard designs reshape the keyboard and place their keys so that the user's hands are in a more natural, or ergonomic, position. Figure 18-14 shows a sample of these natural keyboards.

Portable PC Keyboards

Notebook computers, by design and definition, must be smaller than normal keyboards. Thus, some adjustments must be made in terms of key arrangement, layout, and even function to fit all of the keys users require. Typically, the notebook PC is running the same software the user has on their desktop computer. This means that the same keys used by the application software must be available on both PCs, so the notebook PC manufacturer is faced with a size and space problem. The result is that notebook PC keyboards are small and cramped, the keys are more closely placed, and the arrangement of the keys,

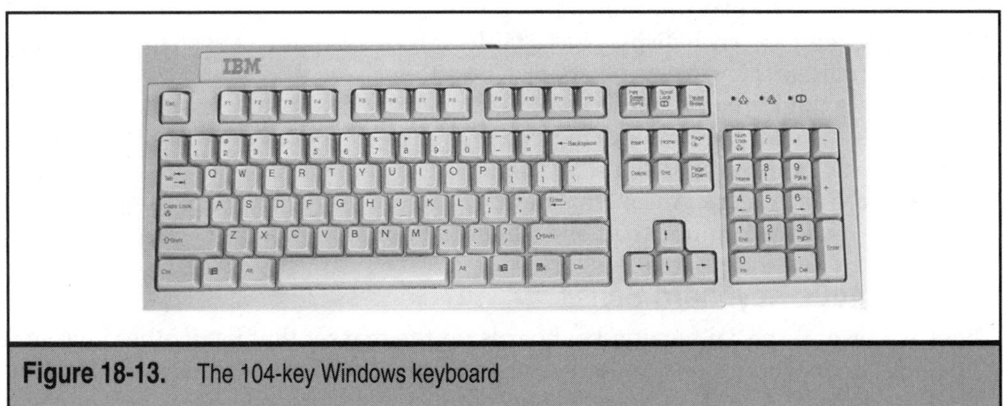

Figure 18-13. The 104-key Windows keyboard

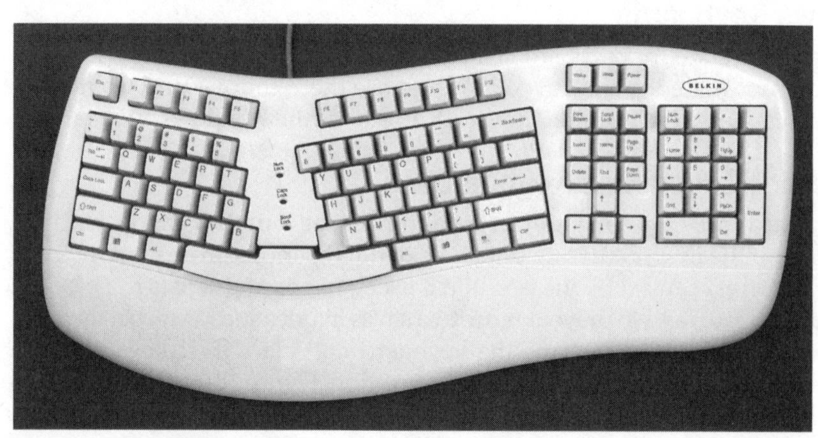

Figure 18-14. A natural, ergonomic style keyboard. Photo courtesy of Belkin Components

which can vary from manufacturer to manufacturer or even from model to model, is normally nonstandard. This is especially true of the cursor control and number pad keys. Most notebook PCs also include a special function (FN) key that is used to control display, sound, and other I/O actions of the PC.

Figure 18-15 shows the keyboard of a very recent notebook design. With portable PCs, the bigger the display, the more room there is for a better keyboard arrangement. A notebook PC with a 12-inch display has a fairly limited space for a keyboard dictated by the PC's overall size. However, a notebook with a 15-inch display has more overall size to accommodate the keyboard and a better arrangement of the keys. Notice the mouse control (called a Glidepoint mouse) in the center of the keyboard in Figure 18-15.

Notebook PCs also provide PS/2 and USB ports that can be used for an external standard keyboard and mouse. An external number pad can also be added to compensate for the lack of a dedicated number pad on virtually all portable PCs.

Miscellaneous Keyboard Styles

There are several special version keyboards on the market that have other keys and buttons that, depending on the keyboards specialty, perform a variety of functions. Internet keyboards include buttons to connect to the Internet, open a browser, or check e-mail. Multimedia keyboards include audio controls such as sound volume and CD controls (play, stop, pause, previous, next, and others). Figure 18-16 shows a multimedia keyboard with its extra buttons. Several new designs have buttons that duplicate the actions of the mouse buttons and some now even have a mouse, trackball, or touch pad built into the keyboard. Some keyboards have all of the above.

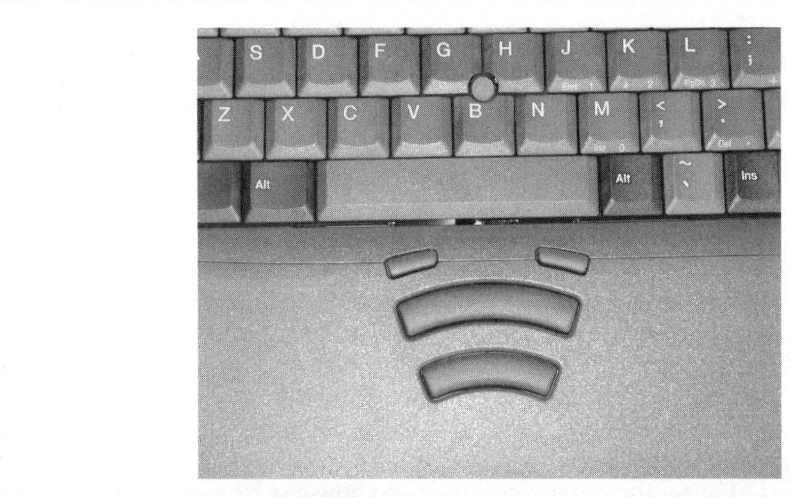

Figure 18-15. The keyboard on a notebook PC

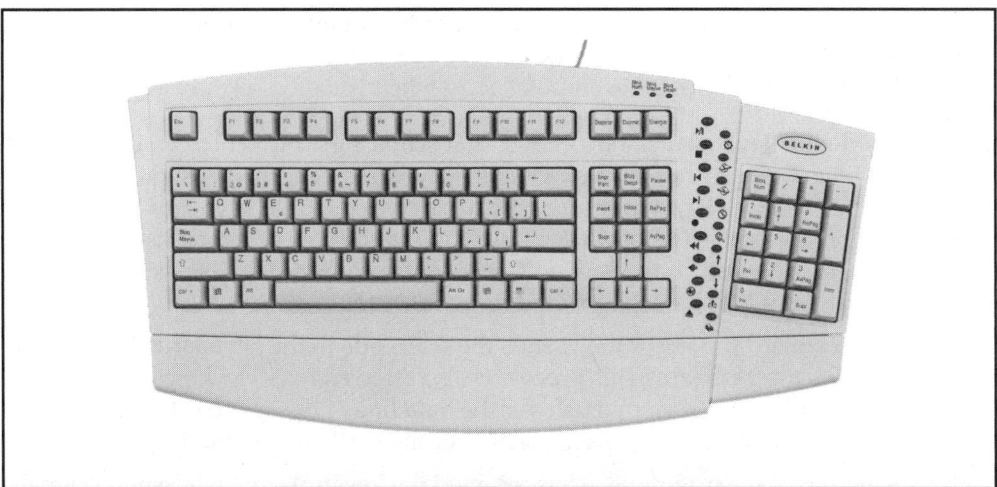

Figure 18-16. A multimedia keyboard. Photo courtesy of Belkin Components

Keyboard Technology

The function of the keyboard is to translate the movement of the user's fingers into text characters that are sent to the PC. It may seem like a fairly simple action—you press the letter *A* and an *A* appears on the screen—but there is a lot of activity that takes place to accomplish this simple feat.

Keys

At the center of keyboard's function is the keyswitch. When a key is pressed, it closes a keyswitch and creates a change in the electricity of the keyboard. Each key on the keyboard is a combination of a keycap and a keyswitch. The keycap provides a comfortable surface for your fingers to press and the keyswitch registers the pressure on the key.

Different keyboards can give a different feel to the user, which is caused by a variety of characteristics of the keys used in the keyboard. These characteristics, which include travel, tactile feedback, audible signal, and activation pressure, combine to provide the feel of the keyboard. How far the key travels down and how hard the key must be pressed to activate it can both affect the user's speed. Some users prefer a key that provides a touch "click" when the key is pressed and some prefer an audible click.

When a key is pressed, the keyswitch is pressed down and signals the keyboard that a key has been struck. The location of the key must be translated into a code that the computer recognizes and can translate into the appropriate value. The value associated with the key is then stored in the PC's keyboard buffer and eventually passed to the application with which the user is working.

Here is a simplification of the events that occur when you press a key on the keyboard:

1. Inside the keyboard is a processor that scans a grid to which all of the keyboard's keys are attached. When a key is pressed, the keyswitch makes contact with the keyboard grid, which is detected by the keyboard processor. The processor then determines a scan code for the key based on its position on the grid. The scan code assigned to the key represents only its position on the grid and not the character printed on its key cap.
2. The keyboard processor then sends the scan code to the keyboard interface on the PC's motherboard. This process is also referred to as clocking because the scan code is sent as serial data over the data line of the keyboard cable at the same time that clock signals are sent over the clock line of the cable.
3. After the keyboard interface has received the keystroke data, it issues a signal to IRQ 1 (the IRQ reserved for the keyboard interface), which starts the keyboard service routine. The keyboard service routine uses the keyboard

status byte (which indicates if the SHIFT, CTRL, or ALT keys are in use) and the scan code to generate a two-byte key code that is put into the keyboard buffer in RAM.

4. The two bytes of the key code are used separately to indicate the key's identity. For a normal character, the first (low) byte is the ASCII (American Standard Code for Information Interchange) code of the character and the second (high) byte contains the scan code. A special character is represented with zeroes in the low byte and the scan or other coding in the high byte.
5. The ASCII code of the key is passed to the application which completes its processing.

Make and Break Codes

The keyboard processor is constantly scanning the keyboard grid to detect if any key being pressed, released, or held down. When one of these actions is detected, the keyboard processor sends a scan code to the PC. Two different types of scan codes are used: make codes and break codes. A make code is sent when a key is pressed or held down. A break code is sent when a key is released. Each key location on the grid (which means each key) is assigned unique make and break codes, which allow the PC to determine the action and the key involved by the scan code sent from the keyboard controller.

The PC has no real way of knowing when a key is pressed or released. The make and break codes indicate when the key was pressed and released, which provides the PC with the information it needs. This allows the PC to detect repeating keys (a key held down to repeat it) and how many to generate. Table 18-2 lists a few of the scan codes used on 101-key and 104-key keyboards.

To type an uppercase *A*, the following keystrokes would be entered:

1. The Right SHIFT key is pressed.
2. The *A* key is pressed.
3. The *A* key is released.
4. The Right SHIFT key is released.

This causes the following actions to be taken by the keyboard controller:

1. The make code for the Right SHIFT key (59) is sent to the keyboard interface.
2. The make code for the *A* key (1C) is sent to the keyboard interface.
3. The break code for the *A* key (F0 1C) is sent to the keyboard interface.
4. The break code for the Right SHIFT key (F0 59) is sent to the keyboard interface.

Key	Make Code	Break Code
1	16	F0 16
2	1E	F0 1E
0	45	F0 45
BACKSPACE	66	F0 66
Q	15	F0 15
E	24	F0 24
A	1C	F0 1C
ENTER	5A	F0 5A
Right SHIFT	59	F0 59
Left CTRL	14	F0 14
SPACE	29	F0 29
ESC	76	F0 76
F1	05	F0 05
NUM LOCK	77	F0 77
INSERT	E0 70	E0 F0 70
PAGE UP	E0 7D	E0 F0 7D
DELETE	E0 71	E0 F0 71
UP ARROW	E0 75	E0 F0 75
PRTSCRN	E0 12 E0 7C	E0 F0 7C E0 F0 12
CTRL-BREAK	E0 7E E0 F0 7E	None

Table 18-2. Sample Keyboard Make and Break Codes

The keyboard interface translates the scan code into its ASCII equivalent, which is then stored in the keyboard buffer area of the system RAM. Like scan codes, ASCII codes are also hexadecimal values. For more information on hexadecimal, see Chapter 2. A sampling of the ASCII values for the characters on the keyboard is in Table 18-3.

Keyswitches

Keyswitches in a PC keyboard are typically one of two general types: contact switches and capacitive switches. The type of switch used in a keyboard may make little difference to the user, but there are differences among the various types.

Character	Hexadecimal	Decimal
SPACE	20	32
!	21	33
"	22	34
0	30	48
1	31	49
2	32	50
=	3D	61
>	3E	62
?	3F	63
A	41	65
B	42	66
C	43	67
H	48	72
I	49	73
J	4A	74
a	61	97
b	62	98
c	63	99

Table 18-3. A Sampling of ASCII Codes

Contact Keyswitches Contact keyswitches require two parts of the switch to make contact in order to complete a circuit. There are three types of contact keyswitches used in PC keyboards:

- **Mechanical contact keyswitch** A very simple switch in which two metal contacts are brought into contact or a metal plunger is pressed against contacts on a circuit board when the switch is pressed. This type of switch is not common on current keyboards.
- **Foam and foil contact keyswitch** This keyswitch is made up of a plunger that is connected to a foam pad that has a piece of foil on its underside. A circuit board (which provides the keyswitch grid) with a pair of copper contacts for each keyswitch sits underneath the keyswitches. When a key is pressed, the foam pad is pressed down and the foil contacts the contacts, completing the

circuit. Keyboards with this type of switches tend to have a soft feel and have had some durability problems.

- ▲ **Rubber dome keyswitch** Also called a carbon-contact keyswitch, this design is very much like the foam and foil contact switch. In each rubber dome switch is a small rounded dome of rubber that has a pad of carbon material on its underside. When the key is pressed, a plunger presses down on the rubber and the carbon contacts the circuit board completing the circuit. This type of keyswitch is the most common type used in current keyboards.

Capacitive Keyswitches A capacitor is an electronic device that stores an electrical charge between two plates. The charge in the capacitor is measured as its capacitance. When the plates of the capacitor move closer or further away, the capacitance changes. It is on this principle that capacitive keyswitches operate.

A capacitive keyswitch is built very much like a foam and file switch except that the plunger has a metal plate attached to its bottom. When the plunger is pressed down, the space between the plate and another plate located below the plunger is reduced. In some designs, the distance between the plates actually increases, but either way a change takes place. The keyboard's circuitry detects the change in the keyswitch's capacitance and a keystroke is detected. This type of keyswitch is very expensive and is usually found only in proprietary or high-end devices.

Keycaps

Keycaps serve a couple of fairly important functions: they provide the service for your finger to press, and they identify the keys so users can find the character they wish to enter. Keycaps can be removed from the keyboard, but depending on the keyboard and the type of switch in use, this is not typically recommended. The keyboard can be cleaned without removing the keycaps and once removed, it is not always easy to replace them.

Keyboard Controller

The keyboard controller is the circuitry inside the keyboard that processes keystrokes and exchanges information with the PC. The keyboard controller is a microprocessor and a ROM (read-only memory) that holds the keyboard processor's instructions. The controller constantly scans the key grid for keystrokes and then translates the scan codes for the keystrokes it finds and transmits the data to the PC.

Keyboard Cable

The cable that connects the keyboard to the PC is a four-wire cable that provides the four signals carried between the PC and the keyboard: data, clocking, ground, and power. A metal grounding sheath binds the four wires of the keyboard cable, and the whole bundle is covered with a thick plastic or rubber outer sheath. The keyboard cable is usually four to six feet in length and is usually straight. If the cable is not long enough for a particular application, keyboard cable extensions are available to lengthen it.

Keyboard cables can be replaced. At the keyboard end, it is attached to a four-wire flat connector that is used to connect the cable to the keyboard. If a cable is pinched or broken, it can cause intermittent errors. It may be easier to simply replace the keyboard completely. However, if you have keyboards from which you can get a good cable, it is a simple operation to replace the cable.

Keyboard Connectors

Keyboards attach to a PC through one of four connector types:

- **5-pin DIN connector** This connector, often called the AT style connector, has been in use since the very first PCs. DIN (Deutsche Industrie Norm) is a German standards organization that developed the round connector style used on this and the 6-pin version of this connector. Only four of the five pins are used; they carry the clocking (pin 1) and data (pin 2) and provide a ground (pin 4) and +5V of power (pin 5).
- **6-pin mini-DIN (PS/2) connector** This is a smaller DIN connector that uses four of the six pins to connect the data signal (pin 1), ground (pin 3), +5V of power (pin 4), and a clocking signal (pin 5). This connector, which is now the de facto standard for all cabled keyboards, was first introduced on the IBM PS/2, which is why it is commonly referred to as the PS/2 connector. Figure 18-17 shows a PS/2 connector.
- **USB (Universal Serial Bus) connector** Many keyboards (and mice) are now available with a USB connector. This type of connector is especially useful when your notebook computer has only one PS/2 port and you wish to connect both a keyboard and mouse to it. Figure 18-18 shows a USB connector.
- **IrDA (infrared) connector** Several keyboard styles are available with an infrared (wireless) interface. Several models of full-sized and even multimedia keyboards are available for use with either desktop or notebook PCs that support the Infrared Data Association (IrDA) standard interface.

Figure 18-17. A 6-pin mini-DIN (PS/2) connector is standard on most PC keyboards

Figure 18-18. A USB connector and port

▲ **Radio frequency (RF) connection** The most common form of cordless devices uses digital radio technology to connect a keyboard (or mouse) to the PC. The advantages of RF cordless devices include that they do not require a line of sight to work and have a range of up to six feet from the receiver. The keyboard actually communicates to the PC through a transceiver unit that attaches to the PC through either a PS/2 or USB port. The transceiver usually has a five- to six-foot cord with it so that it can connect to the port in the rear of the PC and still sit in front of the PC.

THE MOUSE

What is probably the most amazing thing about a PC mouse such as the one shown in Figure 18-19 is that it took so long to become a standard part of the PC's equipment. It is perfectly natural for a user to point at objects on the display instead of typing in a command, and many attempts were made to develop such a tool for the PC. Light pens, touch screens, graphics tablets, and joysticks, among other devices, were all tried, but none satisfied the user as a workable, intuitive pointing device.

The mouse was introduced with the Apple Macintosh and was an immediate success. The mouse was the natural, intuitive, inexpensive pointing device users wanted. But, it wasn't until the early 1980s, when Windows and its graphical user interface (GUI) was released, that the PC had an operating system that could work with the mouse. Since that time, the mouse has become a standard equipment on virtually all PCs.

There are three types of mouse units used with PCs:

▼ **Mechanical mouse** This is the older style of mouse used with early Macintosh and PC GUI systems. In a mechanical mouse, the movement of a rubber ball causes a pair of wheels to spin that sensors detect to send data signals to the PC.

Figure 18-19. A PC mouse

- **Optomechanical mouse** This type of mouse uses light-emitting diodes (LEDs) to sense mouse movements. This is the most common type of mouse used with PCs today.
- **Optical mouse** The optical mouse eliminates the use of mechanical devices (balls, rollers, and wheels) and uses optical scanning to detect the movement of the mouse over virtually any surface.

While there have been any number of attempts to vary the design of the mouse, including the new optical mice, the optomechanical mouse continues to be the most popular style in use. The following discussion focuses on the optomechanical mouse, but the other types of mice are discussed later in this section.

Inside the Mouse

A mouse translates the motion of the user's hand into electrical signals that the PC uses to track a pointer across the monitor's display. To capture the motion of the user's hand, an optomechanical mouse uses six primary components:

- **Ball** The ball is the largest and central part of the mouse. When the user grasps the mouse and moves it over a mousepad or the desktop, the ball rolls inside the mouse.
- **Rollers** As the ball rolls inside the mouse, two rollers that touch the ball track its rotation side to side and up and back.
- **Roller shafts** The rollers are each connected to a shaft; as the rollers turn in conjunction with the ball, each shaft turns an optical encoding disk that is attached to it.

- **Optical encoding disk** As the ball rolls, the rollers turn the shafts that spin the optical encoding disks. The optical encoding disk has 36 holes along its outside edge.
- **Infrared LED and sensor** On one side of each optical encoding disk is a light-emitting diode (LED) that shines an infrared light beam on the disk. On the other side of the disk is a light-sensitive transistor that serves as an infrared sensor. As the disk turns, the solid areas between the holes on the disk break the LED's infrared beam and the infrared sensor sees pulses of light. The rate and duration of the light pulses indicate the speed and distance of the mouse's travel. Figure 18-20 illustrates the placement of the infrared LED and sensor to the optical encoding disk.
- **Processor** The mouse has a processor that reads the pulses sent from the infrared sensors and converts them into binary data, which is sent to the PC's interface over the mouse's connecting cord.
- **Buttons** The mouse also has one, two, three, or more buttons (two is the most common number of buttons on PC mice) that are connected to small switches that also connect to the mouse's processor. As the user clicks the buttons to select an object on the screen or start a program or applet, the processor converts the clicks into binary data that is sent to the PC. Windows systems use two-button mice; Macintosh systems have gotten by very nicely with a single mouse button; and UNIX and Linux systems have functions that require the use of a third mouse button. Mice that have buttons on top as well as on the side and elsewhere require special software device drivers to enable the function of these buttons.

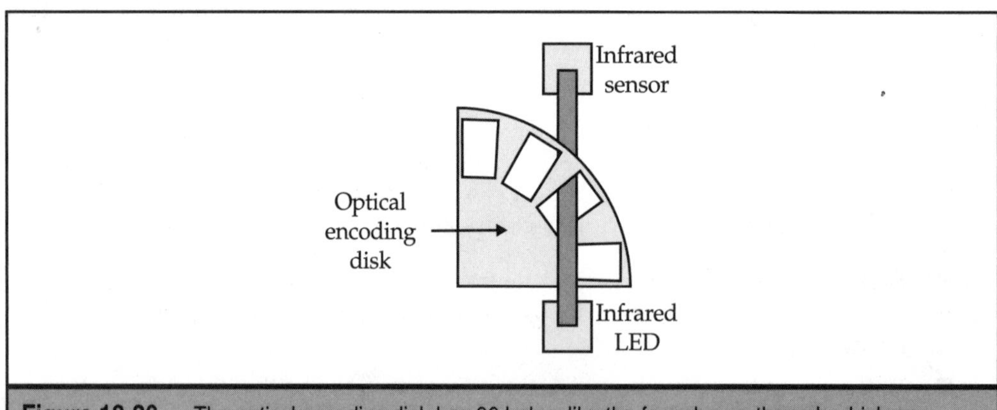

Figure 18-20. The optical encoding disk has 36 holes, like the four shown, through which an infrared beam is sensed

A mouse with a ball that is 21 millimeters (mm) in diameter has rollers that are 7mm in diameter. As stated above, the optical encoding disk has 36 holes. So if the user moves the mouse one inch (25.4mm), the ball rotates slightly more than once; the rollers rotate a little more than three times and cause the disk to spin a little more than one complete revolution, matching the movement of the ball, which results in the sensor detecting about 40 light pulses. The PC is sent 40 bits of data to indicate the mouse's movement.

The process used by the mouse to convert movement into light pulses (and eventually binary data) is called optomechanical. The ball, rollers, and disk move mechanically, and the LED and sensor convert light pulses optically. A mouse may have two sets of LEDs and sensors on each optical encoding disk, one on the left side of the disk and one on the right. Having two LED and sensor sets allows the processor to detect the direction of the disk's rotation.

Although not shown in Figure 18-20, there is also a small plastic window placed between each LED and disk to aim the LED's infrared light beam so that the sensor can be focused on it. The plastic windows on each side of a disk are set at slightly different heights so that the sensors see light pulses at different times. Figure 18-21 shows the effect this has on the infrared light beams. As the disk rotates, the beams show through the disks' holes at slightly different times. The processor can detect the direction of the rotation (and the mouse) by which beam is detected first.

Mouse Connectors

Nearly all mice sold today have a six-pin mini-DIN (PS/2) connector, shown earlier in Figure 18-17, on the PC end of their cable. This connector, which was first introduced with the IBM PS/2 system, has essentially replaced the DB-9 serial connector that was used before that. Serial mice are still available, but since newer PC systems rarely offer more than a single serial port and include PS/2 connectors for both the keyboard and mouse, the serial mouse has all but disappeared.

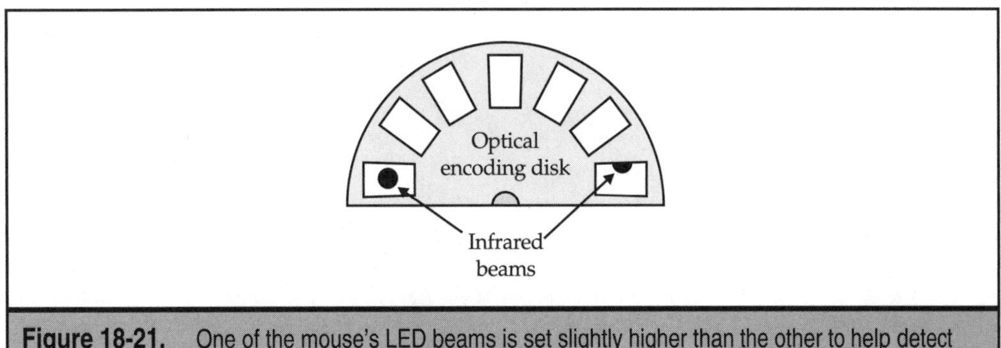

Figure 18-21. One of the mouse's LED beams is set slightly higher than the other to help detect the mouse's travel direction

The PS/2 connector on the mouse uses four pins to connect and communicate to the PC. The mouse sends data and clocking signals to the PC using very much the same techniques as the keyboard. A mouse uses pins in the connector and wires in the cable for +5V power (pin 2), the clocking signal (pin 4), a ground (pin 5), and a data signal (pin 6). The power connection supplies +5V of electricity to the processor and LEDs.

Mice are now available with USB, infrared (IrDA), and radio frequency (RF) connections as well. The USB connector, shown earlier in Figure 18-18, is becoming a popular choice among notebook PC users who wish to connect an external keyboard into a notebook's single PS/2 connection and still use an external mouse. Figure 18-22 shows a USB mouse.

Cordless mice communicate with a PC through either an infrared or an RF receiver. Many PCs now come with an IrDA receiver included, but RF connections require an external receiver. External RF and infrared receivers can also be added to a PC through a PS/2 or USB port. An optomechanical mouse gets its power (+5V) from the PC over its interface cable, but cordless mice do not have a power connection and, regardless of the type of connection in use, run on a pair of AAA batteries.

Infrared connections are line of sight and have a limited effective operating distance. The infrared connection must have a clear, unobstructed line of sight to the receiver, which must be in a clear, open location; a radio frequency connection doesn't require a line of sight.

Data Interface

Three bytes of data are sent as a packet from the mouse to the PC each time the user moves the mouse. The first byte contains data on the mouse buttons and the direction and speed of the mouse. The second and third bytes have the number of pulses detected for the side to side (*x* axis) and up and back (*y* axis) movements of the mouse since the last packet was sent.

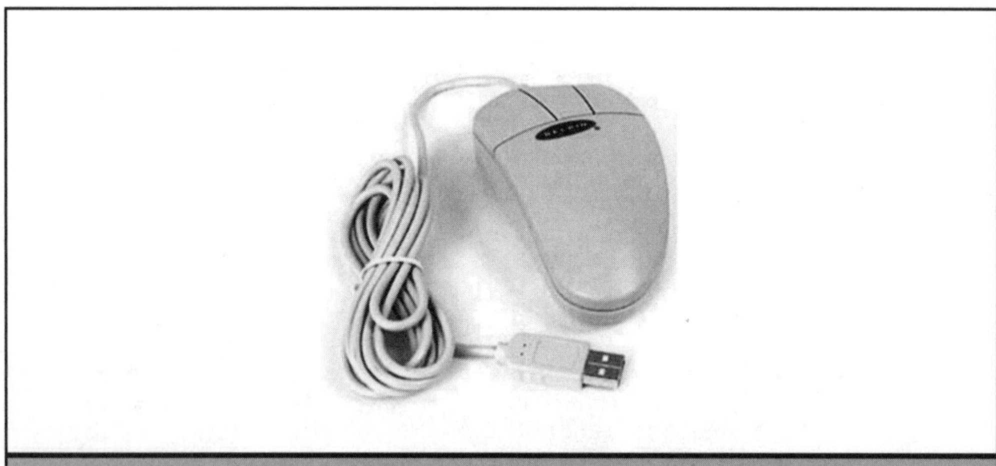

Figure 18-22. A mouse with a USB connector. Photo courtesy of Belkin Components

The first byte of the mouse's data packet contains:

1. Two bits that indicate if either the right or left mouse button was clicked (0 = not clicked, 1 = clicked).
2. Two bits for packet ID (01).
3. Two bits for the x and y axis' direction (0 = negative (backward/left) and 1 = positive (forward/right)).
4. Two bits that indicate the mouse's speed along the x and y-axes was faster than 255 pulses in 0.025 seconds.

The packet is sent to the PC over the data line of the connector as a serial data transmission with clocking signals used to indicate when each bit begins and ends. Eleven bits are actually sent by the mouse to the PC for each byte of data, which include 1 start bit, the 8 data bits, 1 parity bit, and 1 stop bit. The standard PS/2 mouse sends data at a rate of 1,200 bits per second, which translates to about 40 packets sent to the PC to report the mouse's status each second. While this is fast enough for most situations and applications, extremely fast movement of the mouse can overwhelm the mouse's ability to report it accurately.

Wheel Mouse

A newer version of the standard optomechanical mouse is the wheel mouse. As shown in Figure 18-23, the wheel mouse has a finger wheel located on its top, typically between the two buttons. The wheel allows the user to scroll forward and backward through a document in place of clicking on a window's scroll bar or using the PAGE UP and PAGE DOWN keys or the cursor control arrow keys.

Figure 18-23. An example of a wheel mouse. Photo courtesy of Logitech, Inc.

Optical Mouse

The optical mouse eliminates the mouse ball, replacing it with a optical sensors that track the movement of the mouse against the background of the mousepad or whichever flat surface it's on. Figure 18-24 shows the bottom of an optical mouse—notice the ball is missing.

Optical mice have been around for a few years. The older design for the optical mouse required a highly reflective mousepad that had a printed grid on it. The real drawback to this mouse, besides the fact it was slow, was that if you lost the mousepad, the mouse would not work on a normal flat service that had a bit of texture or detail to it. Some surfaces, such as glass, mirrors, or smooth, shiny, solid-color surfaces without detail, do not work well with even the new optical mice.

The latest optical mouse designs include an optical process that captures images of the surface underneath the mouse (called the mousing surface) at a rate of up to 2,000 images per second. The mouse includes a digital signal processor (DSP) that analyzes these images and is able to detect even the slightest movement. The optical system of the mouse eliminates the need for a mousepad and works on virtually any flat surface except those that are very shiny or reflective.

One real advantage to the optical mouse over the optomechanical mouse is that it does not require internal cleaning. Because it has eliminated all moving parts, the optical mouse does not pick up dust and other debris that could clog up the optomechanical mouse and require it to be regularly cleaned. Another advantage is that, according to manufacturer claims, an optical mouse is at least 33 percent faster and many times more accurate than an optomechanical mouse.

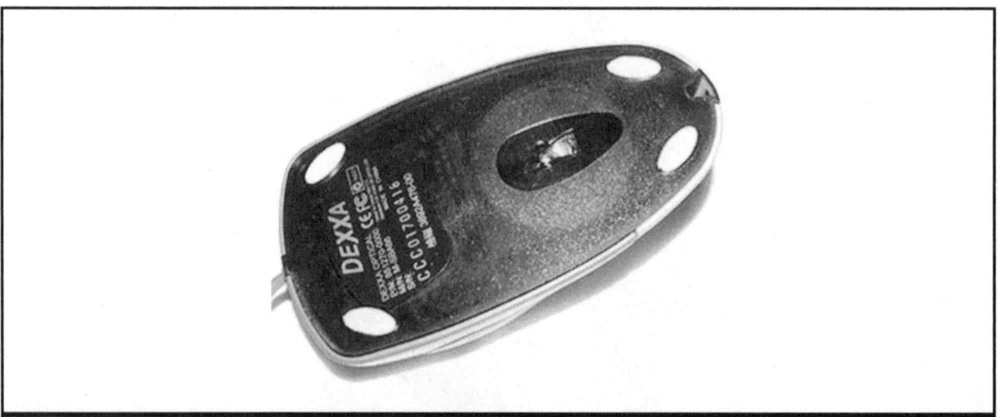

Figure 18-24. The business side of an optical mouse. Photo courtesy of Logitech, Inc.

Other Pointing Devices

Many types of pointing devices exist, but the four that have some popularity beyond the mouse are the touchpad, the trackball, glidepoint, and the joystick.

Touchpads

A touchpad is a fixed-place pointing device that has become very common in notebook computers. A touchpad, like the one shown in Figure 18-25, is a small, flat square or rectangular surface on which you slide (touch) your finger to move the cursor on the display, select objects, and run programs. A touchpad provides the same actions as a mouse.

A touchpad works on the principle of coupling capacitance that uses a two-layer grid of electrodes to hold an electrical charge. The upper layer of the grid has small vertical electrodes, and the lower layer has small horizontally placed electrodes. An IC is attached to the grid that detects any changes in the capacitance of the pad. The chip is constantly monitoring the capacitance between each of the horizontal electrodes and a corresponding vertical electrode. The user's finger when placed over a pair of the electrodes serves as a conductor and alters the capacitance of the electrode pair, since a human finger has a very different dielectric property than air. The chip detects the change and data is sent to the PC using the same techniques that are used by a mouse. As the finger moves over the grid, each of the electrode pairs affected are converted into *x-y* placements for the PC.

Like an optical mouse, the touchpad has no moving parts and does not require preventive maintenance. Touchpads are being integrated into desktop PC keyboards as well as notebook computers. An external touchpad can be added to a PC via its PS/2 port.

Figure 18-25. A touchpad integrated into a notebook PC

Trackballs

A trackball is essentially an upside-down mouse. As shown in Figure 18-26, a trackball is a mouse-like tool that has two or more buttons and a ball on top of the device. The ball, which can be located on the top or side of the trackball, is manipulated with either a thumb or finger to move the cursor on the screen. A trackball, which can be either a corded or cordless device (the one in Figure 18-26 is a cordless unit), uses essentially the same technology as an optomechanical mouse to communicate its movements to the PC and connects through the PS/2 and USB connections.

In a trackball, the rubber-coated ball used in a mouse is replaced with a smooth ball that is about the size of a golf ball. When the trackball is moved, two rollers that touch the trackball are rotated and ultimately movement data is sent to the PC. Only the ball on a trackball pointing device moves, which means a trackball requires less space on the desktop.

Glidepoint Mouse

Glidepoint mice are predominantly found on notebook PCs, but there are a few keyboards available that include this type of pointing device. A glidepoint mouse, shown in Figure 18-27, is the pivoting rubber-tipped device that looks like an eraser tip and is located between the G and the H keys on a notebook PC keyboard. A glidepoint mouse works like a very small joystick (see below), but acts like a mouse on the screen. Glidepoint technology allows the user to leave their hands on the keyboard, assuming they are using the notebook's internal keyboard.

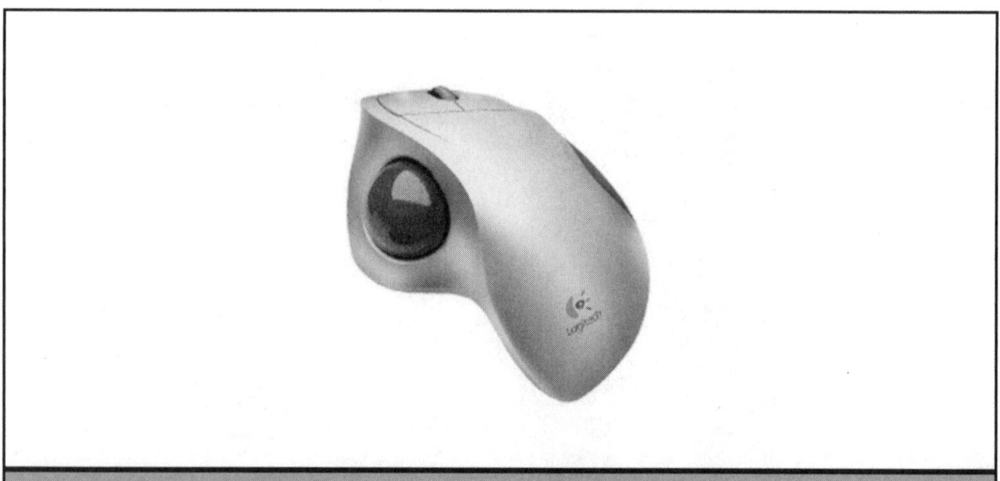

Figure 18-26. A trackball pointing device. Photo courtesy of Logitech, Inc.

Figure 18-27. A glidepoint mouse in a notebook computer keyboard

Joysticks

A joystick is a type of pointing device that is used primarily with game software on a PC. A joystick consists of a handle that is connected to a yoke inside its base. The yoke is set on a pivoting mechanism that allows the joystick to move in any direction from a center point. Sensors are attached to the yoke that detect the movement of the handle and yoke on an *x-y* axis and send data signals to the adapter card to which the joystick is attached. Most joysticks attach to a game port located on a game, video, or sound card, but many new models also support a USB connection as well. A software device driver then interprets the data signals sent from the joystick and transfers the actions onto the screen.

Some joysticks are *force-feedback* devices that simulate pressure and forces on the joystick to make the game more realistic, like the 3D joystick shown in Figure 18-28. Joysticks with 3D capabilities include an *r*-axis that simulates rotational movement in addition to moving up and down and from side to side. On force-feedback units, the game software sends signals back to the joystick that instruct it when to apply force or resist or remove resistance from the motion of the handle. On the handle of the joystick are usually a number of triggers and button that are programmed by the game software to shoot, brake, turn, accelerate, jump, or whatever action the game allows. Most game software includes routines to allow the user to reprogram the settings for the joysticks triggers and buttons.

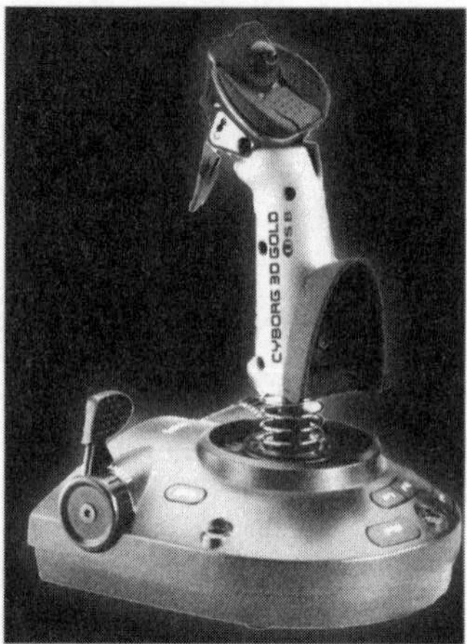

Figure 18-28. A fully featured joystick can make playing a game more fun. Photo courtesy Saitek Industries

CHAPTER 19

Ports and Connectors

It is virtually impossible to design a personal computer with all of the peripheral devices attached to suit the needs of every user. There are as many potential PC configurations as there are potential computer users. Yes, the essential services of the PC, those included inside the system unit such as the motherboard, disk drives, and memory, can be standardized, but beyond that each PC user wants some say in the video, sound, keyboards, printers, and other peripheral devices attached to the PC. The user's particular mix of peripheral devices is what can turn the standard PC core components into a customized workstation, entertainment unit, and publishing center.

The user's group of peripheral devices must attach to the PC in order to be of service to the user. This is where ports and connectors come in. A port is the part of the connector hardware that is attached to the PC itself. The connector is on the end of the cable attached to the peripheral device. The connector is inserted into the port to make the connection between the PC and the peripheral device, which makes the peripheral available to the user.

Each of the various port types—parallel, serial, USB, FireWire, and even wireless—has a purpose for which it is best suited. Parallel ports carry many times more data than serial ports in the same amount of time. USB and FireWire provide a Plug-and-Play compatibility for their peripheral devices, and wireless ports free the user from the constraints of the four-foot cable. Which port is used for what is really a question of the system's design, capabilities, and the devices the user has purchased.

CONNECTORS ON THE MOTHERBOARD

Probably the best place to start when discussing PC connectors is with the motherboard. Nearly all newer PCs have many internal and external interface connectors integrated into the motherboard. Not all motherboards have all of the connectors discussed in this section, but most Pentium-class motherboards have most of the connectors discussed.

The connectors on the motherboard can be classified into three groups: back panel connectors, midboard connectors, and front panel connectors. Not all of these connectors support peripheral devices, either internal or external. Some provide connections between the motherboard and other internal devices, such as the power supply, system speaker, and the front panel switches and LEDs.

Back Panel Connectors

As illustrated in Figure 19-2, the back panel of the motherboard contains several I/O connectors that can be used to connect peripheral devices to the PC. This group of connectors is the focus of this chapter, and each of the connectors shown is discussed in more detail later in the chapter.

Onboard Connectors

Several connectors are located on the central part of the motherboard away from the edges that are used by internal peripheral devices.

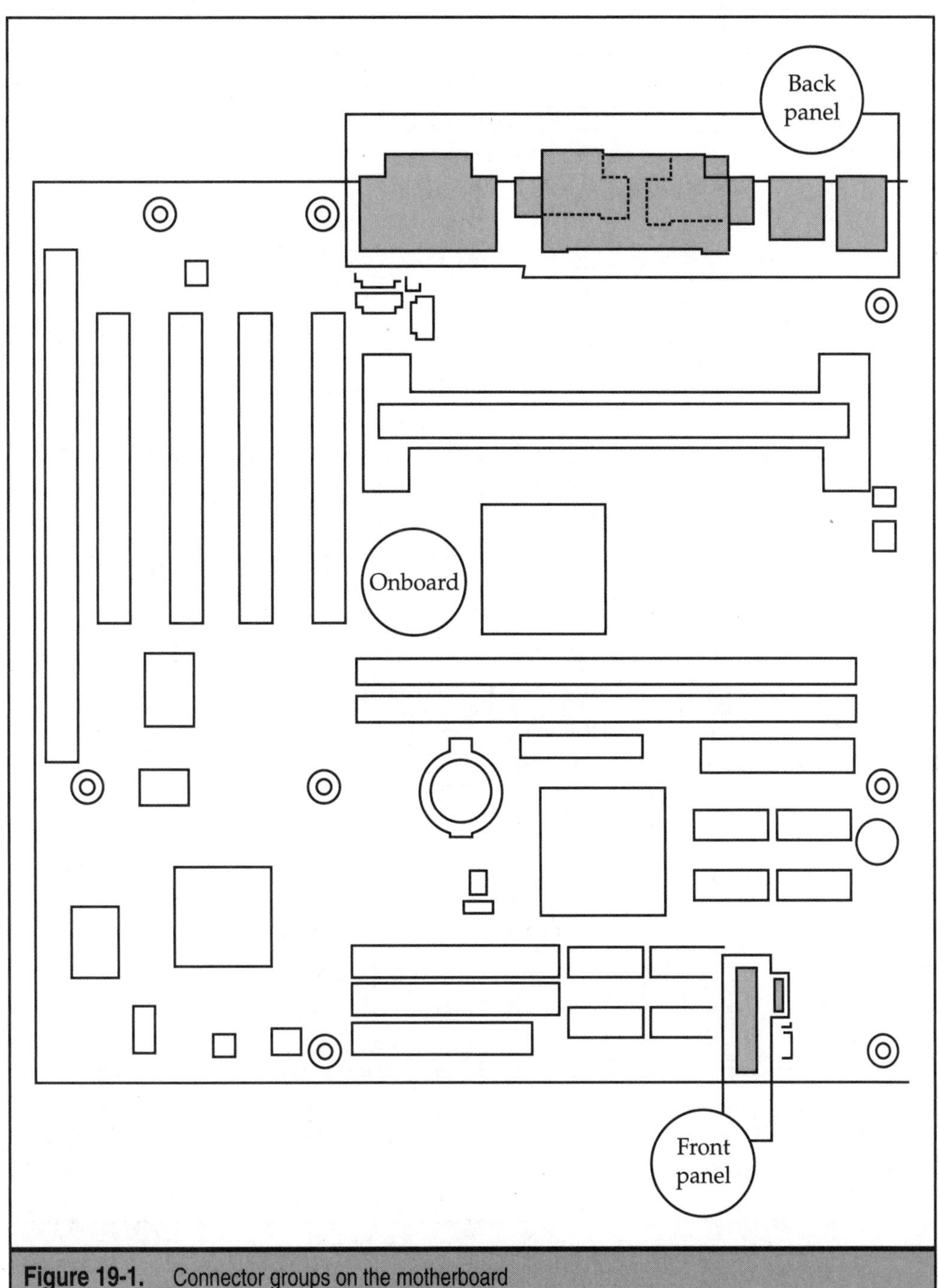

Figure 19-1. Connector groups on the motherboard

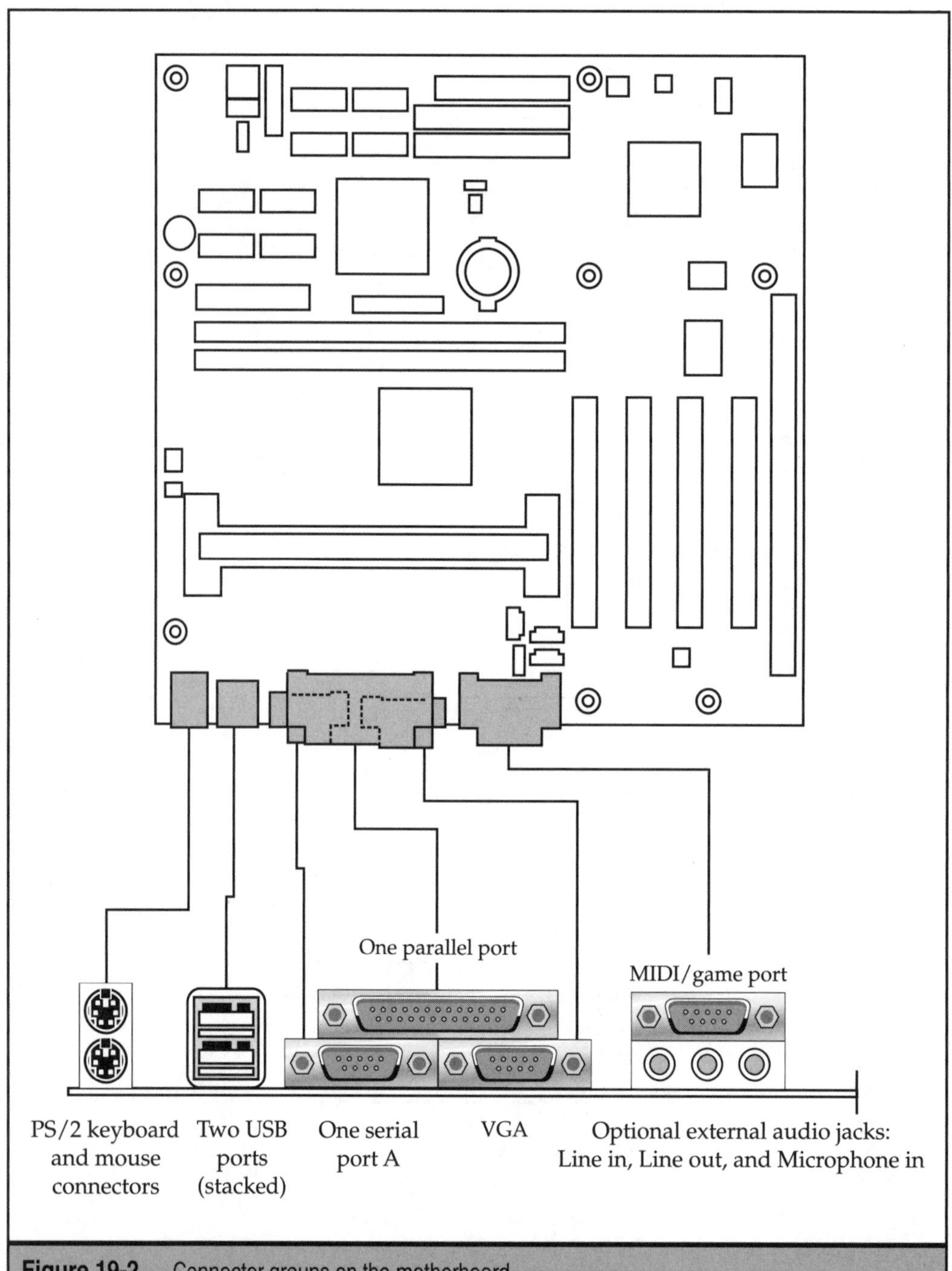

Figure 19-2. Connector groups on the motherboard

The midboard connectors are divided into the following functional groups:

- **Audio/video** This group of connectors is included on motherboards that have sound, video, and CD-ROM support integrated into the motherboard. The connectors included in this group typically include an auxiliary sound line in, a telephony connection, a legacy CD-ROM connector, and an ATAPI (AT Attachment Packet Interface) CD-ROM connection. These connectors and their use are explained in more detail in Chapter 21.
- **Peripheral device interfaces** Most newer motherboards and chipsets include support for some peripheral devices to connect directly to the motherboard through connectors mounted on the motherboard. These connections, shown in Figure 19-3, include the primary and secondary IDE connectors used for hard disk and CD-ROM drives and the floppy disk controller. These connectors are discussed in more detail in Chapters 4 and 5.
- **Hardware power and management** The connectors in this group are used to attach the power supply to the motherboard, to provide support for Wake on LAN or Wake on Ring technology, and to connect system and processor fans to the system.
- **Memory slots** While technically not a peripheral device connector, every motherboard includes some form of connector, mounting, or slot for memory chips or modules. Newer boards have slots for RIMMs (RDRAM inline memory modules) and DIMMs (dual inline memory modules). Older motherboards have slots for SIMMs (single inline memory modules) or DIP (dual inline packaging) sockets.
- **Expansion slots** Every PC motherboard includes at least a few expansion slots that are used to add peripheral device adapter and interface cards to the PC. As explained in Chapter 11, motherboards support a variety of expansion slot types, but ISA (Industry Standard Architecture), PCI (Peripheral Components Interconnect), and AGP (Accelerated Graphics Port) are the most common.

Front Panel Connectors

As described in more detail in Chapter 15, the front panel of the system case can have a variety of LEDs and switches that are attached to the motherboard for power or signals that indicate various activities. Most motherboards include connectors for the hard disk (power and activity), a main power on/off button, possibly a reset button, +5V DC power connections, and grounding circuits. Most motherboards also have connections for the system speaker (the one that sounds beeps and other tones, not the one used to play music). Some motherboards also support an infrared or IrDA (Infrared Data Association) serial port connector as well (more on IR connections later in the chapter).

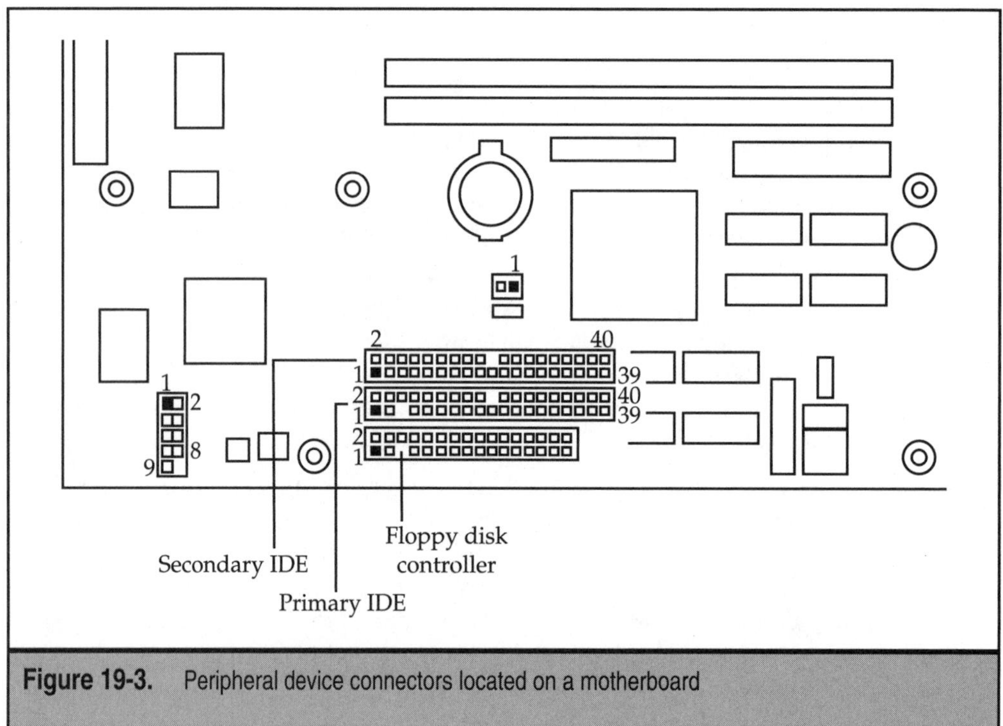

Figure 19-3. Peripheral device connectors located on a motherboard

EXTERNAL PORTS AND CONNECTORS

Although the basic set of external ports on a PC has settled into a sort of standard, it can vary from PC to PC. The standard set includes a serial port or two, a parallel port or two, USB ports or FireWire ports, a video port, a game device port, and speaker and microphone jacks, as illustrated in Figure 19-4. These are the ports and connectors that are the focus of this chapter.

These interfaces are each explained, right after some background information that will help you to understand how the interfaces work.

CHARACTER DATA

So, what does character data have to do with ports and connectors? Well, in order to understand many of the principles of data communications, you must first understand the data being communicated. Data on a PC is stored in a format defined in the American Standard Code for Information Interchange or ASCII (pronounced "askie"). ASCII defines the standard character set used on PCs, which includes special command, inquiry, and graphics characters along with the upper- and lowercase alphabetic characters, spe-

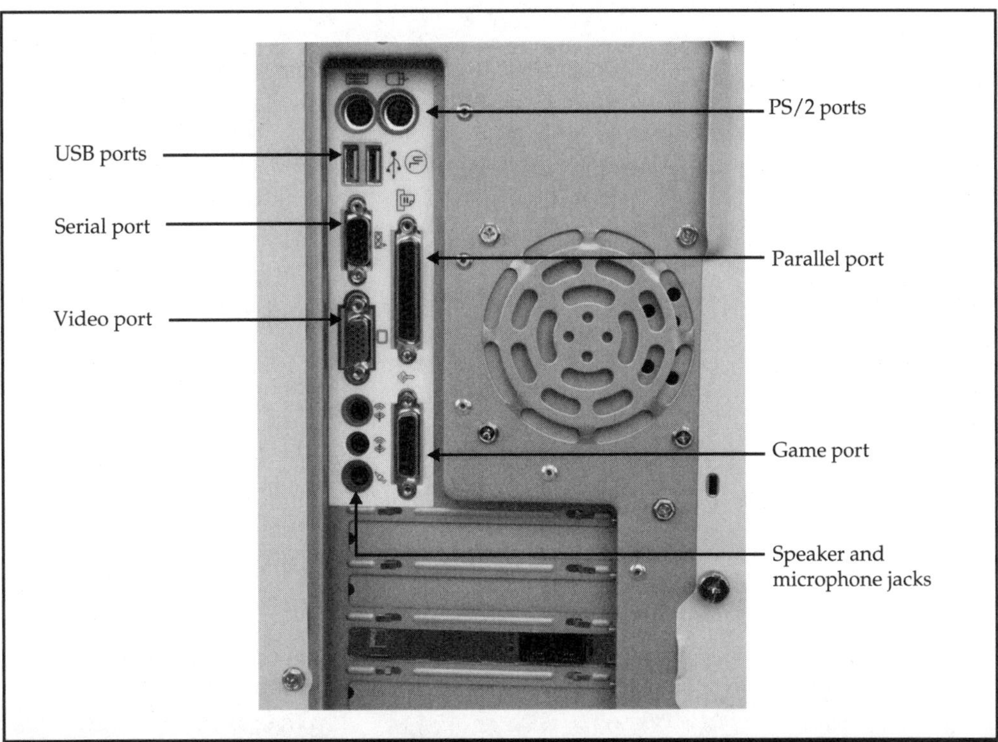

Figure 19-4. The standard interface ports on a modern PC

cial characters, and numbers of American English. Table 19-1 includes a sampling of ASCII characters showing the binary and decimal values for each. The reason for including the binary format should become clearer later in the chapter.

Character	Decimal	Binary
Null	0	00000000
BACKSPACE	8	00001000
Line Feed	10	00001010
Form Feed	12	00001100

Table 19-1. Sample ASCII Characters

Character	Decimal	Binary
SPACE	32	00100000
!	33	00100001
$	36	00100100
0 (zero)	48	00110000
1	49	00110001
2	50	00110010
:	58	00111010
;	59	00111011
?	63	00111111
A	65	01000001
B	66	01000010
C	67	01000011
X	88	01011000
Y	89	01011001
Z	90	01011010
a	97	01100001
b	98	01100010
c	99	01100011
x	120	01111000
y	121	01111001
z	122	01111010

Table 19-1. Sample ASCII Characters *(continued)*

SERIAL AND PARALLEL DATA

Data is transmitted and moved in one of two formats: parallel or serial. Parallel data is sent one character at a time with all of its bits moving at the same time over parallel wires. Serial data is transmitted one bit at a time over a single wire. Figure 19-5 illustrates the difference between these two transmission modes.

As is discussed later, more than 8 bits are actually sent for a character regardless of the mode used to transmit it. The added bits are used for data integrity, identification of data blocks, and synchronization, if used.

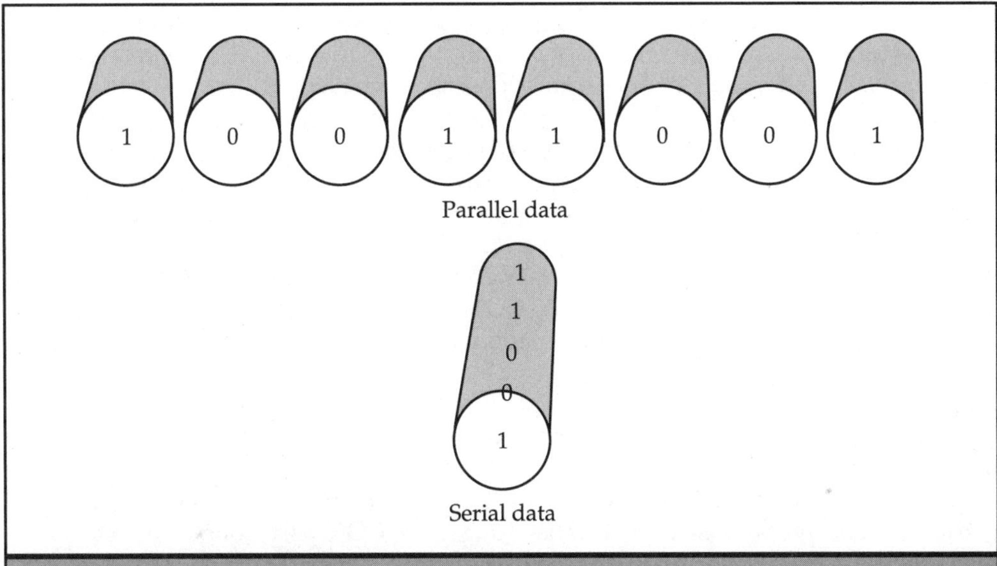

Figure 19-5. Characters bits are sent at the same time in a parallel transmission and one bit at a time in a serial transmission

FULL, HALF, AND SINGLE MODES

Depending on the mode of the communications line, two devices may be restricted or completely free as to when they can transmit. There are three transmission modes a communications line can be configured with. They are

- **Simplex** A simplex line is one that can communicate in only one direction. An example of a simplex communications line is a speaker wire.
- **Half-duplex** A duplex line is one that can carry data in two ways. A half-duplex line is one that can carry data in two directions, but only in one direction at a time. A CB (citizen's band) radio is an example of a half-duplex line—one party must wait until the other party is finished before speaking.
- **Full-duplex** A full-duplex line can carry data into two directions with both directions flowing simultaneously. A very good example of a full-duplex communications line is the telephone system.

SERIAL PORTS AND CONNECTORS

Serial ports and their connectors have been around since the original PCs, when they were used to connect to modems and early dot matrix printers. Serial ports send data as a stream of bits that is transmitted one bit after the other in a series. All serial devices, cables, ports, and communications are based on the principle that serial data is transmitted one bit at a time. To transmit a single byte of data through a serial port, eight separate one-bit transmissions are needed. Serial transmissions are somewhat like a single-lane country road with all traffic lining up to travel over the road single-file.

Serial devices are external devices that connect to the PC via a serial port, which is also referred to as a COM port or an RS-232 port. The term COM originated from early designations of serial ports as communications ports. Before network adapters and other connector types that can be used to connect a PC to a communications link, only the serial port was available for this purpose. On many systems, the serial ports are designated as COM ports, with the first serial port being COM1 and subsequent serial ports designated as COM2, COM3, etc. RS-232 is an abbreviation for "reference standard number two hundred and thirty-two," which was so named by the Institute of Electrical and Electronic Engineers, Inc. (IEEE—pronounced "I triple E"). This is the designation for a wiring pattern used for communications lines, ports, and connectors used to transmit standard serial data communications.

Originally, serial ports were added to the PC through an expansion board that added one to four serial ports. Most newer PCs have one serial/COM port mounted directly on the motherboard. Serial ports are easy to recognize on the back panel of the PC because they are either a 9- or 25-pin male D-type connector. These connectors are designated as DB-9 and DB-25 connectors. There are two versions of what *DB* means. One version is that it means *data bus* with the number representing the number of pins in the connector. The other version is that the first D-shaped connectors were designated as a series that included DA-15, DB-25, DC-37, DD-50, and DE-9 connectors. A male version of the DB-25 connector, shown earlier in Figure 19-4 as a male parallel port, was first used as a serial connector on early PCs. Eventually all D-shaped connectors were designated with the DB prefix. Either way, all serial connectors are DB-type D-shaped connectors, but not all DB-type connectors are used for serial connections.

Pinouts and Cable Connections

A serial transmission requires only nine pins and wires to communicate between the device and the PC serial port adapter, which is why many PCs now use the DB-9 port in place of the DB-25. The DB-9 connector is smaller and has fewer pins, which reduces the potential for damaged or bent pins. Older PC models usually included a single serial DB-25 port on a multipurpose card that also included a second serial port, typically a DB-9 port, a parallel port, or game port. The DB-25 connector is also popular on external modems and serial printers.

Table 19-2 shows the pinouts for the DB-25 and DB-9 serial connection. Notice that there is a difference in the pin assignments between the two connectors; if a cable has a DB-25 connector at one end and a DB-9 at the other end, care must be taken to match up the pins at each end.

DB-25 Pin	DB-9 Pin	Use
1		Ground
2	3	Transmit
3	2	Receive
4	7	RTS (Request to Send)
5	8	CTS (Clear to Send)
6	6	DSR (Data Set Ready)
7	5	Signal Ground
8	1	Carrier Detect
20	4	DTR (Data Terminal Ready
22	9	Ring Indicatorv

Table 19-2. DB-25 and DB-9 Connector Pinouts

A serial cable, like all PC cables, is made up of a wire cable that has as few as 2 wires and usually not more than 20 wires, but this can vary with special applications. A cable with 8 wires is very common. The wires in the cable are colored to make it easier to find the same wire on each end of the cable. This is important because on each end of the cable a connector is attached by soldering the necessary wires to the back of pins in the connector. When the connector is plugged onto a matching, but opposite, port, the pins of the connector make contact with the holes of the port to complete the connection. The PC and the peripheral device attached to the cable can then send signals back and forth to communicate and control the transmission of data.

Asynchronous Communications

Asynchronous communications is what a PC uses to connect with a printer, modem, fax, and other peripheral devices. Loosely translated, *asynchronous* means without synchronization, which on the PC means without regard to clocking signals. The transmitter and receiver of an asynchronous communications session operate independently and are not synchronized to a common clock signal or each other. Data blocks are separated by arbitrary idle periods on the line, as illustrated in Figure 19-6.

Asynchronous Data Blocks

The data blocks in asynchronous communications are fixed in size and format. The eight bits of ASCII characters is preceded by a start bit and followed by one or two stop bits.

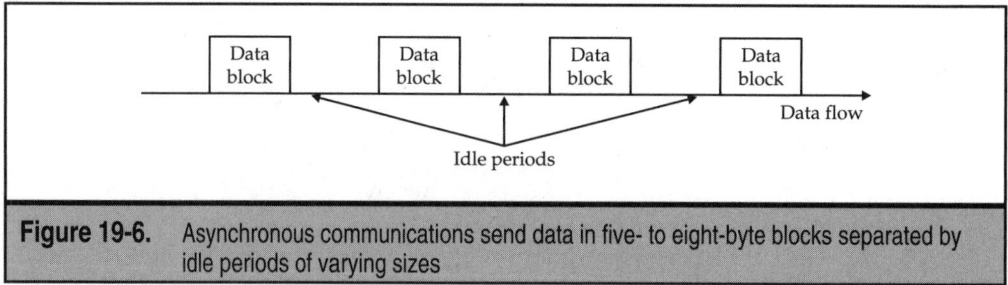

Figure 19-6. Asynchronous communications send data in five- to eight-byte blocks separated by idle periods of varying sizes

These bits mark the beginning and ending of each character transmitted. The start bit has a value of 0, and the stop bit is set to a 1.

If parity is in use, a parity bit is added to the data block to help ensure that the data sent is what arrives. Parity forces the count of 1 bits in the transmitted character to either an even or an odd number. For example, if an uppercase *A* is transmitted, the binary format of 01000001 is what is actually transmitted. If even parity is in use, the parity bit that is added to the end is set to 0 because an even number of 1 bits are present in the character. If odd parity is in use, the parity bit is set to a 1 to force an odd number of 1 bits in the character. If the receiving device detects the wrong number of 1 bits in a character in comparison to its parity method, it requests the sending device to resend the character.

So, with everything added to the ASCII binary character, the data block ends up being 11 bits long, as follows:

Transmitted character: **A**

Start bit:	**0**
ASCII binary data pattern:	**01000001**
Even-parity bit:	**0**
Stop bit:	**1**

Transmitted data block: **00100000101**

The UART

A universal asynchronous receiver/transmitter (UART, pronounced "you-art") controls serial ports and devices. This specialized integrated circuit is found either on the device adapter card or on the motherboard. The UART chip controls all actions and functions of the serial port, including:

- Controlling all the connectors' pins and their associated signals
- Establishing the communication protocol
- Converting the parallel format bits of the PC's data bus into a serial bit stream for transmission

▲ Converting the received serial bit stream into parallel data for transmission over the PC's internal data bus

On the PC, the data coming and being sent through a serial port is interpreted and translated by the UART, which examines incoming data for the correct values in the start and stop bits and verifies the parity bit, if parity is in use. It also encodes outgoing data with start and stop bits and applies the parity bit, if needed.

There is a UART chip in every serial communications device. It is the UART that controls the data speed that a serial port or device is able to support. Table 19-3 lists the UART chips, by their identity numbers, which have been used in PCs, modems, and other serial devices over the years. Most modern PCs use the 16550 UART chip, which supports serial data transmissions with speeds up to 115,200 bits per second (bps) or as it is more commonly stated, 115.2 Kilobits per second (Kbps).

The buffer size of a UART is directly related to its actual data speeds. UART buffer sizes are tied to the MS-DOS requirement that an interrupt process not last longer than one millisecond. The buffer size reflects how many bits the UART can transfer during each one millisecond interrupt plus the number of bits the UART can receive before sending what it already is holding in the buffer. UART buffers operate on a first-in-first-out or FIFO (pronounced "fi-foe"), which means it sends out the bits that came in first and places later arriving bits at the back of the buffer.

The buffer size of the UART also helps to prevent a condition called UART overrun. This condition occurs when a UART is unable to process and send the bits that just came in fast enough to prevent them being clobbered by the next set of bits to arrive. Most PC modems have at least a 16-bit buffer to prevent UART overrun. Older UARTS can randomly lose characters because data arrives too fast for it to process the bits already in the buffer. However, this is really not a problem unless you are trying to use a UART older than a 16550.

Chip	Buffer Size (bytes)	Maximum Speed (bps)
8250	1	19,200
16450	1	38,400
16550	16	115,200
16650	32	430,800
16750	64	921,600
16850	128	1.5Kbps
16950	128	1.5Kbps

Table 19-3. UART Chip Characteristics

The UARTs above the 16550 are used in various types of high-speed and multiport adapter cards and devices, such as ISDN and DSL modems or four-serial port cards.

Synchronous Communications

Synchronous transmissions are coordinated to a common clock, which fixes the length of the interval between data blocks. The transmitting device synchronizes its clock to that of the receiving device and sends the clocking signal right along with the data. The communicating devices complete one operation before beginning the next, which involves acknowledgements that a data block is received and correct before the next block is sent.

RS-232 Communications

The RS-232-C standard (the official name of this standard is the EIA/TIA-232-E standard or the "Interface Between Data Terminal Equipment and Data Circuit Termination Equipment Employing Serial Binary Data Interchange" standard) defines the protocol used by two devices to communicate remotely over a serial connection. EIA is the Electronics Industry Association and TIA is the Telecommunications Industry Association Recommended Standard. A protocol establishes the rules that the devices must follow to carry out a communications session. Under the RS-232 standard, when a modem (or another communications device) is attached to a serial port, it is designated as *data communications equipment* (DCE), and the PC is designated as *data terminal equipment* (DTE). The importance of these designations is that under the RS-232 standard, the DTE initiates and controls some parts of the transmission, and the DCE initiates and controls others. The official name of DCE equipment is *data circuit-termination equipment*, but in common usage it is referred to as data communication equipment.

The pins and wires in the serial port and connector carry signals between the DTE and DCE to create what amounts to a conversation between the two devices. The signals are actually low-voltage charges of DC (direct current) power that flow from one device to the other, where it is detected and interpreted based upon which wire the signal is on (see Table 19-1). RS-232 communications prescribe a signal series that is followed by devices to establish what is called a handshake. The DTE controls some of the pins (and wires) of the serial connection, and the DCE controls the remainder. During the handshake process, the DTE uses its pins to communicate requests, status, and acknowledgements to the DCE. The DCE responds to the DTE and sends its own set of requests and acknowledgements over its pins.

The sequence of signals that flows between the DTE and DCE in RS-232 communications is as follows:

1. The DTE (PC) sends a signal on the Data Terminal Ready (DTR) wire, indicating that it is ready to communicate.
2. The DCE (modem) acknowledges the DTR signal by sending a signal over the Data Set Ready (DSR) wire to indicate that it too is ready to communicate.

3. The DTE signals over its Request to Send (RTS) line requesting the DCE to send any data it has.
4. The DCE replies with a signal over the Clear To Send (CTS) wire to alert the DTE that it ready to send data.
5. The data flows from the DCE over its Transmit line, which is the DTE's Receive line, one bit at a time and is placed in a receiving buffer in the main memory of the PC (DTE).
6. If the data comes in faster than the PC can process it or moves it to another location in memory, the receiver turns off the RTS, which the sender detects, and stops transmitting data until the receiver has been able to process some of the data in the buffer. When it has room in the buffer again, the receiver turns on the RTS and the sender resumes transmitting data. If the sender needs to halt the transmission for any reason, the CTS signal is turned off and back on when it wishes to resume the transmission.

CABLING THE CONNECTION

The cable used to connect a PC to a modem is called a serial cable, a modem cable, or a straight-through cable. In this cable, all the pins are connected one-to-one without any twists, crosses, or other fancy arrangements (that is, unless you need to use a 9- to 25-pin converter should the modem cable come with a 25-pin connector and the PC have a 9-pin serial port).

Although few serial port questions are on the A+ Core Hardware exam, there are some. Expect at least one with "null modem cable" as its answer. On occasion, two PCs are connected in a DTE-to-DTE arrangement. When this happens, the cable's pinouts is changed to simulate the action of the modem by cross-connecting a number of the pins and creating what is called a null modem, or modem eliminator, cable. Both the modem cable and the null modem cable are generic, and you can purchase them at any electronics store.

Configuring a Serial Port

Nearly all PCs include at least one serial port, which is designated as COM1. Additional ports are designated by the BIOS as COM2, COM3, and COM4. Multiple serial ports can be added to the PC individually or in sets of two or four with multiport expansion cards. Individual serial ports require individual system resource assignments, which may cause conflicts with already installed devices. A multiport serial card typically shares a single IRQ (interrupt request) among the ports with an onboard processor handling the traffic management duties. So, if a PC requires multiple serial ports, it may be more efficient for the system to install a multiport card (or consider USB—more on this later in the chapter).

Configuring the serial port on a PC involves setting its system resource assignments. Luckily, most PCs use the default assignments for the COM ports. Table 19-2 lists the default system resource assignments used for the serial ports on most PCs. Notice that COM1 shares an IRQ with COM3 and COM2 shares an IRQ with COM4. What this means is that you must be careful when assigning devices to COM ports so that you don't end up with devices competing for the same interrupt. Chapter 13 has more information on system resources. Chapter 20 includes information on configuring a modem to a serial port.

The COM designation of a serial port is its logical device name, which allows the system and software programs to refer to devices like the serial ports by a common name instead of its physical address, which vary by PC.

On most PCs and on serial port expansion cards, COM1 is typically a DB-9 connector and COM2 is a DB-25 connector. However, there are no standards for these assignments, so you may need to look at the card to see how the connections are labeled. In most instances, COM1 is labeled "COM1" and COM2 is labeled... well, you get it.

Troubleshooting a Serial Port

Most serial port problems are caused by a system resource conflict. These problems show up as a serial device that fails intermittently or doesn't work at all, as another device that stops working when the serial device is installed, or as the PC locking up during the boot sequence.

To troubleshoot a serial port problem, check the following:

- **Inspect the port for bent pins.** Certain pins must be absolutely straight in order for the device to work properly.
- **Ensure that the cable is the appropriate cable for the device.** Some serial devices can't use a straight-through or null modem cable.
- **Check the Windows Device Manager for system resource conflicts.** An IRQ conflict is the most common error in this area. Remember, only one customer to an IRQ at a time.
- **Be sure that the serial cable is not more than 50 feet long.** Beyond this distance, you lose data integrity, which shows up any number of ways, none of which are good.

Logical Device Name	IRQ	I/O Address
COM1	IRQ 4	3F8h
COM2	IRQ 3	2F8h
COM3	IRQ 4	3E8h
COM4	IRQ 3	2E8h

Table 19-4. Serial Port System Resource Assignments

PARALLEL PORTS

Parallel ports are much more straightforward than serial ports. Because all of a character's data moves over a parallel link at one time, the data transmits faster than it does on a serial connection. This is the reason the PC's internal bus structures use the parallel format; it's also another reason why a serial port needs a device like the UART to convert the internal parallel data format to a serial format for transmission over a serial line.

Parallel ports on a PC are female DB-25 connectors that connect to male DB-25 connectors, as shown in Figure 19-7. The PC's parallel ports were originally designed for use by printers. However, other devices have been adapted to them, including other types of output devices, input devices, and storage devices, all taking advantage of the bidirectional capabilities of most of the newer parallel ports and devices. These include some external CD-ROMs, external tape drives, and Zip drives, as well as file transfer software over proprietary cabling.

Parallel Port Standards

The Institute of Electrical and Electronics Engineers (IEEE) has standardized the parallel port protocols. The IEEE standard is formally titled the "IEEE Standard Signaling Method for a Bidirectional Parallel Peripheral Interface for Personal Computers," but it is

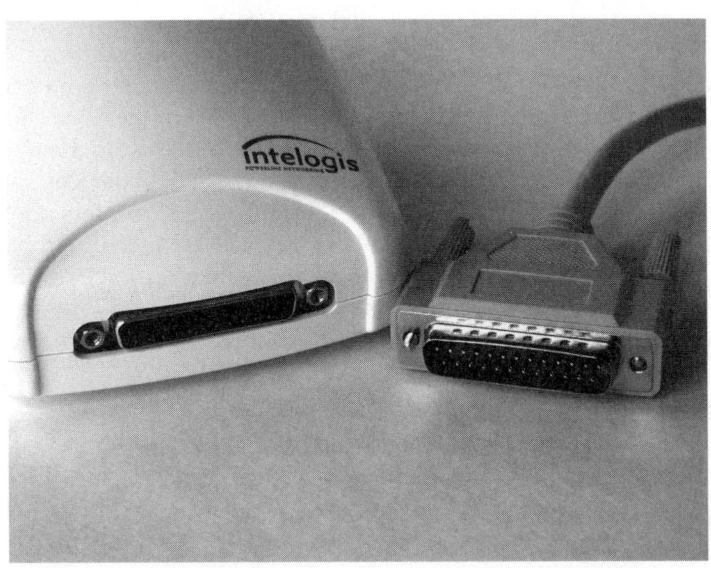

Figure 19-7. A networking device with a parallel port and a cable with a DB-25 male connector

better known as the IEEE 1284 standard. IEEE 1284 incorporates the two pre-existing parallel port standards that were already in use with a new protocol to create an all-encompassing parallel port model and protocol standard.

The IEEE 1284 standards are as follows:

- **Standard Parallel Port (SPP)** This standard defines a simplex parallel port that allows data to travel in one direction only—from the computer to the printer. This standard is included to support very old legacy printers.
- **Enhanced Parallel Port (EPP)** This standard defines a half-duplex parallel port that allows data to flow in two directions, but only in one direction at a time. This allows the printer to communicate with the PC or a network adapter to signal that it is out of paper, its cover is open, and so on.
- **Enhanced Capabilities Port (ECP)** If a PC lists that it has an IEEE 1284–compliant parallel port, it typically means that it has an ECP port. The ECP standard allows bidirectional, simultaneous communications between the printer or parallel device to the PC or network. The IEEE 1284 standard also defines a special cable that is required by the ECP standard. The EPP standard is technically bidirectional, but remember that it is only a half-duplex standard. So, when shopping for a printer cable, be sure you get an ECP cable to work with your ECP parallel port.

Configuring and Troubleshooting a Parallel Port

In a majority of cases, problems with a parallel port are in the device attached to it. A parallel port is virtually featureless and it either works (and it usually does) or it doesn't. Any problem that is specific to the parallel port is either in the connector or port (bent pins or blocked holes), the cable (wrong type—SPP, EPP, or ECP), or the device itself.

There is always an outside chance that a system resource conflict may exist, but this problem is caused by new devices being added to the PC. ECP devices, including some printers, use IRQs and DMA channels (see Chapter 13). Most printers don't use the system resource allocations made to a parallel port. However, when a problem shows up that you have isolated to the parallel port, check for system resource conflicts, especially if a new piece of hardware has just been added to the PC.

The following table lists the default system resource assignments for parallel ports used on most PCs:

Port	IRQ	I/O Address	DMA Channel
LPT1	IRQ 7	378h	DMA 3 (ECP Capabilities)
LPT2	IRQ 5	278h	n/a

THE USB INTERFACE

When the PC had only a printer or a modem connected to it, one or two serial and parallel ports were enough to provide the support required. However, today's PC world has scanners, portable hard disks, Zip and Jazz drives, and no-serious-PC-gamer-should-be-without-one force-feedback joysticks. As a result, there are situations where there are not enough serial and parallel ports for everything you wish to connect to your PC. Another problem is that for many of the newer peripheral devices, standard serial and parallel ports aren't fast enough anyway.

Attempts were made to provide systems with all of the ports a user could possibly use. PCs were configured with as many as eight serial ports, but the problem was that not every new device used a serial port. The next great interface was to be the SCSI (Small Computer System Interface) standard (covered later in this chapter), but it is expensive and the lack of an early standard hurt its chances for global acceptance. Into the void came two new high-speed serial data interconnection standards, USB (Universal Serial Bus) and the FireWire (more on this later).

The Universal Serial Bus (USB) is a newer hardware interface standard that supports low-speed devices such as keyboards, mice, and scanners as well as higher speed devices such as digital cameras. USB, which is a serial interface, provides data transfer speeds of up to 12Mbps for faster devices and a 1.5Mbps subchannel speed for lower speed devices. A newer version of the USB standard, USB 2.0, supports up to 480Mbps for data transfer speeds. Figure 19-8 shows a comparison of the data transfer speeds for the more common interface types.

A USB port offers the following features:

- The flexibility of Plug-and-Play devices.
- Standard connectors and cables with a wide variety of devices available, including keyboards, mice, floppy drives, hard disk drives, Zip and Jazz drives, inkjet printers, laser printers, scanners, digital cameras, modems, and hubs.
- Automatic configuration of USB devices when they are connected.
- Hot swapping—USB devices can be connected and disconnected while the PC is powered on.
- The capability to support up to 127 devices on one channel.

Connecting with USB

USB uses a unique pair of connectors and ports, as shown in Figure 19-9. USB Type A connectors are used to connect devices directly to a PC or USB hub. You'll find USB Type A connectors on devices with permanently attached cables. USB Type B connectors are found on those devices that have a detachable cable. The cable uses a squarish Type B port on the device and connects to either a Type A or Type B socket (the cable usually has both on the other end) on the PC or hub.

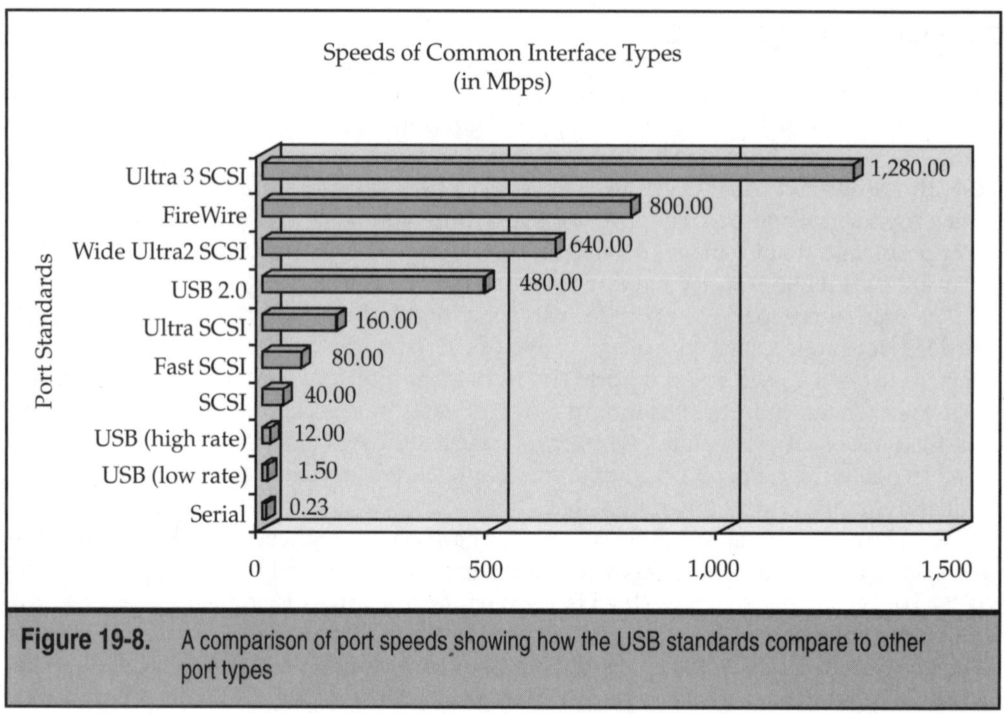

Figure 19-8. A comparison of port speeds showing how the USB standards compare to other port types

The USB interface supports up to 127 devices on a single channel. Most PCs have only one or two USB connectors, as illustrated in Figure 19-10, and not all 127 can directly connect to these ports. These devices connect both to the PC directly or into one or more USB hubs, as shown in Figure 19-11. The fact that each USB port carries .5 amps of electrical power, which is enough to power most low-power devices such as a mouse or keyboard, provides a great deal of flexibility for adding additional devices to the system regardless of its location. USB devices that require higher power usually use their own AC adapters.

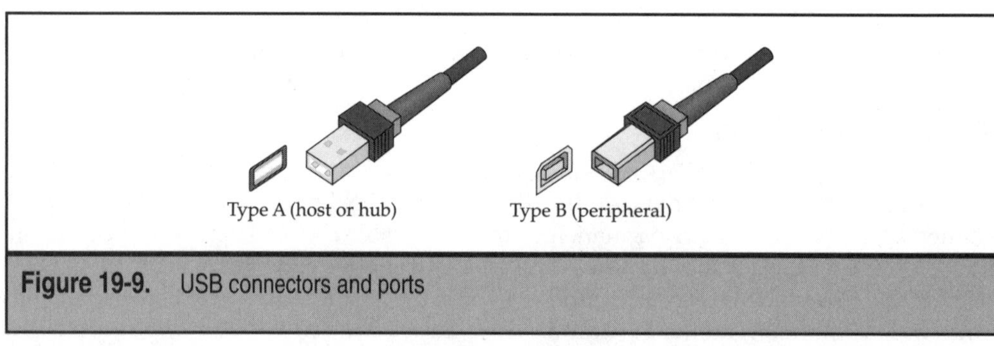

Figure 19-9. USB connectors and ports

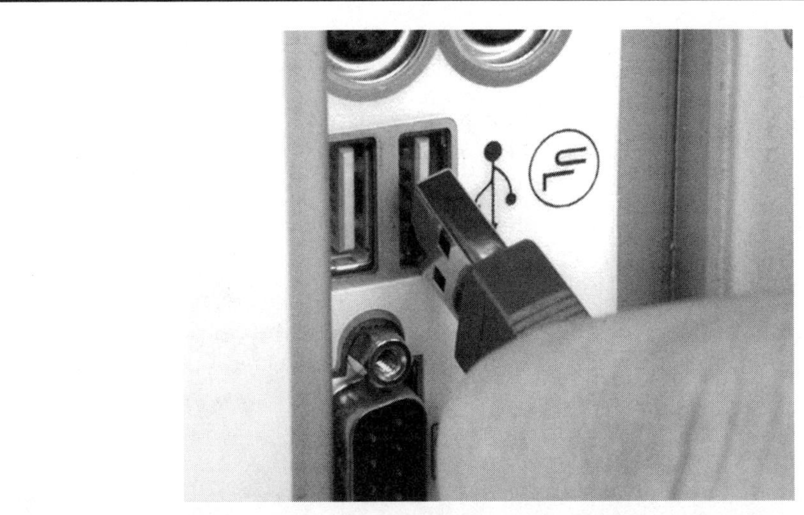

Figure 19-10. Connecting to a USB port on a PC

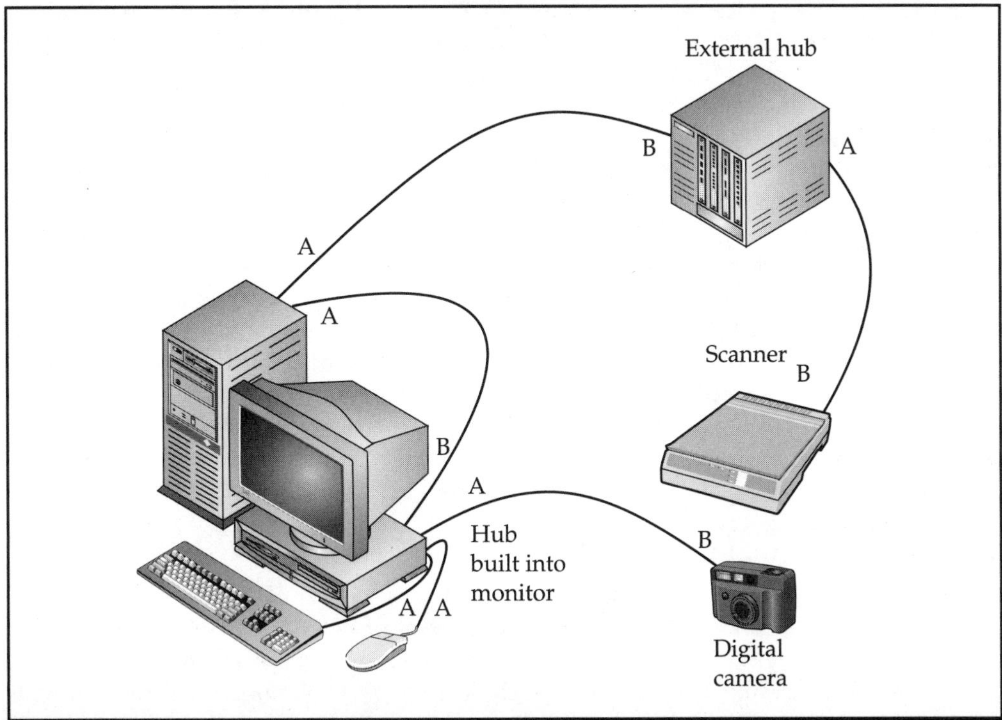

Figure 19-11. Multiple USB devices can be connected to a single PC

The USB Interface

A USB interface has three essential components: a host, a hub, and peripheral devices.

- **USB host** A PC is the USB host device that carries the operating system, chipset, and BIOS that support the USB interface.
- **USB hub** USB interfaces can be built in a tiered fashion. A hub can be plugged into the host. Other hubs can be plugged into that hub and USB devices can be plugged into each of the second-tier hubs. As long as the whole bus has only 127 devices, including the hubs, there should not be any problems.
- **USB devices** In most cases, you will have only one or two USB devices plugged into your PC, and these will be directly connected to the PC itself. However, as described in the preceding bullet, USB devices can be connected to hubs as well. In fact, if a PC has two USB ports, one can have a directly connected device and the other a hub.

How USB Works

When a USB device is plugged into a USB port, the host or the hub detects a change in the voltage on the interface. The host asks the new device to identify itself, a process USB calls enumeration. The device replies with its type, its manufacturer, what it does, and the amount of bandwidth it requires. The device is given an address code that identifies it uniquely from any other USB devices already on the bus. Each USB device attached to the bus, even two of the exact same device, gets a unique address ID so it can be referenced and addressed by the host.

Once the device has its ID, its device driver is loaded. If one cannot be found, the user is asked to supply a disk or CD-ROM with the driver. Unlike a serial or parallel port, any resource conflicts are resolved by the host, which frees the user from configuring IRQs, I/O addresses, or DMA channels. Each USB channel uses only one set of system resources. If the USB port is supporting more than one device, the devices all share the system resources of the USB port. When a USB device is unplugged from the system, the reverse takes place. Once again, the host detects the voltage difference, retires the address ID, and notifies the operating system to unload the device driver.

For more information on the Universal Serial Bus, visit the official USB homepage at **www.usb.org**.

THE FIREWIRE INTERFACE

Another of the newer high-speed serial interface buses is the IEEE 1394 standard that defines a serial bus protocol with data transfer speeds of between 100Mbps to 400Mbps (around 12 to 50 megabytes per second). Newer versions of the 1394 standard, which are being developed by the 1394 Trade Association (**www.1394ta.org**), will provide data speeds of 800Mbps to 1.6Gbps.

Several manufacturers have implemented the IEEE 1394 standard largely as proprietary and licensed interfaces. The more popular of these are i.Link (Sony), Lynx (Texas Instruments), and FireWire (Apple Computer). Of these, the FireWire has been the most commonly implemented, having been licensed by PC manufacturers for use on non-Apple computers. The generic version of the 1394 standard is called the High Performance Serial Bus (HPSB).

An IEEE 1394 connector looks something like a USB connector, except that it is a bit larger and about halfway between rectangular and square. Figure 19-12 shows a FireWire connection from a Nintendo Gameboy.

Defining the 1394 Bus

The IEEE 1394 port has become the standard link between PCs and consumer electronics. Using a 1394 port, a digital video camera can be used to capture video content and then play back the video after it has been edited on a PC.

The IEEE 1394 bus shares several characteristics with the USB interface. They are both high-speed, Plug–and-Play, hot-swappable interface buses. However, 1394 supports isochronous (or real-time) data transfers. In an isochronous transfer, data is transferred within very tight time constraints. This type of data transfer ensures that all parts of the image arrive together. This is very important for data with audio and video elements, such as with multimedia data or images directly from a video camera.

The 1394 is faster and more expensive than the USB interface, which is why it is used primarily for devices that require larger data transfers in a shorter time, such as a digital video camera. Another and perhaps more dramatic difference is that 1394 is a peer-to-peer interface that does not require a host system. The 1394 interface bus can operate quite well with no PC at all. A video camera can easily support and power several devices on a common interface, as illustrated in Figure 19-13. In fact, the IEEE 1394 bus is able to support up to 63 external devices.

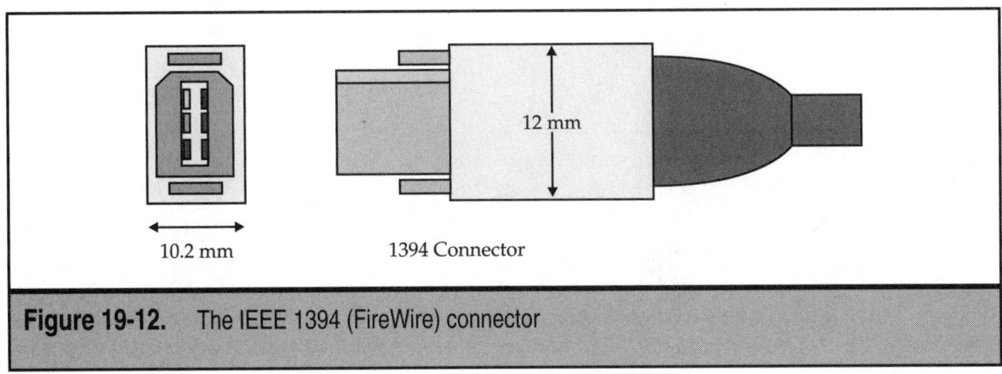

Figure 19-12. The IEEE 1394 (FireWire) connector

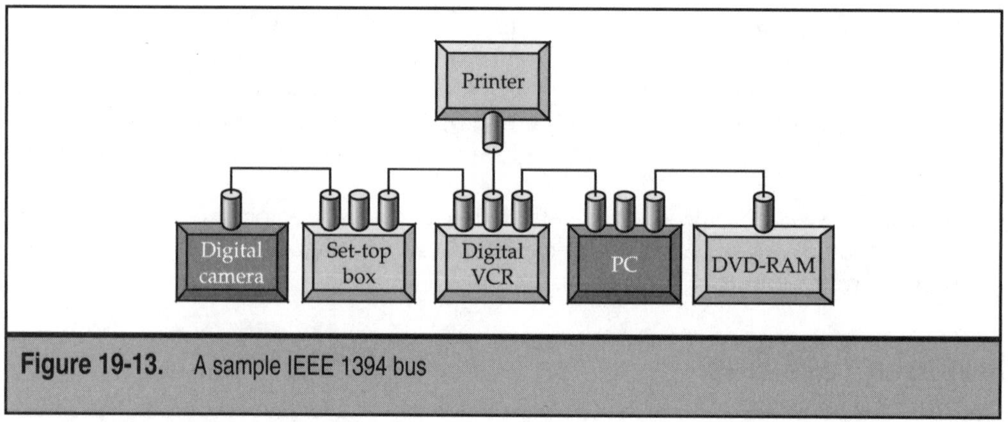

Figure 19-13. A sample IEEE 1394 bus

FireWire Device Drivers

Virtually all of the later versions of popular operating systems, including Windows 98 and 2000, support IEEE 1394, but only if the device controller attached to the port supports the Open Host Controller Interface (OHCI) standard. Windows 2000 supports IEEE 1394 devices through its Serial Bus Protocol (SBP-2) drivers.

WIRELESS PORTS

Wireless or cordless interfaces are becoming more popular for PCs. There are two types of wireless connection technologies in use on PCs: infrared (IR) and radio frequency (RF).

Infrared Ports

An infrared (IR) port uses an invisible band of light from the lower end of the electromagnetic spectrum to carry data between a peripheral device and the PC. IR light is just outside of the light spectrum that humans can see. Infrared contrasts with ultraviolet (UV), which is another invisible band of light, but at the other end of the spectrum. One use of UV light, besides tanning your body, is that it will erase an EPROM after about ten minutes of exposure.

Using the invisible IR beam, IR devices, which are also called IrDA (Infrared Data Association) devices, can be connected to a PC without the use of a physical cable. IrDA is the trade organization for the infrared device industry that has established a number of standards defining and prescribing the use of the IrDA connection. IrDA ports, which are the small oval-shaped dark red plastic windows built into cases, are common on notebook and other portable computers.

IR devices are line-of-sight devices, which means that they must have a clear, unobstructed path between their transmitters and receivers. IR devices are not new; IR is the wireless mode most often used by TV remotes and other wireless controllers. If anything is blocking the path, you must move either the obstruction or the controller to reopen the line-of-sight. Using an IR connection, a portable PC or a PDA (personal digital assistant) can connect to another PC, keyboard, mouse, or printer without the need for a physical cable connection. Most IR ports (receivers) are built into the case of the PC or notebook, but external IR receivers can be attached to the PC through a serial port or USB port.

Here are some tips for working with IR devices:

- Two IR devices must have a clear, unobstructed line-of-sight between them.
- The devices you are trying to connect via IR must be at least six inches apart, but not more than three feet.
- The transmission pattern of the IR signal is a cone about 30 degrees wide. Make sure the devices are oriented to one another inside the transmission cone.
- Make sure there are no competing IR devices in the vicinity that may interfere with the connection, such as a TV remote control.

Radio Frequency Interfaces

Many cordless peripheral devices, especially those that are typically used in close proximity of the PC's system case, use radio frequency (RF) transmitters, receivers, and transceivers (the combination of a receiver and transmitter) to send data to the PC. RF devices include mice, keyboards, modems, and even network adapters for desktop and portable PCs.

RF Keyboards and Mice

Cordless RF mice and keyboards transmit data to a base receiver that is attached to the PC through either a serial or PS/2 connection (discussed in the next section). The operating range of these devices, despite claims of good performance as much as 50 feet away, is more like 6 to 10 feet. In that range, the performance of the cordless RF keyboard and mouse is as good as a wired device. Figure 19-14 shows a cordless RF keyboard and mouse.

RF networking devices, which are covered by the IEEE 802.11 wireless networking standard and the new Bluetooth technology, are discussed in more detail in Chapter 20.

PS/2 AND DIN CONNECTORS

The two most popular connectors for connecting keyboards, mice, and external IR and RF receivers are the PS/2 and the 5-pin DIN connector. For more information on these two connector types, see Chapter 18.

Nearly all mice sold today use the PS/2 connector. This connector has essentially replaced the DB-9 serial connector that was used in the past. Serial mice are still available, but since newer PC systems rarely offer more than a single serial port and do include PS/2 connectors for the keyboard and mouse, the serial mouse connector has all but disappeared, except on legacy systems.

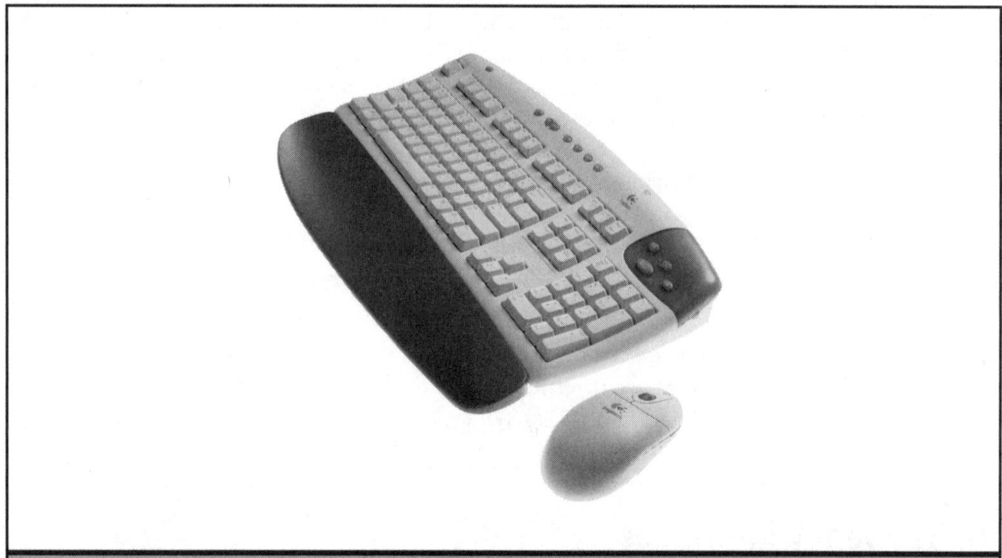

Figure 19-14. A cordless keyboard and mouse that connects to the PC through an RF transmitter and receiver. Photo courtesy of Logitech

VIDEO INTERFACES

Video interfaces, which are explained in more detail in Chapter 12, provide a connection interface for the video adapter that provides a connection to the monitor. On most Pentium-class PCs, a PCI-interface video adapter function is built into the motherboard. The other popular video interface is the Accelerated Graphics Port (AGP). Two legacy architectures that are used on older systems for video interfaces are the ISA and VL Bus interfaces.

- **Peripheral Component Interconnect (PCI)** Support for the PCI interface bus is included in the system chipset on all Pentium-class computers. PCI is commonly used for 2D graphics cards, sound cards, network interface cards, and other expansion cards that attach directly to the motherboard. Of course, a PCI card slot is required. PCI is a bus structure and as such can support a number of different devices. PCI slots, shown in Figure 19-15, are found on virtually all Pentium-class motherboards boards.
- **Accelerated Graphics Port (AGP)** The AGP interface was designed specifically for use as a video system interface. AGP, which runs twice as fast as the PCI interface, creates a high-speed link between the video card and the PC's processor. The AGP interface is also directly linked to the PC's system memory, which makes it possible for 3D images to be stored in main memory and 2D systems to use system RAM for some calculations. All AGP video cards require that the motherboard have an AGP slot. AGP is a port and as such can support only a

single device. The AGP slot (see Figure 19-15)—there is usually only one on a motherboard—is reserved for the graphics card.

- **ISA (Industry Standard Architecture)** The ISA expansion bus (pronounced "eye-ess-aye," not "ice-a") is now generally obsolete, but most motherboards still have at least one ISA slot to provide backward compatibility for older hardware. You can still buy ISA expansion cards, but they are becoming hard to find. On most motherboards, the ISA bus slots are 16-bit that will also support 8-bit cards. Older video cards use ISA, but because it is an 8-bit architecture, it cannot support the speed and throughput demanded by modern video adapters.

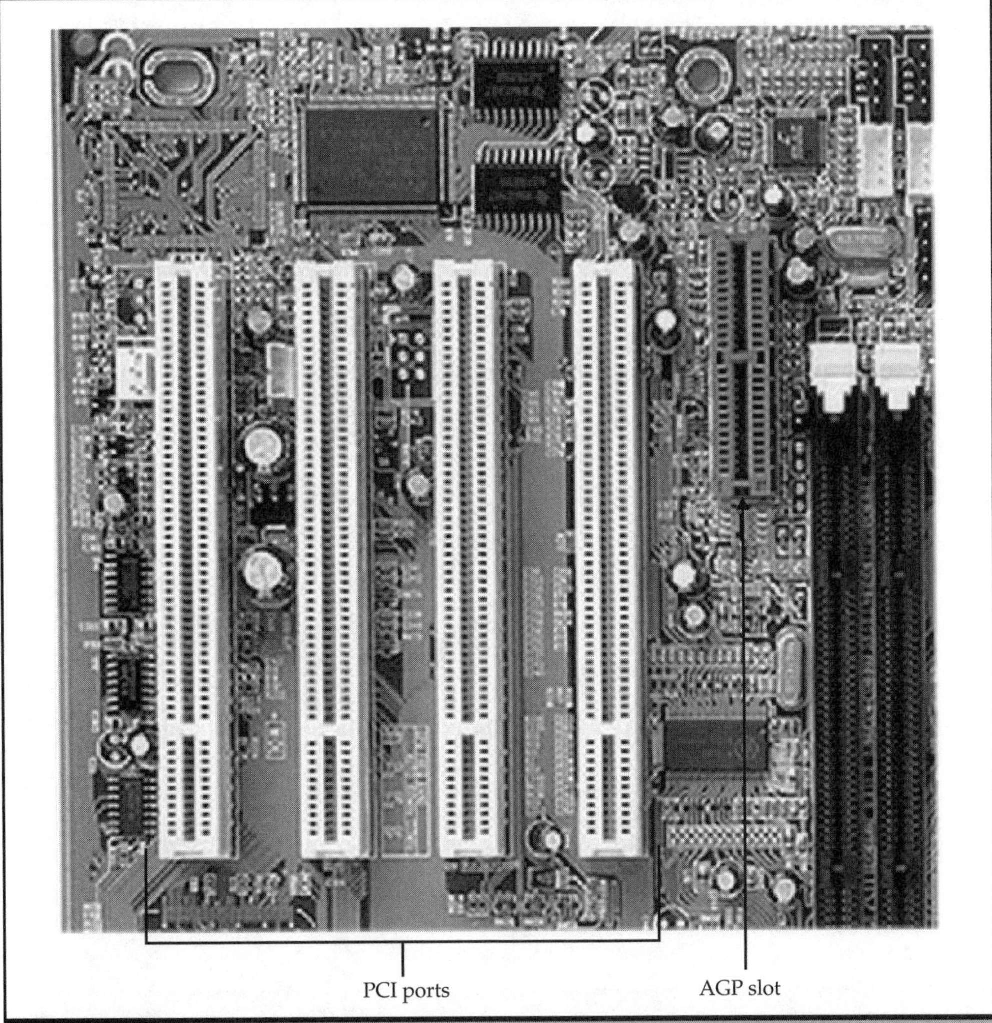

Figure 19-15. A motherboard with PCI and AGP interface slots

- **VESA Local Bus (VL-Bus)** VL-bus is a bus architecture developed by VESA (Video Electronics Standards Association) for use with the 486 processor and video cards. A local bus is one that is attached to the same bus structure used by the CPU. VL-bus is a 32-bit bus that supported bus mastering. The PCI bus has essentially replaced the VL-bus on modern PCs. If your PC has a VL-bus expansion slot, it is the one next to the ISA and EISA slots that has the extra slot added to the end and is about four inches long in total.

AGP is fast replacing PCI as the interface of choice for video cards because of its faster transfer rates. In fact, AGP has evolved into several standard versions, each noting its multiple of the original standard. For example, AGP 1X has a data transfer rate of 266MBps (compared to PCI's 133MBps), AGP 2X supports 533MBps, and AGP 4X transfers data at 1.07GBps.

Video Connectors

Regardless of the type of internal interface a video card uses, virtually all video ports use a female 15-pin DB port and connector. This port is shown in Figure 19-16.

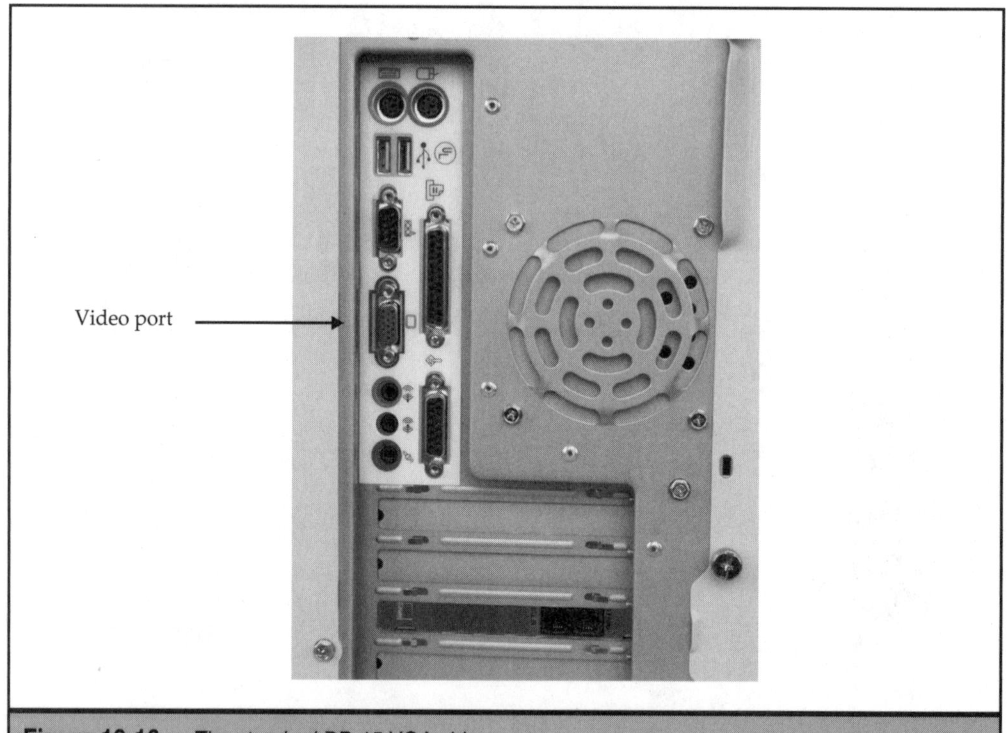

Figure 19-16. The standard DB-15 VGA video port

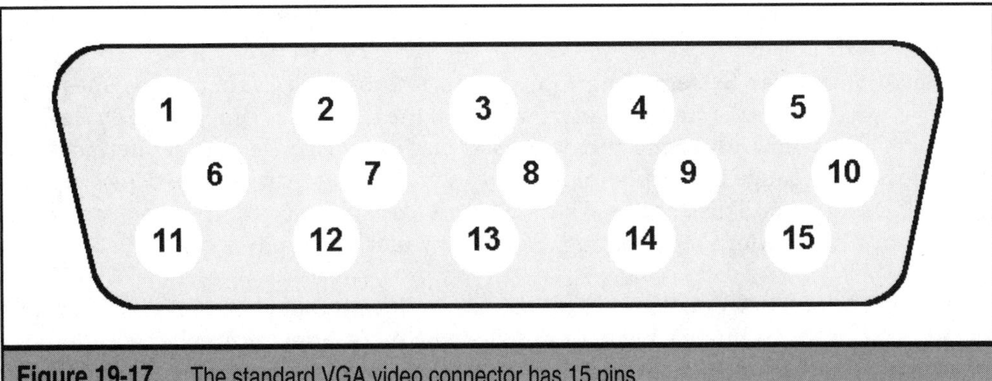

Figure 19-17. The standard VGA video connector has 15 pins

The standard port and connector used for VGA, SVGA, and XGA monitor connections is the DB-15, which is also called a mini-sub D15 connector. Figure 19-17 shows the pin configuration of this connection and Table 19-5 lists its pin assignments.

Pin	VGA/SVGA/SGA
1	Red video
2	Green video
3	Blue video
4	Monitor ID 2
5	Ground/Not used
6	Red video return
7	Green video return
8	Blue video return
9	Not used
10	Ground
11	Monitor ID 0
12	Monitor ID 1
13	Horizontal sync
14	Vertical sync
15	Not used

Table 19-5. Pin Assignments in a Video Connector

SCSI INTERFACE

The Small Computer Systems Interface (SCSI), pronounced "skuzzy" (rhymes with fuzzy), is not an interface standard in the way that the IDE/ATA (Integrated Drive Electronics/AT Attachment) architecture is. SCSI is made up of a collection of interface standards covering a range of peripheral devices, including hard disks, tape drives, optical drives, CD-ROMs, and disk arrays. The SCSI bus is capable of connecting many devices, both internal and external, to a single SCSI controller and share a common SCSI bus interface.

Like IDE/ATA devices, SCSI controllers are built into the devices. As SCSI devices are added to the SCSI bus, each device is assigned a unique device number to differentiate it from the other devices. The SCSI controller communicates with the devices on the bus, by sending a message encoded with the unit's device number, which is also included in any replay sent by the device. A SCSI bus must be terminated to prevent unclaimed or misdirected messages from bouncing back onto the bus.

External SCSI Connectors

There are several different SCSI standards available, each with its own protocols and connectors. Table 19-6 lists the various SCSI standards that are in use and the external connector used by each to connect an external SCSI device to the bus. Figures 19-18 and 19-19 illustrate the connectors referenced in the table.

Some early SCSI standards used 25-pin Centronics and DB-25 connectors. The SCA (Single Connection Attachment), which is a high-density connector that also includes the power connection as well, is now being used for some higher-end SCSI systems.

SCSI Standard	External Connector	Internal Connector
SCSI – 1	50-pin Centronics	50-pin IDC
SCSI – 2	50-pin high density	50-pin IDC
Ultra SCSI	50-pin high density	50-pin IDC
Fast SCSI	50-pin high density	50-pin IDC
Wide SCSI	68-pin high density	68-pin high density
Fast Wide SCSI	68-pin high density	68-pin high density
Ultra SCSI - 3	68-pin high density	68-pin high density
Ultra2 SCSI - 3	68-pin very high density	68-pin high density

Table 19-6. SCSI Standards

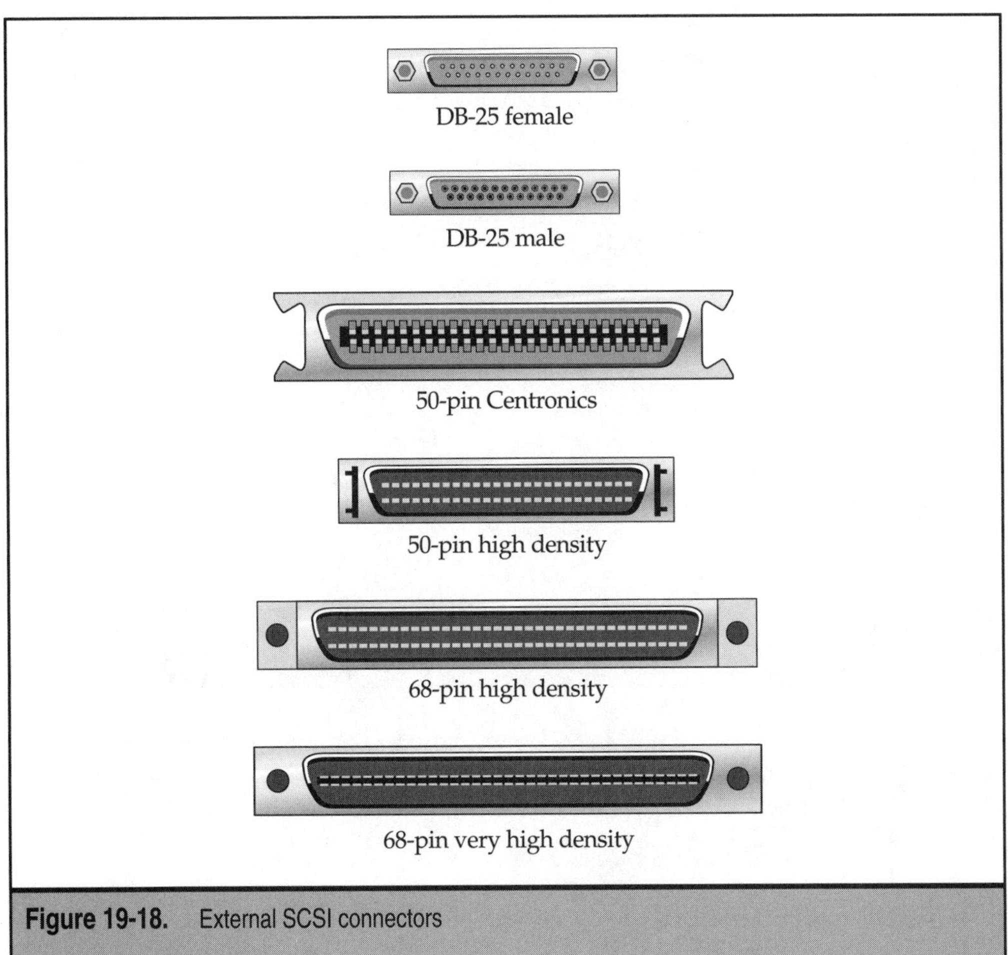

Figure 19-18. External SCSI connectors

SCSI Standards

Here is a brief overview of the various SCSI standards:

- **SCSI (SCSI-1)** This standard is obsolete. It supported up to 16 devices on a single SCSI chain and required each chain (internal and external) to be terminated.
- **SCSI-2** This is also called Fast SCSI. SCSI-2 improved the speed of the original standard to 20MBps. It allowed for either active or passive termination and used a high-voltage differential (HVD) bus.

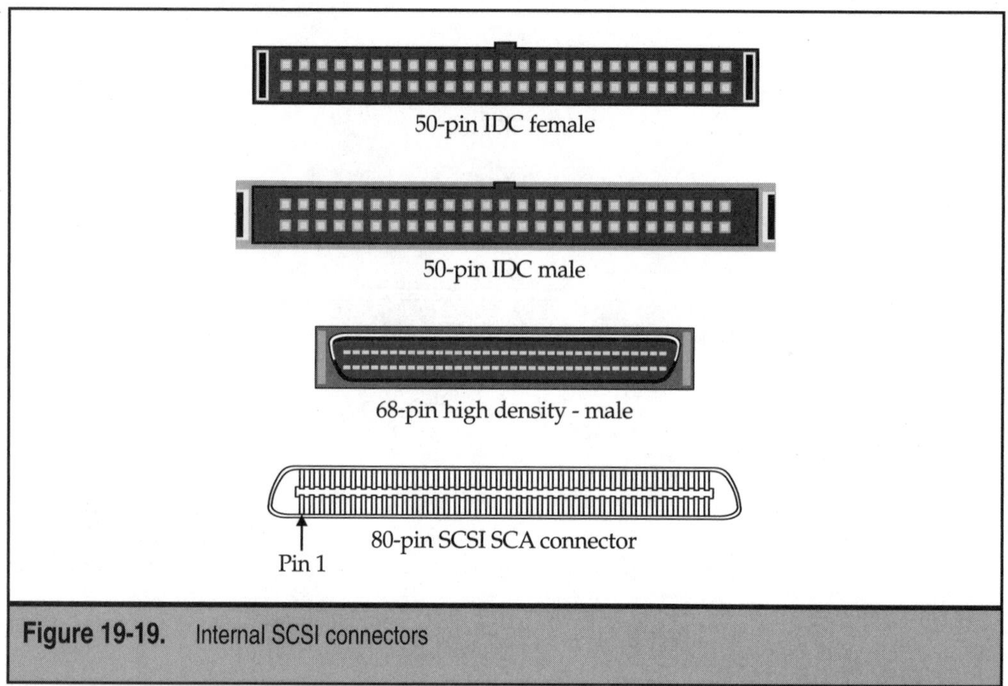

Figure 19-19. Internal SCSI connectors

- **SCSI-3** This standard is referred to as SCSI today. It includes the SCSI Parallel Interface (SPI), which defines the 68-pin high-density connection or SCSI-3 connector. SPI-2 and SPI-3 have improved the connection to include the SCA and the very high-density connectors and speeds up to 160MBps.

SCSI Voltage Differentials

There are three types of signaling used on a SCSI network:

- **Single-ended (SE) SCSI** This type of signaling is used in Fast and Ultra SCSI and allows devices to attach to a terminated SCSI bus chain with a total length of not more than three to six meters.
- **High-voltage Differential (HVD) SCSI** This signaling technology allows the SCSI chain to spread out a bit more by lengthening the total bus length to 25 meters.
- **Low-voltage Differential (LVD) SCSI** This less-costly signaling technology builds the data transceivers into the device controllers. The overall distance of the SCSI bus is reduced to 12 meters, however.

Configuring SCSI Devices

SCSI devices, such as hard disk drives, CD-ROM drives, scanners, and others, must be configured to be a part of a SCSI chain when installed in a PC. The SCSI chain may have only one device, but the configuration is the same as when the chain is hosting 16 or 32 devices. Figure 19-20 illustrates a SCSI bus with two chains: one internal and one external.

Two essential configuration steps must be performed on all SCSI devices. However, depending on the manufacturer or the intended use of the device, such as a disk drive to be used in a RAID (Redundant Array of Independent Disks) configuration, you may have other steps to perform. Check the device's manual or contact the manufacturer for more information. The two required steps are as follows:

- **Termination** If the new device sits on the end of the SCSI chain, the device that occupied the end of the chain prior must have its termination disabled, or you will never see the new device.
- **Device ID** The device ID must be set. This may require changing the setting of a jumper on the device itself. Check the device's manual for instructions.

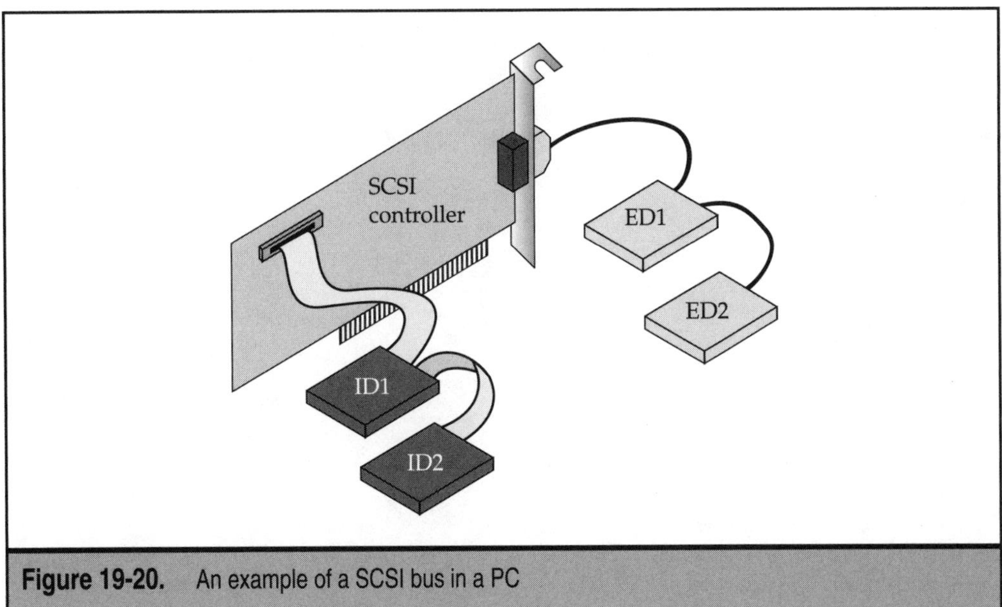

Figure 19-20. An example of a SCSI bus in a PC

CHAPTER 20

Networks and Communications

Nearly everything surrounding communications involves a network of one kind or another these days. The telephone system, technically the Public Switched Telephone Network (PSTN), and the PC can be used together to connect to other computers using local and global networks. The rapid growth of the Internet has dramatically increased the use of computer-based communications in several forms.

This chapter discusses the common means used to connect a PC to networks, including dial-up networks, local area networks (LANs), wide area networks (WANs), the Internet, and takes a brief look at wireless networks.

NETWORK BASICS

Networking has a language all of its own and, depending on how much you want to get into its technology, you can learn what amounts to a foreign language. So, before getting into the specifics of networking, a quick overview of some general network terms and concepts is a good idea.

What Is a Network?

In its most basic form, a network is two or more computers that are connected with a communications line for purposes of sharing resources. Figure 20-1 illustrates a basic network that connects Tom's PC to Sally's PC so that they can share each other's files. So, if two (or more) computers connect to each other over a telephone line or through a piece of cable or even through a wireless connection and the users are able to access ad share files and peripheral devices on the other computers, a network is formed. Most networks are a little more complicated than this, but essentially the arrangement just described is all that is really necessary.

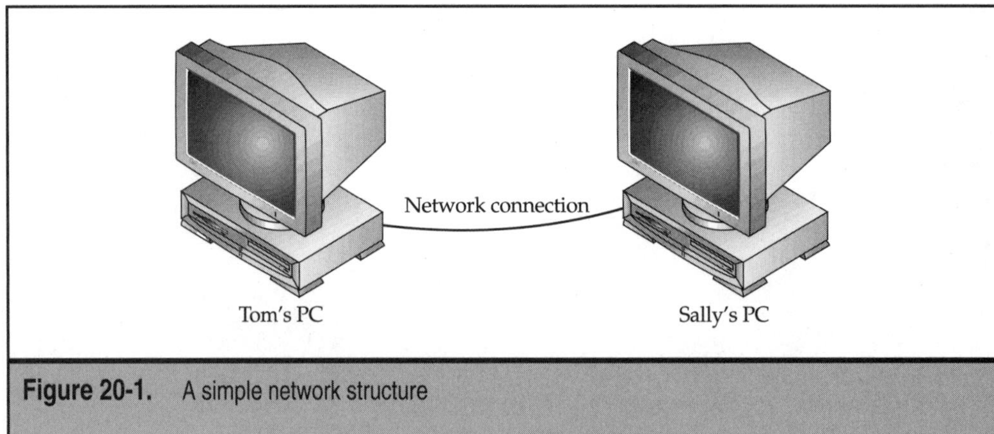

Figure 20-1. A simple network structure

As you might guess, there are different levels and types of networks. Networks are classified by the size and scope of the area they serve. The most common classifications for networks are as follows:

- **Local area network (LAN)** Usually computers connected to a network that is confined to a single office or building. The network in an office or a school's computer lab is typically a LAN.
- **Campus area network (CAN)** A variation of a LAN that extends to include computers in buildings that are in close proximity to one another, such as in an office park or campus setting. The network that connects the buildings of a college or a manufacturing company's buildings is an example of a CAN.
- **Wide area network (WAN)** Interconnects LANs and computers that are located over a large geographical area. Typically, the WAN is built on dedicated high-speed communications lines. The big WAN is the Internet, which is actually a network of networks (something called a nexus), but the network that connects the New York office of a company to its plant in Washington State is also a WAN.
- **Metropolitan area network (MAN)** A type of WAN that interconnects LANs and computers within a specific geographical area, such as a city or a cluster of campuses or office parks. Several cities, including Cleveland, Chicago, and Spokane, have established MANs to provide connectivity to downtown businesses.

Network Structures

As indicated above, creating a network can be as simple as connecting two PCs together or connecting together thousands, even millions, or other networks. Depending on the needs of the users, a network can be quite simple or it can be very complex. There are two basic network structures:

- **Peer-to-peer (peer-based) networks** Two or more computers directly connected to one another for the sole purpose of directly sharing data and hardware resources. The very simple network shown in Figure 20-1 shows a peer-to-peer network. Tom and Sally are directly connected by a cable and are able to grant permission to each other to open and use files and programs stored on their PCs and to share CD-ROM drives, printers, and other hardware. On a peer-based network, each user is responsible for the security and access of his or her PC because there is no central administrator. A peer-to-peer network is practically limited to not more than ten PCs arranged as a LAN.
- **Server-based (client/server) networks** A network of connected computers and peripherals with a centralized server that facilitates the sharing of network data, software, and hardware resources. A client/server network typically has

a central administrator that manages the permissions and access to the resources of the network. This structure is used for the majority of LANs and virtually all WANs and other network types that connect over a WAN.

Any computer that requests services, such as a file, a program, or printing from the network is a client, and any computer that services the requests made to the network is a server. Depending on the request, any computer on the network can be a client for one type of request and a server for another. If Tom's PC has a nifty new laser printer attached to it and Sally has been given permission to use it, Tom's PC becomes a print server for printing requests from Sally's PC client. On a larger network, centralized computers process a variety of services for the computers connected to the network, as shown in Figure 20-2. Typically, on larger networks clients are clients and servers are servers.

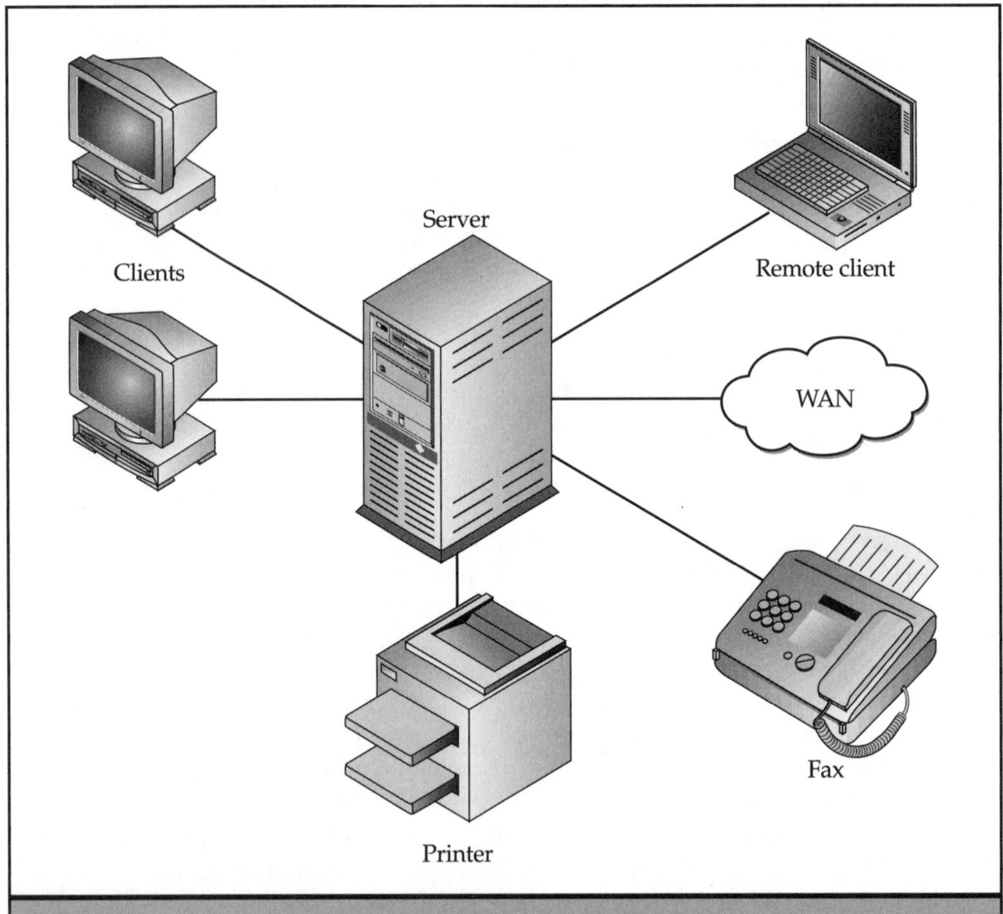

Figure 20-2. A server can provide many services to a network

Network Components

The most basic components of any network are servers, workstations (computers), and other network nodes (printers, modems, etc.), the network operating system (NOS), and the cabling or media used to connect them all together. Each one of these components has a vital part to play in the construction of the network. The role of the servers and workstations (computers) are apparent and easily defined, but the contributions of the other components are equally essential to the operation of the network. Here's what each piece of the puzzle provides:

- **Server** A network computer from which workstations (clients) access and share files, printing, communications, and other services. Servers can be dedicated to a single service such as file servers, print servers, application servers, Web servers, and so on. A server can also be a client for services that it does not provide itself.
- **Workstation** A personal computer that is connected to a network. Workstations are also known as a clients and nodes.
- **Network nodes** Any addressable network device, including workstations, peripherals, or network devices. This term is commonly used interchangeably with workstation.
- **Network operating system** The system software that runs on a network server and provides server, network, and user management, administration, and control functions to the network administrator.
- **Cable or media** The physical medium over which information is transmitted between the computers or other devices of a network. The main types of cable used in networking are coaxial, copper twisted pair, and fiber optic. Networks do not require a physical cable. As is discussed later in this chapter, wireless network technology can also be used to interconnect network elements.

SERVERS

Servers are networked computers that perform a special task to service the resource needs of the workstations (clients) on the network. A server can perform a variety of functions on behalf of a network. A server can be a printer server, a file server, an application server, a fax server, a World Wide Web server, and so on.

Several different types of servers can exist on a network, each one performing a different sort of task for the network and its workstations. Servers are usually thought of as the hardware that houses it, but the server is actually the software that performs, controls, or coordinates a service or resource. One computer can actually provide many different (software) servers to network clients. Table 20-1 lists the most common types of servers implemented on a network.

Function	Description
File server	A centralized computer that stores common network files and users' data files
Print server	A centralized computer that manages the printers connected to the network, the print queues, and the printing of user documents on the network printers
Communications server	A centralized computer that handles common communications functions for the network, such as e-mail, fax, dial-up modem, or Internet services
Application server	A centralized computer that shares network-enabled versions of common application software, eliminating the need for the software to be installed on each workstation
Database server	A centralized computer that manages a common database for the network, handling all data storage, database management, and requests for data

Table 20-1. The Common Server Types Implemented on a Local Area Network

CABLING

The part of a network cable that carries data is normally one of two materials: copper or glass. Both copper and glass are relatively inexpensive and abundant, but more importantly they are excellent conductors. A conductor is a material through which electricity easily passes. Copper is a great conductor of electricity, and glass is a very good conduit for light.

In order for one computer to carry on a conversation with another computer, both computers must be able to transmit and receive electrical impulses representing commands or data. In a networked environment, the computers and peripherals of the network are interconnected with a transmission medium (usually a cable—more on this later) to enable data exchange and resource sharing. Cable media is the foundation on which networks exist—literally.

Cable Types

A network typically uses one of three standard cable types: coaxial, twisted pair, or fiber optic. Twisted pair is by far the most commonly used network medium, but the other cable types have their place as well.

- **Coaxial (coax) cable** Coax cable is similar to the cable used to connect a television set to the cable outlet. There are two types of coax cable used in networks: thick and thin. Thin coax (also called thinnet and thin wire) remains common for many networking environments, such as in damp and dusty places, but it is slowly giving way to twisted pair. Thick coax (also called thicknet, thick wire, and yellow wire) is rarely used today in LAN situations.

  Coaxial cable is constructed with a single solid copper wire core, which is surrounded by an insulator made of plastic or Teflon material. A braided metal shielding layer (and in some cables, another metal foil layer) covers the insulator, and a plastic sheath wrapper covers the cable. The metal shielding layers act to increase the cable's resistance to electromagnetic interference (EMI) and radio frequency interference (RFI) signals. Figure 20-3 shows a piece of coaxial cable and its construction. The connector shown in Figure 20-3 is a BNC (Bayonet Neil-Concelman) type, which is the common connector for coaxial cable.

- **Twisted pair copper** Twisted pair cable is also available in two types: unshielded twisted pair (UTP) and shielded twisted pair (STP). UTP is similar to the wiring used to connect your telephone. STP is the cable media of choice in certain situations where the wire must pass near other electrical components and is preferred for token ring networks (see "Network Topologies" later in this chapter).

Figure 20-3. BNC (Bayonet Neil-Concelman) type cable

- **Fiber optic** Glass fibers carry modulated pulses of light to represent digital data signals. Light travels through a fiber optic cable much faster than electrical impulses through a copper cable, which is why fiber optic cable is used for the long line portion of WANs and carrying signals between cities.

Cable Characteristics

All network cabling has a set of general characteristics that can be used to pick the right cable for a given networking situation. For a wide majority of networks the cable choice is UTP, but there are instances when UTP may not be appropriate. Here are the characteristics you should consider when making a cable choice:

- **Bandwidth (speed)** This is the number of data in bits, typically kilobits or megabits, a cable can transmit in a second. For example, UTP cable is nominally rated at 10 Mbps, or ten million bits per second.
- **Cost** This is always a major consideration when choosing a cable type. Twisted pair cable is the least expensive, but it has limitations that require other hardware to be installed. Coaxial cable is a little more expensive than twisted pair; it doesn't require additional equipment and it is inexpensive to maintain. Fiber optic cabling is the most expensive, requires skilled installation labor, and can be difficult to install and maintain.
- **Maximum segment length** When data is transmitted over any cable, there is a distance at which the transmitted signal begins to weaken and needs to be reenergized to prevent data errors. This is called *attenuation*, and it is the natural tendency for a signal to weaken as it travels over a cable. This distance (normally expressed in meters) is the maximum segment length for a cable medium or the distance at which signals on the cable must be regenerated.
- **Maximum number of nodes per segments** Adding a node to the network cable reduces its attenuation point, much like punching holes in a water hose eventually causes no water to reach the end of the hose. Each cable type limits the number of nodes it can support in a given distance (its maximum segment length) so it can provide its full bandwidth to all nodes.
- **Resistance to interference** The different cable media resist electromagnetic interference (EMI) or radio frequency interference (RFI) in varying degrees. EMI and RFI are caused by electric motors, fluorescent light fixtures, and other electrically noisy devices located near the network cable. As the construction of the cable and its cladding (covering) varies, so does its resistance to EMI and RFI signals.

Table 20-2 lists the characteristics of thin and thick coaxial cable, unshielded twisted pair cable, and fiber optic cable.

Cable Type	Bandwidth	Max. Segment Length	Max. Nodes/ Segment	Resistance to Interference
Thin coaxial	10 Mbps	185 meters	30	Good
Thick coaxial	10 Mbps	500 meters	100	Better
UTP	10–100 Mbps	100 meters	1,024	Poor
STP	16–1,000 Mbps	100 meters	1,024	Fair to good
Fiber optic	100–10,000 Mbps	2,000 meters	No limit	Best

Table 20-2. Network Cable Media Characteristics

Ethernet Cable Designations

In the Ethernet world, cable media is designated with a code that is descriptive of the cable's characteristics. Thick coax cable is designated as 10Base5, thin coaxial cable is 10Base2, and UTP is generally 10BaseT. The 10Base part indicates that these cables carry 10 Mbps bandwidths and that they carry baseband (digital) signals. For coax cable, the 5 and 2 mean 500 meters and 200 meters, respectively, the approximate maximum segment length of the cable. The *T* in 10BaseT refers to twisted pair cable. Fiber optic cable is designated as 10BaseF.

There are also 100 Mbps versions for faster network designations, including:

- **100BaseT** Along with 100BaseX, the generic term for *Fast Ethernet*
- **100BaseTX** A two-pair wire version of 100BaseT
- **100BaseT4** A four-pair wire version of Fast Ethernet
- **100BaseFX** Fast Ethernet using two-strand fiber optic cable
- **100BaseVG** A 100 Mbps standard over Category 3 cable (see the next section for an explanation of the categories of cable)
- **100BaseVG-AnyLAN** Hewlett-Packard's proprietary version of 100BaseVG

Broadband versus Baseband

Baseband networks use only one channel to support digital transmissions. This type of network signaling uses twisted pair cabling. Most LANs are baseband networks.

Broadband networks use analog signaling over a wide range of frequencies. This type of network is unusual, but many cable companies now offer high-speed Internet network access over broadband systems.

Twisted Pair Wire

Unshielded twisted pair (UTP) or 10BaseT cabling, shown in Figure 20-4, is the cable type most commonly used on LANs. Of the three most popular cabling media choices, UTP provides the most installation flexibility and ease of maintenance.

The Electronics Industries Association and the Telecommunications Industries Association (EIA/TIA) defines UTP cable in five categories, or "cats" as they are commonly referred to (as in *Cat 3* or *Cat 5*). The cables defined in Categories 1 and 2 are not used in networking, but here is a description of the three that are.

- **Category 3** A 4-pair (8-wire) cable that supports bandwidth up to 10 Mbps—the minimum standard for 10BaseT networks
- **Category 4** A 4-pair cable commonly used in 16 Mbps token ring networks
- **Category 5** A 4-pair cable with bandwidth up to 100 Mbps used for 100BaseT networks

The RJ-45 connector used with twisted pair cable is very much like the one used on your telephone. Figure 20-5 shows an RJ-45 connector.

The other type of twisted pair is shielded twisted pair (STP) cable. It is easy to tell shielded cable from unshielded cable: STP has each wire pair wrapped with a grounded copper or foil wrapper (see Figure 20-6) that helps to shield it from interference. The shielding makes STP more expensive than UTP, but it does support higher transmission speeds and carry signals over longer distances.

Fiber Optic Cable

Fiber optic cable carries data in the form of modulated pulses of light. To simulate how data travels through a fiber optic cable, you would need to turn a flashlight on and off about two million times in one second. The core of fiber optic cable consists of two (or

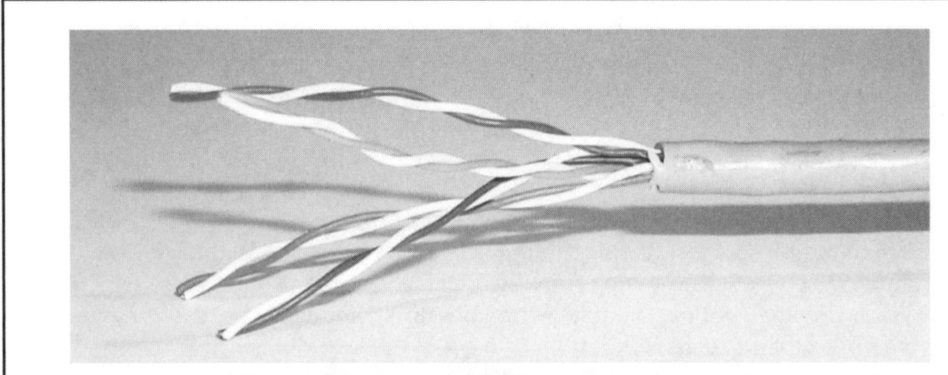

Figure 20-4. Unshielded twisted pair wire (UTP)

Figure 20-5. An RJ-45 connector is used with twisted pair cabling

more) extremely thin strands of glass. Glass cladding covers each strand, helping to keep the light in the strand. Light is carried one way only on each strand because there is no way to send light in two directions simultaneously on a single strand. The two core strands carry light either up or down the cable run. A plastic outer jacket covers the cable. Figure 20-7 shows the makeup of a fiber optic cable.

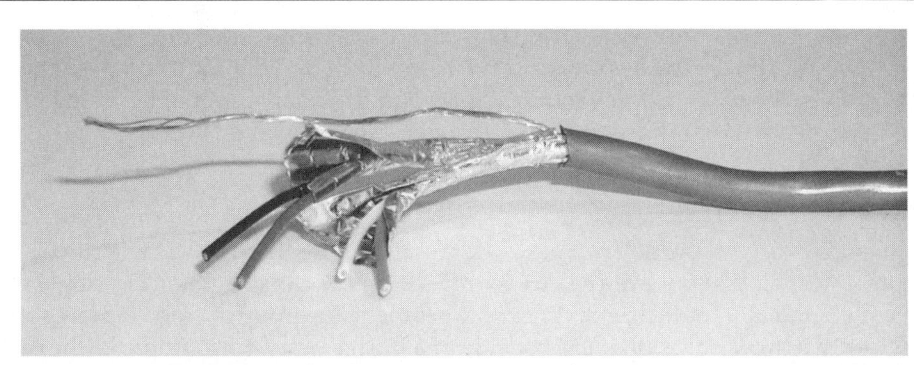

Figure 20-6. The foil wrapper of shielded twisted pair (STP) cable

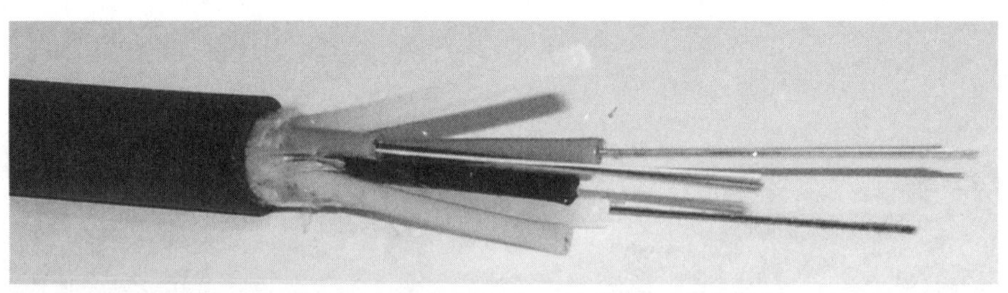

Figure 20-7. The makeup of a fiber optic cable

Because it uses light and not electrical signals, fiber optic cable is not susceptible to EMI or RFI, which gives it incredibly long attenuation and maximum segment lengths. Network backbones commonly use fiber optic cable.

BACKBONES AND SEGMENTS

The cable that runs the entire length of a LAN and interconnects all the computers, printers, servers, and other devices of the network is called the backbone. The network backbone connects and interconnects all of a network's resources and serves as the trunk line for the entire network. Cables commonly used for backbones are 10Base5, 10BaseF, 10BaseT, 100BaseFX, and 100BaseTX.

FDDI

Network backbones commonly use Fiber Distributed Data Interface (FDDI) technology. FDDI is commonly pronounced "F-D-D-I," but some pronounce it "fiddy." FDDI is a 100 Mbps fiber optic network access method that is excellent for moving traffic around the trunk of a network.

FDDI implements networks as two rings. You can attach workstations to one or both rings of the backbone. The two rings serve as redundant network trunks—if one ring breaks or fails, the other takes over, routing around the trouble spot. If both rings break, the remaining pieces bond together to form a new ring.

Segments

A segment is a discrete portion of a network, usually represented by a single run of cable, a group of workstations, or even a LAN within a WAN. A cable segment is a single run of cable with terminators at each end. A network segment is a group of workstations, servers, or devices that are isolated on the other side of a bridge or router to improve the overall network's performance or security.

Segments are created on a network to improve network performance or security. Installing a bridge, router, or switch (see the following section for information on these networking devices) at strategic locations on a network creates network segments.

NETWORKING DEVICES

A variety of networking devices is used on networks to improve the network's performance, to extend the effective range of its media, or to overcome hardware limitations. The following sections cover the most commonly used networking devices.

Repeaters

A repeater is the simplest of the networking devices. A repeater is an electronic echo machine that has no other function. It simply retransmits whatever it receives on one port out the other port, reenergizing the signal's strength. Repeaters are used to extend the maximum segment length of the network cabling and protect against attenuation. By regenerating the signal before the maximum segment length of the cable media is reached, the reenergized signal is able to reach its destination.

Hubs

As illustrated in Figure 20-8, a hub is a networking device used to connect PCs, workstations, and peripheral devices to the network. Each workstation or device is plugged into one of the hub's ports along with a connection to the network's backbone. In general, a hub receives a signal from one port and passes it on to all of its other ports and to whatever is attached to these ports. For example, if an 8-port hub receives a signal on port 4, it immediately passes the signal to ports 1, 2, 3, 5, 6, 7, and 8.

Hubs are commonly used on Ethernet twisted pair networks, especially 10BaseT and 100BaseT configurations. A typical hub is configured with 8, 16, or 24 ports. There are four types of hubs used on networks:

- **Active hub** Acts like a repeater to amplify the signal being passed on and serves as a traffic cop to avoid signal collisions.
- **Passive hub** Passes along the signal without amplifying it.
- **Hybrid hub** Can mix media types (thin coax, thick coax, and twisted pair) and serve as an interconnect for other hubs. Fiber optic cable requires a transceiver, so hubs do not typically support it.
- **Smart (intelligent) hub** An active hub with a bigger brain. Smart hubs include some administrative interface, often SNMP (Simple Network Management Protocol) support or the ability to segment the ports into different logical networks.

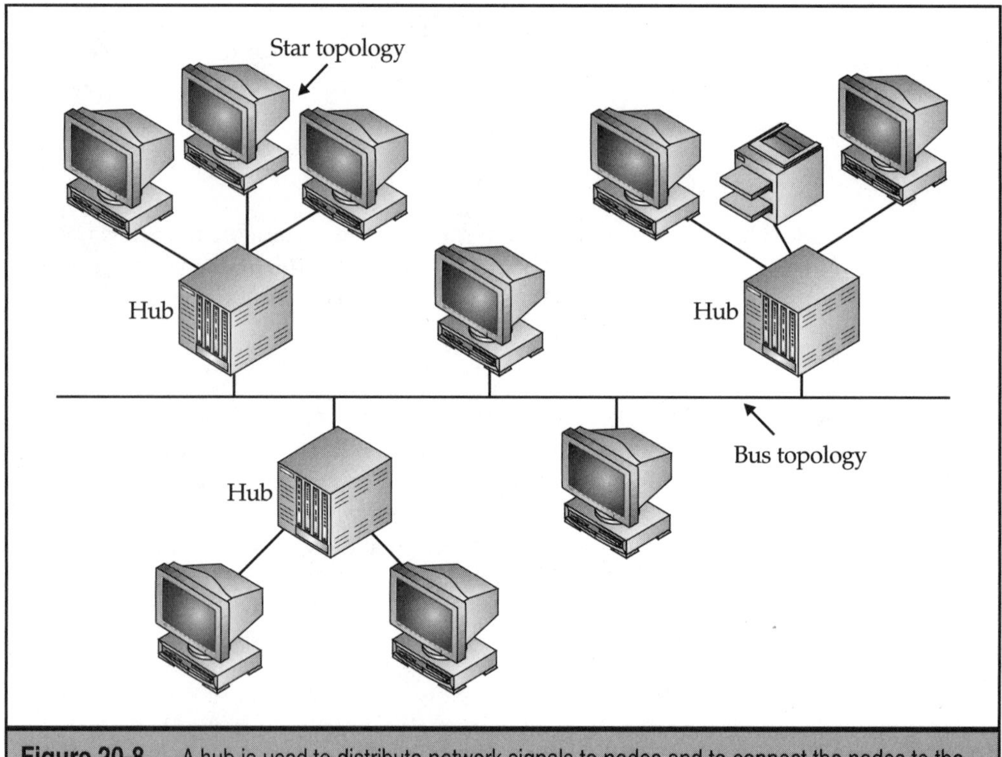

Figure 20-8. A hub is used to distribute network signals to nodes and to connect the nodes to the network backbone

Bridges

A bridge is used to connect two different LANs or two similar network segments so that they appear to be one network. A bridge builds a bridging table of the addresses located on each side of itself, so it can intelligently send messages to the correct network or network segment for delivery. Network node addressing is covered later in this chapter.

Because a bridge sends messages only to the part of the network on which the destination node exists, the overall affect of a bridge on a network is reduced network traffic and a reduction of message bottlenecks.

Switches

A network switch is used like a bridge to connect network segments together to form a single network or larger network segment. A switch can be characterized as a very smart hub. Switches are steadily gaining ability and the newer versions perform some of the same bridging and router functions of bridges and routers.

Routers

A router directs, or routes, network messages across one or more networks. A router determines the best path a message should take to its destination based on the address of the destination.

Routers are also used to control broadcast storms on a network. Network nodes often do not know the address of a workstation or node to which it wants to send data, so it sends a broadcast message to the network addressed to no specific node, but to all nodes at the same time. When too many workstations broadcast too many messages to the whole network, the result is a *broadcast storm*. A router helps prevent broadcast storms by routing messages only to certain segments of the network.

Gateways

A gateway, which is usually a combination of hardware and software, enables two networks using different transmission protocols to communicate with one another. Gateways are used in a number of situations involving the conversion of the characteristics on one network to another, including architecture, protocols, and language.

Three different types of gateways exist:

- **Address gateway** Connects networks using different addressing schemes, directory structures, and file management techniques, such as a Microsoft network to a Novell NetWare network.
- **Protocol gateway** Connects networks that use different protocols. This is the most common gateway. An example of a protocol gateway is a router that interconnects a LAN to the Internet.
- **Format gateway** Connects networks using different data format schemes, for example, one using the American Standard Code for Information Interchange (ASCII) and another using Extended Binary-Coded Decimal Interchange Code (EBCDIC). This type of gateway is used to connect a PC to a mainframe computer.

Network Interface Cards (NICs)

The most basic of network connectivity devices is the network interface card (NIC), also called a network adapter. A NIC, which is pronounced as "nick," is the device that is installed in every PC or peripheral device to attach it to the network cabling and to connect it to the network operating system and protocols. The primary purpose of the NIC is to transmit and receive data to and from other NICs.

Here are some of the major characteristics of a NIC:

- **MAC (Media Access Control) address** Each NIC is physically encoded with a unique identifying address when it is manufactured. A NIC's MAC address is used to identify it on the network.

- **System resources** A NIC is configured to the computer with an IRQ, an I/O address, and a DMA channel. A NIC commonly uses IRQ3, IRQ5, or IRQ10 and an I/O address of 300h.
- **Transceiver type** Some NICs are capable of attaching to more than one media type, such as UTP and coaxial. Each different cable medium requires a different type of transceiver, the device that transmits and receives data from the network.
- **Data bus compatibility** NICs are designed with compatibility to a particular data bus architecture. Most newer NICs are PCI (Peripheral Component Interconnect), but there are still many ISA (Industry Standard Architecture) legacy NICs still in use.

NIC Connectors

Often the media type in use on the network controls other hardware decisions, such as the NIC itself and the type and style of connectors linking it to the network media. Table 20-3 lists the connectors used by each of the popular media types.

NETWORK TOPOLOGIES

A network's topology defines two things. The first is the network's general shape and arrangement. The second is the technologies used to support the network. The most common topology in use is the bus (which is generally referred to as Ethernet, the most common type of bus network) and ring (most commonly called Token Ring, after the IBM implementation that is commonly used) topologies.

Here is a brief description of each of the most common network topologies:

- **Bus/Ethernet** Nodes are connected to hubs or switches, which are in turn connected to a central backbone cable that runs the length of the network. The bus topology is commonly used for Ethernet networks. Refer back to Figure 20-8 for an illustration of how the bus topology is typically implemented.

Media	Connectors Used
Thinnet	BNC (Bayonet Neil-Concelman) connectors
Thicknet	AUI (Attachment Unit Interface) connectors
UTP	RJ-45
Fiber optic	ST connectors

Table 20-3. Cable Media and Associated Connectors

- **Ring/Token Ring** The primary network cable is installed as a loop, or *ring,* and the workstations are attached to the primary cable at points on the ring. The ring topology is the basis for the token ring network structure. Figure 20-9 illustrates a ring topology. On a token ring network, PCs are attached to devices called multiaccess units, which are very similar to a hub, as in the arrangement shown in Figure 20-8.
- **Star** Each workstation is connected directly to the central server with its own cable, creating a starburst-like pattern. The star topology, common to ARCNet networks, is used today with both Ethernet and token ring networks to cluster workstations with hubs, which are then attached to the primary network cable. Figures 20-8 and 20-10 illustrate this arrangement.

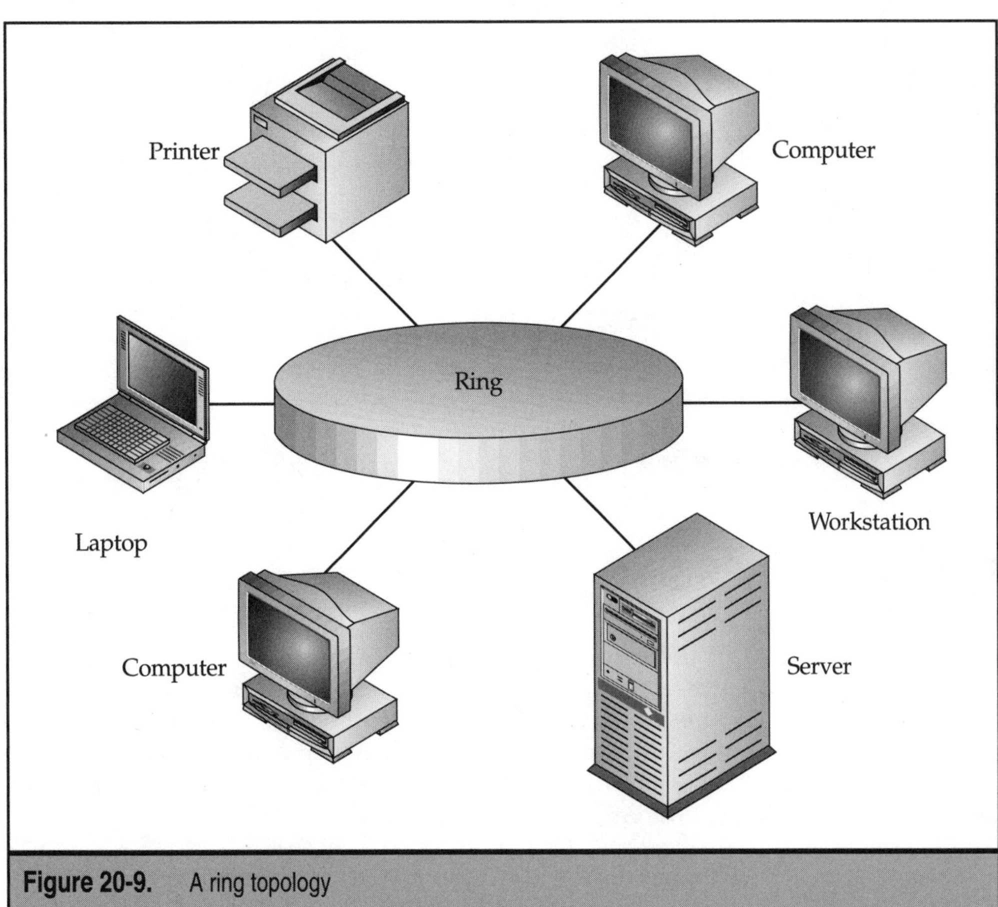

Figure 20-9. A ring topology

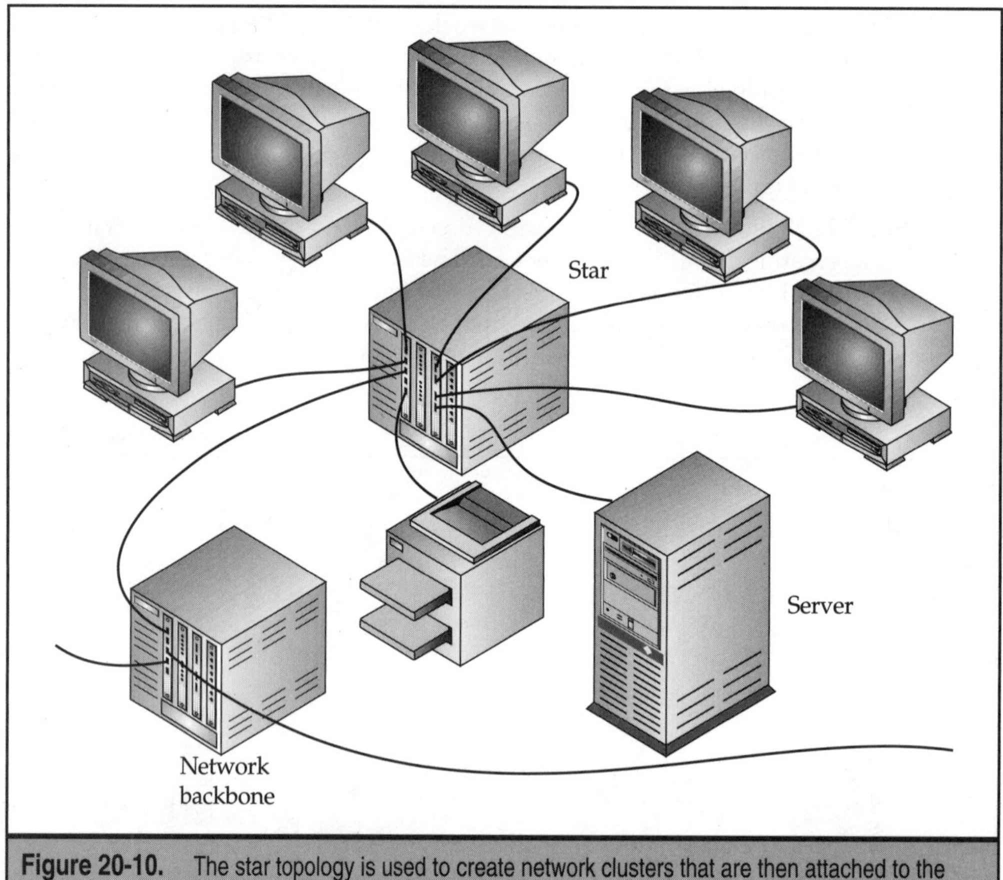

Figure 20-10. The star topology is used to create network clusters that are then attached to the network backbone

NETWORK ADDRESSING

Although this is a hardware book, the network addressing scheme used is something that should be included in any discussion on networking. There are essentially two levels of addressing used on a network: physical and logical. The physical addressing is the MAC (media access control) address that is burned into a NIC or network adapter by its manufacturer. The elements of logical addressing are the share names assigned to devices on the network and, if the TCP/IP (Transmission Control Protocol/Internet Protocol) protocols are in use, the IP (Internet Protocol) address of each network node.

MAC Addresses

Every NIC and network adapter is assigned an ID code that is unique to the world, called the MAC (media access control) address, by its manufacturer. The MAC address is burned into the firmware of the NIC and cannot be changed. The MAC address is the basis for all LAN addressing, and all other address types are cross-referenced to it. A MAC address is a 48-bit address that is expressed as 12 hexadecimal digits (4 bits to a hex digit). Figure 20-11 shows the display from a WINIPCFG (Windows 98) command that includes the MAC address (listed as the adapter address) of a NIC installed on a PC. The MAC address of this PC is 44-45-53-54-00-00. The first three segments identify the manufacturer and the remainder is a serial number for the NIC.

To display the MAC address on your Windows 98 PC, choose Start | Run and, in the Open box, enter WINIPCFG and click OK.

IP Addresses

Many LANS and virtually all WANs use IP (Internet Protocol) addresses to identify their nodes. An IP address for a network workstation combines the address of the network and the node into a 32-bit address that is expressed in four 8-bit octets (which means sets of eight). Figure 20-12 shows the display of an IPCONFIG command that includes the IP addressing information for a networked PC. IPCONFIG displays the IP address assigned to the workstation (in this case, 192.168.1.100), its subnet mask (which is used to determine how much of the address is used to designate the network or the node), and the default gateway of the node.

IP addresses consist of four numbers separated by periods (dots). An IP address is 32 bits long with each of the four numbers being eight bits long. The highest possible IP address is 255.255.255.255, because the highest value that can be represented in eight bits is 255. Each of the four numbers is called an octet, and they are referred to as the first, second, third, and fourth octets.

IP addresses can be assigned as a static IP address (a fixed PC location) or as a dynamically assigned IP address (changeable). A static IP address is permanently assigned to a node when it is added to the network. Static IP addresses work as long as the network or the node doesn't change; for example, a static IP address would not work if a PC's NIC card changed or the network was reconfigured. Dynamic IP addresses are assigned each

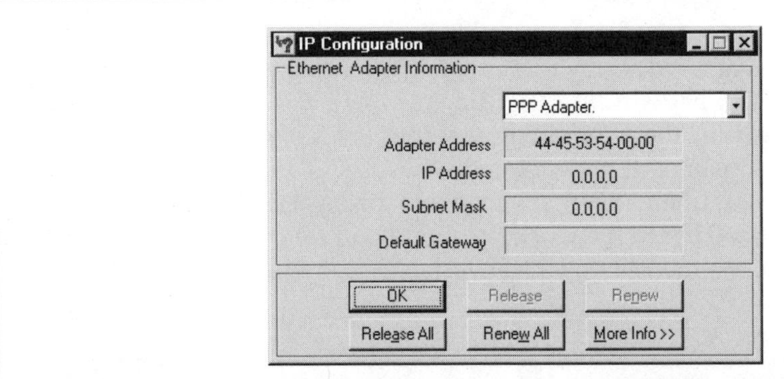

Figure 20-11. The WINIPCFG command displays the MAC (Adapter) address of a PC's NIC

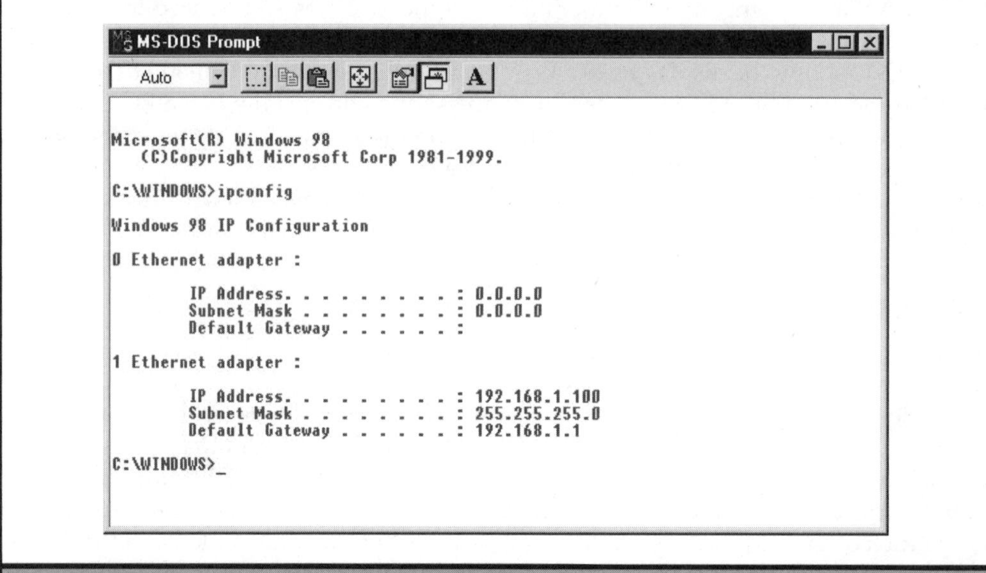

Figure 20-12. The IPCONFIG command is used to display the IP address configuration of a PC

time the PC is booted through the Dynamic Host Configuration Protocol (DHCP). The DHCP server assigns each workstation an IP address to use for that session. All versions of Windows 9*x* and Windows NT/2000 have built-in DHCP clients.

To check the IP address assignment on your networked PC, open an MS-DOS command prompt and enter IPCONFIG on the command line.

Network Names

Every PC and most of the other devices on a Windows network are assigned a NetBIOS (Network Basic Input Output System) name, which is also called a network name. The most common form of a network name is the share name assigned to a workstation and used to identify it to other network users wishing to share its resources over the LAN. Windows builds a table using the WINS (Windows Internet Name Service) that correlates the IP and NetBIOS names of each network node.

The NetBIOS name is a unique 15-character name that is periodically broadcast over the network to be cataloged by the Network Neighborhood function. The NetBIOS name is the one that shows up on the Windows Network Neighborhood.

CONFIGURING A PC FOR NETWORK CONNECTION

Windows 2000 will automatically configure a PC with a typical network setup during its installation processes. However, a Windows 9*x* PC does not have that feature, and the software side of the configuration must be performed by hand. Actually, the NIC is configured to the network; the PC communicates only to the NIC through its device driver.

Four network components can be configured from the Network window:

- **Adapter** This choice identifies and loads the device drivers for a NIC. To configure a PC to a network, a NIC must be installed.
- **Protocol** A protocol is a set of rules that communicating devices must follow when transmitting data, controls, and commands to one another. To communicate with a network, the PC must be using the same protocols as the network.
- **Client** Network clients allow a PC to communicate with specific network operating systems, like Windows NT/2000 or Novell NetWare. To communicate with the network, a PC must have at least one client configured.
- **Service** Network services include specialized drivers that facilitate specialized capabilities, such as file and print Sharing, and support for file systems on non-Windows systems.

DIALING UP A NETWORK

A modem (which is an acronym for modulator/demodulator) converts the digital data signal of the PC into the analogy data signal used on the POTS (plain old telephone system, also called the *public telephone switched network* [PTSN]). Modems can be installed inside the PC in an expansion slot or attached to the PC externally through a serial or USB port.

Modem Types

Nearly all modems used with a PC perform the same tasks and use the same protocols. Where they differ is in the device drivers they use. There are two general types of modems, standard and Windows-only modems:

- **Standard modem** A standard modem can be an internal or external device. It can also be Plug and Play or legacy. Standard modems are operating system–neutral and use generic device drivers.
- **Windows modem** A Windows modem is an internal Plug-and-Play device that requires a device driver provided by the Windows operating system to function properly.

The best way to differentiate one type of modem from another is through the documentation that comes with the system or to visit the manufacturer's Web site.

Internal versus External Modems

An internal modem is installed like any other expansion card into a compatible expansion slot. Most of the internal modems currently sold do not require much physical configuration, but there are some that still require DIP switches or jumpers to be set to select the transmission speed and to designate the COM port to be used. It is common for most of the configuration of an internal modem to be done through the operating system. For example, Windows has the Modem Wizard that can be used to install a non-Plug and Play (PnP) modem. PnP modems are typically installed and configured automatically by the operating system and BIOS.

An external modem is attached to the PC through one of its COM ports. About the only configuration issue involved with installing and configuring an external modem is possible system resource conflicts, especially conflicts with the IRQ (interrupt request).

External modems are connected to the PC through a cable called a null modem cable. Many external modem kits include this cable; if it doesn't, all computer stores sell them.

AT Commands

Virtually all PC-compatible modems are also Hayes Standard AT command set–compatible. This command set provides you with the ability to control the functions and settings of the modem directly through a modem interface or from a scripted set of commands.

AT does not mean Advanced Technology, as it would with a motherboard or power supply. On a modem, AT refers to "attention," which is used to precede each command given the modem from the AT command set. Table 20-4 lists some of the more commonly used AT commands. Remember that each command is preceded with AT.

Command	Action
A0	Answer incoming call
A/	Repeat last command
DT XXX-XXX	Dial the telephone number using touch-tone dialing
H	On hook (hang up)
L	Speaker loudness (volume)
M	Mute (speaker off)
Z	Reset the modem to default settings
&X	Advanced configuration commands, where X is a command letter

Table 20-4. Sample Commands in the Modem AT Command Set

Dial-up Connections

Windows PCs control a modem through the Dial-up Networking (DUN) utility. DUN has a built-in dialer applet that is invoked whenever an application, such as a browser or an e-mail client, is opened. The dialers send to the modem the commands needed to dial up a remote modem and make a connection. The speed of a dial-up connection is typically between 28.8 Kbps and 56 Kbps.

When two PCs directly connect over a modem-to-modem connection, a process called a handshake must take place to set up the connection for the length of the session. The handshake process includes a series of signals that are passed between the two modems. See Chapter 19 for more information on the handshaking process.

When you call your ISP, you are assigned an IP address through its NAS (network access services) or modem banks and the ISP's RADIUS (Remote Authentication Dial-In User Service) services. Once you have been authenticated through a username and password combination, an IP address is assigned to your PC and you are able to communicate over the Internet WAN.

Messages are sent from one PC to another over a network in the form of network packets, regardless of whether the network is a LAN, WAN, or another type of network. A packet holds one portion of the whole message along with the IP addresses of the sender and the destination PC. The TCP/IP protocols break up the original message and create the packets so that the message can be transmitted over the network media. At the receiving end, the protocols reassemble the message from the packets and send it to the destination PC.

Dial-up networking uses the Point-to-Point Protocol (PPP) to send packets over PSTN lines. PPP inserts the packet created by the sending protocols into a PPP packet and carries it over the transmission. At the receiving end, the original packet is removed from the PPP packet and passed to the processing protocols. PPP is merely the intermediary that carries the data packet over the telephone line. If the packet begins the journey as a packet from TCP/IP, IPX (Internetwork Packet Exchange), or another protocol, it arrives at its destination as a packet from that protocol.

Troubleshooting Modem Connections

A dial-up connection that will not connect has several areas that should be included in the troubleshooting:

- **Phone connection** Nearly all modems use sound to allow the user to track the action of the connection (handshake) as it is being made. The first of these sounds is the dial tone from the phone line. If the modem is not connecting and you do not hear a dial tone, chances are there is a problem with the wall jack connection or the phone line itself. You will probably get an error message to the effect that you have no dial tone.
- **Modem problems** If the modem cannot complete the handshake with the other end, it could be that the modem is configured incorrectly in terms of its character length, start and stop bits, and speed.

- **Protocols** Another common problem, especially for new modems, is that TCP/IP or other protocols have not been properly configured. Dial-up connections typically require the PPP protocol. Verify that the protocols are enabled and that the proper bindings are set for the protocols.
- **Remote response** It could be that the NAS you are attempting to connect to is down or having problems. Call the ISP to check.
- **Telephone company problems** If there is sufficient static or crosstalk on the telephone line, it can cause the modem to disconnect very soon after completing the connection or cause enough data retransmissions that the line appears exceptionally slow.

DIGITAL SUBSCRIBER LINES (DSL)

DSL transmits high-speed Internet data over a standard telephone line. Depending on the type of DSL service subscribed to, data speeds can range from 128 Kbps (for IDSL—ISDN over DSL) to 1.1 Mbps (for SDSL—symmetrical DSL). The most common DSL service is ADSL (asymmetrical DSL), which is available to many more homes and businesses than the other forms of DSL.

DSL service is very distance dependent. All DSL services emanate from a telephone company (called the ILEC or Incumbent Local Exchange Carrier) central office. The central office (CO) is where the telephone switching takes place in a town or a portion of a city; the CO is where you connect to other exchanges and long distance service. Your distance from the CO (as measured along the path of the copper wiring that runs from the CO to your house or office) determines the type of DSL service you are able to get. Although distances vary by ILEC, in general SDSL is available up to about 10,000 feet away; ADSL is available up to about 18,000 feet away; and IDSL up to 24,000 feet away. ADSL is a best-effort service, which means that although a data speed is given, the speed realized will depend on a number of network factors. SDSL and IDSL are committed-information-rate (CIR) services that carry guarantees of data transmission rates.

DSL is available only to those locations that have twisted pair copper wiring all the way from the CO. In many situations, the phone companies have used fiber optic cable to run to a distribution box in an area and then run copper wire to each home or building. Any circuit that has fiber optic cabling is not eligible for DSL service—at least, not yet.

One difference between DSL and a legacy dial-up connection is that DSL is always on. The connection is a permanent circuit back to the CO and then through the DSL provider's DSLAM (DSL Access Multiplexer—pronounced "dee-slam") and out to the Internet. The bad news about it being always on is that is it is also always open, which is why a PC connected to a DSL connection should be running firewall software. A firewall protects the PC from unwanted outside intrusions.

When DSL is installed in your home or business, there may be as many as three companies involved in the installation: the local phone company (the ILEC), the DSL provider (the company that placed the DSLAM in the CO), and a local or regional ISP. The phone company verifies that a twisted pair copper line is available for the location; the DSL provider installs the inside wiring to your PC; and the ISP provides the Internet service. If you buy your DSL from the ILEC, you are dealing with a single entity, but the price may be higher and the installation time longer—DSL is not the ILEC's primary business. Most DSL providers do not sell directly to consumers and use ISPs to resell their services. In these cases, the ILEC still must do its part, but the other companies provide the DSL and Internet. This arrangement results in faster installations and in most cases, lower prices.

Many areas now have a technology called "line-sharing" that allows you to use a single phone line for both voice (telephone) and data (DSL). This results in much lower costs, since a second phone line is no longer required and relatively instantaneous installations are available.

DSL Modems, Bridges, and Routers

Most home users who use DSL subscribe to ADSL (asymmetrical DSL), which transmits and sends at different speeds. The customer premise equipment (CPE) for ADSL service is typically an external DSL modem, or bridge, that is attached to a PC through a twisted pair cable and an RJ-45 connector into a NIC installed in the PC. The NIC, the cable, and the connector are the same as would be used for a PC on a LAN. The DSL modem bridges the data from the phone line to a format usable by the NIC and PC. The DSL modem can also be an internal card that is installed in a PCI slot inside the PC. An internal DSL modem does not require a NIC.

SDSL (symmetrical DSL), which sends and receives at the same speed, is usually used to connect a network to DSL and uses a router as its CPE. ADSL service can also be connected through a router, but in most cases the bandwidth is not sufficient for this purpose. A router allows several PCs to share the DSL bandwidth.

CABLE MODEMS

Another way to access the Internet is through a cable modem connection using the cable TV system that most likely already is connected to your home. Cable service is similar to ADSL service, in that it provides higher download speeds and lower upload speeds. Cable Internet access uses a modem, usually an external device, that connects the PC to the cable lines that carry the signal back to what is called the cable head-end where it connects to the Internet.

The real benefit of a cable modem is that you can get high-speed Internet access and keep your phone line free—and you can still watch TV while you are surfing the Net. It is very rare to find a cable company that does not also require you to subscribe to cable TV service to also get the cable Internet service. A device called a signal splitter that is supplied by the cable company separates the two signals. The bad news about cable Internet service is that the cable system is a shared system, and when there is heavy cable TV demand, it can impact the speed of Internet data. However, in most cases, the bandwidth is high enough to offset for slow-down on the system.

ISDN TERMINAL ADAPTERS

Before there were DSL or cable modem systems, there was ISDN (Integrated Services Digital Network). ISDN was once thought to be the end-all high-speed access alternative to accessing the Internet over a POTS line.

There are two types of ISDN services: BRI (Basic Rate Interface) and PRI (Primary Rate Interface). BRI is the type of ISDN used for home or small office connections and PRI is used to provide high bandwidth connections for voice and data to larger companies and telecommunications providers.

BRI is also known as single-line service or single-user ISDN. It is configured for home and small-business use and is typically what is referred to as ISDN. BRI connects through a device called a terminal adapter that connects the ISDN line (provided by the phone company) to the ILEC's CO. From there the circuit is connected to an ISP that provides a connection to the Internet.

The ISDN terminal adapter feeds the digital data from the PC directly to the ISDN. The BRI service uses two bearer channels (called B channels) that carry the data signals and one digital channel (called a D channel) that carries the control signaling and other information about the transmission. Each of the B channels carries 64 Kbps or combines to carry 128 Kbps. The B channel carries 16 Kbps, which combines with the D channels to complete the BRI's rate of 144 Kbps. ISDN is capable of transmitting both voice and data signals over the D channels.

WIRELESS NETWORKING

A wireless network uses radio frequency (RF) devices to transmit and receive data between computers and peripheral devices. Because they do not require a physical cable installation to connect nodes to the network, a wireless local area network, or a WLAN (pronounced "W-lan"), provides a great deal of flexibility and a greatly simplified network installation process. To add a new node to the network does not require more cable to be strung through the walls. The node is simply installed with a wireless network adapter card. A WLAN can also be used to overcome structural barriers that may block the installation of cable in a building or area.

Access Points and Network Adapters

The standard that governs wireless networking is the IEEE 802.11, also called the WI-FI (which stands for wireless fidelity) standard. Devices that meet this standard are guaranteed to be interoperable with devices from other manufacturers. The network adapters used to connect a PC to a wireless LAN are called 802.11 cards (see Figure 20-13).

The model for a wireless network is very much like that used for any Ethernet network in which hubs are used to cluster workstations and to connect them to the network backbone. In the case of a wireless network, the hub is an access point (AP). An access point is typically connected to a conventional hard-wired computer network using a

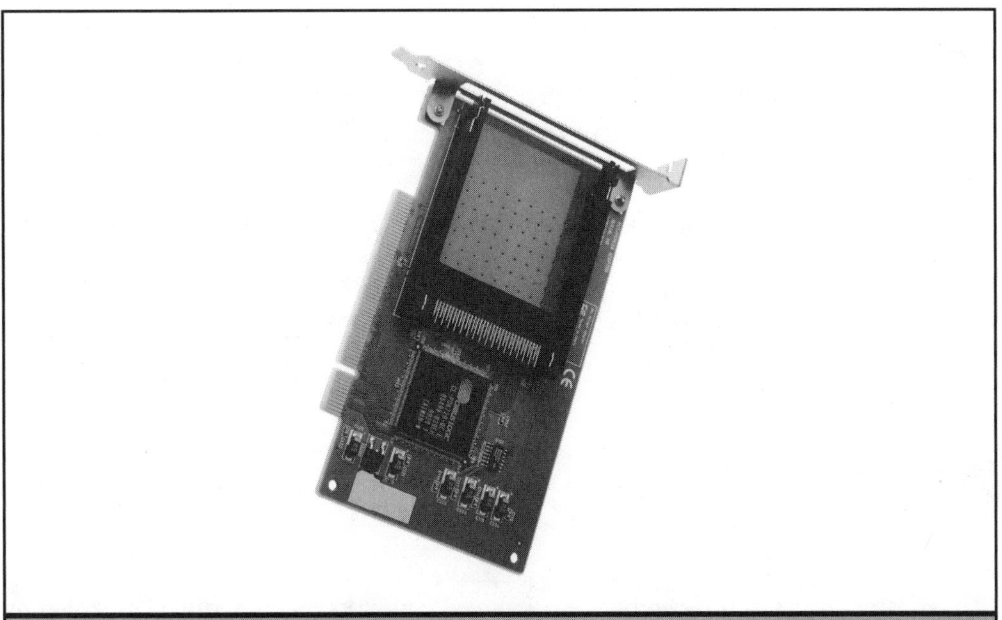

Figure 20-13. An 802.11 (WLAN) network adapter card. Photo courtesy of Nokia

standard 10BaseT (Cat 5) cable. The AP serves as a master station and hub. It transmits and receives data to and from the 802.11 PCI cards in the networked PCs. There are internal cards for PCs, like the one shown in Figure 20-13, as well as 802.11 PC Cards used for notebook and other portable PCs, shown in Figure 20-14. Figure 20-15 shows a WLAN access point, which is typically about the size of an external modem. Access points can be mounted on tabletops, walls, and even ceilings.

The more access points on a network, the better the wireless coverage for the network. In fact, if the access points slightly overlap, it is conceivable that a user could actually walk down a street, move about a conference center, or sit in a café and remain connected to the network and even the Internet.

Another wireless network device, the wireless bridge, is used to connect two hard-wired computer networks that are up to one mile apart. Wireless bridges are used to connect buildings together to form a single network. Wireless network bridges are normally connected to an antenna that is mounted outdoors with a clear line of site to the other bridge's antenna, located on another building.

Bluetooth

Another emerging wireless technology is Bluetooth, which is used to create what is called a wireless personal area network or WPAN (pronounced "W-pan"). (This technology is

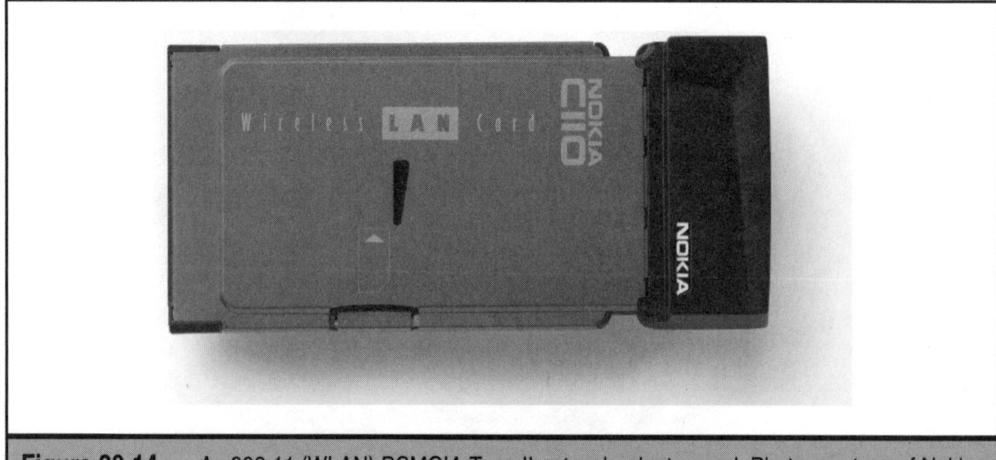

Figure 20-14. An 802.11 (WLAN) PCMCIA Type II network adapter card. Photo courtesy of Nokia

named after the ancient Scandinavian king who united the Scandinavian states by Ericsson, the Swedish communications giant.) Bluetooth is used to connect PCs with external peripheral devices, such as modems and printers. The devices must be within a ten-meter area of the PC, but they do allow for a great deal of flexibility in how personal

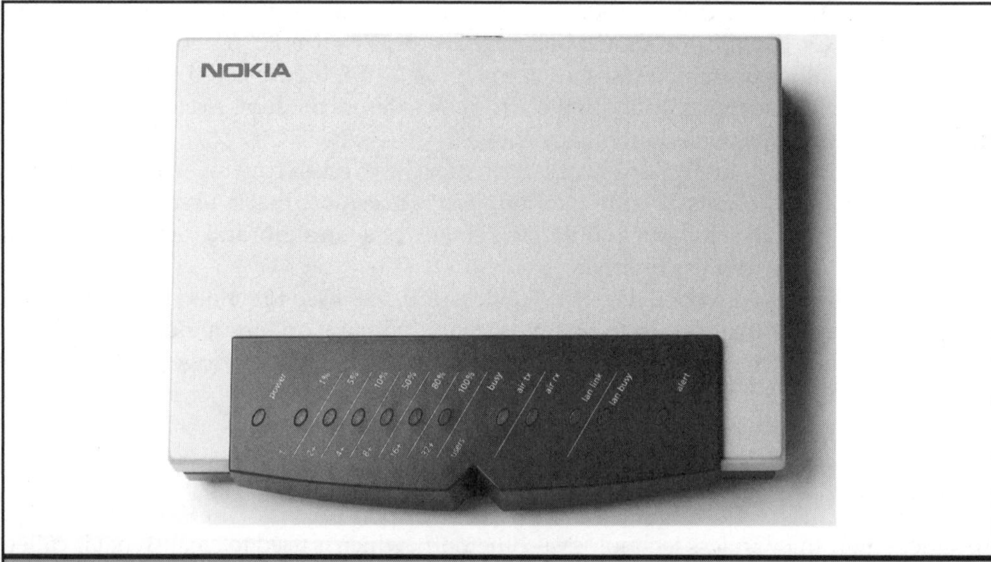

Figure 20-15. An 802.11 (WLAN) network access point. Photo courtesy of Nokia

computing is carried out. Bluetooth technology is capable of being transmitted at 721 Kbps and is very popular with PDAs (personal digital assistants) such as the Palm Pilot and Visor. Bluetooth transceivers are connected to the PC via a USB or serial port. Many devices now come with built-in Bluetooth receivers and transmitters.

One advantage of Bluetooth technology is that the transmissions between Bluetooth devices are encrypted and use frequency hopping (changing frequencies for each transmission), which combine to provide privacy and security for the PC or PDA user.

CHAPTER 21

Audio/Visual Devices

It wasn't all that long ago when the only sounds a PC could produce—other than the noise from the fan and hard disk drives, that is—were a few beeps and tones. Its lone speaker was designed more to signal the user with diagnostic POST (Power-On Self-Test) beep codes and operating system alerts than it was to reproduce high fidelity state-of-the-art sound. Luckily, very few PCs today do not include an adequate to good sound card and a set of speakers. PC sound systems vary from the simple playback of games and system sounds to full-fledged Digital Audio Workstations (DAW) and PC-based entertainment centers available that are capable of professional audio and video production and post-production editing.

Video capability is something still new to the PC. Using the PC as a telephone where you can hear the voice of the other party is one thing, but to actually participate in a real-time see-and-say conversation, now that's something right out of science fiction. Today's computers can be configured to produce simple small frame video playback using special software players, or they can be configured as a DAW for full motion video reproduction. Many PCs now come standard with a DVD (Digital Versatile Disc) player that allows the user to watch full-length theatrical films right on their PC with all the sound quality they can afford.

SOUND ON THE PC

Today, sound is an inherent part of the PC. There are a variety of components common to virtually all PC sound systems: a sound card, an amplifier, speakers, shielding, and drivers and specialized software.

Sound Card

The sound card, also known as an audio adapter, is an expansion card that adds the ability to record and play back sound from internal or external sources. The sound card integrates all of the elements required to capture and reproduce sound. The elements of the sound card are the inputs, outputs, and signal processors, which are the digital to audio converters (DACs) and analog to digital converters (ADCs) required to convert sound into or from digital data.

The sound card typically includes jacks (connectors) to accept sound inputs from a microphone or another sound source, such as a CD player or the like, and output jacks for speakers, amplifiers, or other sound recording equipment. Figure 21-1 shows how the jacks on a sound card are placed so they extend outside of the system case.

Most sound cards, like the one in Figure 21-1, are typically ISA or PCI adapter cards. However, the recent trend is to directly mount a sound chip on the motherboard, which eliminates the need for an audio adapter card.

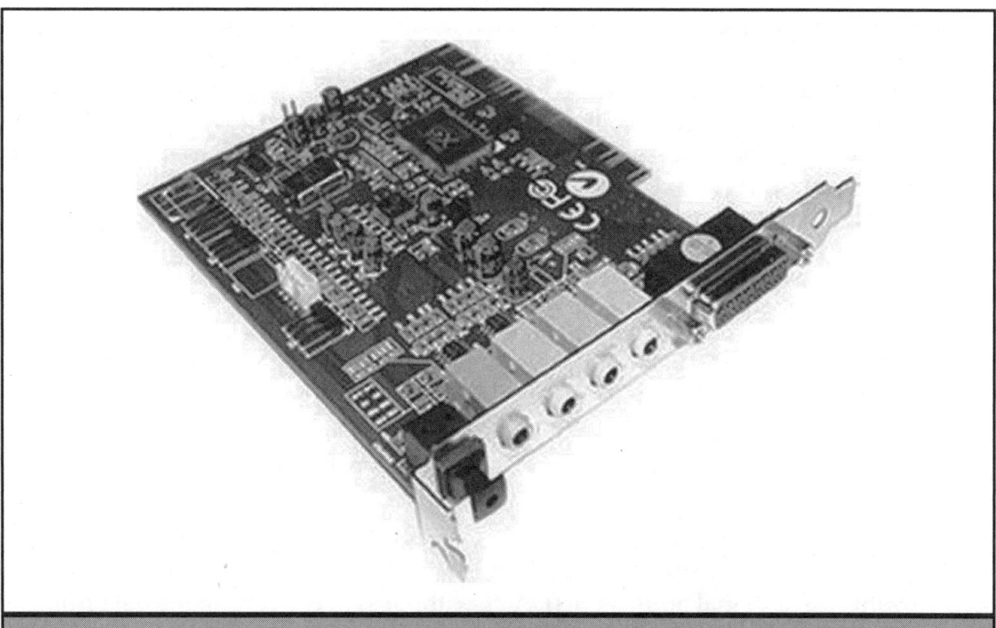

Figure 21-1. The AOpen AW744 Pro sound card. Photo courtesy of AOpen America, Inc.

The components included on the sound card to convert sound into and out of digital data formats are as follows:

- **Digital to analog converter (DAC)** The DAC converts digital audio data from a hard drive or another storage medium into analog sound (normal everyday sound waves) that can be played back on the speakers or a set of headphones.
- **Analog to digital converter (ADC)** An ADC converts analog sound waves, such as a voice or a musical instrument, into digital data so it can be stored, edited, and transmitted. A little later in the chapter, I'll go into why this device and the preceding device are necessary when you work with sound recording and playback on the PC.
- **Analog inputs** Sound cards have two separate analog sound inputs: line-level and microphone-level (a.k.a. mic-level). Line-level inputs accept sound signals from electronic sources such as CD players or tape decks or signals that are directly input from a musical instrument, such as an electronic piano or a synthesizer. There are two separate inputs because microphones produce signals with a much lower voltage level than those from line-level sources. Mic-level inputs are generated from a stand-alone microphone or an unamplified electric guitar plugged into the mic-level input. Line-level inputs are designed to handle the higher voltage signal produced by amplified electronic devices.

The most common connector on analog inputs is the standard 1/8-inch phone jack that is just like those on the earphones of your portable CD or tape player. Professional or more specialized sound cards may include left and right stereo RCA jacks, which are 1/4-inch phone jacks like the ones used to connect earphones to your home stereo components. The RCA jack, named for the early sound pioneering company, is the standard for professional studio equipment.

Other important features and components found on most PC sound cards include:

- **Analog outputs** Most sound cards have two analog output jacks. One, which is usually identified as Phones Out or Speaker Out, (or is marked with a picture to that effect) is powered by a small amplifier on the sound card that is capable of producing the sound for headphones or passive speakers. The other jack, usually labeled as the Line Out jack, produces a line-level signal that can be used as an input to a home-stereo receiver, for example. Like the analog input jacks, 1/8-inch phone jacks are the most common, but higher-end cards use RCA (1/4-inch) phone jacks.
- **Digital I/O (input/output)** This type of connector on a sound card makes it possible to accept input or send output directly to a digital device, such as a MiniDisc or digital audio tape (DAT), without ever converting the data from digital to analog. This eliminates the need for the data to pass through either a DAC or an ADC, which always has the potential to degrade or distort the sound signal. It won't mean much to anyone except a sound engineer, but the most common digital interfaces used on sound cards are S/P-DIF (Sony/Philips Digital Interface) and AES/EBU (Audio Engineering Society/European Broadcasting Union).
- **Game/MIDI port** This connector is commonly used for game controllers such as joysticks or game pads. However, with a special type of cable, this port can be connected to any external MIDI (Musical Instrument Digital Interface) device to send and receive MIDI data. More on MIDI later.
- **Digital Signal Processor (DSP)** Once found only on expensive high-end sound cards, the DSP chip serves only one purpose: to relieve the PC's CPU of the burden for processing audio data. As DSP chips become less expensive and are included in more and more devices, they are now finding their way onto less expensive sound cards. DSP chips are the fastest growing segment of the semiconductor industry as more demand is being generated for sound reproduction in smaller and smaller devices. Among the tasks performed by the DSP chip on a sound card are resampling (changing the bit depth and sample rate of audio data) and adding digital effects such as reverb and echo to an audio piece. Sampling and resampling are discussed later in the chapter.
- **Synthesizer** Unlike digital data that is sent through the DAC to be converted to sound, MIDI signals tell the sound card which sounds to make, at what frequency, and for how long. In order to play back MIDI sounds, the sound

card must be able to generate these sounds using a synthesizer chip. Through MIDI signals, an external MIDI device can control the sound card's synthesizer chip. Synthesizer chips vary widely in capabilities and sound quality, but many newer sound cards now incorporate Wavetable synthesis that produces a higher quality sound by using digital samples of actual instruments in place of other synthesized sounds.

Amplifier

After digital audio data is converted into an audible (analog) signal, it must be amplified before it can be played back on speakers or headphones. Nearly all sound cards have an amplifier that can produce a sound level compatible with a set of headphones or a set of small PC speakers. Because the amplifier on the sound card is usually weak, PC speaker systems may include an amplifier in one or both of its speakers to enhance the sound. By adding the correct cabling and jacks, the sound card's output signal can be sent to your home stereo or home theater, in case you desire very high quality sound reproduction.

Speakers

Like all speakers, PC speakers are categorized into two general groups: passive and active. Passive speakers do not include an amplifier; active speakers do. A passive speaker, which is what most standard PC speakers are, receives a signal that has been amplified enough to generate motion in the speaker's diaphragm and produce sound. An active speaker includes a built-in amplifier and typically does not require external amplifiers. An active speaker can accept low-level (line-level) signals.

Nearly all PC speakers are passive speakers, with the exception of subwoofers. Subwoofers are speakers that generate only very low frequency sounds, like bass tones. A subwoofer usually includes a large built-in amplifier, which makes it an active speaker. The benefit of having a subwoofer on your system is that it will handle all of the low bass sounds, leaving the system's passive speakers and the amplifiers driving them to handle higher-level sounds, which are much easier to reproduce.

Exactly how audio speakers work is beyond the scope of this book, but if you're curious about it, check out Joel Antonini's Audio Visual 101 Web site at **www.audiovideo101.com/learn**.

PC speakers come in a wide range of configurations, from small passive systems powered by the sound card's headphone output to active three-way and surround-sound systems that would rival many home theaters. Some PC monitors have integrated speakers either incorporated into their cases or designed to attach to its sides.

The speakers I have been discussing to this point all connect to the PC via the sound card using 1/8-inch jacks. However, the USB (Universal Serial Bus) speaker system is a recent development. USB speaker systems do not require that a sound card be installed in the PC. Digital audio is sent directly to the speakers via the USB cable, and all signal processing is done within the speaker enclosure itself, outside of the PC. There are many advantages to this type of system, not the least of which are the available expansion slot and reduced sound distortion from the other components inside the PC, but there are also disadvantages. One major disadvantage of USB speakers is that there are no input jacks that can be used to connect external or internal devices like a CD-ROM or DVD player.

Magnetic Shielding

PC speakers typically sit fairly close to the PC. This is for two primary reasons: one, the cords on the speakers are not very long, and two, the PC user wants the sound pointed directly at him or her. Because of their closeness to the PC, PC speaker systems must be magnetically shielded so that their magnets don't distort the screen image on the PC's monitor or possibly damage the monitor permanently. This, more than any other reason, is why you should use caution when using speakers not specifically designed for use on a PC.

Software

Software for audio devices comes on two levels: device control and playback control. Playback control software is used to control a PC device much like you would a stand-alone playback device like a CD or DVD player. Device control software consists of the device drivers that interface to the system BIOS and operating system on behalf of the audio device.

Playback Software

Until recently, CD-ROM drives have had the basic CD-ROM controls on their front panels. These controls include Play, Pause, Stop, Eject, and various forward and reverse controls (see Figure 21-2). However, most of the newer CD-ROM and DVD-ROM drives no longer have these controls, leaving control of the playback to software. Virtually all PC operating systems, including all of Microsoft's Windows versions and the many distributions of Linux, include basic software tools that can be used for recording, playing, and mixing audio from different sources. Advanced tools for recording and manipulating digital audio are available from a variety of software publishers.

Figure 21-2. The display of the Creative Labs PlayCenter playback software

Some of the better-known audio software publishers include:

- **Sonic Foundry** www.sonicfoundry.com
- **Steinberg** www.steinberg.net
- **Cakewalk** www.cakewalk.com
- **RealNetworks** www.real.com
- **Waves** www.waves.com
- **Nullsoft** www.winamp.com
- **Microsoft** www.microsoft.com/windows/windowsmedia

Device Drivers

Another piece of software that must be installed before your PC can be turned into a jukebox is the device driver for the sound card and any other audio devices on your system. Typically, device drivers are included with the device on either a diskette or a CD-ROM. You should also check the Web site of the manufacturer of the sound card or audio device for updates or newly released drivers.

Here are some excellent sites that you can use to track down device drivers for sound cards, as well as device drivers for any other device:

- **The Driver Guide** www.driverguide.com
- **The Driver Zone** www.driverzone.com
- **Windrivers.com** www.windrivers.com
- **WinFiles.com** www.winfiles.com

SOUND CAPTURE AND PLAYBACK

After you have installed the sound card into the PC and installed the appropriate device drivers and playback control software, you can begin recording or playing sound files on your PC. Technically, these actions are called capture (recording) and playback (listening).

Capture

A sound card typically is able to capture audio data from a number of different audio data sources. Exactly which input is used to capture the audio varies depending upon the source of the sound data. If the source is an electronic device like a CD player, stereo receiver, or synthesizer, a line-level input is used. If the source is a live human voice or an acoustic musical instrument captured by a microphone, the source is connected to the sound card through a mic-level jack.

Most sound cards use 1/8-inch phone jacks for their inputs, but very few sound playback devices use these jacks and instead use 1/4-inch or RCA jacks. In order to connect a stand-alone playback device, you will need to use a special cable or adapter that can be found at any electronics supply store. In most situations, connecting your PC to a home stereo source requires a cable with left and right male RCA plugs on one end and a single stereo male 1/8-inch phone plug on the other. A synthesizer or an electronic keyboard typically uses 1/4-inch phone jacks, so the adapter cable to use is one with left and right male 1/4-inch phone plugs on one end and a single stereo male 1/8-inch phone plug on the other.

For capturing live sound, there are a number of inexpensive PC microphones available. PC microphones are designed with 1/8-inch phone plugs to connect directly to the mic input of most sound cards. A higher-end microphone will typically have either a 1/4-inch phone plug or an XLR (eXternal/Live/Return) connector, which require a jack adapter or an adapter cable to connect into the sound card's 1/8-inch jack.

If the source is a device with digital I/O, such as a MiniDisc or DAT device, and the sound card is a digital device, the cabling you should use depends on the type of ports available. Directly connecting these devices requires cables that are specifically designed for digital data. S/P-DIF (Sony/Philips—Digital Interface Format) cables, for example, look almost identical to the standard RCA audio cables but are actually quite different. The same is true of AES/EBU (Audio Engineering Society/European Broadcasting Union) cables, which look like standard XLR microphone cables but are in fact very different underneath the wrapper. It is not likely that you will run into these cables working with your PC unless you plan to do professional-level sound recording, engineering, and editing on your PC.

With the appropriate connections made using the proper cabling and jacks, the rest of the sound capture operation is controlled by software. There is a wide variation in the capabilities and controls in audio capture software. However, on all levels of sophistication, it all boils down to when you wish to record a sound, you click the Record button and start the noise. When you have captured as much of the noise as you desire, you click the Stop button. It is before and after these steps that the complexity of this task exists.

Here are some of the considerations you should address when capturing audio on a PC:

- **File type** Before you capture your sounds, you should have some idea of which of the available audio file formats you wish to use. There is a variety of audio file types to choose from; the most common audio capture format for Windows systems is the WAV file. The different audio file formats use different methods of encoding and compressing the sound data. The WAV format provides the most flexibility for later converting the sound file to another file format. Many audio capture applications will only capture to WAV files.
- **File size** Audio files are large, especially if the sound is captured at a CD-quality sample rate and resolution (sample rates will be discussed shortly). For example, just ten seconds of stereo sound recorded at 44.1 kHz (kilohertz) and 16 bits (what is referred to as "CD-quality") requires about 2MB of disk space. If disk space is an issue, then you can decide which is more important, the quality of the sound recording or whether the sound needs to be in stereo or mono. The latter can cut the size of the file by half.
- **Input level** Recording sound at a very quiet level will produce a very noisy playback at normal volume levels. On the other hand, recording sound too loud can result in clipping. *Clipping* means that the digital waveform peaks of the sound

are literally cut off, which produces distortion in the playback. This is why sound capture software includes some form of visual recording level gauge.

- **Sample rate** Although it is expressed in kilohertz (kHz), the sample rate is the distance between samples captured in a sound file. So, indirectly the sample rate refers to the number of samples, or short bites of the sound, that are taken from the audio in a second. The sample rate used by CD-quality sound is 44.1 kHz, and it produces good results for most applications. Audio recorded for professional applications may be sampled at a higher rate to increase fidelity and provide more headroom for audio editing. Lower sample rates will use less disk space at the cost of audio quality. The maximum and minimum sample rate available is subject to the limitations of both the sound card and the software being used. The standard Windows Sound Recorder provides you with slide controls that allow you to balance the sound file's playback quality to its disk size on its advanced features tab, shown in Figure 21-3.
- **Sample resolution** Expressed in bits, sample resolution refers to the size of the samples taken. CD audio is stored at a resolution of 16 bits. This means that 16 bits of binary data are used to describe the sound that should result from the sample being analyzed by the sound card and DSP. Sample resolution involves the same trade-offs with regard to file size and sound quality that apply to sample rate.

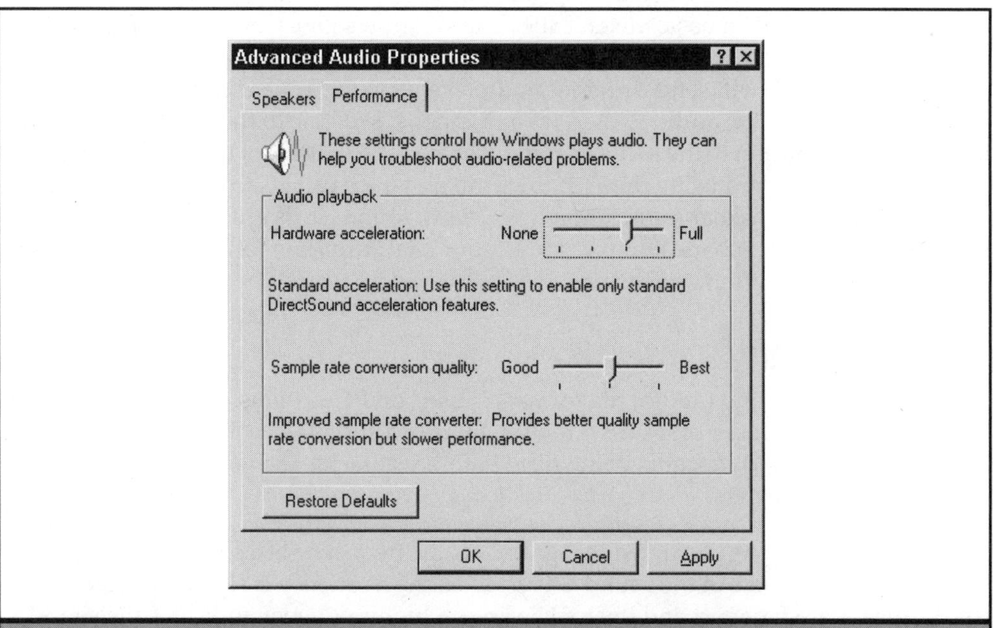

Figure 21-3. The Windows Sound Recorder's advanced features settings

Digital Audio Extraction

Digital audio extraction (DAE) is a method of capturing sounds from an audio CD using a completely digital process. DAE does not require the use of a sound card, and you can make an exact copy of an audio CD without the signal loss typical in most digital to analog conversions. DAE is a feature supported by many new CD-R drives that write to CDs. In addition to a CD-R drive, special software is also required, which is usually bundled with CD writing software. DAE output is typically stored in the form of a WAV file.

Playback

Your Windows system is likely configured to play back certain sounds for system events like error messages, running an application, minimizing a window, or indicating that new mail has arrived. These sounds can be configured using the Sounds icon in the Windows 98 Control Panel or the Sounds and Multimedia icon in the Windows Me/2000 Control Panel. These sounds are the most basic form of playback on your PC.

Other playback events involve more active participation from the user. A Web site or a multimedia title such as an encyclopedia may include icons that the user clicks to hear an audio file describe a topic. The audio capture software used to record sounds, such as the Windows Sound Recorder, typically includes a set of tools for playing back a variety of sound files. The Windows Media Player (see Figure 21-4), which is the companion software to the Windows Sound Recorder, will play back virtually any sound file that can be stored on a PC.

Windows includes a basic mixer, called the Windows Play Control (see Figure 21-5). This software tool can be used to adjust the volume level of various sound events. Some games, for instance, will send different audio events to separate channels on the sound card: speech and digital audio to the Wave channel, CD music to the CD Audio channel, and synthesizer output to the MIDI channel. The relative volume of these different sound sources can be balanced using the Windows mixer, which can be accessed via the yellow speaker icon in the taskbar notification tray. Many sound cards are bundled with a proprietary and usually enhanced mixer application that duplicates and often improves on the functions of the Windows mixer.

Sound File Formats

A wide variety of sound (audio) file formats is used on PC systems. The type of file used depends on the hardware and software used to record and play back the sound. Here are a few of the terms and concepts you'll need before you tackle the various file formats for sound and video data:

- **Frequency** As illustrated in Figure 21-6, the frequency of a sound wave indicates the tone or note of the sound wave. When the frequency is slow, the sound wave peaks are far apart and the tone is low. A high frequency indicates the sound wave peaks are closer together and the tone is high.

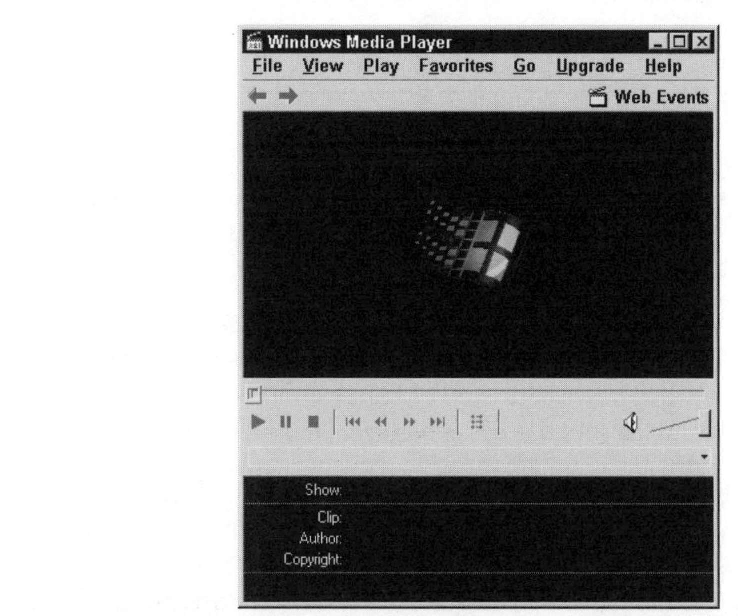

Figure 21-4. The Windows Media Player

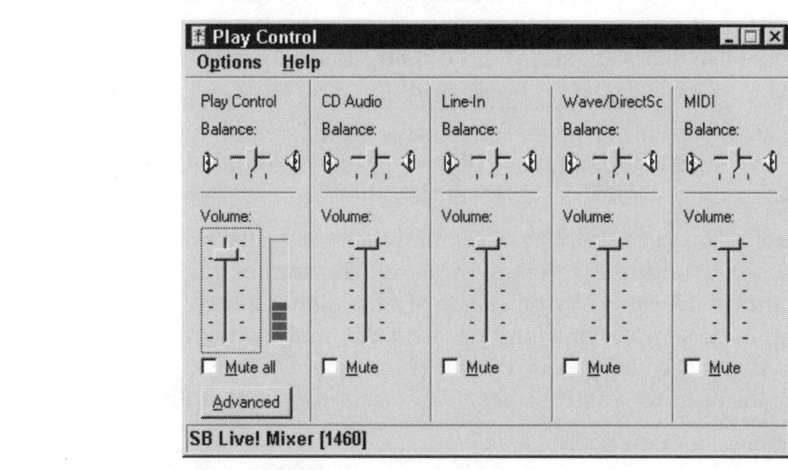

Figure 21-5. The Windows Play Control mixer

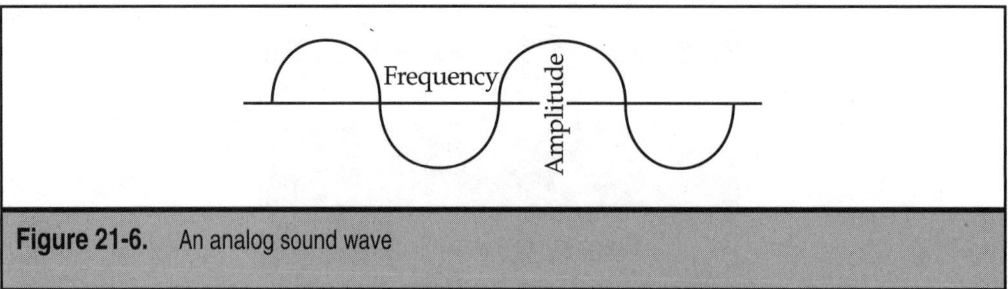

Figure 21-6. An analog sound wave

- **Amplitude** As illustrated in Figure 21-6, the height of the sound wave is its amplitude. This indicates the volume or loudness of the sound. If the sound waves are tall, the volume is loud; shorter waves indicate a softer sound.
- **Sample** As the analog sound is being digitized, it is separated in a series of samples (see Figure 21-7) that measure its frequency and amplitude at different points along the sound wave. The sample records the frequency and amplitude of the sound wave at each point. The precision of the sound's specification is directly affected by the number of bits used to digitally represent the samples.
- **Sample size** The sample size is measured in bits and governs the difference in volume between the softest sound and the loudest sound that can be recorded and played back. The sample size of a standard audio CD is 16 bits; for standard broadcast radio it is 8 bits. Combined with sample rate, the sample size provides a measure of how closely a sound file will match the original sound source.
- **8-bit sound** 8-bit sound is recorded using eight bits to encode its values, allowing 256 levels of specification per sample. 8-bit sound cards offer poor sound quality that is comparable to broadcast AM radio. 8-bit audio allows 256 loudness levels.
- **16-bit sound** 16-bit sound uses 16-bits to specify the values of a sound sample providing 16,000 levels per sample. This is the most common type of sound card available; its sound is comparable to CD audio. 16-bit audio allows 65,536 loudness levels.
- **Sample rate** The sampling rate of a sound file represents how often a sample of a signal is taken. Sample rates are measured as samples per second. A standard audio CD uses a sampling rate of 44.1 kilohertz (kHz), which captures 44,100 amplitude samples of sound per second. Combined with the sample size of a sound file, the sampling rate provides a measure of how closely a sound will match the original sound source. Other examples of sampling rates are:
    - Telephone service—8 kHz
    - 8-bit audio file formats—22 kHz
    - 16-bit file formats—44.1 kHz
    - DAT (digital audio tape)—48 kHz

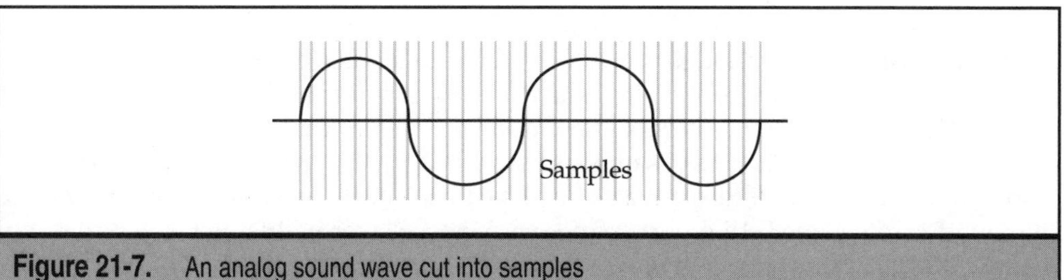

Figure 21-7. An analog sound wave cut into samples

- **Analog sound** Analog sound waves, like those in Figures 21-6 and 21-7, are represented by a continuous signal that fluctuates with the frequency and amplitude of the actual sound it represents.
- **Digital sound** Digital sound files encode a characterization of the original sound using a scheme that varies with the file format and compression techniques used. The encoded data describes the frequency and amplitude fluctuations of the original sound. Because it contains only samples of the sound, the original sound cannot be completely reproduced.

AIFF

AIFF (Audio Interchange File Format) is a digital audio file format developed by Apple and used on the Macintosh. AIFF is the Macintosh equivalent of the Windows WAV format. It breaks sound objects into parts called chunks. The common chunk holds data such as the sound's sampling rate and size, and the sound data chunk contains the digitized sound samples.

AU

The AU standard is very similar to the WAV file format. It was originally developed for the Unix and NeXT platforms and is fairly common on the Internet. Nearly all Windows audio players and Web browsers support the AU file format. AU is the audio file standard on UNIX systems. PC users may encounter AU (audio) files on Internet sites.

MIDI

The MIDI (Music Instrument Digital Interface) file format stores a synthesized sound that is reproduced on the personal computer by sound cards equipped with a synthesizing chip. A MIDI-capable sound card is able to accept commands that specify the instrument originating the sound, the note being played, and the duration of the sound. MIDI is a standard adopted by the electronic music industry for controlling devices, such as synthesizers, keyboards, and other devices that create music. A MIDI file includes values representing a note's pitch, length, and volume, but it can also include additional characteristics, such as attack and delay time. Because a MIDI file stores only how to reproduce sounds, the actual sound's data is not stored in the file, and MIDI files are much smaller than other sound data files such as WAV or AIFF files.

MIDI files, which have the file extension MID, are not actually audio files but contain MIDI data. MIDI can be thought of as a language, a standard for sharing information about musical events such as the pitch and duration of a note between multiple devices. How a PC handles MIDI files is dependent upon the system's configuration. Often MIDI files are routed to the sound card's onboard synthesizer, which in turn generates the corresponding sounds. MIDI files can also be played back on an external device attached to the sound card's game/MIDI port. Windows Media Player will launch MIDI files, but dedicated MIDI sequencing software is required to create and edit MIDI music.

MPEG

MPEG audio uses a similar compression technique to that used for MPEG (Moving Pictures Experts Group) graphic images (covered a little later in the chapter). It compresses CD-quality sound by as much as a 12 to 1 ratio and produces reasonable sound quality. The MPEG audio standard has three layers (Layers I, II, or III) that increase in complexity and sound quality as the layer number increases. Currently, only Layers I and II are commonly used. Because of its size and quality, the MPEG audio format, in the form of MP2 and MP3 (MPEG Layer 2 and 3, respectively) is gaining popularity on the Internet and Web.

Sound file formats that use compression techniques (like MPEG) are emerging to help producers reduce audio file sizes. Most of the compression techniques employed use what is called lossy compression. Lossy means that in the compression process, part of the original sound is lost and the reproduced sound will not sound exactly like the original sound. Some compression techniques have attempted to improve this situation by eliminating only the sounds that are beyond human hearing ranges.

MP3 Audio compression is a means of reducing the size of WAV files to make them more portable and to take up less storage space. MP3 compression has become popular in recent years because file sizes can be reduced dramatically while retaining most of the original WAV file's audio quality. For example, a 50MB WAV file stored at 44.1 kHz and 16 bits can be reduced to around 5MB and maintain a sound quality comparable to that of a CD. Less compression results in larger file sizes but also higher sound quality. The portability of MP3 has led to an explosion of music trading on the Internet and has caused considerable controversy surrounding the potential for copyright infringement.

MP3 files require specialized software for playback, and a number of free MP3 applications are available on the Internet. Nullsoft's Winamp is one of the most popular of these applications. MP3 files are also sometimes available as streaming content on Internet sites, meaning that the file need not be copied to the local system before it can be played. Streaming audio is commonly handled by Web browser plug-ins.

MP2 MPEG-1 Layer 2 is an earlier MPEG compression format that produces lower quality results than MP3; MP2 files can be played back with any MP3 player.

AAC The MPEG compression standard expected to succeed MP3, AAC (Advanced Audio Coding) is another name for MPEG-2, not to be confused with MP2.

RA or RAM

RA or RAM file formats are RealAudio files, a streaming audio format developed by RealNetworks. The quality of RealAudio files varies with the speed of the Internet connection. RealAudio files targeted for high-bandwidth connections like DSL or T1 can approach CD quality, while files designed for modem downloads are similar to the quality of an AM radio signal. RealAudio files require a dedicated RealAudio player or browser plug-in for playback.

3-D Audio

3-D audio is an emerging sound playback technique used to give more depth to traditional 16-bit or higher stereo sound. Typically, it is reproduced with a special device that adjusts the sound coming from the speakers to create the impression that the speakers are further apart. 3-D audio devices are particularly popular where speakers tend to be small and close together.

WAV

The WAV (waveform audio) file format, developed by Microsoft, is the de facto file format standard for nonstreaming audio files. It is supported on nearly all platforms and requires no special software beyond that associated with nearly all sound cards. A WAV file contains a digital representation of an analog sound signal and like most digital sound formats, the better the recording quality, the larger the file. WAV files can be very large. For example, an 8-bit recording can use as much as 1.5MB per minute of original sound, and a 16-bit recording can require 3MB per minute.

WMF

Windows Media File is Microsoft's answer to RealAudio. Like RealAudio, WMF sound quality is bandwidth dependent. WMF files can be played back on Windows Media Player.

Streaming Audio

A very common means of transmitting large audio files over the Internet is streaming audio. The RealPlayer client and the Windows Media Player are the most popular playback software tools, both supporting streaming audio and video (discussed later in the chapter). Streaming audio, which was specifically designed for the Internet, compresses a standard audio file (such as a WAV file) and sends it as a stream of bits to the user. Instead of waiting to download the entire file before you can hear it, as would normally be required for a WAV file, the playback software plays back the file as it is received. The quality of the sound playback is about equal to the radio, provided you have enough bandwidth to drive the stream without interruption.

Streaming media trades convenience for sound quality, especially when there are many sounds at the same time. Streaming architectures are able to compress a 10MB WAV file to less than 300KB, a reduction that allows sound files to be transmitted across the

Internet conveniently. RealPlayer files carry file name extensions of RA or RAM, and Windows Media Player files are designated as WMA files.

CD-ROM AND DVD INTERFACES

CD audio (CD-A) is unique among PC audio formats in that the computer does not process the output from an audio CD. Instead, both CD-ROM and DVD drives send CD audio directly to the sound card via a specialized cable that connects the disk drive directly to the sound card. Although it may appear that the computer is processing CD audio because volume levels can be adjusted with a software mixer, all you are really controlling is the sound card's output level. Digital audio from a CD is converted to analog sound by the DAC on the CD-ROM or DVD drive itself or, less commonly, a digital output on the CD-ROM or DVD drive is cabled to a digital input on the sound card to allow the card's DAC to handle the conversion. While digital outputs on CD-ROM and DVD drives are fairly common, digital CD audio inputs on sound cards are still somewhat rare. Cabling between a CD-ROM or DVD drive and a sound card can be pretty straightforward, especially if the drive shipped with its own audio cable (and most do).

INSTALLING A SOUND CARD

Sound card installation is subject to the same safety considerations discussed in detail in Chapter 10. Here is a review:

- Power down the system before opening the case. On ATX systems you may have to press and hold the power button for several seconds before it turns off. Check that there are no lights illuminated on the front of the case and no fans spinning.
- Always use an antistatic wrist strap when working inside the PC to prevent damage from ESD (electrostatic-discharge).
- Avoid using magnetized screwdrivers while working inside the PC.
- Do not contact the surface of the printed circuit board (PCB) on the motherboard or other adapter cards with your tools, or you may damage the boards.
- Before closing the case, check to see that all expansion cards, RAM modules, and cable connections are still firmly in place.

ISA Sound Cards

Like other ISA expansion cards, ISA sound cards usually require some manual configuration to set the system resource assignments such as I/O port address, DMA, and IRQ for the card. These values are typically set with a series of jumper blocks on the card. Some cards require a combination of jumper settings and some entries in the AUTOEXEC.BAT and CONFIG.SYS files located in the root directory of the hard disk drive. The documentation and installation instructions that come with the card will specify the exact entries needed.

ISA sound cards can be especially complicated to configure because they often use a separate set of values for different functions. For example, there are sound cards that require a separate port address, DMA, and IRQ for general use, another set of values for Sound Blaster emulation, and a third set of values for MPU-401 emulation. That's nine resources to configure for a single expansion card!

As you can see, there is no universal set of steps for configuring an ISA sound card. The only way to know exactly what values need to be assigned and how to assign them is to refer to the manufacturer's documentation. If the manual for the card is unavailable, many sound card manufacturers publish installation guides on their Web sites.

PCI Sound Cards

Many of the difficulties associated with configuring an ISA sound card are eliminated with PCI sound cards. Although there are still a number of resources that need to be assigned, this is typically accomplished by the Plug-and-Play BIOS in conjunction with an operating system that supports Plug and Play, like Windows 95/98/2000. In most of these cases, certain system resources, such as IRQ and DMA, cannot be assigned manually.

A few conditions must be met before a PCI card can be installed:

- There must be an available PCI slot.
- Many older motherboards use an earlier revision of the PCI BIOS that may not be compatible with newer sound cards. Check with the motherboard manufacturer if you have an older PCI motherboard and are not certain that the PCI BIOS revision may be less than version 2.1.
- Motherboard manufacturers commonly develop system BIOS updates after the motherboard is released. Sometimes these updates are designed to address issues such as Plug-and-Play device enumeration that can affect whether or not a card is successfully installed. Check with your motherboard manufacturer to see if there are any critical BIOS updates available. Always use caution when upgrading a system BIOS (see Chapter 4 for more details about BIOS upgrades).

To install a PCI sound card, you will typically follow these steps:

1. Insert the card into an available PCI slot (see Chapter 10 for the precautions that should be observed when dealing with expansion cards).
2. Connect the audio cable following the manufacturer's instructions.
3. Power on the system.
4. When the operating system prompts you for an installation disk, insert the manufacturer's driver disk and point to the directory specified in the manufacturer's documentation.

Although Windows 98/2000 includes drivers for a handful of PCI sound cards, in most cases you will need the manufacturer's drivers to set up the card correctly. If a driver disk is unavailable, drivers can often be found on the manufacturer's Web site. Frequently a manufacturer will release updated drivers that include features or bug fixes not found on the original installation disk, so it is always good practice to check the Web site for updates.

VIDEO AND GRAPHIC FILES

It is not likely that you would videotape a birthday party with the camera's sound turned off. Full-motion video images are rarely recorded without sound because the result would lack meaning and context. This is why the majority of the multimedia architectures used to store and transfer video images on the PC are the same as those that are used to store audio data. Combining video images with sound and storing them in the same file requires more sophisticated file formats and compression algorithms than are required just for audio data. Of course, the major drawback of combining audio with video is that it results in larger, more complex files.

The three more popular video file formats are AVI, MPEG, and QuickTime (MOV).

AVI

AVI (audio/visual interleaved), which is also called Video for Windows and ActiveMovie, is Microsoft's proprietary digital audio-visual architecture. It is actually more of an interface to a set of Windows graphic display routines than it is a video file format. Nonetheless, AVI files produce good video and sound reproduction.

Its drawbacks include the smaller window sizes used for playback and the larger file sizes it can generate. For example, a 30-second AVI file requires about 1.4MB of disk storage space. AVI is no longer supported by Microsoft and is being replaced by DirectShow/ActiveMovie, which supports playback of multimedia from the Web, CD-ROM, and DVD.

MPEG

MPEG (Moving Picture Experts Group) is a nonproprietary, digital audio-visual architecture, developed by the same organization that created the JPEG standard (on which MPEG is based). MPEG was born from the desire for full-motion video on personal computers; using MPEG, computer filmmakers have the ability to create a full-screen, full-motion video with a frame rate of 30 frames per second, the same frame rate used in television.

The size of the MPEG file depends upon the amount of compression used. Because it is a derivation of the JPEG standard, MPEG is a very popular compression method for video data files. Like its cousin JPEG, however, higher compression rates usually result in poorer image quality.

Most browsers and video cards support MPEG viewing without additional software, but many freeware and shareware plug-ins and player applications are available. MPEG files carry either a MPEG or MPG file extension.

QuickTime Movie

QuickTime movies are very popular for video on both CD-ROM and the Internet. QuickTime is a proprietary digital audio-visual architecture developed by Apple Computer. It has become one of the most popular multimedia formats in use and is widely supported. In fact, Apple reports proudly that many millions of copies of the QuickTime player have been downloaded to Windows computers (see Figure 21-8).

QuickTime, like AVI, is a series of graphic display interfaces that are used to encapsulate supported audio and video file formats with instructions for playback. There are several different versions of QuickTime, including QuickTime VR (virtual reality) that lets viewers navigate in 3D and look around 360 degrees from a fixed point in space. QuickTime creates good quality video clips in files with reasonable size. QuickTime files carry a MOV file extension.

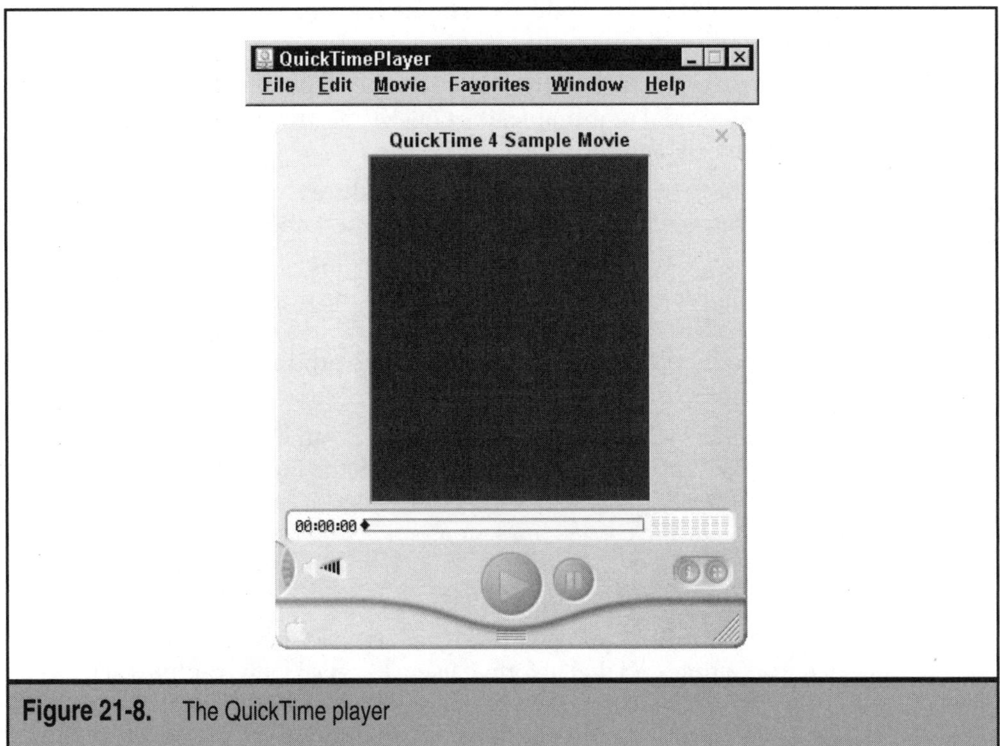

Figure 21-8. The QuickTime player

Video Terminology

Here are some of the terms and concepts that you should know to work with video on the PC:

- **Architecture** Controls how media is handled by the computer, including how movies are displayed to the screen and the creation, storage, and playback of media. It also defines the standard formats used to store media and supports codecs for audio and/or video. QuickTime, RealSystem, and Video for Windows are examples of multimedia architectures.
- **Codec** Short for both coder/decoder and compressor/decompressor. Which meaning is in use depends on the action in use. A coder/decoder is hardware or software that is used to convert analog sound, speech, or video into digital code (analog to digital) and vice versa (digital to analog). Hardware codecs are used in digital telephones and videoconferencing units. Software codecs are used to record and play audio and video over the Web utilizing the CPU for processing. A compressor/decompressor is hardware or software that compresses digital data into smaller files, sometimes encrypted.
- **Flatten** The action used to reduce the frame rate of a video movie to facilitate its conversion into a digital form.
- **Format** The part of an architecture that sets the actual file description in which files are stored. For example, the QuickTime architecture contains the QuickTime MOV file format.
- **Frame** One image in a series that together produce a movie. Multimedia movies consist of a sequence of still images (frames) and an audio track.
- **Frame rate** The number of frames of a video that is captured per second. Similar to the capture rate of sound files. This is the primary measure of reproduction quality. The more frames per second in a movie, the better the image reproduction will be. A low frame rate produces a jerky image since pieces of the action motion are missing.
- **Resolution** Refers to the sharpness and clarity of an image displayed on a graphics monitor. The screen resolution signifies the number of pixels on the entire screen. For example, a 640 × 480 pixel screen is capable of displaying 640 distinct dots on each of 480 lines, or about 300,000 pixels. Resolution can also be stated as dots per inch (dpi). A 15-inch VGA monitor (640 × 480) uses about 50 dots per inch to display an image.
- **Video capture** Converts analog video signals, such as those generated by a video camera, into a compressed digital format using a special video capture card.

Streaming Video

The latest development in multimedia file formats is streaming technology. Streaming audio and video files are experienced in near real-time. Typically, enough of the file is downloaded so that the playback can begin while the remainder of the file is still downloading. This allows the user to see and hear the file without waiting for the complete file to be received. The alternatives to streaming data are files in a nonstreaming format, such as WAV or MPEG files. Nonstreaming files must be downloaded entirely before they can begin playing. Your browser could include support for streaming files, but most likely will require a plug-in player for each separate format on the Web.

Media Player

Microsoft has recently combined its streaming data formats (Advanced Streaming Format (ASF) and Advanced Authoring Format (AAF), and NetShow) into the Windows Media Player architecture. The file formats of this architecture are recognized by their file extensions, ASF and WMA.

RealNetworks

RealNetworks combined two pre-existing technologies (RealAudio and RealVideo) to create a streaming media architecture that is focused exclusively on delivering media on the Internet. The RealPlayer, shown in Figure 21-9, supports both live interactive and on-demand video and audio.

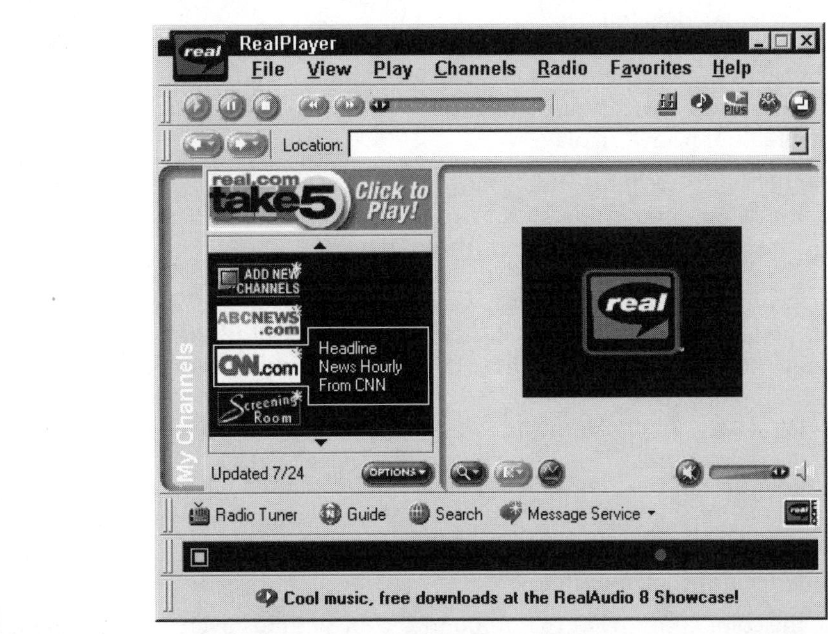

Figure 21-9. The RealPlayer streaming media client

RealVideo relies upon a video server to send data, which makes better use of the bandwidth and improves the overall performance of the streaming video. RealVideo supports both live interactive and on-demand video and includes a number of tools to help the producer and the server and improve the video file's reproduction. The more important tools in RealVideo are:

- **Stream thinning** Dynamically adjusts the video frame rate in real-time to the lowest rate that will accommodate the type of content, which reduces the need to pause the transmission and buffer data. This is particularly effective for activity during peak load periods.
- **Smart networking** Allows RealVideo to deliver a streaming signal across any network. It is compliant with firewall standards and will communicate on internal networks and intranets using a variety of protocols including HTTP.
- **TV mode** Plays a video stream in a television-like window on the viewers desktop while they work with other applications, including a browser. This is a feature Yahoo's Broadcast.com uses in their live television feed over the Internet.

File Sizes

Video files store a lot of data and can become very large. As an illustration of how large they can get, consider that a 24-bit, full screen, 30 frames per second video file would consume around 1.6GB of file space. How so?

Its file size is calculated as follows:

1. Three bytes (representing the 24 bits used for video encoding) times 640 (width of the frame) times 480 (the height of the display frame), which equals the number of pixels in a full frame display.
2. The number of pixels in the full frame display times 30 (the frame rate) times 60 (the number of seconds the video file will run) equals 1,658,880,000 bytes or 1.6GB of storage space for each minute of video.

This doesn't include the audio track which would add another 5 to 10MB. This is why the AVI files distributed on the Windows 98 CD range from 25 to 50MB for 16-bit video files that run an average of two minutes. A video file contains the equivalent of 15 to 30 JPEG files for each second of video.

There are several ways in which the size of a video file can be reduced:

- Decrease the size of the playback window. For example, video files played over the Internet use a standard 160 ×120 pixels. But remember that the smaller the window, the harder it will be to see any text or detailed movements in the video, especially on a 14-inch monitor.
- Reduce the color count from 16 million to 256, or perhaps even 16 colors. Better yet, if possible, convert the video to black and white. Of course, the visual quality of the file will also be reduced right along with the color count.

- Slow the frame rate from 30 to 15 or less frames per second. However, the slower the frame rate, the more jerky the video motion becomes.
- Compress the file. There are compression techniques available that can shrink the file size of a video file using a ration of 100:1. But, once again, video compression is lossy compression, and the file may never look the same again.

Codecs

Many streaming format systems are codecs, a software system that both compresses and decompresses sound or video files. A codec compresses the file using software known as an encoder and reproduces the image or sound with a player that performs the decoding and decompression. The functions of a codec are similar to those of a modem and how it works with data communications: it both modulates and demodulates the signal to control the analog to digital conversions. Some codecs support a range of file formats, but most support only their own proprietary formats.

A codec uses one of two lossy compression techniques, temporal (image) or spatial (size). Temporal compression looks to eliminate the part of the image (or sound) not needed for continuity to the human eye or ear. The video images are examined frame by frame for changes between frames. For example, in a video of a talking head (a clip of a person sitting or standing with little motion), much of the image remains the same from frame to frame. The background never changes and the motion is only head and lip movements. Temporal compression compares the first frame (the key frame) with the next (the delta frame) to see if anything has changed. The key frame is stored and only the information that changes in the delta frame is kept. This eliminates a large portion of the file. Spatial compression deletes information that is common to the entire video or a sequence within the file. It looks for redundant information that repeats at coordinate points from frame to frame.

Teleconferencing Systems

When the Web first got started, threaded discussions and live chats were included on a Web site more for fun that serious business. Today, online conferencing, in one form or another, has a prominent position on many Web sites. In fact, some of the Web's most active sites are devoted to live chat discussions. The technologies of the Internet and Web now offer a wide range of conferencing options. There are numerous online conferencing options, but in general, your choices narrow down to text-based or streaming audio-visual conferencing; for some smaller groups, there is the option of using an Internet phone system.

Video Conferencing

It is only a very slight step up from streaming audio and video systems to video conferencing over the Internet. Online video-conferencing systems are the audio-visual equivalent of a long distance telephone call on the public telephone system. Just as a voice conversation is so much more content-rich than a text-based chat, a live videoconference provides much more than the voice-only conference.

High-end videoconferencing cards can be added to a PC system to make it into an interactive videoconferencing stations. The typical system will have a digital camera, which plugs into the videoconferencing card, and a microphone, which most PC systems are already equipped with. Low-end systems designed for personal use over the Internet are available for less than $200 virtually everywhere computer supplies are sold.

IMAGE CAPTURE

The objectives of image capture are not unlike those of audio capture. In both cases, the purpose is to convert analog information such as a photograph or a human voice into digital data that can be stored and edited on a computer. While not yet as universal as PC sound systems, image capture devices have increased in popularity with the rise of the Internet and have quickly become essential tools for developing visual content for Web pages.

Scanners

Scanners are devices for capturing still images. The scanner uses a light source that reflects off the image being captured, and information about the reflected image is digitized and sent to software where it can be stored, edited, or printed. Scanners are available in a wide variety of configurations, which can be categorized according to different imaging methods, how the scanner's interface with the PC, and how the original image is delivered to the scanner:

Imaging Method

A scanner, regardless of whether it is handheld or flatbed, uses one of three methods to capture and reproduce the image of the document it scans. The three imaging methods used are:

- **Photomultiplier Tube (PMT)** This type of scanner uses a vacuum tube to convert light reflected from the scanned image into an amplified electrical signal that is sent to the PC. PMT scanners are more expensive and generally more difficult to use than CCD scanners (discussed next). They are typically reserved for high-end applications.
- **Charge-Coupled Device (CCD)** This category of scanner includes the general-purpose scanners used in homes and offices. A CCD is a small solid-state sensor that converts light into an electric charge, which is then converted into digital data that can be stored on a PC. A CCD scanner uses literally thousands of CCDs in an array that scans the entire surface of the image. More CCDs in the array translates into a higher maximum resolution for scanned images.
- **Multipass vs. Single Pass** Multipass scanners collect color data using multiple passes of the light source and CCD array over the surface of the image. Multiple scans are required because a single scan is required for the red, green, and blue information on the page. At the end of the three passes, the collected color

information is combined to make a full color image. The drawbacks of this method are that in addition to the time it takes to make three passes, the image quality can suffer from tiny inaccuracies in the alignment of the three sets of data that were combined to create the composite image. A single-pass scanner collects all of the color data in one pass. The result is usually a faster scan with less potential for image distortion than a multipass scan.

Interface

Scanners, like most external peripheral devices, attach to the PC through one of its available ports. The most commonly used connector is the parallel port, but several newer versions are now available with a USB interface as well. Higher-end scanners connect to the PC through the SCSI interface.

- **SCSI** SCSI (Small Computer System Interface) scanners work with either a standard SCSI interface or with their own proprietary adapter card. SCSI scanners are often faster than their parallel counterparts but can cost more when the price of the SCSI adapter is included. Because a SCSI adapter is required, installing a SCSI scanner can be more difficult than other types.
- **Parallel** These scanners connect to the PC's parallel port with a standard DB-25 cable. Most parallel scanners include a pass-through connector to allow a printer to share the same port. An advantage of parallel scanners is that they do not involve the additional expense and trouble of a SCSI adapter, but there is usually a trade-off in speed. In addition, some printers and other parallel devices like Zip drives can have problems with a scanner's pass-through port.
- **USB and IEEE 1394 (FireWire)** These Plug-and-Play scanners eliminate most of the problems of the SCSI and parallel port scanners. Their speeds are comparable to SCSI scanners, and they have a lower price and a simpler installation. USB and IEEE 1394 scanners will only work on systems with operating systems that support these interfaces. All versions of Windows 98/2000 support USB and IEEE 1394, but some USB scanners will not work with Windows 95, no matter what is tried.

Delivery Method

A scanner uses a variety of delivery methods, which means the way it captures the image of a document, that range from partial page, single-sheet, or automatic sheet feeders that can scan a multi-page document. The delivery methods used are:

- **Drum scanners** PMT scanners in which the original document to be scanned must be mounted to a transparent cylindrical drum to capture its image.
- **Handheld scanners** Popularized by Logitech in the early 1990s, these must be moved across the surface of the original by hand. Because they are often narrower than a typical page, more than one scan is usually needed to capture a full-page image. Usually some image manipulation is required to stitch the images together using software.

- **Sheet-fed scanners** These use rollers to move an image past the light source and CCD array. Some sheet-feeders can automatically feed one page after another, making it possible to scan multiple images in a single event. Commonly used for OCR (optical character recognition) on scanned printed documents, they do not work well for scanning books, magazines, or rigid objects. Sheet-fed, or as they are also called, sheet-feed scanners work well only with loose-leaf cut-sheet paper documents.
- **Flatbed scanners** The most popular type of scanner because of its flexibility and ease of use. The material to be scanned is placed on a flat glass surface, and the light source and CCD array pass underneath it. Because the dimensions of flatbed scanner area can vary significantly, the scanner should be chosen with some consideration of the size of the material it is likely to be scanning. Flatbed scanners are typically the best value for home or small office scanning purposes.

Image Software

Like a digitized sound, a visual image must be sent to software before it can be manipulated and stored. Scanners come bundled with software for controlling the scanning process and typically include some basic tools for image editing. Advanced tools for image editing are available from a number of publishers, including:

- **Adobe** www.adobe.com
- **Corel** www.corel.com
- **Jasc** www.jasc.com
- **Ulead** www.ulead.com
- **Xara** www.xara.com

Video Capture Devices

The term "video capture" can be misleading since it suggests that what is captured is always a moving image. Many video capture devices do capture full-motion video, but many others, like the popular Snappy from Play Inc., only capture still images, just like a scanner. Video capture devices, then, are devices that use video cameras or VCRs as a source for still or moving images. In addition to whether or not moving images can be captured, video capture devices can also be categorized according to how they attach to the PC (internally or externally), whether they accept a digital signal, and the type of compression used.

Internal vs. External

Video capture devices typically connect to the PC in one of three ways:

- An adapter card (usually PCI)

- An external parallel interface
- An external USB/IEEE 1394 interface

The distinction between internal and external video capture devices may be blurred by the fact that many capture cards use a *breakout box*, a separate piece of hardware that attaches to the rear of the card and contains all of the connectors for interfacing with the input device (video camera, VCR). Some video cards also double as video capture devices, with varying capabilities.

Digital vs. Analog

Some video capture devices only accept an analog signal like that supplied by a legacy camcorder or VCR through a Composite or S-Video input port. Digital video capture devices use high-speed IEEE 1394 interfaces and accept data directly from digital video cameras. There are video capture cards that include a combination of digital and analog inputs.

CODEC

As with digital audio, the file sizes associated with digital video are huge. One second of uncompressed, full-motion video and audio captured at 24-bit, 640 × 480 resolution will take up approximately 30MB of disk space. Because of this, all video capture devices use at least one compression method to reduce the amount of storage space required. The compression method used has a direct bearing upon the applications for which the captured video can be used, so it should be considered carefully.

These are the most common compression schemes used by video capture devices:

- **MJPEG** A motion video compression method based on the JPEG (Joint Photographic Experts Group) still image compression method. MJPEG (moving JPEG) is optimized for transfer to and from videotape but is used less for multimedia and Internet applications because it requires specialized hardware for playback. Image quality is high, but like most lossy schemes, the quality varies with the amount of compression used.
- **MPEG-1** One of two common video compression schemes developed by the Moving Pictures Experts Group. MPEG-1 is popular for multimedia and Internet video because playback is software-based and file sizes can be reduced while maintaining a good image quality.
- **DV** Digital video (DV) is the compression method used by digital video cameras, which perform their own compression during recording. DV capture cards connect to digital cameras over an IEEE 1394 interface, which is able to transfer the digital video at very high speeds with no signal loss.
- **MPEG-2** The newest compression scheme that supports image resolutions up to four times higher than MPEG-1. MPEG-2 compression is scalable, so it can be used for multimedia or Web-based applications with broadcast quality video. Of course, higher data rates translate to larger file sizes.

Digitizers

Digitizers, which are also called *digitizing tablets, drawing tablets,* or just *tablets,* are drawing tools that capture the movements of the operator's hand. Their operation is similar to that of a mouse, but there are major differences. The input from a mouse is always relative to where the cursor is on the screen. If you draw a line with a mouse and then pick up the mouse and move it to a different position on the desk, the input will continue from the last position of the cursor. However, a digitizing pad relates each position on the tablet to a specific position on the screen. This makes it possible to accurately trace an existing drawing, or to create original drawings, such as an architectural design, which must correspond to precise dimensions.

A digitizer is made up of two main components: an electronic tablet and one of two types of drawing devices. One type is a *pen* (also called a *stylus*), which is held like an ordinary pen and used to "draw" directly on the tablet. These movements are captured and translated into a corresponding drawing on the PC. The other type of drawing device is called a *puck* (or a *cursor*), which closely resembles a mouse and is used in much the same way. A small window with crosshairs makes the puck ideal for very precise tracing of existing drawings. In both cases, the tablet detects the exact position of the drawing device and sends *x* and *y* (left and right and up and down) coordinates to the PC. Pens and pucks are available with and without cords.

Like scanners, digitizers connect to the PC in a variety ways. Most digitizers connect through a proprietary controller card. There is no standardization among the types of cables used between theses proprietary interfaces and the tablet, so the manufacturer must be contacted for replacements should one become necessary. Some digitizers use the serial port, with one end of the connecting cable attaching to the PC with a standard DB-9 or DB-25 connector. However, the other end of the cable, the one connecting to the digitizing tablet, is usually a proprietary connector. There are newer models that now use a USB or IEEE 1394 connectors as well.

PART IV

System Care and Troubleshooting

CHAPTER 22

PC Care and Maintenance

It is only logical that if you take care of your PC and properly maintain it, it will last longer. A PC does not require all that much in the way of general housekeeping and maintenance, and if you make its care part of a regular preventive maintenance routine, it's not even a bother for the most part.

This chapter is a bit different than most of the other chapters in this book because it discusses things you should do rather than technical information about PC components. The presentation is divided into three general parts. The first deals with what you should do and when to keep the PC running. The second part deals with the tools, cleaners, and other supplies you need to use to properly clean and maintain a PC. The third and final part details the specific steps you should take when cleaning and maintaining the PC, inside and out.

PREVENTIVE MAINTENANCE OF A PC

Much as for the scheduled maintenance for an automobile, the reason you perform preventive maintenance (PM) on a PC is to avoid failures and costly repairs and to extend the life of the machine. However, this can only be accomplished if your PM program is performed regularly. The owners' manuals for nearly all PCs include a maintenance chart that details the maintenance, adjustments, and cleaning activities that should be performed, with some indication of when these tasks should be done.

Table 22-1 is my version of what the maintenance guide should include.

PC Maintenance Schedule Guide

Schedule	Component	Maintenance Activity
Daily	PC	Run a virus scan of the memory and hard disk
	Windows	Restart or shut down Windows
	Hard disk	Create a differential backup
Weekly	Hard disk	Create a full backup
	Hard disk	Remove all .tmp files and clear C:\TEMP and C:\WINDOWS\TEMP
	Web browser	Clear browser cache, history, and temporary Internet files

Table 22-1. Preventive Maintenance Schedule

PC Maintenance Schedule Guide

Schedule	Component	Maintenance Activity
	Antivirus Software	Update antivirus data files
	Windows Desktop	Empty the Windows Recycle Bin
Monthly	Hard disk	Defrag the drive and recover lost clusters
	Hard disk	Uninstall all unnecessary applications
	Keyboard	Clean the keyboard with compressed air and check for and repair stuck keys
	Mouse	Clean ball and rollers and check for wear
	Monitor	Turn off and clean screen with soft cloth or antistatic wipe
	Printer	Clean with compressed air to remove dust and bits of paper
On failure	Floppy disk drive	Clean floppy drive head
	System	Troubleshoot and replace, if necessary, failed component
Yearly	Case	Clean with compressed air to remove dust and other debris
	Motherboard	Check chips for chip creep and reseat if needed
	Adapter cards	Clean contacts with contact cleaner and reseat
As required	CMOS	Record and back up CMOS setup configuration
	System	Keep written record of hardware and software configuration of PC system
	Printer	Check ink and toner cartridges or ribbons and replace, if needed
	Hardware	Clean the keyboard, mouse, monitor, and case

Table 22-1. Preventive Maintenance Schedule *(continued)*

Of course, you should not drop or kick the PC. You should try to keep it in a relatively dust and smoke-free environment and avoid spilling liquid into any of its components, especially inside the system case.

Here is a list of other general and common sense tips for keeping your PC in tip-top working condition:

- Place your PC in a room that is both cool and dry. Heat and humidity are hard on electronics.
- Make sure that there is ample air space around the PC to enable it to have a free airflow, but avoid drafty and dusty areas.
- Keep the PC's cords and cables together and tucked out of the way to protect the cords, the PC, and you.
- Avoid powering the system on and off frequently. In addition to cycling between heating and cooling, it puts stress on its electronics.
- Enable any energy saving features on the PC, such as suspending the hard disk and monitor to save electricity and extend the life of these components.
- Connect the PC to the AC power source through a surge suppressor or an uninterruptible power supply (UPS) to protect the PC against the problems associated with electrical spikes, blackouts, and brownouts. (See Chapter 23 for more information on electrical power issues.)
- Always wear an antistatic wrist or ankle strap when working inside the system unit (case) to avoid possible damage from electrostatic discharge (ESD).
- Before beginning work on your PC or its peripherals, close any open applications, shut down the PC, and unplug it from the wall.
- Avoid placing the PC, especially the monitor and speakers, near strongly magnetized objects to avoid distortion or performance problems.
- Never connect or disconnect a serial, parallel, or video device while the system is running.
- Always use the Shut Down option to close the Windows operating system before powering down the PC.

Input Devices

Input devices, such as the keyboard and mouse, get dirty faster than most of the other parts of the PC because your hands are constantly touching them. Not that your hands are particularly dirty, but they do have oil that is deposited on the keys and the mouse. In addition, food crumbs, dirt, and other bits get between and under the keys of the keyboard and are picked up by the mouse ball and can cause it to not roll smoothly.

Keyboard

If dirt, food, or liquid gets under its keycaps, a keyboard can develop all sorts of problems, including keys that stutter, get stuck, or just stop working. The very best maintenance tip for a keyboard is to keep food and beverages away from it completely. After the monitor, the keyboard should be cleaned more frequently than any other component on the PC. The keyboard, like the one shown in Figure 22-1, is an open-faced device that collects whatever falls or spills on it.

To clean a keyboard and perform preventive maintenance, use the following steps:

WARNING: Avoid removing the keyboard cover, especially on older PCs with mechanical switch keys (see Chapter 18). If the keyboard is that seriously dirty or damaged, it might be better just to replace it altogether.

1. The easiest and best way to clean a keyboard is to turn it upside-down and shake it. Just about anything that has fallen under the keycaps should fall out, unless it is a larger item that is stuck behind the keys, such as a paperclip.
2. You can open a cleaning hole so that larger items can fall out by removing the keycaps of the last three keys on the right-hand end of the keyboard, which are the -, +, and ENTER keys of the Numeric keypad. To remove a keycap, gently pry it up with a small flat-bladed screwdriver.

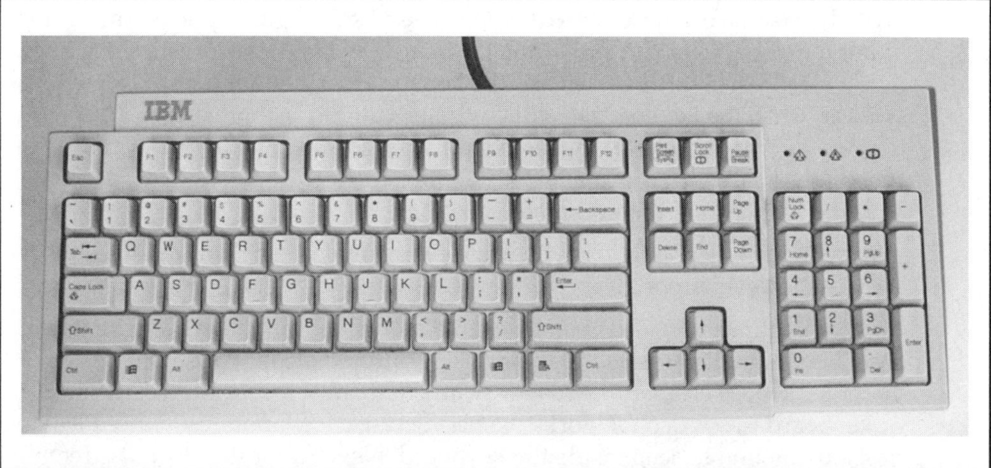

Figure 22-1. A standard 104-key keyboard

3. Use a can of compressed air to blow out the keyboard. Use the air stream to sweep the debris toward the removed keys or toward one end of the keyboard.

> ***TIP:*** You should always wear safety glasses or other eye protection when using compressed air.

4. Use a nonstatic blower brush, brush vacuum, or a probe to lightly loosen any large or stubborn debris and then shake the keyboard or use compressed air to blow it out.
5. If one or two keys are sticking or have stopped working, disconnect the keyboard from the PC and pry off the keycap (the part with the letter or number printed on it) with a screwdriver or another thin flat-bladed tool. Clean under and around the keyswitch using a cotton swab with a small amount of isopropyl alcohol on it. Use compressed air to blow it dry and replace the key(s).
6. Anytime liquid spills on a keyboard, immediately disconnect it from the PC (it gets its power from the PC cable) and turn it upside down.
7. If the keyboard has had soda pop, fruit juice, or some other sticky liquid spilled into it and the keys are beginning to stick and stutter, your choices are to replace the keyboard or wash it. Understand that introducing water into an electronic device is always risky, but if you use proper care, you can wash a keyboard. As explained in Chapter 18, newer keyboards are sealed under the key switches to protect the keyboard grid. Anything that spills in the keyboard is likely to settle on the keyboard membrane as sticky gunk. Use warm, clean water to rinse the residue out of the keyboard. By continually testing the keys, you can tell when you have rinsed the keyboard long enough. In extreme cases, you can wash the keyboard in a dishwasher with no soap. Even after the dishwasher's dry cycle, let the keyboard sit facedown for a few hours and then blow it out with compressed air. Before connecting it to the PC, be very sure that the keyboard is completely dry.
8. After you have cleaned the keyboard, replace any keycaps you removed or replace the keyboard's cover.
9. Most of the time, you also need to clean the outsides of the keys and keyboard case. Use a soft, lint-free cloth and a little isopropyl alcohol or a nonsudsing general-purpose cleaner to wipe away any body oils, ink, or dirt on the keys or keyboard case. Alcohol works the best because it evaporates without leaving moisture behind to seep inside the keyboard. Never pour the alcohol directly on the keys or case. Pour a small amount on the cloth and then wipe the keys and case. The same goes for the cleaner, if you choose to use one. A cotton swab dipped in cleaner or alcohol will get tight spots. Again, be absolutely sure that the keyboard is dry before connecting it to the PC and powering it up.

The 3M Corporation makes a special clean, soft, lint-free cloth that is an excellent tool to clean virtually any part of the PC. This cloth, the Scotch-Brite® High Performance Electronics Cloth (HPEC) (see Figure 22-2), can be purchased at any store that carries home cleaning supplies. In fact, 3M makes special versions of this product for electronics and for cleaning CDs and DVDs. This cloth allows you to clean without the need for alcohol or cleaners.

10. After you've cleaned the keyboard and are absolutely sure that the keyboard is dry, reconnect it to the PC and reboot the system. Watch the POST process carefully for keyboard errors. After the PC is running, test the keyboard by pressing each key and verifying its action.

Mouse

On a conventional balled mouse (see Figure 22-3), if the ball gets dirty, the mouse may not work right. Dirt can get on the ball and be transferred to the sensors and rollers inside the mouse that are used to detect the movement of your hand and the mouse and translate it to movement of the pointer on the screen.

Figure 22-2. Scotch-Brite® High Performance Cleaning Cloth can be used to clean much of the PC without water or cleaning solutions. Photo courtesy of 3M Corporation

Figure 22-3. A conventional ball mouse

The biggest single problem with a balled mouse (the kind that has a ball mechanism on its bottom) is the mouse pad. If the mouse ball is dirty, more than likely the mouse pad is also dirty and needs cleaning. The mouse pad sits in the open where it can get dusty, dirty, wet, and subjected to any accidents that occur on the desktop. If the mouse pad is not cleaned regularly, the mouse picks up the dirt and transfers it inside to the rollers and sensors when the ball rolls over the mouse pad. So, in addition to the steps on how to clean a mouse listed below, you should clean or replace the mouse pad regularly as well. To clean the mouse pad, wipe it with a damp cloth.

Check the mouse pad for wear in its fabric or plastic surface and for places where a track, dent, or dip may have been worn into it. A worn-out mouse pad can cause lint, bits of rubber, or threads to get pulled up inside the mouse.

You may even want to consider using an optical mouse, like the one shown in Figure 22-4, and eliminate both the mouse pad and the dirty mouse ball altogether. See Chapter 18 for more information on conventional and optical type mice.

To clean and care for a conventional balled mouse, use the following steps:

1. It is a good idea to shut down the PC when cleaning the mouse. Any open applications, including Windows, could do some weird things as you clean the mouse.

   You should definitely shut down the PC if you are planning to disconnect the mouse (assuming you have a cabled mouse) from the PC. If the mouse is a USB (Universal Serial Bus) mouse, you can disconnect the mouse while the system is running. USB ports are hot-swappable. However, if the mouse has a serial or PS/2 connector, you should shut down the PC before disconnecting, or reconnecting, the connector.

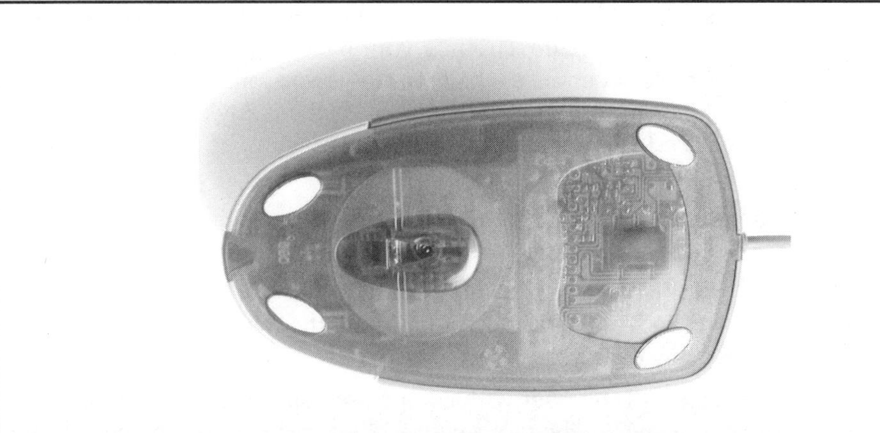

Figure 22-4. An optical mouse, which does not have a ball or moving rollers and sensors, eliminates most of the cleaning required for a ball mouse

2. Roll the mouse over onto its back and remove the ball access slide cover. As illustrated in Figure 22-5, the mouse ball is held in place by a locking cap that rotates to its locking or release positions. Turn the cap in the direction of the arrows printed or molded on it.

Figure 22-5. A mouse ball is held inside the mouse by a locking cap that can be rotated to release the ball

3. Wash your hands thoroughly before touching the mouse ball. Tip the mouse and drop the ball into your palm, cupping your hand so the mouse ball doesn't fall on the floor or table. Examine the ball for pits, cracks, or flat spots. Make sure that the ball is not lopsided or oval-shaped. If the ball has any of these problems, it needs to be replaced. Spare mouse balls are not easy to get, so your best bet is to replace the mouse.
4. Inspect the mouse ball's chamber, shown in Figure 22-6, for lint, dirt, and threads and carefully remove any you find with tweezers or a cotton swab with just a drop of alcohol on it.
5. Inspect the rollers inside the ball chamber and use the tweezers or swab and alcohol to remove any dirt or lint.
6. Blow out the mouse ball chamber with compressed air. To avoid damaging the small electronic parts inside the mouse, direct the air stream off to one side and try not to blast the rollers. You shouldn't try to blow out the dust inside the mouse ball chamber with your mouth for two reasons: saliva may get in the chamber and you may get dust in your eyes.
7. Use a very slightly damp, lint-free cloth or a Scotch-Brite HPEC cloth to clean the mouse ball. If you use a damp cloth, use only water with no cleaners and especially no alcohol. Cleaners and alcohol can shrink or distort the ball. Don't soak it or scrub it, just wipe it clean, let it dry, and then reinsert it in the chamber and replace the locking cap.
8. If needed, you can use isopropyl alcohol or a general-purpose no-rinse cleaner to clean the exterior of the mouse.
9. Restart the PC and watch for any POST problems with the mouse or connector. Give the mouse a complete test, including its buttons.

Figure 22-6. The mouse ball chamber must be inspected for lint, dirt, and other debris

Other Input Devices

If there are other input devices on the PC, you should clean them periodically as well. How frequently you do this depends on the device and how often it is used. Here are some cleaning hints for several of the more common input devices:

- **Scanner** The biggest issue with a flat-bed scanner is its inside glass surface. Use either a nonammonia glass cleaner and a lint-free cloth or the Scotch-Brite HPEC for electronics.
- **Digitizing tablet** Unless the digitizing surface (see Figure 22-7) is a rubber-like material, you can clean it with a general-purpose cleaner and a damp lint-free cloth. Take care not to get the unit too wet and dry it completely.
- **Digital camera** Use a lens cleaner solution that you would use for eyeglasses and a soft lint-free cloth to clean the lens. Use either isopropyl alcohol or a general-purpose cleaner to clean the exterior of the camera. Avoid getting the unit very wet.
- **Microphone** Use the same procedure as for the digitizing tablet. Be very careful not to get water or alcohol in the openings and down inside the microphone.

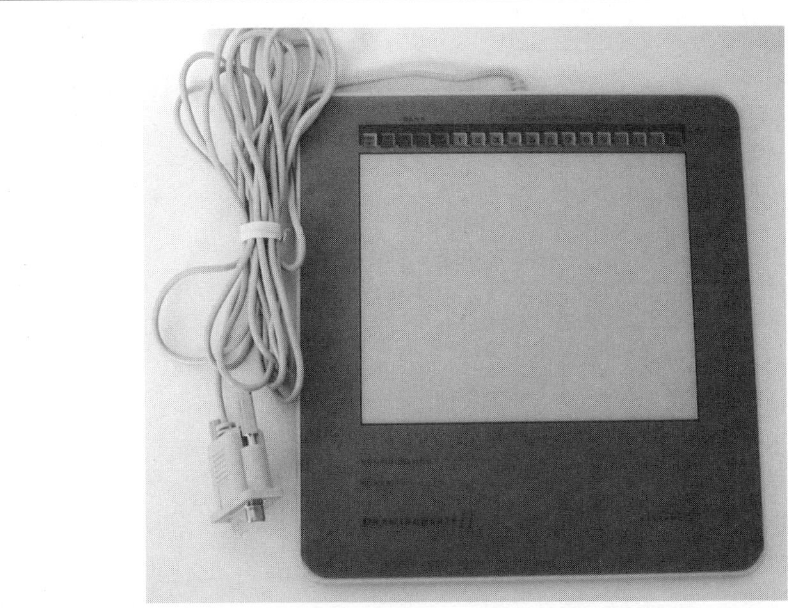

Figure 22-7. A digitizing tablet

Output Devices

Output devices receive more attention in general, probably because if they get dirty it impacts the quality of their products. This section deals with the steps you should use to clean and care for monitors, printers, and speakers.

Monitor

The monitor's glass screen (see Figure 22-8) is the component on a PC that should be cleaned the most often. The monitor screen produces a lot of static electricity that attracts and holds dust and flying lint. If the screen becomes covered with dust, it can strain your eyes to view the screen for extended periods.

Unfortunately, most people take too many safety chances when they clean the monitor screen. The following steps detail how you can safely keep the glass screen and the monitor itself clean and bright:

1. Before cleaning the monitor, switch its power off and unplug it from its power source. There is really no need to disconnect it from the PC. After turning the monitor off, wait a few minutes before beginning to clean it. **Do not wear an ESD ground strap when working with a monitor, even to clean it.**

Figure 22-8. The monitor screen collects dust and should be cleaned regularly. Photo courtesy of ViewSonic Corporation

2. Using compressed air, clean away any dust on the top of the monitor's case. Point the air stream to blow across the top of the monitor, not directly down on it, to prevent dust from blowing into the monitor's vents.
   Never open and remove the cover of a monitor! There is an extremely high voltage hazard inside every monitor, regardless of its size.
3. Use a soft cloth and either isopropyl alcohol or a general-purpose no-rinse cleaner to clean the outside of the monitor case. The alcohol is probably a better choice because it will not create a safety hazard if it's inadvertently dripped inside the case.
4. Use an antistatic cleaner or a Scotch-Brite HPEC for electronics cloth to clean the glass of the monitor. Never use an ammonia-based glass cleaner on the monitor glass. The monitor screen is coated with filtering chemicals to help improve the image and reduce eyestrain. Using a harsh cleaner can remove these coatings, harming the monitor and potentially harming you.
   Never use water or a liquid cleaner to wash the monitor's glass with the power on. Water is an excellent conductor of electricity and if your hand makes sufficient contact with the screen you could be the ground for the electricity in the monitor.
5. Reconnect the monitor and test the video. If nothing displays, check the power switch, the power cord, the video connection, and the brightness and contrast settings, any of which could have been accidentally dislodged, moved, or turned while you were cleaning the case.

Printer

The cleaning procedures and the supplies used vary by the type of printer in use. Laser printers have completely different cleaning and maintenance requirements from inkjets and dot matrix printers. This section gives a general overview of the cleaning and preventive maintenance steps you can use for each type of printer. However, you should follow the specific instructions provided by the manufacturer of your printer in the owner's manual or from the manufacturer's Web site.

Laser Printer The general process for cleaning a laser printer (see Figure 22-9) follows. However, because there are many different designs for how the laser toner and drum cartridge fit into a printer, the process used for any specific printer may be slightly different.

1. Gather the tools you will need. To clean a laser printer thoroughly, you need to have a laser cleaning kit for your make and model and a small vacuum cleaner that is designed to handle laser printer toner. If the cleaning kit does not include cleaning sheets, you should get a pack also.

   Toner, as described in Chapter 17, is made up of ferrous oxide (iron) particles that are coated with a plastic resin material. During the printer's fusing process, the plastic resin is melted to bond the toner to the paper. This great

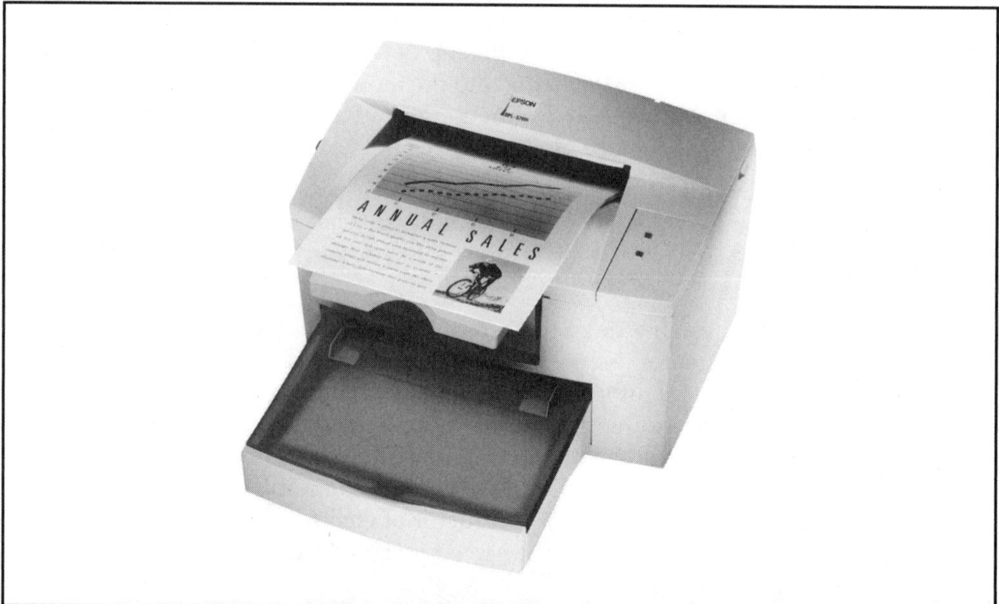

Figure 22-9. A laser printer. Photo courtesy of Epson America, Inc.

adaptation of technology can become a nightmare in your vacuum cleaner if you are using a standard model in which the toner passes near or through the very hot motor where it can melt and gum up the works. Special models of vacuum cleaners are available for working just with toner. You can also contract with an office supplies company to have somebody come in to clean the laser printer for you.

Cleaning kits typically contain cartridge cleaning sheets, cleaning solution, lint-free swabs, an antistatic cloth, plastic gloves, and a few ink and toner remover hand wipes.

2. If the printer has been in use very recently, let the printer sit idle for at least 15 minutes to allow the fusing assembly to cool before removing or opening the covers.
3. Switch off the power on the laser printer and unplug it to prevent the power from being accidentally switched back on. Remove any paper or paper cartridges from the printer.
4. Open the part of the printer's case that exposes the fusing assembly. Follow the printer's instructions to clean the fusing rollers. Typically, this is done with a lint-free cloth and denatured alcohol (which is not the same as isopropyl alcohol). Wipe the rollers lightly and do not rub. Do not touch any of the gears inside the printer.

5. Using an appropriate vacuum with a soft brush attachment, clean the fusing area of any debris; if you do not have a vacuum, at least use compressed air to blow out any debris in this area. In either case, you should wear eye protection. Be very careful not to snag or pull any wires in the fusing area.
6. The next area to clean is the transfer roller area (see the printer's documentation for the specific instructions on how to clean the transfer rollers). This is typically under the toner cartridge, so you must remove the toner cartridge and set it on some newspaper or other large sheets of paper in case the toner spills.
7. Laser printer cleaning kits contain a soft brush with which to clean the transfer rollers. After brushing the rollers, use a vacuum or compressed air to clean away any debris in this area of the printer.
8. Check the paper path and use a soft brush to clean the feed rollers if needed. Replace the toner cartridge if needed and replace the cartridge and any of the printer's cover parts that were removed in earlier steps.
9. Before reconnecting the printer to its AC power source, clean the exterior. The best cleaner is a mild liquid detergent, such as dish soap. Mix a solution of the detergent with water, dampen a cloth with the solution, and wipe the printer clean. Never pour or spray water or cleaners directly on the printer. If you are using a prepared cleaner, spray or pour a small amount on the cloth and wipe the printer with the cloth.
10. If you cleaned the printer's exterior, wait a few minutes to make sure the printer is dry before replacing the paper supply and reconnecting the printer to its power source.
11. If you have laser printer cleaning sheets, run one or two through the printer, following the instructions on the sheet pack to clean the components inside the cartridge. You should run a cleaning sheet each time you change the toner cartridge. If the printer is smearing or smudging the print, use a cleaning sheet to clean out the toner cartridge and perhaps switch to a laser printer type paper.

Inkjet Printer Chapter 17 explains the inkjet printing process in detail, including how the inkjet cartridge works to print a page. Probably the biggest problem you can have with an inkjet printer is a clogged print head on the inkjet cartridge. Beyond that, the inkjet printer, like the one shown in Figure 22-10, is a simple affair that is considered disposable technology. Several inkjet models are now on the market that cost between $40 and $100, which is not all that much more than the ink cartridge itself. Should anything major happen to an inkjet printer, such as the feed rollers getting misaligned or the cartridge gearing that moves the print cartridge side-to-side failing to operate, it is usually less expensive to get a new printer than it is to fix it.

Many inkjet printers have a built-in print head cleaning routine. There are two types of inkjets available, those with the print head built into the ink cartridge, such as Hewlett

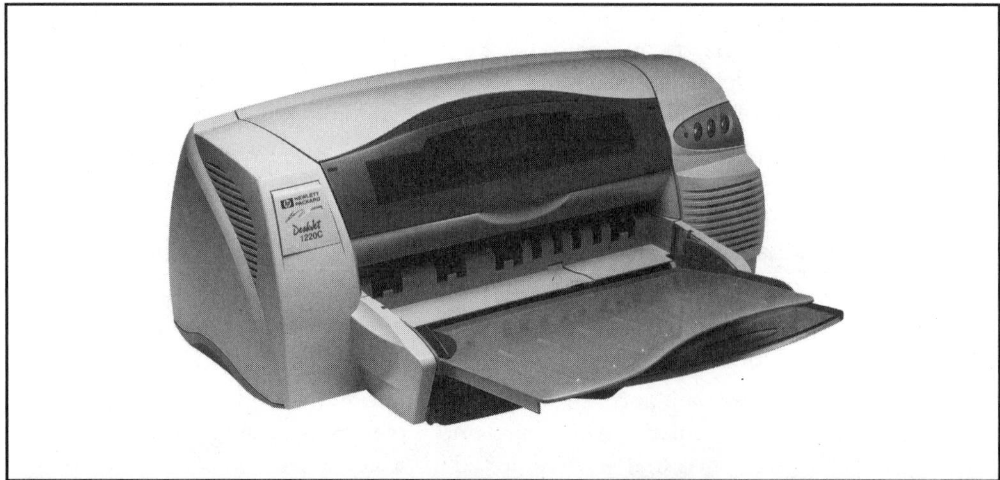

Figure 22-10. An inkjet printer. Photo courtesy of Hewlett Packard Corporation

Packard and Canon printers, and those that separate the print head and ink reservoir, such as an Epson.

Here are some cleaning and maintenance tips that can extend the life of an inkjet printer:

- Clean the print nozzles regularly. Most inkjet printers have a built-in utility to clean or unclog the print head nozzles. You should do this fairly regularly, especially if the printer sits idle for a couple of weeks. If this doesn't work, you can remove the ink cartridge and use a swab or lint-free cloth (that you don't mind staining permanently) dampened with a small amount of isopropyl alcohol and wipe the print head lightly. Don't rub back and forth across the nozzles. Reinstall the print cartridge and rerun the print head cleaning utility. If the cartridge is still clogged, replace it.
- Never turn the printer off at a plug strip or surge suppressor or other power source. Always use the printer's power switch to turn it off. The printer has some built-in functions, such as parking the print head, that are tied to the power-off function of the printer's on/off switch.
- Use inkjet quality paper. Standard bond paper, which is not treated for inkjet inks, absorbs too much ink. On black and white printing, the result may be a fuzzy or blurry print image. On color prints, the result may be light or blurred images. Inkjet paper is treated to provide the best possible image. The printer's owner's manual most likely has a recommendation for the paper that should be used.

- ▲ Dust and paper scraps and bits can collect in the bottom of the paper path in an inkjet printer. On a fairly regular basis, you should check out the inside of the paper path and remove the paper scraps and blow out any dust or paper bits that have accumulated with compressed air. Always wear eye protection when using compressed air, especially when blowing about bits of paper.

Dot Matrix Printer Two primary components cause a dot matrix printer to need to be cleaned regularly: the inked ribbon and the forms tractor.

The downside of a dot matrix printer, after its noise and slow speed, is the ribbon. The ribbon is messy to install and replace and messy to operate. In addition, ribbons are not evenly coated with ink and can drop bits of dried ink down inside the printer's case. The forms tractor is the mechanism that pulls tractor feed paper, the kind shown in the printer in Figure 22-11, through the printer by the holes along the sides of the paper. As the paper is pulled through, the bits of paper from the holes fall down inside the printer.

The paper bits and the dried ink bits should be cleaned out of the printer regularly with a vacuum or compressed air. To get down into the printer and perform any maintenance prescribed by the manufacturer on the print head, you need to remove the ribbon. Typically, a ribbon release lever unlocks the ribbon cartridge so it can be lifted straight up and out. However, since dot matrix printers and their setup vary greatly by manufacturer, check the documentation before cleaning the printer, especially the print head.

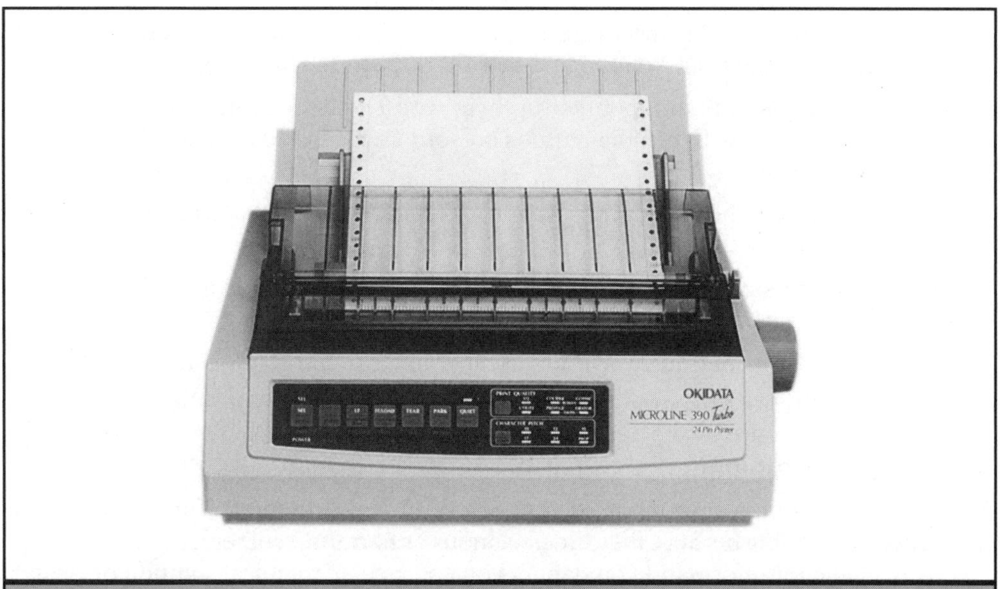

Figure 22-11. A dot matrix printer. Photo courtesy of OkiData Americas, Inc.

Cleaning and Maintenance Supplies

To keep your PC in good working condition, you should have a few simple tools, some cleaning supplies, a boot disk from the PC's installed operating system, an Emergency Repair Disk (ERD), and a PC maintenance schedule. The tools and supplies can be gathered from computer supply stores and even the grocery store. The maintenance schedule is likely in the documentation for the PC, and a sample schedule was included earlier in this chapter (see "Preventive Maintenance for a PC").

Here is a list of the tools and supplies you should have on hand to care for and maintain your PC:

- A bottle of 70 percent isopropyl alcohol (a quart bottle is probably more than enough). This is used to clean many of the smaller parts of the PC, keyboard, printer, and mouse.
- A can or two of compressed air. This is used to clean just about everything on the PC, especially the areas that are hard to reach and those that cannot have water or liquid on them.
- A package of nonshredding cleaning tissues, a soft lint-free cloth, or a Scotch-Brite HPEC cloth. The Scotch-Brite cloth is recommended.
- A package of high-quality cotton swabs. These are used for cleaning just about any small object inside or outside of the PC.
- A #8 Chinese bristle artist's brush, which has bristles about two inches long and is one inch in diameter. You can find these at craft stores that sell painting supplies.
- An inexpensive pair of pointed-tip tweezers. These are useful for removing bits of debris from between the buttons on your keyboard or from inside the mouse ball chamber.
- A small brush-head vacuum cleaner for cleaning the keyboard and inside the system case.
- A medium-size Phillips screwdriver for case, keyboard, and adapter board screws.
- A bottle of nonammonia window cleaner to clean the glass on the monitor.
- An ESD grounding strap. You can also get ESD mats to place the PC on.

Know Your Chemicals

Many liquid cleaning compounds present safety and environmental problems and require special handling because they are poisonous or harmful in other ways. The best reference available for information on dangers of a particular chemical solution or cleaner, including household cleaners, is its Material Safety Data Sheet (MSDS). An MSDS is prepared for every potentially hazardous chemical product.

The contents of a standard MSDS are

- **Section 1** Chemical Product Section
- **Section 2** Composition/Information on Ingredients
- **Section 3** Hazard Identification
- **Section 4** First Aid Measures
- **Section 5** Firefighting Measures
- **Section 6** Accidental Release Measures
- **Section 7** Handling and Storage
- **Section 8** Exposure Control/Personal Protection
- **Section 9** Physical and Chemical Properties
- **Section 10** Stability and Reactivity
- **Section 11** Toxicological Information
- **Section 12** Ecological Information
- **Section 13** Disposal Considerations
- **Section 14** Transportation Information
- **Section 15** Regulatory Information
- **Section 16** Other Information

The following two Web sites list most of the products you might need information about or to look up a product you're not completely sure of:

- The Northwest Fisheries Science Center of the National Oceanic & Atmospheric Administration: **http://research.nwfsc.noaa.gov/msds.html**
- The Vermont Safety Information on the Internet (SIRI): **http://siri.org/msds/index.html**

The first place to look for product safety information is its label. If a hazard exists from using a product, the label will usually include this information. The types of cleaning supplies you should be concerned about include solutions that are used to clean the contacts and connections of adapter cards, glass cleaners, and plastic or metal case cleaning products.

Inside the Case

One of the last places many users think to clean is the inside of the PC's case, because most users never open the PC case. However, the inside of the case should be cleaned regularly, especially if the PC is in a dusty or dirty environment with lots of airborne particles.

The system cooling fan in the power supply either pulls air into or pushes air out of the system case. In either situation, the air is sucked into or pushed out of air vents on the case. A mid-tower PC sitting on the floor in an office, bedroom, or family room will accumulate dust around its air vents, on the grill or blades of the fan, or both.

In extreme examples, the dust inside the case can accumulate on the processor's fan or heat sinks or on the motherboard itself. If enough dust, oil, water, or even metal bits are accumulated inside the case, the motherboard or processor can develop cooling or electrical problems.

So, it is an excellent idea to clean the inside of the PC's case at least every six months. You can use a soft brush vacuum cleaner (the standard type is okay) or compressed air to blow the dust out of the case.

While you have the case open, also check any adapter cards, memory modules, chips, cables, wires, and other motherboard components for fit and connection. As the PC heats up and cools down when turned on and off, integrated circuits, connectors, and expansion cards can creep out of their sockets or connections. This phenomenon is called "chip creep," and it is another good reason to check inside the PC case on a regular basis.

Always wear ESD wrist or ankle straps when working inside the PC case. It is always a good idea to ground yourself with one of the metal chassis parts even when wearing ESD gear.

Here are the steps you should use to perform preventive maintenance inside the system case:

1. After powering off the PC and removing the power cord from the AC power source, carefully remove the case cover.
2. Perform a visual inspection of the inside of the case to assess the need for cleaning or adjustments. On most cases, the inside and outside vents probably have at least a little dust accumulated on them. However, if dust is collecting in a place it shouldn't be, the cooling system may not be working as effectively as it could. The case may be cracked or a part (perhaps an expansion slot filler) may be missing. Examine the interior of the case thoroughly for dust, corrosion, leaking battery acid, and other problems. If the case has only a light accumulation of dust, use compressed air to clean it. Use a vacuum with a brush head to clean away any larger accumulations of dust.
3. Check the data and power cables on the motherboard, power supply, disk drives, and so on for loose connections. Check the adapter cards to make sure they are properly seated.
4. Using compressed air, blow off first the outside vents and then the inside vents of the power supply. Use the compressed air to clean the drive bays, adapter cards, and finally, the outside vents of the case.
5. Replace the case cover, taking care not to snag any cables.

6. Using a general-purpose cleaner, clean the outside of the case, being careful not to get any moisture inside the case.
7. Power on the PC and monitor the POST process for errors.

Hard Disk Drives

There isn't too much you can physically do for a hard disk drive to keep it running, beyond keeping an area of free airflow around it and keeping its cables and power connections snug. Because hard disk drives are sealed units, no physical cleaning needs to be done. The preventive maintenance on a hard disk drive centers around optimizing the storage space.

Here are the preventive maintenance activities you should perform for the hard disk drive:

- Create full and partial backups of the data on the hard disk.
- Run ScanDisk to the surface of the hard disk for errors.
- Run the Disk Defragmenter optimization program.
- Empty the Recycle Bin at least monthly.
- Run the Disk Cleanup utility to remove unneeded files, such as temporary files, Internet content, and installation files, from the hard disk weekly. You can file this tool on the Accessories | System Tools menu.

Data Backups

Backing up your hard disk data to another storage media that can be stored outside of the PC and perhaps outside of the building is definitely preventive maintenance. A data backup protects you against hard disk failure, PC problems, and worse. Hardware can be replaced, but often your data cannot be, at least not very easily. Making a backup copy of your files is a safety precaution that ensures your data can outlive the device on which it's stored. A cardinal rule of computing is to back up files regularly, and then back up the backups.

Any removable medium can be used to make a backup copy of your hard disk's data. Which medium you should use depends mostly on the amount of data you have to back up. If you are backing up a 40GB hard disk, you probably should consider tape, but if you are backing up a 100MB hard disk, a Zip disk will work nicely.

Most operating systems include utilities for creating a backup, and a backup utility is usually included with most tape, recordable CD, and other writable media drives. A variety of software packages specifically designed to perform backups are also available for purchase. Figure 22-12 shows the Windows Backup utility that is included on the Accessories | System Tools menu.

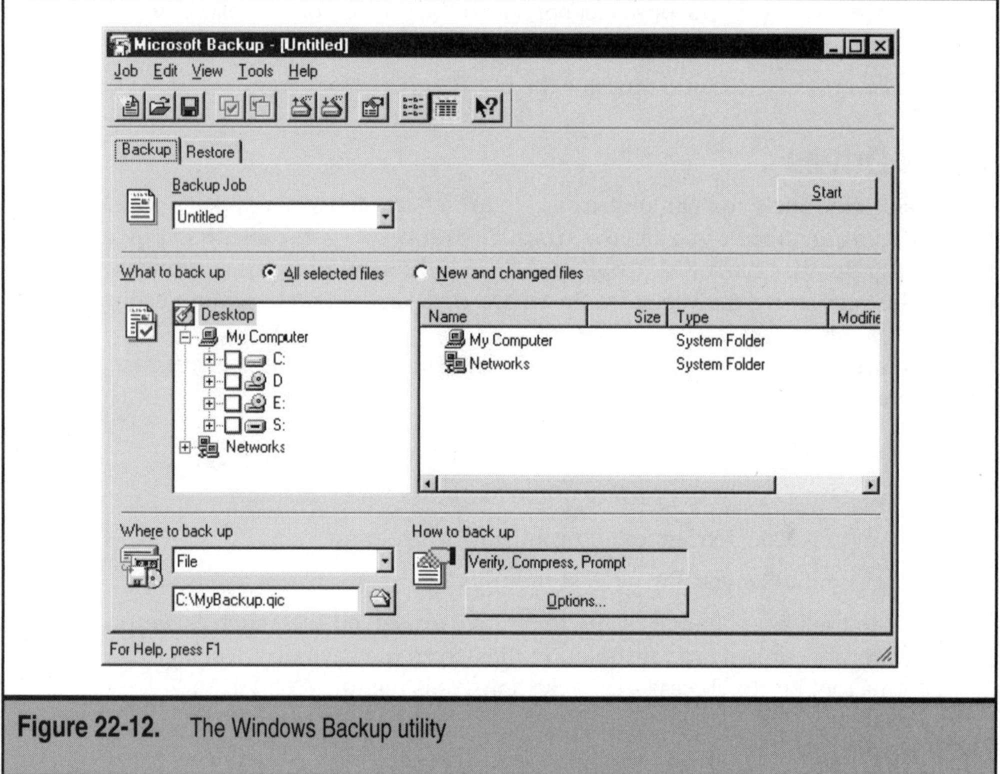

Figure 22-12. The Windows Backup utility

Backup software offers some advantages over just copying a file to a removable medium. Most offer data compression techniques to reduce the number of disks or tapes needed to hold the archived data. Many also offer cataloging routines and single directory or file restore capabilities.

You can create four different types of backups:

- A full backup (or archive backup) includes every directory, folder, file, and program from the hard disk.
- An incremental backup includes only those files that have been modified since the last backup. An incremental backup clears the archive bit of the files it copies to the backup medium.

Each directory and file on the hard disk has an archive bit associated with it. This bit is used by backup utilities to determine which files should be included in the backup.

- A differential backup includes the files that were created or modified since the last full backup. A differential backup does not clear the archive bit.

▲ A copy backup copies specified files and directories to a specified location or drive. When you copy a file from the hard disk to a diskette to safeguard it, you have created a copy backup. The DOS command XCOPY is commonly used to create copy backups because it will copy a directory along with its files and subdirectories.

Optimize the Disk

Windows includes a variety of applets that you can use to improve the performance of the hard disk drive. These tools are found on the Accessories | System Tools menu shown in Figure 22-13. The primary tools available are ScanDisk and Disk Defragmenter.

ScanDisk This utility can be used to scan the disk surface for media errors, scan files, and folders for data problems, or both. ScanDisk runs each time Windows and your PC is not

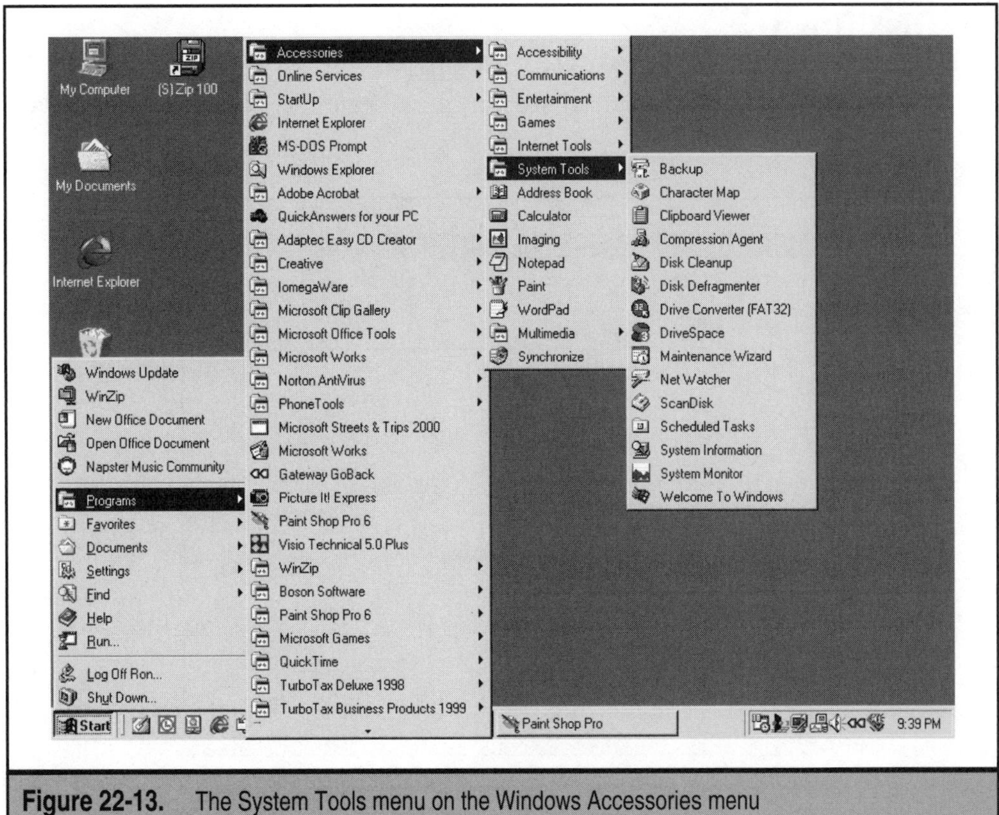

Figure 22-13. The System Tools menu on the Windows Accessories menu

shut down properly. In addition, you should run ScanDisk at least weekly to find and repair small errors on the disk before they become major problems. Figure 22-14 shows the ScanDisk utility running on a Windows 98 system.

Disk Defragmenter The Disk Defragmenter utility is used to rearrange your disk files and combine and organize unused disk space so applications run faster. As you open, modify, and delete files on the hard disk, files become fragmented. The Defragmenter eliminates the fragmentation so that the data in a file is readily available to programs asking for it. Figure 22-15 shows the startup screens of the Disk Defragmenter.

Delete Unused Files A Windows System Tool applet you can use to remove unnecessary files from your hard disk is the Disk Cleanup utility. This tool scans the disk you designate (it works on every disk drive, including diskettes and Zip disks) to find files that can be removed without seriously impacting the operation of the PC and Windows operating system. Figure 22-16 shows the dialog box of the Disk Cleanup applet.

Floppy Disk Drive

There really isn't much that can go wrong with a floppy disk drive beyond verifying that the disk is working. Over-cleaning the floppy disk drive can destroy the read/write

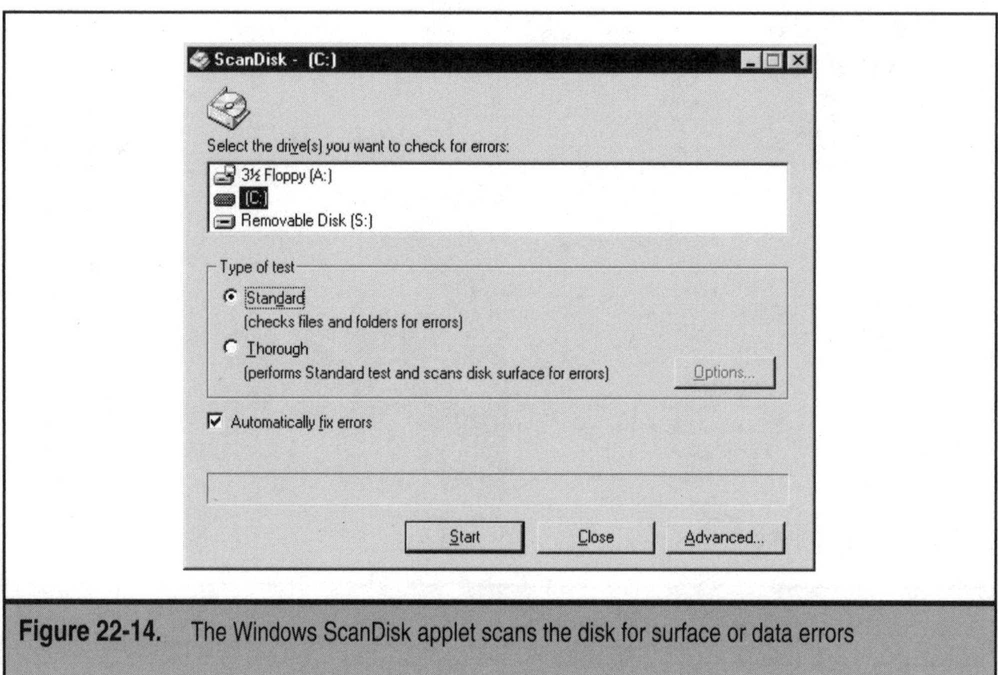

Figure 22-14. The Windows ScanDisk applet scans the disk for surface or data errors

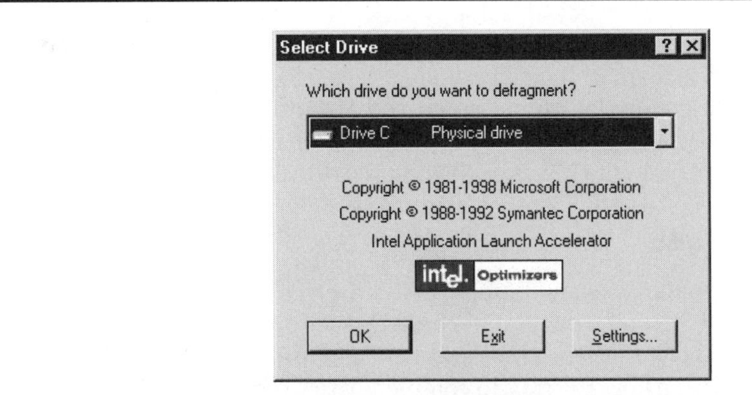

Figure 22-15. The Windows Disk Defragmenter organizes data and free space on the disk

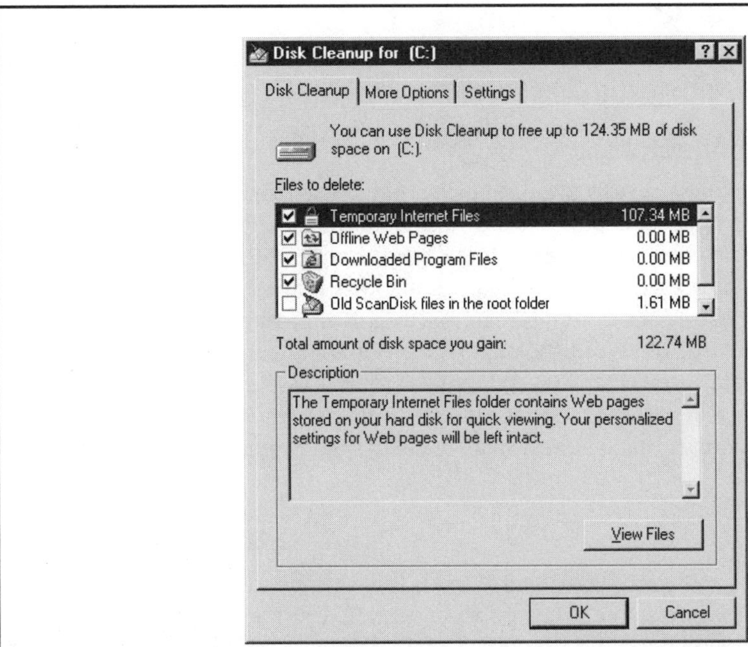

Figure 22-16. The Windows Disk Cleanup utility is used to remove unnecessary files from a disk

heads of the drive. You should only clean a floppy disk drive when it begins having read or write problems. Every so often you may want to blow any dust or debris out of the drive by blowing compressed air in the drive slot.

A floppy disk drive cleaning kit can be purchased at virtually all computer supply stores. When the drive begins exhibiting signs of reading or writing problems, use the cleaning kit to clean the read/write heads, following the directions on the kit.

CD-ROM and DVD Drives

Two things should be regularly cleaned on a CD-ROM or DVD: the disk tray and the lens. The tray is cleaned with some general purpose cleaner or isopropyl alcohol by applying the solution to a soft, lint-free cloth and gently wiping down the tray. Avoid pressing down on the tray. Allow the tray to completely dry before closing it.

To clean the lens, you need to purchase a CD drive cleaning kit that is designed for tray-based CD players. There are many versions of CD cleaning kits available, including some for caddy drives, automobile drives, and others. In the cleaning kit will be a CD disk that has a set of very small brushes on it that clean the lens as the disk spins. Follow the directions on the package exactly to avoid damaging your CD drive.

Miscellaneous Components

Two other components mounted on the motherboard that require attention are expansion slots and external ports.

Expansion Slot Connectors

The connectors in an expansion slot should be cleaned at least twice a year. You can use contact cleaner that is made especially for cleaning metallic electronic connectors, but in most cases, you don't need to go that far. Typically, you only need to remove the expansion card without touching its contacts and use a soft cloth, like the Scotch-Brite HPEC, to wipe the contacts off. Wipe each contact from top to bottom rather than across to avoid dislodging it from the card. Blow out the expansion slot using compressed air.

If you see any discoloration on the card's contacts or on those in the slot, which are referred to as gold fingers, it is either oxidation or a chemical reaction of the metals. Use contact cleaner to clean the contacts. Use a swab to clean gold fingers; avoid rubbing them with a cloth.

External Ports

About all you can do for an external port that extends through the case is to keep it from collecting dust. A very dusty port may make a poor connection. Use compressed air to clean off any unused external ports, especially USB ports. Do not use water or alcohol on female ports because it can get down inside the pinholes and possibly corrode the connection.

Portable PCs

Portable PCs, including laptops, notebooks, and palmtops, have many of the same preventive maintenance requirements as a full-sized PC. Most of the peripheral devices, such as the hard disk, floppy disk, CD-ROM, keyboard, mouse, and ports, use the same cleaning and maintenance activities. The components that have special care requirements are batteries, the video display, and case.

Batteries

The batteries used in portable PCs do not last the life of the PC. They are expendable and eventually lose their ability to be recharged. Today's PC batteries are far better than those used only a few years ago, but they still need to be replaced at some point. Many portable PC users do not understand this.

The most popular battery type is the nickel metal-hydride (NiMH) battery. This battery can be recharged around 600 times before it will begin having recharge problems, which means it will last about a year. The best way to get the most out of a battery is to discharge it completely before you recharge it.

The newest form of battery for portable PCs is the Lithium-Ion (Li-Ion) battery that has a life of about 1200 charges. However, because of its cost, this battery is found only on the most expensive systems.

The best preventive maintenance for portable PC batteries is another battery, but here are some tips on how to get the most out your portable PC battery:

- Use a port replicator or the AC power adapter whenever possible.
- The biggest drains on the battery are the disk drives. Avoid disk access whenever possible.
- If your portable PC includes built-in power-saving features or software, use it. The power-saving features include such things as slowing the processor speed, suspending the hard disk when idle, and others. When you don't need the speed, conserve the power.
- If the portable PC is designed for the Green Star energy standard, it reduces its power consumption as much as 99 percent when it goes into Sleep or Suspend modes, which simulate a shutdown of the PC. The downside to suspending the PC is the time it takes the PC to reawaken when you are ready to work again.

LCD Display

Just like with a standard PC monitor, you should not use harsh cleaners on an LCD display. LCD displays can be scratched very easily and you should not use anything more harsh than a general window cleaner (without ammonia) on a soft, lint-free cloth (such as an old T-shirt). Even better is the Scotch-Brite HPEC cloth I obviously favor.

Case

Portable PC cases, except those on ruggedized portables, are fragile, having been designed for lightness rather than strength. Dropping a portable PC can damage all of the components of the PC.

To clean the portable PC's case, avoid using any liquid in or around the keyboard. Use a soft, damp, lint-free cloth to wipe over the keyboard and the exterior of the case. Use compressed air to clean the keyboard and diskette and CD-ROM slots.

Virus Detection and Protection

A computer virus is a nasty piece of software that attacks a PC with the intent of disrupting its operations, destroying its data, or erasing part or all of its disk drives.

A virus attaches itself to another file or piece of code on a floppy disk, downloaded file, e-mail attachment, or it takes the form of an executable file and runs when it's opened on the target system. A virus replicates itself and infects other systems, propagating itself from one computer to another on a file or by e-mail.

Once on the PC, a virus manifests itself in a variety of ways, including (but not limited to):

- Spontaneous system reboots
- System crashes
- Application crashes
- Sound card or speaker problems
- Distorted, misshapen, or missing video on the monitor
- Corrupted or missing data from disk files
- Disappearing disk partitions
- Boot disks that won't boot
- All of the entries in your e-mail address boot receiving copies of the virus via e-mail

The best defense against a virus on your PC is antivirus software. There are several antivirus offerings on the market, such as Norton Antivirus, McAfee Vshield, and Trend Micro's PC-cillan. These companies provide you with the ability to update the virus database about as often as new viruses show up, which is almost daily.

Electrical Protection

Several levels of protection are available to protect a single PC, a group of PC equipment, or an entire network. How much protection you need is based on the amount of equipment you are trying to protect against electrical over-voltage and under-voltage conditions.

The first line of defense is a surge suppressor. The entry-level surge suppressor is a plug-strip that includes a varistor that is designed to fail should a spike of electricity be sensed to protect anything plugged into it. There are higher end models that will protect your phone lines, modems, and network connections. The best protection from electrical problems is an uninterruptible power supply (UPS), which also provides backup power if the power fails or runs below normal voltages for a while. See Chapter 23 for more information on electrical protection.

Environmental Issues

By law, several of a PC's components require special handling or disposal procedures. The components that you must take care with are batteries, mercury switches, and the monitor's CRT.

Like all batteries, PC batteries, which are usually the lithium battery that powers CMOS memory, should not be disposed of in either fire or water. Batteries should not be casually discarded but should be disposed of according to local restrictions and regulations covering the disposal or recycling of all batteries. Leaking batteries should be handled very carefully. If you must handle a leaking battery, make sure you do not get the electrolyte, the stuff on the inside of the battery, in your eyes or mouth.

A monitor contains the following contaminants: solvents and solvent vapors, metals (including a very high level of lead), photoresist materials, deionized water, acids, oxidizers, phosphor, ammonia, aluminum, carbon slurry, and a long list of other chemicals and caustic materials. Because of this, a monitor should not simply be thrown in the dumpster. It should be disposed of carefully—probably the best way is through a disposal service that handles computer equipment.

Because nearly 70 percent of the CRT's components contain lead, the CRT comes under the Land Disposal Ban Program of the Resource Conservation and Recovery Act (RCRA). This law requires that old CRTs (and old TVs, by the way) be dismantled, crushed, and encapsulated in cement. Salvage companies exist that properly dispose of CRTs for a fee.

Other PC and peripheral components that should be disposed using special procedures are laser printer toner cartridges and refill kits and the used or empty containers of chemical solvents and cleaners. The best place to find information on the proper way to dispose of an item is in its documentation or the MSDS or WHMIS information on a chemical product.

CHAPTER 23

Electrical Power Issues

In one of the true ironies of the computing world, a PC's biggest enemy is the very thing it must have to operate: the electricity it gets from the public power system. The public power system is an imperfect river of electricity that has periods of high, low, and no voltage. The high voltages, referred to as over-voltage or spikes and surges, can fry the PC's power supply and eventually the motherboard and all attached to it. Low voltage periods, also called under-voltage and brownouts, can also inflict damage on the power supply and the other components of the PC. A sudden loss of power, a.k.a. a blackout, loses data and valuable processing time. In addition, a spike in the voltage typically follows a blackout that can fry the fragile components inside the PC.

The two types of damage that can be done to a PC by its electrical supply and electrostatic discharge (ESD) are catastrophic and degradation. Catastrophic damage is when a component or device is destroyed all at once in a single event, such as a direct lightning strike on a building burning out all of the electrical devices plugged into its AC mains. Degradation is when a device is damaged over a period of time, a little at a time, and eventually, usually much later, begins to fail or have intermittent problems. While a catastrophic failure is very serious, most damage to a PC and its components and peripherals is degradation, the result of hundreds and thousands of small electrical events that have slowly degraded the ability of a device to perform. People tend to focus on the catastrophic events, but you should protect your system against degradation.

POWER LINE PROBLEMS

A PC's power supply is quite a heroic device when you consider all that it must contend with day in and day out. One thing that can be said for the public electrical supply system is that it is not consistent. Not all of the inconsistency is the electrical company's fault. Many different situations, many beyond the electric company's control, can cause the electricity received at your home or office to fluctuate up or down. The fluctuations on the electrical supply line are what cause the PC (and its power supply) the most trouble.

Six general types of electrical events occur on an electrical power line and reach your PC: line noise, power surges, power spikes, power sags, brownouts, and blackouts. Each of these has its own varying level of impact on the PC power supply, but the PC can be protected from each successfully. It's mostly a matter of how much you want to spend to protect your system.

Line Noise

Every electrical circuit has a certain amount of electrical line noise, which is electromagnetic interference (EMI) caused by many sources, both from nature and electrical equipment. Most EMI comes from electrical equipment, such as a motor, welder, fluorescent lighting, and radio transmitters. An electrical supply line that is shared with noisy electrical equipment very often carries the electrical noise of the equipment over the circuit to other devices connected to the circuit. An example is what happens to your AM radio or the TV set when a vacuum cleaner is operated on the same electrical circuit. The static you hear is electrical noise. Nearby electrical storm can also be picked up by the electric supply and transmits EMI over the supply lines.

Nearly all PC power supplies are built to handle normal levels of line noise, but excessive line noise often passes through the power supply to the motherboard, disk drives, and any other devices connected to the power supply. Line noise can cause serious problems for a PC or a server if it is not protected. The types of problems that can develop from electrical line noise include memory errors, data loss, circuit connection loss, data transmission problems, and frequent system lockups.

Power Surges

The nominal operating voltage of the AC (alternating current) electricity supplied to the wall outlets in your house or office is 110 volts, and that's what the power company will tell you is the voltage of your wall outlets. However, in real life, the actual voltage on the line can vary between 85 and 135 volts, and most PC power supplies have a strong enough operating range to handle power fluctuations within a certain range. Most ATX form factor power supplies (see Chapter 14 for more information on the PC power supply) have operating ranges like 92 to 130 volts AC or 90 to 135 volts. Systems designed to operate on 220 volts AC or that can be switched between 110-volt service and 220-volt service typically have an operating range of 180 to 270 volts AC.

Certain disturbances in the area, such as a lightning storm, distant lightning strikes, or problems on the electrical power supply grid such as a major factory shutting down all at once or a sudden drop in the load on the supply lines can cause the voltage on the line to suddenly increase. This sharp increase of voltage is an over-voltage event called a surge. An electrical surge is a temporary increase of voltage on the line. A surge is like a rogue wave of electricity that can increase the voltage to as much as 1,000 volts. It typically does this for only a few thousandths of a second, but that's plenty of time to damage anything in its path. Power surges are very common when the power returns from a blackout (see "Blackouts" a little later in this section).

PC power supplies are designed to withstand voltage surges to certain levels, and most are subjected to a few a year. However, even the best power supply will begin to lose its ability to withstand a power surge and can in time begin to fail or begin passing the surge on to internal PC devices connected to it. It is also common for power surges to happen in clusters, which can be fatal for an unprotected system.

Power Spikes

A power spike is a sudden, usually one-time, extremely high-voltage peak of over-voltage on the electrical line. A typical cause of a power spike is lightning striking within a few miles of your vicinity. Lightning carries millions of volts, and if your home or office takes a direct hit, your PC is very likely to be heavily damaged, right along with everything else electrical in the building. Lightning directly striking a building is a fairly rare event, but even a strike within several miles can create an electrical current in metal objects near the strike. This means that any wires or cables in the area can pick up an electrical spike and pass it to whatever is connected to it. The wire or cable could be a power cable on a PC, a telephone wire, the electricity supply to a house or building, and so on. The chances are slim that your home or office will be directly struck by lightning any time soon, but the odds of a lightning strike near you are pretty good.

Power Sags or Dips

Sudden demands for power on the power grid can create a wave of low-voltage on the electrical supply system, which is called a sag or a dip. As the name suggests, a power sag is the opposite of a power surge—it's a temporary dip in the voltage on the supply line that usually lasts only a fraction of a second. Power sags that extend below the normal operating voltage range of a system are rare, but they can happen.

Most of the components in the PC are not designed to operate at very low voltages, even for a very short time. The PC's power supply has some power in reserve to pull up short power sags. However, a series of power sags in a short time can affect the power supply's ability to provide the correct voltages to internal PC components and could weaken, damage, or destroy them.

Brownouts

When the demand for electrical power exceeds the capability of the electrical supply system, the result is reduced voltage for everyone, or what is called a brownout. Brownout is meant to indicate that while there is enough power on the grid to prevent a blackout, or a total loss of power, there isn't enough power to meet the current demand. Brownouts frequently occur during extreme weather conditions, such as a sudden abnormally cold or hot spell, when everyone is running their heat or air conditioning.

A brownout is when the voltage on the electrical supply circuit is less than 105 volts AC for an extended time, which could be minutes or hours. A brownout strains the PC in the same way as a power sag, but because a brownout lasts longer, the result can be immediate failure of some components, a burned out power supply, or in an extreme case, the corruption or loss of data. Brownouts are a tool employed by the power companies to shift supply around the grid to meet the demands in specific areas on a rolling basis, or what is called rolling brownouts, and the damage to a PC is often not noticed right away. However, the strain on a PC's components accumulates and eventually results in a failure that is nearly impossible to troubleshoot. Brownouts are far harder on computer equipment than blackouts.

Blackouts

A blackout is a complete loss of a PC's electrical source. Typically, you think of a blackout as a failure of the power supply grid over an entire area, but a blackout can occur in just a part of a building, an entire building, a block, a section of a city, or an even larger area. A blackout event is a sudden complete drop-off of the power source, which can cause a wide range of problems on a PC or a network. At minimum, all of the data in RAM is usually lost, but depending on the applications or utilities running on the PC, much worse could happen. For example, if you are in the middle of flashing the BIOS on a PC when the power fails, the PC must be recovered through the boot block and the BIOS flashing operations repeated. In the interim, the PC is not usable. Or, if the PC is performing a defrag operation, updating the file system tables, or any other system maintenance activity, the PC may be compromised.

Blackouts are caused by electrical storms; car accidents involving utility poles; the electrical utility company being unable to meet user demands, such as the recent problems in California when they used rolling blackouts to try to satisfy user demands; or a total collapse of the power system due to user overload.

Typically, a blackout doesn't just happen, and a series of surges and spikes occurs both before the crash and when the power is restored. The damage to a PC happens not from the power failing, but from the power surge on the power supply system when the power is restored.

PROTECTING AGAINST POWER PROBLEMS

There are several devices you can use to protect your PC and its peripheral devices. This is one PC area where you get what you pay for, so how much protection you get depends on how much you have to spend. At the low end are plug strips that include a fuse, and on the extremely high end are standby generator and line conditioners. Most people protect individual PCs with products toward the lower end of this scale, and enterprise networks and Internet service providers (ISPs) tend to implement power equipment at the higher end.

The power protection equipment used for a home or small office system doesn't need to be very sophisticated or costly to provide the level of protection required for most situations. Depending on a number of factors, such as the quality of the electrical service available and how often it fails, most home PCs can usually get by with surge protection or a small uninterruptible power supply (UPS). More on the UPS later in this chapter. The following sections look at each of the options available to a home or small office user.

No Power Protection

While certainly not the wisest option, using no power protection equipment is definitely the least expensive way to go, at least in the short term. However, power protection equipment must be viewed as an insurance policy against the almost certain power-related problems on your PC. The cost of the lowest-end protection is usually less than $20, which is a small price to pay to protect your investment in your PC, printer, and other peripheral devices.

If you do choose to not use power protection equipment, at least use common sense with the electrical cords. *Never* cut off the grounding pin on a three-prong plug on the PC's power cord to plug the PC into a two-hole outlet. This removes the earth ground circuit from the PC, which is dangerous to both the PC and you and can cause electrical problems all around.

Surge Suppressors

The most commonly used power protection device is a surge suppressor. This device, which provides protection that ranges from mostly psychological to good, is generally available and sold in virtually any store that also sells extension cords, including drug, grocery, hardware, and computer stores.

At the psychological level of protection are power strips that cost less than $10. These devices are not much more than fancy extension cords and offer very little in the way of surge protection or suppression capability. Be aware that although you will hear surge suppressors called power strips or power bars, you should not expect to get decent protection from these. There are devices that are *only* power strips and power bars and do not include surge suppression at all; again, these are just extension cords.

A good selection of surge suppressor strips is available in the price range of $15 to $35 that provides some level of protection. However, after any severe power event, such as lightning nearby or a power surge strong enough to affect your house or office lighting, be sure to check its MOV's LED, fuse, or circuit breaker for damage. Surge suppressors in this price range are considered disposable technology.

Surge suppressors that also include some line conditioning capabilities, like the one shown in Figure 23-1, will provide good protection. Expect to pay $40 or more for a quality device. For the most part, a surge suppressor is a high-grade extension cord with a plastic block that typically has 4 to 12 three-prong grounded outlets. The surge suppressor is plugged into the nearest AC power outlet and your PC, monitor, printer, and other peripherals plug into the surge suppressor.

Line conditioning ability, which is included in the high-end surge suppressor shown in Figure 23-1, means the device is able to smooth out EMI and other electrical noise on the circuit. Not all surge suppressors include line conditioning, so you need to carefully check the device's specifications if you wish to have this feature. No surge suppressor includes

Figure 23-1. A high-end surge suppressor also includes line conditioning capabilities. Photo courtesy of American Power Conversion Corporation

the level of line conditioning performed by a separate line conditioning unit, but a high-end surge suppressor should be able to handle most of the normal line noise that can be found on virtually every electrical line.

A surge suppressor uses a component called a metal-oxide varistor (MOV) to suppress power surges on the electrical line. Anytime the voltage gets above a specified level, even if only for a millionth of a second, the MOV redirects the current to the ground circuit and is not passed on to the device plugged into the suppressor. The specified level of the surge or spike that the varistor can handle is somewhat limited (a surge suppressor is not designed to handle the surge caused by a lightning strike). If the level is exceeded, the MOV is destroyed and, from that point on, the surge suppressor is nothing but an expensive plug strip and all spikes and surges are passed on to the PC's power supply.

What to Consider When Buying a Surge Suppressor

When purchasing a surge suppressor, remember that a good unit typically costs a bit more. Don't let price be your only guide, but a quality surge suppressor will not be the least expensive one on the shelf. There are $30 surge suppressors that promise complete protection that will be worthless after even the slightest spike on the line. Here are the features you should consider when purchasing a surge suppressor:

- **Amount of energy absorbed** You are buying a surge suppressor to have it absorb over-voltage events and continue to protect your equipment. A surge suppressor is rated by the amount of energy it absorbs, which is stated in a quantity of joules. The higher the number of joules the surge suppressor is rated at, the better the unit. The rule of thumb is that 200 joules is the minimum protection, 400 joules is average protection, and 600 or more is excellent protection.
- **Voltage let-through** Underwriters Laboratories (UL) has defined a standard for surge suppressors, UL 1449, that rates surge suppressors by the amount of electricity they pass through to the equipment plugged into the surge suppressor. This rating states that if a big surge or spike hits the surge suppressor, it will be able to absorb all of the energy except a certain amount that will be passed on to its outlet plugs. A low number in this specification indicates a better quality unit. There are three levels defined in the UL 1449 standard: 330 volts, 400 volts, and 500 volts. When you consider that the device is tested with over 6,000 volts, 330 volts doesn't sound so bad, but that's three times more than the typical electrical outlet nominally supplies.
- **Clamping voltage and speed** Clamping voltage is the voltage at which the suppressor begins to protect the computer. In other words, it's the high-voltage level at which the surge suppressor begins redirecting the over-voltage portion of the electrical circuit to a ground. The clamping speed is the time delay before the surge suppressor begins providing its protection or how much time elapses between detection and protection.

- **Protection LED** Eventually, nearly all MOVs meet with the spike or surge that it cannot absorb and fail. When this happens, the equipment connected to the surge suppressors is no longer protected. Most quality surge suppressors have an LED that is lighted when the MOV is intact and operating. If the MOV blows, the LED stops shining, and it is time to get a new surge suppressor. Don't mistake a power-on LED for a protection LED. The power-on LED merely says that the suppressor is switched on. Many suppressors include the power-on light in the on/off switch.
- **Line conditioning** If this is an important feature to you (and it should be), you must determine the line conditioning capabilities of the surge suppressor from whatever specifications are available on a particular unit. A quality surge suppressor should have a rating between 35 decibels (dB) and 70 dB, with more always better.
- **Power switch** Most surge suppressors have an on/off switch that controls the plugs on the unit. However, some units have plugs that are hot (meaning on) whenever the suppressor is connected to a power source, regardless of whether the on/off switch is on or off. The unswitched plugs can be useful for recharging a notebook PC's battery, or running a clock, radio, or lamp while the devices plugged into the other plugs are switched off. A surge suppressor offering hot plugs is a matter of preference. If you have devices that do need to be on all the time, then you should look for a surge suppressor with hot plugs.
- **Overload circuit breaker or fuse** Most of the better surge suppressors have either a circuit breaker or a fuse that will protect the MOV from being blown should there be an electrical problem with a device plugged into the suppressor or a severe power surge or spike on the line. A breaker is the better choice, as it can be reset and the suppressor will be back in use immediately; when a fuse goes, it must be replaced.
- **Modem/fax/telephone protection** It is common for a surge suppressor to have two RJ-11 jacks that pass a telephone circuit that may be connected to a modem, fax, or a telephone through the MOV circuit. When lightning strikes nearby, the energy seeks out any metal, and a copper telephone line, which is a very good conductor of electricity, is just as likely as the electrical lines to carry some of the millions of volts suddenly on the lines.
- **Protection warranty** More reputable manufacturers provide a warranty that protects your equipment while it is plugged into their surge suppressors (and other power protection equipment). The warranty will pay up to a certain dollar amount to repair or replace your equipment should it be damaged while connected to their device. Before you bet your PC and other equipment on such a warranty, make sure you understand its terms and conditions.

Power Controllers

Typically, a surge suppressor is placed on the floor and out of sight of the user. A variation on the surge suppressor is the power controller, a.k.a. power station or power manager. A power controller is typically placed either between the system unit and the monitor on a desktop PC or beneath the monitor and on the desk for tower-style cases. The power controller (see Figure 23-2) has several electrical outlets on the back, each of which is connected to a separate and dedicated on/off switch on the front. There is typically a master on/off switch as well. This design allows the PC user to control exactly which devices are on or off at any time. The real benefit of power controllers is that they nearly all have full surge suppression capabilities, and the surge suppression extends to every outlet on the unit. Many also have one or two unswitched outlets that allow devices to be on regardless of the status of the master on/off switch.

Other Surge Suppressor Types

Other types of surge suppressors can be used to protect your system, including some that protect your PC by protecting everything in the building. Here are a few other types of surge suppressors available:

- **Single outlet plug** If you wish to plug a single device into a different circuit so that it will be controlled by a different circuit breaker in the electrical control panel of your home or office, you can use a single outlet plug.
- **Multiple outlet plug** Should you wish to plug multiple devices directly into a wall outlet, at least use what is known as a surge suppressing plug block. These devices cost about $40 and usually have most of the features of the plug strip style surge suppressor including the warranty and LEDs.
- **Whole building protection** You can protect an entire building with a single not-too-expensive device. One way to do this is to place a surge suppressor between your electric meter and the main electrical supply to your building. For about $80, you can stop many power surges and spikes before they enter your house. Another way is to install what is called a "whole house" surge suppressor. For about $200, your electric utility or a licensed local electrician can install a unit that provides surge, spike, and electrical noise protection on both the 110 and 220-volt AC lines and the telephone and cable or satellite television feeds. This device is installed in the main service panel of your building. However, these devices do not provide any protection against noise problems that are generated inside the building, so to be completely safe you would need to also use the plug strip type of surge suppressor for your PC equipment.

Line Conditioners

Line conditioners, also called power conditioners (see Figure 23-3), filter the electrical stream to control surges and spikes and to eliminate any line electrical noise on the line.

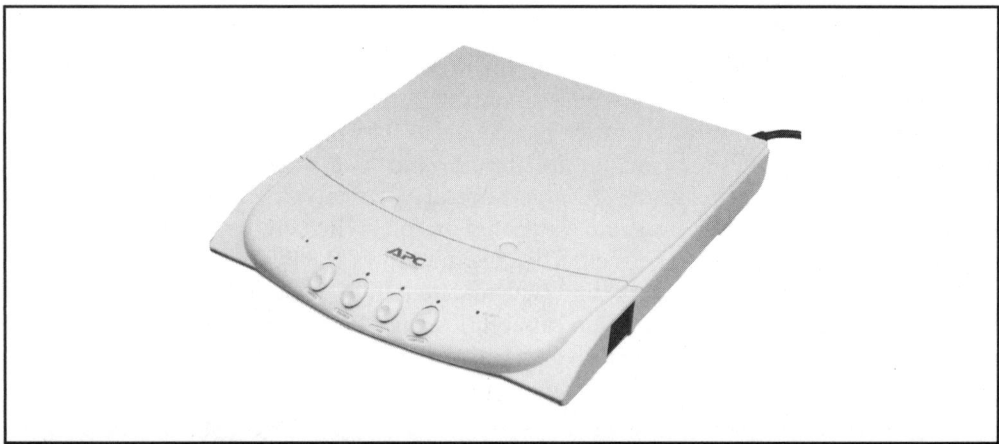

Figure 23-2. A power controller is a surge suppressor that allows the user to control each electrical outlet separately. Photo courtesy of American Power Conversion Corporation

Because they are typically expensive, few PC users use a true line conditioner and use the line conditioning capabilities of a surge suppressor or uninterruptible power supply (UPS) instead. Most line conditioners also provide surge suppression, but they are not designed to provide standby power like a UPS (see the section "Uninterruptible Power Supply (UPS)" later in the chapter).

Figure 23-3. A power line conditioner filters electrical noise on the power line in addition to surge suppression. Photo courtesy of American Power Conversion Corporation

EMI and RFI (radio frequency interference) and electric motor noise are the primary electrical interferences from which you need to protect your PC. Electrical line noise is measured in decibels, the same measurement that's used for audio sound volume. If there is an excessive amount of electrical noise on the power supply, you can often hear it on a TV, radio, or stereo. The good news is that nearly all surge suppressors and UPS units filter out certain levels of line noise. However, if your system is located near a generator or compressor, like those found in a soda pop vending machine, it is unlikely that your surge suppressor or UPS will be able to filter all of the electrical noise on the circuit unless it is a very high-end model. In this type of environment, it may be wise to invest in a line conditioner and use it in place of a surge suppressor to protect your PC and peripheral devices.

Uninterruptible Power Supply (UPS)

Although its name perhaps promises more than the unit is actually able to deliver, an uninterruptible power supply (UPS) is designed to provide a number of power-related services to the devices connected to it:

- **Power source** The UPS unit is placed between the devices you wish to protect from blackouts, brownouts, and other power line events and the electrical outlet from the normal AC electrical service.
- **Line conditioning** Virtually all but the very least expensive UPS units provide line conditioning to filter line noise from the electrical supply.
- **Surge suppression** UPS units provide protection from power surges and spikes on the electrical line.
- **Brownout and sag protection** UPS units fill in the power loss during a power sag or a brownout. Most UPS units cannot make up the power loss of a brownout indefinitely, but unless the brownout is severe they can replace most of the power loss for a short period.
- **Backup power** The primary purpose of a UPS is to provide backup electricity to the devices plugged into it for a certain amount of time.
- **Alarm system** Most of the quality UPS units now available include a means to connect the UPS unit to some means of notifying you of an electrical event serious enough to invoke the UPS. On most units, this is a network connection, but some also offer a telephone line connection used to send an e-mail, a paging call, or the like to notify you of the event. Some also include software that is installed on the protected PC that will initiate shutdown procedures when notified by the UPS over a serial line connection of a serious electricity supply system event.

UPS Technologies

The basic structure of a UPS is an incoming power source, typically an AC wall outlet, a switch that detects the incoming power level, a battery that is constantly being recharged for use should the power source fail, and an outlet to which a device, such as a PC can connect with its power cord. Figure 23-4 illustrates this structure.

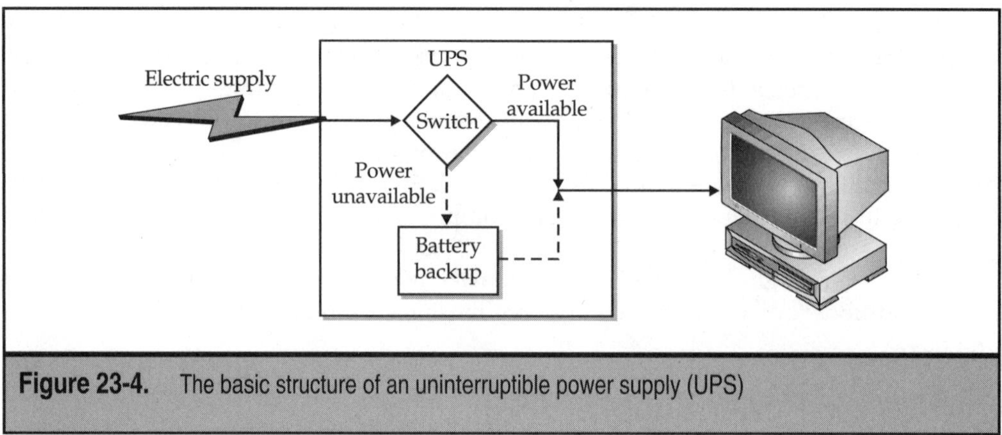

Figure 23-4. The basic structure of an uninterruptible power supply (UPS)

One thing that is common to all UPS technologies is that the incoming AC power must be converted into DC power for use inside the UPS and then converted back into AC power for use by the PC (which will convert it back to DC for use by its internal components). All of this power conversion may seem redundant, but keep in mind that the UPS is there to simulate the normal AC power source.

There are three basic UPS technologies, along with several hybrids, used to protect against or solve different types of power issues: standby power supply (SPS), line-interactive UPSs, and on-line UPSs.

Standby Power Supply (SPS) A standby power supply (SPS), also known as an off-line power supply, is a pass-through unit that is inactive until the power fails. It shares the incoming power with its devices to charge its batteries and, as long as the electrical power source is available, power is passed through the unit to its outlets and the devices plugged into them. Figure 23-4, in the preceding section, illustrates the general configuration of an SPS unit. When a brownout or blackout occurs, the unit switches over to the battery to provide power to its outlets. Because of the time involved to switch its modes, which varies by manufacturer and model, SPS units are not good for dealing with power sags because the reaction time of the unit is usually longer than the duration of these events. This type of UPS is an inexpensive solution for stand-alone, noncritical PCs and peripherals and is generally not suitable for servers. However, because of their lower cost, they are often used to protect desktop workstations.

Standby UPS technology is typically very reliable and switches modes fast enough to prevent serious problems when the power source blacks out. The key specification when considering a standby UPS is the voltage range that the UPS accepts as its normal operating range. Whenever the voltage level of the incoming power is outside this range, the UPS begins drawing on its battery. You want a standby power supply to have a wide operating range, but not too wide. If the voltage range is too wide, your PC may be running on low or high voltage for extended periods. However, you want the range wide enough to minimize the number of times the UPS switches and draws on its battery. Each time the standby UPS switches to its battery backup, it shortens the battery's life. Most standby UPS units use an operating range of 103 volts AC to 132 volts AC, which means that whenever the power sags below 103 volts or surges above 132 volts the unit goes "on-battery."

Line-Interactive UPS A line-interactive UPS unit is especially well-suited to environments where there are few brownouts and blackouts but where surges, spikes, or sags are common. When the power supply is available, the line-interactive UPS provides line conditioning and produces a steady level of output voltage from a fluctuating input voltage level. This type of UPS also provides good protection from EMI, RFI, and other forms of line noise. As shown in Figure 23-5, this type of UPS adds line conditioning to the battery backup capability of the UPS.

In terms of providing battery backup, a line-interactive UPS works just like a standby power supply and is able to switch to its battery backup faster than any connected equipment can detect the power loss. Remember that the PC's power supply has a small amount of reserve power on which it can draw when the power suddenly drops, and most UPS units switch faster than this reserve can be exhausted. The benefit of a line-interactive UPS over a standard SPS is that because it also filters the incoming power, it can reduce the amount of times the UPS switches to its battery.

Use the same criteria used for an SPS unit to judge a line-interactive UPS. However, remember that a blackout is normally preceded by a swarm of surges and spikes before the power is lost completely. Before purchasing a line-interactive UPS, investigate how much over-voltage the unit can withstand before it needs to switch to its battery because a UPS draws on its battery to neutralize over-voltage events.

On-line UPS To many, an on-line UPS is the true uninterruptible power supply. This type of UPS provides all of the services of a surge suppressor, a line conditioner, and a battery backup in a single package. On-line UPS units provide the best protection of all of the UPS technologies but they also cost more than the other technologies.

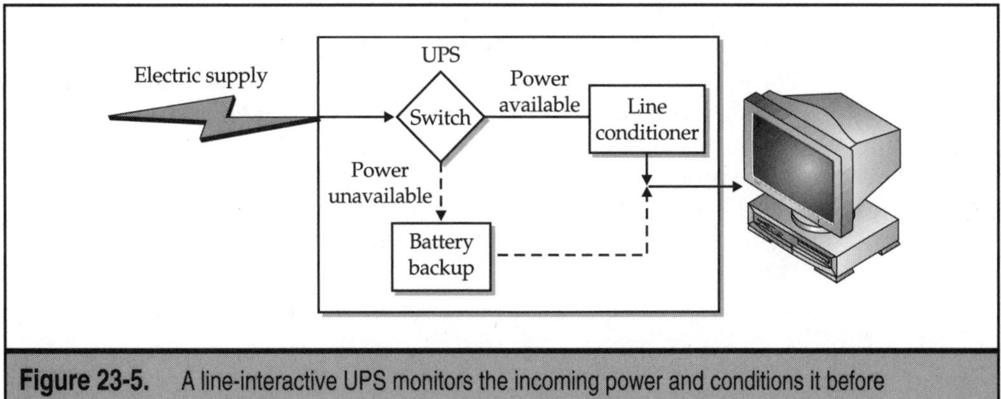

Figure 23-5. A line-interactive UPS monitors the incoming power and conditions it before passing it on

An on-line UPS supplies power continuously from an AC to DC power inverter. There is no switchover when the power fails because the outlets on the UPS are powered from the battery at all times. The incoming power source is conditioned to protect the circuitry of the UPS, but the result is that any device connected to the on-line UPS is isolated from power problems.

An on-line UPS produces the best quality power of any of the UPS technologies. It produces a near-perfect power stream that is free of even the smallest fluctuations. Standby (off-line) and line-interactive UPS technologies reduce the severity of spikes, surges, and sags by clamping them down into the normal operating voltage range of the unit, but fluctuations within the normal range are unaffected. The on-line UPS is able to deal with over- and under-voltage events without using its battery, which can extend the battery's life. Like the line-interactive UPS, the on-line UPS draws a small amount of the incoming power to keep its battery charged. This type of UPS technology is usually applied to mission-critical networks and high-availability devices, such as disk arrays and network access servers.

Sizing a UPS

Typically, a UPS needs to be able to provide between 5 and 15 minutes of good power or enough power for a long enough period to allow the systems to be successfully shut down, either manually or automatically, or for the power source to be restored. The UPS is chosen for a given use based on its technology, load size, and its battery's capacity.

The load size, or the amount of power a UPS can deliver, is specified in volt-amperes (VA), which are commonly called volt-amps. Virtually all PC power supplies are rated in watts. Technically, a watt is one amp of electrical current flowing at 1 volt. However, the power rating of a PC power supply is typically only around 70 percent of the volt-amp rating of the UPS.

To calculate the load size needed for a particular situation, you must first calculate the volt-amp requirements of each device to be protected. To do this, multiply a device's voltage requirement by its ampere requirement. Or, if the device's power requirements are given in watts, multiply the watts required by 1.4, or to be truly safe, by 1.5. Once you have the total volt-amp requirements of the devices to be attached to the UPS, you can begin shopping for a UPS.

A number of UPS size calculators are available on-line on UPS manufacturers' Web sites. American Power Conversion has several interactive calculators available at **www.apcc.com/sizing/selectors.cfm**, and Tripp Lite Power Protection has an interactive sizing guide at **www.tripplite.com/sizing/**. You can use the VA rating of the products recommended by these proprietary tools as an indication of the UPS you need for your situation. More than likely your budget will determine which technology you will choose, but carefully consider the electrical environment of your location and match it to the technology that best suits your needs.

UPS Warnings

There are at least two devices that you should never plug into a UPS: a laser printer or a surge suppressor. A laser printer draws a tremendous amount of power when it starts up and takes power in "gulps" during its fusing processes. Very few UPS units can handle the amount and style of this demand. A laser printer can also inject noise back into the UPS or surge suppressor. Check the documentation of the UPS before connecting a laser printer to it. Some are rated specifically for this purpose.

Surge suppressors are also extremely hazardous to plug into a UPS. You will see this warning in the owner's manuals of both devices.

Generators

If you expect you need backup power and protection beyond the 15 to 20 minutes provided by a UPS, you may want to consider another form of standby power, a power generator. Whether you are in a home, small office, or large data center, there are power generators to fit your needs.

A home or small office that absolutely must have a PC available at all times may want to consider a portable power generator. There are portable and rechargeable models, such as the X-Power device, shown in Figure 23-6, made by Xantrex Technology (**www. statpower. com**). There are also portable gasoline models available from Honda Motors (**www. hondapowerequipment.com/gen.htm**), Coleman Powermate (**www.colemanpowermate. com**), and several other manufacturers. A portable power generator, like the one in Figure 23-7, can provide you with enough power to run a PC for one to eight hours, depending on the PC and the size of the gas tank on the generator. Of course, you will need to have a UPS that lasts long enough for you to get the portable generator on-line. High-end standby power generators are also available, but these are more typically used as emergency power sources to large data centers and service provider operations. A small portable generator typically costs between $300 to $1,000 and a large emergency generator can cost $50,000 or more, plus the cost of the construction and electrician labor to install one.

Protecting Modems and Networks

If lightning strikes within a few miles of your PC and its peripherals, the resulting electrical spike can be transmitted over any metal wire available, including the power lines and telephone lines. So, in addition to protecting your PC from the dangers on the power line, you should consider protecting your dial-up modem, DSL bridge or router, or ISDN terminal adapter from power problems. This same risk extends to the network cable to which your PC may be connected.

Most of the better surge suppressors, and some UPS units as well, now include jacks that provide line conditioning services on telephone and network connections. Typically, there are two RJ-11 and two RJ-45 connectors on the unit. The incoming line is connected to one of the jacks, and the PC or modem is connected to a line attached to an output jack on the surge suppressor or UPS. Passing this line through the protection device allows the unit to condition the line and provide over-voltage protection. Many UPS units are network-ready, and the network adapter can be directly connected to the UPS, which in turn is connected to the network backbone. This also allows the UPS to communicate over the network in the case of a severe electrical event.

Figure 23-6. A small portable power supply can provide a notebook or small PC with enough power to operate for a short time and be shutdown properly. Photo courtesy of Xantrex Technology, Inc.

Figure 23-7. Portable power generators can provide enough emergency power to run your PC. Photo courtesy of Coleman Powermate

You can also protect a phone line with a separate phone/modem isolator, which is an inexpensive device you can buy at any electronics or computer store.

SAVING THE PLANET

Power issues should be a two-way street, with some of the solutions coming from the PC as well as the surge suppressor or UPS. In fact, several governments around the world are working to find ways to reduce the amount of power a PC and its peripherals uses and developing regulations to provide safeguards against the electrical hazards associated with using a PC and its peripheral devices.

To reduce the amount of electricity consumed by computers, the U.S. Environmental Protection Agency (EPA) established guidelines for energy efficiency under a program called U.S. Green Star, also known as Energy Star. On Green Star systems, the power supply works with the computer's components and some peripherals to reduce the power they use when idle.

Green Star devices have a standby program that puts them into sleep mode after the device has been idle for a certain period. In sleep mode, the device reduces 99 percent of its power consumption and uses no more than 30 watts of power.

DC POWER

There are also power protection devices that provide surge suppression and UPS services to equipment requiring direct current (DC) electrical power. PCs, printers, and virtually all other peripheral devices require AC electricity, which is why the discussion in this chapter is focused on AC power protection equipment. Many networking devices, such as routers, switches, and access servers, especially those used in large enterprise or service provider networks, are powered by DC electricity. Typically, this equipment is protected by large arrays of battery backups, data center level power protection equipment, and standby power generators.

CHAPTER 24

Troubleshooting PC Hardware

When a PC starts to malfunction, sometimes it's obvious what the problem is and other times it is not. If the mouse or keyboard isn't working, resolving the problem is as easy as installing a new one. However, if the hard disk drive is intermittently producing read or write errors, the problem could be in the hard disk, power supply, memory, motherboard, cables, or software. Isolating problems on a PC is what troubleshooting is all about.

On a modern PC, a majority of the problems are software-related and can easily be solved by reconfiguring or reinstalling the software. Some problems that at first appear to be software issues can be caused by hardware incompatibilities with the software, but these typically show up almost immediately after new software is installed. In fact, most problems on a PC tend to happen right after new hardware or software is installed or reconfigured.

No magic formula exists for solving all of the problems that can occur on a PC, but there are general troubleshooting processes you can use to isolate what may be causing the problem. This chapter contains a few of these processes as well as some helpful tips and hints you can use to troubleshoot problems on your PC.

POWER SOURCE AND ENVIRONMENTAL ISSUES

Some problems are caused by the PC's environment and especially its electrical setup. One of the best places to start when troubleshooting an unidentified PC problem is at the source—the power source. Here are some questions that you should answer:

- **Is the PC plugged in and switched on?** This may seem like a silly question, but it's not if it is really the problem.
- **What is the PC's power source?**
  - **If the PC is plugged directly into a wall socket** One of the first places to begin troubleshooting is the power supply (see Chapter 14).
  - **If the PC is plugged into a plug strip or surge suppressor** Is the protection circuit still in place and effective? The protection circuit can fail and the protection LED can burn out. If this has happened, the PC may as well be plugged directly into the wall outlet (see Chapter 23).
  - **If the PC is plugged into a UPS (uninterruptible power supply)** Is the UPS working properly? A bad UPS can do more harm than good. Verify that the UPS is working (see Chapter 23).
- **How many devices are sharing the electrical supply?** It could be that too many devices are sharing a plug strip, surge suppressor, or UPS. If this situation has been in use for any period, then it may be likely that the damage is already done, but try removing a few devices from the power source to see if the problems go away. If the problems persist, check out the power supply.

Problems with the power source will usually show up as power supply problems. The power supply is the cause for a majority of PC hardware problems. If the power supply begins going bad, it can pass along power surges, spikes, and low-voltage conditions directly to the devices connected to it. The internal devices run on 12 or fewer volts of direct current (DC) power. Any more or less than this for a prolonged period can cause a device to degrade slowly and eventually fail.

Even when a PC is properly protected against power source issues, its environment can cause problems. The conditions in the PC's environment can strain its cooling system and eventually effect the power supply. As a part of your troubleshooting processes, check out the PC's environment by asking these questions:

- **Is the environment dust-free and otherwise clean?** The PC is an air-cooled device, and airborne dust and other particles are pulled into the PC's case where it can accumulate on the fan, air grills, motherboard components, processor, and expansion cards. If the inside of a PC's case is not cleaned regularly, this dust can, at minimum, clog up the air flow and defeat the cooling system and directly affect the functions of the processor, memory, and other integrated circuits on the motherboard. Depending on the makeup of the dust, such as small metal filings or solvent or chemical mists, it can also cause what appear to be power-related problems by shorting the electrical distribution on the motherboard and expansion cards.
- **Is the environment humid or overly dry?** Too much humidity in the PC's environment can cause the water in the air to condense inside the PC and cause electrical problems. On the other hand, if the air is too dry, static electricity can be produced. It doesn't take very much static electricity, in the form of an electrostatic discharge (ESD), to damage the components of a PC, especially those on circuit cards like the motherboard and expansion cards. PCs do not need perfect operating conditions, but they do better in moderate conditions. Regardless of whether the air is humid or dry, you should always wear an ESD protective device, such as a wrist or heel strap, when working inside the PC.

LEARNING FROM THE PAST

One of the most overlooked tools in the PC repair kit is a record of past problems, troubleshooting, installations, upgrades, and repairs that have been made on a PC, if for no other reason than to remind you that a certain problem has happened before and what you did to troubleshoot it. This record doesn't need to be very formal or extensive. A small spiral notebook with dates and a few notes on anything that has been done to the PC can be a very valuable troubleshooting resource.

Each time you have a PC problem that requires troubleshooting, a quick review of your PC record will remind you of past actions that could be part of the current problem. For example, when software you use very seldom suddenly cannot read the hard disk, it would be helpful to be reminded that a second hard disk drive was installed a month ago as the new primary master. The solution may be to change the software's disk drive reference rather than to replace the hard disk.

The PC record can also come in handy when dealing with warranty issues. Your memory and recollection of a problem will not carry as much credibility as a written journal of problems and actions relating to a particular problem or the PC in general.

When a PC problem is not apparent and needs troubleshooting, you should avoid jumping to conclusions. Review the environment of the PC, review the PC's record, and answer a few simple questions and jot them down in your notebook:

- **When did the problem first happen?** It is important to note when a problem happens: during the boot or startup, when the PC is up and running, or during shutdown.
- **Is this the first time this problem has happened?** If a problem has happened before, is there anything different about it this time?
- **What were you doing when the problem first showed up?** The problem could be caused by a particular application or file.
- **Can you re-create the problem?** As any PC user knows, sometimes stuff just happens that never shows up again. If you are unable to re-create a problem, make a note of it, just in case it does happen again in the future.
- **Did you add hardware or software to the PC right before the problem appeared?** This is when most problems occur. If you have just added new hardware or software, you can be sure the problem is related to this action in some way. Even if everything to do with the new hardware component or software program is perfect, you may have inadvertently dislodged a connector or power cable or installed a different version of a system file used by other software.
- **Is anything happening in the environment?** For example, a blackout, brownout, or lightning storms.
- **Did smoke come out of the PC or monitor?** If the answer is yes, it probably will not be difficult to find the problem. If the smoke came from the monitor, take it to a repair shop—***do not work on it yourself!*** If the smoke came from inside the case, put on your ESD protection, open the case, and carefully examine the motherboard, power supply, and expansion cards for smoke or burned marks. If none are apparent, the best advice is to take it to a repair shop. Don't power it up again to see if you can re-create the smoke. You may just fry the next component down the line.

TROUBLESHOOTING FRMS

A PC is made up of a number of larger components that can be replaced outside of the factory. Each of these components is referred to in the PC hardware business as a field replaceable module (FRM). Troubleshooting a PC is really an exercise in identifying common symptoms and isolating problems on the major FRMs:

- BIOS and CMOS
- CPU
- Floppy drive
- Hard drives
- Memory
- Modems
- Monitor and video cards
- Power supply
- Sound card and speakers

Troubleshooting the BIOS

Except for the extremely rare problem during a BIOS (Basic Input/Output System) flashing operation (see Chapter 6), there isn't much that can go wrong with the BIOS itself. However, during a cold start (when the PC is first powered up), a number of problems can occur while the PC is under the control of the BIOS. Here are some BIOS problems that can happen:

- **Upgrading the BIOS** Too many FRM problems are automatically linked to the BIOS being out of date. A solution to an FRM problem should not be an automatic BIOS upgrade, although it is one thing to be considered. The BIOS should be treated with the philosophy, "if it isn't broke, don't fix it." The BIOS should only be upgraded to solve a specific (and documented) compatibility or performance issue on the PC, typically with new hardware or software, such as a new hardware technology or a new release of the operating system.

  If you do decide to upgrade the BIOS, first enter the BIOS Setup program and record the configuration information in the CMOS. Document the basic setup data completely and any of the advanced menus on which you have made changes. Before you begin the flashing operation, go to the BIOS or motherboard manufacturer's Web site for instructions and the proper flashing utility software. Apply only the BIOS versions (obtainable from the manufacturer only) that are listed as compatible to your motherboard, processor, and chipset.
- **Troubleshooting after a BIOS update** After you have flashed the BIOS, the CMOS settings will be at the default settings of the new version. If you do not enter the settings you documented before flashing the BIOS, it is likely that the boot will fail with a missing device. One or more CMOS settings probably needs to be adjusted. Using the written record of the CMOS settings created before you flashed the BIOS, enter the Setup program and verify that all of the BIOS configuration settings are correct. If after resetting the CMOS information, the system will not boot, it could very well be that the BIOS version you have installed

is not compatible with your system and you will need to reinstall the BIOS. Check your system documentation for instructions on using the boot block or to replace a bad BIOS (see Chapter 6).

- **Matching up the OS and the BIOS** If you are installing a Windows 2000 operating system, the type and compliance of the PC's BIOS is very important. Windows 2000 requires that the BIOS be compliant to the Advanced Configuration and Power Interface (ACPI). If the BIOS is not ACPI-compliant, expect Windows 2000 to have boot errors and crash frequently. ACPI includes the *OnNow* standard that can start the PC from a single keystroke. Without this compatibility, the Windows 2000 setup program may not be able to communicate with the PC's hardware devices. To verify that the BIOS is ACPI-compliant, check the BIOS or motherboard's documentation, the manufacturer's Web site, or the Windows 2000 Hardware Compatibility List (HCL), or contact the PC's manufacturer. Windows Me (Millennium Edition) is also ACPI-compliant, but has a bit more tolerance of systems without it.

POST Errors

If the BIOS is current and compatible, any problems encountered during the boot process are generated by the POST (Power-On Self-Test) process. See Chapter 6 for information on the details of the boot sequence.

During the POST process, the BIOS uses two different ways to notify you of a problem:

- **Error beep codes** The system speaker, which is the one inside the system case, is used to sound out short and long tones in a unique pattern to indicate a problem in a system component that is essential to starting up the PC. During the early phases of the boot process, the monitor is not available, so only sound can be used to signal a problem.
- **Error messages** After the video BIOS (many of the major FRMs have their own BIOS as well) is loaded, the boot process is able to display error messages on the monitor for any problems that occur in the final stages of the boot cycle. The error messages issued from each different BIOS are fairly standard and should describe the problem well enough.

Error Beep Codes Every BIOS system has at least one beep code in common—a single beep tone at the end of the POST process to signal an all clear. However, a single beep can also mean a memory problem on an AMI (American Megatrends, Inc.) BIOS. The following are some general guidelines on the kind of problem identified by a few of the more common POST beep codes:

- **0 beeps** The purpose of the one-beep all clear signal is to let you know that the system is booting. If no beeps are sounded and nothing is displayed on the monitor, the problem is most likely power:
  - Make sure the PC is plugged into a safe AC power source.

- Check to see if the motherboard is getting power. Use the motherboard's documentation to locate the Power LED connector and verify that the connection is good.
- Use a multimeter to check the power of the motherboard's power connectors or plug an LED attached to a wire into the power connector to test that the motherboard is getting power.
- If all else is okay, the power supply may be bad. See Chapter 14 for more information on the power supply.

- **1 beep, 2 beeps, or 3 beeps** These typically indicate a memory error of some form:
  - If you have just installed memory, make sure it is properly seated in the socket.
  - Verify that you used the same type and speed memory and that you have filled a bank before installing memory in another bank.
  - Replace the memory with known good chips and reboot.

  The term "known good" is used frequently in troubleshooting guides to describe FRMs, components, and software configurations that are tested and known to be in good working order.
- **4 beeps, 5 beeps, 7 beeps, or 10 beeps** Reboot the PC a few times to verify the count on these errors because these codes indicate that the motherboard has a serious problem and may need to be replaced or sent to the manufacturer for repairs. See Chapter 4 for more information on the motherboard.
- **6 beeps** The common code for a keyboard failure. During the boot cycle, the keyboard controller is what is being tested.
  - If the motherboard has a separate keyboard controller chip, make sure it is properly seated. A condition called "chip creep," where the heating and cooling of a circuit board can cause a chip to push out of its socket, can affect the seating of an individually mounted integrated circuit (IC). Often, gently but firmly pressing it back into its socket can solve this problem.
  - Check the keyboard connection and the keyboard itself. It is unlikely that the Super I/O chip in the chipset (see Chapter 5) is bad, so the problem must be with the physical components of the keyboard.
- **8 beeps** This code indicates a problem with the video adapter card:
  - Reseat the video card and check its onboard memory to ensure it is also seated properly on the card.
  - If the problem persists, try a replacement video card.
- **9 beeps** Like the motherboard beep codes, you need to be very sure of the count and that the number of beeps is not 8 (video problems) or 10 (motherboard problems). Nine beeps indicate a bad BIOS chip that is not a chip creep problem.

Unless the system has taken a strong electrical hit, this problem should only show up if a BIOS update failed.

- Check with the motherboard or BIOS manufacturer for any known problems.
- The BIOS may need to be updated.

Deciphering BIOS error messages A BIOS error message displayed on the monitor, regardless of the BIOS manufacturer, means that there is a serious problem with a system FRM that is preventing the startup of the PC. The following are some of the more common error messages displayed during the boot cycle (the messages vary by manufacturer slightly):

- **BIOS ROM checksum error—system halted** This is a serious error and you need to contact the motherboard or BIOS manufacturer for recovery procedures, if any. This could be caused by an incomplete faulty flash upgrade and there may be recovery procedures available.
- **CMOS battery failed** The CMOS battery is dead and needs to be replaced. Remember that with the CMOS battery dead, the Setup program's configuration data will be reset to its default values and you will need to re-enter the system configuration from your manual records.
- **CMOS checksum error—defaults loaded** This message indicates that the CMOS has become corrupt and the Setup configuration data has been reset to the default values. The cause is likely a weak CMOS battery that needs to be replaced and the CMOS data reentered from your records.

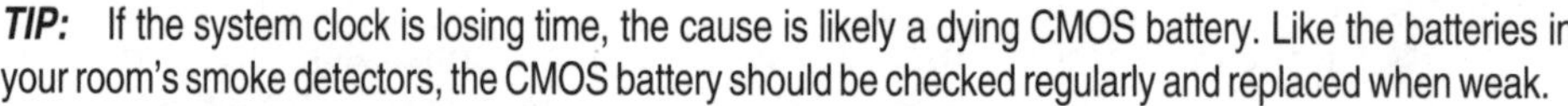

TIP: If the system clock is losing time, the cause is likely a dying CMOS battery. Like the batteries in your room's smoke detectors, the CMOS battery should be checked regularly and replaced when weak.

- **Display switch is set incorrectly** Many older motherboards have a jumper that sets the type of video display being supported. If this error displays, the video jumper setting and the video configuration in CMOS are at odds. Adjust the jumper or the CMOS data accordingly.
- **Floppy disk failure** The BIOS POST is looking for a floppy disk controller (FDC) that is indicated in the CMOS. If the PC does not have a floppy disk drive, you need to change the Diskette Drive value to None (or Auto) in the Setup configuration data. If the FDC is included in the chipset, make sure the floppy disk drive's cables are properly connected.
- **Hard disk failure** The BIOS POST cannot find or initialize a hard disk controller (HDC) included in the CMOS configuration. Make sure the adapter card, if any, is seated snuggly and that the drive cables are properly connected.

- **I/O card failure** This error indicates an expansion card has failed or has a parity error at a certain address. Try reseating the card or moving it to a different slot. If that fails to correct the error, replace the card with a known good card and reboot. If it still fails, and in several slots, the problem may be on the motherboard.
- **Keyboard error or no keyboard present** Make sure the keyboard is attached correctly and no keys are pressed during POST. Check for anything, like a book, lying on the keyboard.
- **Memory test fail** This message displays when an error has been detected during memory testing (indicated by the memory count displayed on the screen). The message should also include information about the type and location of the memory error, such as a memory parity error at *xxxx*, where *xxxx* is the location of the error.
- **Primary/secondary master/slave hard disk fail** This message displays when the BIOS POST process has detected an error in either the primary or secondary master or slave IDE hard disk drive. Check the cabling and the master/slave jumpers.

BIOS Error Messages Most BIOS systems display a three or four-digit error code along with the error message to help pinpoint the apparent source of the problem. The documentation for the BIOS system or your motherboard should list the exact codes used on your PC's make and model.

The BIOS POST error codes are categorized by FRMs and services and numbered in groups of 100. For example, a 600-series error, such as a 601, 622, or 644 error code, indicates a problem with the floppy disk drive or the floppy disk drive controller. Table 24-1 gives examples of the more common error codes.

Series	Category
100	Motherboard errors
200	RAM errors
300	Keyboard errors
600	Floppy disk drive errors
900	Parallel printer adapter errors
1100	COM1 errors
1300	Game port adapter errors

Table 24-1. POST Boot Error Codes

Series	Category
1700	Hard disk drive errors
1800	Expansion bus errors
2400	VGA errors
3000	NIC errors
8600	PS/2 mouse errors

Table 24-1. POST Boot Error Codes *(continued)*

Troubleshooting the CPU

If a PC's processor fails, it can only be replaced. However, most problems that appear to be processor problems are usually a problem with another component. What may show up as a processor problem is more likely a problem with either the cooling of the processor or the system (or both), the power supply, or a compatibility issue between the motherboard and chipset (which would show up after the processor is upgraded).

Here are the most common symptoms that a processor is about to fail:

- The PC will not boot
- The PC does boot, but will not start the operating system
- The PC crashes during startup and if it does boot, crashes frequently when running applications
- The PC suddenly has POST parity error problems in many devices
- The PC locks up after a few minutes of operation

If you experience any of these systems, check the cooling on the processor and on the system, clean the inside of the case, and check the motherboard's power connection. Chapter 3 provides more information on processors and their environments.

Processor Cooling

If a PC boots without problems but consistently halts or freezes after only a few minutes of operation, it is likely that the processor is overheating and shutting itself down. To test for this condition, shut down the PC and power it off. After a few minutes (long enough for the processor to cool down), cold-start the PC. If the same problem occurs, it is likely the pro cessor is not being cooled sufficiently. You may need to add a fan or heat sink to the processor or add supplemental cooling fans to the system case. If that is not possible, replace the system case with one that supports multiple system fans.

If the processor is Pentium-class and does not have a heat sink or a cooling fan, it is definitely overheating. A heat sink and fan, which typically come as a single add-on unit, should be attached using liberal amounts of thermal paste (aka thermal glue).

To troubleshoot the processor, heat sink, and fan, use the following steps:

1. Examine the processor's heat sink and fan to verify that they are installed properly and are not cracked or broken.
2. After making sure the heat sink is not hot, attempt to move it slightly back and forth to check for looseness. If it is loose, it may not have the proper seal between the heat sink and fan. Follow the directions of the manufacturer to seal the heat sink and fan to the processor.
3. Remove the heat sink and fan (it typically unclips from the top of the processor) and verify that the processor is properly secured in its socket or slot. If a ZIF (zero insertion force) socket is in use, make sure that the ZIF arm is locked and anchored. Reseat a Slot 1 or Slot A processor package. Reattach the heat sink and fan, making sure it is attached securely and properly.
4. Make sure that all of the unused expansion slots on the back of the PC's case are filled with slot covers.

System Clock Jumpers

If the PC has symptoms of overheating but everything seems to be in order, the problem could be that the system clock jumpers located on the motherboard or the CMOS settings for the system timers are not set correctly for the processor. This would cause the processor and motherboard to use different clock rates and timings, which would become more out of sync as the system ran and eventually would cause a system failure. Check your motherboard and processor documentation for the proper clock settings and adjust them accordingly.

Processor Power Problems

If the POST process is signaling a processor fault, another problem could be that the processor is not getting the proper power it needs. Use a multimeter to check the power connection to the motherboard. If any of the leads are low (according to the motherboard's documentation) or dead, the power supply should be replaced. Otherwise, you may have a dead processor or a bad socket or slot mounting, which would require replacing the motherboard or the processor itself. If you install a new processor and it fails to solve the problem, the problem is isolated to the motherboard.

Troubleshooting the Floppy Disk Drive

Troubleshooting a floppy disk drive is essentially pinpointing that the floppy disk drive is the source of a problem, and if so, replacing it.

Problems When Booting from the A: Drive

If you encounter problems with attempting to boot from a floppy disk, check the following:

- **Diskette media** The diskette may not be a bootable disk, which means it does not contain the system files needed to boot the system. Use the SYS A: command to copy the system boot files to the diskette.
- **CMOS settings** The boot device setting in CMOS may not be configured with the floppy disk drive as the first boot disk or it may not be listed as a boot device at all. Enter the Setup program and change the boot disk sequence or add the floppy disk drive to the boot device list.
- **Drive problems** A very common problem is that during work inside the system case, a drive's power supply connector or data cable becomes partially disconnected, which results in intermittent errors. Typically, this would be caught during the POST process, but it can show up in operation as well.

Floppy Disk Drive Failures

If the POST process signals a floppy disk drive is bad or missing with either a beep code or a 600-series error message (see Table 24-1 earlier in the chapter), the problem could be a general failure of the floppy disk drive. Here are some things to check out:

- **Power connector** Verify that the power supply connector on the floppy disk drive is snuggly connected. Also check that the cables in the connector are not loose, frayed, bent, or crimped. Try using a different power supply connector or checking the connector's voltage with a multimeter. If the power in the cable is not correct, the problem is the power supply.
- **Cabling** It is easy to install the data cable with the wrong alignment or to shift it one or more pins off. The cable should have a red or blue stripe down the edge of the cable to indicate Pin 1. If the cable is installed backwards or incorrectly, the floppy disk drive's LED will light during the boot and stay lit solid all the time.
- **Installing two floppy drives** As a general rule, the A: drive (first floppy disk drive) is installed after (behind) the twist in the cable, and the B: drive (second floppy disk drive) is installed before (ahead) of the twist in the cable. Figure 24-1 illustrates a floppy disk data cable. The floppy disk drives may have a jumper to configure it for the twist or without the twist. Check the cable and the drives against the drives' documentation.
- **CMOS** The floppy disk controller (FDC) may be disabled in the CMOS setup data. Verify that the controller is enabled. Also check that the CMOS has the correct drive types indicated for the A: and B: drives.
- **Resource conflicts** Floppy disk resource conflicts are very rare, since virtually every PC system reserves IRQ6 and DMA channel 2 for the floppy

disk controller. However, devices that work on the floppy drive interface and with the floppy controller, such as a tape drive adapter, may also try to use these resources.

- **Motherboard issues** If the floppy disk controller is built into the motherboard or its chipset, the problem could be a motherboard issue. In this case, there's not much you can do except to disable the floppy disk controller in the CMOS and install an FDC.

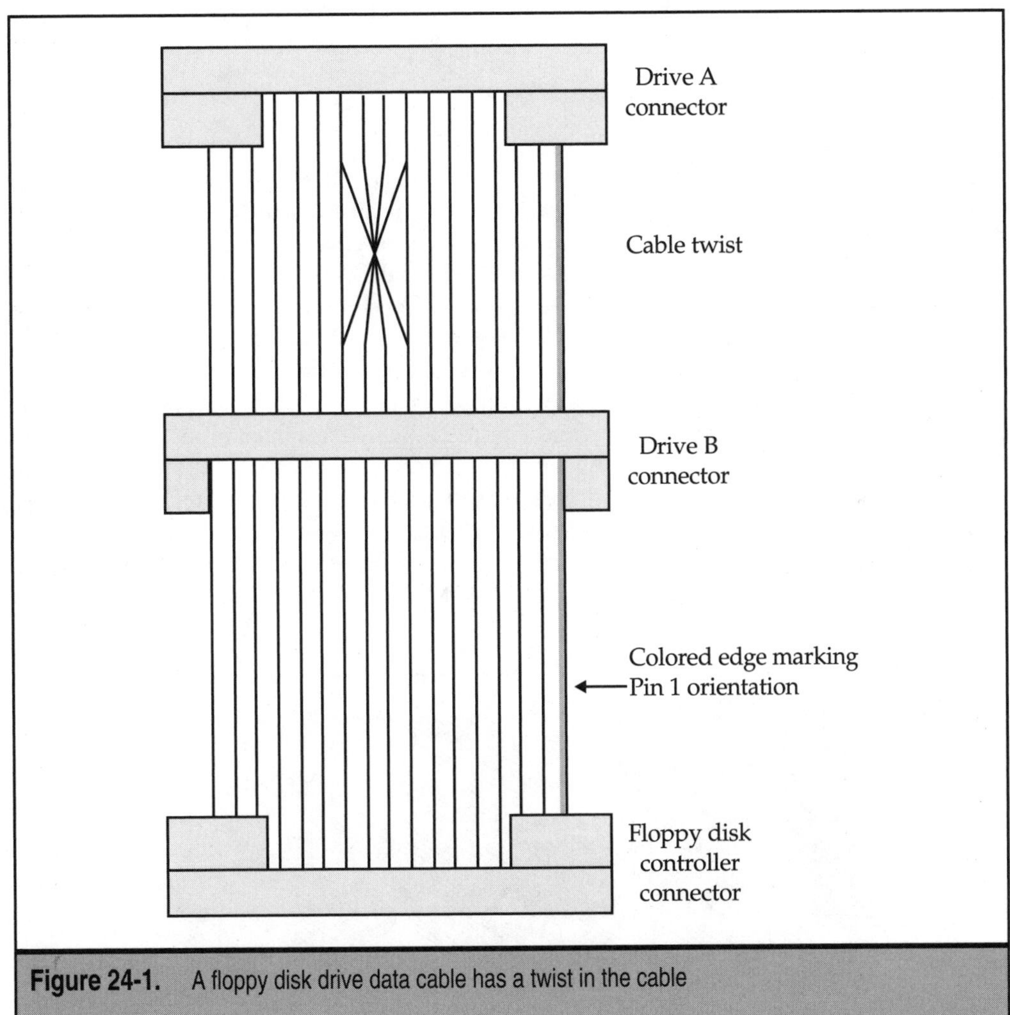

Figure 24-1. A floppy disk drive data cable has a twist in the cable

Troubleshooting Hard Disk Drives

When a hard disk error occurs, it is usually a cause for real concern. Not only will the PC not boot, but there is the threat that all your data and programs could be lost. A hard disk problem can be caused by the hard disk drive, the hard disk controller, a SCSI host adapter, cabling, and in many situations, the power supply.

There is always the risk when troubleshooting a hard disk drive that any data stored on it could be destroyed. This is why you should always create and verify a full backup of the hard disk before you begin to work. To verify a disk backup, restore a few random files from it. All of this assumes that you can access the disk drive to make a backup or to perform troubleshooting.

IDE Hard Disk Drives

Most current PC motherboards include support for either one or two IDE/ATA (Integrated Drive Electronics/AT Attachment) channels. Each IDE/ATA channel supports up to two disk drives, which must be designated with one as a master and one as a slave.

On an IDE/ATA disk, the designation of master represents disk0; slave indicates disk1. Neither is actually in charge of the other. The BIOS uses the disk0 and disk1 designations to assign logical device names (C:, D:, etc.) to disks. The master on the primary channel is assigned a drive letter first (typically C:), followed by the primary slave, and the master and slave, if any, on the secondary channel. Disk0 is typically the boot drive.

The master/slave designation is set with a jumper on the disk drive. Figure 24-2 shows the jumpers from a typical hard disk drive, and Figure 24-3 illustrates the jumper positions used to configure the device. The two IDE/ATA drives on a channel are connected to the same data cable in series. It doesn't matter which drive is designated as the slave or the master. See Chapter 9 for more information on hard disk drives and their jumper settings.

To begin troubleshooting any disk drive problem, you should boot the system from a floppy disk drive. The AUTOEXEC.BAT and CONFIG.SYS files on the boot disk should

Figure 24-2. Jumpers on a hard disk drive

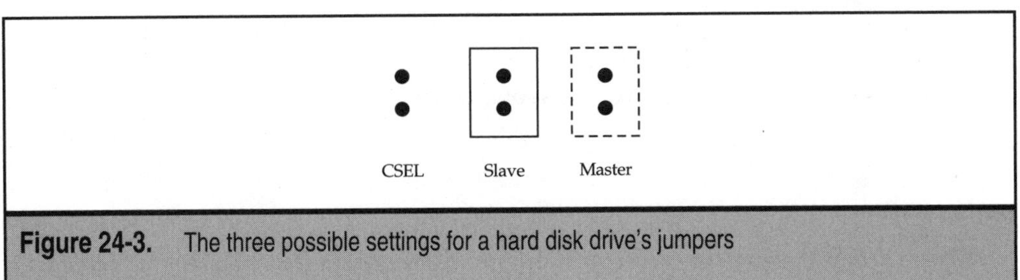

Figure 24-3. The three possible settings for a hard disk drive's jumpers

contain no or minimal device driver support. This allows the system to boot with what is called a clean boot.

Here are some things to check to troubleshoot IDE/ATA hard disk problems:

- **The CMOS configuration is incorrect** This message indicates that something in the BIOS' Startup configuration information stored in CMOS is not consistent with what the POST or boot process is finding. Verify the CMOS configuration of each hard disk drive installed in the system. The information you need regarding the number of heads, platters, etc., should be in the documentation of each drive.
- **Hardware resource conflicts** Messages reporting some form of resource conflict are typically indicating an IRQ (interrupt request) conflict. Use the Windows Device Manager to verify that a resource conflict has not been created for the hard disk drive controllers by the installation of a new piece of hardware.
- **Boot partition is corrupted** If the system files on the boot partition are corrupted, the system cannot boot properly. Use the SYS C: command (from a MS-DOS command prompt) to transfer the system files to the hard drive. If this doesn't solve the problem, use ScanDisk to check for media defects and file problems and then reformat the boot partition and reinstall the operating system. Also verify that the boot partition has not been accidentally removed.
- **The hard disk may have a virus infection** Another reason the system may not be able to find a boot sector is that the boot disk is infected with a computer virus. Many viruses can corrupt the master boot record on the hard drive and cause errors that show up as hard disk errors. If an antivirus program is not installed on the PC, install one and scan the hard disk.
- **The hard disk cable may be bad or not connected properly** A message along the lines of "No hard disk" indicates that the hard disk is probably installed incorrectly. If the front panel hard drive LED lights up and stays on constantly, the drive data cable is not properly connected. This condition should cause a POST error message indicating that no boot device is available. Check both ends of the cable, at the device and on the motherboard or adapter card. Also check the power supply connectors.

- **The hard drive may be defective** It can and does happen. Every disk drive makes some noise and users get accustomed to it. However, the spindle motor or the drive bearings can wear out and seize up.
- **Drive incompatibilities** If two drives will not work with each other in any configuration or combination as master and slave, there is something wrong with the drives. Try replacing one or both and retesting.

Here are some of the common POST and system error messages for hard disk problems:

- **Hard disk configuration error** Typically indicates an incorrect CMOS configuration or a loose, missing, or incorrectly installed data cable.
- **Hard disk 0 failure** Disk0 is the master drive on the primary IDE/ATA channel. This message indicates an incorrect CMOS configuration or a bad connection to the power supply.
- **Hard disk controller failure** Indicates power or data cable connection problems. Check the data cable connection and the power connectors on the drive and the hard disk controller.

SCSI Hard Disk Drives

SCSI hard disk drives can have many of the same problems as an IDE/ATA, especially relating to power and drive failure. However, SCSI drives do not use masters and slaves and are uniquely identified to the system.

Here are some things to look for when troubleshooting a SCSI hard disk drive:

- **CMOS setup** The hard disk drive settings in CMOS should be set to None or Auto-detect. The SCSI host adapter provides BIOS-level support to the hard disk drive.
- **SCSI device drivers** Because SCSI devices require device drivers, make sure the latest drivers are installed. Visit the manufacturer's Web site to download the latest device drivers for the PC's operating system.
- **Host adapter and hard disk IDs** The SCSI host adapter is always designated as Device 7 on the SCSI bus and the first SCSI hard disk drive (the boot disk) on the bus should be assigned SCSI ID 0. If two or more SCSI hard disks are installed on the same bus, which means on the same SCSI cable, each must have a unique SCSI ID number. The ID is set through a jumper on the device.
- **Termination** If the SCSI hard disk is the only internal device or if it is the last device on the SCSI bus, it must be terminated. Use a multimeter to verify that the termination block is good.

IDE/ATA and SCSI Drives Together

A PC that has both SCSI and IDE/ATA hard disk must have a BIOS that supports both types of drives and allows the SCSI to be designated as the boot device, a choice you want to make because the SCSI is usually a higher performance disk drive. If the PC's BIOS doesn't allow a SCSI drive to be the boot disk, check with the BIOS manufacturer for an upgrade that will allow this configuration.

Troubleshooting Memory

Typically, three general types of memory (RAM) problems on a PC require troubleshooting, and for the most part, these problems happen just after new memory has been installed. See Chapter 7 for general information on memory systems. Memory problems also occur because of electrical problems on the motherboard or, on older systems that use DIP (dual inline packaging) memory, chip creep can be a problem. Troubleshooting memory problems is complicated because many FRMs give out symptoms that appear to be memory problems. If you're having memory problems, you should check the following:

- **Configuration** If you have just added new or additional memory to a PC, the amount of memory installed may be more than the PC or operating system is able to support or the BIOS CMOS settings may be incorrect.
- **Hardware** All of the memory installed must be compatible and installed in complete banks. If slower memory is installed in one bank, all of the memory will operate at the slower speed. The problem could also be that at least one memory module or chip is defective.
- **Installation** Most memory problems are caused by the memory chips or modules not being completely or properly seated in their sockets. It could be that a socket is bad, has a bent or broken lead, or just needs cleaning.

Identifying a Memory Problem

Knowing when a memory problem happens is very valuable information. A memory problem that happens during startup is a much different problem than one that happens while an application is running and each is resolved quite differently. Memory problems can occur in these situations:

- **The first time a new PC is started** This common problem is caused by the rigors of shipping a PC. The memory chips may need to be reseated or may be missing. A problem that appears to be memory-related could also be a bad motherboard. Check with the manufacturer or the vendor.
- **Immediately after new memory is installed** Check the part numbers and speed of both the new and the old memory modules. Verify the memory was properly installed or configured in memory banks. If DIP or SIMM (Single Inline Memory Module) memory is in use, check that each bank is filled before memory is placed in another bank. You should also verify that the memory is appropriate for the motherboard, chipset, and processor. For example, the memory bus on a Pentium III PC is usually PC133-compliant, so the memory installed on this system must be PC133.

The part number of a memory module or chip is used to match up memory on a PC. If the memory's part number ends with a dash and a number, such as "-60," it is industry standard EDO (Extended Data Output) or FPM (Fast Page Mode) memory. If the part number ends with a slash and a number, such as "/32," it is industry standard SDRAM (Synchronous DRAM). SDRAM part numbers also indicate the standard to which they conform. For example, a Kingston Technology memory with the part number KTM66X64/128 is compliant with the Intel 66 MHz standard and is a 128 MB DIMM, and a KVR-VC133/128 is a 128 MB, PC133 DIMM. Other manufacturers, such as Viking, Micron, and others have very similar part numbering to allow memory to be matched easily.

- **Immediately after new software or operating system is installed** Later versions of applications and operating systems can require more memory than their older versions. New software, especially beta versions, can have several bugs that produce memory errors on the PC. The way to solve these errors, other than uninstalling or reinstalling the software, is to check for a BIOS upgrade or a service patch for the software.
- **Immediately after hardware is installed or removed** When new hardware is installed incorrectly or a connector that is connected to the motherboard is dislodged or missing, the errors that result can appear to be memory errors, complete with memory error messages. Check the cables and connectors and, if that is not the problem, check for newer device drivers or BIOS updates.
- **For no apparent reason** If a PC has been running okay and suddenly begins having memory problems, reseat the memory modules and check for corrosion on the contacts of the memory modules and the slot connectors. If the PC is running too hot, it may have damaged the motherboard, memory, or processor to the point of errors. And then there is always the power supply to check.

Memory Errors

The following are common instances of memory failures and errors:

- **The POST sounds a single beep code** Remember that a single beep code can either sound an all clear or signal a memory failure. If the boot continues, the beep was the all clear. If it stops, check the memory to ensure it is properly installed and is configured in the BIOS properly.
- **The PC boots with a blank display** If the PC is able to boot but the display is blank, it means that an error may have occurred at the beginning of the memory check. The types of conditions to look for are a dislodged expansion card, a memory module not fully seated, or an unsupported memory module. Confirm that all expansion cards and memory modules are seated in their sockets and verify that the memory installed is compatible with the system by checking its part numbers. Putting nonparity RAM in a PC that has error-

checking code (ECC) memory, or SDRAM in a PC that supports only EDO (Extended Data Output) memory will definitely cause the boot sequence to halt. See Chapter 7 for more information on memory types.

- **The memory count displayed by the POST is wrong** If the memory count displayed by the POST is less than it should be, the BIOS isn't recognizing all of the installed memory. A wrong memory type being installed is a common cause for this error, as well as memory banks not being completed. Another problem is incompatible memory or more memory than the system is able to address.
- **The PC displays a memory error message**, such as:
    - Memory mismatch error
    - Memory parity interrupt at nnnnn
    - Memory address error at nnnnn
    - Memory failure at nnnnn, read nnnnn, expecting nnnnn
    - Memory verify error at nnnnn, where nnnnn is the physical address in RAM of the memory fault.

  These errors typically point out problems between old memory and new memory or a failing memory module. If removing a newly installed memory module eliminates the error, replace the old memory with the new memory. If the error shows up again, the new memory is either defective or not compatible with the system. Another cause for these messages can be a motherboard problem.
- **ESD damage** Intermittent memory problems—those that show up sporadically as an error message, system crash, or a spontaneous system reboot— have a number of possible causes, but one of the leading suspects should be ESD (electrostatic discharge). If you are not properly grounded with effective ESD protection when working inside the system unit, you can cause enough damage to either completely fry a component or to create intermittent problems that result from the circuit slowly degrading over time. Other problems for intermittent memory problems are overheating, corrosion, or a faulty power supply.
- **Software-related memory problems** The problems under this category include registry errors, general-protection and page faults, and exception errors. Registry errors happen when the Windows operating system writes parts of the registry to a defective portion of RAM. Software bugs cause faults and exception errors. For example, an application may release its memory when completed or it may try to occupy the same memory address as another. Rebooting the PC usually solves these problems.

Troubleshooting the Video System

The PC's video system consists of the monitor and the video card. Most video system problems are easily detected because they are visual and show up on the monitor. While the monitor can have problems, the video card is the cause of most video problems on a PC. One thing to remember when troubleshooting the video system is that no matter how high-end the video card may be, it is limited by the abilities of the monitor.

- If the screen is blank or dark, check to see if the monitor is plugged into a power source, the power cord is connected to the monitor, and the monitor cable is connected to the PC. Many newer monitors use a double-ended VGA cable that has a HD-15 connector at the monitor end as well as the video card end. If the cables are okay, reseat the video card.
- The most common video problems are refresh rates, resolution, and color depth settings. These problems are easily solved through the Display Properties applet on the Windows system. See Chapter 21 for information on setting these properties.
- If the monitor's display is blank, scrambled, distorted, or has multiple layers of the same images, the monitor is unable to handle the video card's output. Another very irritating symptom of a mismatch between the monitor and video card is a high-pitched tone coming from the monitor. Use the Windows Display Properties applet to change the color depth and the resolution levels to a more compatible setting. Your monitor and video card documentation should have a recommended refresh rate for the monitor. The tools you need to change the refresh rate are accessed through the Advanced button on the Windows Display Properties window.
- If after changing the refresh rate the monitor image is unreadable, reboot the PC into Windows Safe Mode and change the refresh rate to a lower setting and reboot the PC into normal mode. To boot a Windows system into Safe Mode, choose Shutdown from the Start button's menu and select Restart from the option list. When the Windows screen appears during the boot (the LOGO.SYS screen), press the F8 key.
- It is very common that the device driver included with Windows or shipped with a video card is obsolete. Visit the manufacturer's Web site for a current device driver for the video card.

Troubleshooting the Power Supply

A weak or faulty power supply can create a number of problems for the peripheral devices installed inside the system unit, especially the motherboard and disk drives. Unexplained or intermittent memory or hard disk errors are commonly caused by a faulty or failing power supply. Extended periods of low voltage can damage the hard disk drive as much as over-voltages can burn out the motherboard and memory.

To troubleshoot a PC's power supply, test each of the power connectors for their proper voltages. Test the +12VDC and +5VDC supplies with a multimeter. Many power supplies have adjusting screws to set and adjust the voltages produced by the power supply. Typically, turning the screw clockwise increases the voltage and turning it counter-clockwise decreases it. Dial in the power connectors to their appropriate levels. Check the power supply's documentation for information on the proper voltage levels of the pins. If the pins cannot be adjusted to the correct voltages, replace the power supply.

Troubleshooting the Sound System

It can be very difficult to isolate the source of a sound system problem. Here are some troubleshooting steps to use to track down an audio problem:

- **Resource conflicts** Use the Windows System Information applet (see Figure 24-4) from the Accessories | Systems Tools menu to determine if there are any resource conflicts (IRQ, DMA, or I/O address) between the sound card and other devices. If a conflict exists, reassign the conflicting device or the sound card. The most common conflict is an IRQ.
- **Speakers** Troubleshooting the speakers is a fairly straightforward process:
    1. Make sure the sound card is connected to the speakers and the correct cable is plugged into the correct jack on the sound card. Match up the color-coded plugs to the jacks or look carefully at the little pictures on the jacks.
    2. Make sure the volume on the sound card and the speakers is turned up. The sound card's volume can be set either with an adjustment knob or dial on the sound card or by clicking on the speaker symbol in the tray on the right end of the Task bar to open the Play Control panel. Make sure that the volume on the speakers is turned up.
    3. Make sure that the speaker wires are not crimped or broken and that all of the jacks are seated in the appropriate plugs.
- **Device drivers** Sound cards are completely dependent on their software device drivers. Verify that the latest version of the sound card's driver software is installed by checking the manufacturer's Web site.
- **EMF (Electromagnetic Field)** Sound cards are very susceptible to EMF emissions from other devices and cards. Make sure that the sound card is not placed too close to a disk drive or the power supply inside the system case. For best results, place the sound card in an expansion slot as far away from other components as possible.

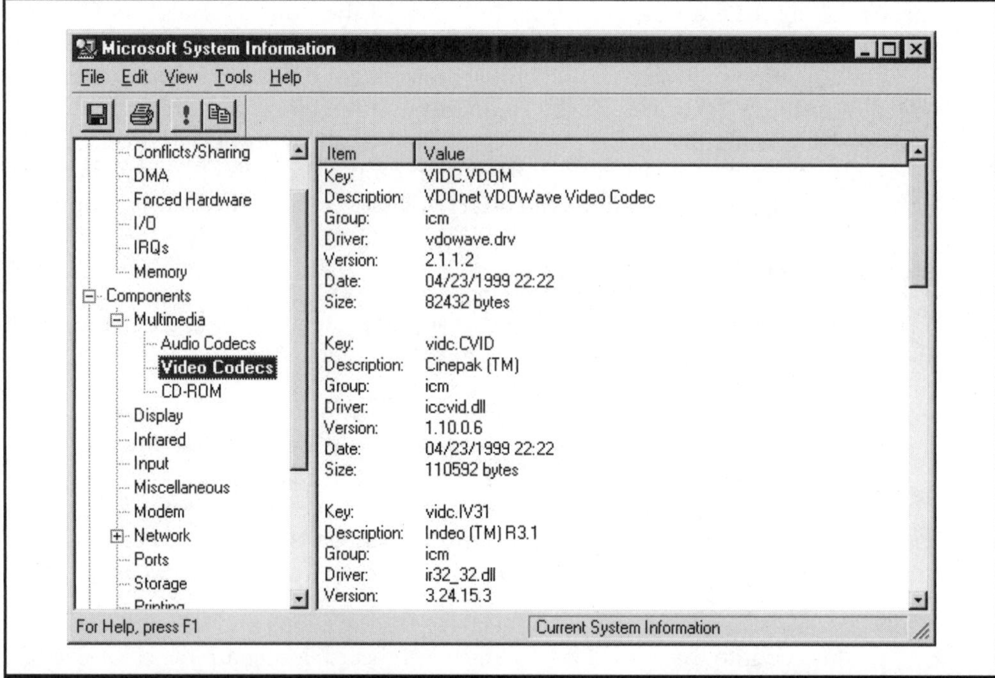

Figure 24-4. The Windows System Information window can be used to display information on the audio system in a PC

Index

A

B

C

D

 E

 F

G

H

I

J

K

L

M

N

O

P

 Q

 R

S

 T

 U

 V

W

X

Y

Z

INTERNATIONAL CONTACT INFORMATION

AUSTRALIA
McGraw-Hill Book Company Australia Pty. Ltd.
TEL +61-2-9417-9899
FAX +61-2-9417-5687
http://www.mcgraw-hill.com.au
books-it_sydney@mcgraw-hill.com

CANADA
McGraw-Hill Ryerson Ltd.
TEL +905-430-5000
FAX +905-430-5020
http://www.mcgrawhill.ca

GREECE, MIDDLE EAST, NORTHERN AFRICA
McGraw-Hill Hellas
TEL +30-1-656-0990-3-4
FAX +30-1-654-5525

MEXICO (Also serving Latin America)
McGraw-Hill Interamericana Editores S.A. de C.V.
TEL +525-117-1583
FAX +525-117-1589
http://www.mcgraw-hill.com.mx
fernando_castellanos@mcgraw-hill.com

SINGAPORE (Serving Asia)
McGraw-Hill Book Company
TEL +65-863-1580
FAX +65-862-3354
http://www.mcgraw-hill.com.sg
mghasia@mcgraw-hill.com

SOUTH AFRICA
McGraw-Hill South Africa
TEL +27-11-622-7512
FAX +27-11-622-9045
robyn_swanepoel@mcgraw-hill.com

UNITED KINGDOM & EUROPE (Excluding Southern Europe)
McGraw-Hill Education Europe
TEL +44-1-628-502500
FAX +44-1-628-770224
http://www.mcgraw-hill.co.uk
computing_neurope@mcgraw-hill.com

ALL OTHER INQUIRIES Contact:
Osborne/McGraw-Hill
TEL +1-510-549-6600
FAX +1-510-883-7600
http://www.osborne.com
omg_international@mcgraw-hill.com